AF782865

HANDBOOK OF RESEARCH ON COMPLEXITY

Handbook of Research on Complexity

Edited by

J. Barkley Rosser, Jr.

Professor of Economics and Kirby L. Cramer, Jr. Professor of Business Administration, James Madison University, USA

Edward Elgar

Cheltenham, UK • Northampton, MA, USA

© J. Barkley Rosser, Jr. 2009

All rights reserved. No part of this publication may be reproduced, stored in a retrieval system or transmitted in any form or by any means, electronic, mechanical or photocopying, recording, or otherwise without the prior permission of the publisher.

Published by
Edward Elgar Publishing Limited
The Lypiatts
15 Lansdown Road
Cheltenham
Glos GL50 2JA
UK

Edward Elgar Publishing, Inc.
William Pratt House
9 Dewey Court
Northampton
Massachusetts 01060
USA

A catalogue record for this book
is available from the British Library

Library of Congress Control Number: 2009922748

PEFC
PEFC/16-33-111
CATG-PEFC-052
www.pefc.org

ISBN 978 1 84542 089 5 (cased)

Printed and bound by MPG Books Group, UK

Contents

PART V INTERNATIONAL ECONOMICS

PART VI EVOLUTIONARY AND ECOLOGICAL-ENVIRONMENTAL ECONOMICS

PART VII BROADER HISTORICAL PERSPECTIVES

Contributors

Peter Allen, Professor, Complex Systems Management Centre, School of Management, Cranfield University, Bedfordshire, UK

W. Brian Arthur, External Professor, Santa Fe Institute, USA

Kevin E. Bassler, Professor of Physics, University of Houston, USA

Hans-Peter Brunner, Senior Economist, Asian Development Bank, Manila

David Colander, Christian A. Johnson Distinguished Professor of Economics, Middlebury College, USA

Ross Cressman, Department of Mathematics, Wilfrid Laurier University, Ontario, Canada

Richard H. Day, Emeritus, Department of Economics, University of Southern California, USA

Herbert Gintis, Santa Fe Institute and Central European University, Budapest, Hungary

Gemunu H. Gunaratne, Professor of Physics, University of Houston, USA

Cars H. Hommes, Center for Nonlinear Dynamics in Economics and Finance (CeNDEF), School of Economics, University of Amsterdam, Netherlands

Alan Kirman, Groupement de Recherche en Economie Quantitative d'Aix Marseille (GREQAM), Ecole des Hautes Etudes en Sciences Sociales (EHESS), University d'Aix Marseille, France

Michael Kopel, Vienna University of Technology, Institute of Management Science, Austria

Roger Koppl, Institute for Forensic Science Administration, Fairleigh Dickinson University, Madison, New Jersey, USA

Thomas Lux, Department of Economics, University of Kiel and Kiel Institute for the World Economy, Germany

Joseph L. McCauley, Professor of Physics, University of Houston, USA

J. Barkley Rosser, Jr., Professor of Economics and Kirby L. Cramer, Jr. Professor of Business Administration, James Madison University, USA

Thijs Ruijgrok, Mathematics Department, Utrecht University, Netherlands

K. Vela Velupillai, Department of Economics, University of Trento, Italy and Girton College, Cambridge, UK

Frank H. Westerhoff, Department of Economics, University of Bamberg, Germany

PART I

CONCEPTUAL OVERVIEWS

1. Introduction

J. Barkley Rosser, Jr.

> In the earlier times the profession was trying to focus on empirical discipline. They felt that if you didn't have so many equilibria, you would have more discipline with your analysis. So I had to hide any multiple equilibria in footnotes where future researchers could find them but where referees were less likely to see them. (William A. ["Buz"] Brock in Colander, Holt, and Rosser, 2004, p. 162)

What is complexity research about?

Complexity research is about complexity in various disciplines. It can be argued that ultimately this is a transdisciplinary view of the world, but it gets applied in specific disciplines. This book will focus on its applications in economics in particular, which means that we need to know what we mean by *complexity*, itself a complex issue, and one that is at the heart of several chapters in the first part of this book.

Let us posit three different levels of complexity. The lowest level, labeled "small tent" complexity by Rosser (1999), and also as "Santa Fe complexity," involves a focus on interacting heterogeneous agents. In a widely noted formulation, Arthur, Durlauf, and Lane (1997) provided a list of six characteristics that this lowest level tends to exhibit: 1) dispersed interaction among heterogeneous agents acting on each other locally in some space, 2) no global controller that can exploit all opportunities or interactions, despite the possibility of some weak global interactions, 3) cross-cutting hierarchical organization with tangled relations, 4) continual adaptation and learning by evolving agents, 5) perpetual novelty as new markets, technologies, behaviors, and institutions create new niches in the ecology of the system, and 6) out-of-equilibrium dynamics with either zero or many equilibria existing, and the system unlikely to be near a global optimum. This then is an imperfect world of bounded rationality and unexpected events and processes.

This lowest level of complexity can be viewed as the central workhorse and focus of much of complexity research that has gone on and continues to go on, with various examples and discussions of this view in several of the chapters in this book. Although it had existed previously in such outposts as Brussels and Stuttgart, it was at Santa Fe that it achieved its breakthrough of recognition and focus. In economics this was symbolized by three volumes out of the Santa Fe Institute, appearing every nine years

(Anderson, Arrow, and Pines, 1988; Arthur, Durlauf, and Lane, 1997; Blume and Durlauf, 2006). These saw the development of this concept of complexity from an initial revolutionary phase through an expanded set of applications to a consolidation of the approach,[1] especially as the editors of the final volume argued the concept of complexity had been reconciled with neoclassical economics. Rosser (2008) argued that this represented the selection of papers in the volume and the avoiding of more controversial material and researchers, although it must be admitted that ideas considered heretical 20 years ago have come to be viewed as more acceptable today, if not completely so.

The next level of complexity up is what Rosser (1999) labeled "big tent" complexity, which was defined following Day (1994) in dynamic terms, as processes that for endogenous reasons fail to converge to either a point, a limit cycle, or a simple expansion or contraction. This definition will be discussed more in the third chapter of this book, but suffice it for now to note that it included a set of other views based on nonlinear dynamics that had historically preceded the appearance of this later interacting agents complexity, although they were not called complexity (and some would argue that they are not actually complexity). These were the first three of what Horgan (1997) derisively labeled "the four Cs," the fourth being complexity. These first three were *cybernetics*, *catastrophe theory*,[2] and *chaos theory*, each of which was seen as having been an intellectual fad that experienced a bubble and then deservedly crashed. In Rosser (2004) these were represented by important past papers applying them to a wide variety of fields of economics.[3] Rosser argued that they grew out of each other, reaching a critical mass of intellectual weight in the most recent period. It may be this accumulation of intellectual weight to the point where most observers must now credit the complexity concept with a degree of seriousness that may justify the remarks of Blume and Durlauf (2006) regarding the acceptance of the idea, or some parts of it anyway, by neoclassical economics.

Finally, the highest level of complexity I shall now call here for the first time, *meta-complexity*. This is the level at which Seth Lloyd has long been located, famous for having gathered at least 45 different definitions of complexity (Horgan, 1997, Ch. 11). The dynamic definition noted above, which contains the four Cs, is but a small part of this, even if it is arguably the most widely used perspective in economics. But the movement of research has more recently moved into some of these other definitions and perspectives. An important alternative is the computational perspective, arguably first introduced into economics by the late Peter Albin (1982). Chapter 4 of this volume focuses on this approach to complexity. At the cutting edge of complexity research these alternative views of complexity have become increasingly important, and the computational view is deeply linked to the widely used algorithmic perspective in broader, transdisciplinary complexity. However, it must be recognized that as one moves to the level of meta-complexity, the definition of what it is becomes much less distinct. Nevertheless, this book presents perspectives at this broader and higher level of current cutting-edge research in complexity in various areas of economics.

Where did complexity come from?

The question of where the idea of complexity came from has a simple answer: it came from mathematics. In this regard, Weintraub (2002) has argued that revolutions in the history of economics have reflected revolutions in the history of mathematics. So, as Mirowski (1989) has argued, late 19th-century neoclassical economics arose from the mathematics used in the physics of the mid-19th century. The formalistic and axiomatic approach associated with the proofs of the existence of general equilibrium and early game theory was associated with the ultra-formalism of the Bourbakist school of mathematics in France, out of which milieu Gérard Debreu came. The more recent relaxation of this axiomatism and the move to greater use of computer simulations that has been integral to much recent complexity research reflected trends in mathematics as well. In this regard, mathematical developments are the link between related developments occurring across many disciplines.

Thus, just as Buz Brock complained about how he used to have to hide his multiple equilibria in footnotes so that referees would not notice them, so it is that the mathematical foundations of modern complexity theory arose out of the deep past, with many of the discoverers shying away from the "monsters" they had discovered, preferring an orderly universe without such complications. A supreme example of this was Poincaré (1899), who arguably invented the qualitative theory of differential equations and bifurcation theory. From these he would observe the possibility of endogenously irregular dynamics, later known to be chaotic, which he rejected and shied away from. But the origins run deeper, even as they were often largely ignored.

Thus, Rössler (1997, Ch. 1) has argued that one can find the idea of self-similarity as it appears in fractal geometry in the work of the pre-Socratic philosopher, Anaxagoras. This may be a stretch, but Arnol'd (1992) argues that Poincaré was preceded in his understanding of bifurcation theory by Huygens in 1654, who studied the stability of cusp points in caustics and wave fronts. Mandelbrot (1983, p. 4) pinpoints a crucial discovery by Weierstrass in 1872 of a function that is continuous but non-differentiable everywhere. In 1879 Cayley would study path dependence in the form of the question of when would a simple cubic equation converge to which of its three roots. In 1883 Cantor would discover transfinite sets and with his famous Cantor set, the possibility of sets of zero measure that nevertheless were at the level of the continuum and exhibited fractal dimensionality. In 1892 Lyapounov would initiate the study of the stability of dynamical systems, and in the 20th century, the Russian School (Andronov, 1928; Kolmogorov, 1941; Sharkovsy, 1964) would follow this to develop much of the apparatus of modern complexity mathematics. Electrical engineers would discover in reality actual complex dynamics, such as chaos (van der Pol and van der Mark, 1927). It would only be later that these developments would find their manifestation in economic research, although again there would be pioneers ahead of their time with little recognition in their day (Kalecki, 1935; Goodwin, 1951; Schelling, 1971).[4]

In any case, just as in economics there would long be resistance to the newer approach, so in mathematics it first took a long time for these "monsters" to be accepted as house pets that are really quite ordinary, arguably more ordinary than the perfected mathematical objects of ancient Euclidean geometry. Thus, as Benoît Mandelbrot (1983, p. 1) has put it: "Clouds are not spheres, mountains are not cones, coastlines are not circles, and bark is not smooth, nor does lightning travel in a straight line."

What is in this book?

Three further chapters occupy this opening Conceptual Overviews part of this book. The first of these is by an important figure from the Santa Fe complexity group, W. Brian Arthur. He emphasizes the themes noted in the characteristics listed above of the "small tent" complexity view, such as perpetual novelty and interacting agents. He notes also the important role of nonlinearity, particularly in the form of positive feedbacks in systems, which can both destabilize dynamics while bringing about the emergence of higher forms of order. Indeed, he poses an important and deep theme of complexity research, that order can come out of chaos. Complex systems can be self-ordering, against all apparent odds, as he demonstrates in his famous El Farol Bar example.

The next chapter is the first of a pair that can be seen as engaging in a debate over the proper definition of complexity. It is by J. Barkley Rosser, Jr. and poses and works through the contrast between the computational and dynamic views of complexity, ultimately arguing for the greater usefulness in economics of the dynamic view, while granting the greater rigor associated with the computational view.

The chapter following that one is by K. Vela Velupillai and presents an overview of the new computable economics view, which in turn rests on computational or algorithmic definitions of complexity. Velupillai argues that this developing perspective rests on deep roots in mathematical logic and probability theory. He links these to the deep unavoidability of bounded rationality in the face of the multiform problems of computability and solvability of systems. He poses deeper questions about the axiomatic foundations of mathematics and the implications for economic theory of these problems and issues.

The second part of this volume focuses on Market Dynamics with two chapters. The first of these is by Cars H. Hommes, who further pursues the problem of bounded rationality and learning in complex markets. He considers problems of expectation formation, posing adaptive learning as a key to evolutionary selection and dynamics. The performance of different forecasting rules in systems with interacting heterogeneous agents is considered, and evidence from recent economic experiments is presented and reviewed. He notes the deep interaction between simple rules of thumb and more costly methods of forecasting, with dynamics often driven by this alternation as the former can destabilize a system and push it into more complex dynamical patterns, while the latter may induce periods of stability and simplicity.

The second chapter in this part is by Michael Kopel who reviews models of oligopoly dynamics. This is an important area in complexity research as well as more broadly in mathematical economics. After all, it was in studying duopoly that Cournot was the first to apply calculus to economic theory, and it would be to the same problems conceived dynamically that David Rand (1978) would be the first to consciously apply chaos theory to the study of economics. Kopel covers these matters but brings in the more advanced models of multidimensional chaos and multistability in which multiple basins of attraction in a system coexist. The complexities involved can include fractal basin boundaries and riddled basins. He provides both a historical perspective on these approaches as well as distinguishing how each apply differently to Cournot, Bertrand, and Stackelberg problems.

The third part of the book moves to Macroeconomic Issues, again with two chapters. The first by Alan Kirman deals with complexity and aggregation. Coming originally out of general equilibrium theory, Kirman was among the first to point out the depth of problems involved in attempting to aggregate so that an economy would be modeled by a representative agent. Thus, he has been a major herald and advocate of the hetereogeneous agents approach to complexity research. In this chapter he reviews these original theoretical concerns and then moves on to a variety of applications of heterogeneous agent modeling from public goods games to the Schelling model of urban segregation to the evolution of market networks, drawing on his famous work on the Marseille fish market.

Richard H. Day then follows with a chapter on simplicity and macroeconomic complexity. He emphasizes the deep complexity concept of the emergence of higher-order structures out of lower-level systems, applying this to problems of multilevel causality in economics from the micro through the meso to the macro. He considers various issues such as reducibility and discretization in the relationship between simplicity and complexity, eventually presenting some models of macroeconomic dynamics based on nonlinear foundations.

The fourth part deals with the newly emerging field of Econophysics and its application to financial markets. The first chapter in this part, and the longest in the entire volume, is by Thomas Lux on applications of statistical physics in finance and economics. He presents a broad overview of econophysics methods and approaches. While deeply sympathetic, he does not hesitate to point out problems with certain approaches, echoing the critiques he put forth with others quite recently (Gallegati et al., 2006). A centerpiece of this chapter is showing how when econophysicists fall into using orthodox economic theory as a foundation for their modeling, this can lead them into making drastically incorrect forecasts about financial market dynamics and futures.

The second of the two chapters is by Joseph L. McCauley, Kevin E. Bassler, and Gemunu L. Gunaratne, on the analysis of time series with nonstationary increments. They challenge a variety of established views in this chapter on time series analysis, drawing on ideas from physics. They argue that Hurst coefficients exhibit serious problems and they dispute the existence of kurtotic "fat tails" in certain market data. They pose the log return as a central conceptual focus to study Markov processes, scaling Ito processes, and financial market problems of liquidity, noise, and crashes of speculative bubbles. This chapter constitutes a challenge not only to orthodox economic theory and econometrics, but to what has emerged as more standard approaches used in econophysics as well.

The fifth part of the book focuses on International Economics. The first of the two chapters is by Frank H. Westerhoff, who surveys recent work on nonlinear modeling of exchange rate dynamics, which have long been notorious for being the most difficult of economic variables to model or forecast. A major thrust of this chapter is on the interaction between fundamentalists and chartists, or technical traders, in the foreign exchange markets, and how heterogeneous agents can move back and forth between strategies. While generally, technical traders tend to destabilize and complexify dynamics, they can also serve to some degree as stabilizers in these markets. The emphasis on learning and adaptation links this chapter to some of the others in the book and shows how the extreme volatility and unpredictability in these markets has made those studying them more open than many to considering the use of models using complexity approaches.

The second chapter in this part is by Hans-Peter Brunner and Peter Allen, who consider complex systems modeling and international development. They focus on autocatalytic processes in developing economies and how a complexity perspective alters the approach to policy. Rather than imposed top-down interventions, the concept is that interventions must cohere well with the networks and structures of the socioeconomic system. The emphasis is on self-organization of these processes as stimulated by careful policy interventions. It presents an example of the approach using an input–output model of the poor state of Orissa in northeastern India, with its trade relations with other states and nearby countries, considering the possible outcomes from different levels of transportation infrastructure investment.

Part VI of this volume is on Evolutionary and Ecological-Environmental Economics. The first chapter is in the vein of evolutionary game theory by Herbert Gintis, Ross Cressman, and Thijs Ruijgrok on subgame perfection in evolutionary dynamics with recurrent perturbations. Under conditions of perturbation in finite noncooperative games with unique subgame perfect equilibria, they show how often there will not be convergence to this equilibrium; indeed that convergence may go quite far away from it. This fits in well with the theme of out-of-equilibrium dynamics in complex systems.

The second chapter by Rosser is on complex dynamics in ecologic-economic systems. This considers the peculiar complexities that can arise from the interaction of biology and economics in such coupled systems with their inevitable nonlinearities. Models of fisheries and forests are studied, as are models of climate change dynamics. The problem of hierarchy and broader evolutionary dynamics are also looked at.

The final part of the book moves on to broader historical perspectives of economic thought. The first chapter is by Roger Koppl and considers complexity and Austrian economics. Portions of his discussion echo the earlier chapter by Velupillai with a concern for the limits of computability and the implications for bounded rationality that he argues the Austrian perspective of Hayek and others implies for economic analysis. He poses the key to the links between complexity and Austrian economics to be "BRICE," bounded rationality, rule following, institutions, cognition, and evolution. He points out in particular the role of Hayek as an early, conscious complexity theorist.

The final chapter in the volume is by David Colander on complexity and the history of economic thought. After considering alternative visions of economics as the complexity perspective contrasted with a more conventional or orthodox view, including a consideration of the boundaries of economics and how these might change as a result of complexity research, he engages in a re-evaluation of past thinkers in economics in regard to how they fit in with the emerging complexity perspective. Among those moving up are Adam Smith, John Stuart Mill, Karl Marx, Alfred Marshall, and Friedrich Hayek. Those moving down include David Ricardo and Léon Walras. Those neutrally affected include both Thomas Robert Malthus and John Maynard Keynes, although each of them is partly moving up and partly moving down. He concludes by elevating both Charles Babbage and John von Neumann, whom he sees as important precursors of the later development of complexity research more generally.

Notes

1. Curiously the one person to appear in all three of these volumes was William Brock, quoted at the beginning of this Introduction.
2. Catastrophe theory in particular came in for much ridicule from Horgan and others. See Rosser (2007) for further discussion.
3. The least represented was the first, although it has arguably resurfaced most clearly in the newer heterogeneous agents complexity. It had two branches: cybernetics proper, founded by Norbert Wiener (1961), and system dynamics founded by Jay W. Forrester (1961). See Richardson (1991) for a discussion of the relationship between these two.
4. See Rosser (2000, Ch. 2) for a fuller discussion of the mathematical underpinnings of these developments.

References

Albin, Peter S. (1982), "The Metalogic of Economic Predictions, Calculations, and Predictions," *Mathematical Social Sciences*, **3**(4), 329–58.

Anderson, Philip W., Kenneth J. Arrow, and David Pines (eds) (1988), *The Economy as an Evolving Complex System*, Redwood City, CA: Addison-Wesley.

Andronov, A.A. (1928), "Poincaré's Limit Cycles and the Theory of Oscillations," *Doklady Akademii Nauk*, **6**.

Arnol'd, Vladimir I. (1992), *Catastrophe Theory*, 3rd edn, Berlin: Springer-Verlag.

Arthur, W. Brian, Steven N. Durlauf, and David A. Lane (eds) (1997), *The Economy as an Evolving Complex System II*, Reading, MA: Addison-Wesley.

Blume, Lawrence E. and Steven N. Durlauf (eds) (2006), *The Economy as an Evolving Complex System III: Current Directions and Future Prospects*, New York: Oxford University Press.

Cantor, Georg (1883), "Über unendliche, lineare Punktmannigfatigkeiten V," *Mathematische Annelen*, **21**, 545–91.

Cayley, Sir Arthur (1879), "The Newton-Fourier Imaginary Problem," *American Journal of Mathematics*, **2**, 97.

Colander, David, Richard P.F. Holt, and J. Barkley Rosser, Jr. (2004), *The Changing Face of Economics: Conversations with Cutting Edge Economists*, Ann Arbor: University of Michigan Press.

Day, Richard H. (1994), *Complex Economic Dynamics, Volume I: An Introduction to Dynamical Systems and Market Mechanisms*, Cambridge, MA: MIT Press.

Forrester, Jay W. (1961), *Industrial Dynamics*, Cambridge, MA: MIT Press.

Gallegati, Mauro, Steve Keen, Thomas Lux, and Paul Ormerod (2006), "Worrying Trends in Econophysics," *Physica A*, **370**(1), 1–6.

Goodwin, Richard M. (1951), "The Nonlinear Accelerator and the Persistence of Business Cycles," *Econometrica*, **19**(1), 1–17.

Horgan, John (1997), *The End of Science: Facing the Limits of Scientific Knowledge in the Twilight of the Scientific Age*, New York: Broadway Books.

Kalecki, Michal (1935), "A Macrodynamic Theory of Business Cycles," *Econometrica*, **3**(3), 327–44.
Kolmogorov, Andrei N. (1941), "Local Structure of Turbulence in an Incompressible Liquid for Very Large Reynolds Numbers," *Doklady Akademii Nauk SSSR*, **30**(4), 299–303.
Lyapounov, A.N. (1892) [reprinted 1950], *Obshchaya Zadacha ob Restoichivosti Dvizheniya*, Mosow-Leningrad: Gosteklhizdat, (English translation, 1947, *The General Stability of Motion*, Annals of Mathematical Studies No. 17, Princeton: Princeton University Press).
Mandelbrot, Benoît B. (1983), *The Fractal Geometry of Nature*, 2nd edn, San Francisco: W.H. Freeman.
Mirowski, Philip (1989), *More Heat than Light: Economics as Social Physics, Physics as Nature's Economics*, Cambridge, MA: Cambridge University Press.
Poincaré, Henri (1899), *Les Méthodes Nouvelles de la Mécanique Celeste, Vols I–III*, Paris: Gauthier-Villars.
Rand, David (1978), "Exotic Phenomena in Games and Duopoly Models," *Journal of Mathematical Economics*, **5**(2), 173–84.
Richardson, George P. (1991), *Feedback Thought in Social Science and Systems Theory*, Waltham, MA: Pegasus Communications.
Rosser, J. Barkley, Jr. (1999), "On the Complexities of Complex Economic Dynamics," *Journal of Economic Perspectives*, **13**(4), 169–92.
Rosser, J. Barkley, Jr. (2000), *From Catastrophe to Chaos: A General Theory of Economic Discontinuities, Vol. I: Mathematics, Microeconomics, Macroeconomics, and Finance*, 2nd edn, Boston/Dordrecht: Kluwer Academic.
Rosser, J. Barkley, Jr. (ed.) (2004), *Complexity in Economics, Vols I–III: The Internationational Library of Critical Writings in Economics 174*, Cheltenham, UK and Northhampton, MA, USA: Edward Elgar.
Rosser, J. Barkley, Jr. (2007), "The Rise and Fall of Catastrophe Theory Applications in Economics: Was the Baby Thrown out with the Bathwater?," *Journal of Economic Dynamics and Control*, **31**(8), 3255–80.
Rosser, J. Barkley, Jr. (2008), Book Review of *The Economy as an Evolving Complex System III*, *Journal of Economic Behavior and Organization*, **61**(3–4), 797–800.
Rössler, Otto E. (1997), *Endophysics: The World as an Interface*, Singapore: World Scientific.
Schelling, Thomas C. (1971), "Dynamic Models of Segregation," *Journal of Mathematical Sociology*, **1**(2), 143–86.
Sharkovsky, A.N. (1964), "Coexistence of Cycles of a Continuous Map of a Line into Itself," *Ukrainskii Matemacheskii Zhurnal*, **16**, 61–71.
van der Pol, Balthasar and J. van der Mark (1927), "Frequency Demultiplication," *Nature*, **120**(3019), 363–4.
Weintraub, E. Roy (2002), *How Economics Became a Mathematical Science*, Durham, NC: Duke University Press.
Wiener, Norbert (1961), *Cybernetics: Or Control and Communication in the Animal and the Machine*, 2nd edn, Cambridge, MA: MIT Press.

2. Complexity and the economy*

W. Brian Arthur

Complexity

What exactly is complexity? Different people have different definitions and none is absolute. But common to all studies on complexity are systems with multiple elements adapting or reacting to the pattern these elements create. The elements might be cells in a cellular automaton, or ions in a spin glass, or cells in an immune system, and they may react to neighboring cells' states, or local magnetic moments, or concentrations of B and T cells—"elements" and the "patterns" they respond to vary from one context to another. But the elements adapt to the world—the aggregate pattern—they co-create. Time enters naturally here via adjustment and change: as the elements react, the aggregate changes, as the aggregate changes, elements react anew. Barring some asymptotic state or equilibrium reached, complex systems are systems in process, systems that constantly evolve and unfold over time. Thus, complexity in the sciences is not a discipline. It is a movement that takes process seriously.

Why did the complexity movement come along in the late 1970s and early 1980s? The answer is simple. Generally, complex systems have no analytic "solution." The patterns that are in the process of being formed are too complicated to be worked out analytically and hence are beyond analytic study. But with the computer we can do agent-based modeling: we can treat each element in the system as a computational object that responds to the pattern created by the others, and thereby observe how the overall pattern forms. Complexity as a movement came along in the late 1970s and early 1980s because at that time scientists got workstations.

Complex systems arise naturally in the economy. Economic agents, whether they are banks, consumers, firms, or investors, continually adjust their market moves, buying decisions, prices, and forecasts to the situation these moves or decisions or prices or forecasts together create. But unlike ions in a spin glass that react dumbly to their local magnetic field, economic "elements"—human agents—react with strategy and foresight by considering outcomes that *might* result as a consequence of behavior they *might* undertake. This adds a layer of complication to economics not experienced in physics or immunology.

Like most other sciences in pre-computer days, conventional economic theory chose not to study the unfolding of patterns its agents create, but rather to seek analytical solutions. To do this it needed to simplify its questions. Thus, conventional theory—the economic theory of the last 200 years—asks what behavioral elements (actions, strategies, expectations) are *consistent with* the aggregate patterns these behavioral elements co-create. For example, general equilibrium theory asks: What prices and quantities of goods produced and consumed are consistent with—would pose no incentives for change to—the overall pattern of prices and quantities in the economy's markets? Game theory asks: What strategies, moves, or allocations are consistent with—would promote an optimal outcome for an agent (under some criterion)—given the strategies, moves, allocations his or her rivals might choose? Rational expectations economics asks: What forecasts (or expectations) are consistent with—are on average validated by—the outcomes these forecasts and expectations together create? Conventional economics thus studies patterns in behavioral *equilibrium*, patterns that would induce no further reaction. In the last few years, economists, at the Santa Fe Institute, Stanford, Wisconsin, MIT, Chicago, and other institutions, have begun to broaden this equilibrium approach by turning to the question of how actions, strategies, or expectations might react in general to—might endogenously change with—the aggregate patterns these create (Anderson, Arrow, and Pines, 1988; Arthur, Durlauf and Lane, 1997; Blume and Durlauf, 2005; and Tesfatsion and Judd, 2006). And so, this complexity approach is not an adjunct to standard theory, but theory at a more general, out-of-equilibrium level. At this more general level, economic patterns sometimes simplify into a simple, homogeneous equilibrium; more often they are ever-changing, showing perpetually novel behavior and emergent phenomena.

Let me illustrate perpetual novelty with a classic study of Karl Lindgren (1991). Lindgren sets up a computerized tournament where strategies compete in randomly chosen pairs to play a repeated prisoner's dilemma game. Strategies that do well replicate and mutate. Ones that lose eventually die. Strategies can "deepen" by using deeper memory of their past moves and their opponent's. A strategy's success of course depends on the current population of strategies, and so the elements here—strategies—in a sense react to, or change with, the competitive world they together create.

In his computerized tournament Lindgren discovered that the simple strategies in use at the start went unchallenged for some time. Tit-for-tat and other simple strategies dominated at the start. But then other, deeper strategies emerged that were able to exploit the mixture of these simple ones. In time, yet deeper strategies emerged to take advantage of those, and so on. If strategies got "too smart"—too complicated—sometimes simple ones could exploit these. In this computer world of strategies, Lindgren found periods with very large numbers of diverse strategies in the population, and periods with few strategies; periods dominated by simple strategies, and periods dominated by deep strategies. But nothing ever settled down. In Lindgren's world, the set of strategies in use evolved and kept evolving in a world of perpetual novelty. This is unfamiliar to us in standard economics. Yet there is a realism about such dynamics with its unpredictable, emergent, and complicated sets of strategies. Chess play at the grand master level for example, evolves over decades and never settles down. Lindgren's system is simple, yet it leads to a dynamic of endless unfolding and evolution. This is typical of complex system studies.

Positive feedbacks

The type of systems I have described, where elements react to the pattern the elements create, become interesting if they contain nonlinearities or positive feedbacks. To get some idea of how positive and negative feedback work, imagine a tray with water poured on it. First consider negative feedback: under gravity alone, the water flows away from any accumulation of water. And trivially a single, equilibrium water level is reached. A physicist would say that a single phase or single mode emerges—the equilibrium level of the water. This outcome is unique and perfectly predictable. Now let us add positive feedback. Take the same tray, polish it, and spread a thin film of water on it. Now surface tension—a form of positive feedback—becomes important. Under surface tension an agglomeration of water tends to attract neighboring molecules, so we have a mixture of positive and negative feedback of molecules attracting one another and flowing away from water. What happens? Droplets form. Do the experiment once and you get a pattern of droplets; do the experiment again and in all likelihood you get a different pattern of droplets, even though you're careful to start out with the same conditions. When there are positive feedbacks, small differences in temperature, small quantum effects, get magnified and change the outcome. It's therefore history dependent. It's also a pattern: it can't be described by a single phase variable. It's not predictable. The presence of positive feedback leads to properties we associate with complexity.

In economics, positive feedback arises from increasing returns (Arthur, 1990b, 1994a). Standard economics usually assumes negative feedback, or diminishing returns, so as to ensure a unique, predictable equilibrium. If one firm gets too far ahead in the market, it runs into higher costs or some other negative feedback and the market is shared at a predictable, unique equilibrium. When we allow positive feedbacks or increasing returns, a different outcome arises. Suppose a new technology becomes available, nuclear power for example, in alternative versions A or B or

C (light water, heavy water, gas-cooled, and so on). And suppose each technology improves as it becomes more adopted—there are increasing returns. Then if one technology gets far enough ahead it gains advantage and eventually may dominate. (In the nuclear case, light-water reactors almost completely dominate in the United States.) Alternatively, consider the market for online services of a few years back, in which three major companies competed: Prodigy, CompuServe, and America Online (now AOL). As each gained in membership base it could offer a wider menu of services as well as more members to share specialized hobby and chatroom interests with—there were increasing returns to expanding the membership base. Prodigy was first in the market, but by chance and strategy American Online got far enough ahead to gain an unassailable advantage. Today it dominates. Under different circumstances, another rival might have taken the market. Notice the properties here: a multiplicity of potential "solutions"; the outcome actually reached is not predictable in advance; it tends to be locked in; it is not necessarily the most efficient economically; it is subject to the "adoption path" taken; and while the technologies may start equal, the outcome is asymmetrical. These properties have counterparts in nonlinear physics where similar positive feedbacks are present. What economists call multiple equilibria, nonpredictability, lock-in, inefficiency, historical path dependence, and asymmetry, physicists call multiple meta-stable states, nonpredictability, phase- or mode-locking, high-energy ground states, non-ergodicity, and symmetry breaking.

Increasing returns problems have been discussed in economics for a long time. More than 100 years ago in his *Principles*, Alfred Marshall (1890) noted that if firms gain advantage as their market share increases, then "the market goes to whichever firm first gets off to a good start." But the conventional, static equilibrium approach gets stymied by indeterminacy: if there is a multiplicity of equilibria, how might one be reached? The process-oriented, complexity approach suggests a way to deal with this. In the actual economy, "small random events" happen—in the technology case "random" design improvements, word-of-mouth recommendations. Over time, increasing returns magnify the cumulation of such events to "select" the outcome randomly. Thus, increasing returns problems in economics are best seen as dynamic *processes* with random events and natural positive feedbacks—as nonlinear stochastic processes. This shift from a static outlook into a process orientation is common to complexity studies. Increasing returns problems are being studied intensively in market allocation theory (Arthur, 1994a), economic network theory (Wilhite, 2006), the evolution of technology choice (Arthur, 1989), economic geography (Arthur, 1990a; Krugman, 1991), and the evolution of patterns of poverty and segregation (Durlauf, 1996). The common finding that economic structures can crystallize around small events and lock in is beginning to change policy in all these areas toward an awareness that governments should avoid both extremes of coercing a desired outcome or keeping strict hands off, and instead seek to push the system gently toward favored structures that can grow and emerge naturally. Not a heavy hand, not an invisible hand, but a nudging hand.

Expectational problems in economics

Once we adopt the complexity outlook, with its emphasis on the *formation* of structures rather than their given existence, problems involving prediction in the economy look different. The conventional approach asks what forecasting model (or expectations) in a particular problem, if given and shared by all agents, would be consistent with—would be on average validated by—the actual time series this forecasting model would in part generate. This "rational expectations" approach is valid. But it assumes that agents can somehow deduce in advance what model will work, and that everyone "knows" that everyone knows to use this model (the *common knowledge* assumption). What happens when forecasting models are not obvious and must be formed individually by agents who are not privy to the expectations of others?

Consider as an example my Bar or El Farol Problem (Arthur, 1994b). One hundred people must decide independently each week whether to show up at their favorite bar (El Farol in Santa Fe). The rule is that if a person predicts that more that 60 (say) will attend, he or she will avoid the crowds and stay home; if he or she predicts fewer than 60 he or she will go. Of interest are how the bar-goers each week might predict the numbers showing up, and the resulting dynamics of the numbers attending. Notice two features of this problem. Our agents will quickly realize that predictions of how many will attend depend on others' predictions of how many attend (because that determines their attendance). But others' predictions in turn depend on their predictions of others' predictions. Deductively there is an infinite regress, no "correct" expectational model that can be assumed to be common knowledge, and from the agents' viewpoint, the problem is ill-defined. (This is true for most expectational problems, not just for this special case.) Second, and diabolically, any commonalty of expectations gets broken up: if all use an expectational model that predicts *few* will go, *all* will go, invalidating that model. Similarly, if all believe *most* will go, *nobody* will go, invalidating that belief. Expectations will be *forced* to differ.

In 1994 I modeled this situation by assuming that as the agents visit the bar, they act inductively—they act as statisticians, each starting with a

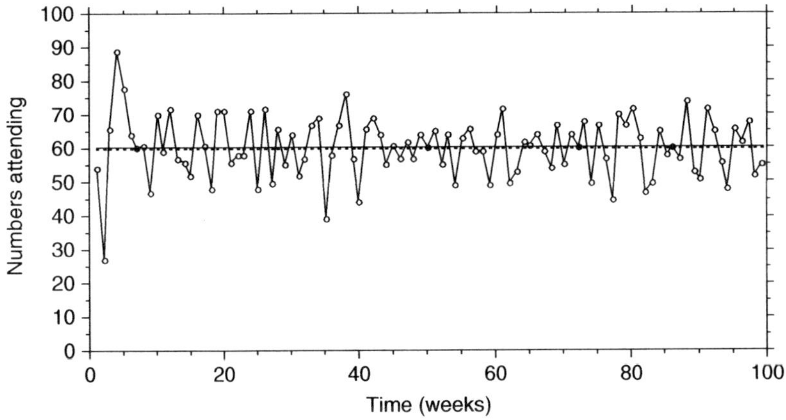

Source: Arthur, 1994b.

Figure 2.1 Bar attendance in the first 100 weeks

variety of subjectively chosen expectational models or forecasting hypotheses. Each week they act on their currently most accurate model (call this their *active* predictor). Thus, agents' beliefs or hypotheses compete for use in an *ecology* these beliefs create. Computer simulation (Figure 2.1) showed that the mean attendance quickly converges to 60. In fact, the predictors self-organize into an equilibrium pattern or "ecology" in which of the active predictors, on average 40 percent are forecasting above 60, 60 percent below 60. This emergent ecology is organic in nature. For, while the population of active predictors splits into this 60/40 average ratio, it keeps changing in membership forever. Why do the predictors self-organize so that 60 emerges as average attendance and forecasts split into a 60/40 ratio? Well, suppose 70 percent of predictors forecasted above 60 for a longish time, then on average only 30 people would show up. But then this would validate predictors that forecasted close to 30, restoring the "ecological" balance among predictions. Even though different predictors are used continually, over time the 40–60 percent "natural" combination becomes an emergent structure. As an expectational economy in miniature, the Bar Problem has become popular for study among physicists (Challet, Marsili, and Zhang, 2004; Coolen, 2005).

Financial markets

One important application of these ideas is in financial markets. Standard theories of financial markets assume rational expectations—that agents adopt uniform expectations (or forecasting models) that are on average validated by the prices these forecast (Lucas, 1978). The theory works well to first order. But it does not account for actual market "anomalies" such as unexpected price bubbles and crashes, random periods of high and low volatility (price variation), and the heavy use of technical trading (trades based on the recent history of price patterns). Holland, LeBaron, Palmer, Tayler, and I (Arthur et al., 1997) have created a model that relaxes rational expectations by assuming, as in the Bar Problem, that investors cannot assume or deduce expectations but must discover them. Our agents continually create and use multiple "market hypotheses"—individual, subjective, expectational models—of what moves the market price and dividend within an artificial stock market on the computer. These "investors" are individual, artificially intelligent computer programs that can generate and discard expectational "hypotheses," and make bids or offers based on their currently most accurate of these. The stock price forms endogenously from the bids and offers of the agents, and thus ultimately from their expectations. So this market-in-the-machine is its own self-contained, simple, artificial financial world, like the bar, a "mini-ecology" in which expectations compete in a world these expectations together create.

Within this computerized market, we found two phases or regimes. If parameters are set so that our artificial agents update their hypotheses slowly, the diversity of expectations collapses quickly into homogeneous rational expectations ones. The reason is that if a majority of investors believes something close to the rational expectations forecast, then resulting prices will validate it, and deviant or mutant predictions that arise in the population of expectational models will be rendered inaccurate. Standard finance theory, under these special circumstances, is upheld. But if the rate of updating of hypotheses is turned up, the market undergoes a phase transition into a "complex regime" and displays several of the "anomalies" observed in real markets. It develops a rich "psychology" of divergent beliefs that don't converge over time. Expectational rules such as "If the market is trending up, predict a 1 percent price rise" that appear randomly in the population of hypotheses can become mutually reinforcing: if enough investors act on these, the price will indeed go up. Thus, subpopulations of mutually reinforcing expectations arise, agents bet on these (therefore technical trading emerges) and this causes occasional bubbles and crashes. Our artificial market also shows periods of high volatility in prices followed randomly by periods of low volatility. This is because if some investors "discover" new, profitable hypotheses, they change the market slightly, causing other investors to also change *their* expectations. Changes in beliefs therefore ripple through the market in avalanches of all sizes, causing periods of high and low volatility. We conjecture that actual financial markets, which show exactly these phenomena, lie in this "complex" regime.

Conclusion

After two centuries of studying equilibria—static patterns that call for no further behavioral adjustments—economists are beginning to study the general emergence of structures and unfolding of patterns in the economy. In the actual economy, agents continually adjust their behaviors to the aggregate "pattern" these behaviors create. Economic theory has always recognized this, but until recently has simplified its approach to the identification of equilibrium states, where agents' behaviors are consistent with the aggregates these behaviors imply. In the last few years, economists are turning to the wider question of how agents might continually respond endogenously to the patterns they create. Complexity economics is not a minor adjunct to static economic theory, it is economics done out-of-equilibrium—economics done in a more general way.

The complexity approach has made itself felt in every area of economics: game theory (Lindgren, 1992; Blume, 1997); the theory of money and finance (Marimon, McGratton, and Sargent, 1990; Hommes, 2006; LeBaron, 2006); learning in the economy (Sargent, 1993; Darley and Kauffman, 1997); the evolution of networks (Ioannides, 1997; Wilhite, 2006); the stability of the economy (Bak et al., 1993); and political economy (Kollman, Miller, and Page, 2006). And several collections of papers have now appeared, most prominently those of Anderson, Arrow, and Pines (1988); Arthur, Durlauf, and Lane (1997); Blume and Durlauf (2005); and Tesfatsion and Judd (2006). The approach is helping us understand phenomena such as market instability, the emergence of monopolies, and the persistence of poverty in ways that will help us deal with these. And it is bringing an awareness that policies succeed better by influencing the natural processes of formation of economic structures than by forcing static outcomes.

When viewed in out-of-equilibrium formation, economic patterns sometimes simplify into a simple, homogeneous equilibrium of standard economics. More often they are ever-changing, showing perpetually novel behavior and yielding emergent phenomena. Complexity therefore portrays the economy not as deterministic, predictable, and mechanistic; but as process-dependent, organic, and always evolving.

Note

* This chapter is an extended version of a paper that appeared in *Science*, 2 April 1999, **284**(5411), 107–9.

References

Anderson P., K.J. Arrow, and D. Pines (eds) (1988), *The Economy as an Evolving Complex System*, Reading, MA: Addison-Wesley.

Arthur, W.B. (1989), "Competing Technologies, Increasing Returns and Lock-in by Historical Events," *Economic Journal*, **99**(394), 106–31.

Arthur, W.B. (1990a), "Silicon Valley Locational Clusters: When do Increasing Returns Imply Monopoly?," *Mathematical Social Sciences*, **19**(3), 235–51.

Arthur, W.B. (1990b), "Positive Feedbacks in the Economy," *Scientific American*, **262**(2), 92–9.

Arthur, W.B. (1994a), *Increasing Returns and Path Dependence in the Economy*, Ann Arbor: University of Michigan Press.

Arthur, W.B. (1994b) "Bounded Rationality and Inductive Behavior (the El Farol Problem)," *American Economic Review Papers and Proceedings*, **84**(2), 406–11.

Arthur, W.B. (1999) "Complexity and the Economy," *Science*, **284**(5411), 107–9.

Arthur, W.B., S.N. Durlauf, and D.A. Lane (eds) (1997), *The Economy as an Evolving Complex System II*, Reading, MA: Addison-Wesley.

Arthur, W.B., J.H. Holland, B. LeBaron, R. Palmer, and P. Tayler (1997), "Asset Pricing Under Endogenous Expectations in an Artificial Stock Market," in W.B. Arthur, S.N. Durlauf, and D.A. Lane (eds), *The Economy as an Evolving Complex System II*, Reading, MA: Addison-Wesley, pp. 15–44.

Bak, P., K. Chen, J. Scheinkman, and M. Woodford (1993), "Aggregate Fluctuations from Independent Sectoral Shocks," *Ricerche Economiche*, **47**(1), 3–30.

Blume, L.E., (1997), "Population Games," in W.B. Arthur, S.N. Durlauf, and D.A. Lane (eds), *The Economy as an Evolving Complex System II*, pp. 425–60.

Blume, L.E. and S.N. Durlauf (eds) (2005), *The Economy as an Evolving Complex System III*, New York: Oxford University Press.

Challet, D., M. Marsili, and Y-C. Zhang (2004), *Minority Games*, Oxford: Oxford University Press.

Coolen, A.C.C. (2005), *The Mathematical Theory of Minority Games*, Oxford: Oxford University Press.

Darley, V.M. and S.A. Kauffman (1997), "Natural Rationality," in W.B. Arthur, S.N. Durlauf, and D.A. Lane (eds), *The Economy as an Evolving Complex System II*, pp. 45–80.

Durlauf, S.N. (1996), "Statistical Mechanics Approaches to Socioeconomic Behavior," in W.B. Arthur, S.N. Durlauf, and D.A. Lane (eds), *The Economy as an Evolving Complex System II*, pp. 81–104, and in *Journal of Economic Growth*, **1**(1), 75.

Hommes, C. (2006), "Heterogeneous Agent Models in Economics and Finance," in L. Tesfatsion and K. Judd (eds), *Handbook of Computational Economics, Vol. 2*, pp. 1109–86.

Ioannides, Y.M. (1997), "The Evolution of Trading Structures," in W.B. Arthur, S.N. Durlauf, and D.A. Lane (eds), *The Economy as an Evolving Complex System II*, pp. 129–68.

Kollman, K., J. Miller, and S. Page (2006), "Computational Methods and Models of Politics," in L. Tesfatsion and K. Judd (eds), *Handbook of Computational Economics, Vol. 2*, pp. 461–90.

Krugman, P.R. (1991), *Geography and Trade*, Cambridge, MA: MIT Press.

LeBaron, B. (2006), "Agent-based Computational Finance," in L. Tesfatsion and K. Judd (eds), *Handbook of Computational Economics, Vol. 2*, pp. 1187–233.

Lindgren, K. (1992), "Evolutionary Phenomena in Simple Dynamics," in C.G. Langton, C. Taylor, J.D. Farmer, and S. Rasmussen (eds), *Artificial Life II*, Reading MA: Addison-Wesley, pp. 295–312.

Lucas, R.E. (1978), "Asset Prices in an Exchange Economy," *Econometrica*, **46**(6), 1429–45.

Marimon R., E. McGrattan, and T.J. Sargent (1990), "Money as a Medium of Exchange in an Economy with Artificially Intelligent Agents," *Journal of Economic Dynamics and Control*, **14**(2), 329–73.

Marshall A. (1890), *Principles of Economics*, London: Macmillan.
Sargent T.J. (1993), *Bounded Rationality in Macroeconomics*, Oxford: Clarendon Press.
Tesfatsion, L. and K. Judd (eds) (2006), *Handbook of Computational Economics, Vol. 2: Agent-based Computational Economics*, Amsterdam: Elsevier/North-Holland.
Wilhite, A.W. (2006), "Economic Activity on Fixed Networks," in L. Tesfatsion and K. Judd (eds), *Handbook of Computational Economics, Vol. 2*, pp. 1035–45.

3. Computational and dynamic complexity in economics

*J. Barkley Rosser, Jr.**

3.1 Introduction

As reported by Horgan (1997, p. 305), Seth Lloyd has gathered at least 45 definitions of complexity. Rosser (1999) argued for the usefulness in studying economics of a definition he called *dynamic complexity* that was originated by Day (1994). This is that a dynamical economic system fails to generate convergence to a point, a limit cycle, or an explosion (or implosion) endogenously from its deterministic parts. It was argued that nonlinearity was a necessary but not sufficient condition for this form of complexity,[1] and that this definition constituted a suitably broad "big tent" to encompass the "four Cs" of *cybernetics, catastrophe, chaos*, and "small tent" (or heterogeneous agents) *complexity*. Other approaches used in economics have included *structural* (Pryor, 1995; Stodder, 1995),[2] *hierarchical* (Simon, 1962), and *computational* (Lewis, 1985; Albin with Foley, 1998; Velupillai, 2000).

In recent years (Markose, 2005; Velupillai, 2005a, b, c) there has been a tendency to argue that the latter concept is superior because of its foundation on more well-defined ideas, such as *algorithmic* complexity (Chaitin, 1987) and *stochastic* complexity (Rissanen, 1989, 2005). These are seen as founded more deeply on work of Shannon (1948) and Kolmogorov (1983). Mirowski (2007) argues that markets themselves should be seen as algorithms that are evolving to higher levels in a Chomskyian (1959) hierarchy of computational systems, especially as they increasingly are carried over computers and become resolved through programmed double-auction systems and the like. McCauley (2004, 2005) and Israel (2005) argue that such dynamic complexity ideas as *emergence* are essentially empty and should be abandoned for either more computational-based ones or more physics-based ones, the latter especially relying on *invariance* concepts.

In contrast, this chapter will argue that while these ideas serve useful purposes, dynamic complexity and such concepts as emergence are useful for understanding economic phenomena and are not as incoherent and undefined as has been argued. A sub-theme of some of this literature, although not all of it, has been that biologically based models or arguments are fundamentally unsound mathematically and should be avoided in more analytical economics. Instead, this chapter will argue that such approaches can be used in conjunction with the dynamic complexity approach to explain emergence mathematically and that such approaches can explain certain economic phenomena that may not be easily explained otherwise.

3.2 Computationally based arguments

Velupillai (2000, pp. 199–200) summarizes the foundations of what he has labeled "*computable economics*",[3] in the following:

> Computability and randomness are the two basic epistemological notions I have used as building blocks to define computable economics. Both of these notions can be put to work to formalize economic theory in effective ways. However, they can be made to only on the basis of two theses: the Church-Turing thesis, and the Kolmogorov-Chaitin-Solomonoff thesis.

Church (1936) and Turing (1937) independently realized that several broad classes of functions could be described as "recursive" and were "calculable" (programmable computers had not yet been invented). Turing (1936–37) was the first to realize that Gödel's (1931) incompleteness theorem provided a foundation for understanding when problems were not "calculable," called "effectively computable" since Tarski (1949). Turing's analysis introducing the generalized concept of the Turing machine, now viewed as the model for a rational economic agent within computable economics (Velupillai, 2005c, p. 181). While the original Gödel theorem relied upon a Cantor diagonal proof arising from self-referencing,[4] the classic manifestation of non-computability in programming is the *halting problem*, that a program will simply run forever without ever reaching a solution (Blum et al., 1998).

Much of recent computable economics has involved showing that when one tries to put important parts of standard economic theory into forms that might be computable, it is found that they are not effectively computable in any general sense. These include Walrasian equilibria (Lewis, 1991), Nash equilibria (Prasad, 1991; Tsuji, da Costa, and Doria, 1998), more general aspects of macroeconomics (Leijonhufvud, 1993), and whether a dynamical system will be chaotic or not (da Costa and Doria, 2005).[5]

Indeed, what are viewed as dynamic complexities can arise from computability problems that arise in jumping from a classical and continuous, real number framework to a digitized, rational numbers-only framework. An example is the curious "finance function" of Clower and Howitt (1978) in which solution variables jump back and forth over large intervals discontinuously as the input variables go from integers, to non-integer rationals to irrational numbers and back. Velupillai (2005c, p. 186) notes the case of a Patriot missile missing its target by 700 meters and killing 28 soldiers as "friendly fire" in Dhahran, Saudi Arabia in 1991 due to a computer's non-terminating cycling through a binary expansion on a decimal fraction. Finally, the discovery of chaotic sensitive dependence on initial conditions by Lorenz (1963) because of computer round-off error is famous, a case that is computable but undecidable.

There are actually several computability based definitions of complexity, although Velupillai (2000, 2005b, c) argues that they can be linked as part of the broader foundation of computable economics. The first is the Shannon (1948) measure of information content, which can be interpreted as attempting to observe structure in a stochastic system. It is thus derived from a measure of entropy in the system, or its state of disorder. Thus, if p(x) is the probability density function of a set of K states denoted by values of x, then the *Shannon entropy* is given by

$$\mathrm{H(X)} = -\sum_{x=1}^{\mathrm{K}} \ln(\mathrm{p}(x)). \tag{3.1}$$

From this it is trivial to obtain the *Shannon information content* of $\mathrm{X} = x$ as

$$\mathrm{SI}(x) = \ln(1/\mathrm{p}(x)). \tag{3.2}$$

It came to be understood that this equals the number of bits in an algorithm that it takes to compute this code. This would lead Kolmogorov (1965) to define what is now known as *Kolmogorov complexity* as the minimum number of bits in any algorithm that does not prefix any other algorithm a(x) that a universal Turing machine (UTM) would require to compute a binary string of information, x, or,

$$\mathrm{K}(x) = \min |\mathrm{a}(x)|, \tag{3.3}$$

where | | denotes length of the algorithm in bits.[6] Chaitin (1987) would independently discover and extend this *minimum description length* (MDL) concept and link it back to Gödel incompleteness issues, his version being known as algorithmic complexity, which would get taken up later by Albin (1982) and Lewis (1985) in economic contexts.[7]

While these concepts usefully linked probability theory and information theory with computability theory, they all share the unfortunate aspect of being non-computable. This would be remedied by the introduction of stochastic complexity by Rissanen (1978, 1986, 1989, 2005). The intuition behind Rissanen's modification of the earlier concepts is to focus not on the direct measure of information but to seek a shorter description or model that will depict the "regular features" of the string. For Kolmogorov a model of a string is another string that contains the first string. Rissanen (2005, pp. 89–90) defines a likelihood function for a given structure as a class of parametric density functions that can be viewed as respective models, where θ represents a set of k parameters and x is a given data string indexed by n:

$$M_k = \{f(x^n, \theta): \theta \in \mathbf{R}^k). \tag{3.4}$$

For a given f, with $f(y^n)$ a set of "normal strings," the *normalized maximum likelihood function* will be given by

$$f^*(x^u, M_k) = f(x^n, \theta^*(x^n))/[\int_{\theta(yn)} f(y^n, \theta(y^n))dy^n], \tag{3.5}$$

where the denominator of the right-hand side can be defined as being $C_{n,k}$.

From this the stochastic complexity is given by

$$-\ln f^*(x^n, M_k) = -\ln f(x^n, \theta^*(x^n)) + \ln C_{n,k}. \tag{3.6}$$

This term can be interpreted as representing "the 'shortest code length' for the data x^n that can be obtained with the model class M_k" (Rissanen, 2005, p. 90). With this we have a computable measure of complexity derived from the older ideas of Kolmogorov, Solomonoff, and Chaitin. The bottom line of Kolmogorov complexity is that a system is complex if it is not computable. The supporters of these approaches to defining economic complexity (Israel, 2005; Markose, 2005; Velupillai, 2005b, c) point out the precision given by these measures in contrast to so many of the alternatives.

3.3 Dynamic complexity and emergence

In contrast with the computationally defined measures described above, the dynamic complexity definition stands out curiously as essentially for its negativity: dynamical systems that do *not* endogenously and deterministically generate certain "well-behaved" outcomes. The charge that it is not precise carries weight. However, the virtue of it is precisely its generality guaranteed by its vagueness. It can apply to a wide variety of systems and processes that many have described as being "complex." Of course, the computationalists argue with reason that they are able to subsume substantial portions of nonlinear dynamics with their approach, as, for example, with the already mentioned result on the non-computability of chaotic dynamics (da Costa and Doria, 2005).

However, most of this recent debate and discussion, especially by Israel (2005), McCauley (2005), and Velupillai (2005b, c) has focused on a particular outcome that is associated with some interacting agents models within the smaller tent complexity part of the broader big tent dynamic complexity concept. This property or phenomenon is *emergence*. It was much discussed by cyberneticists and general systems theorists (von Bertalanffy, 1962), including under the label *anagenesis* (Boulding, 1978; Jantsch, 1982), although it was initially formalized by Lloyd Morgan (1923), drawing upon the idea of *heteropathic laws* due to Mill (1843, Book III).[8] Much recent discussion has focused on Crutchfield (1994) because he has associated it more clearly with processes within computerized systems of interacting heterogeneous agents and linked it to minimum length computability concepts related to Kolmogorov's idea, which makes it easier for the computationalists to deal with. In any case, the idea is of the dynamic appearance of something new endogenously and deterministically from the system, often also labeled *self-organization*.[9] Furthermore, all of these cited here would add another important element, that it appears at a higher level within a dynamic hierarchical system as a result of processes occurring at lower levels of the system. Crutchfield (1994) allows that what is involved is symmetry breaking bifurcations, which leads McCauley (2005, pp. 77–8) to be especially dismissive, identifying it with biological models (Kaufmann, 1993) and declaring that "so far no one has produced a clear empirically relevant or even theoretically clear example." The critics complain of implied *holism* and Israel identifies it with Wigner's (1960) "mystical" alienation from the solidly grounded view of Galileo.

Now the complaint of McCauley amounts to noting an apparent lack of invariance, a lack of ergodicity or steady state equilibria, with clearly identifiable symmetries whose breaking brings about these higher-level reorganizations or transformation:

> We can understand how a cell mutates to a new form, but we do not have a model of how a fish evolves into a bird. That is not to say that it has not happened, only that we do not have a model that helps us to imagine the details, which must be grounded in complicated cellular interactions that are not understood. (McCauley, 2005, p. 77)[10]

While he is probably correct that the details of these interactions are not fully understood, a footnote on the same page points in the direction of some understanding that has appeared, not tied directly to Crutchfield or Kaufmann. McCauley notes the work of Hermann Haken (1983) and his "examples of bifurcations to pattern formation via symmetry breaking." Several possible approaches suggest themselves at this point.

The first is a direct argument by biochemists Eigen and Schuster (1979) ironically enough regarding the preservation, reproduction, and transmission of information content in genetical systems. They label the first appearance of self-reproducing biochemical structures as the *hypercycle*, "the simplest system that can allow the evolution of reproducible links" (ibid., p. 87). They propose a *threshold of information content*. Below this threshold the system can stabilize itself against the accumulation of errors in self-reproduction. Above it will occur an *error catastrophe* that results in the "disintegration of information due to a steady accumulation of errors" (op. cit., p. 25). Assuming that V is the number of symbols, $\sigma > 1$ is the degree of "superiority of the master copy," and q is the quality of symbol copying, then the threshold below which the number of symbols must remain is given by

$$V < \ln \sigma/(1 - q). \qquad (3.7)$$

Hypercycle formation has been simulated by Mosekilde, Rasmussen, and Sorenson (1983) and the concept has been applied to the evolution of market structures based on differential rates of learning among firms by Silverberg, Dosi, and Orsenigo (1988).

It has also been linked with the concept of *autopoesis*, defined as the stable reproduction of a space–time structure (Varela, Maturana, and Uribe, 1974). While Turing defined *morphogenesis* as structural differentiation due to bifurcation at a single level, anagenesis within a hierarchical system of a new, self-reproducing hierarchical level that is self-reproducing has been labeled *hypercyclic morphogenesis* by Rosser (1991, 1992) or the *anagenetic moment* by Rosser et al. (1994). Some of the early models of hypercycle formation required the absence of parasites, however with appropriate mixing, they may be stable against parasites (Boerlijst and Hogeweg, 1991).

This raises parallels within evolutionary game theoretic models of the issue of multilevel evolution (Henrich, 2004), with the Price-Hamilton equations providing sufficient conditions for this to occur, although the original version of these was due to Crow (1955). For its discrete form, if ΔC is the single generation change mean value of the trait in the whole population, B_w and B_b are the within- and between-group genetic regressions of fitness on the value of the trait, V_w and V_b the within and between-group genetic variances, and W the mean population fitness, then

$$\Delta C = (B_w V_w + B_b V_b)/W. \qquad (3.8)$$

This allows for a statement of Hamilton's (1972) condition for an altruistic trait to increase (the equivalent of cooperation at a higher level) as

$$B_w/(B_b - B_w) < r, \qquad (3.9)$$

where r is the Sewall Wright coefficient of relationship (Crow and Aoki, 1984). The left-hand side can be interpreted as a cost-of-fitness to benefit-minus-cost-of-fitness ratio.

Another approach is that of *synergetics* due to Haken (1983), alluded to above. This deals more directly with the concept of entrainment of oscillations via the *slaving principle* (Haken, 1996), which operates on the principle of *adiabatic approximation.* A complex system is divided into order parameters that are presumed to move slowly in time and "slave" faster-moving variables or subsystems. While it may be the that the order parameters are operating at a higher hierarchical level, which would be consistent with many generalizations made about relative patterns between such levels (Allen and Hoekstra, 1992; Holling, 1992), this is not necessarily the case, and the variables may well be fully equivalent in a single, flat hierarchy, such as with the control and state variables in catastrophe theory models. Stochastic perturbations can lead to structural change near bifurcation points.

If slow dynamics are given by vector **F**, fast dynamics generated by vector **Q**, with **A, B**, and **C** being matrices, and $\boldsymbol{\varepsilon}$ a stochastic noise vector, then a locally linearized version is given by

$$\mathrm{d}\mathbf{q} = \mathbf{Aq} + \mathbf{B(F)q}\ \mathbf{C(F)} + \boldsymbol{\varepsilon}. \tag{3.10}$$

Adiabatic approximation is given by

$$\mathrm{d}\mathbf{q} = -(\mathbf{A} + \mathbf{B(F)})^{-1}\mathbf{C(F)}. \tag{3.11}$$

Fast variable dependence on the slow variables is given by $\mathbf{A} + \mathbf{B(F)}$. Order parameters are those of the least absolute value.

The symmetry-breaking bifurcation occurs when the order parameters destabilize by obtaining eigenvalues with positive real parts, while the "slave variables" exhibit the opposite. Chaos is one possible outcome. However, the most dramatic situation is when the slaved variables destabilize and "revolt" (Diener and Poston, 1984), with the possibility of the roles switching within the system and former slaves replacing the former "bosses" to become the new order parameters. An example in nature of such an emerging and self-organizing entrainment might be the periodic and coordinated appearance of the slime mold out of separated amoebae, which later disintegrates back into its isolated cells (Garfinkel, 1987).

Finally there is the model of Nicolis (1986), derived from the work of Nicolis and Prigogine (1977) on frequency entrainment. Rosser et al. (1994) have argued that this can serve as a possible model for the anagenetic moment, or the emergence of a new level of hierarchy. Let there be n well-defined levels of the hierarchy, with $\mathbf{L}_1$ at the bottom and $\mathbf{L}_n$ at the top. A new level, $\mathbf{L}_{n+1}$, or dissipative structure, can emerge at a phase transition with a sufficient degree of entrainment of the oscillations at that level. Let there be k oscillating variables, x_j and $z_i(t)$ be an i.i.d. exogenous stochastic process with zero mean and constant variance, then dynamics are given by the coupled, nonlinear differential equations of the form

$$dx_i/dt = f_i(x_j, t) + z_i(t) + \Sigma_j{=}_1{}^k \int_1{}^k x_j(t')\mathbf{w}_{ij}(t' + \tau)dt', \qquad (3.12)$$

with $\mathbf{w}_{ij}$ representing a cross-correlation matrix operator. The third term is the key, either being "on" or "off," with the former showing frequency entrainment. Nicolis (1986) views this in terms of a model of neurons, with a *master hard nonlinear oscillator* being turned on by a symmetry breaking of the cross-correlation matrix operator when the probability distribution of the real parts of its eigenvalues exceed zero.[11] Then a new variable vector will emerge at the $\mathbf{L}_{n+1}$ level that is y_j, which will dampen or stimulate the oscillations at level $\mathbf{L}_n$, depending on whether the sum over them is below or above zero.

3.4 Discussion and conclusions

Needless to say, most of the models discussed in this last section would not impress most of the adherents of the computability approach to complexity. To the extent that the models discussed have axiomatic foundations rather than being merely ad hoc, which many of them ultimately are, these foundations are strictly within the non-constructivist, classical mathematical mode, assuming the axiom of choice, the law of the excluded middle, and other hobby horses of the everyday mathematicians and mathematical economists. To the extent that they provide insight into the nature of dynamic economic complexity and the special problem of emergence (or anagenesis), they do not do so by being based on axiomatic foundations[12] that would pass muster with the constructivists and intuitionists of the early and mid-20th century, much less their more recent disciples, who are following the ideal hope that "The future is a minority; the past and present are a majority," to quote Velupillai (2005b, p. 13), himself paraphrasing Shimon Peres from an interview about the prospects for Middle East peace.

In any case, even if the future belongs to computable complexity, there is a considerable array of models available for contemplating or modeling emergent phenomena operating at different hierarchical levels. I would suggest at this point that a potentially interesting area to see which of the approaches might prove to be most suitable may well be in the study of the evolution of market processes as they themselves become more computerized. This is the focus of Mirowski (2007) who goes so far as to argue that fundamentally markets *are* algorithms. The simple kind of posted price, spot market most people have traditionally bought things in is at the bottom of a Chomskyian hierarchy of complexity and self-referenced control. Just as newer algorithms may contain older algorithms within them, so the emergence of newer kinds of markets can contain and control the older kinds as they move to higher levels in this Chomskyian hierarchy. Futures markets may control spot markets, options markets may control futures markets, and the ever higher order of these markets and their increasing automation pushes the system to a higher level towards the unreachable ideal of being a full-blown universal Turing machine (Cotogno, 2003).

Mirowski brings to bear more recent arguments in biology regarding coevolution, noting that the space in which the agents and systems are evolving itself changes with their evolution. To the extent that the market system increasingly resembles a gigantic assembly of interacting and evolving algorithms, both biology and the problem of computability will come to bear and influence each other (Stadler et al., 2001). In the end the distinction between the two may become irrelevant.

In that regard what may become more important as the system moves to higher-order levels will be the old struggle between the continuous and the discrete, with such intermediate compromises such as those posed in Blum et al. (1998) looming as more important over time. While this struggle may result in system-wide crashes or failures due to the sorts of computer errors that pushed the Patriot missile 700 meters off in 1991, more likely will be an outcome in which the way that a particular algorithm or system behaves or interacts with the other parts will depend on how it looks at the system and from which level. In that regard, I conclude with a quote from Joseph Schumpeter (1939, pp. 226–7).

> Our theory of the mechanism of change stresses discontinuity. It takes the view that, as we may put it, evolution proceeds by successive revolutions, or, that there are in the process jerks or jumps which account for many of its features. As soon, however, as we survey the history of society or of any particular sector of social life, we become aware of a fact which seems at first sight to be incompatible with that view: every change seems to consist in the accumulation of many small influences and events and comes about precisely by steps so small as to make any exact dating and any sharp distinction of epochs almost meaningless. . . Now it is important to note that there is no contradiction whatever between our theory and a theory of history which bases itself on those facts. What difference there is, is a difference of purpose and method only. This becomes evident if we reflect that any given industrial development, for instance the electrification of the household, may involve many discontinuities incident to the setting up of new production functions when looked at from the standpoint of individual firms and yet appear, when looked at from other standpoints as a continuous process proceeding

steadily from roots centuries back. By one of the many roughnesses or even superficialities forced upon us by the nature of the task this volume is to fulfill, we may characterize this as a difference between microscopic and macroscopic points of view: there is as little contradiction between them as there is between calling the contour of a forest discontinuous for some and smooth for other purposes.

Notes

* The author wishes to thank K. Vela Velupillai for providing materials and discussion of interest and also for his hospitality and that of his colleagues at the University of Trento. He also wishes to thank Joseph L. McCauley and E. Roy Weintraub for providing materials and interesting discussion and Philip Mirowski for providing useful materials. The usual caveat applies.

1. This is incorrect. Goodwin (1947) showed such endogenous dynamic patterns in coupled linear systems with lags. Similar systems were analyzed by Turing (1952) in his paper that has been viewed as the foundation of the theory of morphogenesis, a complexity phenomenon par excellence. However, the overwhelming majority of such dynamically complex systems involve some nonlinearity, and the uncoupled normalized equivalent of the coupled linear system is nonlinear.
2. Structural complexity appears in the end to amount to "complicatedness," which Israel (2005) argues is merely an epistemological concept rather than an ontological one, with "complexity" and "complicatedness" coming from different Latin roots (*complecti*, "grasp, comprehend, or embrace" and *complicare*, "fold, envelop"), even if many would confuse the concepts (including even von Neumann, 1966). Rosser (2004) argues that complicatedness as such poses essentially trivial epistemological problems, how to figure out a lot of different parts and their linkages.
3. "Computable economics" was neologized by Velupillai in 1990 and is distinguished from "computational economics," symbolized by the work one finds at conferences of the Association for Computational Economics and its journal, *Computational Economics*. The former focuses more on the logical foundations of the use of computers in economics while the latter tends to focus more on specific applications and methods.
4. Implications of self-referencing as related to Gödel's incompleteness theorem have been studied by Binmore (1987) and Koppl and Rosser (2002). One issue that can arise is multiple levels of conscious playing, one player thinking about the other player thinking about the first player thinking about the other player and so on up to n-levels (Bacharach and Stahl, 2000).
5. Another main theme of computable economics involves considering which parts of economic theory can be proved when such classical logical axioms are relaxed as the axiom of choice and the exclusion of the middle. Under such *constructive* mathematics, problems can arise for proving Walrasian equilibria (Pour-El and Richards, 1979; Richter and Wong, 1999; Velupillai, 2002, 2006) and Nash equilibria (Prasad, 2005), although, we shall not pursue such themes here further.
6. It should be understood that whereas on the one hand Kolmogorov's earliest work axiomatized probability theory, his efforts to understand the problem of induction would lead him to later argue that information theory precedes probability theory (Kolmogorov, 1983). McCall (2005) provides a useful discussion of this evolution of Kolmogorov's views.
7. Closely related would be the universal prior of Solomonoff (1964) that puts the MDL concept into a Bayesian framework. From this comes the rather neatly intuitive idea that the most probable state will also have the shortest length of algorithm to describe it. Solomonoff's work was also independently developed, drawing on the probability theory of Keynes (1921).
8. I thank K. Vela Velupillai for making me aware of these arguments. Lloyd Morgan was a key part of what is now known as the "British emergentist" school of thought (McLaughlin, 1992).

9. This term has been especially associated with Bak (1996) and his *self-organized criticality*, although he was not the first to discuss self-organization in these contexts.
10. McCauley's argument is based on Moore's (1990, 1991a, b) study of low dimensional, iterated maps that are Turing machines without attractors, scaling properties, or symbolic dynamics. McCauley argues that this view provides a foundation for complexity as ultimate surprise and unpredictability.
11. In a related model, Holden and Erneux (1993) show that the systemic switch may take the form of a slow passage through a supercritical Hopf bifurcation, thus leading to the persistence for a while of the previous state even after the bifurcation point has been passed.
12. While this movement focuses on refining axiomatic foundations, it ultimately seeks to be less formalistic and Bourbakian. This is consistent with the history of mathematical economics, which first moved towards a greater axiomatization and formalism within the classical mathematical paradigm, only to move away from it in more recent years (Weintraub, 2002).

References

Albin, Peter S. (1982), "The metalogic of economic predictions, calculations and propositions," *Mathematical Social Sciences*, **3**(4), 329–58.

Albin, Peter S. with Duncan K. Foley (1998), *Barriers and Bounds to Rationality: Essays on Economic Complexity and Dynamics in Interacting Systems*, Princeton: Princeton University Press.

Allen, T.F.H. and Thomas W. Hoekstra (1990), *Toward a Unified Ecology*, New York: Columbia University Press.

Bacharach, M. and Dale O. Stahl (2000), "Variable-frame level-n theory," *Games and Economic Behavior*, **32**(2), 220–46.

Bak, Per (1996), *How Nature Works: The Science of Self-organized Criticality*, New York: Copernicus Press for Springer-Verlag.

Binmore, Ken (1987), "Modeling rational players I," *Economics and Philosophy*, **3**, 9–55.

Blum, Lenore, Felipe Cucker, Michael Shub, and Steve Smale (1998), *Complexity and Real Computation*, New York: Springer-Verlag.

Boerlijst, M.C. and P. Hogeweg (1991), "Spiral wave structure in pre-biotic evolution," *Physica D*, **48**(1), 17–28.

Boulding, Kenneth E. (1978), *Ecodynamics: A New Theory of Social Evolution*, Beverly Hills: Sage.

Chaitin, Gregory J. (1987), *Algorithmic Information Theory*, Cambridge, UK and New York: Cambridge University Press.

Chomsky, Noam (1959), "On certain formal properties of grammars," *Information and Control*, **2**(2), 137–67.

Church, Alonzo (1936), "A note on the *Entscheidungsproblem*," *Journal of Symbolic Logic*, **1**(1), 40–41, correction 101–2.

Clower, Robert W. and Peter W. Howitt (1978), "The transactions theory of the demand for money: a reconsideration," *Journal of Political Economy*, **86**(31), 449–65.

Cotogno, Paolo (2003), "Hypercomputation and the physical Church-Turing thesis," *British Journal for the Philosophy of Science*, **54**(2), 181–223.

Crow, James F. (1955), "General theory of population genetics: synthesis," *Cold Spring Harbor Quantitative Symposium on Biology*, **20**, 54–9.

Crow, James F. and Kenichi I. Aoki (1984), "Group selection for a polygenic behavioral trait: Estimating the degree of population subdivision," *Proceedings of the National Academy of Sciences U.S.A.*, **81**(19), 2628–31.

Crutchfield, James (1994), "The calculi of emergence: computation, dynamics and induction," *Physica D*, **75**(1–8), 11–54.

da Costa, Newton C.A., and Francisco A. Doria (2005), "Computing the future," in Velupillai (2005a), pp. 15–50.

Day, Richard H. (1994), *Complex Economic Dynamics, Volume I: An Introduction to Dynamical Systems and Market Mechanisms*, Cambridge, MA: MIT Press.
Diener, Marc and Tim Poston (1984), "The perfect delay convention and the revolt of the slaved variables," in Hermann Haken (ed.), *Chaos and Order in Nature*, 2nd edn, Berlin: Springer-Verlag, pp. 249–68.
Eigen, Manfred and Peter Schuster (1979), *The Hypercycle: A Natural Principle of Self-organization*, Berlin: Springer-Verlag.
Garfinkel, Alan (1987), "The slime mold *Dictosteliam* as a model of self-organization in the social systems," in F. Eugene Yates (ed.), *Self-organizing Systems: The Emergence of Order*, New York: Plenum Press, pp. 181–212.
Gödel, Kurt (1931), "Uber formal unentscheidbare satze principia mathematica und verwandter systeme I", *Monatshefte für Mathematik und Physik*, **38**, 173–98.
Goodwin, Richard M. (1947), "Dynamical coupling with especial reference to markets having production lags," *Econometrica*, **15**(3), 181–204.
Haken, Hermann (1983), *"Synergetics:" An Introduction. Nonequilibrium Phase Transitions in Physics, Chemistry, and Biology*, 3rd edn, Berlin: Springer-Verlag.
Haken, Hermann (1996), "The slaving principle revisited," *Physica D*, **97**(1–3), 95–103.
Hamilton, W.D. (1972), "Altruism and related phenomena, mainly in the social insects," *Annual Review of Ecology and Systematics*, **3**, 192–232.
Henrich, Joseph (2004), "Cultural group selection, coevolutionary processes and large-scale cooperation," *Journal of Economic Behavior and Organization*, **53**(1), 3–35.
Holden, Lisa and Thomas Erneux (1993), "Understanding bursting oscillations as periodic slow passage through bifurcation and limit points," *Journal of Mathematical Biology*, **31**(4), 351–65.
Holling, C.S. (1992), "Cross-scale morphology, geometry, and dynamics of ecosystems," *Ecological Monographs*, **62**(4), 447–502.
Horgan, John (1997), *The End of Science: Facing the Limits of Knowledge in the Twilight of the Scientific Age*, New York: Broadway Books (paperback edition).
Israel, Giorgio (2005), "The science of complexity: epistemological problems and perspectives," *Science in Context*, **18**, 1–31.
Jantsch, Erich (1982), "From self-reference to self-transcendence: The evolution of self-organization dynamics," in William C. Schieve and Peter M. Allen (eds), *Self-organization and Dissipative Structures*, Austin: University of Texas Press, 344–53.
Kaufmann, Stuart A. (1993), *The Origins of Order: Self-organization and Selection in Evolution*, Oxford: Oxford University Press.
Keynes, John Maynard (1921), *A Treatise on Probability*, London: Macmillan.
Kolmogorov, A.N. (1965), "Three approaches to the quantitative definition of information," *Problems of Information Transmission*, **1**(1), 4–7.
Kolmogorov, A.N. (1983), "Combinatorial foundations of information theory and the calculus of probabilities," *Russian Mathematical Surveys*, **38**(4), 29–40.
Koppl, Roger and J. Barkley Rosser, Jr. (2002), "All I have to say has already crossed your mind," *Metroeconomica*, **53**(4), 339–60.
Leijonhufvud, Axel (1993), "Towards a not-too-rational macroeconomics," *Southern Economic Journal*, **60**(1), 1–13.
Lewis, Alain A. (1985), "On effectively computable realizations of choice functions," *Mathematical Social Sciences*, **10**, 43–80.
Lewis, Alain A. (1991), "On Turing degress of Walrasian models and a general impossibility result in the theory of decision making," Mimeo, School of Social Sciences, University of California-Irvine.
Lloyd Morgan, C. (1923), *Emergent Evolution*, London: Williams and Norgate.
Lorenz, Edward N. (1963), "Deterministic non-periodic flow," *Journal of Atmospheric Sciences*, **20**(2), 130–41.
Markose, Sheri M. (2005), "Computability and evolutionary complexity: Markets as complex adaptive systems (CAS)," *The Economic Journal*, **115**(504), F159–F192.
McCall, John J. (2005), "Induction," in Velupillai (2005a), pp. 105–31.

McCauley, Joseph L. (2004), *Dynamics of Markets: Econophysics and Finance*, Cambridge, UK: Cambridge University Press.
McCauley, Joseph L. (2005), "Making mathematics effective in economics," in Velupillai (2005a), pp. 51–84.
McLaughlin, Bryan P. (1992), "The rise and fall of British emergentism," in A. Beckerman, H. Flohr, and J. Kim (eds), *Emergence or Reduction? Essays on the Prospects of Nonreductive Physicalism*, Berlin: Walter de Gruyter, pp. 49–93.
Mill, John Stuart (1843), *A System of Logic: Ratiocinative and Inductive*, London: Longmans Green.
Mirowski, Philip (2007), "Markets come to bits: evolution, computation and markomata in economic science," *Journal of Economic Behavior and Organization*, **63**(2), 209–42.
Moore, Christopher (1990), "Undecidability and unpredictability in dynamical systems," *Physical Review Letters*, **64**, 2354–7.
Moore, Christopher (1991a), "Generalized shifts: Undecidability and unpredictability in dynamical systems," *Nonlinearity*, **4**, 199–230.
Moore, Christopher (1991b), "Generalized one-sided shifts and maps of the interval," *Nonlinearity*, **4**, 727–45.
Mosekilde, Erik, Steen Rasmussen, and Torben S. Sorenson (1983), "Self-organization and stochastic re-causalization in systems dynamics models," in J.D.W. Morecroft, D.F. Anderson, and J.D. Sterman (eds), *Proceedings of the 1983 System Dynamics Conference*, Chestnut Hill, MA: Pine Manor College, pp. 128–60.
Nicolis, Grégoire and Ilya Prigogine (1977), *Self-organization in Nonequilibrium Systems: From Dissipative Structures to Order through Fluctuations*, New York: Wiley-Interscience.
Nicolis, John S. (1986), *Dynamics of Hierarchical Systems: An Evolutionary Approach*, Berlin: Springer-Verlag.
Pour-El, Marian Boykan and Ian Richards (1979), "A computable ordinary differential equation which possesses no computable solution," *Annals of Mathematical Logic*, **17**, 61–90.
Prasad, Kislaya (1991), "Computability and randomness of Nash equilibria in infinite games," *Journal of Mathematical Economics*, **20**(5), 429–42.
Prasad, Kislaya (2005), "Constructive and classical models for results in economics and game theory," in Velupillai (2005a), pp. 132–47.
Pryor, Frederic L. (1995), *Economic Evolution and Structure: The Impact of Complexity on the U.S. Economic System*, New York: Cambridge University Press.
Richter, M.K. and K.C. Wong (1999), "Non-computability of competitive equilibrium," *Economic Theory*, **14**(1), 1–28.
Rissanen, Jorma (1978), "Modeling by shortest data description," *Automatica*, **14**(5), 465–71.
Rissanen, Jorma (1986), "Stochastic complexity and modeling," *Annals of Statistics*, **14**(3), 1080–100.
Rissanen, Jorma (1989), *Stochastic Complexity in Statistical Inquiry*, Singapore: World Scientific.
Rissanen, Jorma (2005), "Complexity and information in modeling," in Velupillai (2005a), 85–104.
Rosser, J. Barkley, Jr. (1991), *From Catastrophe to Chaos: A General Theory of Economic Discontinuities*, Boston: Kluwer, Vol. I, 2nd edition, 2000, Mathematics, Microeconomics, Macroeconomics, and Finance series. Boston: Kluwer.
Rosser, J. Barkley, Jr. (1992), "The dialogue between the ecologic and the economic theories of evolution," *Journal of Economic Behavior and Organization*, **17**(2), 195–215.
Rosser, J. Barkley, Jr. (1999), "On the complexities of complex economic dynamics," *Journal of Economic Perspectives*, **12**(4), 169–92.
Rosser, J. Barkley, Jr. (2004), "Epistemological implications of economic complexity," *Annals of the Japan Association for Philosophy of Science*, **13**(1), 45–57.
Rosser, J. Barkley, Jr., Carl Folke, Folke Günther, Heikki Isomäki, Charles Perrings, and Tönu Puu (1994), "Discontinuous change in multilevel hierarchical systems," *Systems Research*, **11**(3), 77–94.

Schumpeter, Joseph A. (1939), *Business Cycles*, New York: McGraw-Hill.
Shannnon, C.E. (1948), "A mathematical theory of communication," *Bell Systems Technical Journal*, **27**(3), 379–423, 623–56.
Silverberg, Gerald, Giovanni Dosi, and Luigi Orsenigo (1988), "Innovation, diversity and diffusion: a self-organization model," *The Economic Journal*, **98**(393), 1032–54.
Simon Herbert A. (1962), "The architecture of complexity," *Proceedings of the American Philosophical Society*, **106**(6), 467–82.
Solomonoff, R.J. (1964), "A formal theory of inductive inference Parts I and II," *Information and Control*, **7**(1), 1–22, 224–54.
Stadler, Barbel, Peter Stadler, Gunter Wagner, and Walter Fontana (2001), "The topology of the possible: Formal spaces underlying patterns of evolutionary change," *Journal of Theoretical Biology*, **213**(2), 241–74.
Stodder, James P. (1995), "The evolution of complexity in primitive economies: theory," *Journal of Comparative Economics*, **20**(1), 1–31.
Tarski, Alfred (1949), Abstract, "On essential undecidability," *Journal of Symbolic Logic*, **14**(1), 75–6.
Tsuji, Marcelo, Newton C.A. da Costa, and Francisco A. Doria (1998), "The incompleteness theories of games," *Journal of Philosophical Logic*, **27**(6), 553–68.
Turing, Alan M. (1936–37), "On computable numbers, with an application to the *Entscheidungsproblem*," *Proceedings of the London Mathematical Society*, *Series 2*, **42**, 230–65, correction 1937, ibid., **43**, 544–6.
Turing, Alan M. (1937), "Computability and λ-definability," *Journal of Symbolic Logic*, **2**, 153–63.
Turing, Alan M. (1952), "The chemical basis of morphogenesis," *Philosophical Transactions of the Royal Society B*, **237**(641), 37–72.
Varela, Francisco G., Humberto R. Maturana, and R. Uribe (1974), "Autopoesis: the organization of living systems, its characterization and a model," *Biosystems*, **5**(4), 187–96.
Velupillai, K. Vela (2000), *Computable Economics*, Oxford: Oxford University Press.
Velupillai, K. Vela (2002), "Effectivity and constructivity in economic theory," *Journal of Economic Behavior and Organization*, **49**(3), 307–25.
Velupillai, K. Vela (ed.) (2005a), *Computability, Complexity and Constructivity in Economic Analysis*, Victoria: Blackwell.
Velupillai, K. Vela (2005b), "Introduction," in Velupillai (2005a), pp. 1–14.
Velupillai, K. Vela (2005c), "A primer on the tools and concepts of computable economics," in Velupillai (2005a), pp. 148–97.
Velupillai, K. Vela (2006), "Algorithmic foundations of *computable* general equilibrium theory," *Applied Mathematics and Computation*, **179**(1), 360–69.
von Bertalanffy, Ludwig (1962), *General Systems Theory*, New York: Braziller.
von Neumann, John (1966), *Theory of Self-reproducing Automata*, edited and compiled by Arthur W. Burks, Urbana: University of Illinois Press.
Weintraub, E. Roy (2002), *How Economics Became a Mathematical Science*, Durham, NC: Duke University Press.
Wigner, Eugene (1960), "The unreasonable effectiveness of mathematics in the natural sciences," *Communications in Pure and Applied Mathematics*, **13**(1), 1–14.

4. A computable economist's perspective on computational complexity

*K. Vela Velupillai**

4.1 Prologue

> There are many levels of complexity in problems, and corresponding boundaries between them. Turing computability is an outer boundary, . . . any theory that requires more power than that surely is irrelevant to any useful definition of human rationality. A slightly stricter boundary is posed by computational complexity, especially in its common 'worst case' form. We cannot expect people (and/or computers) to find exact solutions for large problems in computationally complex domains. This still leaves us far beyond what people and computers actually CAN do. The next boundary . . . is computational complexity for the 'average case' . . . . That begins to bring us closer to the realities of real-world and real-time computation. Finally, we get to the empirical boundary, measured by laboratory experiments on humans and by observation, of the level of complexity that humans actually can handle, with and without their computers, and – perhaps more important – what they actually do to solve problems that lie beyond this strict boundary even though they are within some of the broader limits. (Herbert Simon, letter to the author, 25 May 2000)

As it happens, Herbert Simon's lucid letter to me, delineating a rough ordering along the complexity scale for problem-solving by means of a machine model of computation, was dated 25 May 2000. The day before, on 24 May 2000, Arthur Jaffe, as the then President of the Clay Mathematical Institute, had announced the seven millennium problems,[1] the solutions for which – in the form of a proof or a counterexample – would earn prizes of a million dollars each. It was also fittingly, at least in the context of this brief chapter, announced to commemorate the centennial of Hilbert's famous lecture on 'Mathematical Problems', given at the meeting of the International Congress of Mathematicians in Paris, in August, 1900. Fittingly, because the most enduring model of computation underpinning almost all the frontier developments in computational complexity theory is the Turing machine. This device was conceived and implemented by Alan Turing in the process of answering the *Entshceidungsproblem*, formulated by Hilbert, as a way of answering unambiguously and decisively, Brouwer's sustained criticisms of standard mathematics and its methodological bases, particularly its proof theoretical underpinnings. The earliest formulation, at least by Hilbert, of the *Entshceidungsproblem* can be traced back to the tenth of Hilbert's 23 problems in that famous Paris Lecture of 1900.

The fourth in the alphabetic list of seven problems is the quintessential problem of computational complexity theory: P = ?NP. Computational complexity theory is doubly related to mathematical economics and economic theory:[2] first, as a theory of the efficiency of computations, it is best viewed as the economic theory of computations; second, having at its central core the paradigmatic combinatorial, intractable, NP-complete, (in)famous TSP: the travelling salesperson's problem.[3] In the former case, it must first be remembered that the pure theory of computations abstracts away from all kinds of resource constraints; computational complexity theory, the 'applied' theory of computation, is its finessing, taking explicit account of resource constraints, typically time and space constraints.

Computational complexity theory considers problem-solving, with a model of computation explicitly underpinning it, as *decision problems*.[4] In these two aspects it differs fundamentally from economics: in economics, whether in its mathematical modes or not, there is no explicit model of computation underpinning its optimization problem formulation – which is the second sense in which it differs from economic theory; that is, in economics the quintessential problem-solving framework is one of *constrained optimization*, albeit without ever incorporating a model of computation that underpins the construction, detection or computation of the optimum. Generally, the latter can be transformed into a form of the former (see below for an explicit and paradigmatic example of converting an integer linear programming (ILP) problem into a conjunctive normal form (CNF) decision problem).

Anyone who tries to learn a programming language is introduced to it, in the very first lesson or lecture, via instructions on how to write a simple program, such as: Print, 'Hello, World'; or: Print, '*n*', where '*n*' is an arbitrary, given, integer. But anyone who tries to learn the theory of programming is taught, again in the very first lecture, that *there is no algorithm for finding the shortest program for printing such an integer, 'n', and halting*! Put another way, this negative answer is for the following absolutely simple 'minimization' problem:

Problem 1 Find the (or one of the) shortest programs for printing a given integer *n*, and halting.

At a much more sophisticated level of abstract computational complexity theory, there is a kind of analog of this simple non-maximization result.

Theorem 2 Blum's speedup theorem[5]

$\forall$ complexity measures – that is, criteria of optimization, $\exists$ total recursive functions such that, $\nexists$ optimal programs – that is, algorithms – to compute them.

Whatever the underlying model of computation, my own view is that the best way to introduce the subject of computational complexity theory to economists would be by way of a three-stage process. First, an introduction to economics in the computational mode;[6] this entails an underpinning of economic theory in the mathematics of recursion theory or constructive analysis, both of which are intrinsically algorithmic. Second, a discussion of the intrinsic complexity of the kind of functions and sets that are in the domain of recursion theory and constructive analysis; that is, the intricacy of the functions and sets, quite apart from the difficulty of actually computing them. Finally, an analysis of the computational complexity of the functions and sets; that is, the actual difficulty of computing the functions or deciding membership or other properties of the sets. But such a strategy is clearly not feasible within the limited scope of one chapter. Therefore, I will have to forego any and all discussions of the abstract approach to computational complexity theory, an area pioneered by Manuel Blum. I will also have to eschew any attempt at introducing an economic theory in its computational mode. Instead, I will have to remain at a fairly superficial level of the concrete, applied part of recursion theory. Regrettably, therefore, I shall not be able to develop the full implications of the above kind of fundamental theorems – the speedup, the gap and the compression theorems – in this chapter. The perceptive reader will know how to keep these results at the back of the mind – and if such an elusive person also equips him or herself with an idea of Simon's behavioural economic research program – or to seek them out, when, and if, the issues I will actually discuss lead to questions about orthodox formulations of mathematical economics in general, and choice theory in particular.

The three most important classes of decision problems that almost characterize the subject of computational complexity theory are the P, NP and NP-complete classes. Concisely, but not quite precisely, they can be described as follows. P defines the class of computable problems that are solvable in time bounded by a polynomial function of the size of the input; NP is the class of computable problems for which a solution can be verified in polynomial time; and a computable problem lies in the class called NP-complete if every problem that is in NP can be reduced to it in polynomial time.

It is important to observe the following features characterizing these three classes (and will, eventually, come to characterize every finer, nuanced, classification, too). First, the classification is of computable problems; second the ubiquity of 'polynomial' in the definitions; third the role of the two notions of 'verify' and 'reduce'. Finally, conspicuous by its absence is any mention of how, in the case of the class NP, one arrived at a solution that is verifiable in polynomial time. Magic, intuition, leap of faith, appeal to oracles, ESP, whatever, is allowed in finding solutions; only algorithmic means are allowed in verifying their truth status. One of the greatest 'solution finders' was Srinivasa Ramanujan; one of the great algorithmic problem-solvers was George Polya. There was once, in fact, an interesting encounter between the 'magician' and the problem-solver (albeit – as befits a magician – many years after his death). It illustrates the real life conundrums of verifying solutions versus devising them, in the first place (Srinivasa, 1998, p. 13, emphasis added):

> One day in 1951 while Polya was visiting Oxford, he borrowed from Hardy his copy of Ramanujan's notebooks. A couple of days later, Polya returned them in almost a state of panic explaining that however long he kept them he would have to keep attempting to *verify* the formulae therein and never again would have time to *establish* another original result of his own.

4.1.1 Preamble

> The 'P versus NP' question . . . focuses on a simplified view of the goals of (efficient) computations. Specifically, [this focuses] on efficient procedures that *always* gives the *exact* answer. In practice, one may be content with efficient procedures that 'typically' give an 'approximate' answer. (Goldreich, 2001, p. 522, emphasis in original)

Economists, flushed with the wide and easy availability of powerful symbol-manipulating software packages, such as Mathematica and Matlab, and the ubiquity of the computer, approximate, compute and evaluate almost indiscriminately. Is there any issue, of any reputable journal in economics, with a modicum of computations, estimations or simulations, let alone serious mathematical calculations, devoid of arbitrary Taylor series expansions, thoughtless linearizations and gratuitous statements about choosing analytically simple functions ('without loss of generality', as the cliché goes!) that facilitates computations without approximations?

Efficiency of computations and approximations are highlighted in the questions posed in Borwein and Borwein (1988), given below in the opening quote of the next section. They are the two decisive features characterizing the theory of computational complexity. Moreover, it must be kept in mind that economic theory is predominantly mathematized in terms of real analysis. Hence, any consideration of the computational complexity of economic processes, economically motivated functional assumptions and economic computations must focus on some kind of real number model of computation. I shall also try to discuss some aspects of such issues in this chapter.

The chapter is divided into four main sections, in addition to this Prologue. Each of the main sections are sub-divided into further subsections dealing with more focused topics.

The next section, 4.2, 'Preliminaries', is sub-divided into three subsections. In the first subsection, some of the terminological and conceptual ideas and hurdles are outlined with examples. In the next sub-section, I look at decision problems as optimization problems. In the following sub-section, titled 'Exotica', I illustrate some conceptual issues that figure crucially in computational complexity theory; notions such as easy and fast verification of a proposed result or theorem, the speed of convergence, the nature of the growth of functions and the subtle and nuanced differences between deriving a theorem and verifying its truth value.

Section 4.3 is a mixture of historical settings for classic problems of computational complexity theory and frontier topics in the subject.

Section 4.4 is a telegraphic presentation and critical discussion of a model of real computation, recently advocated with tremendous conviction in Blum et al. (1998).

In the concluding Section 4.5, there is an attempt to reflect on the future of a more computationally oriented economic theory, where questions of the efficiency of computations and approximations can be posed and discussed more coherently and consistently. Related speculative thoughts on alternative, constructively founded, mathematical economics suggests that Herbert Simon's research programme is the only hope for those of us who want to be able to analyse the efficiency of computations.

Appendix A at the end of the chapter takes a closer look at algorithmic complexity theory.

4.2 Preliminaries

4.2.1 Approximating π, Deciding γ, Calculating 2^{64} and all that!

> The kinds of questions we pose are:
> (1) How much work (by various types of *computational* or *approximation* measures) is required to *evaluate n* digits of a *given function* or *number*?
> (2) How do analytic properties of a function relate to the *efficacy* with which it can be *approximated*?
> (3) To what extent are analytically *simple* numbers or functions also easy to *compute*?
> (4) To what extent is it easy to *compute analytically simple functions*? Even partial answers to these questions are likely to be very difficult.
> (6) Why is the Taylor series often *the wrong way to compute familiar functions*?
> (Borwein and Borwein, 1998, p. 589, emphasis added)

'Given function' is a phrase that would make sense to most analytically minded people, especially those who are in the habit of interpreting the notion of a function as a rule (rather than the Dirichlet-Kuratowski inspired interpretation as a 'graph'). But what is the meaning of a 'given number', particularly a 'given *real* number'? Take, for example, π. By definition, it is 'the ratio of the circumference to the diameter of a circle'. Given this definition, n digits of it can be evaluated – that is, $\exists$ an algorithm to evaluate it, say, to $n = 20$ digits: 3.14159265358979323846. Is there any other way a real number can be 'given', except by a rule defining it? Suppose the defining rule for a real number – or, even a function – is non-constructive; what can be done to 'evaluate' it? What, indeed, can be done to 'approximate' it? Archimedes inscribed polygons to approximate the circumference of the inscribing circle. Is there, then, a 'fastest' algorithm to inscribe a polygon to a 'given' circle? How fast does an algorithm to evaluate the circumference of a given circle converge?

A slightly more exotic example is Euler's constant,[7] usually denoted by γ. To the best of my knowledge, to this day, we do not even know whether it is rational or not, even though the formula defining it has the appearance of being a well-defined algorithm.[8]

Most readers will be aware of the famous example of the request for just one grain of rice on the first square of a chessboard and, then, a doubling, sequentially, on each of the remaining 63 squares, by the winner of a game of chess against a mythical King.[9] We all know – depending on the initial condition – that the 64th square would require the King to place 2^{64} grains of rice on that final one! This monstrosity emerges naturally in a 'simple' and 'small' typical combinatorial economic problem. There is no more paradigmatic example of intractability than that quintessential economic combinatorial problem: the travelling salesperson's problem (TSP). Consider the following TSP[10] (see Figure 4.1).

The distance between each of the nodes is ten miles. Then:

Problem 3 Can the salesman start at node 1 and visit each of the nodes in a journey of 70 miles?

This classic TSP problem can be converted to the following equivalent satisfiability problem of the prepositional calculus:

Problem 4 Assign truth values to A_t^m such that the following prepositional formula is true:

$$E = J \& V \& N \& A_1^0 \tag{4.1}$$

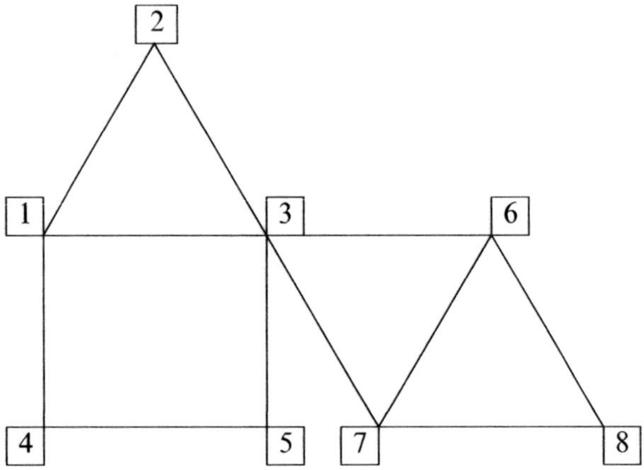

Source: Austin, 1983, p. 398.

Figure 4.1 TSP

Where:

A_t^m: the salesman is at node t, after $10 \times m$ miles;
$J_y^x \doteq (A_i^m \rightarrow (A_1^{m+1} \vee A_2^{m+1} \vee \ldots \vee A_{i-1}^{m+1} \vee A_{i-1}^{m+1} \vee \ldots \vee A_7^{m+1}))$;
and each A_i^m is true.

Put:

$$J = J_1^0 \& J_2^0 \& \ldots . \& J_8^0 \& J_1^1 \& J_2^1 \& \ldots .. \& J_8^1 \& \ldots ... \& J_8^6$$

Each node has to be visited:

$$A_i^0 \vee \ldots ... \vee A_i^7; \forall i = 1, \ldots, 7$$

Put:

$$V = \wedge \ (A_i^0 \vee \ldots ... \vee A_i^7); \forall i = 1, \ldots, 8$$

Denote the condition that the salesman can only be at one node at a time by:

$$N_i^j = (A_i^j \rightarrow \sim A_1^j) \ \& \ (A_i^j \rightarrow \sim A_2^j) \ \ldots .. \ (A_i^j \rightarrow \sim A_8^j)$$

Put:

$$N = \bigwedge (N_i^j); \forall i = 1,\ldots,8; j = 0,\ldots,7$$

How many possible truth value assignments have to be tried for (4.1)? There are 64 different values of A_t^m, for which truth assignments of T, F have to be tried: that is, 2^{64}!

Frankly, almost all the questions of computability, computational complexity and approximation theories can be framed in the context of the above seemingly simple problems. The hallmark of the weird and wonderful world of complexity theory is its feature – which I have tried to illustrate with the above examples – of hiding intricacies and intractabilities behind a facade of simplicities. Lurking behind the simple formulations, assertions and frames are the curses of dimensionality, exponential growth and logical depth.

4.2.2 Decision problems as optimization problems

> Alternatively, you might *find* a polynomial-time algorithm for an NP-complete problem. If you do, then you have, in effect, found polynomial-time algorithms for *all* NP problems, and the Clay Mathematics Institute will make you a millionaire. But that million will pale beside what you you'll gain by cracking all the cryptographic systems based on the difficulty of NP problems.
> (Cipra, 2002, p. 87, original emphasis)

Consider the following three-variable Boolean formula:

$$\neg x_3 \wedge (x_1 \vee \neg x_2 \vee x_3) \tag{4.2}$$

Just as in the case of equations with integer (or rational) values, given a truth assignment $t(x_i) = 1$ or 0 for each of the variables x_i $(i = 1, \ldots 3)$, the above Boolean formula can be evaluated to be true or false, globally. For example, the following assignments gives it the value *true*: $t(x_1) = 1$; $t(x_2) = 1$; $t(x_3) = 0$. Boolean formulas that can be made true by some truth assignments are said to be *satisfiable*.

Now consider the Boolean formula:

$$(x_1 \vee x_2 \vee x_3) \wedge (x_1 \vee \{\neg x_2\}) \wedge (x_2 \vee \{\neg x_3\}) \\ \wedge (x_3 \vee \{\neg x_1\}) \wedge (\{\neg x_1\} \vee \{\neg x_2\} \vee \{\neg x_3\}) \tag{4.3}$$

Remark 5 Each subformula within parenthesis is called a clause; the variables and their negations that constitute clauses are called literals; it is 'easy' to 'see' that for the truth value of the above Boolean formula to be true all the subformulas within each of the parenthesis will have to be true. It is equally 'easy' to see that no truth assignments whatsoever can satisfy the formula such that its global value is true. This Boolean formula is *unsatisfiable*.

Problem 6 SAT – the satisfiability problem

Given m clauses, $C_i(i = 1, \ldots, m)$, containing the literals (of) $x_j(j = 1, \ldots, n)$, determine if the formula $C_1 \wedge C_2 \wedge \ldots \ldots \wedge C_m$ is satisfiable. Determine means 'find an (efficient) algorithm'. To date it is not known whether there is an efficient algorithm to solve the satisfiability problem – that is, to determine the truth value of a Boolean formula. In other words, it is not known whether SAT $\in$ P. But:

Theorem 7 SAT $\in$ NP

Now to go from here to an optimization framework is a purely mechanical affair. Denoting the union operator as ordinary addition and the negation operator related to arithmetic operators as: $\neg x = (1 - x)$ and noting that it is necessary, for each clause C, there should, at least, be one true literal, we have, for any formula:

$$\sum_{x \in C} x + \sum_{x \in C} (1 - x) \geq 1 \tag{4.4}$$

With these conventions, the previous Boolean formula becomes the following integer linear programming (ILP) problem:

$$x_1 + x_2 + x_3 \geq 1 \tag{4.5}$$

$$x_1 + (1 - x_2) \geq 1 \tag{4.6}$$

$$x_2 + (1 - x_3) \geq 1 \tag{4.7}$$

$$x_3 + (1 - x_1) \geq 1 \tag{4.8}$$

$$(1 - x_1) + (1 - x_2) + (1 - x_3) \geq 1 \tag{4.9}$$

$$0 \leq x_1, x_2, x_3 \leq 1, \text{ and integer} \tag{4.10}$$

Definition 8 A Boolean formula consisting of many clauses connected by conjunction (that is, $\wedge$) is said to be in conjunctive normal form (CNF).

Remark 9 A CNF is satisfiable iff the equivalent ILP has a feasible point.

Clearly, the above system of equations and inequalities does not, as yet, represent an ILP since there is no 'optimization'. However, it can be turned into a complete ILP in the ordinary sense by, for example, replacing the first of the above inequalities into:

$$Max\ y, \text{ such that: } x_1 + x_2 + x_3 \geq y \tag{4.11}$$

Remark 10 The formula is satisfiable iff the optimal value of y, say $\hat{y}$ exists and satisfies $\hat{y} \geq 1$.

Finally, we have Cook's famous theorem, rounding off all these connections and bringing into the fold of computational complexity theory, the quintessential combinatorial economic optimization problem:

Theorem 11 Cook's theorem

SAT is NP-complete.

4.2.3 Exotica

4.2.3.1 The question of 'fast and easy verifiability' In the Preface to Mersenne's *Cogitata Physico-Mathematica*, a proposition about perfect numbers[11] implies, $\forall p \leq 257$, $(p \in \mathbb{N})$, $2^p - 1$ is prime only for $p = 2, 3, 5, 7, 13, 17, 19, 31, 67, 127$ and 257. This proposition, made in 1644, was falsified five times between 1883 and 1922, for 61, 67, 89, 107 and 257. The most memorable of the falsifications, at least anecdotally, (Wigderson, 2006),[12] was the one by F.N. Cole in a talk given to the American Mathematical Society on 31 October 1903. Apparently, without uttering a word, he is reputed to have gone to the blackboard and written:

$$2^{67} - 1 = 193707721 \times 761838257287$$

Professor Cole is then supposed to have proceeded 'to perform the long multiplication of the integers on the right-hand side to derive the integer on the left'. Given the probable mathematical calibre of the audience, it is not surprising that no questions were asked!

This example highlights six aspects of a key issue in computational complexity theory, remembering that its mathematical foundations lie in computability theory. First of all, the falsification of the proposition can be achieved by showing, as Cole did with $p = 67$ (and Kraïchik did with $p = 257$), that one of the 11 values of p is composite; or, second, by showing that some of the other 245 possible values for p are, in fact prime (as was done for $p = 61$ by Pervusin, in 1883, and, for $p = 89$ and 167, by Powers, in 1914).[13] Third, by devising a general formula that provides a rigorous criterion, $\forall p > 2$, for verifying primality of $2^p - 1$, as was provided by D.H. Lehmer in 1931. Fourth, the correctness of Cole's factorization is easy to verify quickly: easy because long multiplication is an elementary process; quick, since the required multiplication can be speeded up almost indefinitely. Fifth, the 'proof' of Cole's result is almost scandalously short. Finally, how Cole (and Kraïchik) arrived at their results seems to be a non-issue; it may or may not have been hard.[14] On the other hand, the Lehmer criterion, built up from the method developed by Edouard Lucas, follows the usual mathematical development of a criterion or result as a theorem.

4.2.3.2 Approximation, convergence and divergence Smorynski (1985a, pp. 360–61) refers to Hardy's (1910) classic text on *Orders of Infinity* for the following two series and their convergence and divergence behaviours. First consider the following convergent series:

$$A{:}\sum_{n=3}^{\infty}\frac{1}{n\log n(\log\log n)^2}$$

This series converges to 38.43; however, it requires $10^{3.14 \times 10^{86}}$ terms before even a two-decimal accuracy can be achieved! What, under such circumstances, is the numerical content and computational meaning of 'convergence'?

Next, consider the series:

$$B{:}\sum_{n=3}^{\infty}\frac{1}{n\log n(\log\log n)}$$

This series diverges; however, 'the partial sums exceed 10 only after a googolplex of terms have appeared'! Does it matter, for an applied science, that this series diverges? Years ago, the distinguished Cambridge applied mathematician and polymath, Sir Harold Jeffreys, made a pertinent observation regarding divergent series in the context of applied sciences:

> Enough work has been done on asymptotic and other divergent series to prove that an infinite series may be useful in physical applications *without being convergent* in the sense defined in works on pure mathematics. It is less generally realized that the converse is equally true, that *a series may be convergent and yet be totally useless for the purpose of calculating the value of the function represented*...
>
> In evaluating a function one is limited to expansions that can be actually summed *numerically in the time available*, and it is therefore necessary that the first few terms shall give a good *approximation* to the function. Those terms once obtained, the rest of the series is of no interest to the physicist. (Jeffreys, 1926, pp. 241–2, emphasis added)

Jeffreys conflates, from the point of view of the applied sciences, the issues of numerical computation, convergence, divergence, approximation and the time constraint that should be considered in a numerical evaluation. All of these issues are explicitly and abundantly evident in the behaviour of the two series above, *A* and *B*. Computational complexity theory shares both the vices and virtues here. Being an asymptotic theory, computational complexity theory tends to disregard the kind of common-sense factors mentioned by Jeffreys. But when viewed as the economics of computability theory – that is, theories of the efficiency of computations – and against the backdrop that all efficiency theorems in economic theory are 'asymptotic theories', this is not necessarily an incongruence. Moreover, the efficiency criteria for computation considered in computational complexity theory is very explicit in a fundamental way about time resources. Finally, there is the issue of approximation. Here, even in computational complexity theory – but, perhaps, not in algorithmic complexity theory[15] – the important distinction between the theory of exact approximation and the approximations intrinsic to numerical analysis is never made explicit, even in the new and innovative theory of computational complexity of real computations developed by Blum and Smale and their associates (Blum et al., 1998).

4.2.3.3 Growth of functions and orders of growth

> If we drop the requirement of computability – well, there is Tibor Rado's Busy Beaver Function. This irrepressible little fellow grows more rapidly than any theoretically computable function – a feat of not particularly great magnitude.
> (Smorynski, 1985b, p. 377)

In economics the implications of exponential expansion is most vividly illustrated in the 'power of compound interest',[16] via neoclassical models of pure growth[17] and in Malthusian population theory. In the theory of computational complexity theory the key wedge between P and NP is driven by the difference between polynomial and exponential growth rates of resources required for computation. In a sense, economists do not seem to realize that the difference between the modesty of 'simple interest' and the 'power of compound interest' is exactly analogous to the mathematical difference between countable and uncountable sets, in a precise sense:

> The finite-infinite analogy . . . states that polynomial vs. exponential growth corresponds in some sense to *countability vs. uncountability*. The basis for this analogy is that exponential growth and uncountability both frequently arise from *the power set construction*. (Sipser, 1983, p. 62, emphasis added)

Put succinctly, for the purposes of computational complexity theory one must be able to understand the sense in which 2^n grows faster than n^2!

In the following definition, formulae and theorems,[18] f, g are functions from $\mathbb{N} \rightarrow \mathbb{N}$:

Definition 12 $f(n) = O(g(n))$, if $\exists\ c, n_0 \in \Re$, such that, $f(n) \leq cg(n)$, $\forall n \geq n_0$.

Definition 13 If $f(n) = O(g(n))$ and if $g(n) = O(f(n))$, then f and g have the same rate of growth.

Proposition 14 Let p be a polynomial of degree r. Then p and n^r have the same rate of growth.

Theorem 15 $\forall k > 1$, k^n grows faster than any polynomial p.

4.3 Computational complexity theory: a setting

> Complexity . . . is . . . a weaselword used to avoid commitment to a definite and clear thought. (*pace* Fritz Machlup)[19]

The world of theories of complexity is many-splendoured. Quite apart from 'orthodox' computational complexity theory, there is the weird and wonderful world of algorithmic complexity theories, diophantine complexity theory, topological complexity theory – to mention a few of the fields that are especially and explicitly based on a formal model of computation. I am not convinced that algorithmic complexity theory should have been referred to with the soubriquet 'complexity' adorning it in its 'title'. A brief discussion of this view, bordering on an extended comment, is attempted in Appendix A at the end of the chapter. The background necessary to discuss diophantine complexity – essentially providing an economic context for the unsolvability of Hilbert's tenth problem – will make this already over-long and fractured chapter even more so. The best I can do at this point is to refer to the brief remarks in Velupillai (2000, ch. 7). As for topological complexity, even a brief definition and motivating discussion of this concept would require an extended presentation of the model of real computation in Blum et al. (1998) (referred to, occasionally, as the BCSS model). All I can do here is to give a telegraphic definition of topological complexity in the brief discussion of the BCSS model, given in the next main section.

Rosser's interesting outline (2007) of this world gives a much broader and far more illuminating perspective on complexity theory and I refer the interested reader to it for a concise overview. In this section, after what I call a 'potted proto-history' for the setting, a version of orthodox[20] computational complexity theory, largely against the familiar backdrop of linear programming, is outlined. As a result of the conundrums arising in this discussion, a brief sketch of a complexity theory for models of real computation continues the themes in the next main section.

4.3.1 Potted proto-history

> The fact is that every writer creates his own precursors. (Borges, 1964, 'Kafka and His Precursors', in *Labyrinths*, p. 201)

On Spring Equinox day, 20 March 1956, Gödel wrote, in his last letter to von Neumann:

> It is evident that one can easily construct a Turing machine which, for each formula F of the predicate calculus and for every natural number n, will allow one to decide if F has a proof of length n. Let $\Psi(F, n)$ be the number of steps that the machine requires for that and let $\varphi(n) = \max_F \Psi(F, n)$. The question is, how fast does $\varphi(n)$ grow for an optimal machine? *One can show that* $\varphi(n) \geq Kn$. *If there actually were a machine with* $\varphi(n) \sim Kn$ *(or even only with* $\sim Kn^2$*), this would have consequences of the greatest magnitude.* That is to say, it would clearly indicate that, despite the unsolvability of the *Entshceidungsproblem*, the mental effort by the mathematician in the case of yes-or-no questions could be completely replaced by machines. One would indeed have to simply select an n so large that, if the machine yields no result, there would then also be no reason to think further about the problem. (Gödel, 1956, p. 10, emphasis added)

Essentially, Gödel is conjecturing on the implications of the existence of a polynomial time algorithm for the satisfiability problem! As always this 'greatest logician since Aristotle', as von Neumann referred to him (Feferman et al., 1986, p. 218), had an uncanny prescience about new directions in applied recursion theory – on the eve of the emergence of the newly codified fields of computational complexity theory and algorithmic complexity theory.

Furthermore, the important concepts of reducibility and completeness were first introduced in Post's seminal paper (1944) and had become, by the time these concepts were fruitfully harnessed in the codifying of computational complexity theory at the frontiers, part of what has come to be called 'higher recursion theory', or the study of recursively enumerable sets and degrees.[21] Thus, there is, at least with hindsight, a natural transition from classic recursion theory – from the Gödel, Church, Turing, Rosser, Kleene, Post period of 1931–44 – to the gradual implementation of 'Post's program' on degrees of solvability, say maturing around the period 1965–80, to the overlapping and intertwined conceptual development of the theoretical framework of modern computational complexity theory.

Alexander Schrijver's monumental three-volume, encyclopaedic treatise on *Combinatorial Optimization* (2003) will remain the classic on many things, but, surely, above all, on the history of every possible concept of relevance for complexity theory from the point of view of combinatorial optimization. In particular, I can do no better than refer any serious scholar of the history of the ideas that shaped classical computational complexity theory to these three exhaustive and excellent volumes for full details of every possible source, placed, described and explained in impeccable context.

A Whig interpretation of the history of computational complexity theory would mean a retracing of the past from the vantage point of the P = ?NP question; or, more accurately, from the point of view of the polynomial-time computability versus NP-completeness point of view. From this latter point of view, the modern history of computational complexity theory will have to be told as originating in two traditions: one, the tradition of mathematical logic, particularly recursion theory and proof theory; the other, accepting a model of computation only implicitly, and often even on an ad hoc basis, along the special traditions, emerging from, solving special purpose problems: the travelling salesperson's problem, problems in graph theory, linear and integer linear programming problems, network flows and transportation problems, and so on. It is the codification of the notion of the efficiency of computations that provided the impetus for the merging of the two traditions, almost by accident. The explicit recognition of the model of computation in the second tradition, and the need to go beyond degrees of undecidability in the first tradition, were brought together and fused into the one powerful and fruitful field of computational complexity theory. The five pioneers who achieved this 'unification' of the two traditions – I think, unwittingly, but serendipitously – were Edmonds, Constable, Cook, Levin and Karp, standing, of course, on the shoulders of giants of the past (and the future, even if it may sound paradoxical to be able to stand on the shoulders of giants yet unborn). The former two codified and etched the notion of polynomial-time as the standard of efficiency of computation; the latter three codified the conundrums of non-deterministic computations by defining and characterizing the NP-complete class, both theoretically and with imaginative and exhaustive examples.

It will be a salutary lesson for economists, who will be disabused of optimization in the decision model tradition of computational complexity theory, to learn that efficiency in this computational tradition and vision simply means 'good', not the 'best'! The computer scientists and their mathematicians were mindful of that old adage: *the best is the enemy of the good*![22] Edmonds, the almost undisputed pioneer in the codification of polynomial-time computation as the criterion for efficiency introduced the notion and, indeed, the whole subject, as follows (in 1965; see also Cobham, 1965):

> For practical purposes computational details are vital. However, my purpose is only to show as attractively as I can that there is an *efficient algorithm*. According to the dictionary, 'efficient' means 'adequate in operation or performance.' This is roughly the meaning I want . . . *Perhaps a better word is 'good.'*
>
> There is an obvious finite algorithm, but that algorithm increases in difficulty exponentially with the size of the graph. It is by no means obvious whether *or not* there exists an algorithm whose difficulty increases only algebraically with the size of the graph. . .
>
> For practical purposes the difference between algebraic and exponential order is often more crucial than the difference between finite and non-finite. (In Schrijver, 2003, p. 56, last set of italics in original)

Three remarks on these perceptive comments by Edmonds may not be out of place. First of all, the notion of efficiency is more akin to Simon's visions of satisficing processes than anything from orthodox economics; second, by 'algebraic' Edmonds refers, obviously, to 'polynomials'; third, it may be useful to recall Sipser's analogy between the polynomial–exponential divide and the countable–uncountable one, whereby the exponential-uncountable nexus comes about due to power-set constructions.

Finally, in line with the aims of being a 'potted proto-history', I shall make just one salient remark on Cook's seminal paper (1971), which highlighted the crucial role the satisfiability problem was to play in the development of computational complexity theory. I think the consensus is that the most important point of Cook's paper was the following proposition:

$$P = NP \text{ iff } SAT \subset P$$

Cook's contribution achieved a neat synthesis of the two traditions I referred to above; SAT is a quintessential problem of mathematical logic. By using the concept of reducibility from computability theory he was able to show that any instance of a problem in NP can be reduced to an appropriate instance of a problem in SAT. Therefore, the instance of the NP problem is solvable if, and only if, the SAT instance is solvable. Finally, he also showed that the reducibility can be achieved in polynomial time.[23]

Karp (1972), who felicitously coined the suffix 'complete', built on Cook's framework and, in a sense, codified the subject of computational complexity theory to what it has since become. In particular, his characterization of NP-complete was decisive. Karp's results showed that almost all garden-variety combinatorial optimization problems encountered in economics are – and will forever remain – intractable, unless P = NP. Herein lies the significance of its inclusion in the Clay millennium seven.

My final comment in this context is the following: these conceptual innovations, mathematical formalizations and computational structures gave rise to exact results on feasible computations – or, efficient computations – precisely in the sense of Herbert Simon's overall research programme. In particular, the last mentioned Karp result on the implications of $P \neq NP$ compels the economic theorist and the mathematical economist to resort to 'near-optimal', 'satisfactory', 'satisficing' solutions and processes. That the Simon visions have not been underpinned more formally by the results from computational complexity theory remains an unwritten intellectual chapter in behavioural economics.

4.3.2 An LP interregnum

Linear programming, LP, with the variables and the coefficients defined over $\Re$, had been the classic optimization problem in economics – until recently, when it seems to have been dethroned by DP, dynamic programming, particularly in macroeconomics – that was also coupled, almost intrinsically, with an eminently practical numerical algorithm to implement it: the simplex method. A couple of intertwined landmark results on the LP problem can possibly be given the sobriquet, 'proto-history of computational complexity theory': the Klee-Minty (1972) result on the intractability of the simplex method, then the re-absorption of LP into the theoretically tractable fold by Khachiyan's (1979) seminal results on LP, where Shor's (1970) earlier work on the ellipsoid algorithm was imaginatively exploited, and finally consolidated by Karmarkar's interior point method, which was also (claimed to be) practically tractable. It is important to remember that in all three algorithms the variables are defined on $\Re$, even though the complexity criteria were developed for discrete variable or combinatorial decision problems.

The simplex algorithm for the LP problem with a constant coefficient matrix **A** of dimension $m \times n$ can theoretically visit the following number of vertices:

$$2\left(\frac{m}{n}\right) = \frac{n!}{m!(n - m!)} > \left(\frac{n}{m}\right)^m \tag{4.12}$$

$$\Rightarrow \geq 2^m : \forall n \geq 2m$$

Thus, there is the possibility that intractability – that is, computational complexity – is intrinsically embedded within the structure of the simplex algorithm. It was a recognition of this intrinsic possibility and then an exploitation of it that enabled Klee and Minty to devise their (artificial) problem to show the intractability of the simplex algorithm. They showed intractability in a class of LP problems with $m = n$ equality constraints in $2n$ non-negative variables in which the simplex required $2^n - 1$ iterations; that is, a 'visit' to every vertex of the problem. How was this achieved? Why was it attempted? The latter question can be answered by saying that the framework of computational complexity theory had been formulated and, therefore, an analyst knew what had to be sought to show non-tractability. As for the 'how', the following geometric approach suggests, intuitively, the way intractability was constructed:

1. Recall, first, that the simplex algorithm moves from vertex to vertex; therefore, find a polytope that has an exponential number of vertices. For example, a 3-*d* cube has 6 faces (2×3) and 8 vertices (that is, 2^3). Thus, a cube with $2d$ faces has 2^d vertices.
2. Next, orient the polytope such that the direction of decreasing cost is 'upwards'; that is, orient the sequence of the exponentially many vertices (2^d), adjacent to one another, each higher than the previously visited vertex.
3. Then: $\forall d > 4$, $\exists$ a LP with 2^d equations, 3^d variables, and integer coefficients with absolute values bounded by 4, such that, the simplex algorithm can take $2^d - 1$ iterations to find the optimum.

Not much later, Khachiyan's seminal result appeared and settled decisively the polynomial time status of LP. Let me first show where exactly the need for precise numerical analysis – that is, analysis in $\Re$ – enters the ellipsoid method.[24] Locating the source of the appeal to precise arithmetic, in $\Re$, is crucial in knowing where and what kind of approximation has to be used in any particular instance of an application of the ellipsoid method[25] so that it is consistent with its underlying model of computation.

Definition 16 An ellipsoid, $\mathbb{E}$, *Ellip* [**z**, D], is a set of vectors $\mathbf{x} \in \Re^n$, such that:

$$Ellip\,[\mathbf{z}, D] := \{\mathbf{x} \mid (\mathbf{x} - \mathbf{z})^T D^{-1} (\mathbf{x} - \mathbf{z}) \leq 1\} \tag{4.13}$$

where:

D: a positive definite matrix of order n;
z: the centre of *Ellip* [**z**, D].

Remark 17 A set $\mathbb{E}$ is an ellipsoid iff $\mathbb{E}$ is an affine transformation of the unit ball, $\{\mathbf{x} \mid \mathbf{x}^T \mathbf{x} \leq 1\}$.

The basic idea of 'binary search' consists of 'halving' a set, a domain, at each iteration of the 'search' process. This is encapsulated for the ellipsoid method in the following proposition:

Proposition 18 Let **a** be a row vector of the given *Ellip* [**z**, *D*], and let $\mathbb{E}' \supset$ *Ellip* [**z**, *D*] $\cap$ $\{\mathbf{x}|\mathbf{ax} \leq \mathbf{az}\}$, such that $\mathbb{E}'$ has smallest volume. Then $\mathbb{E}'$ is unique and $\mathbb{E}' =$ *Ellip* [**z**$'$, *D*$'$], where:

$$\mathbf{z}' := \mathbf{z} - \frac{1}{n+1} \cdot \frac{D\mathbf{a}^T}{\sqrt{\mathbf{a}D\mathbf{a}^T}} \tag{4.14}$$

$$D' := \frac{n^2}{n^2-1}\left(D - \frac{2}{n+1} \cdot \frac{D\mathbf{a}^T\mathbf{a}D}{\mathbf{a}D\mathbf{a}^T}\right) \tag{4.15}$$

and:

$$\frac{vol\,\mathbb{E}'}{vol\,\mathbb{E}} < e^{-\frac{1}{2}\frac{1}{(n+1)}} \tag{4.16}$$

The point to note is the square root term in (4.14). No underlying model of computation that is not capable of precise real number computation will be able to implement the ellipsoid algorithm consistently. There are three alternatives to circumvent the problem of precision:

- appeal to, and utilize, relevant approximation results, as is done in, for example, Schrijver (1986, pp. 166–7);
- build an underlying model of exact real number computation, as claimed to have been done in Blum et al. (1998);
- or, finally, resort to careful and informed ad hockery, as is expertly resorted to in Papadimitriou and Steiglitz (1982, Section 8.7.4).

There is a problem with the first of the alternatives. The second of the two approximation lemmas on which Schrijver (1986) relies on, to circumvent the problem of numerical imprecision, entailed by the inconsistency between the ellipsoid method invoking real number domains and the implicit model of computation relying on rational or integer number domains, is based on a non-constructive argument at a crucial point in the proof (op. cit, bottom, p. 167).[26] A similar infelicity plagues the method of 'informed ad hockery'; for example, in Papadimitriou and Steiglitz (1982, p. 182), when a claim holding '$\forall x \in \Re, |x - \hat{x}|/|x| \leq 2^P$, for a given precision *P*'. As for relying on an underlying real number model of computation, in a sense the whole research programme represented by Blum et al. (1998) could be said to have emanated from the conundrums posed by the LP problem. My own reservations about this method are given below.

An outline of the Khachiyan solution is as follows. Consider the problem of finding a feasible point satisfying the following system of inequalities:

$$\langle \mathbf{h}_i, \mathbf{x} \rangle \leq g_i, i = 1,\ldots,p \tag{4.17}$$

$$\mathbf{h}_i \in E^n, p \geq 2, n \geq 2$$

Khachiyan's algorithm finds a feasible point, or establishes its nonexistence, in a finite number of iterations, polynomial in its input variables.

Denote by L: the length of the binary encoding of the input data; then:

$$L = \sum_{i,j=1}^{n,p} \log_2(|h_{ij}| = 1) + \sum_{j=1}^{p} \log_2(|g_j| + 1) + \log_2 np + 2 \tag{4.18}$$

where: h_{ij} is thc jth element of vector $\mathbf{h}_i$. Then, Khachiyan's algorithm is, schematically:

Step 1: Set $x_0 = 1$; $H_0 = 2^{2L} I$, $k = 0$.
Step 2: Terminate the algorithm with $\mathbf{x}_k$ as the feasible point. If $\mathbf{x}_k$ satisfies:

$$\langle \mathbf{h}_i \mathbf{x}_k \rangle < g_i + 2^{-L}, \forall i = 1,\ldots,p \tag{4.19}$$

Step 3: If $k < 4(n + 1)^2 L)$, then go to Step 4; otherwise, terminate the algorithm with the negative, tractable, answer that no solution exists.
Step 4: Choose any inequality for which:

$$\langle \mathbf{h}_i \mathbf{x}_k \rangle \geq g_i + 2^{-L} \tag{4.20}$$

Now, set:

$$\mathbf{x}_{k+1} = \mathbf{x}_k - \frac{1}{(n+1)} \frac{H_k \mathbf{h}_i}{\langle \mathbf{h}_i, H_k \mathbf{h}_i \rangle^{1/2}} \tag{4.21}$$

and:

$$H_{k+1} = \frac{n^2}{n^2 - 1} \left[H_k - \frac{2}{n+1} \frac{H_k \mathbf{h}_i \mathbf{h}_i^T H_k}{\mathbf{x}_p \mathbf{h}_i, H_k \mathbf{h}_i} \right] \tag{4.22}$$

Step 5: Set $k = k + 1$ and go to Step 2.

Remark 19 The Khachiyan algorithm returns a feasible solution or establishes its non-existence in $4(n + 1)^2 L$ iterations.

Remark 20 With minor modifications the algorithm can be adapted to handle the system above in the presence of an additional system of linear equalities: $N^T \mathbf{x} = \mathbf{b}$.

Remark 21 It is clear that the 'villain of the piece' appears in the denominator of the iteration linking $\mathbf{x}_k+_1$ to $\mathbf{x}_k$ in equation (4.21).

Next, consider the iteration in (4.21)–(4.22) as a dynamical system – in this case a map. Suppose using one of the two approximation schemes referred to above the initial conditions are guaranteed to be rational numbers; that is, computable numbers. Thus, the sequence of numbers generated by the iteration in (4.21)–(4.22), can be guaranteed to be computable, that is, a recursive real number. Does this guarantee that the limit is a recursive real number? I think not and my conjecture is that a proof is relatively easy. I shall leave it as an unproved conjecture for the moment.

Finally, anyone who examines in detail the complete structure of the proof can be certain to find that it is replete with non-constructivities – that is, appealing to undecidable disjunctions. Moreover, the detailed proof given in Schrijver (1986) appeals, at a crucial point, to the proof of Farkas's lemma; which, in turn, appeals to a theorem that is proved using an algorithm equivalent to the simplex method, whose intractability was our starting point in this saga on the interregnum! In any case, it is best to underpin these kinds of problems on a model of 'real computation', as in Blum et al. (1998) (see, in particular, ch. 6). Fred Richman perceptively observed, years ago (1990, p. 125, emphasis added):

> Even those who like algorithms have remarkably little appreciation of the thoroughgoing algorithmic thinking that is required for a constructive proof. . . . I would guess that most realist mathematicians are unable even to recognize when a proof is constructive in the intuitionist's sense.
>
> It is a lot harder than one might think to recognize when a theorem depends on a nonconstructive argument. One reason is that *proofs are rarely self-contained, but depend on other theorems whose proofs depend on still other theorems. These other theorems have often been internalized to such an extent that we are not aware whether or not nonconstructive arguments have been used, or must be used, in their proofs.* Another reason is that the law of excluded middle [LEM] is so ingrained in our thinking that we do not distinguish between different formulations of a theorem that are trivially equivalent given LEM, although one formulation may have a constructive proof and the other not.

What is the meaning – and the point – of proving polynomial time computability of a method that relies on non-constructive proofs, invoking undecidable disjunctions?

4.4 The problem of computational complexity of real numbers and real functions

> The 'computable' numbers may be described briefly as *the real numbers whose expressions as a decimal are calculable by finite means.* Although the subject of

> this paper is ostensibly the computable numbers, it is almost equally easy to define and investigate computable functions of an integral variable or a *real* or computable variable, computable predicates, and so forth. The fundamental problems involved are, however, the same in each case, and I have chosen the computable numbers for explicit treatment as involving the least cumbrous technique. I hope shortly to give an account of the relations of the computable numbers, functions, and so forth to one another. This will include a development of *the theory of functions of a real variable* expressed in terms of computable numbers. According to my definition, a number is computable if its decimal can be written down by a machine. (Alan Turing, 1936–37, p. 230, emphasis added)

These fascinating and prescient opening sentences in Turing's classic paper indicate, clearly and unambiguously, that the model of computation that he developed – now felicitously and justly called the Turing machine model of computation – was intimately linked with, and underpinned by, real numbers and real functions. These links were explored, developed and expanded, in the immediate post-war years, even while orthodox computational complexity theory was in its infancy, in a series of seminal books and papers by Goodstein, Grzegorczyk, Lacombe, Mazur and Specker.[27] Their modern successors are Pour-El and Richards, Ko and Friedman, Weihrauch, Aberth[28] and Shepherdson.[29] Both prior to and parallel with these developments, in what is now broadly referred to as recursive or computable analysis, there was the rich vein of algorithmic analysis emanating from the Brouwer-Heyting tradition of intuitionistic constructive analysis; its definitive codification – at least as a constructive, even if not intuitionistic, variant – was achieved with Errett Bishop's classic work of 1967 on the *Foundations of Constructive Analysis*. There have, thus, been available a variety of supremely elegant, comprehensive and rigorous foundations for models of real number and real function computations for the whole of the period since the Turing model has been in existence. Computer science – both theoretically and in its applied versions, and even practically – has developed, *pari passu*, with these theories as its foundation. Yet, numerical analysis and numerical analysts have gone about their traditional and noble business, a tradition that can be traced back at least to Newton and Gauss, without paying any attention to these developments. This remains a paradox, especially since the ubiquity of the digital computer has meant that the numerical analyst's theories have to be implemented on these machines. Numerical analysts have always been concerned with the efficiency of algorithms, for example in terms of approximation criteria for convergence of numerical methods, but the connection between their concerns with efficiency and those of the computer scientist's with computational complexity theory has never had more than a tangential connection with each other. These issues have been raised to a new level of awareness in the work around the BCSS model and its origins and development. However, they – the originators of the BCSS model, Smale in particular – seem not to have paid sufficient attention to the algorithmic tradition in real analysis; not even to the clearly related tradition of analog computation.[30] Space constraints prevent me from a proper discussion and evaluation of the technical merits and conceptual priorities in the two approaches – the recursive analysis and the BCSS model. I shall, instead, simply outline – in the next subsection – some salient features of the BCSS model and the way orthodox complexity theoretic concepts are defined in it. However, I remain sceptical of the need for considering real number and real function computation from the perspective of the BCSS model; some of my reasons are also sketched out.

4.4.1 Complexity theory of real computation: notes on the BCSS model

> In the late 17th century, when Newton and Leibniz were first inventing calculus, part of their theory involved *infinitesimals* – i.e., numbers that are infinitesimal but nonzero. . . . Indeed, Leibniz and Newton had infinitesimals in mind when they invented calculus. (Schechter, 1997, pp. 394–6; emphasis in the original)

Yet the whole rationale and motivation for the development of the BCSS model of real computation seems to be based on ignoring this historical fact! Smale, in particular, has tirelessly propagated the view that the Newtonian 'vision' of the universe is underpinned by a 'continuous real number model'. I shall return to these issues in the concluding section. For now, let me simply outline just the bare bones BCSS model to enable me to define the classes P and NP for real number and real function computations in this framework. Anyone interested in delving into the deeper reaches of the BCSS model can easily do so via the extremely readable and clearly presented monograph by Blum et al. (1998).

Contrary, also, to Turing's original approach, whereby the real numbers are expressed as decimal expansions, in the BCSS model they are taken as abstractly and axiomatically given entities:

> [C]ontinuing from a very different point of view, I will devise a notion of computation taking the real numbers as something axiomatically given. So, a real number to me is something *not* given by a decimal expansion; a real number is just like a real number that we use in geometry or analysis, something which is given by its properties and not by its decimal expansion. (Smale, 1991, p. 62, emphasis added)

One would wonder, then, how properties replete with undecidable disjunctions could be implemented on any kind of computer, if also the axioms are not recursively presented. Moreover, if the starting point is an axiomatic representation of real numbers, why stop there? Why not take an axiomatic approach to the P = ?NP problem? I shall return to this particular theme in the concluding section.

The BCSS model is presented, at least in Blum et al. (1998), as a 'mathematical foundation of the laws of computation of numerical analysis' (and the Turing model is generated as a special case). But the 'main goal' of Blum et al. is 'to extend the [the classical theory of computational complexity] to the real and complex numbers' in a special context:

> A cornerstone of classical complexity theory is the theory of NP-completeness and the *fundamental* P ≠ NP? problem.
>
> A main goal of [Blum et al.] is to extend this theory to the real and complex numbers and, in particular, to pose and investigate the fundamental problem within a broader mathematical framework. (Blum et al., 1998, p. 24)

With this aim in focus, the following general framework of computations over a ring (or field) – in contrast to the starting point in natural numbers, according to BCSS, of the traditional[31] 'Turing theory' – is set up:

Definition 22 Machines over $\mathbb{R}$ (say a commutative ring with unit).

A machine $\mathbb{M}$ over $\mathbb{R}$ is a finite connected directed graph, containing the following five types of nodes:

1. input, with underlying input space $\mathbb{I}_{\mathbb{M}}$;
2. computation, in state space, $\mathbb{S}_{\mathbb{M}}$;
3. branch;[32]
4. output, with underlying output space, $\mathbb{O}_{\mathbb{M}}$;
5. shift nodes, $\Sigma_{\mathbb{M}}$.

Where the input space, $\mathbb{I}_{\mathbb{M}}$, and output space, $\mathbb{O}_{\mathbb{M}}$ are defined in $\mathbb{R}^{\infty}$, which is the disjoint union:

$$\mathbb{R}^{\infty} = \sqcup_{n \geq 0} \Re^{n}$$

and the state space, $\mathbb{S}_{M}$, is defined in $\mathbb{R}_{\infty}$, the bi-infinite direct sum space over $\mathbb{R}$, such that, typical elements of it, $x \in \mathrm{R}_{\infty}$, are of the form:

$$x = (\ldots\ldots x_{-2}, x_{-1}, x_0 \circ x_1, x_2, \ldots\ldots)$$

and:

$x_i \in \mathbb{R}$, $\forall i \in \mathbb{Z}$ (and each such x_i is referred to as a coordinate of x) and $x_k = 0$ for $|k|$ sufficiently large;

$\circ$ is a distinguishing marker between x_0 and x_1.

Remark 23 The space R_∞ has natural left and right shift operations:

$$\sigma_l(x)_i = x_{i+1} \text{ and } \sigma_r(x)_i = x_{i-1}$$

Remark 24 Anyone familiar with the definition of the Turing machine, say as given in the classic book by Martin Davis (1958) (see also the appendix in Velupillai, 2000), will find it easy to interpret the above definitions in their specific, more general, domains. The mechanism is exactly identical.

Two 'reminders', particularly to economists, are apposite at this point: the first is to keep in mind that in computational complexity theory of any hue, one is dealing with decision problems; the second is that in this field the primary interest is in decidable problems, that is, problems for which their characteristic functions are computable. The complexity of the former is usually measured by the complexity of the latter.

Definition 25 A decision problem over $\mathbb{R}$ is a set $\mathbb{S} \subset \mathbb{R}^\infty$

Definition 26 $\forall x \in \mathbb{R}^\infty$, its characteristic function is defined as:

$$\chi_{\mathbb{S}} = \begin{cases} 1 & \text{if} x \in \mathbb{S} \\ 0 & \text{otherwise} \end{cases}$$

Definition 27 Polynomial functions over $\mathbb{R}$

Suppose h: $\mathbb{R}^m \rightarrow \mathbb{R}$ is a polynomial function of degree d over $\mathbb{R}$.
Then h defines a polynomial function, $\hat{h}$, on $\mathbb{R}_\infty$, of dimension m and degree d:

$$\hat{h} = \mathbb{R}_\infty \rightarrow \mathbb{R}$$

where: $\forall x \in \mathbb{R}_\infty, \hat{h} = h(x_1, x_2, \ldots., x_m)$

Definition 28 Polynomial time

$\mathbb{M}$ over $\mathbb{R}$ works in polynomial time if, $\forall x \in \Re^n \subset \Re^\infty$, and for some fixed $c, q \geq 1$:

$$cost\,(x) \leq cn^q$$

where $cost\,(x)$: the number of nodes traversed during the computation.

Corresponding to a measure of bits over $\mathbb{Z}_2$, there is *height*, $ht_{\mathbb{R}}(x) = 1$, $\forall x \in \mathbb{R}$.

Definition 29 $\forall x \in \Re^n \subset \Re^\infty$, *length* $(x) = n$ and *size* $(x) = n \cdot ht_{\mathbb{R}}(x)$

where

$$ht_{\mathbb{R}}(x): \mathbb{R} \to \mathbb{Z}_{0 \cup +} \text{ and } ht_{\mathbb{R}}(x) = \max ht_{\mathbb{R}}(x_i)$$

Definition 30 $\forall x \in \Re^n \subset \Re^\infty$:

$$cost_{\mathbb{M}}(x) = T(x) \times ht_{\max}(x)$$

where $T(x)$: the halting time of $\mathbb{M}$ on input x.

Definition 31 Polynomial-time machine, $\mathbb{M}$ over $\mathbb{R}$

$\mathbb{M}$ over $\mathbb{R}$ is a polynomial-time machine on $X \subset \mathbb{R}^\infty$ if $\exists\, c, q \in \mathbb{Z}_+$ such that:

$$cost(x) \leq c(size(x))^q, \forall x \in X$$

Definition 32 $\varphi: X \to Y \subset \mathbb{R}^\infty$ is said to be polynomial time computable – or a p-morphism – over $\mathbb{R}$, if φ is computable by a polynomial time machine on X.

Finally, for the main relevant definitions, that is, of the class P over a ring, $\mathbb{R}$:

Definition 33 The class P

A decision problem $S \subseteq \mathbb{R}^\infty$ is in class P over $\mathbb{R}$ – that is, $S \in \mathrm{P}_{\mathbb{R}}$ – if χ_S is a p-morphism over $\mathbb{R}$.

Before we proceed to the NP world, the notion of reducibility has to be defined:

Definition 34 p-reduction p-reducible

A morphism φ is a p-reduction, if:

$$\varphi: \mathbb{R}^\infty \to \mathbb{R}^\infty, \text{ such that, } \varphi(S) \subseteq S' \text{ and } \varphi(\mathbb{R}^\infty - S) \subseteq \mathbb{R}^\infty - S'$$

where the decision problem S is, then, said to be p-reducible to the decision problem S'.

Definition 35 The class NP

A decision problem $S \subseteq \mathbb{R}^\infty$ is in class NP over $\mathbb{R}$ – such that, $S \in NP_{\mathbb{R}}$ – if $\exists\, \mathbb{M}$ over $\mathbb{R}$, with (input space), $\mathbb{I}_{\mathbb{M}} = \mathbb{R}^\infty \times \mathbb{R}^\infty$, and $c, q \in \mathbb{Z}_+$, such that:

1. if $x \in S$ then $\exists w \in \mathbb{R}^\infty$, such that, $\Phi_{\mathbb{M}}(x, w) = 1$ and $cost_{\mathbb{M}}(x, w) \leq c\,(size\,(x))^q$;
2. if $x \notin S$ then $\nexists w \in \mathbb{R}^\infty$ such that, $\Phi_{\mathbb{M}}(x, w) = 1$.

The obvious question about TSP is immediately answered:

Proposition 36 TSP is in class NP_R

Definition 37 NP-hard

A decision problem $\hat{S}$ is $NP_{\mathbb{R}}$-hard if every $S \in NP_{\mathbb{R}}$ is p-reducible to it.

Finally, we have the important definition of NP-completeness.

Definition 38 NP-completeness

A decision problem $\hat{S}$ is said to be NP-complete over $\mathbb{R}$ if it is $NP_{\mathbb{R}}$-hard and $\hat{S} \in NP_{\mathbb{R}}$

Remark 39 By considering the 'special' case of $\mathbb{Z}_2$ the orthodox domain of computational complexity theory based on the Turing model of computation over binary sequences, it is immediate that Cook's theorem holds.

Remark 40 The earlier LP feasibility problem, when specialized over $\mathbb{Q}$ is easily shown, in the above framework, to be in class P.

4.4.2 Sceptical notes on the BCSS model

> What is not so clear is that *continuous processes* (*with differential equations*) may also be regarded as trial and error methods of solution to static equations. The reason why it is not so easy to see is that no human being can make continuous trials infinite in number. This gap in our grasp of the problem has been closed by the perfection of electronic and electro-mechanical computers – sometimes called zeroing servos – which continuously 'feed back' their errors as a basis for new trials until the error has disappeared. *Such a machine is an exact analogue of a continuous dynamic process.* Therefore it seems entirely permissible to regard the motion of an economy as a process of computing answers to the problems posed to it. (Goodwin, 1951, pp. 1–2, emphasis added)

What Goodwin is suggesting here is that the economic system can be felicitously interpreted using the metaphor and model of the analogue computer

– a metaphor that had, with equal finesse, been invoked by Walras, Pareto and Hayek. My sceptical notes on the BCSS model revolve around four perplexities:

1. What is wrong with the analogue model of computation over the reals and why was it not invoked to provide the mathematical and physical foundation for numerical analysis by the authors of the BCSS model?
2. What is wrong with the computable and recursive analytic model, with its rich complexity theoretic analysis of classic optimization operators routinely used in economic theory (optimal control, dynamic programming, and so on), of the perennial paradoxes of the initial value problem on ordinary differential equations and their solution complexities and of much else in a similar vein?
3. I don't think there is any historical or analytical substance to the Newtonian vision frequently invoked as a backdrop against which to justify the need for a new mathematical foundation for numerical analysis.
4. Finally, there is an important strand of research that has begun to interpret numerical algorithms as dynamical systems; from this kind of interpretation to a study of undecidability and incompleteness of numerical algorithms is an easy and fascinating frontier research topic within the framework of computable analysis, which owes nothing to – and has no need for – the BCSS kind of modelling framework – even though there are claims to the contrary in Blum et al. (1998) regarding such issues.[33]

The last of the perplexities, has, at present, not considered the problem of computational complexity of numerical algorithms via an analysis of equivalent dynamical systems; but, surely, it is only a question of time before that step is taken. There is a cryptic acknowledgement to an important strand in this new tradition, pioneered by da Costa and Doria, in Blum et al. (1998, p. 35): 'An undecidability result, related to chaotic dynamics . . . but very different in methodology and spirit is in [da Costa and Doria].'[34]

4.4.2.1 Real computation with analogue computers One of the recurrent themes in the BCSS modelling approach is the need for a model of computation over the reals so that classic mathematical physics – or applied mathematical – problems like those posed by the need to solve, numerically, ordinary differential equations, defined over R can be justified theoretically. Consider the following reasonably 'complex' dynamical system, the so-called Rössler system:

$$\frac{dx}{dt} = -(y + z)$$

$$\frac{dy}{dt} = x + 0.2y$$

$$\frac{dz}{dt} = 0.2 + z(x - 5.7)$$

Suppose a general purpose analogue computer (GPAS) is defined in terms of the usual adders, multipliers and integrators as the elementary units, similar to the elementary operations for M defined above for the BCSS model, which, in turn, are analogous to the elementary operations defining a Turing machine or a partial recursive function (μ-recursion, minimalization, and so on). Then it can be shown that a GPAS consisting of three adders, eight multipliers and three integrators can simulate the above Rössler system. What kind of functions can be constructed by combining such elementary units to build a GPAS to simulate continuous functions, defined over R? A series of results, beginning with Shannon in 1941, and culminating in Rubel's fundamental results on GPAS in 1988, give precise answers to this question. I have summarized the GPAS framework and results pertaining to them in Velupillai (2004). The main theorem is the following:

Theorem 41 (Rubel's theorem): There exists a nontrivial fourth-order, universal, algebraic differential equation[35] of the form:

$$P(y', y'', y''', y'''') = 0 \tag{4.23}$$

where P is a homogeneous polynomial in four variables with integer coefficients.

The exact meaning of 'universal' is the following:

Definition 42 A universal algebraic differential equation P is such that any continuous function $\varphi(x)$ can be approximated to any degree of accuracy by a C^∞ solution, $y(x)$, of P. In other words:

If $\varepsilon(x)$ is any positive continuous function, $\exists y(x)$ such that

$$|y(x) - \varphi(x)| < \varepsilon(x), \forall x \in (-\infty, \infty). \tag{4.24}$$

There is, then, a ready-made framework in which to study the real functions traditionally used in modelling physical (and, dare I say, economic processors). Why not develop a computational complexity theory for GPAS rather than replicate the Turing model for $\Re$?

4.4.2.2 Real computation within the Turing model of computation I have described Chris Moore's construction of a smooth map simulating a 'Minsky program' machine, that is, a minimal Turing machine, in Velupillai (2000, pp. 47–8). This is an exercise going in the reverse direction to the one pursued in BCSS modelling. But it is directly relevant here, because the computational complexity results for the Turing model will carry over to the constructed, equivalent, smooth map. In an e-mail message to me, of 20 January 1995, Chris Moore wrote as follows: 'I consider the systems [I have constructed] highly contrived, so I'm not sure how relevant [they] really [are] to economics, but enjoy.' My feeling is that the BCSS model is also 'highly contrived' and its relevance to economics very dubious.[36]

On the more concrete problem of the computational complexity of ODEs, there have been research and impressive results within one or another recursive analysis model for at least 40 years. For example Cleave (1969, p. 447), working within Goodstein's recursive analysis, showed, already in 1969, how 'to estimate the computational complexity of the solution of an ordinary differential equation in terms of its position in the Grzegorczyck hierarchy of primitive recursive functions'. The extra finesse here, from a practical, computing point of view, is not only its basis in the Turing model of computation; but also based on first constructivizing the classical non-constructive Cauchy-Lipschitz existence theorem. In my own work, when I use ODEs, I try to rely on a constructivized version of the Peano existence theorem to replicate the kind of analysis and results achieved by Cleave and others. Even more pertinent to the claims in Blum et al. (1998), on building mathematical foundations for numerical methods, there is Miller's work (1970) aimed precisely at providing a recursive function theoretic analysis of numerical methods.[37]

4.4.2.3 The contrived Newtonian vision

> Isaac Newton made a continuous mathematical model of a discrete universe using differential equations to explain how things in that universe move. . . . Real numbers are crucial to Newton's universe of a continuous universe. Real numbers give the picture of a continuous set of numbers between zero and one. (Smale, 1988, pp. 90–91)

Clearly, the authors of Blum et al. (1998) have not done their homework on Newton (and Leibnitz). That these two pioneers of the differential and integral calculus struggled to found their mathematics on the non-standard numbers, rather than the conventional real number continuum, is part of the folklore of the history of analysis – at least since Veronese, Skolem and, more recently, Abraham Robinson and Edward Nelson. Quite apart from the historically unsubstantiable assertion that Newton's calculus was based on what is now called real analysis – and, thus, the real number continuum – rather than non-standard analysis, there is the even more contentious suggestion, in the general program enunciated and propagated via the BCSS model, that continuous time modelling of physical processes in the natural sciences is, somehow, more 'realistic' or accurate. I can do no better than to remind these authors of one of Kolmogorov's perceptive observations in this regard:

> Until recently, in the mathematical treatment of natural science. . . the prevailing way of modelling real phenomena was by means of mathematical models constructed on the mathematics of the infinite and the continuous. For example, in studying the process of molecular heat conductivity, we imagine a continuous medium in which the temperature is subject to the equation
>
> $$\frac{\partial u}{\partial t} = K\left(\frac{\partial^2 u}{\partial x^2} + \frac{\partial^2 u}{\partial y^2} + \frac{\partial^2 u}{\partial z^2}\right) \qquad [4.25]$$
>
> Mathematicians usually regard the corresponding difference scheme
>
> $$\Delta_t u = K(\Delta_{xx}u + \Delta_{yy}u + \Delta_{zz}u) \qquad [4.26]$$
>
> Only as arising out of the approximate solution of the 'exact' equation [4.25]. *But the real process of heat conduction is no more similar to its continuous model expressed by [4.25] than to the discrete model directly expressed by [4.26].* (Kolmogorov, 1983, p. 30, emphasis added)

Not very recently, Richard Feynman (1982, p. 467) wondered: 'Can physics be simulated by a universal computer?' Feynman, in his characteristically penetrating way, then asked three obviously pertinent questions to make the above query meaningful:

- What kind of physics are we going to *imitate*?
- What kind of *simulation* do we mean?
- Is there a way of simulating rather than imitating physics?

Before providing fundamental, but tentative, answers to the above queries, he adds a penetrating caveat (ibid., p. 468; emphasis in original): 'I want to talk about the possibility that there is to be an *exact* simulation, that the computer will do *exactly* the same as nature.'

Feynman's answer to part of the first question was that the kind of physics we should simulate are 'quantum mechanical phenomena', because (op. cit. p. 486):

> I'm not happy with all the analyses that go with just the classical theory, because nature isn't classical, dammit, and if you want to make a simulation of

> nature, you'd better make it quantum mechanical, and by golly it's a wonderful problem, because it doesn't look so easy.

But he was careful to point out, also, that there was a crucial mathematical difference between 'quantizing' and 'discretizing' (op. cit, p. 488; emphasis added):

> *Discretizing is the right word.* Quantizing is a different kind of mathematics. If we talk about *discretizing* . . . of course I pointed out that we're going to *have to change the laws of physics.* Because the laws of physics as written now have, in the classical limit, a continuous variable everywhere.

He was not the only giant in the natural sciences who wondered thus: Einstein, Schrödinger, Hamming, Toffoli, Fredkin and most recently, Penrose, too, have had speculative thoughts along similar lines. Einstein, in perhaps his last published work, seems to suggest that a future physics may well be in terms of the discrete: 'One can give good reasons why reality cannot be represented as a continuous field' (Einstein, 1955, p. 166).

Roger Penrose, in his recently published, massive, vision of *The Road to Reality*, was even more explicit:

> [W]e may still ask *whether the real-number system is really 'correct' for the description of physical reality at its deepest level.* When quantum mechanical ideas were beginning to be introduced early in the 20th century, there was the feeling that perhaps we were now beginning to witness *a discrete or granular nature to the physical world* at its smallest scales . . . . Accordingly, various physicists attempted to build up an alternative picture of the world in which discrete processes governed all action at the tiniest levels . . . .
>
> In the late 1950s, I myself tried this sort of thing, coming up with a scheme that I referred to as the theory of 'spin networks', in which the discrete nature of quantum-mechanical *spin* is taken as the fundamental building block for a *combinatorial* (i.e. a discrete rather than real-number-based) approach to physics. (Penrose, 2004, pp. 61–2; emphasis in the second paragraph as in original)

These speculations on the granular structure of 'reality' at some deep level arose out of purely theoretical developments in the subject, but in continuous interaction with the epistemology of measurement in well-designed and sound experimental environments. Where these reflections by Feynman, Einstein and Penrose leave the loose epistemology and wild methodological claims in Blum et al. (1998), I am not at all sure.

4.5 Lessons from the past; visions for the future

> [Takeuti says]: I am now very much interested in proving $P < NP$.
>
> [Kreisel says]: I am interested in the subject only if $P = NP$.

(*Pace* Gaisi Takeuti). ('Kreisel and I' in *Kreiseliana: About and Around Georg Kreisel*, edited by Piergiorgio Odifreddi, A.K. Peters, 1996)

To this I may add:[38] [da Costa and Doria say]: S + [P = NP] is a consistent theory where, S: a 'reasonably strong consistent axiomatic system that includes arithmetic and has a recursively enumerable set of theorems'.

Where does all this leave a computable economist and his or her perspectives on computational complexity theory. Da Costa and Doria summarize metamathematical approaches to the P = ?NP question, even suggesting that S could well be ZFC. I, as a computable economist, shudder to think how a non-computable economist, non-competent in metamathematics, justifies invoking this kind of exotic result to claim that TSP is tractable, in theory – as they do with equilibria and efficiency postulates, with no hope ever of deciding or computing any such thing.

Any analysis of the computational complexity of any theory requires that the investigated theory should be underpinned by a model of computation. As it is in economic theory today, not a single respectable formalization – whether orthodox or not – is underpinned by a formal or informal model of computation. Ad hoc, ex post, approximations of uncomputable, non-constructive economic theories, indiscriminate approximations using expansions and contractions without any understanding of the computable structure of a model are routinely resorted to, and far-reaching policy conclusions are inferred. Non-constructive contraction mappings, uncomputable local equilibria, undecidable efficiency postulates – these are the staple features of analytical economics. The advent of the digital computer, and its ubiquity, has lent a veneer of respectability to computation and, hence, there seems to be licence to talk about the computational – and other – complexities of such essentially non-computable models.

Is there a way out of this morass and confusion? My own view, from the point of view of computable economics, is uncompromising: one has to formulate theories with a model of computation underpinning them. There is no point in proving the existence of a solution to the IVP of an ODE, without also knowing how to constructivize[39] the solution so that one can investigate how easy or hard it is to determine it.

The lessons from the past are depressing. I have, myself, been bamboozled by the dazzling beauty of a mathematical format that appears to be meaningfully numerical. This happened to me in the particular case of the ellipsoid algorithm. When I was taught it, and then came to apply it, in particular, in policy-oriented contexts, I was not sufficiently alert to the fact that there was serious question of consistent approximation involved (see the discussion above, in the section on LP. I do not know of any advanced textbook in mathematical economics that deals with the theory of exact approximation. Neither is there any meaningful teaching of constructive mathematics, even of a rudimentary kind. Thus, no able young graduate student is ever trained to think algorithmically; instead, the substitute is indiscriminate computation and blind approximations.

The way I have structured the chapter, and the idiosyncratic – almost psychedelic – way the discussion proceeded, was with the intention of providing a series of vignettes of, and brief glimpses into, a world of quantitative adventures where approximations, computations and constructions rule absolutely. Moreover, the opening quote from the letter Simon wrote to me was given the prominence it deserves, because my conviction is that the only kind of economic theory amenable to a consistent analysis in terms of computational complexity theory is the Simon version of behavioural economics. In particular, satisficing is a natural concept within the framework of decision problems (in the sense in which that phrase is defined in metamathematics, recursion theory and model theory); bounded rationality, too, is best understood in a theory that is underpinned by a model of computation, as it was the case with anything Simon modelled.

The new behavioural economics is devoid of an underlying model of computation; so are game theory and experimental economics. That the latter is not underpinned by a model of computation is, for me, a sad indictment of the puzzling hold that orthodox ways of thinking about mathematics can strangle the richness of a fresh subject. It is also puzzling that the subject that defines itself as that which 'studies efficient allocation of scarce resources', and that which has made much of having brought into this fold the study of information and its husbanding, has not done so with respect to computation, computational resources and computational structures.

In his thoughtful Foreword to Chaitin's magnum opus, Jacob Schwartz made the perceptive observation that (Schwartz, 1987, p. vii):

> This quantitative theory of description and computation, or Computational Complexity Theory as it has come to be known, studies the various kinds of resources required to describe and execute a computational process. Its most striking conclusion is that there exist computations and classes of computations having innocent-seeming definitions but nevertheless requiring inordinate quantities of some computational resource.

But there are possible worlds and visions that may make them also realizable. It is possible that the eternal charm of 'innocent-seeming definitions' and simple assumptions leading to unfathomable depths of computations and unimaginably difficult approximations may lure the sinners away from facile computations and faulty theorizing.

In my visions for the future I envisage a new generation of graduate students willing to learn the mathematics of the computer, the philosophy of computations and the engineering of numerical analysis. They are being taught by an older generation innocent of the metamathematical way of thinking about computations. They are also being inundated with the axiomatic way of reasoning – which I, not having been brought up on the much vaunted Greek mathematical tradition, have never had to unlearn. I think the most important vision for the future is to find a way to teach economics from a consistently and uncompromisingly algorithmic mode.

Yiannis Moschovakis, one of the outstanding frontier scholars of mathematical logic – in its recursion theoretic, set theoretic and model theoretic modes – concluded his highly stimulating essay on the provocative question of 'What Is an Algorithm?' with the following observation, (2001, p. 935, emphasis added):

> I would guess that many results in the analysis of algorithms are, in fact, *discovered by staring* at recursive equations (or *informal procedures* which can be expressed by systems of recursive equations), and then proofs are re-written and grounded on some specific model of computation for lack of a rigorous way *to explain an 'informal' argument*.

Herbert Simon was the ultimate – even, perhaps, in the sense of being the 'last', 'final' – maestro of proceeding to theorize about decision processes in economics in this way. In my visions of the future of and for economics, there will be reincarnations of Simon who may make the subject intrinsically algorithmic so that computational complexity can become a routine part of the subject that '*efficiently* allocates scarce resources' – where the notion of 'efficiency' is that of the 'good' and the 'practical'. I end with visions, also, of Keynesian dentists dominating the subject with their eminent practical sense of the possible.

Appendix A Algorithmic complexity theory

> There is also *a technical sense of 'complexity'* in *logic*, variously known as Kolmogorov complexity, Solomonoff complexity, Chaitin complexity . . . algorithmic complexity, information-theoretic complexity, and program-size complexity. The most common designation is 'Kolmogorov complexity' . . . this is probably a manifestation of the principle of 'Them that's got shall get,' since Kolmogorov is the most famous of these mathematicians.[40] (Franzén, 2005, p. 137, emphasis added)

This biblical reason for naming these variations on the theme of complexity may well be plausible from some points of view. However, it appears that Kolmogorov himself suggested that what is usually referred to as 'Kolmogorov complexity' should be called 'Kolmogorov entropy':

> [W]e call 'Kolmogorov entropy' what is usually called 'Kolmogorov complexity.' *This is a Moscow tradition suggested by Kolmogorov himself.* By this tradition the term 'complexity' relates to *any* mode of description and 'entropy' is the complexity related to an *optimal* mode (i.e., to a mode that, roughly speaking, gives the shortest description). (Uspensky and Shen, 1996, p. 271; italics in the original; emphasis line 2 added)

Current orthodoxy of the field of algorithmic complexity theory, linking all of the different variations of the themes mentioned above, is elegantly and comprehensively discussed, explained and described in the almost encyclopaedic treatise by Li and Vitanyi. The 'Moscow tradition', referred to above, is also amply discussed in works by Kolmogorov's students and co-authors (for example, Uspensky, 1992 and Uspensky and Shen, 1996). I have myself had a stab at a concise outline of the field, from the point of view of randomness and induction (cf. Velupillai, 2000, ch. 5), to which I may refer the interested reader[41] for a potted survey of the field. There is no point in rehashing easily available visions and comprehensively presented interpretations.[42] In this brief Appendix I want to suggest that algorithmic complexity theory, even by any other name, has no intrinsic connection with computational complexity theory.

The orthodox story, in an ultra-brief – almost scandalous – nutshell, is that the origins of the field of algorithmic complexity theory lie in the work of Kolmogorov, Chaitin and Solomonoff,[43] in their approaches to, respectively, the quantity of information in finite objects, program-size descriptions of the information content of a finite object and induction. For an economist the most interesting approach is that by Solomonoff, whose starting point, in fact, was the *Treatise on Probability* (1921) by Keynes. These original aims developed into, and linked with the earlier research on, the von Mises attempt to define a frequency theory approach to probability, randomness[44] and Bayesian estimation. All this is part of the folklore of the subject, easily gleaned from any of the indicated references, above.

In all three traditions – that is, the Kolmogorov, Chaitin and Solomonoff – the intentions were to measure the amount of information necessary to *describe* a given, finite, binary sequence (or string). A little more precisely, the idea is as follows: given a string x, its algorithmic complexity is defined to be the shortest string y from which a universal Turing machine[45] can 'produce' the given x. On the other hand, in computational complexity theory – particularly as a result of adherence to 'Post's program' – attention is *not* focused on *individual finite strings*. Instead the fundamental questions are about the computational difficulty – that is, complexity – of recognizing *sets*. Thus, the problem is about *deciding* whether a given finite string belongs to a particular set or not. From the main part of the chapter it will be evident that in computational complexity theory one tries to associate a function $\tau_{\wp}: \mathbb{N} \rightarrow \mathbb{N}$, to a recursive set, $\wp$ such that $\wp$ is accepted by those Turing Machines, say Θ, that run in *time* $\Omega(\tau_{\wp}(n))$. Therefore, one way to link algorithmic complexity theory with computational complexity theory will be to define a notion of the former that is *time-bounded* and is able to capture aspects of the complexity of the set $\wp$. In other words, it is necessary to add a time-bounded complexity component, as is routine in computational complexity theory, to the standard measure of algorithmic complexity. If this is done, the complexity of the finite string, x, will now be defined by the minimum of the sum of the description length and a measure of the time required to produce that x, from the given description.

Thus, it is clear that algorithmic complexity theory is as separate a field from computational complexity theory as information theory or physics – or even economics – are. The main difference is, of course, that algorithmic complexity theory is, *ab initio*, underpinned by the Turing model of computation. Hence, it is natural to define time-constrained generation of the descriptive complexity of members of sets. For example, as a computable economist, I construct economic theories underpinned by Turing's model of computation. Given a computable economic theory, there will be naturally definable time-bounded measures to describe the theory and, hence, immediate considerations of computational complexity of such descriptions. This is the way the complexity of solutions to ODE is studied, in the references given in the main part of the chapter. First, the ODE is constructified; then the computational complexity of the constructified solution is evaluated. Again, the difference is that description is intrinsically algorithmized, in algorithmic complexity theory.

In conclusion, the following two remarks add, I hope, further substance to my stance that the soubriquet 'complexity' in algorithmic complexity theory is somewhat unfortunate.

First, I would like to add another point so as to dispel popular misconceptions about correlating or juxtaposing *complexity* with *incompleteness*.[46] Many an unwary reader of Chaitin's important works – and his specific program-size approach to algorithmic information theory, the incarnation of Kolmogorov complexity in Chaitin's independent work – has had a tendency to claim that incompleteness, undecidability or uncomputability propositions are only valid in so-called 'sufficiently complex' mathematical systems. *A fortiori*, that intuitively *simple* computable systems are not computationally complex. This is simply false. Very simple formal mathematical systems are capable of generating incompleteness and undecidability propositions; just as intuitively very simple computable systems are capable of encompassing incredibly complex computational complexities, as some of the above examples have shown. Conversely, there are evidently complex systems that are provably complete and decidable; and, similarly, there exist seemingly complex functions that are capable of being computed, even primitive recursively. As one obvious and famous example illustrating *incompleteness* and *essential undecidability* in an *intuitively simple, finitely axiomatizable, simply consistent*[47] theory, one can take Robinson's arithmetic (Robinson, 1952), as shown in some of the classic books of metamathematics,[48] for example, Kleene (1952, 1967, pp. 280–81) and Boolos, Burgess and Jeffrey (2002, pp. 215ff).

The issues and points raised in the previous paragraph are, in my opinion, relevant as a preface to any discussion of algorithmic complexity, especially because, as indicated in Franzén's perceptive observation in the above opening quote, this whole area is really about 'a technical sense of "complexity" in logic'.[49] I believe it adds substance to the 'Moscow tradition' of not using the word 'complexity' to refer to this vast and fascinating field.

Second, if the distant modern origins of computational complexity theory, via computability theory, can be found in Hilbert's tenth problem, then modern exact approximation theory is even more directly linked to Hilbert's 13th problem.[50] Hilbert's aim in formulating the 13th problem – based on problems of nomography[51] – was to characterize functions in terms of their complexity in a natural way: find those defining characteristics of a function, such that, the given function can be built up from simpler functions and simple operations, rather like – once again – the way partial recursive functions are built up from a collection of base functions and elementary operations, like μ-recursion, minimalization, and so on. Hilbert's honed intuition suggested the formulation of the 13th problem; it was – like the tenth problem – solved 'negatively', by Kolmogorov and Arnold. The point to be emphasized here is, however, not the direct and obvious connection with computational complexity theory;[52] but, to strengthen my thesis that the 'Moscow tradition' of referring to Kolmogorov entropy is entirely justified even from the point of view of his work on approximation theory. Essentially, Kolmogorov introduced the concept of 'ε-entropy' of a metric space[53] 'to evaluate the order of increase of the volume of the [nomographic] table for an *increase in the accuracy* of [nomographic] tabulation' (Vitushkin, 1961, p. xiii, emphasis added). In other words, in his work on approximation theory, preceding his work on algorithmic complexity theory by only a few years, Kolmogorov defined the 'size' of a finite body – actually a subset of a Banach space – in terms of its 'metric entropy'; on the other hand, in his work on algorithmic complexity theory, he defined the information content in a finite string in terms on 'entropy'(in the Shannon tradition), too.

Finally, I don't even think the notion of randomness of finite strings needs to be based on algorithmic complexity theory. I believe the more constructive notion of lawless sequences, first enunciated by Brouwer, provides quite an adequate basis for defining randomness of finite sequences.[54] However, this is quite separate from the use of algorithmic complexity theory to provide rigorous foundations for the von Mises notion of '*Kollektives*' and thereby make it possible to remove the circularities that plagued early definitions of the frequency theory of probability.

Notes

* John McCall, Chico Doria and Stefano Zambelli have been educating me, from different points of view, on many fascinating visions of the thorny concept of complexity. More than a decade and a half of constant, stimulating, discussions with John McCall on Kolmogorov – algorithmic – complexity and theories of probability have been a source of great pleasure and consistent intellectual adventures. Not being particularly competent in the actual programming of theoretically structured computing models, I have had to rely on Stefano Zambelli for instruction and advice on the felicitous link between theory and application that is the hallmark of computational complexity theory. More recently, I have had the pleasure and privilege of being able to pick Chico Doria's fertile brain for exotic ideas about the P = ?NP question. Years ago, now bordering on almost two decades, the decision by Shu-Heng Chen to write his UCLA dissertation on the application of algorithmic and stochastic complexity theories, with me as his main thesis advisor, forced me to try to be at least one step ahead of his incredible learning abilities. Barkley Rosser's stimulating visit to Trento last year provided much inspiration on many topics related to a broader perspective on complexity. I wish I could blame them, and not have to plead guilty, for the infelicities and errors that remain!

1. The seven millennium problems, listed alphabetically, are (Jaffe, 2006, p. 655): 1. the Birch/Swinnerton-Dyer conjecture; 2. the Hodge conjecture; 3. the Navier-Stokes equations has smooth solutions; 4. P is not NP; 5. the Poincaré conjecture; 6. the quantum Yang-Mills theory exists with a mass gap; 7. the Riemann hypothesis.
2. One of the modern pioneers of computational complexity theory, Richard Karp, perceptively noted (1987, p. 464, emphasis added):

   > [I] do think there are some very worthwhile and interesting analogies between complexity issues in computer science and in economics. For example, economics traditionally assumes that the agents within an economy have universal computing power and instantaneous knowledge of what's going on throughout the rest of the economy. Computer scientists deny that an algorithm can have infinite computing power. *They're in fact studying the limitations that have arisen because of computational complexity. So, there's a clear link with economics.*

3. For reasons of 'convenience' I may abscond from gender neutrality when referring to the TSP.
4. A decision problem asks whether there exists an *algorithm* to *decide* whether a mathematical assertion does or does not have a proof; or a formal problem does or does not have a solution. Thus the definition makes clear the crucial role of an underpinning model of computation; second, the answer is in the form of a yes/no response. Of course, there is the third alternative of 'undecidable', too, but that is a vast issue outside the scope of this chapter.
5. The Blum speedup theorem should be presented in conjunction with the equally important gap and compression theorems of abstract computational complexity theory, especially when presenting the subject to an economic audience. These are the kinds of results from abstract computational complexity theory that make Simon's behavioural economics, underpinned by boundedly rational agents satisficing in the face of decision

problems, against a backdrop of a model of computation, the natural framework for the economics of choice under constraints. Instead, economists are weaned in the mathematics of real analysis and pure existence proofs, which are then, at another stage, given computational, cognitive and numerical content, entirely divorced from the original problem formulation.

6. That which I have called 'computable economics'. This is different from the currently fashionable reference to 'computational economics' where, in general, there is no underlying model of computation. The paradigmatic examples of such computational economic models are, in macroeconomics, the recursive computational equilibrium, RCE, model; in microeconomics, the (in-)famous example is, of course, the computable general equilibrium, CGE, model. Neither of these models is underpinned by any formal model of computation. The connection between the mathematics of the theory and the mathematics of the computation (or the mathematics of the numerical analysis) is non-existent.
7. Which is, of course, not the same as its more famous 'cousin', Euler's number, e.
8. γ is defined as the difference between the harmonic series and the natural logarithm, in the limit:

$$\gamma = \lim_{n\to\infty}\left[\left(\sum_{k=1}^{\infty}\frac{1}{k}\right) - \log n\right] = \int_1^{\infty}\left(\frac{1}{\lfloor x\rfloor} - \frac{1}{x}\right)dx$$

Of course, from a fairly young age most of us would have been taught the harmonic series; and even earlier, the natural log. An enlightened or subtle teacher could use the definition to teach students, at an early age, that the notion of a 'given number' may entail eternal perplexities.

9. I was myself taught this fascinating story in childhood as the '*paal payasam*' story of a game of chess between a King and Lord Krishna. The King, having inevitably lost the game to a god – although Hindu gods are not infallible – was requested by Lord Krishna to prepare, and distribute freely, the rice and milk-based drink, '*paal payasam*'. No doubt the story, in other traditions, is narrated with other metaphors.
10. This example is taken from Austin (1983).
11. A number is said to be perfect if it is equal to the sum of all its proper divisors (for example, $6 = 1 + 2 + 3$; $28 = 1 + 2 + 4 + 7 + 14$).
12. This example has become part of the folklore of dramatic examples in computational complexity theory (cf., for example, Pratt, 1975 and Wilf, 1986, too).
13. Characteristically illuminating discussions of all these results and formulas can be found in the wonderfully entertaining book by Rouse Ball and Coxeter (1987, ch. 1).
14. Cole is supposed to have claimed that it took him 'three years of Sundays' to arrive at the result (Wigderson, 2006, p. 8). How long it may have taken Ramanujan to arrive at, for example, the formula for $p(n)$, the number of partitions of n, we do not know; nor do we know whether it was hard or easy for him to 'derive' them. Very little is known about the thought or other processes used by Ramanujan to arrive at his remarkably complex formulas, except for a poignant remark by his 'mentor' at Cambridge, G.H. Hardy, regarding $p(n)$, (Srinivasa, 1998, p. 52, emphasis added): 'Ramanujan was the first and up to now, the only, mathematician to discover any [properties of $p(n)$]; and *his theorems were discovered in the first instance, by observation.*' Incidentally, it took the PC on which I am writing this document, using Mathematica Version 5, 0.016 seconds to factor $(2^{67} - 1)$!!
15. See the remarks and discussions in Appendix A.
16. Keynes, in speculating on the 'Economic Possibilities for our Grandchildren' (1930, p. 361) perceptively noted (emphasis added): 'From [the 16th century] until today the power of accumulation by compound interest,. . . was re-born and renewed its strength. And the *power of compound interest over two hundred years is such as to stagger the imagination.*'
17. On a neoclassical exponential growth path, at the rate of growth of per capita income at g, with an initial value of income at y_0, we have:

$$y(t) = y_0 e^{gt}.$$

Thus, countries like China, India and Brazil, growing at double-digit rates, these days, would double their per capita income in under seven years. How long can this go on and what kind of resources are being used to achieve these kinds of 'growth miracles' (Lucas, 1993)?

18. There is no need to restrict the range of f, g to $\mathbb{N}$; some prefer to work with the range $\mathbb{R}$.
19. Fritz Machlup's original remark was about 'structure' (1958): 'Structure . . . is . . . a weaselword used to avoid commitment to a definite and clear thought.'
20. This may well be the only time in my academic life that I find myself a defender of orthodoxy!
21. An elegant exposition of which can be found in Soare (1987), with a beautiful early treatment in the classic by Hartley Rogers (1967).
22. Apparently the original Voltaire quote is: 'the perfect is the enemy of the good'.
23. All this in a paper that was only seven pages in length!
24. I shall follow Schrijver's characteristically clear presentation here (1986, ch. 13), but Papadimitriou and Steiglitz (1982, ch. 8) is equally felicitous on this issue.
25. Geometrically, the ellipsoid method is very similar to the classic method of 'binary search', for example, Papadimitriou and Steiglitz (1982, p. 171); or, at a popular level, to variations of the '20 questions' game.
26. Moreover, it is not clear to me that the rounding process invoked in the first theorem, op. cit, p. 166, is itself in *P*.
27. The classic references are: Specker (1949), Lacombe (1955), Grzegorczyk (1957), Goodstein (1961), Mazur (1963). Grzegorczyk was continuing the Polish tradition, initiated by Banach and Mazur, that had commenced almost simultaneously with Turing's original contribution. In their Foreword to the unfortunately relatively little acknowledged classic by Mazur (1963), Rasiowa and Grzegorczyk made the melancholy, observation that (emphasis added):

> [Mazur's booklet] is based on the lectures [he gave on] 'Computable Analysis' in the academic year 1949–1950 at the Institute of Mathematics of the Polish Academy of Sciences in Warsaw. These lectures present a systematic exposition of the results obtained by S. Banach and S. Mazur in 1936–1939 and contain a detailed examination of recursive *real numbers*, recursive sequences, recursive functionals and recursive *real functions*. The authors never published their results . . . because the Second World War made this impossible.

28. Aberth's work is a development of the Russian constructivists, but has become a part of the modern theory of real computation based on the Turing model of computation. Russian constructivism is clearly and concisely outlined in Bridges and Richman (1987, ch. 3); copious references to the pioneering Russian contributions, almost simultaneous with the above Polish, French and American pioneering works are given in Aberth (2001).
29. Here the representative references are: Shepherdson (1976), Ko and Friedman (1982), Pour-El and Richards (1989), Ko (1991), Weihrauch (2000).
30. I have tried to 'resurrect' a consideration of this tradition, again from the point of view of a computable economist, in Velupillai (2004). I shall have a little to say about this approach below.
31. My fidelity to orthodox computational complexity theory emanates from my adherence to orthodoxy in computability theory!
32. Topological complexity is defined at this node.
33. Primarily in relation to the decidabilty problems of the Mandelbrot and Julia sets, as posed by Penrose (2004).
34. That in a book published in 1998, the authors of Blum et al. do not even manage to cite the published version of one of the early pioneering results of da Costa and Doria, from

1991 – the early examples are in, da Costa and Doria (1991a, 1991b) – let alone their later work and the related work of Chris Moore, for example (1990), and several others, is, I guess, an indication of the lack of attention paid to these other 'methodologies and spirit'! But these pioneering works are on undecidability of dynamical systems, not the computational complexity of dynamical systems. Perhaps that is the reason why not much attention was paid to these works in Blum et al. (1998).

35. An algebraic differential polynomial is an expression of the form:

$$\sum_{i=1}^{n} a_i x^{r_i} y^{q_{0i}} (y')^{q_{1i}} \ldots (y^{(k_i)})^{q_{k_i i}}$$

where a_i is a real number, r_i, q_{0i}, ..., $q_{k_i i}$ are non negative integers and y is a function of x.

Algebraic differential equations (ADEs) are ODEs of the form:

$$P(x, y, y', y'', \ldots, y^{(n)}) = 0$$

where P is an algebraic differential polynomial not identically equal to zero.

36. Thoughtless appeals to the BCSS model are not unknown in an economic text purporting to provide a framework and an analysis of 'complexity' in *real* economic models underpinned by a model of computation:

> Computing with real numbers offers some important advantages in the context of scientific computing . . . it is also relevant to applications in economic theory. *Economic models typically use real variables and functions of them.* A model of computing in which the elementary operations are functions of real variables allows the model to be directly applied to standard economic models, without requiring an analysis of approximations in each application. (Mount and Reiter, 2002, pp. 1–2, emphasis added)

37. There is a 'grudging nod' to the long and rich tradition of considering computability and complexity of models defined over R, in a variety of recursive and computable analyses, by Smale (1991, p. 61, emphasis added): 'Indeed, some work has *now been done* to adapt the Turing machine framework to deal with real numbers. . . Thus, the foundations are probably being laid for a theory of computation over the real numbers.' This acknowledgement comes in 1991 after almost continuous work by recursive and computable analysts to adapt the Turing model to domains over R. Weihrauch, himself a notable contributor to this adapting tradition that refutes what I can only call a 'preposterous' claim in Blum et al. (1998, p. 23):

> A major obstacle to reconciling scientific computation and computer science is the present view of the machine, that is the digital computer. As long as the computer is seen simply as a finite or discrete object, it will be difficult to systematize numerical analysis. We believe that the Turing machine as a foundation for real number algorithms can only obscure concepts.

I can only endorse, wholeheartedly, Weihrauch's entirely justifiable claim that the 'theory presented in his book (2000, p. 268) 'refutes their [that is, the above] statement'.

38. I am relying on da Costa, Doria and Bir (2007) for these 'exotic' remarks.
39. I have used 'constructivize' very often in this chapter. I think it is safe to assume that I really mean 'algorithmize' whether with a Turing model of computation as the backdrop or not. Constructive mathematics refuses to abide by the Church-Turing thesis, but all its propositions are algorithmic. I have, very gradually, come round to the view that the constructivist's more general vision, which subsumes the recursion theorist's algorithmic world, is superior from many points of view.
40. In their comprehensive and admirable text on this subject, Li and Vitanyi first gave the reason for subsuming all these different variations on one theme by the name

'Kolmogorov complexity' (1993, p. 84): 'Associating Kolmogorov's name with [algorithmic] complexity may also be an example of the 'Matthew Effect' first noted in the Gospel according to Matthew, 25:29–30'

41. John Kelly's famous 'elusive creature'!
42. As in the case of computational complexity theory, there are encyclopaedic treatises, like Garey and Johnson (1979), Papadimitriou (1994) and Schrijver (2003) and many others, that tell the story of the field, both from the point of view of the history of the forming ideas and the exciting work at the frontiers. I am neither summarizing these excellent treatises nor writing a survey. My aim here has been to try to give the various stories a slightly different perspective from the point of view of a computable economist. This entails a perspective from a generalized algorithmic vision – not just a recursion theoretic perspective.
43. I have, in my various related other writings on this subject, also tried to give due credit to the earlier and contemporary independent work of Lars Löfgren and Hilary Putnam. The representative references for Chaitin, Kolmogorov and Solomonoff are, Solomonoff (1964a, b), Kolmogorov (1965), Chaitin (1966).
44. One direct link with the contents of the main part of this chapter, that is, with computational complexity theory, was stated succinctly by Compagner (1964, p. 700, emphasis added): '[T]he mathematical description of random sequences in terms of complexity, which in algorithmic theory leads to the identification of randomness with *polynomial-time unpredictability*.' Once algorithmic complexity theory is viewed as the basis for a definition of finite random sequences, then it is inevitable that the emphasis will be on prediction rather than computation. Thus, the link with orthodox computational complexity theory is not as firm as the inclusion of the soubriquet 'complexity' in the title may suggest.
45. In the Solomonoff tradition the corresponding 'universality' resides in the concept of a 'universal distribution'.
46. Or, *simplicity* with *completeness*. I am, of course, referring to *incompleteness* in the strict metamathematical sense.
47. See Kleene (1952, p. 470, Theorem 53) and Kleene (1967, p. 287, footnote 216). The part played by simple consistency and the analogy with Rosser's result of the essential undecidability of $\mathbb{N}$, (1936) is also discussed in the relevant parts of Rosser (2007). Furthermore, despite some unfortunate misprints and unclarity, Franzén's fine exposition of the use and abuse of Gödel's incompleteness theorems has a good discussion of the way the Rosser sentence (rather than the more famous Gödel sentence) is used in proving – by reference to Smullyan (1992) – undecidability in Robinson's arithmetic (Franzén, 2005, pp. 158–9).
48. I cite this example also because Robinson's arithmetic is sufficient to represent every recursive function. It figures in the very first, 'Introductory', pages of Odifreddi's comprehensive, yet pedagogical, textbooks of classical recursion theory (Odifreddi, 1989, section I.1, p. 23). There are many equivalent ways of setting out the axioms of Robinson's arithmetic (see, for example, the discussion in ibid.); the following is the definition in the exceptionally clear presentation of Boolos, Burgess and Jeffrey (2002, pp. 215ff) (the prime denotes the successor operation):
    1. $x = \mathbf{0} \vee \exists y$, such that, $x = y'$;
    2. $0 \neq x'$;
    3. $x' = y' \rightarrow x = y$;
    4. $x + \mathbf{0} = x$;
    5. $x + y' = (x + y)'$;
    6. $x \cdot \mathbf{0} = \mathbf{0}$;
    7. $x \cdot y' = (x \cdot y) + x$;
    8. $x < y \longleftrightarrow \exists z, (z' + x = y)$.
49. However, I believe Chaitin's reference to his own pioneering work as 'algorithmic information theory' is a much better encapsulation of the contents of the field and the intentions of the pioneers. Indeed, the natural precursor is Shannon, rather than von

Mises, but Whig history is a messy affair and straightening out historical threads is a difficult task, even in a contemporary field.

50. If one reads the main content of the 13th problem by replacing the word 'nomography' with 'algorithm', then the connection with the subject matter of this chapter becomes fairly clear (Hilbert, 1900, p. 424, original emphasis):

    [I]t is probable that the root of the equation of the seventh degree is a function of its coefficients which does not belong to the class of functions capable of nomographic construction, i.e., that it cannot be constructed by a finite number of insertions of functions of two arguments. In order to prove this, the proof would be necessary *that the equation of the seventh degree* $f^7 + xf^3 + yf^2 + zf + 1 = 0$ *is not solvable with the help of any continuous functions of only two arguments.* I may be allowed to add that I have satisfied myself by a rigorous process that there exist analytical functions of three arguments x, y, z which cannot be obtained by a finite chain of only two arguments.

    Kolmogorov and Arnold refuted Hilbert's conjecture by constructing representations of continuous functions of several variables by the superposition of functions of one variable and sums of functions.

51. In the opening lines of the section stating the 13th problem, Hilbert gives an intuitive idea of 'nomography' (ibid.): 'Nomography deals with the problem: to solve equations by means of drawings of families of curves depending on an arbitrary parameter.' Those of us who indulge in drawing vector fields might see the similarities!
52. A beautiful discussion of approximation theory from this point of view – albeit implicitly – is given in an unfortunately little referenced work by Vitushkin (1961); a more technical and comprehensive survey of Kolmogorov's work on approximation theory is in Tikhomirov (1989).
53. See Vitushkin (1961, p. xiii) and Lorentz (1986, chs. 9 and 10). 'Order of increase', 'increase in the accuracy', 'most favourable system of approximation', 'rapidity of convergence' are some of the phrases used in Kolmogorov approximation theory. These are the considerations that make approximation theoretical considerations naturally algorithmic and, therefore, also amenable to computational complexity analysis.
54. This is a distinctly undigested conjecture; but see van Lambalgen (1992) for rigorous suggestions along these lines.

References

Aberth, Oliver (2001), *Computable Calculus*, Academic Press, San Diego and London.

Austin, A. Keith (1983), 'An Elementary Approach to NP-completeness', *American Mathematical Monthly*, **90**(6), 398–9.

Bishop, Errett A. (1967), *Foundations of Constructive Analysis*, McGraw-Hill Book Company, New York.

Blum, Lenore, Felipe Cucker, Michael Shub and Steve Smale (1998), *Complexity and Real Computation*, Springer Verlag, New York.

Boolos, George S., John P. Burgess and Richard C. Jeffrey (2002), *Computability and Logic*, 4th edn, Cambridge University Press, Cambridge, UK.

Borges, Jorge Luis (1964), 'Kafka and His Precursors', *Labyrinths: Selected Stories and Other Writings*, New Directions Publishing Corporation, New York.

Borwein, J.M. and P.B. Borwein (1988), 'On the Complexity of Familiar Functions and Numbers', *SIAM Review*, **30**(4), 589–601.

Bridges, Douglas and Fred Richman (1987), *Varieties of Constructive Mathematics*, Cambridge University Press, Cambridge, UK.

Chaitin, Gregory J. (1966), 'On the Length of Programs for Computing Fintite Binary Sequences', *Journal of the Association of Computing Machinery*, **13**(4), 549–69.

Cipra, Barry (2002), *What's Happening in the Mathematical Sciences, Vol. 5*, edited by Paul Zorn, American Mathematical Society, Providence, Rhode Island.

Cleave, John (1969), 'The Primitive Recursive Analysis of Ordinary Differential Equations and the Complexity of Their Solutions', *Journal of Computer and System Sciences*, **3**(4), 447–55.

Cobham, A. (1965), 'The Intrinsic Computational Difficulty of Functions', in *Logic, Methodology and Philosophy of Science – Proceedings of the 1964 International Congress*, edited by Y. Bar-Hillel, North-Holland, Amsterdam, pp. 24–30.

Cole, F.N. (1903), 'On the Factoring of Large Numbers', *Bulletin of the American Mathematical Society*, **10**(3), 134–7.

Compagner, Aaldert (1964), 'Definitions of Randomness', *American Journal of Physics*, **59**(8), 700–705.

Cook, S.A. (1971), 'The Complexity of Theorem Proving Procedures', in *Proceedings of the 3rd ACM Symposium on the Theory of Computing*, ACM Publications, pp. 151–8.

da Costa, Newton C.A. and Francisco A. Doria (1991a), 'Undecidability and Incompleteness in Classical Mechanics', *International Journal of Theoretical Physics*, **30**(8), 1041–73.

da Costa, Newton C.A. and Francisco A. Doria (1991b), 'Classical Physics and Penrose's Thesis', *Foundations of Physics Letters*, **4**(4), 363–73.

da Costa, Newton C.A., Francisco A. Doria and E. Bir (2007), 'On the Metamathematics of the P vs. NP Question', *Applied Mathematics and Computation*, **189**(2), 1223–40.

Davis, Martin (1958), *Computability and Unsolvability*, McGraw-Hill, New York.

Edmonds, J. (1965), 'Paths, Trees and Flowers', *Canadian Journal of Mathematics*, **17**, 449–67.

Einstein, Albert (1955), 'Relativistic Theory of the Non-symmetric Field', in *The Meaning of Relativity*, 5th edn, Princeton University Press, Princeton, New Jersey, Appendix II, pp. 133–66.

Feferman, Solomon, John W. Dawson, Jr., Stephen C. Kleene, Gregory H. Moore, Robert M. Solovay and Jean van Heijenoort (1986), *Kurt Gödel: Collected Works Volume 1: Publications 1929–1936*, Oxford University Press, New York.

Feynman, Richard P. (1982), 'Simulating Physics with Computers', *International Journal of Theoretical Physics*, **21**(6/7), 467–88.

Franzén, Torkel (2005), *Gödel's Theorem: An Incomplete Guide to its Use and Abuse*, A.K. Peters, Wellesley, Massachusetts.

Garey, Michael R. and David S. Johnson (1979), *Computers and Intractability: A Guide to the Theory of NP-completeness*, W.H. Freeman and Company, New York.

Gödel, Kurt (1956), 'Letter to von Neumann', translated and reprinted in Michael Sipser (1992), 'The History and Status of the P versus NP Question', *Proceedings of the Twenty-Fourth Annual ACM Symposium on the Theory of Computing*, Victoria, British Columbia, pp. 603–18.

Goldreich, Oded (2001), 'Computational Complexity', in *Mathematics Unlimited – 2001 and Beyond*, edited by Björn Engquist and Wilfried Schmid, Springer-Verlag, Berlin and Heidelberg.

Goodstein, R.L. (1961), *Recursive Analysis*, North-Holland Publishing Co., Amsterdam.

Goodwin, Richard M. (1951), 'Iteration, Automatic Computers, and Economic Dynamics', *Metroeconomica*, **III**(1), 1–7.

Grzegorczyk, Andrezej (1957), 'On the Definitions of Computable Real Continuous Functions', *Fundamenta Mathematicae*, **44**, 61–71.

Hardy, G.H. (1910), *Orders of Infinity: The 'Infintärcalcül' of Paul Du Bois-Raymond*, Cambridge Tracts in Mathematics and Mathematical Physics, 12, Cambridge University Press, Cambridge, UK.

Hilbert, David (1900), 'Mathematical Problems', *Bulletin of the American Mathematical Society*, **8**, 437–79; translated from the original German: 'Mathematische Probleme' by Dr Mary Winston Newson.

Jaffe, Arthur M. (2006), 'The Millennium Grand Challenge in Mathematics', *Notices of the American Mathematical Society*, **53**(6), 651–60.

Jeffreys, Harold (1926), 'On the Relation to Physics of the Notion of Convergence of Series', *Philosophical Magazine*, **2**(7), 241–4.

Karp, R.M. (1972), 'Reducibility Among Combinatorial Problems', in *Complexity of Computer Computations*, edited by R.E. Miller and J.W. Thatcher, Plenum Press, New York, pp. 85–104.
Karp, Richard (1987), 'Complexity and Parallel Processing: An Interview with Richard Karp', a Turing Award Interview with Karen A. Frenkel, in *ACM Turing Award Lectures – The First Twenty years, 1966–1985*, ACM Press/Addison-Wesley Publishing Company, Reading, Massachusetts.
Keynes, John Maynard (1921), *A Treatise on Probability*, Macmillan and Company Limited, London.
Keynes, John Maynard (1930), 'Economic Possibilities for our Grandchildren', reprinted in *Essays in Persuasion*, The Norton Library, W.W. Norton & Company, Inc., New York.
Khachiyan, L.G. (1979), 'A Polynomial Algorithm for Linear Programming', *Doklady Akad. Nauk USSR*, **244**(5), 1093–6.
Klee, V. and G.J. Minty (1972), 'How Good is the Simplex Algorithm', in *Inequalities, III*, edited by O. Shisha, Academic Press, New York, pp. 159–75.
Kleene, Stephen C. (1952), *Introduction to Metamathematics*, D. Van Nostrand Company, Inc., Princeton, New Jersey.
Kleene, Stephen C. (1967), *Mathematical Logic*, John Wiley & Sons, Inc., New York.
Ko, Ker-I. (1991), *Complexity Theory of Real Functions*, Birkhäuser, Boston and Basel.
Ko, Ker-I. and Harvey Friedman (1982), 'Computational Complexity of Real Functions', *Theoretical Computer Science*, **20**(2), 323–52.
Kolmogorov, Andrei N. (1965), 'Three Approaches to the Definition of the Concept of the "Amount of Information"', *Problems of Information Transmission*, **1**(1), 1–7.
Kolmogorov, Andrei N. (1983), 'Combinatorial Foundations of Information Theory and the Calculus of Probabilities', *Russian Mathematical Surveys*, **38**(4), 29–40.
Lacombe, D. (1955), 'Extension de la Notion de Fonctions Récursive aux Fonctions d'une ou Plusieurs Variables Réelles, I, II, III', *C.R. Acad., Paris*, **240**, 2478–80, **241**, 13–14, 151–3.
Li, Ming and Paul Vitanyi (1993), *An Introduction to Kolmogorov Complexity and its Applications*, Springer-Verlag, Berlin and Heidelberg.
Lorentz, G.G. (1986), *Approximation of Functions*, AMS Chelsea Publishing, Providence, Rhode Island.
Lucas, Robert E. Jr. (1993), 'Making a Miracle', *Econometrica*, **61**(2), 251–72.
Machlup, Fritz (1958), 'Structure and Structural Change: Weaselwords and Jargon', *Zeitschrift für Nationalökonomie*, **18**, 280–98.
Mazur, S. (1963), *Computable Analysis*, Rozprawy Matematyczne, XXXIII, edited by Andrzej Grzegorczyk and Helena Rasiowa, PWN Publishers, Warsaw.
Miller, Webb (1970), 'Recursive Function Theory and Numerical Analysis', *Journal of Computer and System Sciences*, **4**(5), 465–72.
Moore, Christopher (1990), 'Unpredictability and Undecidability in Dynamical Systems', *Physical Review Letters*, **64**(20), 2354–7.
Moschovakis, Yiannis (2001), 'What is an Algorithm?', in *Mathematics Unlimited – 2001 and Beyond*, edited by Björn Engquist and Wilfried Schmid, Springer-Verlag, Berlin and Heidelberg, pp. 910–36.
Mount, Kenneth R. and Stanley Reiter (2002), *Computation and Complexity in Economic Organization*, Cambridge University Press, Cambridge, UK and New York.
Odifreddi, Piergiorgio (1989), *Classical Recursion Theory: The Theory of Functions and Sets of Natural Numbers*, North-Holland, Amsterdam and New York.
Papadimitriou, Christos H. (1994), *Computational Complexity*, Addison-Wesley Publishing Company, Reading, Massachusetts.
Papadimitriou, Christos H. and Kenneth Steiglitz (1982), *Combinatorial Optimization: Algorithms and Complexity*, Prentice-Hall, Inc., Englewood Cliffs, New Jersey.
Penrose, Roger (2004), *The Road to Reality: A Comprehensive Guide to the Laws of the Universe*, Jonathan Cape, London.
Post, Emil (1944), 'Recursively Enumerable Sets of Positive Integers and their Decision Problems', *Bulletin of the American Mathematical Society*, **50**, 284–316.

Pour-El, Marian B. and Jonathan I. Richards (1989), *Computability in Analysis and Physics*, Springer-Verlag, Berlin, Heidelberg and New York.
Pratt, Vaughan R. (1975), 'Every Prime has a Succinct Certificate', *SIAM Journal of Computing*, **4**(3), 214–20.
Richman, Fred (1990), 'Intuitionism as Generalization', *Philosophia Mathematica*, **14**, 124–8.
Robinson, Raphael M. (1952), 'An Essentially Undecidable Axiom System', in Vol.1 of *Proceedings of the International Congress of Mathematicians*, Cambridge, Massachusetts, 1950; American Mathematical Society, Providence, Rhode Island, pp. 729–30.
Rogers, Hartley, Jr. (1967), *Theory of Recursive Functions and Effective Computability*, McGraw-Hill, New York.
Rosser, J. Barkley (1936), 'Extensions of Some Theorems of Gödel and Church', *Journal of Symbolic Logic*, **1**(3), 87–91.
Rosser, J. Barkley, Jr. (2007), 'Computational and Dynamic Complexity in Economics', available at: cob.jmu.edu/rosserjb/DYNAMIC%20 AND%20COMPUTATIONAL%20 COMPLEXITY%20IN%20ECONOMICS.doc.
Rouse Ball, W.W. and H.S.M. Coxeter (1987), *Mathematical Recreations and Essays*, 13th edn, Dover Publications, Inc., New York.
Rubel, Leo. A. (1988), 'Some Mathematical Limitations of the General-purpose Analog Computer', *Advances in Applied Mathematics*, **9**(1), 22–34.
Schechter, Eric (1997), *Handbook of Analysis and its Foundations*, Academic Press, San Diego.
Schrijver, Alexander (1986), *Theory of Linear and Integer Programming*, John Wiley & Sons, Chichester and New York.
Schrijver, Alexander (2003), *Combinatorial Optimization: Polyhedra and Efficiency: Volumes A, B, C*, Springer-Verlag, Berlin and Heidelberg.
Schwartz, Jacob T. (1987), Foreword to *Algorithmic Information Theory* by Gregory J. Chaitin, Cambridge University Press, Cambridge, UK and New York.
Shannon, Claude E. (1941), 'Mathematical Theory of the Differential Analyzer', *Journal of Mathematics and Physics*, **XX**(4), 337–54.
Shepherdson, J.C. (1976), 'On the Definition of Computable Functions of a Real Variable', *Zeitschrift für Mathematische Logik und Grundlagen der Mathematik*, **22**, 391–402.
Shor, N.Z. (1970), 'Utilization of the Operation of Space Dilation in the Minimization of Convex Functions', *Kibernetika*, **6**, 6–12.
Sipser, Michael (1983), 'Borel Sets and Circuit Complexity', *Proceedings of the 15th ACM Symposium on the Theory of Computing*, Association for Computing Machinery.
Sipser, Michael (1992), 'The History and Status of the P versus NP Question', *Proceedings of the Twenty-Fourth Annual ACM Symposium on the Theory of Computing*, Victoria, British Columbia, pp. 603–18.
Smale, Stephen (1988), 'The Newtonian Contribution to Our Understanding of the Computer', in *Newton's Dream*, edited by Marcia Sweet Stayer, published for *Queen's Quarterly*, by McGill-Queen's University Press, pp. 90–95.
Smale, Stephen (1991), 'Theory of Computation', in *Mathematical Research Today and Tomorrow: Viewpoints of Seven Fields Medalists!*, edited by C. Casacuberta and M. Castellet, Springer-Verlag, Berlin and Heidelberg, pp. 60–69.
Smorynski, Craig (1985a), '"Big" News from Archimedes to Friedman', in *Harvey Friedman's Research on the Foundations of Mathematics*, edited by L.A. Harrington, M.D. Morley, A. Ščedrov and S.G. Simpson, North-Holland, Amsterdam and New York, pp. 353–66.
Smorynski, Craig (1985b), 'Some Rapidly Growing Functions', in *Harvey Friedman's Research on the Foundations of Mathematics*, edited by L.A. Harrington, M.D. Morley, A. Ščedrov and S.G. Simpson, North-Holland, Amsterdam and New York, pp. 367–80.
Soare, Robert I. (1987), *Recursively Enumerable Sets and Degrees: A Study of Computable Functions and Computably Generated Sets*, Springer-Verlag, Berlin and Heidelberg.
Solomonoff, Ray J. (1964a), 'A Formal Theory of Inductive Inference: Part I', *Information and Control*, **7**(1), 1–22.

Solomonoff, Ray J. (1964b), 'A Formal Theory of Inductive Inference: Part II', *Information and Control*, **7**(2), 224–54.
Specker, Ernst (1949), 'Nicht konstruktiv beweisbare Sätze der Analysis', *The Journal of Symbolic Logic*, **14**(3), 145–58.
Srinivasa Rao, K. (1998), *Srinivasa Ramanujan: A Mathematical Genius*, EastWest Books (Madras) Pvt. Ltd., Chennai and Bangalore.
Smullyan, Raymond (1992), *Gödel's Incompleteness Theorems*, Oxford University Press, Oxford.
Tikhomirov, V.M. (1989), 'A.N. Kolmogorov and Approximation Theory', *Russian Mathematical Surveys*, **44**(1), 101–52.
Turing, Alan M. (1936–37), 'On Computable Numbers, with an Application to the *Entscheidungsproblem*', *Proceedings of the London Mathematical Society*, **42**, 230–65, Correction, **43**, 544–6.
Uspensky, Vladimir A. (1992), 'Complexity and Entropy: An Introduction to the Theory of Kolmogorov Complexity', in *Kolmogorov Complexity and Computational Complexity*, edited by Osamu Watanabe, Springer-Verlag, Berlin and Heidelberg, pp. 85–102.
Uspensky, Vladimir A. and A. Shen (1996), 'Relations between Varieties of Kolmogorov Complexities', *Mathematical Systems Theory*, **29**(1), 271–92.
van Lambalgen, Michiel (1992), 'Independence, Randomness and the Axiom of Choice', *Journal of Symbolic Logic*, **57**(4), 1274–1304.
Velupillai, Kumaraswamy (2000), *Computable Economics*, Oxford University Press, Oxford.
Velupillai, K. Vela (2004), 'Economic Dynamics and Computation – Resurrecting the Icarus Tradition', *Metroeconomica*, **55**(2&3), 239–64.
Vitushkin, A.G. (1961), *Theory of the Transmission and Processing of Information*, translated from the Russian by Ruth Feinstein, Pergamon Press, Oxford and London.
Weihrauch, Klaus (2000), *Computable Analysis: An Introduction*, Springer-Verlag, Berlin and Heidelberg.
Wigderson, Avi (2006), 'P, NP and Mathematics – A Computational Complexity Perspective', available at: www.math.ias.edu/~avi/PUBLICATIONS/MYPAPERS/W06/W06.pdf.
Wilf, Herbert S. (1986), *Algorithms and Complexity*, Prentice-Hall, Inc., Englewood Cliffs, New Jersey.

PART II

MARKET DYNAMICS

5. Bounded rationality and learning in complex markets*

Cars H. Hommes

5.1 Introduction

There are two opposing views concerning the expectations hypothesis in economics and finance. According to the traditional, neoclassical view, propagated by Muth (1961) and Lucas (1972), agents form rational expectations (RE) without any systematic forecasting mistakes. In the rational framework it is often assumed that agents have full knowledge of their economic environment, and use all available information from economic theory to compute rational forecast. Moreover, typically it is assumed that *all* agents are fully rational, leading to the representative rational agent benchmark. Friedman (1953) provided an early argument in support of the representative rational agent framework, namely that irrational agents would be driven out of the market, since rational agents earn higher profits or utility. Stated differently, evolutionary selection prevents irrational behavior and the economy may be described *as if* all agents are perfectly rational.

Simon (1957) already criticized this view, arguing that deliberation and information gathering costs should be taken into account. More recently, work on *bounded rationality* in the 1990s, surveyed, for example, in Sargent (1993) and Conlisk (1996), has challenged the traditional view, emphasizing that the extreme assumptions concerning perfect knowledge of the economy and infinite computing capacities are highly unrealistic and in sharp contrast with observed behavior in laboratory experiments with human subjects (for example, Tversky and Kahnemann, 1974). In macroeconomics, much work has been done on *adaptive learning*, as surveyed, for example, in Evans and Honkapohja (2001). A key underlying assumption is that agents do *not* know the underlying "law of motion" of the economy, but instead use time series observations to form expectations based upon their own "perceived law of motion", trying to learn the model parameters as more observations become available. Much of this literature has focused on the stability of rational expectations equilibria (REE) and equilibrium selection, in an attempt to justify rationality by adaptive learning.

Stimulated by work at the Santa Fe Institute, the view that markets are *complex evolving systems* has gained popularity; see, for example, the Santa

Fe conference proceedings, Anderson, Arrow and Pines (1988) and Arthur, Durlauf and Lane (1997), the collection of papers in Rosser (2004) and the recent survey in Arthur (2006). When the economy is viewed as a complex system with many interacting agents, it seems hard to justify perfect structural knowledge about the economy and fully rational expectations, since knowledge about the beliefs of all other agents would be required. A large population of boundedly rational heterogeneous agents, using different forecasting rules ranging from simple to sophisticated, seems much more natural and in line with human behavior. A problem of bounded rationality, however, is that there are many degrees of freedom, and which model of bounded rationality is an accurate description of learning behavior at the individual level?

In this chapter we review some work on bounded rationality, expectation formation and learning in complex markets. We will use the familiar demand–supply cobweb model, exactly the same framework employed by Muth (1961), in his seminal paper introducing rational expectations. We emphasize two stories of bounded rationality, one story of adaptive learning and another story of evolutionary selection; at the end of the chapter we combine both stories. An important point of departure for both stories is that agents do not understand the world in its full complexity, but have some simple perception of this complex world and use relatively simple decision heuristics or forecasting rules. According to the first adaptive learning story, agents are identical, and can be represented by an "average agent", who adapts his or her behavior, trying to learn an optimal rule within a class of simple rules. An example is the consistent expectations equilibrium proposed by Hommes and Sorger (1998), where agents try to learn the best linear rule, minimizing forecasting errors, in an unknown nonlinear economy. The optimal linear rule fits the observable sample mean and sample autocorrelation structure of the nonlinear economy. The second story is concerned with heterogeneous, interacting agents and evolutionary selection of different forecasting rules. Heterogeneous agent models are becoming increasingly popular in finance, where a distinction between fundamentalists and chartist trading strategies can be made; see, for example, Hommes (2006) and LeBaron (2006) for extensive surveys. Here, we consider the *adaptive belief systems* proposed by Brock and Hommes (1997, 1998), where agents can choose between a costly sophisticated forecasting strategy, such as rational expectations, and a freely available simple strategy, such as naive expectations. At the end of the chapter, we will integrate both stories and consider an economy with evolutionary selection between a costly sophisticated adaptive learning rule and a cheap, simple forecasting rule such as naive expectations.

There is a lot of theoretical work on expectations formation and learning when agents are boundedly rational, but surprisingly little experimental work on expectations and learning of human subjects has been done. A controlled laboratory environment is well suited to investigate how individuals form expectations and learn from experience, and how the market aggregates individual forecasting strategies. Recently, Hommes et al. (2007) conducted experiments on expectation formation within a cobweb framework. We confront theoretical work on expectation formation and learning with the observed "stylized facts" in these laboratory experiments.

The chapter is organized as follows. Section 5.2 discusses cobweb dynamics under various expectations rules, such as naive, rational and adaptive expectations. Section 5.3 focuses on laboratory experiments with human subjects on expectation formation. In Section 5.4 we discuss adaptive learning, in particular the notion of consistent expectations equilibrium (CEE) and sample autocorrelation (SAC-)learning. Section 5.5 focuses on heterogeneity and evolutionary competition between different forecasting rules and ends with an example where adaptive learning and evolutionary selection are combined. Finally, Section 5.6 briefly discusses a future perspective.

5.2 The cobweb model

The classical cobweb model is a partial equilibrium model describing commodity price fluctuations of a non-storable good, such as corn or hogs, that takes one time period to produce. It is one of the simplest benchmark models in economic dynamics and can be found in many standard textbooks (for example, Nicholson, 1995, pp. 590–94). Producers must form price expectations one period ahead and derive their optimal production decision from expected profit maximization. Given producers' price forecast p_t^e, optimal supply is given by

$$S(p_t^e) = \text{argmax}_{q_t} \{p_t^e q_t - c(q_t)\} = (c')^{-1}(p_t^e). \tag{5.1}$$

The cost function $c(\cdot)$ is assumed to be strictly convex so that the second-order condition for profit maximization is satisfied. The marginal cost function is then invertible and supply is strictly increasing in expected price. The simplest case arises when the cost function is quadratic, $c(q) = q^2/(2s)$, yielding a linear supply curve

$$S(p^e) = sp^e \quad s > 0. \tag{5.2}$$

In general a strictly convex cost curve leads to a nonlinear, increasing, supply curve. As an example, we will consider an increasing, S-shaped supply curve

$$S(p^e) = b + \arctan(\lambda p^e), \quad \lambda > 0, b > \pi/2, \tag{5.3}$$

where the parameter λ tunes the nonlinearity of the supply curve and $b > \pi/2$ is a parameter tuning the production level ensuring that production is always non-negative.[1]

Consumer demand D depends upon the current market price p_t. The demand curve D can be derived from consumer utility maximization, but for our purposes it is not necessary to specify these preferences explicitly. Throughout the chapter we will simply work with a linearly decreasing demand curve

$$D(p_t) = a - dp_t + \varepsilon_t, \quad a,d > 0, \tag{5.4}$$

where $-d$ is the slope of the demand curve, a determines the demand level and ε_t is an independently and identically distributed (IID) stochastic series representing exogenous random demand shocks. If beliefs are *homogeneous*, that is, all producers have identical price expectations p_t^e, market clearing implies

$$D(p_t) = S(p_t^e) \tag{5.5}$$

yielding the realized market price

$$P_t = D^{-1}(S(p_t^e)) = \frac{a + \varepsilon_t - S(p_t^e)}{d}. \tag{5.6}$$

With an increasing supply curve and a decreasing demand curve, there can only be one price, denoted by $p = p^*$, where demand and supply intersect. The price dynamics in (5.6) thus depends upon the demand and supply curves, as well as on the assumed expectations hypothesis. How do producers form price expectations? We first consider the benchmarks of naive, rational and adaptive expectations.

5.2.1 *Naive expectations*

Before the rational expectations revolution it was common practice to use simple forecasting rules. The simplest case studied in the 1930s, for example, by Ezekiel (1938), assumes that producers have naive expectations, that is, their prediction equals the last observed price $p_t^e = p_{t-1}$. Under naive expectations, the price dynamics (5.6) becomes

$$p_t = D^{-1}(S(p_{t-1})). \tag{5.7}$$

According to the well-known cobweb theorem (see, for example, Ezekiel, 1938), there are essentially two possibilities for the price dynamics under naive expectations, depending upon the ratio of marginal supply and marginal demand at the steady state p^*. When $-1 < S'(p^*)/D'(p^*) < 0$ the steady state p^* is (locally) stable, and prices converge to the steady state. If, on the other hand, $S'(p^*)/D'(p^*) < -1$ the steady state p^* is (locally) unstable, and prices diverge from the steady state. In the case of a nonlinear, bounded supply curve as in (5.3), if the steady state is unstable, prices will converge to a stable two-cycle, with regular up and down oscillations, as illustrated in Figure 5.2 in the next section.

5.2.2 *Rational expectations*

It has been argued that simple forecasting rules, such as naive expectations, lead to *systematic forecasting errors*. This argument seems particularly strong when the model generates a two-cycle, even in the presence of (small) exogenous shocks. When producers expect a high (low) price, they will supply a high (low) quantity and consequently the realized market price will be low (high). Along a "hog cycle" of up and down price oscillations, expectations are thus *systematically wrong*, and forecasting errors are strongly correlated. Rational agents would learn from their systematic errors and revise expectations accordingly, so the argument goes. These considerations led Muth (1961) to introduce *rational expectations*, where producers' subjective price expectations equal the objective conditional mathematical expectation of the market price, that is, $p_t^e = E_t[p_t]$. Using market equilibrium (5.5) with the linear demand curve (5.4), taking conditional mathematical expectation on both sides, we can solve for the rational expectations forecast

$$p_t^e = E_t[p_t] = p^*, \tag{5.8}$$

where p^* is the unique price corresponding to the intersection point of demand and supply. Given producers' rational price forecast $p_t^e = p^*$, the actual law of motion (5.6) becomes

$$p_t = p^* + \frac{\varepsilon_t}{d}. \tag{5.9}$$

The cobweb model therefore has a unique REE, given by an IID process with mean p^*. Along an REE expectations are *self-fulfilling* and producers make no systematic forecasting errors, since forecasting errors are uncorrelated. It is important to note that, in order to form rational expectations, perfect knowledge of underlying market equilibrium equations is required and, in particular, agents must be able to compute the intersection point p^*.

5.2.3 *Adaptive expectations*

It is worthwhile reconsidering the issue of "systematic forecasting errors" in the light of the recent discovery of chaotic dynamics in simple nonlinear deterministic systems and under the more plausible assumption of bounded rationality, where agents do not know underlying market equilibrium equations, but only use time series observations to forecast.[2] As an example, consider the cobweb model with *adaptive expectations*, that is,

$$p_t^e = (1 - w)p_{t-1}^e + wp_{t-1}, \quad 0 \leq w \leq 1, \tag{5.10}$$

where w is the expectations weight factor. The expected price is a weighted average of yesterday's expected and realized prices, or equivalently, the expected price is adapted by a factor w in the direction of the most recent realization. Adaptive expectations may thus be seen as "error learning" with a constant factor. Notice that for $w = 1$, adaptive expectations reduces to naive expectations. Under adaptive expectations and, given the linear demand curve (5.4), the dynamics of expected prices in the cobweb model becomes

$$p_t^e = (1 - w)p_{t-1}^e + w\left(\frac{a + \varepsilon_t - S(p_{t-1}^e)}{d}\right). \tag{5.11}$$

Chiarella (1988) and Hommes (1991, 1994) have shown that, without any random shocks ε_t, for *nonlinear*, but monotonic, demand and/or supply curves, this nonlinear deterministic difference equation can easily generate chaotic fluctuations in expected prices, and therefore also in prices, quantities and forecasting errors. Figure 5.1 shows a bifurcation diagram with respect to the expectations weight factor w, with the nonlinear, S-shaped supply curve (5.3). For high values of w, sufficiently close to $w = 1$ (that is, close to naive expectations) prices converge to a stable two-cycle, whereas for small values of w, sufficiently close to $w = 0$, prices converge to the RE steady state. For intermediate w values however, chaotic price oscillations arise.

When prices fluctuate chaotically, the corresponding forecasting errors will be highly unpredictable and the question arises whether boundedly rational agents would be able to detect any structure in these chaotic forecasting errors and improve upon their simple adaptive forecasts. If patterns are indeed hard to discover, then adaptive expectations with chaotic price fluctuations might be a satisfactory (long-run) boundedly rational equilibrium.

5.3 Laboratory experiments

There is a lot of theoretical work on expectations formation and learning when agents are boundedly rational, but surprisingly few laboratory experiments with human subjects have been performed to study how individuals form expectations and learn from experience, and how the market aggregates individual forecasts.

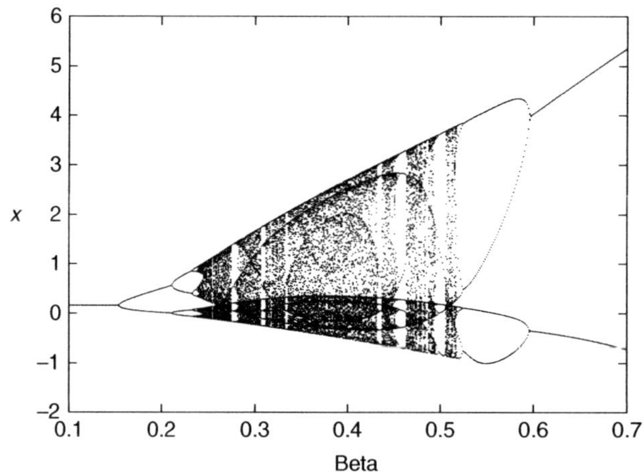

Note: x is the deviation from the inflection point of the nonlinear, S-shaped supply curve (5.3). For large values of w prices converge to a regular two-cycle with large amplitude. As w decreases the amplitude of price fluctuations decreases and a bifurcation route to chaos occurs. When w becomes very small, chaotic fluctuations are stabilized and prices converge to REE

Figure 5.1 Bifurcation diagram with respect to the expectations weight factor w, $0.1 \leq w \leq 0.7$, with the other parameters fixed at $a = 0.7$, $d = 0.25$ and $\lambda = 4.8$

Early experiments on expectations have been done in Schmalensee (1976), who uses historical data on wheat prices and asks subjects to predict the mean wheat price for the next five periods. In Dwyer et al. (1993) and Hey (1994) subjects have to predict a time series generated by a stochastic process such as a random walk or a simple linear first-order autoregressive process. More recently, Kelley and Friedman (2002) consider learning in an orange juice futures price forecasting experiment, where prices are driven by a linear stochastic process with two exogenous variables (weather and competing supply). A drawback of these papers is that subjects are forecasting an exogenous process, and there is no feedback from individual expectations to realizations.

Williams (1987) considers expectation formation in an experimental double auction market, which varies from period to period by small shifts in the market clearing price. Participants predict the mean contract price for four or five consecutive periods. The participant with the lowest forecast error earns $1. Peterson (1993) studies price predictions in repeated double auction experimental asset markets, as in the famous bubble experiments of Smith, Suchanek and Williams (1988), and shows that forecasts tend to be biased and inconsistent with RE, but there is a tendency of forecasts to evolve in the direction of RE.

Marimon, Spear and Sunder (1993) and Marimon and Sunder (1993, 1994, 1995) have studied expectation formation in laboratory experiments in inflationary overlapping generations economies. Marimon, Spear and Sunder (1993) find experimental evidence for expectationally driven cycles and coordination of beliefs on a sunspot two-cycle equilibrium, but only after agents have been exposed to exogenous shocks of a similar kind. Marimon and Sunder (1995) present experimental evidence that a "simple" rule, such as a constant growth of the money supply, can help coordinate agents' beliefs and help stabilize the economy. More recently, Adam (2007) conducted laboratory experiments on inflationary expectations.

Here we discuss some recent laboratory experiments of Hommes et al. (2007) on individual expectations and learning in the cobweb framework. See also Hommes et al. (2005) for similar experiments in an asset pricing framework. The participants in the experiments were asked to predict next period's price of a certain, unspecified, good. The realized price p_t in the experiment was determined by the (unknown) cobweb market equilibrium equation

$$D(p_t) = \frac{1}{K}\sum_{i=1}^{K} S(p^e_{i,t}), \tag{5.12}$$

where $D(p_t)$ is the demand for the good at price p_t, K is the size of the group, $p^e_{i,t}$ is the price forecast by participant i and $S(p^e_{i,t})$ is the supply of producer i depending upon the forecast by participant i. Demand and supply curves D and S were fixed during all experiments (except for small random shocks to the demand curve) and unknown to the participants. We focus on the group experiments with $K = 6$, as in Hommes et al. (2007). Hommes, Sonnemans and van de Velden (2000) ran one-person experiments (that is, $K = 1$); Colucci and Valori (2006) use these one-person experiments to estimate various learning models.[3] Solving (5.12) for the market equilibrium price, with a linear demand curve as in (5.4), yields

$$p_t = \frac{a - \frac{1}{K}\sum_{i=1}^{K} S(p^e_{i,t})}{d} + \varepsilon_t, \tag{5.13}$$

where ε_t are IID demand shocks, which are drawn from a normal distribution N (0, 0.5). In the experiments the parameters were fixed at $a = 2.3$, $d = 0.25$ and $K = 6$, and we used the nonlinear, S-shaped supply curve (geometrically similar to the S-shaped supply curve [5.3]):

$$S(p^e_{i,t}) = \mathrm{Tanh}(\lambda(p^e_{i,t} - 6)) + 1. \tag{5.14}$$

Expectation formation of the producers is the only part of the model that is affected by the participants in the experiments. Participants did not know underlying market equilibrium equations, nor were they informed about the distribution of any exogenous shocks to demand and/or supply. The participants were told that they were advisors to producers of an unspecified good and that the price was determined by market clearing. Based upon this information the participants were asked to predict next period's price. The predicted price had to be between 0 and 10 and the realized price was also always between 0 and 10. Participants' earnings in each period were a quadratic function of their forecasting error. The better their forecast, the higher their earnings. After every period the participants were informed about the realized price in the experiment. Also a time series of the participant's own prediction and a time series of the realized price in the experiment was shown on their computer screen.

Participants in the experiments therefore had little information about the price-generating process and had to rely mainly upon time series observations of past prices and predictions. The information in the experiment was thus similar to the information assumption underlying much of the bounded rationality literature, where agents form expectations based upon time series observations. Our set-up enables us to test the expectations hypothesis in a controlled dynamic environment. The main question was whether agents can learn and coordinate on the unique REE, in a world where consumers and producers act as if they were maximizing utility and profits, but where they do *not* know underlying market equilibrium equations and only observe time series of prices and expected prices. Our choice for a nonlinear, S-shaped supply curve enables us to investigate whether agents can avoid systematic forecasting errors, as would, for example, occur along a two-cycle under naive expectations, or can even learn a REE steady state.

In their experiment, Hommes et al. (2007) considered a stable and an unstable treatment, which only differ in the parameter λ tuning the nonlinearity of the supply curve (5.14). In the stable treatment, if all subjects use naive expectations, prices converge to the RE steady state. In contrast, in the unstable treatment, if all subjects use naive expectations, prices diverge from the RE steady state and converge to the stable two-cycle, with systematic forecasting errors, as illustrated in Figure 5.2 (top left panel). Figure 5.2 also illustrates what would happen in the unstable treatment of the experiment if all subjects would use one of the other well-known benchmark expectations rules, namely adaptive expectations ($w = 0.2$), rational expectations (that is, use the RE price p^* as forecast), learning by average, that is, use the sample average

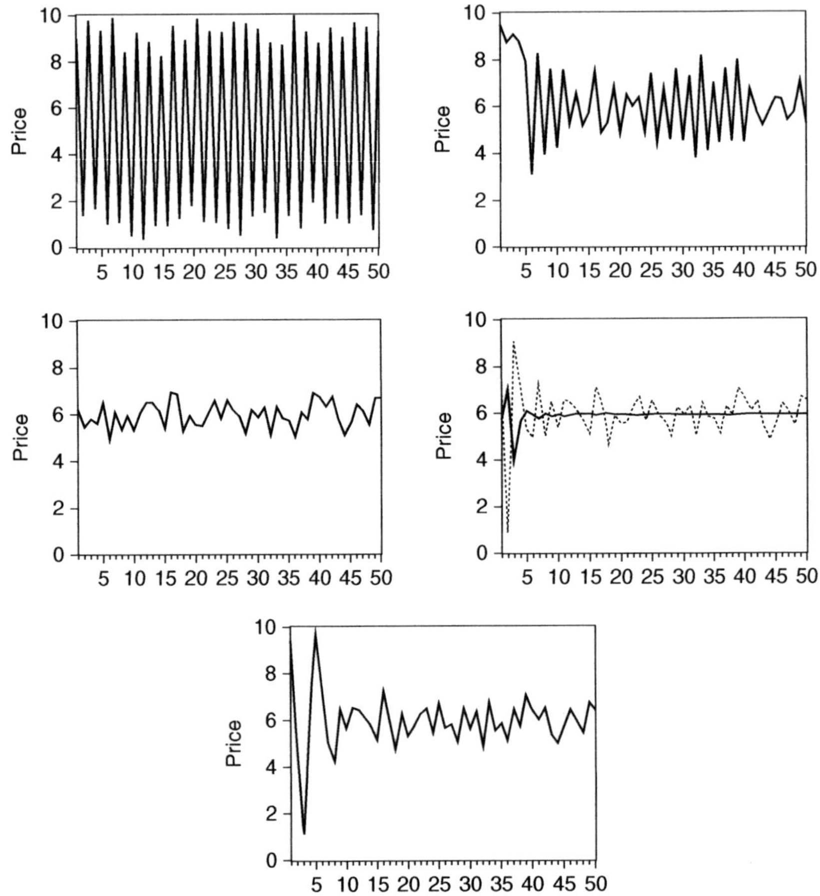

Figure 5.2 Price fluctuations in the cobweb model under naive expectations (top left), adaptive expectations (top right), rational expectations (middle left), average price forecast (middle right) and SAC-learning (bottom)

$$p_t^e = \left(\sum_{j=0}^{t-1} p_j \right) / t, \tag{5.15}$$

for example, as in Carlson (1969), and sample autocorrelation (SAC-) learning (that is, updating sample average and first-order sample autocorrelation coefficient, as discussed in detail in Section 5.4).

Figure 5.3 shows time series of the realized prices in two typical group experiments, one stable and one unstable treatment, and Table 5.1

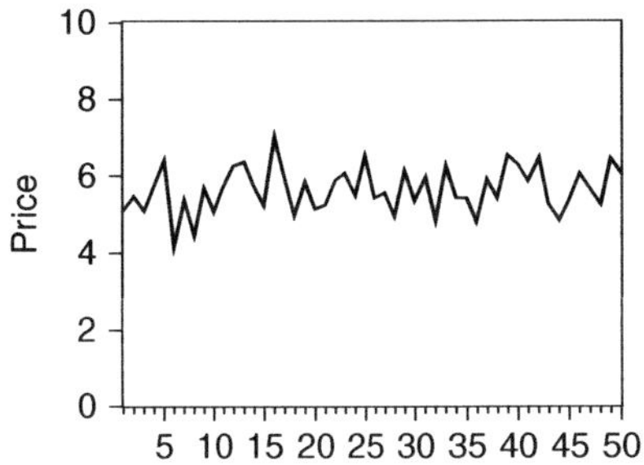

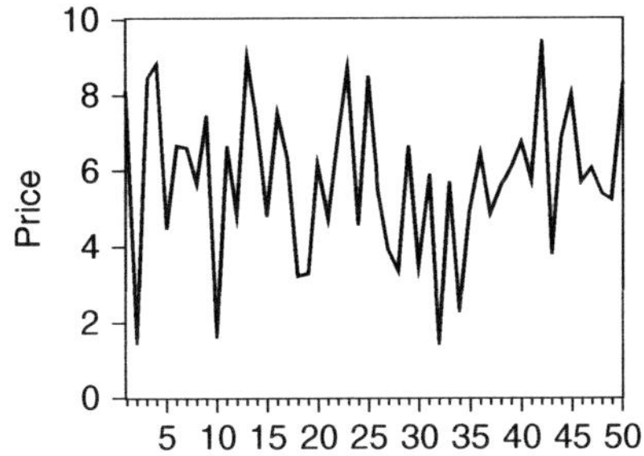

Note: In the stable treatment (left panel; $\lambda = 0.22$) the price quickly converges to the RE price, whereas in the unstable treatment (right panel; $\lambda = 2$) prices do not converge but exhibit excess volatility, characterized by strongly fluctuating prices around the RE price

Figure 5.3 Realized market prices in two different cobweb group experiments

Table 5.1 Sample mean and sample variance of realized market prices in the laboratory experiments for the stable and the unstable treatment, over the full sample of 50 periods and over the subsamples of the first 25 and the last 25 periods, together with rational expectations benchmarks

	1–25		26–50		1–50	
	Sample average	Sample variance	Sample average	Sample variance	Sample average	Sample variance
Stable treatment ($\lambda = 0.22$)						
RE	5.57	0.25	5.57	0.25	5.57	0.25
Experiment	5.59	0.44	5.66	0.29	5.63	0.36
Unstable treatment ($\lambda = 2$)						
RE	5.91	0.25	5.91	0.25	5.91	0.25
Experiment	6.07	4.75	5.50	3.32	5.79	4.04

summarizes the sample mean and sample variances, over the subsamples 1–25, 26–50 and the full sample 1–50, for both treatments and for the corresponding RE benchmarks. For both treatments, the sample mean of realized prices is very close to the (unknown) RE price. Moreover, in the stable treatment, the sample variance (0.44, 0.29 and 0.36 respectively, over the first half, the second half and the full sample) is close to the variance (0.25) of the RE benchmark. In contrast, in the unstable treatment the sample variance (4.75, 3.32 and 4.04 respectively, over the first half, the second half and the full sample) is significantly higher than the variance (0.25) of the RE benchmark, so that the unstable treatment exhibits excess volatility. Hommes et al. (2007) also look at autocorrelations in realized market prices, and find that there is no statistically significant autocorrelations in realized market prices, for both the stable and the unstable treatments. Apparently, the heterogeneous interaction of individual forecasting rules has washed out all linear predictable structure in realized market prices. The stylized facts of realized market prices in the cobweb experiments may thus be summarized as follows:

1. The sample mean of realized market prices is very close to the RE price.
2. The sample variance of realized market prices depends on the treatment:
   (a) in the stable treatment the sample variance is very close to the RE benchmark;
   (b) in the unstable treatment the sample variance is significantly higher than the RE benchmark.
3. There is no linear autocorrelation left in realized market prices.

One may say that the stable treatment converges to RE,[4] whereas the unstable treatment exhibits excess volatility, with prices fluctuating irregularly (no autocorrelations) and with high amplitude around the RE benchmark.

It is useful to compare these experimental results to the theoretical benchmarks illustrated in Figure 5.2.[5] These are *representative agent* benchmarks, where all agents use the same forecasting rule, and demand and supply are exactly the same as in the unstable treatment in the experiment. Naive expectations is clearly very different from the experiments, since it leads to high amplitude price fluctuation with regular, predictable up and down (noisy) period 2 oscillations. Adaptive expectations is also inconsistent with the experiments. Although the amplitude is smaller, the price fluctuations are too regular, with frequent up and down oscillations. In contrast to the experiments, the price series under adaptive expectations, for example, exhibits strong negative first-order autocorrelation. The time series under rational expectations is very similar to the time series in the stable treatment (the exogenous shocks in the experiments are the same as for the RE benchmark simulation), but very different from the unstable treatment, which has a much larger amplitude. RE is therefore a good description in the stable treatment, but not in the unstable treatment. Finally, learning by average or by sample autocorrelation always leads to (quick) convergence to RE, which is inconsistent with the observed excess volatility in the unstable treatment of the experiments. None of these representative agent learning models thus can explain the cobweb experiments, suggesting that *heterogeneous expectations* play a key role in expectation formation of boundedly rational agents. Before turning to heterogeneous expectations models in Section 5.5, we discuss adaptive learning by an "average agent" in Section 5.4.

5.4 Adaptive learning

Adaptive learning usually refers to the situation where agents use some parameterized rule, and update the parameters over time as additional observations become available. Agents thus try to learn the parameters of their rule, for example behaving as a time series econometrician using a recursive ordinary least squares (OLS) updating rule. Marcet and Sargent (1989) contains early examples of such an approach; Evans and Honkapohja (2001) contains an extensive and excellent overview of adaptive learning in macroeconomics. Within the cobweb framework, adaptive learning has been applied, for example, by Bray and Savin (1986).

Adaptive learning may provide a learning story how agents may learn an REE, without structural knowledge of market equilibrium equations but based on time series observations. In fact, we have seen an example already, since the average price forecast rule (5.15) can be obtained from OLS regression of prices on a constant. As we have seen, the average price forecast rule enforces convergence to the unique REE in the cobweb model. In cases when there are multiple REE, adaptive learning may be used as an equilibrium selection device, providing a justification of RE equilibria that are stable under learning.

However, adaptive learning need not always converge to REE. In particular, when the perceived law of motion (that is, the law of motion agents believe in) is *misspecified* (that is, different from the true law of motion), the learning process need not converge to an REE steady state, but may lead to some *boundedly rational learning equilibrium*, leading to expectations-driven periodic or even chaotic fluctuations. Well-known examples are Bullard (1994), Schönhofer (1999),[6] and Bullard and Duffy (1998); Grandmont (1998) contains a discussion of (in-)stability conditions of adaptive learning rules. Evans and Honkapohja (2001) use the notion of *restricted perception equilibria* to describe a situation where agents' perceived law of motion is misspecified, and agents try to learn a rule that is optimal within a limited class of misspecified rules. Branch (2006) wrote a stimulating recent review on restricted perception equilibria, and their importance for macro.

The purpose of this section is to discuss a simple adaptive learning scheme, sample autocorrelation (SAC-)learning, as introduced by Hommes and Sorger (1998). In this setting agents are trying to learn the best *linear* rule (according to forecasting performance) in an unknown, *nonlinear* economy. In equilibrium the linear rule has the same autocorrelation structure as the unknown nonlinear system, and Hommes and Sorger (1998) called this situation a consistent expectations equilibrium. Within the cobweb model, we will see that SAC-learning may sometimes converge to an REE steady state, but may also fail to converge and even lead to chaotic fluctuations and excess volatility.

5.4.1 Consistent expectations equilibrium (CEE)

We start from a motivating example in chaos theory. Consider the dynamics

$$x_{t+1} = T_\beta(x_t), \tag{5.16}$$

where $-1 < \beta < +1$ and $T_\beta(x)$: $[0, 1] \to [0, 1]$ is the 1-D piecewise linear *asymmetric tent map* (see the graphs in Figure 5.4)

$$T_\beta(x) = \begin{cases} \frac{2}{1+\beta}x, & 0 \leq x \leq \frac{(\beta+1)}{2} \\ \frac{2}{1-\beta}(1-x), & \frac{(\beta+1)}{2} < x \leq 1. \end{cases} \tag{5.17}$$

This piecewise linear map is expanding, that is, $|T'_\beta(x) > 1$, and typical trajectories are chaotic. In particular, the following properties of the dynamics are well known (Bunow and Weiss, 1979; Sakai and Tokumaru, 1980):

1. Almost all time paths $\{x_t\}_{t=0}^{\infty}$ are chaotic and dense in [0, 1].
2. For almost all initial states $x_0 \in [0, 1]$, *the sample average* of the (chaotic) time path is $\bar{x} = \lim_{T\to\infty}\frac{1}{T+1}\sum_{t=0}^{T}x_t = \frac{1}{2}$.
3. For almost all initial states $x_0 \in [0, 1]$, the *sample autocorrelation coefficient* at lag j is $\rho_j = \beta^j$.

These properties imply that the nonlinear dynamical system (5.16) has the same autocorrelation structure as a stochastic AR(1) process. Boundedly rational agents observing time series generated by the unknown nonlinear process (5.16) and using linear statistical techniques, might wrongly believe that the time series is generated by a stochastic AR(1) process. This example motivated the concept of consistent expectations equilibrium, introduced in Hommes and Sorger (1998), building on earlier work in Hommes (1998) and Sorger (1998), and the concept of *self-fulfilling mistake* of Grandmont (1998).

We discuss the CEE concept within the cobweb model. Assume that agents believe that prices are generated by a stochastic AR(1) process. Given this perceived law of motion and prices known up to p_{t-1}, the predictor for p_t minimizing the mean squared prediction error is

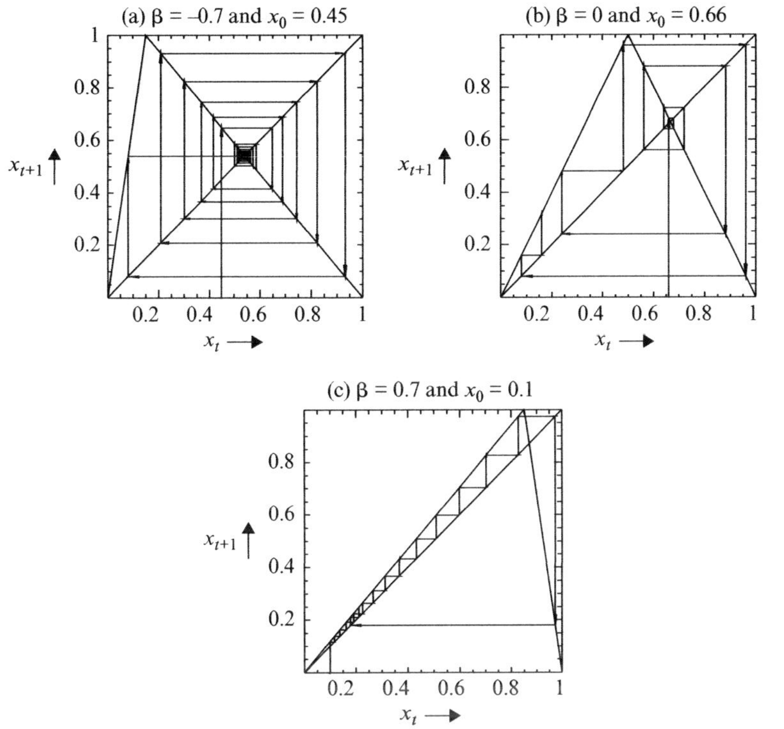

Note: In each case, a typical trajectory is chaotic with sample mean 1/2. The first-order sample autocorellation coefficient of a chaotic trajectory equals β.

Figure 5.4 Graphs of the asymmetric tent map for different values of the parameter β

$$p_t^e = \alpha + \beta(p_{t-1} - \alpha) \tag{5.18}$$

where the parameters α and β, $\beta \in [-1, 1]$ represent the long-run average and the first-order autocorrelation coefficient. Given that agents use the linear predictor (5.18), the implied actual law of motion for the cobweb model becomes

$$p_t = F_{\alpha,\beta}(p_{t-1}) := D^{-1}S(\alpha + \beta(p_{t-1} - \alpha)). \tag{5.19}$$

The sample average of a time series $(p_t)_{t=0}^{\infty}$ is defined as

$$\bar{p} = \lim_{T\to\infty}\frac{1}{T+1}\sum_{t=0}^{T} p_t \tag{5.20}$$

and the sample autocorrelation coefficients are given by

$$\rho_j = \lim_{T\to\infty} \frac{c_{j,T}}{c_{0,T}}, \quad j \geq 1, \tag{5.21}$$

where

$$c_{j,T} = \frac{1}{T+1} \sum_{t=0}^{T-j} (p_t - \bar{p})(p_{t+j} - \bar{p}), \quad j \geq 0. \tag{5.22}$$

A CEE is now defined as

DEFINITION A triple $\{(p_t)_{t=0}^{\infty}; \alpha, \beta\}$, where $(p_t)_{t=0}^{\infty}$ is a sequence of prices and α and β are real numbers, $\beta \in [-1, 1]$, is called a consistent expectations equilibrium (CEE) if

1. the sequence $(p_t)_{t=0}^{\infty}$ satisfies the implied actual law of motion (5.19);
2. the sample average $\bar{p}$ in (5.20) exists and is equal to α; and
3. the sample autocorrelation coefficients $\rho_j, j \geq 1$, in (5.21) exist and the following is true:
   (a) if $(p_t)_{t=0}^{\infty}$ is a convergent sequence, then $\text{sgn}(\rho_j) = \text{sgn}(\beta^j)$, $j \geq 1$;
   (b) if $(p_t)_{t=0}^{\infty}$ is not convergent, then $\rho_j = \beta^j, j \geq 1$.

Stated differently, a CEE is a price sequence together with an AR(1) belief such that expectations are self-fulfilling in terms of the *observable* sample average and sample autocorrelations. Along a CEE, expectations are thus correct in a linear statistical sense.

5.4.2 *Sample autocorrelation learning*

So far, the notion of CEE involves a given AR(1) belief, with fixed parameters α and β. Now consider the more flexible situation of adaptive learning with agents updating their AR(1) belief parameters α_t and β_t over time, as additional observations become available. A natural learning scheme fitting the framework of CEE is based upon sample average and sample autocorrelation coefficients.

For any finite set of past observations $\{p_0, p_1, \ldots, p_t\}$ the sample average is

$$\alpha_t = \frac{1}{t+1} \sum_{i=0}^{t} p_i, \quad t \geq 1 \tag{5.23}$$

and the first-order sample autocorrelation coefficient is

$$\beta_t = \frac{\sum_{i=0}^{t-1} (p_i - \alpha_t)(p_{i+1} - \alpha_t)}{\sum_{i=0}^{t} (p_i - \alpha_t)^2}, \quad t \geq 1. \tag{5.24}$$

When, in each period, the belief parameters are updated according to (5.23) and (5.24) the (temporary) law of motion (5.19) becomes

$$p_{t+1} = F_{\alpha_t,\beta_t}(p_t) = D^{-1}S(\alpha_t + \beta_t(p_t - \alpha_t)), \quad t \geq 0. \qquad (5.25)$$

We call the dynamical system (5.23)–(5.25) the actual dynamics with sample autocorrelation learning (SAC-learning).[7] The initial state for the system (5.23)–(5.25) can be any triple (p_0, α_0, β_0) with $\beta_0 \in [-1, 1]$.

Which type of CEE exist in the cobweb model, and to which of them will the SAC-learning dynamics converge? Hommes and Sorger (1998) show that in the most relevant case, when demand is decreasing and supply is increasing, the *only* CEE is the RE steady state price p^*. This means that, even when underlying market equilibrium equations are *not* known, agents should be able to learn and coordinate on the REE price simply by looking at sample averages and sample autocorrelations. Although other simple forecasting rules, such as adaptive expectations, might lead to chaotic price fluctuations, these forecasting rules are inconsistent in terms of sample autocorrelations. Hence, in a nonlinear cobweb economy with monotonic demand and supply, boundedly rational agents should, at least in theory, be able to learn the unique REE from time series observations.[8]

In general however, given an AR(1) belief, there are at least three possible types of CEE:

- a steady state CEE in which the price sequence $(p_t)_{t=0}^{\infty}$ converges to a steady state p^*, with $\alpha = p^*$ and $\beta = 0$;
- a two-cycle CEE in which the price sequence $(p_t)_{t=0}^{\infty}$ converges to a period 2-cycle $\{p_1^*, p_2^*\}, p_1^* \neq p_2^*$, with $\alpha = (p_1^* + p_2^*)/2$ and $\beta = -1$;
- a chaotic CEE in which the price sequence $(p_t)_{t=0}^{\infty}$ is chaotic, with sample average α and autocorrelations β^j.

Which of these cases occurs in the cobweb model depends on the composite mapping $D^{-1}S$ in (5.19), determined by demand and supply curves. We will discuss a chaotic example below.

5.4.3 CEE in a fishery model with backward-bending supply

As an illustration of chaotic CEE, we briefly discuss the fishery model in Hommes and Rosser (2001), with a backward-bending supply curve derived from optimal management of the fish resources, by a sole owner maximizing discounted revenues from harvesting. The backward-bending supply curve is given by

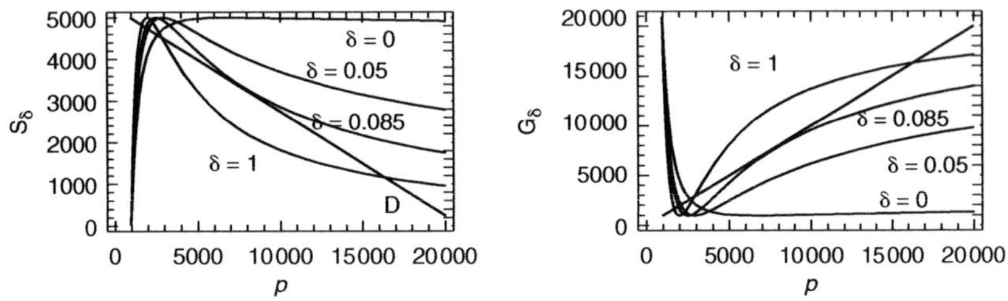

Note: As the discount factor δ increases the supply curve becomes strongly backward bending and two additional steady states are created for $\delta \approx 0.085$.

Figure 5.5 Graphs of the demand and the discounted equilibrium supply curves S_δ in (5.26) (left panel) and graphs of the implied law of motion G_δ in (5.29) under naive expectations (right panel) for several discount factors δ

$$S_\delta(p) = h = F(x_\delta^*(p)) = rx_\delta^*(p)\left(1 - \frac{x_\delta^*(p)}{k}\right). \tag{5.26}$$

Supply equals harvest h, which in sustained yield equilibrium has been set equals to the (logistic) growth of the fish population x. Moreover, $x_\delta^*(p)$ is the optimal bioeconomic equilibrium fish population derived from maximization of discounted future net revenues, which depends on the discount rate δ and the fish price p. In the case of logistic growth of the fish population and a standard specification of the harvesting cost function $c(x) = c/(qx)$, it is given by

$$x_\delta^*(p) = \frac{k}{4}\left\{1 + \frac{c}{pqk} - \frac{\delta}{r} + \sqrt{\left(1 + \frac{c}{pqk} - \frac{\delta}{\mathrm{r}}\right)^2 + \frac{8c\delta}{pqkr}}\right\}. \tag{5.27}$$

For details, the interested reader is referred to Hommes and Rosser (2001), and to Clark (1985, 1990) for an extensive treatment of fishery and other renewable resource models.[9]

We refer to $S_\delta(p)$ in (5.26) as the *discounted equilibrium supply curve.* For consumer demand for fish, we will choose the same linear form (5.4) as before. Figure 5.5 shows plots of the equilibrium demand and supply system, for different values of the discount rate δ.[10] Figure 5.5 (left panel) shows that, as the discount rate δ increases, the supply curve becomes more backward bending. The most backwardly bent supply curve corresponds with the totally myopic case of $\delta = \infty$, which corresponds to the open access bionomic equilibrium case studied by Gordon (1954) and which is associated with overfishing behavior. We note that the supply curve bends backwards quite quickly at values of the discount rate that are empirically and socially meaningful. Figure 5.5 illustrates the fact that a backward-bending supply curve together with a sufficiently inelastic demand curve may lead to multiple steady state equilibria even for the static case. In the extreme case $\delta = 0$ there is a unique steady state equilibrium price, whereas at the other extreme $\delta = +\infty$ there are three different steady state equilibrium prices.

The market equilibrium price at date t is determined by demand and supply, that is,

$$D(p_t) = S_\delta(p_t^e). \tag{5.28}$$

With linear consumer demand D as before in (5.4), the discounted supply curve S_δ in (5.26), and price expectations given by SAC-learning, the implied actual law of motion becomes

$$\begin{aligned} p_{t+1} &= G_\delta(\alpha_t + \beta_t(p_t - \alpha_t)) = D^{-1}S_\delta(\alpha_t + \beta_t(p_t - \alpha_t)) \\ &= \frac{a - S_\delta(\alpha_t + \beta_t(p_t - \alpha_t))}{d}, \end{aligned} \tag{5.29}$$

with α_t given by (5.23) and β_t by (5.24). Figure 5.5 (right panel) shows graphs of the implied actual law of motion $G\delta$, for different values of the discount rate. In our simulations of the adaptive SAC-learning process (5.23), (5.24) and (5.29), we have observed three typical outcomes:

- convergence to the "good" steady state equilibrium with a low price and a high fish stock;
- convergence to the "bad" steady state equilibrium with a high price and a low fish stock;
- convergence to a chaotic CEE, with prices and fish stock irregularly jumping between low and high values.

Simulations of the SAC-learning dynamics suggest that for low values of the discount rate, convergence to the "good" equilibrium steady state is the most likely outcome of the SAC-learning process, whereas for high values of the discount rate convergence to the "bad" steady state is most likely. For intermediate discount rates the outcome of the learning process is uncertain and in general depends on the initial states, that is, on the initial belief parameters α_0, β_0 and the initial fish stock x_0. The system may settle down to either the "good" or the "bad" steady state, possibly after a long (chaotic) transient. However, it may also happen that belief parameters α_t and β_t converge to constants α^* and β^*, while prices never converge to a steady state (or to a cycle), but keep fluctuating chaotically, as illustrated

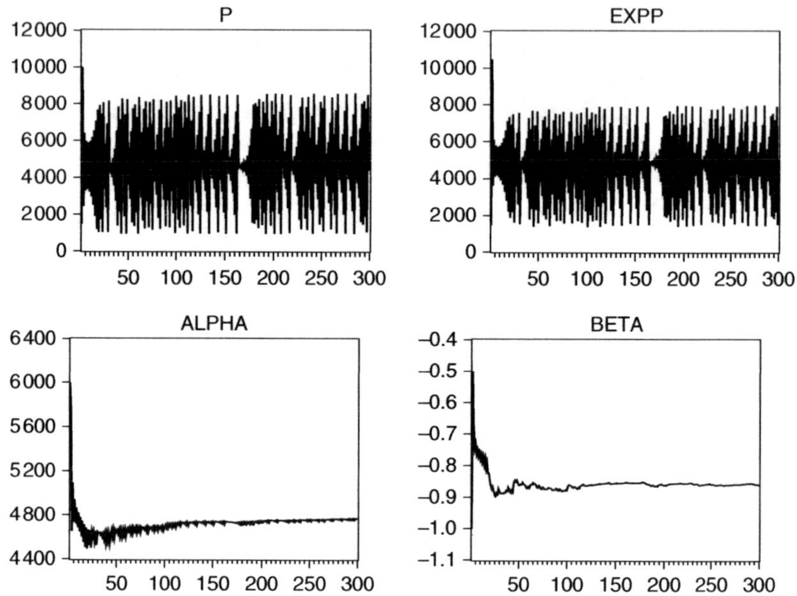

Figure 5.6 *Learning to believe in chaos, that is, belief parameters converge (bottom panels* α *and* β*), while prices and forecasts (top panels) fluctuate chaotically. In this example, belief parameters* $(\alpha_t, \beta_t) \rightarrow (\alpha^*, \beta^*) \approx (4988, -0.87)$

in Figure 5.6 for $\delta = 0.1$. This situation is referred to as *learning to believe in chaos* and it seems to occur with positive probability, that is, for an open set of initial states (x_0, α_0, β_0). Learning to believe in chaos means that the SAC-learning dynamics converges to a chaotic system, when α_t and β_t have converged to constants α^* and β^*, while prices keep fluctuating chaotically.[11]

Next we investigate the effect of noise upon the learning dynamics. SAC-learning with additive dynamic noise is given by (5.23), (5.24), as before, and adding a noise term to the implied actual law of motion, that is,

$$p_{t+1} = G_{\delta,\alpha_t,\beta_t}(p_t) = G_\delta(\alpha_t + \beta_t(p_t - \alpha_t)) + \varepsilon_t, \quad t \geq 0, \qquad (5.30)$$

where ε_t is an independently identically distributed (IID) random process and $G_\delta = D^{-1}S_\delta$ in (5.29) as before. Notice that the noise is not merely observational noise, but dynamic noise, for example, due to exogenous demand or supply shocks, affecting the dynamic law of motion in each period of time. Figure 5.7 illustrates a typical example, with ε_t drawn from

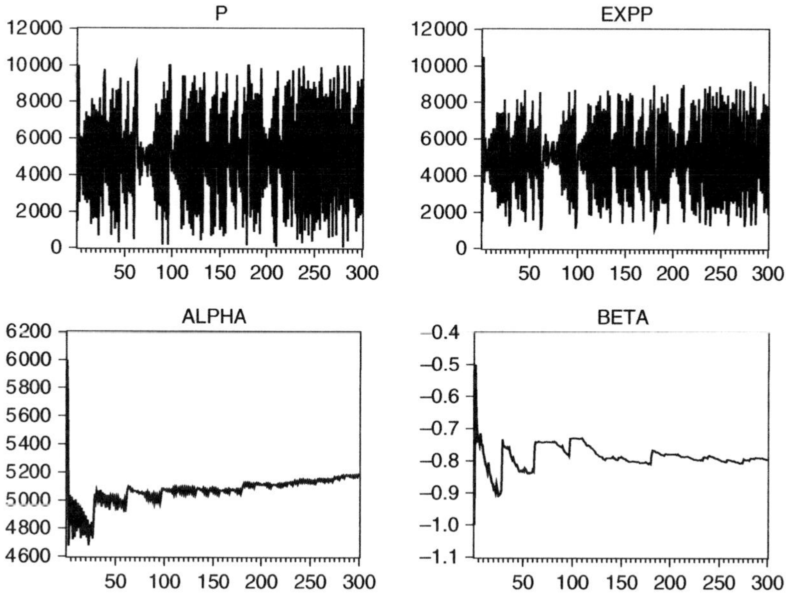

Figure 5.7 *Learning to believe in noisy chaos, that is, belief parameters converge (bottom panels), while dynamics of prices and forecasts (top panels) follow a noisy chaotic process. In this example, belief parameters* $(\alpha_t, \beta_t) \to (\alpha^*, \beta^*) \approx (5200, -0.8)$

a uniform distribution over the interval $[-1000, +1000]$; for this choice of the noise process, the signal to noise ratio, as measured by the ratio $\sigma_p/\sigma_\varepsilon$ of standard deviations of the noise free price series to the noise, is about 5. Surprisingly, even in the presence of dynamic noise, the SAC-learning dynamics still settles down to a chaotic CEE as illustrated in Figure 5.7. The noisy chaotic series has an autocorrelation pattern very similar to that of an AR(1) process with strongly negative first-order autocorrelation. In fact, estimation of an AR(1) process on the noisy chaotic series yields estimated parameters $\hat{\beta}$ and $\hat{\alpha}$, which are close to the coefficients of the underlying chaotic CEE $\beta^* \approx -0.87$ and $\alpha^* \approx 4988$. Standard statistical tests such as the Q-statistic indicate that the null hypothesis that prices follow a stochastic AR(1) process can *not* be rejected, not even at the 10 percent level. Learning to believe in noisy chaos is thus a possibility that is not rejected by linear statistical theory. Agents are therefore satisfied with their linear forecasting rules, and have no reason to abandon their belief and will stick to their AR(1) belief in an unknown stochastic nonlinear economy.

The key feature of a (noisy) chaotic CEE is that learning parameters converge to constants, whereas prices do not converge but fluctuate chaotically on a (noisy) strange attractor, with the correct sample average and sample autocorrelations. A chaotic CEE may be seen as an example of what Sargent (1993) calls an *approximate rational expectations equilibrium*, with optimal misspecified forecasts. A chaotic CEE is not an REE, because expectations do not coincide with the conditional mathematical expectations, which could only be derived if underlying market equilibrium equations would be known. Agents are using a simple, but misspecified model to forecast an unknown, possibly complicated actual law of motion. In the presence of (small) dynamic noise, the misspecification is hard to detect and boundedly rational agents using linear statistical techniques can do no better than stick to their optimal, simple linear model of an unknown stochastic, nonlinear economy.

5.5 Heterogeneous beliefs and evolutionary selection

So far we have focused on a representative agent cobweb model, where all producers have identical expectations. But why would all agents have the same expectations? Laboratory experiments have shown that, even when individuals face the same information, they may disagree and take different decisions. In a complex market it seems more appropriate to model agents as boundedly rational and heterogeneous, using different types of forecasting rules. But this raises an immediate problem: which rules will boundedly rational agents choose from the infinitely many possibilities?

Models with heterogeneous agents are becoming increasingly popular. In particular, finance models with fundamentalists and chartists have received much attention. Examples include Zeeman (1974), Frankel and Froot (1986), DeLong et al. (1990), Kirman (1991), Lux (1995), Brock and Hommes (1998) and DeGrauwe and Grimaldi (2006). Hommes (2006) and LeBaron (2006) have recently reviewed this rapidly expanding literature.

In this section we discuss a model with heterogeneous expectations, as proposed in Brock and Hommes (1997) (henceforth BH) based on three underlying assumptions: (1) agents choose from a class of rules varying from very simple to very sophisticated; (2) more sophisticated rules require more effort and are therefore more costly than simple rules, and (3) agents tend to switch to rules that have performed better in the recent past. Evolutionary selection thus disciplines the forecasting rules to be used. In the cobweb framework, producers can choose between different forecasting rules H_j. The fractions $n_{j,t}$ of producers using predictor H_j at date t, will be updated over time based upon a publically available evolutionary fitness measure, given by realized net profits, associated to each predictor.

BH focus on a simple two-type case with rational expectations, which can be obtained at costs $C \geq 0$ per time period, versus naive expectations, which is freely available. This case may be viewed as an extreme case, with rational expectations representing the most sophisticated forecasting rule, and naive expectations representing the simplest forecasting rule. BH show the occurrence of a *rational route to randomness*, that is, a bifurcation route to strange attractors and chaos as producers become more rational in the sense that they become more sensitive to differences in past performance and switch more quickly to a better predictor.

Rational agents have perfect knowledge about market equilibrium equations and are aware of the fact that the market equilibrium price is affected by the presence of naive traders. Hence, in a heterogeneous world, rational agents have perfect knowledge about prices and quantities, but also about *beliefs* of *all* other traders. Although this case is theoretically appealing, it seems highly unrealistic in real markets that some agents have (perfect) information about beliefs of other agents. Therefore, we will focus here on some perhaps more realistic cases, where agents only use information extracted from observable quantities, such as prices. As a starting point of the discussion, we consider the case of two simple linear predictors. Two special cases will be discussed, the case of *fundamentalists* versus naive expectations and the case of *contrarians* versus naive.

5.5.1 *Linear forecasting rules*

Consider the two linear AR(1) prediction rules

$$H_j(p_{t-1}) = \alpha_j + \beta_j p_{t-1}, \quad j = 1,2, \tag{5.31}$$

with fixed parameters α_j and β_j. Throughout this section we focus on the case where the supply curve is *linear* as in (5.2), with corresponding cost function $c(q) - q^2/(2s)$. The market clearing price in the cobweb model with linear demand and supply and two trader types, with linear predictors as in (5.31), is determined by[12,13]

$$a - dp_t = n_{1t}s(\alpha_1 + \beta_1 p_{t-1}) + n_{2t}s(\alpha_2 + \beta_2 p_{t-1}), \tag{5.32}$$

where n_{1t} and n_{2t} denote the fractions of agents using respectively H_1 and H_2, at the beginning of period t. These fractions will be updated according to an evolutionary fitness measure based on past realized profits. Realized net profit in period t for traders using predictor H_j is given by

$$\pi_{j,t} = sp_t H_j(p_{t-1}) - \frac{s}{2}(H_j(p_{t-1}))^2 - C_j, \tag{5.33}$$

where C_j represents the average costs per time period for obtaining predictor H_j. For a simple habitual rule of thumb predictor, such as naive or adaptive expectations, these costs C_j will be zero, whereas for more sophisticated predictors such as fundamentalists' beliefs based on fundamental analysis, information gathering costs C_j may be positive. The fitness measure underlying evolutionary selection is given by

$$U_{jt} = wU_{j,t-1} + (1 - w)\pi_{j,t}, \tag{5.34}$$

where $0 \leq w \leq 1$ is a memory parameter. A smaller w puts more memory on recent observations and in the case $w = 0$ fitness is given by most recent observed realized net profits.

Brock and Hommes (1997) considered this model with *synchronous* updating of strategies, that is, in each period *all* agents update their strategies. Here we consider the more general case of *asynchronous* updating. Per time unit only a fraction $1 - \delta$ of agents, distributed randomly among agents of both types and independently across time, is assumed to reconsider their strategy on the basis of the most recent information available. The remaining fraction δ sticks to their current strategy. The corresponding dynamics of the fractions is given by a modified version of the discrete choice, logit probabilities:

$$n_{jt} = (1 - \delta)e^{\gamma U_{j,t-1}}/Z_{t-1} + \delta n_{j,t-1}, \tag{5.35}$$

where $Z_{t-1} = \sum_h e^{\gamma U_{h,t-1}}$ is a normalization factor so that fractions add up to 1. For $\delta = 0$, we are back in the case of synchronous updating. In evolutionary games there has been a discussion whether asynchronous updating may lead to more stability (cf. Nowak and May, 1992; Huberman and Glance, 1993 and Nowak, Bonhoeffer and May, 1994). Financial market models with asynchronous updating have been considered by Diks and van der Weide (2005) and Hommes, Huang and Wang (2005). A key feature of this evolutionary predictor selection is that agents are boundedly rational, in the sense that predictors with higher evolutionary fitness attract more followers. The parameter γ is called the *intensity of choice*, measuring how fast producers switch between different prediction strategies. For $\gamma = 0$ the fractions always converge to equal shares $1/H$, whereas for the other extreme $\gamma = \infty$, in each period *all* producers who update in that period (that is, a fraction $1 - \delta$) switch to the optimal predictor. Hence, the higher the intensity of choice, the more rational agents are in the sense that they switch more quickly to the best strategy in terms of past performance.

The timing of the coupling between the market equilibrium equation (5.32) and the evolutionary selection of strategies (5.35) is important. The market equilibrium price p_t in (5.32) depends upon the fractions n_{ht}. These fractions n_{ht} depend upon *past* fitness $U_{h,t-1}$, which in turn depends upon past prices p_{t-1} in periods $t - 1$ and further in the past. After the equilibrium price p_t has been revealed by the market, it is used in evolutionary updating of beliefs and determining the new fractions $n_{h,t+1}$. These new fractions $n_{h,t+1}$ will then determine a new equilibrium price p_{t+1}. Market equilibrium prices and fractions of different trading strategies thus co-evolve over time.

5.5.2 *Fundamentalists versus naive expectations*

The linear predictors (5.39) specialize to the case with fundamentalists versus naive expectations when $\alpha_1 = p^* = a/(d + s)$ (the steady state price), $\beta_1 = 0$, $\alpha_2 = 0$ and $\beta_2 = 1$:

$$H_1(p_{t-1}) = p^* = \frac{a}{d + s} \tag{5.36}$$

$$H_2(p_{t-1}) = p_{t-1}. \tag{5.37}$$

Figure 5.8 shows attractors for different values of the intensity of choice γ and some corresponding time series. The bifurcation diagram and largest LE-plot in Figure 5.9 illustrate a *rational route to randomness*, that is, a bifurcation route from simple to complicated, chaotic dynamics as the intensity of choice increases. The market switches between periods of low volatility, with prices close to the fundamental price, and high volatility, with irregularly fluctuating prices. Prices diverge slowly from the fundamental steady state price, as long as most agents use the simple, freely available naive forecast. When forecasting errors increase, it becomes worthwhile to buy the sophisticated fundamental forecast, and more agents start switching to the fundamental forecast, thus stabilizing price fluctuations, and so on. Due to the asynchronous updating of strategies, agents switch more gradually between strategies, and the time series of fractions of fundamentalists shows much more persistence than in the case with synchronous updating. Figure 5.8 (bottom panel) also illustrates the sample average and first-order sample autocorrelation (SAC) of the price series. Sample average quickly settles down to a value close to 0,[14] whereas the first-order SAC is clearly negative, converging to approximately −0.85.

It is remarkable that both the attractor and the price time series are similar to the case of rational versus naive expectations studied in BH, and in particular for γ large, the system is close to a homoclinic tangency.[15]

5.5.3 *Contrarians versus naive expectations*

In the case of fundamentalists versus naive, price series exhibit strong first-order negative autocorrelations, even when the dynamics is chaotic. This has been illustrated in Figure 5.8 showing that, for $\gamma = 3$, the sample

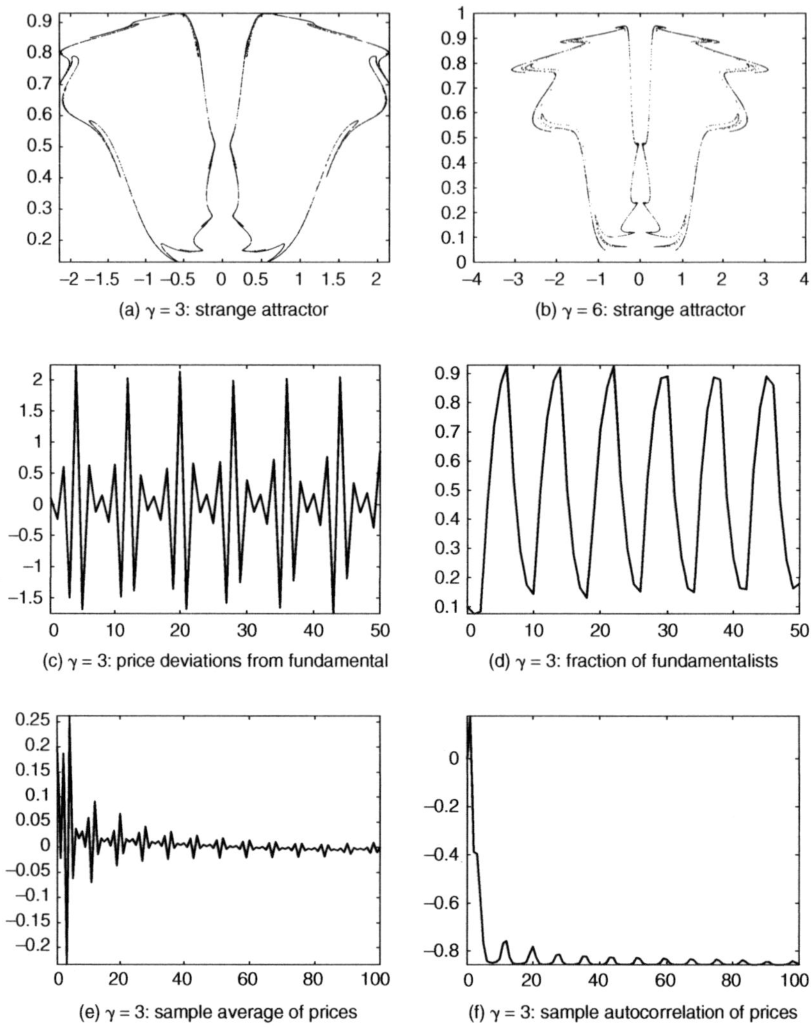

Note: Strange attractors and time series for different γ values, with other parameters fixed at $a = 0$, $d = 0.5$, $s = 1.35$, $\delta = 0.5$, $\alpha_1 = 0$, $\beta_1 = 0$, $C_1 = 1$, $\alpha_2 = 0$, $\beta_2 = 1$ and $C_2 = 0$. Although price dynamics is chaotic, there is still clear linear autocorrelation structure. Sample average of prices converges (close) to fundamental value, while sample autocorrelations converge (close) to -0.85, indicating significantly negative first-order autocorrelation.

Figure 5.8 Fundamentalists versus naive

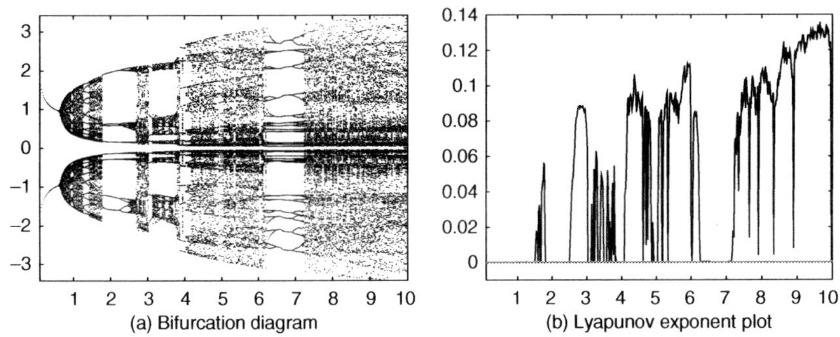

Note: Parameters: $a = 0$, $d = 0.5$, $s = 1.35$, $\delta = 0.5$, $\alpha_1 = 0$, $\beta_1 = 0$, $C_1 = 1$, $\alpha_2 = 0$, $\beta_2 = 1$ and $C_2 = 0$.

Figure 5.9 Fundamentalists versus naive: a rational route to randomness as the intensity of choice increases

autocorrelations of prices converges to a negative value around −0.85. An agent who behaves as a time series econometrician would easily detect this strong negative autocorrelation and adapt his or her forecasts. Even without the use of any statistical software, a smart agent might detect negative autocorrelation, simply by observing that positive (negative) deviations from the average price are always followed by negative (positive) deviations. What would happen if agents recognize this structure from observing realized market prices and attempt to exploit it?

Consider a group of contrarians, who take the negative first-order autocorrelation in prices into account, and predict that next period's deviation from the fundamental price will be on the opposite side, that is, we replace the fundamental forecast by a contrarian rule

$$H_1(p_{t-1}) = p^* + \beta_1(p_{t-1} - p^*). \quad \beta_1 < 0 \tag{5.38}$$

Figure 5.10 illustrates an example with $\beta_1 = -0.85$ (with other parameters as in Figure 5.8), that is, contrarians recognize the autocorrelation structure present in the previous example. The structure of the strange attractors in Figure 5.10 seems more complicated than in the case of fundamentalists versus naive in Figure 5.8. In particular, the negative autocorrelation in prices becomes weaker, since the sample autocorrelation $\rho_t \to -0.57$ (instead of −0.85). Due to the presence of contrarians in the market, the strongly negative first-order autocorrelation has become weaker.[16] In a sense, contrarians have "arbitraged away", at least partly, predictable linear structure in the price time series.[17]

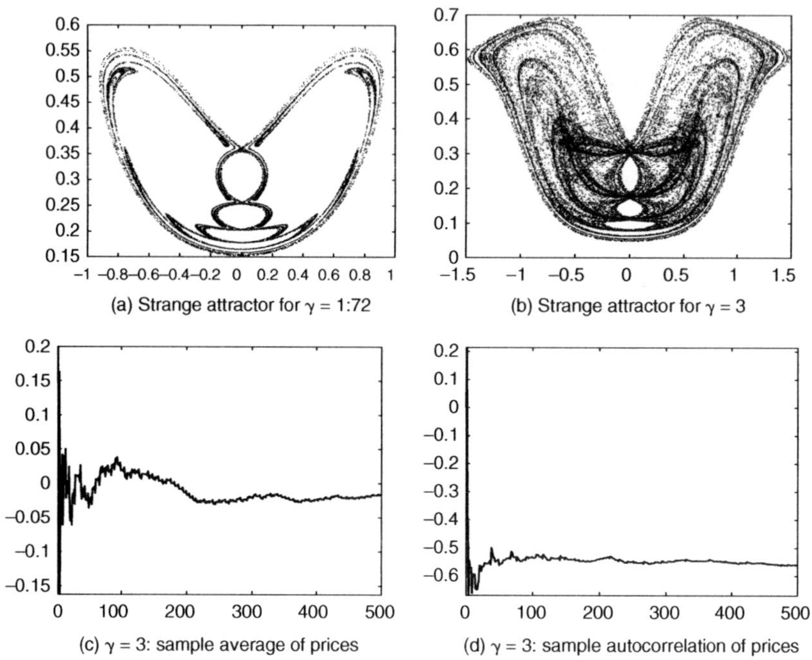

Note: Strange attractors (top panel) for different γ values, with other parameters fixed at: $a = 0$, $d = 0.5$, $s = 1.35$, $\delta = 0.5$, $\alpha_1 = 0$, $\beta_1 = -0.85$, $C_1 = 1$, $\alpha_2 = 0$, $\beta_2 = 1$ and $C_2 = 0$. Time series of sample average and (first-order) sample autocorrelation converge. Compared to fundamentalists, contrarians weaken the negative first-order autocorrelations in prices, and in the long-run sample autocorrelations converge to -0.57.

Figure 5.10 Contrarians versus naive

5.5.4 Adaptive learning versus naive expectations

In this subsection, we combine evolutionary strategy selection and adaptive learning. In the previous example we have seen that the presence of contrarians in the market weakens the negative first-order autocorrelations in realized prices. A time series econometrician might note however, that contrarian behavior is still *inconsistent* with realized prices since contrarians expect strong negative autocorrelation $\beta_2 = -0.85$, while realized prices exhibit weaker SAC, with first-order SAC $\beta_t \to -0.57$. It is natural to go one step further and introduce a type of agent with adaptive learning, trying to optimize the parameters of his or her linear forecasting rule:

$$H_1(p_{t-1}) = \alpha_{t-1} + \beta_{t-1}(p_{t-1} - \alpha_{t-1}), \tag{5.39}$$

where α_t and β_t are determined through SAC-learning as in (5.23) and (5.24) respectively. This approach widens the range of forecasting rules to all linear AR(1) rules. The sophisticated agent type tries to learn the optimal linear rule through adaptive learning, within a heterogeneous agent environment. Recently, Branch and Evans (2006) have studied a related cobweb model with two types of agents, both using OLS-learning of a misspecified model, and allowing for endogenous, evolutionary switching between the two predictors. DeGrauwe and Markiewicz (2006) compare evolutionary learning and adaptive (or statistical) learning in an asset pricing framework, and investigate how these different learning schemes replicate the stylized facts (disconnect puzzles, excess volatility) in exchange rates. Diks and Dindo (2008) consider an asset pricing model with heterogeneous information combining adaptive learning of the growth rate of dividends and evolutionary switching between free riding and costly information gathering.

Figure 5.11 illustrates the dynamics in the case of SAC-learning versus naive expectations. Agents learn to be contrarians, as $\beta_t \rightarrow -0.62$, consistent with the SAC in realized prices. In this example there is still fairly strong negative first-order autocorrelation in prices, but it is consistent with the behavior of the sophisticated type, who have learned the first-order autocorrelation coefficient consistent with realized market prices. Figure 5.12 illustrates an example with memory in the fitness measure, where the (first-order) autocorrelation in prices becomes even weaker ($\beta_t \rightarrow -0.48$).

5.6 Concluding remarks

We have reviewed bounded rationality and learning in the familiar cobweb, hog-cycle framework. Two stories of bounded rationality have been emphasized. The story of adaptive learning assumes a representative "average" agent trying to optimize a simple (linear) misspecified rule in an unknown complex (nonlinear) economy. The other story assumes heterogeneous forecasting strategies and endogenous, evolutionary selection based upon past performance. We have also presented an example where both stories are integrated, with evolutionary selection between an adaptive learning rule and a simple, fixed rule.

In a cobweb economy with nonlinear, monotonic demand and supply curves, many adaptive learning processes enforce convergence to the unique REE steady state price. The steady state price forecast is, for example, the only (linear) forecast, where sample averages and sample autocorrelations of realized market prices are consistent with beliefs. Simply by looking at sample averages and sample autocorrelations, in particular trying to learn the negative first-order autocorrelation so typical for the "hog cycle", boundedly rational agents should be able to learn the unique REE.

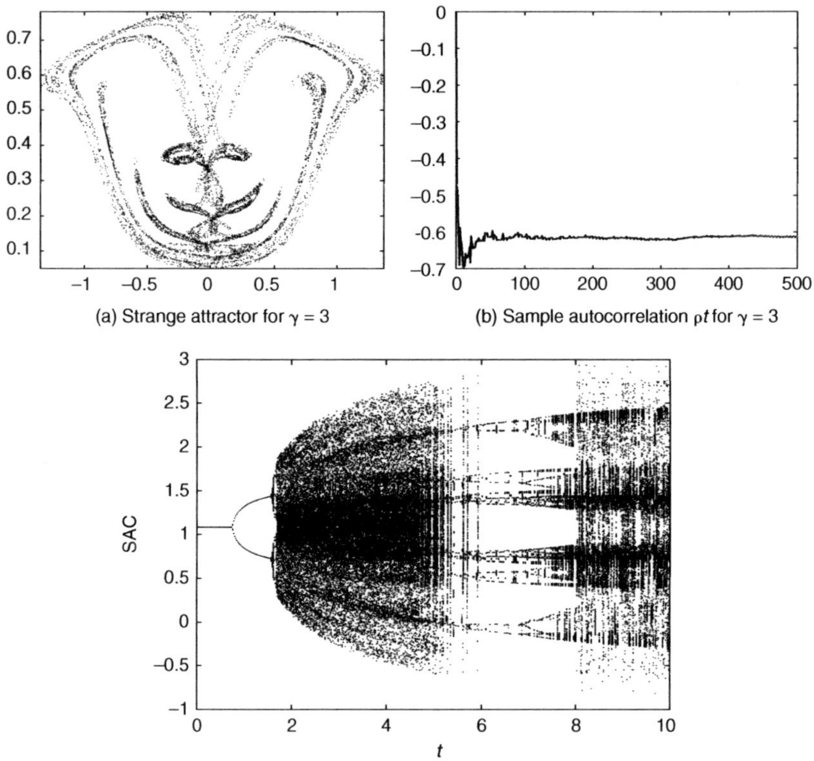

(c) Bifurcation diagram

Note: Agents learn to be contrarians, as the first-order autocorrelation coefficient converges, $\beta_t \to -0.62$. The bifurcation diagram shows a rational route to randomness, as the intensity of choice γ increases. Parameters: $a = 0$, $d = 0.5$, $s = 1.35$, $\delta = 0.5$, $w = 0$, $C_1 = 1$, $\alpha_2 = 0$, $\beta_2 = 1$ and $C_2 = 0$.

Figure 5.11 SAC-learning versus naive

Laboratory experiments with human subjects show, however, that this is not as easy as theory suggests. Only in the stable treatment of the experiment (that is, when the market is stable under naive expectations) do market prices converge to REE. In the unstable treatment of the experiments, realized market prices are characterized by three stylized facts: (1) the sample mean is close to the RE price; (2) there is excess volatility, that is, the sample variance is much higher than the RE variance, and (3) there is no linear predictability (no autocorrelations) in realized prices. The observed excess volatility is inconsistent with convergence of adaptive learning of a representative agent. For other simple expectations rules,

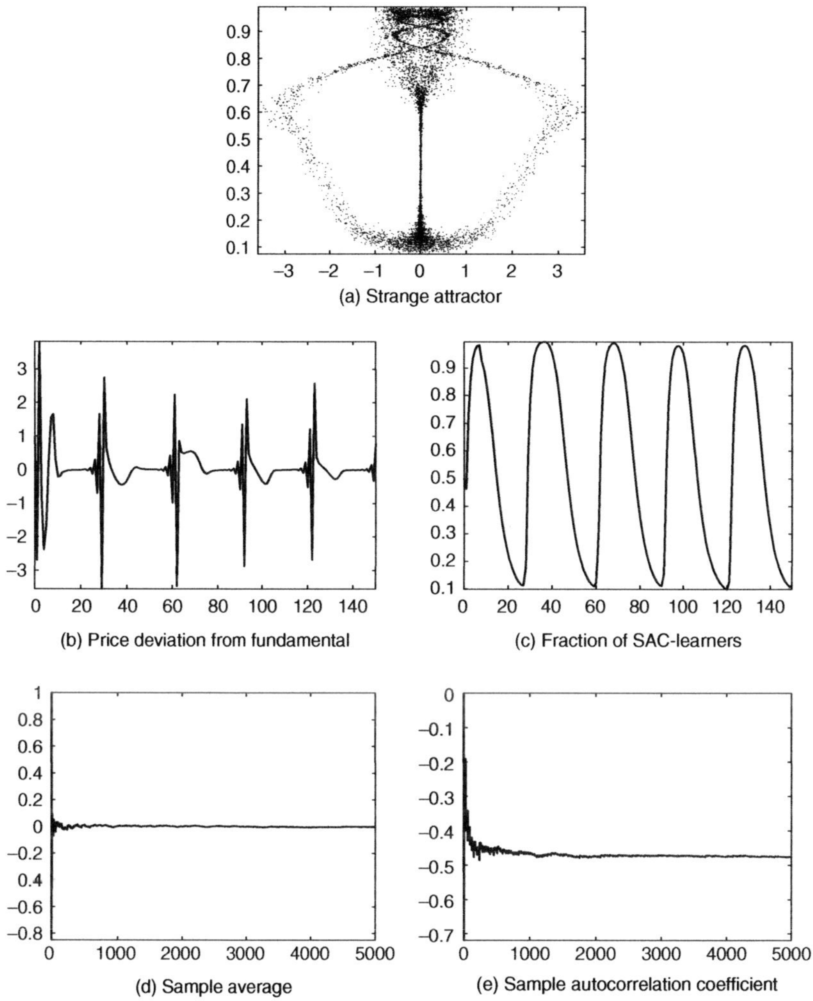

Note: Attractor (a) and time series of prices p_t (deviations from fundamental), fraction n_{1t} of SAC-learners, sample average α_t and sample autocorrelation coefficient β_t. With more memory in the fitness meausure, the remaining autocorrelation in prices is weaker ($\beta_t \to -0.48$). Parameters: $\gamma = 3$, $a = 0$, $d = 0.5$, $b = 1.35$, $\delta = 0.5$, $w = 0.9$, $C_1 = 1$, $\alpha_2 = 0$, $\beta_2 = 1$ and $C_2 = 0$.

Figure 5.12 SAC-learning versus naive expectations with memory in the fitness measure such as adaptive expectations, irregular price fluctuations around the RE benchmark arise, but these fluctuations, even when chaotic, typically still exhibit negative first-order autocorrelations, inconsistent with stylized fact (3) in the experiments. Some form of heterogeneity is therefore needed to explain the laboratory experiments.

We have also reviewed some results on heterogeneous agent models with endogenous, evolutionary strategy selection, including several two-type cases with a costly sophisticated forecasting rule (fundamentalists, contrarians or SAC-learning) versus a free, simple forecasting rule (naive expectations). These two-type models will converge to the RE price in the stable treatment of the experiment, and at the same time may generate instability and excess volatility in the unstable treatment, when agents switch fast enough between strategies, similar to the stylized facts in the experiments. However, it is not clear whether a two-type model can simultaneously explain stylized fact (3), that is, linear unpredictability. A two-type model with fundamentalists versus naive expectations generates strongly negative first-order autocorrelation in prices, even when the system is chaotic. The typical up and down "hog-cycle" oscillations are still present, and would be observable to a careful agent. When fundamentalists are replaced by contrarians, who try to exploit the negative first-order autocorrelation in prices, the first-order autocorrelation gets weaker, but does not disappear completely. When contrarians are replaced by SAC-learning the results are similar: first-order autocorrelation becomes weaker but again does not completely vanish. In the cobweb framework, adaptive agents learn to become contrarians and "arbitrage away" part of the linear predictability, but do not completely wash out the autocorrelations in market prices. These results suggest that, in order to match all stylized facts of the experiments, either the simple strategy (naive expectations) in these two-type models needs to be replaced by a somewhat more complicated strategy (perhaps adaptive expectations or a two-period average forecast), or more heterogeneity, that is, more types of forecasting rules are needed to fully explain the laboratory experiments, see, for example, Hommes and Lux (2009). Matching the stylized facts of laboratory experiments on expectations formation remains an important challenge for theories of bounded rationality and learning, in the simple cobweb framework as well as for other, more realistic expectations feedback settings.

Notes

* Earlier versions of this chapter have been presented at the workshop on Complexity, Aix-en-Provence, 18–20 May 2006, the conference on Heterogeneous Agents in Financial Markets, Nijmegen, 24 January 2007 and the Annual Symposium of the Society for Nonlinear Dynamics and Econometrics, Paris, 15–16 March 2007. I would like to thank the participants for stimulating discussion and particularly Thomas Lux and the Editor, Barkley Rosser, for helpful comments on an earlier draft. This research

has been supported by the Netherlands Organization for Scientific Research (NWO), by a EU STREP-grant "Complex Markets", and by the EU POLHIA grant no. 225408. None of the above are responsible for errors in this chapter.

1. An S-shaped supply curve can, for example, be derived from a fourth or higher-order polynomial convex cost curve $c(q) = \frac{1}{d+1}(q - 1)^{d+1} + q$, where d is an odd integer, for example, $d = 3$. Optimal supply then becomes $q = S(p^e) = (p^e - 1)^{(1/d)} + 1$.
2. At the time of the introduction of rational expectations by Muth (1961) and its introduction into macroeconomics by Lucas (1972) and others, the phenomenon of deterministic chaos was still largely unknown to economists.
3. Sonnemans et al. (2004) conducted strategy experiments to study the long run behaviour of the group experiments and show that for the strongly unstable treatment a large fraction of markets exhibit chaotic price fluctuations.
4. For different market settings, these results may, of course, change. The cobweb model has negative expectations feedback. Heemeijer et al. (2009) show in fact that the results are quite different in markets with positive feedback, such as demand-driven speculative asset markets. Positive feedback may lead to persistent deviations from the fundamental benchmark, with the sample mean of realized prices, for example, much higher than the RE fundamental benchmark.
5. Arifovic (1994) investigates genetic algorithm learning in the cobweb model and compares the results to the cobweb experiments of Wellford (1989).
6. Recently Tuinstra and Wagener (2007) have argued that cycles and chaos are the result of the estimation procedure in Bullard (1994) and Schönhofer (1999). If agents regress inflation rates on a constant, instead of regressing (nonstationary) prices on past prices, adaptive learning does converge to REE. Interestingly, Tuinstra and Wagener (2007) also show that in the case of heterogeneous agents, with agents switching between the two estimation procedures based upon past performance, complicated price fluctuations arise again.
7. SAC-learning is closely related to OLS-learning. For both learning schemes α_t is the same, but β_t has one extra term in the denominator under SAC-learning, ensuring that $-1 \leq \beta_t \leq +1$. Simulations for OLS-learning lead to similar results and would not change our general conclusions below.
8. Bray and Savin (1986) show that OLS-learning also converges to the REE steady state in the cobweb model. Arifovic (1994) shows that agents using genetic algorithms can learn the REE steady state.
9. Parameters will be fixed as follows: the fish carrying capacity $k = 400\,000$, catchability (per vessel per day) $q = 0.000013$, the marginal cost of effort $c = 5000$ and the growth rate of fish $r = 0.05$.
10. The parameters of the demand curve are fixed at $d = 0.25$ and $a = 5240.5$.
11. Schönhofer (1999, 2001) presents a related case of learning to believe in chaos in an OLG-model. In Schönhofer's examples belief parameters of the OLS-learning scheme do *not* converge but keep fluctuating chaotically, while at the same time, due to inflation, prices diverge to infinity.
12. In our simulations we will work in deviations $x_t = p_t - p^*$ from the fundamental RE steady state price p^*. This is equivalent to setting the parameter $a = 0$, so that the RE steady state $p^* = a/(d + s) = 0$.
13. The more general case of nonlinear demand and supply is studied in Goeree and Hommes (2000).
14. Recall that the simulations are in deviations $x_t = p_t - p^*$ from the fundamental, so that the sample average of prices converges to fundamental value.
15. See the original working paper Brock and Hommes (1995) for more details concerning the case of fundamentalists versus naive expectations.
16. The attractors in Figure 5.10 suggest that there are transversal intersections between the stable and the unstable manifolds of the steady state. Apparently homoclinic bifurcations are weakening the autocorrelation structure.
17. See Dindo and Tuinstra (2006) and Dindo (2007) for similar results in the context of the well-known El-Farol Bar problem and related models.

References

Adam, K. (2007), "Experimental evidence on the persistence of output and inflation", *Economic Journal*, **117**(520), 603–36.

Anderson, P.W., K.J. Arrow and D. Pines (eds) (1988), *The Economy as an Evolving Complex System*, Redwood City, CA: Addison-Wesley.

Arifovic, J. (1994), "Genetic algorithm learning and the cobweb model", *Journal of Economic Dynamics and Control*, **18**(1), 3–28.

Arthur, W.B. (2006), "Out-of-equilibrium economics and agent-based modeling", in L. Tesfatsion and K.L. Judd (eds) *Handbook of Computational Economics, Volume 2: Agent-based Computational Economics*, Netherlands: Elsevier Science.

Arthur, W.B., S.N. Durlauf and D.A. Lane (eds) (1997), *The Economy as an Evolving Complex System II*, Reading, MA: Addison-Wesley.

Branch, W.A. (2006), "Restricted perception equilibria and learning in macroeconomics", in D. Colander (ed.), *Post Walrasian Macroeconomics: Beyond the Stochastic General Equilibrium Model*, New York: Cambridge University Press.

Branch, W.A. and G.W. Evans (2006), "Intrinsic heterogeneity in expectation formation", *Journal of Economic Theory*, **127**(1), 264–95.

Bray, M.M. and N.E. Savin (1986), "Rational expectations equilibria, learning and model specification", *Econometrica*, **54**(15), 1129–60.

Brock, W.A. and C.H. Hommes (1995), "Rational routes to randomness", *SSRI Working Paper* No. 9506, University of Wisconsin.

Brock, W.A. and C.H. Hommes (1997), "A rational route to randomness", *Econometrica*, **65**(5), 1059–95.

Brock, W.A. and C.H. Hommes (1998), "Heterogeneous beliefs and routes to chaos in a simple asset pricing model", *Journal of Economic Dynamics and Control*, **22**, 1235–74.

Bullard, J. (1994) "Learning equilibria", *Journal of Economic Theory*, **64**(2), 468–85.

Bullard, J. and J. Duffy (1998), *Learning and Excess Volatility*, Federal Reserve Bank of St. Louis.

Bunow, B. and G.H. Weiss (1979), "How chaotic is chaos? Chaotic and other 'noisy' dynamics in the frequency domain", *Mathematical Biosciences*, **47**, 221–37.

Carlson, J. (1969), "An invariably stable cobweb", *Review of Economic Studies*, **35**(3), 360–62.

Chiarella, C. (1988), "The cobweb model: its instability and the onset of chaos", *Economic Modelling*, **5**(4), 377–84.

Clark, C.W. (1985), *Bioeconomic Modelling and Fisheries Management*, New York: Wiley-Intersceince.

Clark, C.W. (1990), *Mathematical Bioeconomics: The Optimal Management of Renewable Resources*, 2nd edn New York: Wiley-Interscience.

Colucci, D. and V. Valori (2006), "Ways of learning in a simple economic setting: A comparison", *Chaos, Solitons & Fractals*, **29**(3), 653–70.

Conlisk, J. (1996), "Why bounded rationality?", *Journal of Economic Literature*, **34**(2), 669–700.

DeGrauwe, P. and M. Grimaldi (2006), "Exchange rate puzzles: A tale of switching attractors", *European Economic Review*, **50**(1), 1–33.

DeGrauwe, P. and A. Markiewicz (2006), "Learning to forecast the exchange rate: Two competing approaches", *CESifo Working Paper*, No. 1717.

DeLong, J.B., A. Shleifer, L.H. Summers and R.J. Waldmann (1990), "Noise trader risk in financial markets", *Journal of Political Economy*, **98**(4), 703–38.

Diks, C.G.H. and P.D.E. Dindo (2008), "Informational differences and learning in an asset market with boundedly rational agents", *Journal of Economic Dynamics and Control*, **32**, 1432–65.

Diks, C.G.H. and R. van der Weide (2005), "Herding, a-synchronous updating and heterogeneity in memory in a CBS", *Journal of Economic Dynamics and Control*, **29**(4), 741–63.

Dindo, P.D.E. (2007), "Bounded rationality and heterogeneity in economic dynamic models", PhD thesis, *Tinbergen Institute Research Series 396*.

Dindo, P.D.E. and J. Tuinstra (2006), "A behavioral model for participation games with negative feedback", *CeNDEF Working Paper* No. 06-10, University of Amsterdam.
Dwyer, G.P., A.W. Williams, R.C. Battalio and T.I. Mason (1993), "Tests of rational expectations in a stark setting", *Economic Journal*, **103**(418), 586–601.
Evans, G.W. and S. Honkapohja (2001), *Learning and Expectations in Macroeconomics*, Princeton, NJ: Princeton University Press.
Ezekiel, M. (1938), "The cobweb theorem", *Quarterly Journal of Economics*, **52**(2), 255–80.
Frankel, J.A. and K.A. Froot (1986), "Understanding the US dollar in the eighties: The expectations of chartists and fundamentalists", *Economic Record*, special issue, 24–38; also published as NBER Working Paper No. 0957, December 1987.
Friedman, M. (1953), "The case for flexible exchange rates", in *Essays in Positive Economics*, Chicago: Univ. Chicago Press.
Goeree, J.K. and C.H. Hommes (2000), "Heterogeneous beliefs and the nonlinear cobweb model", *Journal of Economic Dynamics and Control*, **24**(37), 761–98.
Gordon, H.S. (1954), "The economic theory of a common-property resource: The fishery", *Journal of Political Economy*, **62**(2), 124–42.
Grandmont, J.-M. (1998), "Expectations formation and stability in large socio-economic systems", *Econometrica*, **66**(4), 741–81.
Heemeijer, P., C.H. Hommes, J. Sonnemans and J. Tuinstra (2009), "Price stability and volatility in markets with positive and negative expectations feedback: An experimental investigation", *Journal of Economic Dynamics and Control*, in press.
Hey, J.D. (1994), "Expectations formation: rational or adaptive or. . .?", *Journal of Economic Behavior and Organization*, **25**(3), 329–49.
Hommes, C.H. (1991), "Adaptive learning and roads to chaos. The case of the cobweb", *Economics Letters*, **36**(2), 127–32.
Hommes, C.H. (1994), "Dynamics of the cobweb model with adaptive expectations and nonlinear supply and demand", *Journal of Economic Behavior and Organization*, **24**(3), 315–35.
Hommes, C. H. (1998), "On the consistency of backward-looking expectations: The case of the cobweb", *Journal of Economic Behavior and Organization*, **33**(3–4), 333–62.
Hommes, C.H. (2006), "Heterogeneous agent models in economics and finance", in L. Tesfatsion and K.L. Judd (eds), *Handbook of Computational Economics, Volume 2: Agent-Based Computational Economics*, Netherlands: Elsevier Science, pp. 1109–86.
Hommes, C.H. and T. Lux (2009), "Individual expectations and aggregate behavior in learning to forecast experiments", *CeNDEF Working Paper*, University of Amsterdam.
Hommes, C.H. and G. Sorger (1998), "Consistent expectations equilibria", *Macroeconomic Dynamics*, **2**(3), 287–321.
Hommes, C.H., H. Huang and D. Wang (2005), "A robust rational route to randomness in a simple asset pricing model", *Journal of Economic Dynamics and Control*, **29**(4), 1043–72.
Hommes, C.H. and Rosser, J. Barkley Jr. (2001), "Consistent expectations equilibria and complex dynamics in renewable resource markets", *Macroeconomic Dynamics*, **5**, 180–203.
Hommes, C.H., J. Sonnemans and H. van de Velden (2000), "Expectation formation in a cobweb economy: Some one person experiments", in D. Delli Gatti, M. Gallegati and A. Kirman (eds), *Interaction and Market Structure. Essays on Heterogeneity in Economics, Lecture Notes in Economics and Mathematical Systems 484*, Berlin/Heidelberg: Springer Verlag, pp. 253–66.
Hommes, C.H., J. Sonnemans, J. Tuinstra and H. van de Velden (2005), "Coordination of expectations in asset pricing experiments", *Review of Financial Studies*, **18**(3), 955–80.
Hommes, C.H., J. Sonnemans, J. Tuinstra and H. van de Velden (2007), "Learning in cobweb experiments", *Macroeconomic Dynamics*, 11(S1), 8–33.
Huberman, B.A. and N.S. Glance (1993), "Evolutionary games and computer simulations", *Proceedings of the National Academy of Sciences* (USA), **90**(16), 7716–18.

Kelley, H. and D. Friedman (2002), "Learning to forecast price", *Economic Inquiry*, **40**(4), 556–73.
Kirman, A. (1991), "Epidemics of opinion and speculative bubbles in financial markets", in M. Taylor (ed.), *Money and Financial Markets*, London: Macmillan.
LeBaron, B. (2006), "Agent-based computational finance", in L. Tesfatsion and K.L. Judd (eds), *Handbook of Computational Economics, Volume 2: Agent-based Computational Economics*, Netherlands: Elsevier Science, pp. 1187–233.
Lucas, R.E. (1972), "Econometric testing of the natural rate hypothesis", in O. Eckstein (ed.), *The Econometrics of Price Determination Conference*, Board of Governors of the Federal Reserve System and Social Science Research Council.
Lux, T. (1995), "Herd behavior, bubbles and crashes", *The Economic Journal*, **105**(431), 881–96.
Marcet, A. and T.J. Sargent (1989), "Convergence of least squares learning mechanisms in self-referential linear stochastic models", *Journal of Economic Theory*, **48**(2), 337–68.
Marimon, R. and S. Sunder (1993), "Indeterminacy of equilibria in a hyperinflationary world: Experimental evidence", *Econometrica*, **61**(5), 1073–107.
Marimon, R. and S. Sunder (1994), "Expectations and learning under alternative monetary regimes: An experimental approach", *Economic Theory*, **4**(1), 131–62.
Marimon, R. and S. Sunder (1995), "Does a constant money growth rule help stabilize inflation?", *Carnegie-Rochester Conference Series on Public Policy*, **43**, 111–56.
Marimon, R., S.E. Spear and S. Sunder (1993), "Expectationally driven market volatility: An experimental study", *Journal of Economic Theory*, **61**(1), 74–103.
Muth, J.F. (1961), "Rational expectations and the theory of price movements", *Econometrica*, **29**(6), 315–35.
Nicholson, W. (1995), *Microeconomic Theory. Basic Principles and Extensions*, 6th edn, Fort Worth: Dryden Press.
Nowak, M. and R.M. May (1992), "Evolutionary games and spatial chaos", *Nature*, **359**(6398), 826–929.
Nowak, M., S. Bonhoeffer and R.M. May (1992), "Spatial games and the maintenance of cooperation", *Proceedings of the National Academy of Sciences* (USA) **91**, 4877–81.
Peterson, S.P. (1993), "Forecasting dynamics and convergence to market fundamentals. Evidence from experimental asset markets", *Journal of Economic Behavior and Organization*, **22**(3), 269–84.
Rosser, J.B. (2004), *Complexity in Economics: The International Library of Critical Writings in Economics 174* (3 volumes), Cheltenham, UK and Northampton, MA, USA: Edward Elgar.
Sakai, H. and H. Tokumaru (1980), "Autocorrelations of a certain chaos", *IEEE Transactions on Acoustics, Speech and Signal Processing*, **28**(5), 588–90.
Sargent, T.J. (1993), *Bounded Rationality in Macroeconomics*, Oxford: Clarendon Press.
Schmalensee, R. (1976), "An experimental study of expectation formation", *Econometrica*, **44**(1), 17–41.
Schönhofer, M. (1999), "Chaotic learning equilibria", *Journal of Economic Theory*, **89**(120), 1–20.
Schönhofer, M. (2001), "Can agents learn their way out of chaos?", *Journal of Economic Behavior and Organization*, **44**(1), 71–83.
Simon, H.A. (1957), *Models of Man*, New York, NY: Wiley.
Smith, V., G.L. Suchanek and A.W. Williams (1988), "Bubbles, crashes and endogenous expectations in experimental spot asset markets", *Econometrica*, **56**(5), 1119–51.
Sonnemans, J., C.H. Hommes, J. Tuinstra and H. van de Velden (2004), "The instability of a heterogeneous cobweb economy: A strategy experiment on expectation formation", *Journal of Economic Behavior and Organization*, **54**(4), 453–81.
Sorger, G. (1998), "Imperfect foresight and chaos: An example of a self-fulfilling mistake", *Journal of Economic Behavior and Organization*, **33**(3–4), 363–83.
Tuinstra, J. and F.O.O. Wagener (2007), "On learning equilibria", *Economic Theory*, **30**(3), 493–513.

Tversky, A. and D. Kahneman (1974), "Judgment under uncertainty: Heuristics and biases", *Science*, **185**(4157), 1124–31.
Wellford, C.P. (1989), "A laboratory analysis of price dynamics and expectations in the cobweb model", *Discussion Paper* No. 89-15, Department of Economics, University of Arizona.
Williams, A.W. (1987), "The formation of price forecasts in experimental markets", *Journal of Money, Credit and Banking*, **19**(1), 118.
Zeeman, E.C. (1974), 'On the unstable behavior of stock exchange', *Journal of Mathematical Economics*, **1**(1), 39–49.

6. Oligopoly dynamics*

Michael Kopel

6.1 Introduction

A market structure in which there are relatively few firms, each of which is large relative to the total industry, is referred to as oligopoly. In contrast to the extreme cases of a monopolistic market and a perfectly competitive market, in an oligopoly the interconnections of one particular firm with the rival firms play a central role and must not be neglected. A firm operating in such a market is certainly the most difficult to manage, since the optimal action depends on the actions of the other firms, and the strategic interactions among the firms have to be taken into account when the optimal decision is determined. Oligopoly theory usually studies the behavior (or conduct) and the performance of firms in a partial equilibrium framework. It is due to the complexity of oligopoly that no single model exists that can describe all the phenomena observed in real-world markets.

The literature on oligopoly has rapidly increased over the last 25 years, and most of the models in the field of industrial organization can be linked to one of the names of Cournot, Bertrand or von Stackelberg (for more exhaustive historical accounts of early work in oligopoly theory the reader is referred to Shapiro, 1989 and Puu and Sushko, 2002). Antoine Augustin Cournot is often considered as the founder of oligopoly theory. In his book, Cournot studies a simple linear oligopoly model in which firms select quantities and he derives production levels, prices, and profits of the firms in equilibrium (see Cournot, 1838). Although it seems that Cournot has been aware of the fact that firms implicitly choose prices, 45 years later Joseph Bertrand (see Bertrand, 1883) was quite critical of Cournot's quantity competition framework and he proposed that firms set prices directly (price competition). He suggested that the outcomes lead to drastically different conclusions. About one century after Cournot, it was Heinrich von Stackelberg who introduced timing issues into a quantity-setting model by assuming that one of the competitors might try to become a "leader" (see von Stackelberg, 1934). His set-up highlights the role of commitment and being the first mover in oligopoly markets. After von Stackelberg it then took until the 1940s, when modern game theory, usually associated with the names of John von Neumann and Oskar Morgenstern, was founded, for these earlier approaches in oligopoly theory to be reconsidered, which thereafter progressively developed into several new directions.

I will consider the quantity-setting model of Cournot, the price-setting framework associated with Bertrand, and the leader–follower model of von Stackelberg in more detail in Section 6.2 of this chapter as these core models are not only important for later developments but also ideally suited for introducing key game-theoretic notions like, for example, Nash equilibrium, reaction functions, Cournot tâtonnement, and stability.

After these early oligopoly models, starting in the 1960s, researchers increasingly focused on the question of whether an equilibrium can be reached over time when the oligopolists act myopically. Actually, it was again Cournot who was the first to investigate this problem. He considered action-response sequences of the duopolists and investigated the question of whether this process will lead to the (unique) equilibrium in the long run. These later papers are developments of Cournot's preliminary work and extended into different directions. I will present various adjustment and expectation formation processes commonly used in oligopoly dynamics in Section 6.3 and then I proceed with a short review of the main contributions in this stream of literature in Section 6.4. I will refer to this work as belonging to the "early phase" in the theory of oligopoly dynamics.

From the 1970s to the early 1990s complexity became an important issue in economics (see Rosser, 1999, 2004), and the field of complex economic dynamics became a new independent research area. New developments in nonlinear dynamical systems theory heavily influenced the social sciences and among them oligopoly theory. It now became clear that nonlinearities can lead to complicated, but bounded, time paths of the economic state variables, that the evolution might sensitively depend on the initial conditions, and that in the long run the trajectories might evolve along distinct objects in phase space, so-called strange or chaotic attractors. The focus of work in this "middle phase" in oligopoly dynamics was the loss of stability of an equilibrium and the emergence of other structures on a larger scale (for example, periodic cycles, quasiperiodic motion, or more complicated attractors). Section 6.5 will be devoted to discoveries along these lines.

Finally, in the last ten years, the focus of research in oligopoly dynamics began to shift towards the topic of global dynamics, that is, researchers got interested in the question of what happens not only locally in a neighborhood around an equilibrium, but in other regions of the phase space away from any equilibrium. As I will illustrate in Section 6.6, contributions in this "late phase" studied the basins of attraction, that is, the set of initial conditions that converge towards an attractor, and the changes these sets undergo when key economic parameters of the oligopoly model change. An investigation of these basins is particularly important in a situation of multi-stability, that is, when several stable attractors coexist. Due to developments of new mathematical methods for nonlinear non-invertible maps, it was now possible to study nonlinear dynamic oligopolies more rigorously. The new insights were that these basins of attraction can be quite complicated sets, despite the fact that the long-run outcomes of the oligopoly model can be very simple.

Summarizing, the chapter will develop along the following lines. I will argue that work belonging to the early phase focused on conditions under which complexity can be ruled out. To make things more precise, I will first use the following simple and broad definition of complexity (henceforth type 1-complexity): "A dynamical system is complex if it endogenously does not tend asymptotically to a fixed point, a limit cycle, or an explosion" (Rosser, 1999, p. 170, after Day, 1994). According to this definition, in the early phase of oligopoly dynamics, when researchers focused on the local and global stability of equilibria, type 1-complexity was ruled out. In contrast to this, in the middle phase of oligopoly dynamics, type 1-complexity became the main issue. Researchers now focused on situations of instability and (local) bifurcations of simple attractors and the emergence of more complicated structures like chaotic or strange attractors. In the late phase it became clear, however, that the simple definition above leaves out one important aspect of complexity in oligopoly dynamics (or, more general, in economic dynamics), the complexity that originates from the global dynamic properties of a dynamical system. Although Day (1994) already illustrated that complex dynamics is related to regime switching, multiple-phase dynamics, and structural change, only later work showed that type 1-complexity and the complexity that originates from the complicated structure of the basins of attractions and their boundaries can be considered separately and that simple attracting sets might have complicated basins and vice versa. Hence, in the late phase it has been illustrated that this new and important type of complexity (henceforth type 2-complexity) can be observed in nonlinear dynamic oligopoly models. Up to now there is no generally accepted definition of type 2-complexity in oligopoly dynamics. Therefore, in this chapter I will first use a rather non-technical definition and discuss more rigorous approaches in the concluding section. I will say that a dynamical system exhibits type 2-complexity if the basins of the attracting sets are multiply connected or non-connected and in a sense "intermingled". A multiply connected basin is pierced by (infinitely many) holes. A non-connected basin is made up of (infinitely many) areas without any connection. The main issue here is that it becomes difficult – at least for initial conditions in some regions of the phase space – to predict the long-run fate of trajectories starting from these initial conditions, resulting in some kind of final state uncertainty. It is obvious that this is particularly important in a case of coexisting stable attractors or in situations where not all initial conditions lead to economically feasible evolutions of the system variables.

6.2 The core models of oligopoly theory

In the following subsections, I will consider the three core models of oligopoly theory, capturing quantity competition, price competition, and commitment issues. These models are usually associated with the names of Cournot, Bertrand, and von Stackelberg, respectively. Due to space restrictions, this introduction will be informal and will neglect many important details like, for example, capacity constraints. I will also not deal with conditions guaranteeing existence and uniqueness of equilibria and I will use game-theoretic concepts like, for example, Nash equilibrium and best-reply functions without providing formal definitions. For a more rigorous treatment of these issues, the reader is encouraged to consult, for example, Tirole (1988), Shy (1995), Vives (1999), Martin (2002), or Bischi et al. (2009). In what follows we will denote an oligopoly as homogeneous if the firms offer identical products and we will call it heterogeneous if the products are differentiated. In a homogeneous oligopoly the products of all firms are sold for a single market price, whereas in a heterogeneous oligopoly the prices for the products differ.

6.2.1 Cournot or quantity competition

Consider an oligopoly market where n firms offer a homogeneous product. The demand function and the inverse demand are denoted by

$$Q = D(p), \quad p = D^{-1}(Q) = f(Q), \tag{6.1}$$

respectively, where p is the market price, q_i, $i = 1, 2, \ldots, n$ denote the quantities offered by the n firms, and $Q = \sum_{l=1}^{n} q_l$ is the industry output. The firms' costs of production are given by $C_i(q_i)$, $i = 1, 2, \ldots, n$. Then the profit of firm i is

$$\pi_i(q_1, q_2, \ldots, q_n) = q_i f(q_i + Q_i) - C_i(q_i), \tag{6.2}$$

where $Q_i = \sum_{l \neq i} q_l$ denotes the sum of the quantities offered by the competitors of firm i. Firms try to select their production levels in order to maximize their profits (6.2). Let us assume that from the first-order condition

$$\partial\pi_i/\partial q_i = f(q_i + Q_i) + q_i f'(q_i + Q_i) - C_i'(q_i) = 0 \tag{6.3}$$

a unique optimal quantity q_i for any given Q_i can be derived, that is,

$$q_i = R_i(Q_i), \tag{6.4}$$

where the function $R_i(\cdot)$ is commonly known as the reaction function, best response, or best reply of firm i. Let us also take it for granted that the second-order conditions guaranteeing a global maximum are satisfied. From the viewpoint of firm i, the reaction function gives the (unique) profit-maximizing response for firm i if (it assumes, predicts, expects, or somehow knows that) the competitors collectively produce Q_i. In a situation of complete information about the demand conditions and cost functions of all firms, each individual firm can derive an equilibrium by introspection and deduction (on this point see, for example, Fudenberg and Tirole, 1992). In a (Cournot-)Nash equilibrium $(q_1^*, q_2^*, \ldots, q_n^*)$ no firm can increase its profit by unilateral deviation, hence

$$q_i^* = R_i\left(\sum_{l \neq i} q_l^*\right) \text{ for } i = 1, 2, \ldots, n. \tag{6.5}$$

As long as firms are out of an equilibrium situation, at least one firm can increase its profit by unilateral deviation from its current production level.

As an example, let us consider a linear duopoly model originally introduced by Cournot. The (inverse) market-demand function is linear and given by $p = f(Q) = a - bQ$, $a > 0, b > 0$. The firms' costs of production are given by $C_i(q_i) = c_i q_i$, $i = 1, 2$, where $0 \leq c_1, c_2 < a$. To simplify the exposition, let us assume that firms have identical costs, $c_1 = c_2 = c$, so that $C(q_i) = cq_i$. Each firm chooses its production level q_i in order to maximize the profit

$$\pi_i(q_1, q_2) = f(q_1 + q_2)q_i - C(q_i) \; i = 1, 2 \tag{6.6}$$

given the production quantity chosen by firm j. Solving the first-order condition yields

$$q_i = R_i(q_j) = \frac{a - c}{2b} - \frac{1}{2}q_j, \; i = 1, 2, \, i \neq j. \tag{6.7}$$

Observe that the reaction functions R_i are downward sloping (that is, the quantities are strategic substitutes) and that if $q_j = 0$, the monopoly output $q_i^M = R_i(0) = (a - c)/2b$ is indeed a best response. The Cournot-Nash equilibrium can be found graphically as the intersection point of the reaction functions and the equilibrium output levels can be analytically calculated by solving the best-response functions, which yields

$$q_1^C = q_2^C = \frac{a - c}{3b}. \tag{6.8}$$

The Cournot equilibrium price is

$$p^C = a - b(q_1^C + q_2^C) = \frac{a + 2c}{3b}$$

and the profits of the firms are

$$\pi_i^C = \pi_j^C = \frac{(a - c)^2}{9b}$$

6.2.2 Von Stackelberg and the value of commitment

In the previous subsection, firms are assumed to choose their production levels simultaneously (or equivalently, that firm i does not know the choices of the competitors when it makes the production decision). We will now turn to a type of market structure often referred to as leader–follower oligopoly based on the idea of von Stackelberg (for a detailed historical account of von Stackelberg's contribution, see Scherer, 1996). Here we consider a two-stage game, where firm 1 (the leader) commits to a production level in stage 1, which is irreversible (that is, it cannot be changed afterwards). Each firm j, $j = 2, \ldots, n$ observes firm 1's production level and subsequently, in period 2, determines how much to produce. This game in extensive form is solved by backwards induction, that is, we first look at the decision problems of the $n - 1$ followers. Firm j chooses q_j to maximize its profit, taking the production level q_1 of firm 1 as given. The profit function of firm j is $\pi_j(q_1, q_2, \ldots, q_n) = f(Q)q_j - C_j(q_j)$, and hence identical to the Cournot case. Solving the first-order condition results in the reaction function

$$q_j = R_j(q_1, .., q_{j-1}, q_{j+1}, .., q_n) \tag{6.9}$$

with the difference that now q_1 is the observed, and not the anticipated or expected, quantity of firm 1. The simultaneous-move game of period 2, where the $n - 1$ followers participate, has the solution

$$q_j = \overline{R}_j(q_1).$$

Since it is assumed that firm 1 possesses all the relevant information, it can calculate the response strategies $\overline{R}_j(q_1)$ the same way the followers do. Using this information, the leader's problem is to maximize

$$\pi_1(q_1) = f\left(q_1 + \sum_{j=2}^{n} \overline{R}_j(q_1)\right)q_1 - C_1(q_1),$$

and from the first-order condition the leader can derive the optimal quantity q_1^S. The followers react to this choice by producing $q_j^S = \overline{R}_j(q_1^S)$.

Considering again the linear model for $n = 2$ and assuming that leader and follower have identical costs, we obtain

$$q_2 = R_2(q_1) = \frac{a - c}{2b} - \frac{1}{2}q_1$$

and

$$\pi_1(q_1) = \left(a - c_1 - b\left(q_1 + \frac{a - c}{2b} - \frac{1}{2}q_1\right)\right)q_1.$$

The leader's profit-maximizing choice is therefore

$$q_1^S = \frac{a - c}{2b} = q_1^M > q_1^C$$

and the follower's production level is therefore

$$q_2^S = R_2(q_1^S) = \frac{a - c}{4b} < q_2^C.$$

It is easy to see that this market structure is more competitive than the Cournot market structure

$$p^S = \frac{a + 3c}{4} < p^C \quad Q^S = \frac{3(a - c)}{4b} > Q^C,$$

and that the following relations for the profits hold:

$$\pi_1^S = \frac{(a - c)^2}{8b} > \pi_1^C \qquad \pi_2^S = \frac{(a - c)^2}{16b} < \pi_2^C.$$

This shows that firm 1, which moves first, earns a higher profit than under Cournot competition, since it could commit itself in period 1 to a higher output level than under Cournot competition, which forces the follower to optimally reduce its production level below q_2^C. The follower's profit is lower than under Cournot competition. Levin (1988) demonstrates that this result also holds in an n-player market with more general demand and cost functions. Gal-Or (1985) discusses the conditions under which a first-mover advantage prevails and Hamilton and Slutsky (1990) consider the endogenous choice of the leader and the follower role.

6.2.3 *Bertrand or price competition*

In a Bertrand market structure, firms set prices instead of quantities. If firms are not capacity-constrained and have identical production costs, then one can show that the outcome in a homogeneous Bertrand duopoly is the same as in a perfectly competitive market. That is, the Bertrand-Nash equilibrium is given by $p_1^B = p_2^B = c$ and $q_1^B = q_2^B = (a - c)/2b$; see, for example, Shy (1995). The reason for this extreme solution is that each firm can undercut the price set by its competitor. This leads to the rather surprising result that with only two firms the competitive outcome is obtained and firms earn zero profits in equilibrium. Since the literature on oligopoly dynamics primarily focused on price competition in a heterogeneous oligopoly, we will turn to markets where firms offer differentiated products.

Consider a price-setting oligopoly with n differentiated products, each produced by a different firm. Because of product differentiation, the demand for firm i's product depends on the prices of all the other firms too, that is,

$$q_i = D_i(p_1, p_2, \ldots, p_n), \quad i = 1, 2, \ldots, n. \tag{6.10}$$

With the same notation as before, the profit of firm i is

$$\pi_i(p_1, p_2, \ldots, p_n) = p_i D_i(p_1, p_2, \ldots, p_n) - C_i(D_i(p_1, p_2, \ldots, p_n)),$$

and (given that the appropriate conditions on the demand and cost functions are satisfied) from the first-order conditions

$$\frac{\partial \pi_i}{\partial p_i} = D_i(p_1, p_2, \ldots, p_n) + (p_i - C_i')\frac{\partial D_i}{\partial p_i} = 0 \tag{6.11}$$

the reaction functions

$$p_i = R_i(P_i) \tag{6.12}$$

can be derived, where $P_i = (p_1, \ldots, p_{i-1}, p_{i+1}, \ldots p_n)$. In a (Bertrand-)Nash equilibrium $(p_1^*, p_2^*, \ldots, p_n^*)$ no firm can increase its profit by unilateral deviation, hence

$$p_i^* = R_i(p_1^*, \ldots, p_{i-1}^*, p_{i+1}^*, \ldots, p_n^*) \text{ for } i = 1, 2, \ldots, n.$$

Observe that from the direct demand system (6.10), the inverse demand system

$$p_i = f_i(q_1, q_2, \ldots, q_n) \text{ for } i = 1, 2, \ldots, n$$

can be derived. For this differentiated quantity-setting oligopoly the same considerations can be made as for the differentiated Bertrand oligopoly.

To demonstrate which type of results can be obtained in a differentiated-products setting, we again look at the linear duopoly model. The firms choose prices p_1 and p_2, and the quantities demanded from the firms are

$$q_1(p_1, p_2) = a - bp_1 + dp_2 \qquad q_2(p_1, p_2) = a - bp_2 + dp_1,$$

$$\text{where } b > 0, b^2 > d^2. \tag{6.13}$$

Observe that according to our assumption the own-price effect dominates the cross-price effect. The products of the duopolists are substitutes, independent, or complements according to whether $d > 0$, $d = 0$, or $d < 0$, respectively. The firms' cost functions are given by $C_i(q_i) = cq_i$, $i = 1, 2$. Both firms simultaneously select their prices such that their profits $\pi_i(p_i, p_j) = (p_i - c)\, q_i(p_i, p_j)$ are maximized (that is, without knowing the price level selected by the competitor). The first-order condition for firm i yields the following best-response function in prices

$$p_i = R_i(p_j) = \frac{a + bc}{2b} + \frac{d}{2b}p_j.$$

The best reply is upward-sloping (the prices are strategic complements) if the products are substitutes ($d > 0$), they are downward-sloping (the prices are strategic substitutes) if the products are complements ($d < 0$). The Bertrand-Nash equilibrium can be found at the intersection of the two best responses or, analytically, by solving the best-reply functions, which yields

$$p_1^{BD} = p_2^{BD} = \frac{a + bc}{2b - d}.$$

This equilibrium can again be determined by the firms through introspection and deduction, if we assume that firms are rational, know that their competitors are rational, and have complete information about prevailing demand and cost structures. The corresponding production levels and profits in equilibrium are

$$q_1^{BD} = q_2^{BD} = \frac{b(a - c(b - d))}{2b - d} \qquad \pi_1^{BD} = \pi_2^{BD} = \frac{b(a - c(b - d))^2}{(2b - d)^2}.$$

For comparisons, the Cournot quantity game with differentiated products is considered in the literature. Inverting the demand system (6.13) yields

$$p_1(q_1, q_2) = \alpha - \beta q_1 - \gamma q_2 \qquad p_2(q_1, q_2) = \alpha - \beta q_2 - \gamma q_1,$$

where $\alpha = (a(b + d))/(b^2 - d^2)$, $\beta = b/(b^2 - d^2)$, $\gamma = d/(b^2 - d^2)$. Observe that $\gamma > 0$ ($\gamma < 0$) if $d > 0$ ($d < 0$). Proceeding in a similar way as above then gives the quantities, prices, and profits in equilibrium for the corresponding quantity game. Singh and Vives (1984) consider such a duopoly model and show that in this (linear) set-up Cournot and

Bertrand competition with differentiated products exhibit a duality property. Cournot (Bertrand) competition with substitute products is the dual of Bertrand (Cournot) competition with complementary products, where dual structures share similar strategic properties. Using this result, they demonstrate that as in the homogeneous case, quantities are lower and prices are higher in Cournot than in Bertrand competition (independent of the fact that products are substitutes or complements); see also Cheng (1985). Hence, price competition is more competitive than quantity competition. They also show that profits are larger in Cournot than in Bertrand competition if products are substitutes. Further results for differentiated oligopolies can be found in Vives (1985), Okuguchi (1987), and morc recently Amir and Jin (2001).

In a differentiated oligopoly setting, one could also consider von Stackelberg competition in prices. Consider, for example, a duopoly market where firms offer differentiated products but firm 1 sets the price first. We have seen that in a quantity-setting game, where we are dealing with strategic substitutes, the first-moving firm earns a higher profit. However, it can be shown that to move first in a price-setting environment, if prices are strategic complements, turns into a disadvantage: the leader's profit is lower than the follower's profit (the profits of both firms are higher though than in a Bertrand setting with differentiated products).

6.3 Adjustment processes, expectations, and stability issues

Up to now we were interested in the equilibrium outcomes obtained under quantity and price competition and we have motivated Nash equilibrium behavior of the players as follows: under the assumption that firms are rational, use their knowledge about demand and cost conditions, and know that their rivals are rational, firms can determine the equilibrium by introspection and deduction. In this subsection I deal with the idea of using learning-type adjustment processes to explain how an equilibrium is reached and I introduce the concept of expectation formation. According to the adjustment or learning approach, firms respond myopically to the choices of other firms, often without trying to fully anticipate their reaction. The question of convergence of such an adjustment procedure corresponds to the question of stability of an equilibrium with respect to this adjustment process, where the concepts of local and global stability can be loosely defined as follows. An equilibrium is locally (asymptotically) stable with respect to a certain dynamic adjustment process if the trajectories generated by this process converge to that equilibrium if the initial selection of the firms' actions are sufficiently close to (that is, in a small neighborhood around) the equilibrium. It is globally (asymptotically) stable if the convergence occurs with arbitrary initial selections.

Adjustment processes can be classified along two lines. First, one can distinguish dynamic processes according to the time concept used, since adjustment can occur in continuous time or in discrete time. In a continuous-time framework, firms adjust their actions at every instant and this behavior can be captured by differential equations. In a discrete-time set-up, actions and expectations are adapted period after period, which is usually modeled using difference equations. The second criterion that can be employed for classification focuses on the issue of rationality or information. We can assume that the (boundedly rational) players in our games know the demand function and the production costs, so that they are able to derive their profits and best responses (with respect to expected actions of the competitors). In such situations the stability of, for example, best-reply dynamics can be investigated. Or, we can argue that this assumption is too demanding and that the players do not know the market demand. In this case, one often considered model is that players only know how profits marginally change when the firms marginally change their actions. In the case of such limited information, the stability of, for example, gradient-adjustment rules can be studied.

In what follows I will mainly focus on time-discrete adjustment processes, although I will make reference to results on continuous-time processes occasionally. One justification for this is that as far as complexity issues are concerned, (nonlinear) dynamical systems in discrete time are more interesting. Apart from this more pragmatic point, the argument that firms rather determine and revise their actions or plans on a weekly, monthly, or maybe quarterly basis, and so a discrete time scale is more fitting, also carries some relevance. I will first start with a situation where firms are informed about the demand and cost conditions and I present a variety of adjustment processes commonly studied in the literature on oligopoly dynamics. Afterwards I will relax this assumption and consider dynamic processes based on marginal profits. This latter situation of less informed players has gained increasing importance in oligopoly dynamics.

6.3.1 *Sequential adjustment*

The idea of using an adjustment process goes back to Cournot, who asked the following question: What happens if firms choose initial production levels different from the equilibrium production levels defined by (6.5)? Cournot studied the following sequence of actions and reactions in a duopoly. Assume firm 1 moves first in period $t = 0$ and chooses $q_1(0)$. Then firm 2 would select the best-reply quantity $q_2(1) = R_2(q_1(0))$ in period $t = 1$, where R_2 is the reaction function defined in (6.4). Continuing, firm 1 would choose $q_1(2) = R_1(q_2(1)) = R_1(R_2(q_1(0)))$, subsequently firm 2 would respond with $q_2(3) = R_2(q_1(2)) = R_2(R_1(q_2(1)))$, and so on. The situation would be as depicted in Figure 6.1a. If this process of sequential adjustment does converge to a steady state (q_1^*, q_2^*), then $q_2^* = R_2(q_1^*)$ and $q_1^* = R_1(q_2^*)$, so the steady state is a Nash equilibrium. Cournot illustrated that in the linear case described above, the discrete-time process of sequential adjustment converges to the Nash equilibrium (6.8). In this case the Nash equilibrium is (locally and globally) stable. Observe that (only) in the duopoly case does sequential adjustment basically consist of two independent adjustment processes of the form

$$q_i(t) = R_i(R_j(q_i(t-2))), \quad i,j = 1,2; i \neq j; t \geq 2,$$

where t denotes the time period and $q_i(t)$ the production quantity in period t. Therefore, this process is (locally) stable for $|R'_1||R'_2| < 1$, and unstable otherwise. Obviously, in order to guarantee stability, the reaction functions have to cross each other "correctly" (see Moulin, 1982; Amir and Wooders, 1998).

Let us consider another example that demonstrates that multiple equilibria might exist in rather simple duopoly models (see also Binmore, 1992; Cox and Walker, 1998). Assume that the inverse demand function is linear, $p = a - b(q_1 + q_2)$ with $a > 0, b > 0$, but that the cost functions are quadratic, $C_i(q_i) = c_i q_i + d_i q_i^2$, with $b + d_i > 0$ and $a - c_i > 0$. Note that we allow marginal costs to be increasing ($d_i > 0$) or decreasing ($d_i < 0$). It is easy to derive the (linear) best replies,

$$R_i(q_j) = \frac{a - c_i}{2(b + d_i)} - \frac{b}{2(b + d_i)} q_j.$$

Figure 6.1a illustrates the situation for $|R_1'||R_2'| = b^2/(4(b + d_1)(b + d_2)) < 1$, which occurs if marginal costs are increasing or even decreasing, but not too strongly. In this case there is a unique interior Nash equilibrium NE 1 and using sequential adjustment all trajectories converge to it. The quantities in the interior equilibrium NE 1 are given by

$$q_1^* = \frac{b(a - 2c_1 + c_2) + 2(a - c_1)d_2}{4(b + d_1)(b + d_2) - b^2}$$

$$q_2^* = \frac{b(a - 2c_2 + c_1) + 2(a - c_2)d_1}{4(b + d_1)(b + d_2) - b^2}.$$

Figure 6.1b demonstrates that for $b^2/(4(b + d_1)(b + d_2)) > 1$, which occurs if marginal costs are decreasing strongly, the interior equilibrium NE 1 is unstable and there exist two "boundary" equilibria, NE 2 and NE 3, which are both stable. If the initial quantity $q_1(0)$ of firm 1 is smaller than

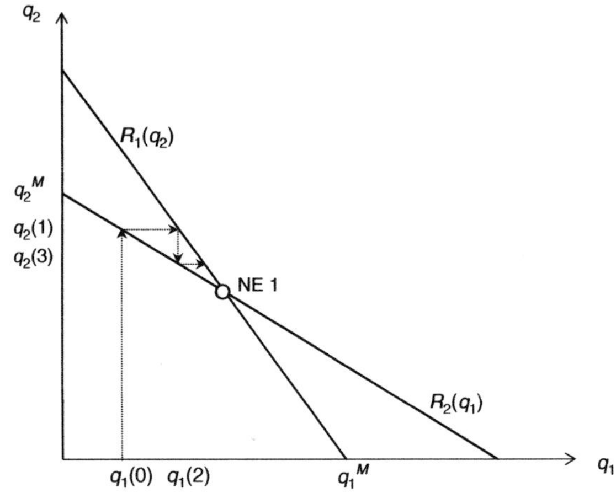

Figure 6.1a Linear best replies and convergence to the interior Nash equilibrium NE 1

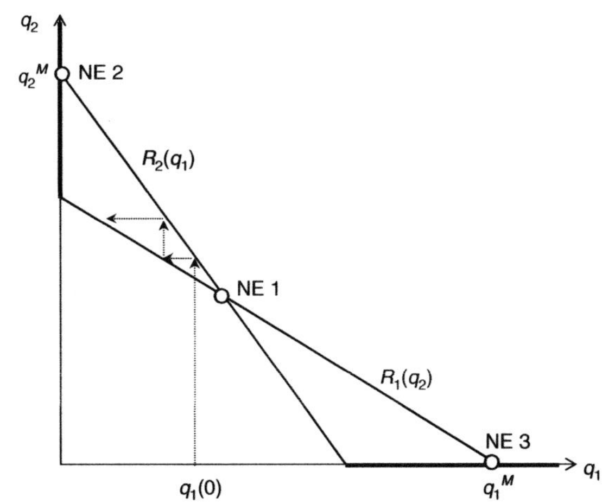

Figure 6.1b Linear best replies and convergence to the boundary Nash equilibrium NE 2

q_1^*, then sequential adjustment eventually leads to a monopoly of firm 2, that is, NE 2 $= (0, q_2^M) = (0,(a - c_2)/(2(b + d_2)))$. If the initial quantity $q_1(0)$ of firm 1 is larger than q_1^*, firm 1 takes over the whole market and eventually offers its monopoly quantity, NE 3 $= (q_1^M, 0) = ((a - c_1)/(2(b + d_1)),0)$. If firm 2 makes the first move, similar considerations can be made.

6.3.2 *Simultaneous adjustment and expectation formation*

I have introduced the Cournot quantity-setting game by saying that firms choose their quantities without knowing the production levels of their competitors (or, equivalently, that they choose their production levels simultaneously). Similarly, in the Bertrand price-setting game with differentiated products, firms choose their own price without knowing the price selections of the other firms. In a dynamic environment where players move simultaneously and (possibly) reach an equilibrium over time, we need to answer two questions. First, we have to clarify how firms make predictions about the production levels or the prices of the other firms. Consider, for example, a quantity-setting model and let us assume that in each period firm i selects its profit-maximizing production level based on information collected up to this period. The information set can contain, for example, past prices, past quantities of all firms, and also expected prices and quantities up to t. Firm i can now try to use this information to derive an expected production level for the upcoming period either for each individual competitor or for the industry output (excluding its own output) and select its own production quantity to maximize its expected profit. Second, we need to define how firms adjust their actions given these predictions or expectations. Before I deal with expectations formation, I will introduce two commonly used adjustment processes.

6.3.2.1 Best-response dynamics As an example, let $Q_i^e(t+1)$ denote the expectation of firm i for the aggregate production level of its competitors in the next period $t+1$, where this expectation has been derived by using past data. Firm i's expected profit is then

$$\pi_i^e = q_i f(q_i + Q_i^e) - C_i(q_i)$$

and the profit-maximizing response is

$$R_i(Q_i^e(t+1)),\ i = 1, 2, \ldots, n, \tag{6.14}$$

where again R_i denotes the reaction function given in (6.4). The best-response dynamics now assumes that firm i adjusts its production level immediately to this new quantity, that is,

$$q_i(t+1) = R_i(Q_i^e(t+1)),\ i = 1, 2, \ldots, n. \tag{6.15}$$

Instead of forming expectations for the aggregate production level of all competitors, firm i can also have individual expectations for each competitor, that is, $q_i^e = (q_{i1}^e, .., q_{ii-1}^e, q_{ii+1}^e, \ldots, q_{in}^e)$ and select the best response to these expectations. In an analogous way expectations in a price-adjusting heterogeneous oligopoly model are introduced. Let $P_i^e = (p_{i1}^e, .., p_{ii-1}^e, p_{ii+1}^e, . . ., p_{in}^e)$ denote the vector of prices firm i expects the other firms to choose, then firm i's best reply is $R_i(P_i^e)$ and the best-response dynamics is

$$p_i(t + 1) = R_i(P_i^e(t + 1)), \; i = 1, 2, . . ., n. \qquad (6.16)$$

6.3.2.2 Partial adjustment to the best response Another adjustment process widely used in oligopoly dynamics is based on the profit-maximizing response. Although firms can calculate the best replies, for reasons of inertia or distrust in their own calculations, they might not be willing to fully adjust their production quantities or prices to this new optimal level. Instead the new production level (price) is determined as a weighted average of the previous production quantity (price) and the best response. For example, the partial adjustment process to the best response with expectations on the aggregate quantity, see (6.14), is given by

$$q_i(t + 1) = (1 - \alpha_i)q_i(t) + \alpha_i R_i(Q_i^e(t + 1)), \; i = 1, 2, . . ., n,$$

where $\alpha_i \in (0, 1]$ are the adjustment coefficients. The continuous-time counterpart to this "proportional adjustment" process reads

$$\dot{q}_i = \frac{dq_i}{dt} = \alpha_i(R_i(Q_i^e) - q_i).$$

The partial adjustment processes to individual quantities or prices are defined analogously. It has been studied in various experiments if subjects actually use adjustment processes of the kind considered above to determine their actions and the answer is affirmative. For example, Huck, Normann, and Oechssler (1999) test various learning theories in the context of a Cournot oligopoly and find that the best replies play an important role (given that the required information is available), but that adjustment is almost always incomplete. Kruse et al. (1994) also find experimental evidence of partial adjustment to the best reply, but in a price-adjusting experiment.

Obviously, in order to obtain full-fledged dynamical systems, we need to specify how firms form expectations on quantities or prices.

6.3.2.3 Naive expectations A rather simple way to make predictions is to assume that the actions of the competitors remain unchanged from one period to the next. This type of expectations is called static or naive. In a quantity-setting model this is captured by

$$Q_i^e(t+1) = Q_i(t) = \sum_{l \neq i} q_l(t). \tag{6.17}$$

Taken together, (6.15) and (6.17) define an n-dimensional dynamical system in discrete time,

$$q_i(t+1) = R_i\left(\sum_{l \neq i} q_l(t)\right), \quad i = 1, 2, \ldots, n, \tag{6.18}$$

to which I will refer as the *best-reply dynamics with naive expectations*. It is easy to see that in the duopoly case ($n = 2$) the simultaneous adjustment process (6.18) and the sequential adjustment process described above are equivalent in the sense that they have the same steady states and the same (local) stability properties. The reason is that for $n = 2$ the dynamical system (6.18) also consists of two independent iterations,

$$q_1(t+1) = R_1(R_2(q_1(t-1)))$$

$$q_2(t+1) = R_2(R_1(q_2(t-1))).$$

Of course, this equivalence does not hold for oligopolies with more than two firms. As far as local stability of the Nash equilibrium in a duopoly game is concerned, a well-known result in oligopoly dynamics can be derived. Consider the best-reply dynamics in (6.18) for $n = 2$. Then an equilibrium is locally stable with respect to the best-reply dynamics with naive expectations if $|R_1'|\,|R_2'| < 1$. Since from the implicit function theorem we get $|R_i'| = |\partial^2\pi_i/\partial q_i q_j| \,/\, |\partial^2\pi_i/(\partial q_i)^2|$, this is equivalent to

$$\left|\frac{\partial^2\pi_1}{(\partial q_1)^2}\,\frac{\partial^2\pi_2}{(\partial q_2)^2}\right| > \left|\frac{\partial^2\pi_1}{\partial q_1 \partial q_2}\,\frac{\partial^2\pi_2}{\partial q_1 \partial q_2}\right|.$$

This result, which can be found in many textbooks on oligopoly or game theory (see, for example, Fudenberg and Tirole, 1992; Vives, 1999; Martin, 2002), is useful for checking stability if the best replies can not be derived in closed form.

Although sequential adjustment and the best-reply dynamics share the same local stability properties for $n = 2$, they differ with regard to their global dynamics. To see this let us consider again the duopoly with linear inverse demand $p = a - b(q_1 + q_2)$ and quadratic costs $C_i(q_i) = c_i q_i + d_i q_i^2$, and let us assume that the firms have identical cost function, that is, $c_1 = c_2 = c$ and $d_1 = d_2 = d$. In this case the oligopoly game is symmetric and the quantities in the interior Nash equilibrium NE 1 are $q_1^* = q_2^* = q^* = (a - c)/(3b + 2d)$. In the case $b^2/(4(b + d)^2) > 1$, the sequential adjustment process leads to NE 2 for all initial conditions

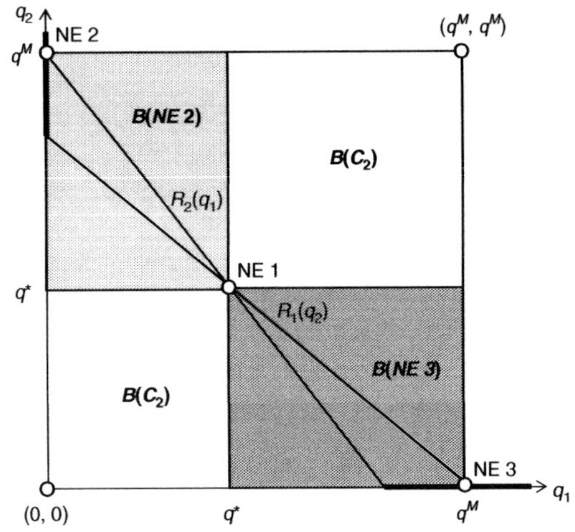

Figure 6.2 Basins of attraction of the two boundary Nash equilibria and the coexisting cycle C_2

$q_1(0) < q^*$ and to NE 3 for all initial conditions $q_1(0) > q^*$. In contrast to this, if firms simultaneously adjust their quantities based on their naive expectations, see (6.18), then even cyclical dynamics can be observed. Figure 6.2 depicts the coexisting stable attractors in this case. For initial quantities located in the light grey (dark grey) region, simultaneous adjustment leads to firm 2 (firm 1) being a monopolist. In addition to that, if the initial quantities are selected in one of the white squares, then simultaneous adjustment leads to cyclic dynamics, where firms choose the monopoly quantity q^M in one period and then choose $q = 0$ in the subsequent period.

From an economic point of view, two objections might be raised with respect to the validity of this two-cycle as a plausible description of real-world behavior. First, note that in the two-cycle the players' expectations are always wrong in the sense that they are always inconsistent with what actually happens (even in the long run). Although players are myopic, they might nevertheless be able to discover a cyclic pattern that is actually caused by their assumption that the rival's action remains unchanged from one period to the next. As a result they might switch to a different rule for predicting the rival's behavior. The second point is even more severe in this example. Observe that the firms do not make any profit if $q = 0$. On the other hand, if both produce the monopoly quantity q^M, then the profit for each firm is

$$\pi(q^M, q^M) = \frac{(a - c)^2 d}{4(b + d)^2},$$

which is even negative due to $d < 0$ (recall that marginal costs are decreasing). Hence, the market price is so low that no firm can make a positive profit. Consequently, this two-cycle is not feasible from an economic point of view. The conclusion is that a global analysis reveals that only initial conditions located in the basins $B(NE\ 2)$ and $B(NE\ 3)$ of NE 2 and NE 3 lead to economically feasible solutions of the oligopoly game, whereas initial conditions in the (non-connected) basin $B(C_2)$ of the two-cycle $C_2 = ((0, 0); (q^M, q^M))$ do not.

Considering a heterogeneous oligopoly, naive expectations can be incorporated in a similar way by letting

$$\begin{aligned} q_i^e(t+1) &= (q_{i1}^e(t+1), .., q_{ii-1}^e(t+1), q_{ii+1}^e(t+1), \ldots, q_{in}^e(t+1)) \\ &= (q_1(t), .., q_{i-1}(t), q_{i+1}(t), \ldots, q_n(t)). \end{aligned}$$

In a price-setting model naive expectations are captured by

$$\begin{aligned} P_i^e(t+1) &= (p_{i1}^e(t+1), .., p_{ii-1}^e(t+1), p_{ii+1}^e(t+1), \ldots, p_{in}^e(t+1)) \\ &= (p_1(t), .., p_{i-1}(t), p_{i+1}(t), \ldots, p_n(t)) \end{aligned} \tag{6.19}$$

that is, firm i assumes that the prices of the competitors remain unchanged. Together with (6.16) this yields the best-reply dynamics with naive expectations in the heterogeneous Bertrand case.

The *partial adjustment process to the best response with naive expectations* is given by

$$q_i(t+1) = (1 - \alpha_i)q_i(t) + \alpha_i R_i\Big(\sum_{l \neq i} q_l(t)\Big), \quad i = 1, 2, \ldots, n, \tag{6.20}$$

where $\alpha_i \in (0, 1]$. Note that for $\alpha_i = 1, i = 1, 2, \ldots, n$ the best-reply dynamics is obtained. The continuous-time analog is

$$\dot{q}_i = \frac{dq_i}{dt} = \alpha_i\Big(R_i\Big(\sum_{l \neq i} q_l(t)\Big) - q_i\Big). \tag{6.21}$$

6.3.2.4 Conjectural variations For the sake of completeness, I also briefly look at the conjectural variations approach, which has been considered infrequently in oligopoly dynamics, but deserves some attention as a historical milestone. In the (static) Cournot and Bertrand models it is implicitly assumed that the competitors of each particular firm do not react to changes in the action of this firm. This can be readily seen from the first-order conditions (6.3) and (6.11), where the effect of variations of firm i's action on the decisions of the other firms is not taken into account. In order to illustrate how the conjectural variations approach tries to remedy this shortcoming, consider a quantity-setting homogeneous duopoly (see also Bresnahan, 1981; Dixit, 1986). If firm i's belief about the relationship between the outputs of the firms is represented by the conjectural variation term $\frac{dq_j}{dq_i} = vi(q_1, q_2)$, then the perceived marginal profit of firm i is

$$\partial \pi_i/\partial q_i = f(q_i + q_j) + q_i f'(q_i + q_j)\left(1 + \frac{dq_j}{dq_i}\right) - C'_i(q_i) = 0.$$

With the concept of conjectural variations, different first-order conditions for various models are obtained, like, for example, the competitive case ($v^i(q_1, q_2) = -1$), the collusive case ($v^i(q_1, q_2) = q_j/q_i$), and also the Cournot model ($v^i(q_1, q_2) = 0$). The conjectural variation approach can be applied in an analogous way to a price-setting framework. In this case the conjectural variation term represents firm i's belief about the effect of a change of p_i on the other prices.

6.3.2.5 Adaptive expectations If firms use naive expectations to predict the future behavior of their competitors, they only take the most recent information on prices or production quantities into account. It might be argued, however, that a more sophisticated rule should also include the actions of previous periods, maybe even adjusted if older data are considered as less relevant than more recent observations. One such expectation formation rule is called adaptive expectation, which builds on the current expectation derived from past data and corrects or adjusts it when a new observation becomes available.

As an example consider the quantity-setting model and let $Q_i^e(t)$ and $Q_i(t) = \Sigma_{l \neq i} q_l(t)$ be the expected and the observed aggregate production level of the competitors, respectively, in period t. If these quantities do not coincide, then the adaptive expectation rule suggests to correct or adjust firm i's expectation in the following way:

$$Q_i^e(t+1) = Q_i^e(t) + \alpha_i(Q_i(t) - Q_i^e(t)), \tag{6.22}$$

with $\alpha_i \in (0, 1]$. Note that for $\alpha_i = 1$ the adaptive expectation scheme reduces to naive expectations. The adaptive expectation scheme takes previous data into account, although with (geometrically) declining weights. Repeated substitution for Q_i^e yields

$$\begin{aligned} Q_i^e(t+1) &= (1 - \alpha_i)Q_i^e(t) + \alpha_i Q_i(t) \\ &= (1 - \alpha_i)^{t+1} Q_i^e(0) + \alpha_i \sum_{j=0}^{t} (1 - \alpha_i)^j Q_i(t - j). \end{aligned}$$

Taken together, (6.15) and (6.22) result in a $2n$-dimensional dynamical system,

$$q_i(t+1) = R_i(Q_i^e(t) + \alpha_i(Q_i(t) - Q_i^e(t)))$$

$$Q_i^e(t+1) = Q_i^e(t) + \alpha_i(Q_i(t) - Q_i^e(t)).$$

Observe that this dynamical system can be written as

$$Q_i^e(t+1) = (1-\alpha_i)Q_i^e(t) + \alpha_i \sum_{l \neq k} R_l(Q_l^e(t)), \qquad (6.23)$$

that is, as an n-dimensional system of difference equations in the expected variables. How do partial adjustment to the best response with naive expectations (6.20) and best-reply dynamics with adaptive expectations (6.23) relate to each other? It is easy to see that the two systems are equivalent in the duopoly case. For $n > 2$ it can be shown that these two processes have the same local stability properties (see Bischi et al., 2009). Of course, as far as global stability is concerned, these two processes differ in general.

The principle of adaptive expectations can also be applied to individual quantities and prices. In a price-setting environment each firm chooses the best reply to the vector of price expectations P_i^e, see (6.16), but now the individual price expectations of firm i are obtained by

$$p_{il}^e(t+1) = p_{il}^e(t) + \alpha_{il}(p_l(t) - p_{il}^e(t)) \quad l = 1, 2, \ldots, n; l \neq i.$$

Again for $\alpha_{il} = 1$ we are back to the case of naive expectations. The continuous-time analog would be

$$\dot{p}_{il}^e = \frac{dp_{il}^e}{dt} = \alpha_{il}(p_l(t) - p_{il}^e) \quad l = 1, 2, \ldots, n; l \neq i.$$

6.3.2.6 Extrapolative expectations Another type of expectation formation much less considered is extrapolative expectations, where only observations from the previous L periods are used to make a prediction for period $t + 1$. As an example consider $L = 2$, then expectations are formed according to

$$Q_i^e(t+1) = Q_i(t) + \alpha_i(Q_i(t) - Q_i(t-1))$$

in a discrete-time framework. In a continuous-time setting extrapolative expectations are captured by

$$Q_i^e(t) = Q_i(t) + \alpha_i \frac{dQ_i}{dt}.$$

6.3.2.7 Gradient adjustment and related processes So far we have assumed that firms have sufficient information so that they can derive the best-response functions and use them to determine their future actions. We will now turn to situations where firms only possess limited information on demand and cost conditions. One possible adjustment process considered in oligopoly dynamics suggests that players change their strategies at a rate proportional to the gradient of marginal profitability. For example, in a quantity-setting framework it seems plausible to assume that firm i will increase its quantity from one period to the next if the marginal profit with respect to the production level is positive, and decrease it otherwise. This is captured by

$$q_i(t + 1) = q_i(t) + \alpha_i \frac{\partial \pi_i}{\partial q_i}, \tag{6.24}$$

where $\alpha_i > 0$ are the adjustment speeds. The continuous-time analog is

$$\dot{q}_i = \frac{dq_i}{dt} = \alpha_i \frac{\partial \pi_i}{\partial q_i}. \tag{6.25}$$

It is easy to see that gradient adjustment and partial adjustment to the best reply lead to similar (linear) dynamical systems if the demand and cost functions are linear. The two systems only differ with respect to their adjustment speeds (by a factor that depends on the slope of the demand function), so that for given values of the adjustment speeds one system might be stable whereas the other one is not.

To conclude this section, it should be mentioned that there has been some criticism of modeling boundedly rational agents in dynamic oligopoly models using adjustment processes of the kind considered above; see, for example, Friedman (1977, 1982). The players ignore the fact that their current actions will have an impact on the future actions of the competitors (that is, the adjustment process itself may not be an equilibrium of the repeated game). Therefore, it has been suggested that it is more reasonable to assume that firms that operate in markets over many time periods wish to maximize a discounted stream of profits over a finite or infinite time horizon taking the strategic behavior of their competitors into account. Beside the fact that such an approach necessarily assumes a high degree of information and rationality of the players, one justification for the interest in such models is given by more recent results that demonstrate that myopic play is (approximately) optimal if the discount factor is very small (see Dana and Montrucchio, 1986, 1987). Moreover, non-equilibrium adjustment processes like, for example, the Cournot sequential adjustment process presented above can be shown to implicitly rely on a combination of "lock-in" and impatience, and this may serve as a further explanation for the players' myopia (see Tirole, 1988; Fudenberg and Levine, 1998). In any case, in this chapter I follow the argument that the kind of adjustment processes considered in this section can "be interpreted as a crude way of expressing the *bounded rationality* of agents" (Vives, 1999, p. 49, emphasis in original). Readers interested in dynamic games where players are more rational and forward-looking might want to consult, for example, the book by Dockner et al. (2000) who present a variety of models and summarize many interesting results.

After these preparations, we are now in a position to turn to the main part of this chapter, the development of oligopoly dynamics in the last 45 years seen through the lens of complexity research. In the next three sections I will briefly review the main contributions in the early, middle, and late phases. The early phase is characterized by a focus on (local and global) stability. Hence, according to the definition of type 1-complexity, these early papers put the emphasis on deriving conditions for which complexity can be ruled out. In contrast to this, in the middle phase attention shifted to situations where local stability of the equilibrium is lost and to the investigation of dynamic oligopoly models where type 1-complexity occurs. In the late phase, although some work is still done on discovering type 1-complexity, more and more contributions deal with the topic of multi-stability, coexistence of attractors, and their basins of attractions. In other words, there is an ongoing shift towards studying type 2-complexity and the change in the degree of complexity when key parameters of the oligopoly models are varied.

6.4 The early phase

6.4.1 Quantity-setting oligopoly models

I start the literature review with the largest group of contributions, namely quantity-setting games. The classical references beside Cournot's early work are Theocharis (1960), Fisher (1961), and McManus and Quandt (1961). In Theocharis' paper it is shown that the Nash equilibrium in the linear model is unstable with respect to the best-reply dynamics with naive expectations (6.18) if the number of firms is larger than $n = 2$. Fisher and McManus and Quandt consider more general homogeneous oligopolies with quadratic costs and partial adjustment to the best reply (with naive expectations), see (6.20) and (6.21), and show that increasing marginal costs or smaller speeds of adjustment have a stabilizing effect.

These papers were the starting point of a series of articles. Hahn (1962) has given a general sufficient condition for global stability for continuous-time dynamic oligopolies and the adjustment process (6.21), which is based on a comparison of the slopes of the market demand function and marginal costs. This result has been generalized by Okuguchi (1964) to situations where the rate of change follows a sign-preserving, monotonic function. Further considerations along these lines can be found in Seade (1980) and also in Al-Nowaihi and Levine (1985). Okuguchi (1970) has introduced adaptive expectations into these models and shows that the Nash equilibrium is stable if the absolute rate of change of marginal profit of the i-th firm with respect to a change in its own output is greater than that with respect to a simultaneous change of all other firms' outputs. For generalizations of the linear oligopoly models to set-ups with adaptive expectations in discrete time, see Szidarovszky and Okuguchi (1988) and Szidarovszky and Yen (1991), who provide more general conditions for (global) stability, which are also based on the speeds of adjustment and the coefficients of output changes. Hadar (1966) has been the first to consider a differentiated oligopoly with best-reply dynamics and naive expectations. His sufficient condition shows that global stability is obtained if the effect of an output change of firm i on marginal costs and marginal revenue dominates the sum of the effects of output changes of all competitors on the marginal revenue. In other words, stability can be guaranteed if the interdependence between the products is sufficiently weak. Sato and Nagatani (1967) and McMillan (1984) study the stability of the equilibrium if firms employ a conjectural variations approach. Okuguchi (1976) and Krelle (1976) provide summaries and further extensions of many of these early results for discrete-time and continuous-time oligopolies. Interesting new aspects into the quantity-setting framework are introduced by Howroyd and Russell (1984) and Russell, Rickard, and Howroyd (1986). They consider partial adjustment to the best reply (6.20) and (6.21), but assume that due to delays in the information flow the adjustment of output is also delayed. They also use more general cost functions, for example (in our notation)

$$C_i(q_1, q_2, \ldots, q_n) = f_i + c_i q_i + \frac{1}{2} d_i q_i^2 + q_i \sum_{j \neq i} h_{ij} q_j, \tag{6.26}$$

in order to allow for cost externalities. The parameters f_i, c_i, and d_i are non-negative, while $h_{ij} < 0$ ($h_{ij} > 0$) corresponds to an external economy (an external diseconomy). Through this last term, changes in the marginal costs as a result of the behavior of the competitors can be taken into account. The authors demonstrate that information delays on output might affect the stability of the system.

Howroyd and Rickard (1981) and Szidarovszky and Yen (1995) consider another specification of the cost function. They assume that firms face (quadratic) production adjustment costs and study the stability of partial adjustment to the best reply and best reply (with naive expectations) respectively. It is demonstrated that adjustment costs have a stabilizing effect since they inhibit large variations in output. The sequential adjustment process has been generalized to oligopoly models with *n* firms, and its stability properties have been investigated, see; for example, Moulin (1982) or Okuguchi and Szidarovszky (1989).

Finally, in more recent years the focus has been on dynamic multi-product oligopolies. For partial adjustment to the best reply with naive expectations, see Szidarovszky, Rassenti and Yen (1992), and for stability results for the best-reply dynamics, see Zhang and Zhang (1996). Szidarovszky and Li (2000) introduce adaptive expectations into the multi-product model, and Szidarovszky and Okuguchi (1993) and Okuguchi and Szidarovszky (1999) provide an array of results for several adjustment processes and multi-product oligopoly models. For stability results on models with extrapolative expectations, see Okuguchi (1976) for single-product oligopolies and Okuguchi and Szidarovszky (1999) for their multi-product counterparts. In all these studies conditions for (local and global) stability of the equilibrium are provided.

In the papers mentioned above it is assumed that the players know the demand and cost structures, and therefore they can derive the best replies. The question arises how stability of the equilibrium is affected if players do not know the demand function. Hosomatsu (1969) was the first to consider this problem in a discrete-time oligopoly framework. He assumes that the misspecified and the true demand functions are both linear and costs are quadratic. At the end of each period, firms can observe the market price and update their estimated demand function. The firms then use these perceived demands to derive their best replies with naive expectations. Hosomatsu demonstrates that stability of an equilibrium for the resulting dynamical process is more likely for higher marginal costs, for a smaller number of firms, and for steeper slopes of the estimated price functions (compared with the actual market price function).

Observe that although the dynamical system converges to some equilibrium, this equilibrium might not coincide with the equilibrium of the "true" model. This has been demonstrated by Kirman (1975); see also Kirman (1983, 1995). A related idea has been studied recently by Bischi, Naimzada, and Sbragia (2007) who assume that firms derive linear approximations of the true demand by local quantity variations neglecting the influence of the competitors. In their model, the adjustment process based on such "local monopolistic approximation" converges to the same Nash equilibrium as the best-reply dynamics. Surprisingly, for a market with isoelastic demand curve it turns out that the model with less information leads to more stability. The concept of gradient adjustment, which assumes that firms adjust their quantities with respect to the marginal profit, see (6.24) and (6.25), is closely related to this idea, since it is based on the assumption that firms can somehow get a local estimate of the slope of the profit function through (price or) quantity variations. For example, Dixit (1986) and Furth (1986) study the local and global stability of equilibria using gradient adjustment in a continuous-time oligopoly model. Furthermore, Furth (1986) illustrates the occurrence of multiple equilibria in oligopoly models with nonlinear cost functions.

6.4.2 *Von Stackelberg oligopoly models*

Dynamic von Stackelberg models have also been studied, although to a much lesser degree. Different paths have been followed in the literature on oligopoly dynamics to obtain dynamic versions of the von Stackelberg model, and some of them seem more reasonable than others. A dynamic version of the static leader–follower-type model introduced above is as follows. Assume that at the beginning of period $t + 1$ the leader (firm 1) determines its production level $q_1(t + 1)$. The $n - 1$ followers (firms 2, . . ., n) observe this production level and subsequently select their production choices $q_j(t + 1)$ simultaneously based on the assumption that the competitors' outputs remain unchanged from period t to period $t + 1$. From the optimization problem of firm j it is easy to derive

$$q_j(t + 1) = R_j\left(q_1(t + 1) + \sum\nolimits_{\substack{l=2 \\ l \neq j}}^{n} q_l(t)\right), \quad j = 2, .., n.$$

Firm 1 (the leader) anticipates the reactions of the followers and determines the production level q_1 such that the profit

$$\pi_1 = f\left(q_1 + \sum\nolimits_{j=2}^{n} R_j\left(q_1 + \sum\nolimits_{\substack{l=2 \\ l \neq j}}^{n} q_l(t)\right)\right) q_1 - C_1(q_1)$$

is maximized. From the first-order condition we get

$$q_1(t + 1) = R_1(q_2(t), q_3(t), . . ., q_n(t)),$$

which together with the equations for the other firms form a dynamical system.

Schoonbeek (1997) incorporates production adjustment costs into a slightly different version of a dynamic von Stackelberg model, where the followers have naive expectations with respect to all the other firms (including the leader) and determine their profit-maximizing production levels. The leader anticipates their reaction and optimally determines its own quantity. It turns out that in this model, stability is obtained for a larger range of the parameter values than for the related Cournot model. Krelle (1976) investigates another dynamic variant of the von Stackelberg model and finds that for linear inverse demand and linear costs the system is stable as long as $n \leq 3$. A quite different set-up of von Stackelberg dynamics is considered by Hathaway, Rickard, and Howroyd (1979). In their model (1) each firm assumes that the competitors are following a Cournot strategy (6.18) and then takes maximum advantage of this assumption, that is, acts like a von Stackelberg leader, and (2) externalities are included in the cost function; see (6.26). They investigate the dynamics of the partial adjustment to the best-response process and find that stability depends on the speed of adjustment, on the magnitude of an existing cost diseconomy, and on the number of competitors. Further work on this set-up has been done by Okuguchi (1979) and Rickard (1980).

6.4.3 Price-setting oligopoly models

The first account of a dynamic price-setting model in oligopoly dynamics is by Quandt (1967), who considers a differentiated oligopoly with linear demand and quadratic costs. He shows that for a continuous-time adjustment process the results on stability are different than the results for quantity-setting models; for example, marginal costs have a destabilizing effect. Several papers have reconsidered Quandt's model and have tried to generalize it. Okuguchi (1968) introduces adaptive expectations and Tarr (1975) subsequently shows that stability in the model with naive expectations is both sufficient and necessary for stability in the model with adaptive expectations. Okuguchi (1969) considers more general cost functions and assumes partial adjustment to the best reply in a discrete-time model. He shows that a decrease in the responsiveness of any firm to other firms' changes in prices is conducive to the stability of the system. Veendorp and Vessal (1978) correct a misleading result in Quandt's paper, which is on stability if the number of oligopolists is increased. Okuguchi (1978) studies the effect of conjectural variations in a discrete-time set-up. Schoonbeek (1996) investigates the influence of higher-order lags on stability in the Quandt model and finds that stability is obtained in the model with higher-order lags if and only if it is obtained in the model with first-order lags only.

Quite independent of all this work, Krelle (1976) considers a variety of set-ups including models with static price expectations (6.19), which he calls "Launhardt-Hotelling-oligopolies," and von Stackelberg models with price-setting firms. Finally, Puu (2001) focuses on a spatial formulation of price competition, now known as the Hotelling model in textbooks on oligopoly theory (see Hotelling, 1929), and discusses various extensions of his preliminary results on stability.

Price-setting models with incomplete knowledge of the market demand have also been analyzed. Bonanno and Zemann (1985) and Bonanno (1988) assume that firms derive linear approximations of the true demand by local price variations. They demonstrate that an equilibrium in such a framework always exists at which each firm makes a positive profit. Chiarella and Szidarovszky (2005) consider a standard Bertrand oligopoly and study the stability properties of this model when firms use simple price-setting strategies (which are based on information about previous prices and quantities). They demonstrate that under realistic conditions global stability of the system is obtained.

The contributions to oligopoly dynamics in the early phase were important and showed under which conditions the Nash equilibrium can be reached by boundedly rational players. On the other hand, some essential issues have not been answered or have been treated in an unsatisfactory way, in particular for *nonlinear* oligopoly games. First, usually conditions were imposed so that multiple equilibria are ruled out. This has been done since often the existence of many possible equilibria were considered a weakness of the model. However, it seems that there is nothing inherently wrong with the fact that a model can give rise to several equilibria as long as it captures the economic forces that it is meant to describe in a satisfactory way (see on this point also Friedman and Mezzetti, 2002). Furthermore, (sufficient) conditions for the global (asymptotic) stability of the equilibrium often turn out to be quite restrictive (see Bischi et al., 2009). Hence, the question arises of what happens when these conditions are relaxed. Second, many papers have concentrated on a local stability analysis based on the linear approximation of the dynamical system around the steady state. However, local (asymptotic) stability means than that the trajectories of the dynamic game converge to the equilibrium in the long run, provided that the initial conditions are sufficiently close to it. Nothing is said about the extent of this neighborhood or about the dynamical properties of the dynamic game if the initial conditions are outside this neighborhood. It has turned out in later years that these issues are particularly important for discrete-time nonlinear oligopolies.

6.5 The middle phase

In the middle phase starting in the late 1970s, quite in contrast to the early phase, the main focus in oligopoly dynamics has been on the loss of (local) stability of the equilibrium and the emergence of attractors different from steady states, for example, periodic orbits or chaotic attractors. Mathematically, (in)stability of the equilibrium and (local) bifurcations can be checked by considering a linearization of the nonlinear dynamical system around the equilibrium and calculating the eigenvalues of the Jacobian (see, for example, Lorenz, 1993; Day, 1994). The trigger for this shift in interest was the discovery that simple, but nonlinear, dynamical systems can, for certain values of the model parameters, exhibit complex dynamics in the sense that the resulting trajectories are erratic-looking with no apparent pattern or regularity and can not be distinguished from stochastic time paths. This seemingly random behavior appears when the state variables are observed over time, whereas in phase space the state variables evolve along compact objects, so-called chaotic attractors. On these attractors, the trajectories show sensitive dependence on initial conditions, which results in a loss of predictability. Researchers in oligopoly dynamics started to reconsider their models with this new agenda in mind and tried to find out if their models showed type 1-complexity, where we recall that a dynamical system is of type 1-complexity if it remains bounded, but does not converge to a fixed point or a limit cycle. In what follows, I will give a brief survey of the main work and point out the differences in the microeconomic assumptions. Since there already exist comprehensive reviews of work done in this area, I will keep this section short. For more elaborate expositions I refer the reader to, for example, Rosser (2000, 2002).

Interestingly, in the middle phase, the majority of papers has focused on the quantity-setting framework, very little work has been done on the von Stackelberg set-up, and no work has been devoted to price-setting models. The first paper dealing with type 1-complexity in a quantity-setting duopoly model is Rand (1978). He studies the qualitative dynamics of discrete simultaneous-move best-reply systems with naive expectations (6.18) under the assumption that the best replies R_1 and R_2 are unimodal. It is clear by now and has been pointed out by economists and game theorists alike that non-monotonic best-reply functions emerge in oligopoly settings for a variety of reasons, for example, because of network effects (Katz and Shapiro, 1985) or because firms are trying to deter the entry of a competitor (Bulow, Geanakoplos, and Klemperer, 1985). Accordingly, from an economic point of view the interest in non-monotonic best-reply functions seems justified, although it still needs to be clarified under which demand and cost conditions such type of best replies can be derived. Dana and Montrucchio (1986, 1987) show that (infinite-horizon) duopoly games in discrete time can exhibit complex dynamics. They also demonstrate that for an isoelastic demand function

$$p = f(Q) = \frac{1}{Q + w} \tag{6.27}$$

where w is a non-negative constant, the best replies are non-invertible. Later on, Puu (1991) investigates the dynamics of the resulting discrete best-reply dynamics with naive expectations and shows that type 1-complexity may occur; see also Puu (2003). A different approach can be found in Kopel (1996), where the (inverse) demand function is still linear like in the original Cournot model, but, similar to Howroyd and Russell (1984) and Russell, Rickard, and Howroyd (1986), it is assumed that the cost function exhibits an externality; see (6.26). Kopel considers homogeneous and heterogeneous Cournot duopolies and illustrates that for particular types of externality the best replies are given by quadratic functions of the form

$$R_1(q_2) = \mu_1 q_2(1 - q_2) \tag{6.28}$$

$$R_2(q_1) = \mu_2 q_1(1 - q_1).$$

It is then demonstrated that type 1-complexity may occur for discrete adjustment processes like best reply and partial adjustment to the best reply (with naive expectations). The partial adjustment to the best-reply process has been further studied in Agiza (1999), where it is also shown that the chaotically fluctuating trajectories can be controlled. For chaos control in an oligopoly framework with three firms, see Richter and Stolk (2004). Bischi and Gardini (1998) analyze in detail the various (local) bifurcations of the best-reply dynamics (6.18) for $n = 2$ and consider quadratic best replies as an example. Matsumoto and Nonaka (2006) study a duopoly model with cost externalities, but assume that the products of the two firms are complementary goods. They demonstrate that the model might exhibit a wide array of dynamics including complex dynamics. Interestingly, they show that for both firms the long-run average profit taken along a chaotic trajectory might be higher than the profits at a Nash equilibrium. Wirl, Kopel, and Feichtinger (1999) investigate a duopoly model where firms use threshold advertising rules to determine their advertising outlays. It is demonstrated that type 1-complexity may occur in this set-up. Finally, a result similar to Dana and Montrucchio's (1986) "anything goes" proposition for discrete duopoly games has been proven by Corchon and Mas-Colell (1996). They show that it is possible to construct a continuous three-player game such that the best-reply system exhibits complex dynamics.

There are few papers dealing with type 1-complexity in a dynamic von Stackelberg model. Puu (1998) considers an isoelastic demand function and compares the resulting dynamics of two set-ups, a simultaneous-move Cournot model with three oligopolists and a "probabilistic" von Stackelberg model, where leadership is assigned to a firm on a probabilistic basis; see also Puu (1996, 2003). He demonstrates that complex dynamics can be observed in both cases. Finally, I am not aware of work on price-setting oligopoly models and type 1-complexity, although Puu (2001) in his paper on spatial price competition points out the possibility of complex dynamics.

The contribution of work that focuses on type 1-complexity is that it shows the array of potential dynamics of oligopoly games. Some authors argue that this is primarily of mathematical interest, however. From an economic point of view non-convergence to and instability of an equilibrium raises a couple of critical issues (see also Amir and Wooders, 1998). First, if an equilibrium is not reached, then this usually goes along with inconsistent expectations in the long run. As we have already briefly discussed in the context of a simple duopoly model, it seems likely that the players would detect these inconsistencies and would switch to different expectation schemes. One might argue that it is difficult for the players to detect any systematic pattern in forecasting errors if the dynamical system exhibits complex dynamics, that is, chaotic consistent expectations equilibria might exist. This question has not been investigated extensively in oligopoly dynamics, but in Bischi and Kopel (2001) it is demonstrated that if the players are able to detect a linear statistical relationship between their own forecasting errors of two consecutive periods, then despite complex dynamics the steady states are the only consistent expectations equilibria.

A second argument why stable equilibria are of interest in oligopolies is based on the observation that an unstable equilibrium in a Cournot oligopoly has economically unintuitive properties (for example, Amir and Lambson, 2000). Third, Slade (1994) focuses on the topic of reducing the task of calculating Nash equilibria (a fixed-point problem) to solving an ordinary optimization problem. She discovers that Nash equilibria of a game that are not maxima of the objective function of such an optimization problem are generically unstable. The fourth and final point that can be mentioned is that experimental evidence demonstrates that a Nash equilibrium predicts play well if the equilibrium is stable, but performs poorly if it is unstable (see, for example, Cox and Walker, 1998).

6.6 The late phase

The evidence presented at the end of the previous section gives support to focusing on the steady states of dynamic oligopoly models. If there is a unique equilibrium, then this equilibrium serves as a prediction of how the game is played. However, often in oligopoly games several equilibria might coexist, giving rise to an equilibrium selection problem (see, for example, Krugman, 1991; Grosser, 1999). In this case, a mechanism is required that allows predictions to be made of which of the multiple equilibria will be more likely to be observed in situations described by the game. One approach to select among the equilibria is to use stability arguments, which consider an equilibrium point as a convention that arises among players interacting repeatedly. As unstable equilibria will not be the result of such an evolutionary process, only stable equilibria have to be considered. If such a stability argument selects a single equilibrium, we can abstract from the process itself with its dependence on historical accident. However, often many equilibria survive this refinement, and a situation of strategic uncertainty prevails. In such situations of *multi-stability*, the selected equilibrium is path-dependent and the selection of the initial conditions is important. As we have already seen in the context of a simple duopoly with linear inverse demand and quadratic costs, in such situations of multi-stability the study of the *basins of attraction* becomes of crucial importance; see Friedman (1991, 1998), Mailath (1998), and also Van Huyck, Cook, and Battalio (1997), who demonstrate empirically how important the basins are for predicting choices in a coordination game.

This has been realized in the late period starting in the mid-1990s. Although type 1-complexity was still studied in many contributions, the global dynamic properties of oligopolies increasingly became the issue of concern. The term "global dynamics" refers to properties of a dynamical system that cannot be characterized by a linearization of the system around the equilibrium. That is, in order to characterize the structure of the basins in situations of multi-stability and their qualitative changes, it is not sufficient to study the local stability properties of the dynamical system in a small neighborhood of the equilibria. Early studies have shown, however, that a global analysis of nonlinear oligopolies is particularly challenging in the case of discrete dynamical systems governed by the iteration of non-invertible maps, for example, a combination of (6.23) and (6.28). Although it has been observed early on in such models that, for example, the basins may be complicated topological objects, like multiply connected or non-connected sets often formed by the union of infinitely many disjoint portions (see, for example, Lorenz, 1992; Day, 1994), the mathematical tools for analyzing (in particular higher-dimensional) dynamical systems based on non-invertible maps were known only to a few mathematicians. In the late phase these methods were introduced into oligopoly dynamics and based on recent results on basin bifurcations in non-invertible maps, mainly the method of critical sets, insights into the structure of the basins and into the creation of complex basin boundaries could be obtained (for an introduction and references, see, for example, Agliari, Bischi, and Gardini 2002; Bischi and Kopel, 2003a; Bischi et al., 2009). As some parameters are varied, such changes in the structure can be characterized by global bifurcations: they are the consequence of *contact bifurcations*, which are due to contacts between critical sets and invariant sets (such as fixed points or cycles or their stable sets).

In order to demonstrate (again) that basins can be quite complicated sets, we present two figures taken from Bischi and Kopel (2001), who analyze a dynamic duopoly model with adaptive expectations. Figure 6.3a shows the state space $[0, 1]^2$ and the two Nash equilibria, E_1 and E_2, which are both stable. The basins are simple sets given by the triangles above and below the diagonal Δ, which is the stable manifold of E_S. After a global bifurcation occurred, the basins suddenly become complicated, multiply

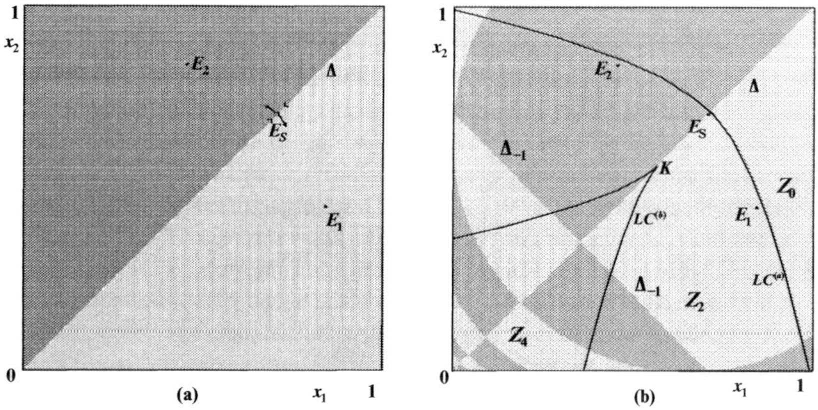

Source: Adapted from Bischi and Kopel (2001).

Figure 6.3a and b *Basins of attraction of the two coexisting Nash equilibria E_1 and E_2. A global bifurcation changes the topological structure of the basins from simple to complex*

connected sets (see Figure 6.3b). The transition from a simply connected to a multiply connected basin can be analyzed by calculating the critical curves denoted by $LC^{(a)}$ and $LC^{(b)}$ in Figure 6.3b, where the determinant of the Jacobian vanishes. These critical sets mark regions with a different number of preimages, that is, each point in region Z_k has k preimages. A global bifurcation occurs when the critical curve $LC^{(b)}$ has a contact with the diagonal Δ (the cusp point K is first in the negative domain and then has a contact with the origin 0), since after this bifurcation has occurred, points around the origin now have four preimages (instead of two) and these preimages are located in disconnected regions of the phase space.

Summarizing, in the literature on oligopoly dynamics two different types of complexity have been studied. Type 1-complexity is related to the complexity of the attracting sets that characterize the long-run evolution of the dynamic process and describe the time paths of players' actions over time. It is mainly based on an investigation of the local stability properties and corresponding local bifurcations of attractors of the dynamical system. The second one, type 2-complexity, focuses on the complexity of the boundaries that separate the basins when several coexisting attractors are present. It is important to realize that the two types of complexity are *not related*! This means that very complex attractors may have simple basin boundaries and, vice versa, boundaries that separate the basins of simple attractors, such as coexisting stable equilibria, may have very complex structure. As I argued above, it seems that for game-theoretic considerations type 2-complexity is more important. This is also confirmed by recent results of Dawid (2007) for evolutionary games, who considers the problem of transferring results that are obtained for a deterministic imitation dynamics to the underlying agent-based model. He shows that a thorough study of the basins of attraction and their bifurcations (under the deterministic dynamics) is very helpful to detect situations where the long-run behavior of the deterministic game dynamics is substantially different from the behavior of the agent-based simulation model.

To give an impression of the progress made so far on type 2-complexity in oligopoly dynamics, I briefly review some of the more recent work. The focus has been on quantity-setting games with and without full information. To my knowledge, von Stackelberg dynamics and price-setting games have not been considered up to now. Let us consider contributions that assume full information first. Bischi, Mammana, and Gardini (2000) study best-reply dynamics with naive expectations in a duopoly setting and show that such dynamic games are usually characterized by multi-stability. They study the global bifurcations the basins undergo when parameters of the model are varied. Anderson, Myran, and White (2005) study a duopoly model introduced by Kopel (1996) and show how the basins of multiple Nash equilibria can be delimited. Bischi and Kopel (2001) study a duopoly model with partial adjustment to the best-reply and adaptive expectations like (6.23). Due to an interfirm externality the best replies are given by the quadratic functions in (6.28). They illustrate that the basins of the (asymmetric) equilibria might be complicated objects and analyze the basin bifurcations by employing the method of critical curves; see also Bischi, Gardini, and Kopel (2006). Agiza, Bischi, and Kopel (1999) analyze a triopoly game with cost externalities, see (6.26), but here the firms are assumed to use partial adjustment to the best reply with naive expectations. Local stability properties of the multiple Nash equilibria are studied, and the global bifurcations of the basins are illustrated by a numerical analysis. Agliari, Gardini, and Puu (2000) study the global dynamics of an oligopoly market with three firms, where the price is reciprocal to total demand like in (6.27). They study the local and global properties of the best-reply adjustment process (with naive expectations). An interesting new issue is raised in Agliari, Gardini, and Puu (2006). Recall that we derived the best replies in (6.4) without taking the non-negativity of quantities into account, that is, we assumed that the profit-maximizing response is unique and in the interior. However, more generally, the best reply is restricted by zero and by a maximum capacity L of the firm, that is,

$$q_i = \min(\max(0, R_i(Q_i)), L).$$

Although this piecewise smoothness of the best replies makes the resulting dynamical system much harder to analyze, it also makes the game more realistic as a representation of real-world situations. Agliari, Gardini, and Puu (2006) now consider partial adjustment to the best reply in a duopoly model with isoelastic demand function, but in contrast to earlier contributions they take into account that the best response has to be non-negative. They demonstrate that in such oligopoly models with lower bounds due to non-negativity constraints a new type of bifurcation, a so-called *border collision bifurcation*, associated with a collision of an invariant set with the border of a region, may occur. This seems to be an important observation since due to such a type of (global) bifurcation the dynamics of the game may suddenly change in a drastic way (for more on this point, see Bischi et al., 2009). Finally, in the paper by Bischi, Gardini, and Kopel (2000) firms are assumed to use simple behavioral rules to determine their marketing expenditures, which subsequently determine the market shares of the duopolists. If the sales revenues are above the (marketing) costs, then marketing efforts are increased from one period to the next, otherwise they are decreased. Bischi, Gardini, and Kopel study the feasible set of initial conditions and, using the method of critical curves, describe the structural changes of this set when parameters are changed.

Quite some attention has been paid to models where players are imperfectly informed about demand and cost conditions. Several papers deal with the global dynamic properties of oligopoly models where players misspecify the demand function. Many of these contributions are based on Léonard and Nishimura (1999), who introduce a Cournot model with imperfect information where the true demand is given by (6.1), but players mistakenly believe that the demand function is $Q = \varepsilon D(p)$, $\varepsilon \neq 1$. Whereas Léonard and Nishimura focus on the local stability of steady states of the (perceived) dynamics, Bischi, Chiarella, and Kopel (2004) study the global dynamics of this game. Again an interfirm cost externality in a duopoly model is assumed and the basins and their (global) bifurcations are analyzed, applying the methods for non-invertible maps. Chiarella and Szidarovszky (2001, 2004) study the continuous-time counterpart and introduce time delays in obtaining information on the output of rivals and prices. They show that limit cycles can occur under these circumstances.

A number of papers have studied gradient learning in oligopoly models. Bischi, Stefanini, and Gardini (1998) start from the standard duopoly model with linear demand and linear costs, but assume that the production level is increased if marginal profit is positive, and decreased otherwise. They analyze the basins (or, more appropriately, the feasible set) and basin bifurcations occurring in this simple set-up; see also Bischi and Naimzada (1999). In addition, Bischi, Gallegatti, and Naimzada (1999) consider the (global) dynamics of the same adjustment process in a model with isoelastic demand. Bischi and Lamantia (2002) assume positive cost externalities in a nonlinear duopoly and show that global bifurcations change the structure of the basins from simple to complex. A dynamic rent-seeking game is studied by Bischi, Kopel, and Naimzada (2001), who demonstrate that in addition to critical curves the concept of so-called *focal points* can be helpful to understand the changes of the structure of the basins as parameters vary. Finally, Bischi and Kopel (2003b) detect multi-stability in a dynamic brand competition model and show that the basins of the coexisting equilibria and other attractors can have a very complicated structure, giving rise to what is referred to as final state sensitivity (see Grebogi et al., 1983).

Also, evolutionary games have been analyzed using the critical curve method. In two papers by Bischi, Dawid, and Kopel (2003a, b), inter- and intra-population cost externalities are introduced and a two-population evolutionary game based on a word-of-mouth dynamics is derived. The resulting discrete dynamical system describes the dynamics of the shares of firms of a population, which are active in a market and produce a certain good. It is demonstrated that several steady states (for the population shares) can coexist and be stable. Moreover, global bifurcations can transform the basins from simple to complex, and these bifurcations can be understood by employing the critical curve approach. This can be observed in Figures 6.4a–d. In Figure 6.4a there are two stable equilibria. In V_I population 1 takes over the whole market, in V_{III} population 2 has a 100 percent market share. The basins are quite simple. For increasing inter-population cost externalities, a new equilibrium P_{III} emerges in addition to the former equilibria; see Figure 6.4b. The basin of P_{III} and V_{III} are now intermingled and convergence to one of these equilibria sensitively depends on the initial population shares serving the market. Figures 6.4c and 6.4d describe another transition, where C_4 is a cycle of period 4 on the horizontal set $x_2 = 1$. Whereas in Figure 6.4c for most of the initial population shares above the diagonal population 2 could take over the whole market, in Figure 6.4d (for slightly higher inter-population cost externalities) we observe cyclic behavior of the shares of population 1 that serve the market.

6.7 Final remarks and future research directions

In a paper by Al-Nowaihi and Levine (1985) on dynamic Cournot games it has been pointed out that the global dynamics of discrete dynamic games is an unresolved issue. As the brief review of contributions from the late phase has demonstrated, since then significant progress has been made. There are, however, some issues that are not yet solved and future work has to address them.

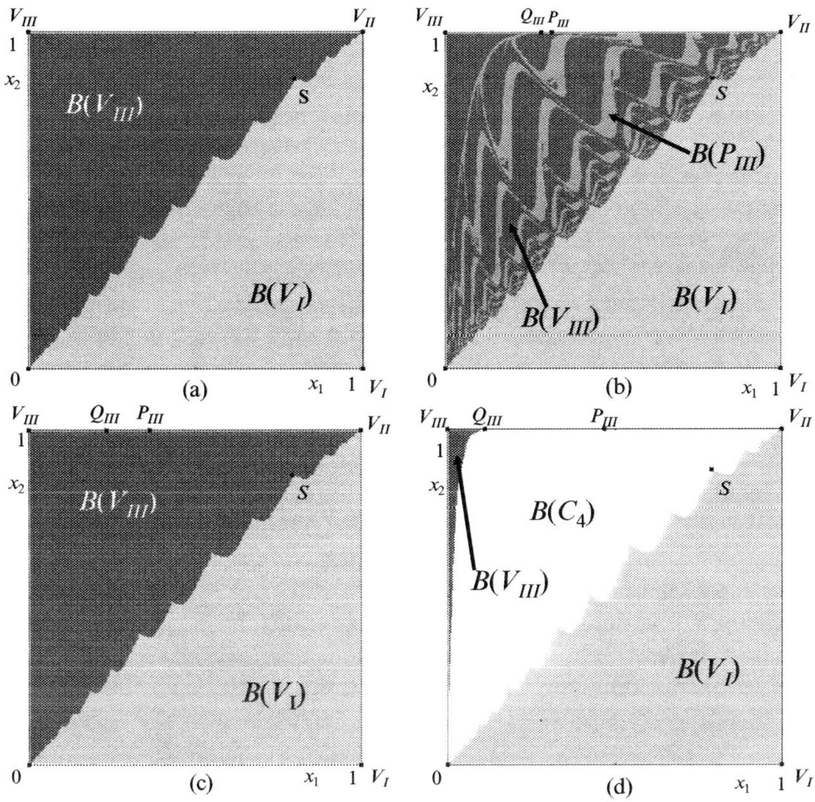

Source: Bischi, David, and Kopel (2003b).

Figure 6.4a, b, c, and d Changes in the basins of attraction of the locally stable equilibria for increasing cost externalities between population 1 and population 2

First of all, there is a lack of work done on dynamic von Stackelberg and price-setting models with respect to global dynamics. It certainly would be interesting to follow the tradition in industrial organization and compare quantity- and price-setting models as far as the global dynamical properties, for example, basins and their extension, are concerned. A further topic that has gained some attention recently is the possibility of border collision bifurcation and their associated sudden changes in the dynamics, which are due to contacts between critical sets or regime boundaries and the equilibria (see Agliari, Gardini, and Puu, 2006; Bischi et al., 2009). Much more work has to be done in this area to fully appreciate the significance of this new type of bifurcation to oligopoly dynamics. Finally, one main topic that deserves particular attention is the question of how to measure the size or extension of a basin and the complexity of its boundaries.

Recall that type 1-complexity deals with the loss of stability and possible convergence to a chaotic attractor. The evolution of the trajectories might sensitively depend on the initial conditions, but they are confined to a single attractor, which is a bounded object in the phase space. Type 2-complexity, on the other hand, deals with the basins of (multiple) attractors and (the complexity of) their basin boundaries. In physics and engineering these issues have been discussed intensively, but many of the definitions for complexity seem too restrictive for applications in economics and game theory. For example, in this body of literature a basin is called "riddled" if every neighborhood around an initial condition converging to an attractor *A* contains initial conditions that converge to another attractor *B* (see, for example, Alexander et al., 1992). However, most of the "complicated" basins found, for example, in oligopoly models, are not riddled according to this definition and the basins would not qualify as being complex. The basins depicted in Figures 6.3b and 6.4b are also not riddled, although from a practical point of view a prediction of the fate of trajectories starting from initial conditions in certain regions of the phase space becomes difficult, if not impossible. Consequently, for most economists or game theorists the complexity of the situations illustrated in these figures is apparent. Two further questions can be asked in this context: (1) can we rank dynamic oligopolies with regard to their type 2-complexity, that is, can we say that one dynamical system has a higher type 2-complexity than the other, and (2) when can we say that the basin of an equilibrium is large or small? To find an answer to all these questions is an important task for the following reason. In order to be able to use the concept of basins of equilibria as some sort of refinement in a situation of multi-stability, we need to decide how to measure the robustness of an equilibrium with respect to exogenous (stochastic) perturbations. In other words, some kind of quantitative measure has to be defined.

In the economics and game-theoretic literature no attention has been paid to these issues, with two exceptions. Ellison (2000) discusses such a quantitative concept in the context of evolutionary games with persistent randomness and introduces the notions of radius and coradius of a basin. Roughly speaking, the radius of a basin is the number of mutations that are needed to leave the basin of a certain equilibrium. Brock and Hommes (1997) consider a deterministic model of adaptive rational equilibrium dynamics and show coexistence of attractors. They point out that these coexisting attractors can be the source of complicated dynamics in the presence of small stochastic perturbation, since the trajectories might be pushed from one basin to another in an irregular way, in particular when the basin boundaries are complicated. They then refer to McDonald et al. (1985), who formalized the notion of final state sensitivity by introducing the uncertainty dimension as a quantitative measure, and provide estimates of the uncertainty dimension for their model.

To illustrate the concept of uncertainty dimension, let us start with a simple idea. Assume that we are interested in the global properties of a dynamical system and that the phase space is given by the unit square $I = [0, 1]^2$. There exists an equilibrium E^* (not necessarily unique) inside I. Consider now a grid of $n \times n$ equally spaced points over I, take each point on this grid as an initial condition, and see if the trajectory generated by the dynamical system converges to E^*. To measure the complexity of the basin of E^* we can use the following metric:

$$\varphi = \frac{\#\, points\ converging\ to\ E^*}{n^2}.$$

Clearly, if E^* is unstable then $\varphi = 0$, and if the generic point belongs to the basin of E^* then $\varphi = 1$. As long as the basin boundaries are not too complicated and the boundaries are smooth, $0 < \varphi < 1$ holds, and this quantity can be used to rank the stability of multiple equilibria.

However, in case of highly complex (that is, fractal) boundaries, measurement errors of the initial conditions would influence this metric to a high degree. Therefore, McDonald et al. introduced a more sophisticated measure based on the extent to which uncertainty in the initial condition leads to uncertainty in the final state (see also Grebogi et al., 1983). Assume now that there are two possible equilibria in I, denoted E_1^* and E_2^*, and that I is divided by the basin boundary Σ into the two basins $B(E_1^*)$ and $B(E_2^*)$ of E_1^* and E_2^*. Consider now a measurement of a point q in I, which is uncertain in the sense that the true point is anywhere in a disk D of radius ε around q. If q is sufficiently far away from the boundary Σ, then all initial conditions inside D will converge to the same equilibrium, that is, there is no final state uncertainty. If, however, q is close to Σ, then initial conditions taken from D may converge either to E_1^* or to E_2^*. In this case q is called an ε-uncertain point, since D now contains initial conditions from different basins. Now assume that initial conditions are chosen randomly with uniform distribution in I and let $f(\varepsilon, I)$ denote the fraction of ε-uncertain points. McDonald et al. demonstrate that if the boundary Σ is regular, then $f(\varepsilon, I)$ is proportional to ε, whereas if Σ is fractal, the scaling law is

$$f(\varepsilon, I) \sim \varepsilon^{\alpha}, \quad 0 < \alpha < 1.$$

The uncertainty exponent α is defined as

$$\alpha = \lim_{\varepsilon \to 0} \frac{\ln(f(\varepsilon, I))}{\ln \varepsilon}.$$

It is then shown that α might be significantly less than 1, so that an increase in the accuracy of the measurement (or a reduction of the "measurement error") by a factor of $2^{1/\alpha}$ only improves the predictability of the final state by a factor of 2. If we consider the quantity $\gamma = 1 - \alpha$, then $\gamma = 0$ indicates that the boundary Σ between the coexisting equilibria is smooth and φ can be used as a metric for comparing the basins of the attractors. If, on the other hand, the boundary is fractal and/or the basins are intermingled, then γ will be closer to 1 and the metric φ becomes less meaningful.

With respect to the other question, namely which measure can be found to determine the size of a basin, we have to use a different concept. For non-intermingled basins, even if the basin boundary is non-smooth, in addition to the uncertainty measure introduced above, we have to pay attention to the fact that it also matters where the considered equilibrium is located. Although the basin itself might be quite large with respect to I, the equilibrium might be close to the basin boundary. Vice versa, the basin might be comparably small, but the equilibrium further away from the boundary. In such a situation, we would consider the former case as "less stable" than the latter (see Bischi, Kopel, and Szidarovszky, 2005). We can make this more precise by considering, for example, the largest radius of a circle with center E_i^* entirely included in its corresponding basin (or feasible set) as a measure for the robustness with regard to random disturbances. In the literature, nothing has been said on this topic. As this brief discussion shows, a lot of work awaits us in future years.

Note

* I would like to thank my co-authors for providing me with insights and ideas on the topic of oligopoly dynamics. The present chapter has particularly benefitted from comments and suggestions by G.I. Bischi, C. Chiarella, H. Dawid, C. Hommes, K. Okuguchi, T. Puu, and F. Szidarovszky.

References

Agiza, H.N. (1999), "On the Analysis of Stability, Bifurcation, Chaos and Chaos Control of Kopel Map," *Chaos, Solitons & Fractals*, **10**(11), 1909–16.

Agiza, H.N., G.I. Bischi, and M. Kopel (1999), "Multistability in a Dynamic Cournot Game With Three Oligopolists," *Mathematics and Computers in Simulation*, **51**(1), 63–90.

Agliari, A., G.I. Bischi, and L. Gardini (2002), "Some Methods for the Global Analysis of Dynamic Games Represented by Iterated Noninvertible Maps," in T. Puu and I. Sushko (eds), *Oligopoly Dynamics: Models and Tools*, Springer, Berlin, Heidelberg, Ch. 3, pp. 31–83.

Agliari, A., L. Gardini, and T. Puu (2000), "The Dynamics of a Triopoly Game," *Chaos, Solitons & Fractals*, **11**(15), 2531–60.

Agliari, A., L. Gardini, and T. Puu (2006), "Global Bifurcations in Duopoly When the Cournot Point is Destabilized via a Subcritical Neimark Bifurcation," *International Game Theory Review*, **8**(1), 1–20.
Alexander, J.C., J.A. Yorke, Z. You, and I. Kan (1992), "Riddled Basins," *International Journal of Bifurcations and Chaos*, **2**(4), 795–813.
Al-Nowaihi, A. and P.L. Levine (1985), "The Stability of the Cournot Oligopoly Model: A Reassessment," *Journal of Economic Theory*, **35**(2), 307–21.
Amir, R. and J.Y. Jin (2001), "Cournot and Bertrand Equilibria Compared: Substitutability, Complementarity and Concavity," *International Journal of Industrial Organization*, **19**(3–4), 303–17.
Amir, R. and V.E. Lambson (2000), "On the Effects of Entry in Cournot Markets," *Review of Economic Studies*, **67**(2), 235–54.
Amir, R. and J. Wooders (1998), "Cooperation vs. Competition in R&D: The Role of Stability of Equilibrium," *Journal of Economics*, **67**(1), 63–73.
Anderson, D.R., N.M. Myran, and D.L. White (2005), "Basins of Attraction in a Cournot Duopoly Model of Kopel," *The Journal of Difference Equations and Applications*, **11**(10), 879–87.
Bertrand, J. (1883), "Theorie Mathèmatique de la Richesse Sociale", *Journal des Savantes*, **48**(883), 499–508.
Binmore, K. (1992), *Fun and Games. A Text on Game Theory*, D.C. Heath, Lexington.
Bischi, G.I. and L. Gardini (1998), "Cycles and Bifurcations in Duopoly Games," in Quaderni dell' Istituto di Mathematica "E. Levi," University of Parma, No. 3.
Bischi, G.I. and M. Kopel (2001), "Equilibrium Selection in a Nonlinear Duopoly Game With Adaptive Expectations," *Journal of Economic Behavior and Organization*, **46**(1), 73–100.
Bischi, G.I. and M. Kopel (2003a), "Long Run Evolution, Path Dependence and Global Properties of Dynamic Games: A Tutorial," *Cubo Matemática Educacional*, **5**(3), 437–68.
Bischi, G.I. and M. Kopel (2003b), "Multistability and Path Dependence in a Dynamic Brand Competition Model," *Chaos, Solitons & Fractals*, **18**(3), 561–76.
Bischi, G.I. and F. Lamantia (2002), "Nonlinear Duopoly Games with Positive Cost Externalities Due to Spillovers," *Chaos, Solitons & Fractals*, **13**(4), 701–21.
Bischi, G.I. and A. Naimzada (1999), "Global Analysis of a Duopoly Game With Bounded Rationality," in *Advances in Dynamic Games and Applications, Vol. 5*, Birkhauser, Boston, pp. 361–85.
Bischi, G.I., C. Chiarella, and M. Kopel (2004), "The Long Run Outcomes and Global Dynamics of a Duopoly Game With Misspecified Demand Functions," *International Game Theory Review*, **6**(3), 343–80.
Bischi, G.I., H. Dawid, and M. Kopel (2003a), "Spillover Effects and the Evolution of Firm Clusters," *Journal of Economic Behavior and Organization*, **50**(1), 47–75.
Bischi, G.I., H. Dawid, and M. Kopel (2003b), "Gaining the Competitive Edge Using Internal and External Spillovers: A Dynamic Analysis," *Journal of Economic Dynamics and Control*, **27**(11), 2171–93.
Bischi G.I., M. Gallegati, and A. Naimzada (1999), "Symmetry-breaking Bifurcations and Representative Firm in Dynamic Duopoly Games," *Annals of Operations Research*, **89**(1), 253–72.
Bischi, G.I., L. Gardini, and M. Kopel (2000), "Analysis of Global Bifurcations in a Market Share Attraction Model," *Journal of Economic Dynamics and Control*, **24**(5–7), 855–79. Reprinted in J. B. Rosser, Jr. (ed.) (2004), *Complexity in Economics, Vol I: Methodology, Interacting Agents, and Microeconomic Models*, Edward Elgar, Cheltenham, UK and Northampton, MA, USA.
Bischi, G.I., L. Gardini, and M. Kopel (2006), "Noninvertible Maps and Complex Basin Boundaries in Dynamic Economic Models With Coexisting Attractors," *Chaos and Complexity Letters*, **2**(1), 43–76.
Bischi, G.I., M. Kopel, and A. Naimzada (2001), "On a Rent-seeking Game Described by a Noninvertible Iterated Map With Denominator," *Nonlinear Analysis*, **47**(8), 5309–24.

Bischi, G.I., M. Kopel, and F. Szidarovszky (2005), "Expectation-stock Dynamics in Multi-agent Fisheries," *Annals of Operations Research – Special Issue on Contributions to the Theory of Games*, **137**(1), 299–329.

Bischi, G.I., L. Stefanini, and L. Gardini (1998), "Synchronization, Intermittency and Critical Curves in a Duopoly Game", *Mathematics and Computers in Simulation*, **44**(6), 559–85.

Bischi, G.I., C. Mammana, and L. Gardini (2000), "Multistability and Cyclic Attractors in Duopoly Games," *Chaos, Solitons & Fractals*, **11**(4), 543–64.

Bischi, G.I., A.K. Naimzada, and L. Sbragia (2007), "Oligopoly Games With Local Monopolistic Approximation," *Journal of Economic Behavior and Organization*, **62**(3), 371–88.

Bischi, G.I., C. Chiarella, M. Kopel, and F. Szidarovszky (2009), *Nonlinear Oligopolies: Stability and Bifurcations*, forthcoming, Springer, Berlin/Heidelberg/New York.

Bonanno, G. (1988), "Oligopoly Equilbria When Firms Have Local Knowledge of Demand," *International Economic Review*, **29**(1), 45–55.

Bonanno, G. and E.C. Zeeman (1985), "Limited Knowledge of Demand and Oligopoly Equilibria," *Journal of Economic Theory*, **35**(2), 276–83.

Bresnahan, T.F. (1981), "Duopoly Models with Consistent Conjectures," *American Economic Review*, **71**(5), 934–45.

Brock, W.A. and C.H. Hommes (1997), "A Rational Route to Randomness," *Econometrica*, **65**(5), 1059–95.

Bulow, J., J. Geanakoplos, and P. Klemperer (1985), "Holding Idle Capacity to Deter Entry," *The Economic Journal*, **95**(1), 178–82.

Cheng, L. (1985), "Comparing Bertrand and Cournot Equilibria: A Geometric Approach," *RAND Journal of Economics*, **16**(1), 146–52.

Chiarella, C. and F. Szidarovszky (2001), "The Nonlinear Cournot Model Under Uncertainty With Continuously Distributed Time Lags," *Central European Journal of Operations Research*, **9**(3), 183–96.

Chiarella, C. and F. Szidarovszky (2004), "Dynamic Oligopolies Without Full Information and With Continuously Distributed Time Lags," *Journal of Economic Behavior and Organization*, **54**(4), 495–511.

Chiarella, C. and F. Szidarovszky (2005), "On the Stability of Price-adjusting Oligopolies with Incomplete Information," *International Journal of Systems Science*, **36**(8), 501–7.

Corchon, L.C. and A. Mas-Colell (1996), "On the Stability of Best Reply and Gradient Systems with Applications to Imperfectly Competitive Models," *Economics Letters*, **51**(1), 59–65.

Cournot, A. (1838), *Researches into the Principles of the Theory of Wealth*, English translation, 1963, Irwin Paperback Classics in Economics, Ch. VII.

Cox, J.C. and M. Walker (1998), "Learning to Play Cournot Duopoly Strategies," *Journal of Economic Behavior and Organization*, **36**(2), 141–61.

Dana, R.-A. and L. Montrucchio (1986), "Dynamic Complexity in Duopoly Games," *Journal of Economic Theory*, **40**(1), 40–56.

Dana, R.-A. and L. Montrucchio (1987), "On Rational Dynamic Strategies in Infinite Horizon Models Where Agents Discount the Future," *Journal of Economic Behavior and Organization*, **8**(3), 497–511.

Dawid, H. (2007), "Evolutionary Game Dynamics and the Analysis of Agent-based Imitation Models: The Long Run, the Medium Run and the Importance of a Global Analysis," *Journal of Economic Dynamics and Control*, **31**(5), 2108–33.

Day, R.H. (1994), *Complex Economic Dynamics, Vol. I: An Introduction to Dynamical Systems and Market Mechanisms*, MIT Press, Cambridge, MA.

Dixit, A. (1986), "Comparative Statics for Oligopoly," *International Economic Review*, **27**(1), 107–22.

Dockner, E., S. Jorgensen, N. van Long, and G. Sorger (2000), *Differential Games in Economics and Management Science*, Cambridge University Press, New York.

Ellison, G. (2000), "Basins of Attraction, Long Run Stochastic Stability, and the Speed of Step-by-step Evolution," *Review of Economic Studies*, **67**(1), 17–45.

Fisher, F.M. (1961), "The Stability of the Cournot Oligopoly Solution: The Effects of Speeds of Adjustment and Increasing Marginal Costs," *Review of Economic Studies*, **28**, 125–35.
Friedman, J.W. (1977), *Oligopoly and the Theory of Games*, North-Holland, Amsterdam.
Friedman, J.W. (1982), "Oligopoly Theory," in *Handbook of Mathematical Economics, Vol. II*, K.J. Arrow and M.D. Intriligator (eds), North-Holland, Amsterdam, Ch. 11.
Friedman, D. (1991), "Evolutionary Games in Economics," *Econometrica*, **59**(3), 637–66.
Friedman, D. (1998), "On Economic Applications of Evolutionary Game Theory," *Journal of Evolutionary Economics*, **8**(1), 15–43.
Friedman, J.W. and C. Mezzetti (2002), "Bounded Rationality, Dynamic Oligopoly, and Conjectural Variations," *Journal of Economic Behavior and Organization*, **49**(3), 287–306.
Fudenberg, D. and D.K. Levine (1998), *The Theory of Learning in Games*, MIT Press, Cambridge, MA.
Fudenberg, D. and J. Tirole (1992), *Game Theory*, MIT Press, Cambridge, MA.
Furth, D. (1986), "Stability and Instability in Oligopoly," *Journal of Economic Theory*, **40**(2), 197–228.
Gal-Or, E. (1985), "First Mover and Second Mover Advantages," *International Economic Review*, **26**(3), 649–53.
Grebogi, C., S.W. McDonald, E. Ott, and J.A. Yorke (1983), "Final State Sensitivity: An Obstruction to Predictability," *Physics Letters*, **99A**, 415–18.
Grosser, J. (1999), "Multiple Equilibria, Equilibrium Selection and Economic Policy," *Zeitschrift für Wirtschafts- und Sozialwissenschaften*, **119**, 191–204.
Hadar, J (1966), "Stability of Oligopoly with Product Differentiation," *Review of Economic Studies*, **33**(1), 57–60.
Hahn, F.H. (1962), "The Stability of the Cournot Oligopoly Solution," *Review of Economic Studies*, **29**(4), 329–31.
Hamilton, J. and S. Slutsky (1990), "Endogenous Timing in Duopoly Games: Stackelberg or Cournot Equilibria," *Games and Economic Behavior*, **2**(1), 29–46.
Hathaway, N.J., J.A. Rickard, and T.D. Howroyd (1979), "Dynamic Stackelberg Stability," *Economics Letters*, **2**(3), 209–13.
Hosomatsu, Y. (1969), "A Note on the Stability Conditions in Cournot's Dynamic Market Solution When Neither the Actual Market Demand Function nor the Production Levels of Rivals are Known," *Review of Economic Studies*, **36**(105), 117–22.
Hotelling, H. (1929), "Stability in Competition," *Economic Journal*, **39**(153), 41–57.
Howroyd, T.D. and J.A. Rickard (1981), "Cournot Oligopoly and Output Adjustment Costs," *Economics Letters*, **7**(2), 113–17.
Howroyd, T.D. and A.M. Russell (1984), "Cournot Oligopoly Models with Time Delays," *Journal of Mathematical Economics*, **13**(2), 97 103.
Huck, S., H.-T. Normann, and J. Oechssler (1999), "Learning in Cournot Oligopoly – An Experiment," *The Economic Journal*, **109**(454), C80–C95.
Katz, M.L. and C. Shapiro (1985), "Network Externalities, Competition, and Compatibility," *American Economic Review*, **75**(3), 424–40.
Kirman, A.P. (1975), "Learning by Firms About Demand Conditions," in *Adaptive Economic Models*, R.H. Day and T. Groves (eds), Academic Press, New York, pp. 137–56.
Kirman, A.P. (1983), "On Mistaken Beliefs and Resultant Equilibria" in *Individual Forecasting and Aggregate Outcomes*, R. Frydman and E.S. Phelps (eds), Cambridge University Press, Cambridge, UK, pp. 147–66.
Kirman, A.P. (1995), "Learning in Oligopoly: Theory, Simulation, and Experimental Evidence," in *Learning and Rationality in Economics*, A. Kirman and M. Salmon (eds), Blackwell, Oxford, pp. 127–78.
Kopel, M. (1996), "Simple and Complex Adjustment Dynamics in Cournot Duopoly Models," *Chaos, Solitons & Fractals*, **7**(12), 2031–48. Reprinted in J.B. Rosser, Jr. (ed.) (2004), *Complexity in Economics, Vol I: Methodology, Interacting Agents, and Microeconomic Models*, Edward Elgar, Cheltenham, UK and Northampton, MA, USA.
Krelle, W. (1976), *Preistheorie, Part 1: Monopol- und Oligopoltheorie*, J.C.B. Mohr (Paul Siebeck), Tübingen.

Krugman, P. (1991), "History Versus Expectations," *Quarterly Journal of Economics*, **106**(2), 651–67.

Kruse, J.B., S. Rassenti, S.R. Reynolds, and V.L. Smith (1994), "Bertrand-Edgeworth Competition in Experimental Markets," *Econometrica*, **62**(2), 343–71.

Léonard, D. and K. Nishimura (1999), "Nonlinear Dynamics in the Cournot Model Without Full Information," *Annals of Operations Research*, **89**(1), 165–73.

Levin, D. (1988), "Stackelberg, Cournot and Collusive Monopoly: Performance and Welfare Comparisons," *Economic Inquiry*, **26**(2), 317–30.

Lorenz, H.-W. (1992), "Multiple Attractors, Complex Basin Boundaries, and Transient Motion in Deterministic Economic Systems," in G. Feichtinger (ed.), *Dynamic Economic Models and Optimal Control*, North-Holland, Amsterdam, pp. 411–30.

Lorenz, H.-W. (1993), *Nonlinear Dynamical Economics and Chaotic Motion*, Springer, Berlin/Heidelberg/New York.

Mailath, G.J. (1998), "Do People Play Nash Equilibrium? Lessons from Evolutionary Game Theory," *Journal of Economic Literature*, **36**(3), 1347–74.

Martin, S. (2002), *Advanced Industrial Economics*, Blackwell Publishing, Oxford.

Matsumoto, A. and Y. Nonaka (2006), "Statistical Dynamics in a Chaotic Cournot Model With Complementary Goods," *Journal of Economic Behavior and Organization*, **61**(4), 769–83.

McDonald, S.W., C. Grebogi, E. Ott, and J.A. Yorke (1985), "Fractal Basin Boundaries," *Physica*, **17D**, 125–53.

McManus, M. and R.E. Quandt (1961), "Comments on the Stability of the Cournot Oligopoly Model," *Review of Economic Studies*, **28**(2), 136–9.

McMillan, J. (1984), "Collusion, Competition, and Conjectures," *Canadian Journal of Economics*, **17**(4), 788–805.

Moulin, H. (1982), *Game Theory for the Social Sciences*, New York University Press, New York.

Okuguchi, K. (1964), "The Stability of the Cournot Oligopoly Solution: A Further Generalization," *Review of Economic Studies*, **31**(2), 143–45.

Okuguchi, K. (1968), "The Stability of Price Adjusting Oligopoly: The Effects of Adaptive Expectations," *Southern Economic Journal*, **35**(1), 34–6.

Okuguchi, K. (1969), "On the Stability of Price Adjusting Oligopoly Equilibrium under Product Differentation," *Southern Economic Journal*, **35**(3), 244–6.

Okuguchi, K. (1970), "Adaptive Expectations in an Oligopoly Model," *Review of Economic Studies*, **37**(2), 233–7.

Okuguchi, K. (1976), *Expectations and Stability in Oligopoly Models, Lecture Notes in Economics and Mathematical Systems*, Springer, Heidelberg.

Okuguchi, K. (1978), "The Stability of Price-adjusting Oligopoly with Conjectural Variations," *Zeitschrift für Nationalökonomie*, **38**, 55–60.

Okuguchi, K. (1979), "On the Stability of the Stackelberg Oligopoly Equilibrium," *Economics Letters*, **3**(4), 321–5.

Okuguchi, K. (1987), "Equilibrium Prices in the Bertrand and Cournot Oligopolies," *Journal of Economic Theory*, **42**(1), 128–39.

Okuguchi, K. and F. Szidarovszky (1989), "On Sequential Stability of Equilibrium," in *Computing and Computers for Control Systems*, P. Borne et al. (eds), J.C. Baltzer, Basel, pp. 357–9.

Okuguchi, K. and F. Szidarovszky (1999), *The Theory of Oligopoly with Multi-product Firms*, 2nd, revised and enlarged edn, Springer, Berlin.

Puu, T. (1991), "Chaos in Duopoly Pricing," *Chaos, Solitons & Fractals*, **1**(6), 573–81.

Puu, T. (1996), "Complex Dynamics With Three Oligopolists," *Chaos, Solitons & Fractals*, **7**(12), 2075–81.

Puu, T. (1998), "The Chaotic Duopolist Revisited," *Journal of Economic Behavior and Organization*, **33**(3), 385–94.

Puu, T. (2001), "Bertrand Oligopoly Revisited," *Discrete Dynamics in Nature and Society*, **6**(1), 1–10.

Puu, T. (2003), *Attractors, Bifurcations & Chaos: Nonlinear Phenomena in Economics*, 2nd edn, Springer, Berlin, Heidelberg.
Puu, T. and I. Sushko (2002), *Oligopoly Dynamics: Models and Tools*, Springer, Berlin.
Quandt, R.E. (1967), "On the Stability of Price Adjusting Oligopoly," *Southern Economic Journal*, **33**, 332–6.
Rand, D. (1978), "Exotic Phenomena in Games and Duopoly Models," *Journal of Mathematical Economics*, **5**(2), 173–84.
Richter, H. and A. Stolk (2004), "Control of the Triple Chaotic Attractor in a Cournot Triopoly Model," *Chaos, Solitons & Fractals*, **20**(2), 409–13.
Rickard, J.A. (1980), "Stability Properties in a Dynamic Stackelberg Oligopoly Model," *Economic Record*, **56**(164), 253–6.
Rosser Jr., J.B. (1999), "On the Complexities of Complex Economic Dynamics," *Journal of Economic Perspectives*, **13**(4), 169–92.
Rosser, J.B., Jr. (2000), *From Catastrophe to Chaos: A General Theory of Economic Discontinuities. Mathematics, Microeconomics, Macroeconomics, and Finance*, 2nd edn, Kluwer Academic Publishers, Boston.
Rosser, J.B., Jr. (2002), "The Development of Complex Oligopoly Dynamics Theory," in Puu, T. and I. Sushko (eds), *Oligopoly Dynamics: Models and Tools*, Springer, Berlin, Heidelberg, Ch. 2, pp. 15–29.
Rosser Jr., J.B. (2004), *Complexity in Economics, Vols. I–III*, Edward Elgar, Cheltenham, UK and Northampton, MA, USA.
Russell, A., J.A. Rickard, and T.D. Howroyd (1986), "The Effects of Delays on the Stability and Rate of Convergence to Equilibrium of Oligopolies," *Economic Record*, **62**(177), 194–8.
Sato, R. and K. Nagatani (1967), "The Stability of Oligopoly with Conjectural Variations," *Review of Economic Studies*, **34**(4), 409–16.
Scherer, F.M. (1996), "Heinrich von Stackelberg's Marktform und Gleichgewicht," *Journal of Economic Studies*, **23**(5/6), 58–70.
Schoonbeek, L. (1996), "Higher Order Lags in Price-adjusting Oligopoly," *Economic Theory*, **7**(3), 547–55.
Schoonbeek, L. (1997), "A Dynamic Stackelberg Model with Production-adjustment Costs," *Journal of Economics*, **66**(3), 271–82.
Seade, J. (1980), "The Stability of Cournot Revisited," *Journal of Economic Theory*, **23**(1), 15–27.
Shapiro, C. (1989), "Theories of Oligopoly Behavior," in *Handbook of Industrial Organization Vol. I*, R. Schmalensee and R. Willig (eds), North-Holland, Amsterdam, Ch. 6.
Shy, O. (1995), *Industrial Organization – Theory and Applications*, MIT Press, Cambridge, MA.
Singh, N. and X. Vives (1984), "Price and Quantity Competition in a Differentiated Duopoly," *RAND Journal of Economics*, **15**(4), 546–54.
Slade, M.E. (1994), "What Does an Oligopoly Maximize?," *The Journal of Industrial Economics*, **42**(1), 45–61.
Szidarovszky, F. and W. Li (2000), "A Note on the Stability of Cournot-Nash Equilibrium: The Multiproduct Case with Adaptive Expectations," *Journal of Mathematical Economics*, **33**, 101–7.
Szidarovszky, F. and K. Okuguchi (1988), "A Linear Oligopoly Model With Adaptive Expectations: Stability Reconsidered," *Journal of Economics*, **48**, 79–82.
Szidarovszky, F. and K. Okuguchi (1993), "Dynamic Oligopoly With Complete Information," *Belgian Journal of Operations Research, Statistics and Computer Science*, **33**, 13–44.
Szidarovszky, F. and J. Yen (1991), "Stability of a Special Oligopoly Market," *PU.M.A. Series B*, **2**(2–3), 93–100.
Szidarovszky, F. and J. Yen (1995), "Dynamic Cournot Oligopolies With Production Adjustment Costs," *Journal of Mathematical Economics*, **24**, 95–101.
Szidarovszky, F., S. Rassenti, and J. Yen (1992), "Modified Cournot Expectations in Dynamic Oligopolies," *PU.M.A. Series B*, **3**(2–4), 143–50.

Tarr, D.G. (1975), "The Effects of Adaptive Expectations on the Stability of Price Adjusting Oligopoly," *Southern Economic Journal*, **41**(4), 673–7.
Theocharis, R.D. (1960), "On the stability of the Cournot Solution on the Oligopoly Problem," *Review of Economic Studies*, **27**(2), 133–4.
Tirole, J. (1988), *The Theory of Industrial Organization*, MIT Press, Cambridge, MA.
Van Huyck, J.B., J.P. Cook, and R.C. Battalio (1997), "Adaptive Behavior and Coordination Failure," *Journal of Economic Behavior and Organization*, **32**(4), 483–503.
Veendorp, E.C.H. and A. Vessal (1978), "Price Adjusting Oligopoly for the n-Seller Case," *Southern Economic Journal*, **45**(2), 502–7.
Vives, X. (1985), "On the Efficiency of Bertrand and Cournot Equilibria with Product Differentiation," *Journal of Economic Theory*, **36**(1), 166–75.
Vives, X. (1999), *Oligopoly Pricing: Old Ideas and New Tools*, MIT Press, Cambridge, MA.
von Stackelberg, H. (1934), *Marktform und Gleichgewicht*, Springer, Wien.
Wirl, F., M. Kopel, and G. Feichtinger (1999), "Threshold Advertising Rules in a Duopoly Framework," *Central European Journal of Operations Research*, **7**, 39–52.
Zhang, A. and Y. Zhang (1996), "Stability of a Cournot-Nash Equilibrium: The Multiproduct Case," *Journal of Mathematical Economics*, **26**(1), 441–62.

PART III

MACROECONOMIC ISSUES

7. Complexity and aggregation

Alan Kirman

7.1 Introduction

Why is the complex systems approach of particular interest currently for economists and how is it related to aggregation? I will try to explain why it may offer a way out of some of the difficulties that have beset economics in general and macroeconomics in particular in recent years. Economic theory has revealed itself to be vulnerable on two fronts. The first is the problem of aggregation; how is the behaviour of the economic system related to that of the individuals that make it up? Can the aggregate be shown to have certain desirable properties? The second is that of why do individuals behave as they do?

The answer to the first question is simple but undermines much of modern macroeconomics. What has been proved is that the standard model of a system composed of isolated indiviuals each satisfying the standard rationality axioms and each solving his or her own maximizing problem does not allow one to show that the system will have a unique and stable equilibrium. To avoid the difficulties that this entails, macroeconomists usually assume that the whole system can be analysed as if it were an individual satisfying the standard rationality axioms.[1] But because of the results just mentioned, in fact the idea that the aggregate will satisfy the assumptions on individual behaviour is reduced to the status of an additional ad hoc hypothesis and one that cannot be derived from assumptions on individuals. This poses problems only because economists want to base their aggregate analysis on "sound microfoundations". But the idea that sound microfoundations are those based on the isolated maximizing individual whose rationality corresponds to the standard Arrow-Debreu axioms is also, itself, an assumption. The fact that this assumption has become standard does not make it legitimate. Had we shown that there was a body of evidence showing that people do, in fact, behave according to these axioms then it would be appropriate to attribute the term "scientific" to them. But, as many distinguished economists, from Pareto to Koopmans, have pointed out, our assumptions about human economic behaviour are based on introspection by economists, not on any observed reality. In particular this means that the choice of the axioms that underlie individual behaviour in modern economic models is not inevitable or endowed with some special scientific status. It is as ad hoc as any other choice of microbasis. Worse, as already mentioned, the use of the representative agent that enables one to pass neatly from individual to aggregate behaviour is purely ad hoc and no reasonable restrictions on individuals' characteristics will guarantee that the aggregate satisfies the assumptions on individuals.

However, all of this brings us to the second question that is posed by behavioural economics, which explicitly questions the idea that individuals do behave according to the standard "sound microfoundations". Pareto devoted a whole chapter of his *General Treatise on Sociology* (1915) to what he described as "irrational behaviour". From Simon (1957) onwards many have suggested that individuals reason in a limited and local way. Experiments, observation and examination of the neural processes utilized in making decisions all suggest that homo economicus is not an accurate or adequate description of human decision-making.[2]

Where does this leave us? Either we continue to try to reconcile aggregate behaviour with that of the standard rational individual, a hopeless task, or we accept that the difference between individual and aggregate behaviour is fundamental and then build models that show this explicitly. Thus, aggregation has to move to the centre of the stage. In this chapter I will give some examples in which aggregate behaviour does not correspond to that of a "rational individual" and suggest that by modelling markets or economies as complex adaptive systems we can make progress in explaining such phenomenon. To start with, however, it is worth examining one of the basic difficulties with aggregation.

7.2 The problem of heterogeneity

One of the major problems for aggregation is that posed by the underlying heterogeneity of individual characteristics. Those brought up in the general equilibrium tradition will argue that heterogeneity is allowed. Indeed, one of the arguments used against the negative results of Sonnenschein (1972), Mantel (1974), and Debreu (1974) mentioned in note 1 is that too much heterogeneity is permitted.[3] It was then argued that by reducing the heterogeneity allowed one could solve the underlying problem. This cannot be done, as Kirman and Koch (1986) have shown that even if all individuals have identical preferences the problem is not solved.

7.2.1 Voluntary heterogeneity: the division of labour

But there is a second difficulty, which is that in many situations there is a voluntary creation of heterogeneity as a result of a collective desire to exploit increasing returns, for example.

The division of labour is a remarkable and fundamental phenomenon that can be found in a wide number of circumstances, particularly in social insects, where different tasks are taken on by different members of the hive or nest. The nature of increasing returns or "non-convexities of the production set", is one that has been widely discussed in economics ever since Adam Smith (1776) gave the example of the pin factory. Whilst the precise modelling of this phenomenon has been very limited, its nature is intuitive. If animals or humans specialize on specific tasks then they require much less cognitive capacity and thus overall productivity is increased since the tasks can be done faster. Specialization means that one can no longer describe overall activity as the result of one typical agent but the phenomenon is so prevalent that we can surely not afford to ignore it.

A fascinating example is given by honeybees who specialize in their tasks. Not only do we find heterogeneity of roles but these roles change. The kind of work performed by the worker depends largely upon her age. The first three weeks of her adult life, during which she is referred to as a house bee, are devoted to activities within the hive, while the remainder of her life is devoted to field work, so that she is called a field bee (see Adjare, 1990). Thus, there is important heterogeneity even within individuals.

The tasks for house bees are varied but temperature control is one of the important duties. When the temperature is low, bees cluster to generate heat for themselves, but when it is high, *some of them* fan their wings to circulate air throughout the hive. The general hive temperature required is between 33° and 36°C, while the brood chamber requires a constant heat of 35°C. Honey has to be cured in order to ripen, and this also requires the help of circulating air. According to Crane (1999), 12 fanning bees positioned across a hive entrance 25 centimetres wide can produce an air flow amounting to 50–60 litres per minute. This fanning can go on day and night during the honey-flow season. Honey bees' wings beat 11,400 times per minute, thus making their distinctive buzz.

What is the lesson here for us? The typical economist's response to this phenomenon would be to consider a representative bee and then study how its behaviour responds to the ambient temperature. This would be a smooth function of temperature, wing beats going up with the temperature. Yet this is not what happens at all. Bees have different threshold temperatures and they are either on (beating at 11,400 beats per minute) or off. As the temperature rises more bees join in. Thus, collectively with very simple 1, 0 rules the bees produce a smooth response. This sort of coordination, with each agent doing something simple, can only be explained by having a distribution of temperature thresholds across bees. Aggregation of individuals with specific local and differentiated simple rules of behaviour produces smooth and sophisticated aggregate behaviour.

When there are non-convexities and specialization is advantageous, it can emerge. The same is true in markets where information is dispersed and agents are not in contact with all the others. Each agent can learn to do something specific and a situation can be obtained in which different individuals are behaving differently. The division of labour is such a longstanding and prevalent feature of our society that the names that people are given often reflect professions. The profession, or specialized activity, one undertakes conditions one's tastes, and one's place, in society. Thus, this voluntary diversification is, to some extent, self-perpetuating. Yet, as a result of this diversification, collectively the system may act in a more sophisticated way than its components. This is the hallmark of a complex system.

7.2.2 Contributions to public goods

This is one type of heterogeneity in which agents or insects undertake different tasks and in so doing distinguish themselves from one another, but contribute jointly to the common good. By varying the tasks of individuals the joint cause is advanced. The result of aggregating over consciously chosen heterogeneity is superior to the result that could be obtained without coordination.

However, a different sort of heterogeity may occur in which people in identical situations, in which there is, apparently, a "rational" way to behave, do, in fact, behave differently from one another. Careful consideration of simple experiments on contributions to public goods games illustrates this point clearly.

The prototype model of this sort of experiment involves each participant choosing how to split his or her initial endowment of money between his or her private consumption and his or her contribution to a public good that is jointly consumed by all the participants. There are two standard reference points. The first is characterized by that level of contributions that maximizes joint welfare as measured by the sum of the individual pay-offs. Call this the social optimum. The second is defined by the contributions that constitute a Nash equilibrium. Here the individual's contribution is the best from his or her own point of view, given the contributions of the others.

Slightly more formally then, the basic game of private contribution to a public good, each subject i, $(i = 1, \ldots, N)$ has to split an initial endowment E into two parts: the first part $(E - C_i)$ represents his or her private share and the other part C_i represents his or her contribution to the public good. The pay-off of each share depends on and varies with the experimental design, but in most experiments is taken to be linear (Andreoni, 1995). The total pay-off π_i of individual i, is given by the following expression, which gives the linear case for $\alpha = 1$:

$$\pi_i = E - c_i + \theta\left(\sum_{j=1}^{N} c_j\right)^{\alpha}$$

In the linear version of these games, the Nash equilibrium involves nobody contributing, whereas in the social optimum everyone would give

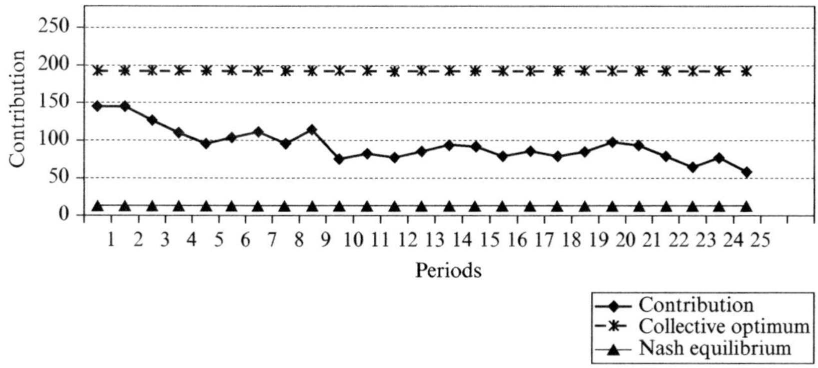

Source: Hichri and Kirman (2007).

Figure 7.1 *Average values of total group contributions with* $\theta = 6.93$

everything, providing $\theta \geq 1$. The results of the experiments, run with this model with several repetitions, reveal that some cooperation emerges early in the game, though, in general, the social optimum is not obtained (see Ledyard, 1997). Yet, over time, the sum of the contributions diminishes towards the Nash non-cooperative solution. The standard explanation is that the players are "learning to play Nash" and that, if the game went on long enough, all the players would be free-riding and all heterogeneity of behaviour would have disappeared. This is reinforced by an examination of the aggregate data from a whole series of experiments. Yet, careful examination of the individuals' behaviour (see Hichri and Kirman, 2007) shows that this is misleading.

In Figure 7.1 we see the average total contribution over all the groups who played the game with a value of $\theta = 6.93$.

This would seem to comfort the idea that "players learn to play Nash". Careful examination of the disaggregated data shows, however, that this is too hasty a conclusion and that heterogeneity does, in fact, persist. Consider now the total contributions of each of the groups in the same treatment as shown in Figure 7.2.

We see that groups behave rather differently both in terms of the level and volatility of their contributions. This suggests that the behaviour of those with whom participants interact does play a role in the outcome and undermines the idea that there is some systematic behaviour that is common to all players. One might take this observation at its face value and suggest that individuals in the same group would behave similarly. However, examination of the individuals' behaviour does not support this idea. Figure 7.3 shows the individual contributions within different groups.

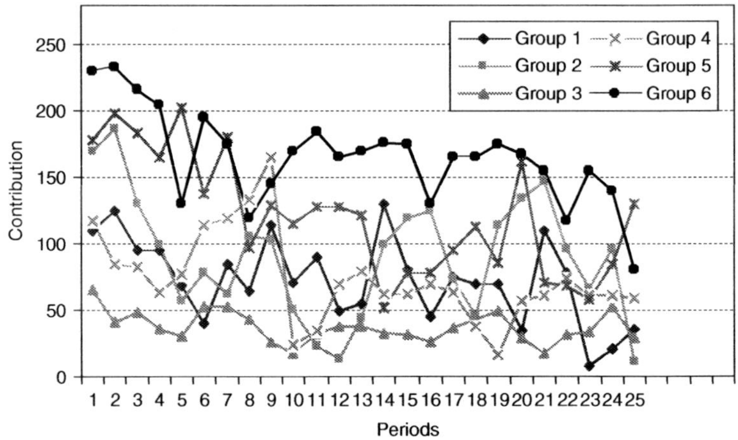

Source: Hichri and Kirman (2007).

Figure 7.2 Contributions of the six groups

What we observe is that even within the same group players behave very differently. Some players play in a rather altruistic way, some are non-cooperative all the time and others seem to signal their intentions to other players. This mixture of behaviour does not disappear. The explanation for this phenomenon is far from clear and the puzzle remains.

An argument that has been used is that people have more or less altruistic preferences (Fehr and Schmidt, 1999), but then one has to explain the origin of this. One suggestion is that altruism is selected for but if we observe differences across individuals this selection cannot be uniform. A large literature on the emergence and persistence of fairness and altruism has sprung up (see Fehr and Gächter, 2000) and the debate is far from closed. Yet within the context of the experiments that we have examined here the altruism explanation does not stand up to close inspection. If participants simply vary in their degree of altruism they should each settle to a fixed level of contribution. However, this is manifestly not the case and how they manage to coordinate on a sum not far from the Nash equilibrium whilst varying their contributions remains to be explained. This is a remarkable example of the complicated relation between the aggregate and individual levels of behaviour.

7.3 Coordination: the Schelling model

One of the important features of complex systems is that the system can coordinate on a solution that could not be predicted from a careful analysis

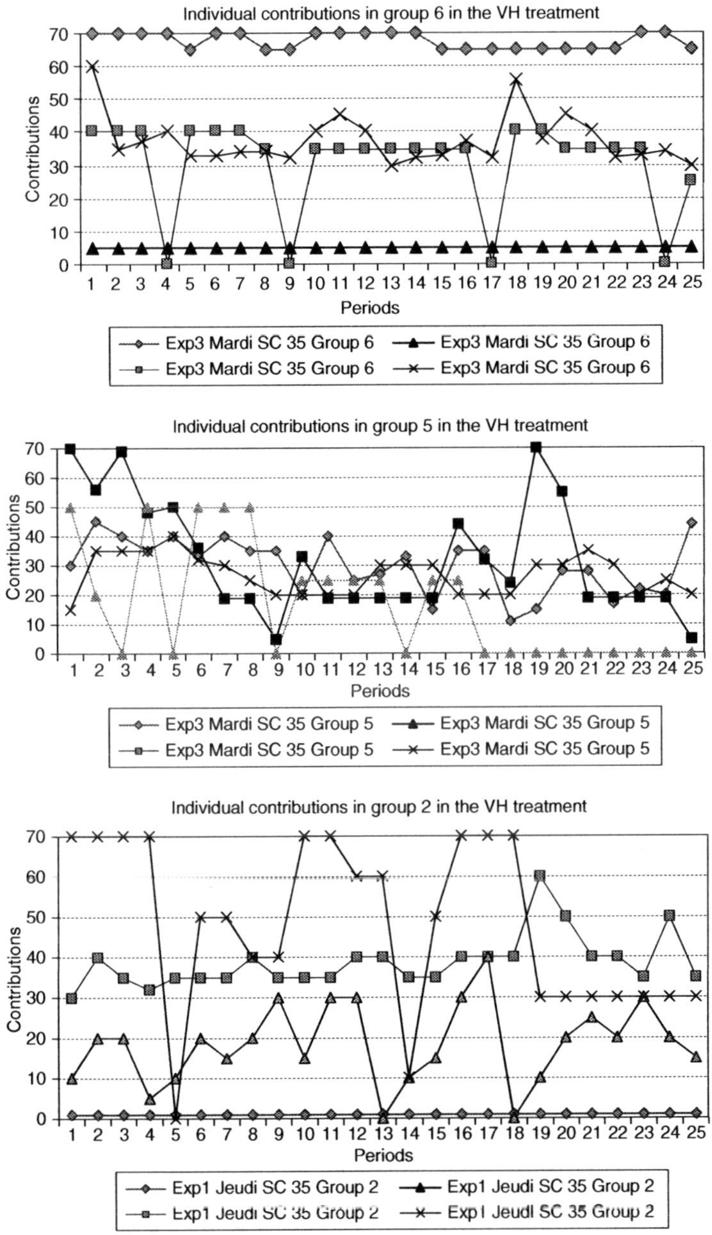

Source: Hichri and Kirman (2007).

Figure 7.3 Individual contributions in the different groups

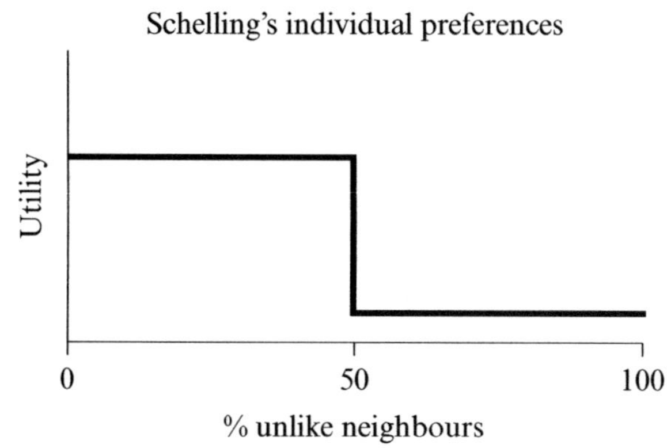

Source: Pancs and Vriend (2007).

Figure 7.4 Schelling's original utility function

of the average or typical individual. At the end of the 1960s, Tom Schelling (for a summary, see Schelling, 1978) introduced a model of segregation that showed that even if people only have a very mild preference for living with neighbours of their own colour, as they move to satisfy their preferences complete segregation will occur. This result was greeted with surprise and has provoked a large number of reactions. Before asking why this was it is worth looking at the model that Schelling introduced.

Take a large chessboard, and place a certain number of black and white counters on the board, leaving some free places. Then take a counter at random. The counter prefers to be on a square where at most four of his or her eight neighbours are of a different colour than his or her own. This "utility function" is illustrated in Figure 7.4.

If the individual is not happy he or she moves to the nearest unoccupied space where he or she is happy. A sequence of moves illustrating this is shown in Figure 7.5 and it is clear that segregation develops rapidly. Thus, the aggregate phenomenon that amounts to complete segregation is not that which might have been predicted from the preferences of the individuals. Indeed, this observation leads us directly to the interesting question as to why people have paid so much attention to this model. Pancs and Vriend (2007) give three explanations. First, it is the "micro motives" of the agents that lead to the aggregate result, in other words a macro phenomenon "emerges" from individual behaviour. Furthermore, as we have said, the result at the aggregate level is more extreme than what would have been necessary to make the individuals happy. Second, the model is remarkably simple and its workings can be understood immediately. Last, the model

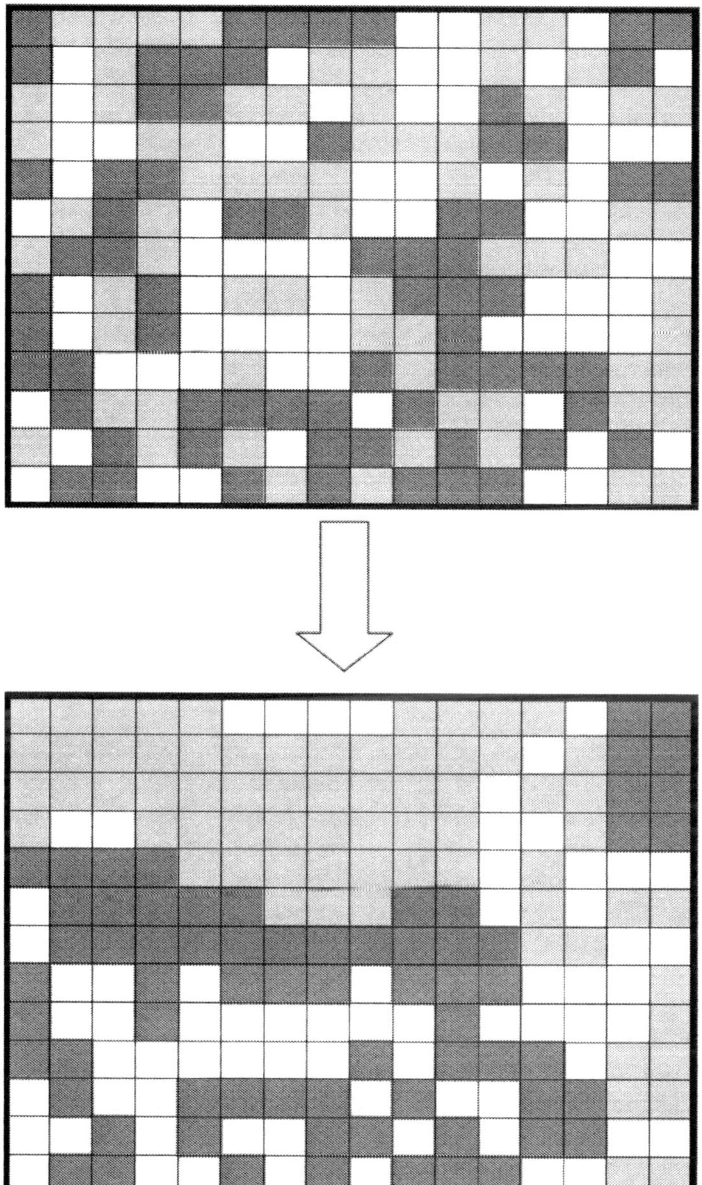

Source: Pancs and Vriend (2007).

Figure 7.5 Sequence of moves by agents to the nearest preferred unoccupied space concerns a topic of great concern in the developed world, that of segregation whether it be on racial or any other grounds.

In a recent paper (Vinkovic and Kirman, 2006), we have developed an argument to suggest that this result is not, in fact, surprising and that some simple physical theory can explain the segregation phenomenon. Numerous papers have been written using Schelling's original model as a starting point and they have used many variants. Typically, the form of the utility function used by Schelling has been questioned, as have the number of neighbours, the rules for moving, the amount of unoccupied space, and all of these have been claimed to be relevant for the results.

Using simulations in general, a number of authors have argued that modifying the parameters just mentioned yields different patterns of segregation. What has been lacking so far is a theoretical structure that can incorporate all of these considerations and then can produce analytic results for each variation. It is precisely this that we propose in the recent paper mentioned above, where we develop a physical analogy to the Schelling model. The agent's happiness or satisfaction in this interpretation corresponds to the energy stored in the agent. An increase in utility would correspond to a decrease in the internal energy. An agent, therefore, wants to minimize his or her energy, and this may be achieved, either by taking some action or through the interaction with his or her environment. In the Schelling model the utility of an agent depends on his or her local environment and the agent moves if the utility declines below a certain value. This analogue is a typical model description of microphysical interactions in dynamical physical systems of gases, liquids, solids, colloids, solutions, and so on. Interactions between particles are described with potential energies, which result in inter-particle forces driving particles' dynamics.

The goal of such models is to study the collective behaviour of a large number of particles. Since the basic tendency of such a physical system is to minimize its total energy, it can do that only by arranging particles into structures (clusters) that reduce the individual internal energy of as many particles as possible. In other words, inter-particle forces attract particles into clustering and the stability of a cluster is determined by this force. Hence, all we need to do is to look at the behaviour of this force on the surface of a cluster to see if the surface will be stable or if it will undergo deformations and tearing. If we think of the Schelling model and the utility function that he chose it is clear that the only individuals who do not have high utility are those on the boundary and it is for this reason that the evolution and final form of the boundary are of particular interest.

The initial configuration of the system may well be out of equilibrium in the sense that some particle can lower its energy, or some individual improve his or her utility by moving to another location. A typical initial state of the Schelling model involves randomized positions of particles in the system. After that we let the system evolve and reach its equilibrium condition. Since we can consider different types of utility functions, the equivalent physical systems can also differ in their underlying definition of inter-particle forces. This, in turn, will lead to different types of "equilibria". Three types of equilibria can be immediately predicted based on physical analogues:

1. Those that are *dynamically unstable*: particles cannot create any stable structure and the whole system is constantly changing, with clusters forming and breaking apart all the time. Water clouds are an example of this equilibrium, where water droplets are constantly forming and re-evaporating. In a society this would correspond to constantly changing neighbourhoods with no propensity to settle to any clear spatial structure.
2. Those that are *dynamically stable*: well-defined clusters are formed. They maintain their size despite constant change of its surface due to rearrangement of the surface particles. This, in the context of spatial arrangements of society, corresponds to the idea that areas on the border between two segregated zones will see movement since it is precisely in these areas that individuals wish to change. The boundary will shift slightly all the time but will not be fundamentally retraced.
3. Those that "*freeze*": all particles stop their movement because all of them reach the energy minimum or do not have any available space to move into. The frozen cluster structure can be either completely irregular (amorphous) or well structured. Glass is an example of the former and crystals of the latter. This sort of frozen structure can happen when there is relatively little free space available and when particles can only move locally.

Thus, we can study the formation and stability of a cluster by considering the energy of particles on its surface. The inter-particle forces derived from the utility function will determine the optimal change of the cluster's surface as it tries to minimize the energy of surface particles. The first step toward this analysis is a transition from the discretized lattice of the Schelling model into a continuous medium by refining the lattice and taking the limit. Next we transform the utility function from counting the individuals in a neighbourhood around an agent into the measurement of the total solid angle covered by different particles around the differential area $d\underset{\cdot}{A}$ (Figure 7.6).

A cluster tries to minimize this surface energy and this is what drives its dynamics. In physics, this force is usually called *surface tension*. By

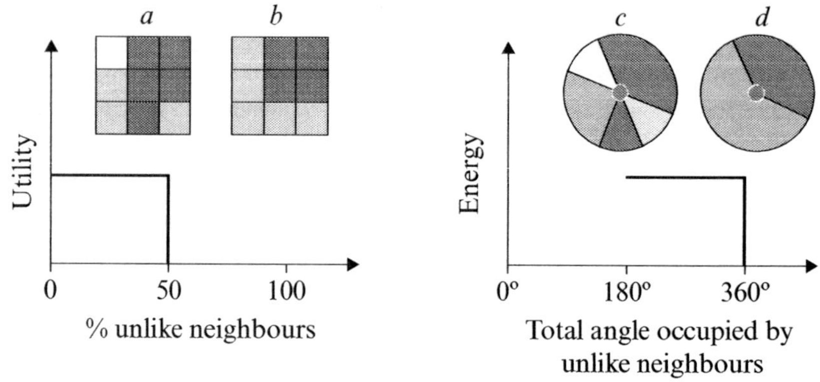

Source: Vinkovic and Kirman (2006).

Figure 7.6 Approximation of the discrete model by a continuum

analysing this we can predict the behaviour of a cluster for a given utility function for the individuals. In the continous version we show that any convex cluster surface experiences a tangential force pushing the surface toward flattening. The outcome of this surface reshaping are clusters that "prefer" flat surfaces, except for parts covered by a boundary layer made of empty space. In Figure 7.6 we can see the approximation of the discrete model by a continuum.

In Figure 7.7 we can see the forces at work on the frontier trying to "flatten" the surface.

When clusters start to grow they compete for particles they can collect. A bigger cluster has a bigger surface for collecting particles, thus also a higher probability of collecting them. Eventually, one cluster grows bigger than others and grows until it collects all available particles. Smaller clusters can exist if they manage to "freeze" their particles, not letting them "evaporate" and travel to the big cluster. If the volume of the big cluster is not much smaller than the total available volume then particles segregate into two distinct clusters separated by a flat surface. Alternatively, a cluster at the centre of the available volume forms. Since particles have the same probability to reach the cluster's surface from any direction, such a cluster will stay close to a spherical shape. In Vinkovic and Kirman (2006) we give detailed illustrations of the sort of cluster patterns that can form under different parameter values.

The growth of one big cluster out of a mixture of particles is a common natural phenomenon and is well known in the physics of metal surfaces, where the evolution of fewer but larger nano-structures out of many

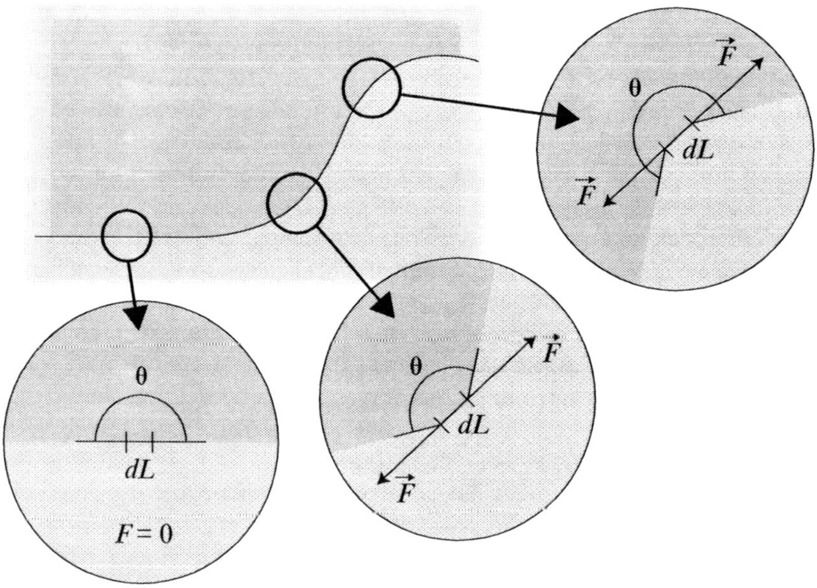

Source: Vinkovic and Kirman (2006).

Figure 7.7 How the forces at work tend to "flatten" the frontier

smaller nano-structures is an actively studied phenomenon generally known as "coarsening". The Schelling model is, therefore, just a discretized model of such physical phenomena.

This analysis allows us not only to obtain the well-known "surprising" result of Schelling but also can show that other configurations can appear depending on the distance that inidviduals can move and how much space is available and the particular utility function that is attributed to them. We can thus find a wide range of aggregate possibilities over and above the pure segregation found in the original model. Nevertheless, the basic point remains: the rather simple behaviour of individuals gives rise to very varied aggregate outcomes, none of which could have been directly predicted by trying to interpret the system as that of an average particle or individual.

7.4 The "El Farol Bar"

Another interesting example of emergent coordination is that provided by Brian Arthur (1994) in his "El Farol Bar" problem. The simple model that he develops and that has been taken up by many physicists under the name of "the minority game", shows how individuals using rules of thumb can come to coordinate in a way that yields a satisfactory social outcome even though no individual had any such intention. The idea of the original example is that there is a bar that can hold 100 people. When there are fewer than 60 people there, being at the bar is, by common consent, better than staying at home. However, once attendance goes over 60 the bar becomes too crowded and home is the preferable alternative. The question then is how will people decide whether to go to the bar or not? Suppose that they all reason strategically. In this case they must decide as a function of what their neighbours will decide. Thus, to anticipate whether there will be more than 60 people at the bar they must reflect on the strategies employed by the others. However, they must also take into account that the others are doing the same and know that the others know that they know that they are behaving in this way. This leads to an infinite regress that poses logical problems for the foundations of such game-theoretic reasoning (see Binmore, 1990).

Rather than attribute such calculating capacities to his agents, Brian Arthur imagined that each was endowed with a small subset of possible forecasting rules based on previous attendance at the bar. Given his or her set of rules, the individual chooses that rule that has forecast best up to the present, where by "best" one means the forecast that has the smallest sum of squared prediction errors, for example. Now, each agent uses, as information, just the attendance observed at the bar, and updates in consequence. There is no coordinating mechanism, yet the model quickly settles to the "equilibrium" solution with 60 people at the bar with occasional small deviations. Furthermore, each agent receives a fixed and limited number of forecasting rules, some of which may be rather stupid. Nevertheless coordination is achieved at the aggregate level.

Some things about this model are worth noting. It is not guaranteed that all agents will learn to forecast correctly; some may persist in erroneous forecasts. The way in which the model is set up means that whenever attendance goes to 61 many people are unhappy, which is not the case when it goes to 59. This asymmetry does not prevent the achievement of collective coordination, however. Thus, the relation between satisfactory performance at the aggregate level and satisfaction at the individual level is tenuous. Whilst many may find this example intriguing, one might enquire as to how it can be directly applied to economic problems. An interesting answer is to be found in a book by some Oxford physicists who specialize in complex systems and who apply the model to financial markets (see Johnson, Jeffries and Hui, 2003, pp. 81–136).

7.5 Market relations

The next example concerns the network of buyer–seller relations on markets. Markets are frequented by agents, buyers and sellers, who establish relationships over time. In various studies of the Marseille wholesale fish market, for which we have full details of every transaction over three years, with a number of co-authors (see Kirman and Vignes, 1991; Härdle and Kirman, 1995; and Kirman and Vriend, 2001), we have performed econometric tests, established some of the stylized facts and built models to explain the network of relations between buyers and sellers. In particular we have developed (Weisbuch, Kirman and Herreiner, 2000), a theoretical framework within which to analyse the emergence of links between agents in such a market. The idea here is to examine the structure of the network of links that emerges as a result of simple behaviour at the individual level.

Consider the simplest market in which there are n buyers i and m sellers j. Buyers visit one seller per day and the quantity that they buy determines the profit they will obtain outside the market. Sellers offer a quantity that is fixed by them each day before the market opens. Thus, when a buyer chooses a seller he or she will either obtain a unit or he or she will be unlucky because the seller that he or she has chosen is out of stock. The cumulated profit that a buyer i obtains from a seller j is given by the following expression,

$$J_{ij}(t) = (1 - \gamma)J_{ij}(t - 1) + \pi_{ij}(t)$$

where obviously the current profit is zero if the seller has already sold all of his or her stock.

Now we have to say how buyers choose sellers. We will assume that the rule that determines the probability that buyer i will purchase from seller j is made on the basis of the profit that they obtained in the past from those sellers. In particular we will assume that the probability p_{ij} that i will visit j in that period is given by:

$$p_{ij}(t) = \frac{\exp \beta J_{ij}(t)}{\sum_k \exp \beta J_{ik}(t)}$$

where β is a reinforcement parameter that describes how sensitive the individual is to past profits. This nonlinear updating rule will be familiar from discrete choice problems and is known as the "quantal response function" in game theory. It is widely used in statistical physics.

This rule can be derived as resulting from a trade-off between "exploration" and "exploitation". Agents in many economic situations have to face a choice between using their past experience as to actions that have been profitable and trying out new actions. Exploration can be thought of as trying to choose those actions that will provide the maximum information about what is profitable and in this case, with no prior information, one would choose probabilities to maximize the entropy of the system. This amounts to sampling the possible actions with uniform probability. Exploitation would involve maximizing expected profit given the performance of the rules in the past. Maximizing a linear combination of the two,

$$\underset{p_j}{Max}\,\beta \sum_j p_{ij} J_{ij}(t) + \sum_j p_j \log p_j$$

yields the rule given above.

Given this rule, we can now derive the equilibrium probabilities for this situation. We shall use a technique adopted from physics called the "mean field" approach. It is clear that if we use our basic approach directly we have to model a stochastic process in discrete time. At each point buyers will visit sellers. Depending on whether they are successful or not they will then sell the quantity, in the simplest case one unit, on the outside market and make a profit. This profit will modify the probability of their choosing different sellers in the next period. Once they have made their choice in that period the process will recommence.

Now the mean field approach makes two approximations. First, it replaces the random variables by their expected values and second it approximates a discrete process by a continuous one. To see how this works consider the following expression where a continuous representation is given and where the profit is now replaced by the expected profit:

$$\frac{dJ_{ij}}{dt} = -\gamma J_{ij} + \langle \pi_{ij} \rangle$$

where the expected profit is given by the following:

$$\langle \pi_{ij} \rangle = Pr(q_j > 0)\pi_{ij} \frac{\exp(\beta J_{ij})}{\sum_k \exp(\beta J_{ik})}$$

where $Pr(q_j > 0)$ represents the probability that seller j still has a unit to sell when buyer i arrives. Now let us consider the very simplest case in which there are two sellers who both charge the same price and therefore who generate the same profit for the buyer and furthermore they always have sufficient fish to satisfy all customers, that is we will assume that

$$Pr(q_j > 0) = 1 \text{ and } \pi_{ij} = \pi \text{ for all } i \text{ and } j$$

Clearly the cumulated profits will evolve over time and the equilibrium will be reached when the probabilities no longer change, that is when,

$$\frac{dJ_{ij}}{dt} = 0$$

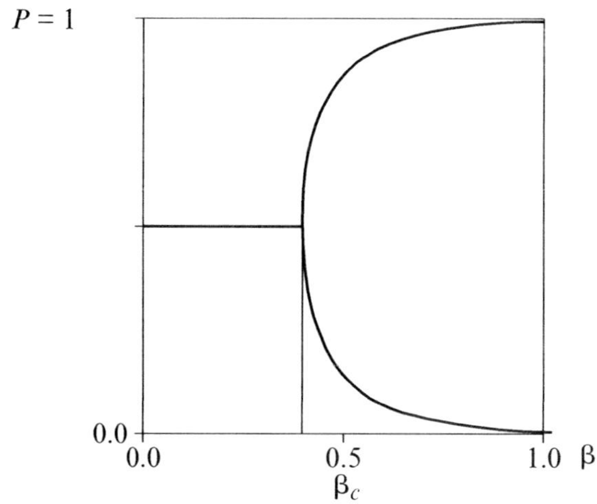

Note: Plot of both equilibrium preference coefficients versus the discrimination rate β. Below the transition rate β_c, preference coefficients are equal, but they rise or plummet sharply when the discrimination rate β increases above the transition. When profits from both sellers are equal (as in this figure), loyalty to one describes the upper branch, while loyalty to the other describes the lower branch.

Source: Weisbuch, Kirman and Herreiner (2000).

Figure 7.8 The order/disorder transition in β

The equilibrium conditions in this case for seller 1 and symmetically for seller 2 are given by,

$$\gamma J_1 = \pi \frac{\exp(\beta J_1)}{\exp(\beta J_1) + \exp(\beta J_2)}$$

$$\gamma J_2 = \pi \frac{\exp(\beta J_2)}{\exp(\beta J_1) + \exp(\beta J_2)}$$

Consider now the difference, that is, $\Delta = J_1 - J_2$ and we have,

$$\Delta = \frac{\pi \exp(\beta\Delta - 1)}{\gamma \exp(\beta\Delta + 1)}$$

What are the solutions? There are two cases to examine. First, if $\beta < \beta_c = (2\gamma/\pi)$ then there is one solution that is given by $\Delta = 0$ and $J_1 = J_2 = (\pi/2\gamma)$. Second, if $\beta > \beta_c$ there are three solutions and the equiprobability solution $\Delta = 0$ is now unstable; furthermore there is a rapid transition to two distinct solutions at $\beta = \beta_c$ as shown in Figure 7.8.

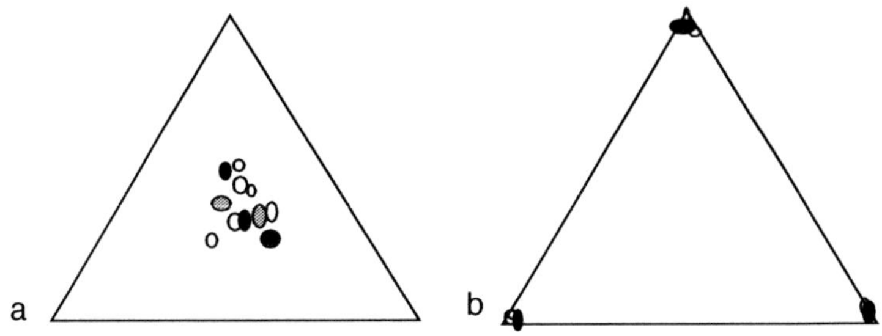

Source: Weisbuch et al. (2000).

Figure 7.9a and b The probabilities of visiting one of three sellers for buyers with a low β *(a) and* β *(b)*

What this says is that if individuals have a β above the critical level then they will have a much higher probability of going to one seller than another even though visiting each seller is equally profitable. Thus, in the market we would expect to see such individuals being very loyal to a particular seller. In the Weisbuch, Kirman and Herreiner (2000) model, as already mentioned, this sort of "phase transition" is derived using the "mean field" approach. The latter is open to the objection that random variables are replaced by their means and, in consequence, the process derived is only an approximation. The alternative is to consider the fully stochastic process but this is often not tractable, and one can then resort to simulations to see whether the theoretical results from the approximation capture the features of the simulated stochastic process.

Consider, for example, the case of three sellers, and 30 buyers. The simplex in Figure 7.9a and b above can be used to represent this situation. Each of the 30 buyers has certain probabilities of visiting each of the sellers and thus can be thought of as a point in the simplex. If he or she is equally likely to visit each of the three sellers then he or she can be represented as a point in the centre of the triangle. If, on the other hand, he or she visits one of the sellers with probability one then he or she can be shown as a point at one of the apexes of the triangle. Thus, at any one point in time, the market is described by a cloud of points in the triangle and the question is how will this cloud evolve? If buyers all become loyal to particular sellers then the result will be be that all the points, corresponding to the buyers, will be at the apexes of the triangle as in Figure 7.9b. This might be thought of as a situation in which the market is "ordered". On the other hand, if buyers learn to search randomly amongst the sellers then the result will be a cluster of points at the centre of the triangle, as in Figure 7.9a. In network terms, the first case corresponds to a situation in which every buyer has a link with

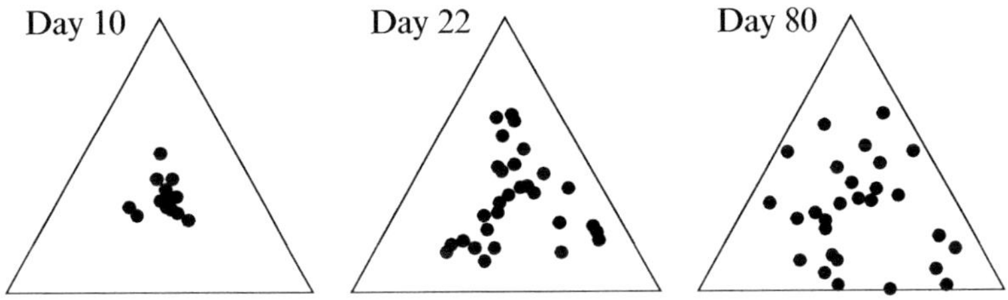

Figure 7.10 The evolution of loyalty when buyers have a low β

every seller and in the second case each buyer has a link to only one seller. Which of these situations will develop depends crucially on the parameters β, γ and the profit Π per transaction. The stronger the reinforcement, the slower the individual forgets, and the higher the profit the more likely it is that order will emerge. In particular, as mentioned, the transition from disorder to order is very sharp with a change in β.

Why is it important to understand the nature of the trading relationships that emerge? The answer is that the aggregate efficiency of the market depends on them. A market where agents are predominantly searchers is less efficient than one with many loyal traders. When searching is pre-eminent, sellers' supply will often not be equal to the demand they face. Some buyers will be unsatisfied and some sellers will be left with stock on their hands. This is particularly important in markets for perishable goods.

To illustrate the evolution of the networks involved in this model, it is worth looking at Figures 7.10 and 7.11. As before we are looking at a situation with three sellers and 30 buyers and the evolution of the loyalty of the individuals and the group can be seen as time passes.

What was done to produce these figures was to simulate the actual stochastic process to see whether the approximate results obtained in the deterministic approximation still held up in the actual process. Thus, at each step the market participants decide which rule to use according to its success and then form their offer prices, for the sellers, and reservation prices for the buyers. This in turn determines the profit the buyers and sellers make in that period and this conditions the buyers' new probability of visiting each seller. They draw a seller according to these probabilities and the process starts again. The only way in which the two figures, 7.10 and 7.11, differ is in the value of β. Figure 7.10 shows the situation in which β is small and below the critical value that is determined by the profit and the rate of discount. The graph corresponding to this situation is one in which each buyer visits several sellers with a positive probability. Although each agent changes his or her probability of visiting the sellers they are essentially still in the centre of the simplex.

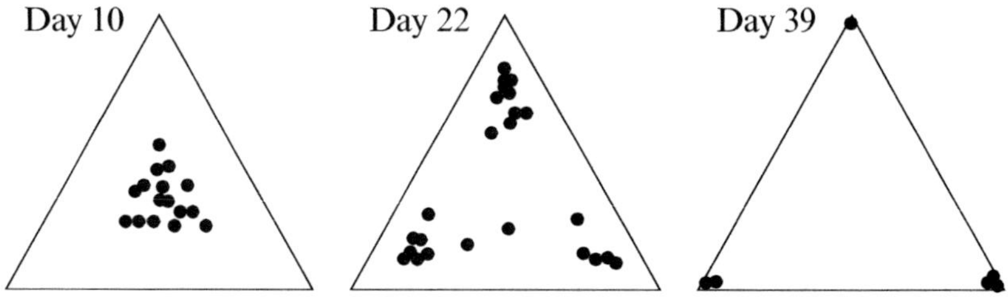

Figure 7.11 The evolution of loyalty when buyers have a high β

In Figure 7.10 however, β is above the critical value and each of the buyers rapidly become loyal to a single seller. Thus, the graph is essentially deterministic and is characterized for each individual by a single link with one seller. It is clear that the graph structure is very different in the two cases.

As has already been observed, the deterministic graph is more efficient in terms of resource utilization. Buyers know where to find what they want and sellers know how much to supply. Now, what predictions could we make about an empirical situation? Recall that we have always talked about high and low values of β itself. Yet, since we know nothing about the β of each individual we must assume that they are all the same. However, the critical value of β is different for each individual and depends on the two parameters, Π the profit per transaction and γ the discount rate. In the Marseille wholesale fish market, where the model was tested, those buyers who have a low critical value of β will be those who have a low γ or a high Π. That is, they will be those who come often to the market and who make large profits.

Yet, for the results of the simulations to be convincing we have to deal with one unsatisfactory feature of the way in which the model was simulated. Why do buyers with high βs always find what they want in the simulated model? It may be because there are no random buyers to interfere with their learning process. Yet what we are claiming is that in a market where both types of buyer are present those with high β develop deterministic links, while the low β continue to shop randomly. Our simulations are of markets with all traders with high β or all traders with low β. Might it not be the case that when mixed our results no longer hold?

To test this we ran a simulation with a mixed population. Half of them had low critical values of β and half high values. The result can be seen in Figure 7.12.

Here the light grey circles represent buyers with a low critical value while the black individuals have high critical value. There is clearly a separation

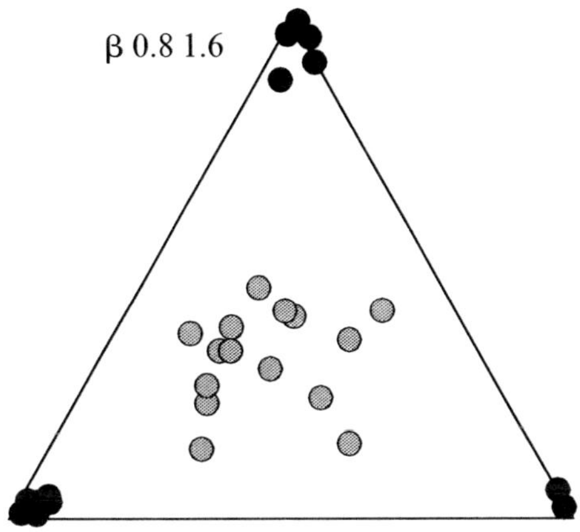

Note: β = 0.8 or 1.6.

Figure 7.12 The evolution of loyalty in a mixed population after 2000 periods

and if the situation were represented as a graph one would have a mixture of links with probability $p_{ij} = 1$ and others with almost $p_{ij} = (1/3)$ but none with intermediate values.

Now what about the empirical evidence? The data, which cover every single transaction over three years, reveal that this is precisely the case: frequent buyers and those who buy large quantities are, indeed, extremely loyal, whilst the others "shop around" and do not become loyal at all. The distribution of the number of sellers visited per month is bimodal with a peak at 1 as shown in Figure 7.13.

Here again we have a situation in which small variations in individual behaviour can lead to significant changes in aggregate behaviour. Using a simple model from physics enables us to understand why the system should organize itself in such a way that buyers are sharply divided into two groups. The existence of these two groups could not be forecast from an examination of the average parameter values of the individuals involved. The aggregate structure is more complicated than would have been suggested by considering individuals in isolation and, indeed, the important feature here is that the system organizes itself in this way.

7.6 Conclusion

The purpose of this chapter has been to argue that economies and markets share an essential characteristic with other complex systems. This is, that there are essential differences between behaviour at the aggregate level and

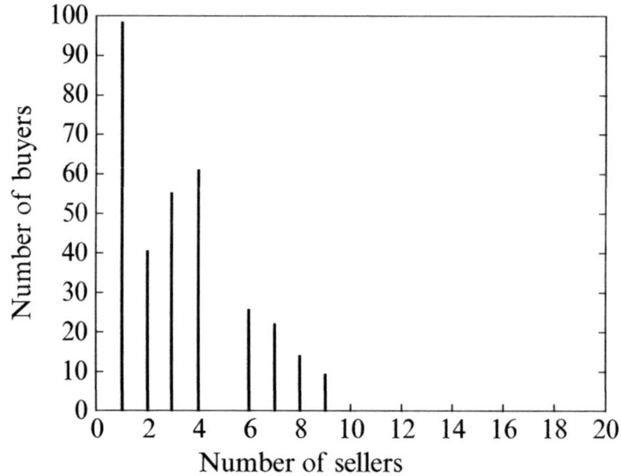

Note: The sample of buyers include those visiting more than once per month, and present in the market for more than six months. The distribution is clearly bimodal, with one peak corresponding to fidelity to one seller, and another peak centred on visiting four sellers on average.

Source: Weisbuch, Kirman and Herreiner (2000).

Figure 7.13 Fidelity histogram of the number of buyers of cod as a function of how many sellers they visit on average during one month in 1990

that of the individuals who make up the system. The aggregate may be "better" or "worse" behaved than its components but it is intrinsically different. Viewing the economy as a complex system allows us to account for phenomena that are not compatible with the frequently used "representative agent" model. Using the complexity approach, which attributes less rationality but more interaction to the components of a system, provides a solution to the aggregation problem that has long plagued economics and that cannot be ignored.

Notes

1. This is not the place to enter into the details of this assertion but the basic argument is given in Kirman (1992) and stems from the results of Sonnenschein (1972), Mantel, (1974) and Debreu (1974).
2. For a good survey of the relevant literature see Rabin (1998).
3. However, Grandmont (1992) following up on earlier ideas first suggested by Cournot (1838) and later developed analytically by Hildenbrand (1983) suggested that appropriate assumptions on the distribution of individual characteristics might solve the aggregation problem. He argued that the more heterogeneity the less important was the aggregation

problem. However, this approach has fundamental difficulties and has given rise to a large but not conclusive literature.

References

Adjare, S.O. (1990), *Beekeeping in Africa*, FAO Agricultural Services Bulletin No. 68/6, Food and Agriculture Organization of the United Nations.

Andreoni, J. (1995), "Cooperation in public-goods experiments: Kindness or confusion?", *American Economic Review*, **85**(4), 891–904.

Arthur, W.B. (1994), "Inductive reasoning and bounded rationality", *American Economic Review*, **84**(2), 406–11.

Binmore, K. (1990), *Essays on the Foundations of Game Theory*, Oxford: Basil Blackwell.

Crane, E. (1999), *The World History of Beekeeping and Honey Hunting*, London: Routledge.

Cournot, A.A. (1838), *Recherches sur les Principes Mathématiques de la Théorie des Richesses*, Paris: Hachette.

Debreu, G. (1974), "Excess demand functions", *Journal of Mathematical Economics*, **1**, 15–23.

Fehr, E. and S. Gächter (2000), "Cooperation and punishment in public goods experiments", *American Economic Review*, **90**(4), 980–94.

Fehr, E. and K. Schmidt (1999), "A theory of fairness, competition, and cooperation", *Quarterly Journal of Economics*, **114**(3), 817–68.

Grandmont, J.-M. (1992), "Transformations of the commodity space, behavioural heterogeneity, and the aggregation problem", *Journal of Economic Theory*, **57**(1), 1–35.

Härdle, W. and A. Kirman (1995), "Nonclassical demand: a model-free examination of price–quantity relations in the Marseille fish market", *Journal of Econometrics*, **67**(1), 227–57.

Hichri, W. and A. Kirman (2007), "The emergence of coordination in public goods games", *European Physical Journal B*, **55**(2), 149–59.

Hildenbrand, W. (1983), "On the law of demand", *Econometrica*, **51**(4), 997–1019.

Johnson, N., P. Jeffries and P.M. Hui (2003), *Financial Market Complexity*, Oxford: Oxford University Press.

Kirman, A. (1992), "What or whom does the representative individual represent?", *Journal of Economic Perspectives*, **6**(2), 117–36.

Kirman, A. and K. Koch (1986), "Market excess demand functions: Identical preferences and collinear endowments", *Review of Economic Studies*, **53**(3), 457–63.

Kirman, A.P. and A. Vignes (1991), "Price dispersion: theoretical considerations and empirical evidence from the Marseilles fish market", in K.G. Arrow (ed.), *Issues in Contemporary Economics*, London: Macmillan.

Kirman, A. and N. Vriend (2001), "Evolving market structure: An ACE model of price dispersion and loyalty", *Journal of Economic Dynamics and Control*, **25**(3–4), 459–502.

Ledyard, J. (1997), "Public goods: A survey of experimental research", in John H. Kagel and Alvin E. Roth (eds), *Handbook of Experimental Economics*, Princeton: Princeton University Press.

Mantel, R. (1974), "On the characterisation of aggregate excess demand", *Journal of Economic Theory*, **7**, 348–53.

Pancs, R. and N.J. Vriend (2007) "Schelling's spatial proximity model of segregation revisited", *Journal of Public Economics*, **91**(1–2), 1–24.

Rabin, M. (1998) "Psychology and economics", *Journal of Economic Literature*, **36**(1), 11–46.

Schelling, T.S. (1978), *Micromotives and Macrobehavior*, New York: W.W. Norton and Co.

Simon, H. (1957), *Models of Man: Social and Rational*, New York: Wiley.

Smith, A. (1776), *An Inquiry into the Nature and Causes of the Wealth of Nations*, London: Methuen & Co.

Sonnenschein, H. (1972), "Market excess demand functions", *Econometrica*, **40**, 549–56.
Vinkovic, D. and A. Kirman (2006), "A physical analogue of the Schelling model", *Proceedings of the National Academy of Sciences*, **103**(51), 19261–19265.
Weisbuch, G., A. Kirman and D. Herreiner (2000), "Market organisation and trading relationships", *Economic Journal*, **110**(463), 411–36.

8. On simplicity and macroeconomic complexity

Richard H. Day

By complexity we mean phenomena generated by interacting parts, all of whose causal connections are not easily discernible, whose behavior over time exhibits disorder and behaves unpredictably or chaotically.[1] Our concern here is with macroeconomic complexity. The remarks that follow briefly consider some sources of complexity involved in science generally and in economics in particular, and the strategies used to overcome them. Then several examples from macroeconomics are summarized.

8.1 Sources of complexity

8.1.1 Multi-level causality

Theoretical analysis requires the identification of variables that describe attributes of a system at a given level in the hierarchy of causal structures. The causal structure that is discerned at a given level emerges from structures at a "lower" level and provides the foundation out of which "higher" levels of causal relationships emerge. As one goes "down" in the hierarchy of relationships to successively more micro, successively more "fundamental" structures, the number of distinct entities becomes larger, at very micro levels so large that the representation and analysis of relationships among individual entities is not possible. The multi-level nature of matter and energy begins with subatomic particles, continues through atoms, molecules, material objects made up of them, planets, solar systems, galaxies, and, some speculate, universes. For each level there is a special set of physical concepts and principles.

The multi-level economic activity of nations rises out of the behavior of individual people interacting with one another in homes, stores, factories, farms, and within a panoply of political and socioeconomic organizations. Individuals' actions emerge from underlying physiological processes, which themselves rest on the underlying molecular phenomena. Thus, action ascends from atoms, to physiologics, to thoughts, to observable human actions, to organizations, to nations, and to the interactions among nations, all involving multi-level interacting flows of information, energy, and materials. Within this hierarchy is the macroeconomic structure of interacting aggregate variables that characterize a national economy. At the national level are a few hundred entities, at the institutional level, thousands or even millions of socioeconomic organizations, and at the human level there are now billions and their number is still growing. Describing the behavior of each one of them, let alone explaining it, is impossible—just as impossible as tracking the behavior of each and every atom in a cup of tea.

The essential implication of these observations for the present discussion is that theory and inference depend on the level in the hierarchy of causal interactions that are of concern. A theory at one level abstracts from causal interactions that occur at a deeper level or at a higher level and, though limited to that level, may be useful.

8.1.2 Causal effect reversal and nonlinearity

Balzac observed that "when the effect produced is no longer in direct proportion to the cause, disorganization sets in," a literary way of saying that linear relationships are predictable but the nonlinear ones may not be.[2] Nonlinearity arises in dynamic relationships when they involve causal effect reversals. In such cases, the effect of a change in a "causing" variable, say x, influences another variable, say y, in a given direction, but when the x continues to change in the same direction, the direction of change in y reverses. The classic example of an economic relationship that exhibits this phenomenon is the total revenue curve for an individual commodity. Given a downward-sloping demand curve, $x = D(p)$, the total revenue curve generated by sales in amount x at the price p is $R = px = pD(p)$. The simplest example, $D(p) = a - bP$, where a and b are positive, yields the single-humped quadratic total revenue curve $R = ap - bp^2$. Total revenue increases when p increases below $a/2b$ and decreases when p increases above $a/2b$, thereby reversing the influence on total revenue of increasing price. Thus, the effect is not "proportional to the cause." An analysis of pure competition out-of-equilibrium based on this phenomenon shows how chaotic fluctuations of market demands and prices are one of the possible consequences.[3]

8.1.3 Multi-phase causality

Another source of complexity in many contexts is the fact that the causal relationships connecting variables in some regions of their domain may be structurally distinct from the causal relationships connecting them in other regions of their domain. The "tent map" and the "baker's transformation" are two of the simplest examples. Both have been used to illustrate dynamic behavior that arises in a wide variety of situations involving nonlinearity. In the former, behavior on the real [0, 1] interval is governed by a positively sloping linear relationship on [0, x'] and by a downward-sloping linear relationship on the interval [x', 1], thus exhibiting both structural change and causal effect reversal. In the baker's transformation on the intervals [0, x'] and [x', 1] both causal structures are positively sloping linear relationships but are discontinuous at x'. In both cases the map defined on [0, 1] is nonlinear even though it is linear on the two separate phase domains [0, x'] and [x', 1]. Both provide examples of the generation of chaotic trajectories that behave essentially like stochastic processes. The implication of these examples is that complex behavior need not be the result of large numbers of interacting parts but may also result from nonlinearity in systems that can be described by very simple nonlinear or multi-phase relationships. It is primarily for this reason that macroeconomics involves complexity in theory as well as in fact.

To summarize: complexity arises from multiple interacting entities, from causal effect reversal or nonlinearity, and from the multi-phase nature of causal relationships.

8.2 Multi-level measurement

Scientific endeavor begins with and rests on empirical observation because observation presents both the phenomena to be explained and the ultimate criterion that validates the explanation. It is obvious that any explanation must be tested empirically at the level of human observation because it is only at that level that human perception can be engaged. In this regard, economics is much better off than physics. *We* are the atoms of economic science; households, firms, and government agencies are the molecules. Data about individual people at the action level can be obtained from questionnaires, surveys, census enumerations, and simply by watching, as in engineering time and motion studies. Moreover, the mental activity that leads to action is immediately accessible in conscious thought: the admonition to "know thyself" emphasizes the first step in understanding the world around us. But this subjective accessibility can only be accessed by others (at least "objectively") only indirectly through speech, psychological experiments, and using the neurophysiological methods now being exploited in neuroeconomics. At the organizational level, data can also be obtained by direct observation, as in Cyert and March, and surveys of people within them, as in Chamberlain,[4] but also from accounting records and from statistical data collected and maintained by various consumer, producer, and other institutes and associations.

Passing from the personal and organizational microeconomic level to the meso and macroeconomic levels, the problem is to measure aggregates of variables that reflect the total or overall activity and characteristics of groups of people within occupational (or otherwise defined) categories, aggregates of input and output flows within various technologically and/or regionally delineated sectors as in Leontief's input–output interindustry models, Jorgenson's[5] industrial investment equations, or in my own recursive programming models of industrial sectors and agricultural regions.

For the economy as a whole, data must also be based on weighted statistical averages of micro data samples that combine all consumer goods into consumption as an aggregate, "*C*," all investment goods into an aggregate investment, "*I*," production of all goods into the GDP index, "*Q*," all prices into an aggregate price index, "*P*," and so on, as in the national income product accounts that provide the empirical basis for estimating and evaluating macroeconomic models of national economies such as those of Fair or Godley. Finally, national data have been used to compose a description of the world economy as a whole, as in the *World Dynamics* of Forrester.[6]

The point to be emphasized is: once the "natural" micro level of the individual, household, and firm is set aside and the meso and macro levels become the levels of inquiry, quantitative data must be *constructed* from samples of micro data. The causal interactions among micro components that generate the original micro data are lost. New causal relationships may emerge among aggregate variables at the meso and macro levels. Research at these levels shows that they do.

8.3 Decomplexifying causal structure

8.3.1 Salience

A salient phenomenon is one that is "prominent in the consciousness," one that stands out, that commands attention. We are never aware of everything, nor do we ever try to explain everything. What is salient depends on what we are doing, what we are thinking about, what problem we are facing. The attraction that the earth exhibits toward all the objects on it was salient to Newton as he thought about motion in the solar system, just as the fading sound of a passing train was salient to Einstein as he thought about the relativity of motion and its geometric implications. To early thinkers about economics the correlation of the price of wheat with its supply, how necessary things might be free while completely unnecessary objects could command great sums, these facts stood out. They commanded an explanation. Thus: identifying the salient is the first step in decomplexifying causal structure.

8.3.2 Controlled experimentation

Experimental sciences deal with complexity by physically isolating specific phenomena so as to limit the number of observable real world interactions to be studied. This intentionally artificial but highly effective strategy is a standard operating procedure in chemistry, engineering, and the biological disciplines. But its strength is the source of its fundamental weakness: its intentional isolation from the complex process within which the controlled phenomena work themselves out *in vivo*, for in the real world the processes of interest may exhibit complex behavior not predicted or explained by the experimentally derived relationships—sometimes with disastrous consequences as with unanticipated "side-effects" of a medical treatment based on laboratory experiments.

8.3.3 Modeling and story-telling

Non-experimental sciences adopt a different strategy for simplifying the study of complex systems. Here, simplification is also achieved by identifying salient features of real world processes but that can be mimicked by artificial methods. They proceed by constructing mathematical, computer, or analogical physical models whose properties can be studied using abstract symbols and pure logic, or by conducting computational, mechanical, or electronic simulations, and whose verisimilitude can be tested by comparing model behavior with real world observations or with data aggregated or composed at the appropriate level. Surely the all-time boldest and perhaps most useful example of such an abstract analog is Newton's model of stellar dynamics, which can not only predict the relative positions of planets in the solar system with great accuracy, but, when aided by numerical approximations, physical observations, and engineering control systems, can guide humans to and from the moon.

As the number of causal interactions to be comprehended increases, modeling necessarily passes from controlled experiments to physical analogs to mathematical similes to computer simulations. For the most complex relationships at the basis of human nature and human history, one enters a realm where science may be restricted to careful observation and historical description, and understanding represented by narrative stories that reflect real relationships but only hint at general truths.

8.3.4 Decomposition and reducibility

In the identification of salient phenomena it is very often the case that cause and effect relationships among some variables seem to be, are, or are approximately independent of—that is, not influenced by—other variables and causal relationships. Such phenomena are (at least approximately) *decomposable* in the sense that they can be studied effectively in isolation. For example, stellar motion can be studied independently of earthly phenomena even though life on earth is entirely dependent on the nature of the solar system. Conversely, human psychology or physical chemistry need not take into account the nature of objects in space.

More general are systems that are influenced by variables "outside" the given system but that do not seem to influence the system outside itself. The "outside variables" are said to be "exogenous," the "inside" ones "endogenous." Systems that can be treated in this way are said to be *reducible*. Or, it could be the case that the endogenous variables do influence the exogenous ones, but in a way difficult to discern. One then treats the system *as if* it were reducible, in this way leaving open a complete understanding of the connection between the two.

8.3.5 Discretization

The physical world seems for the most part to move continuously through time and space so the representation of phenomena as continuously varying seems natural to the theorist. Mathematical modeling in continuous time involves differential and integral equations for which a highly developed mathematical theory is available, but one that cannot be represented exactly in numerical terms because it depends on limiting arguments. The existence of model solutions represented abstractly in these terms must always be approximated. This involves substituting discrete time difference equations and iterative operations (mathematical groups and semi-groups) for continuous time integral and differential equations.[7]

While for purposes of pure theory, the abstract world of real analysis may be simplest, for the purpose of modeling to mimic real world processes, discrete dynamics may be necessary and perhaps more realistic. It has the effect of averaging out change within discrete time periods. The longer in continuous time the discrete period is defined to be, the more coarse is the dynamic explanation obtained from the discrete time model. Discretization, while simplifying the analytical process in a practical sense, pays its price in the coarseness of the approximation of actual change.

8.3.6 Linearization

As noted above, linearity involves uni-directional causation. Approximating relationships by local linearization is a standard method for decomplexifying nonlinear systems. "Local" means "near a given position." Perhaps Samuelson's (1948) *Foundations of Economic Analysis* is still the best reference on comparative dynamics, using local linearities to determine local stability in the neighborhood of a stationary or steady state. Linearization is such a powerful simplifying strategy that it has played a major role in mathematical economics and econometrics, where it facilitated progress so successfully that consideration of nonlinearity received much less attention except in the esoteric world of general equilibrium theory. Nonlinearity is much more widely understood today and progress in exploring nonlinear theory in all fields of science is advancing.

To summarize: complex structures are simplified by confining attention to relatively small numbers of variables and causal relationships, by using controlled experiments where possible, by constructing mathematical, numerical, or physical analogs, by identifying decomposable or reducible systems, by defining change in terms of discrete variables and/or discrete time, and by linearizing causal relationships.

8.4 Simplicity and complexity in macroeconomics

A modern economy is made up of tens or hundreds of millions of people and thousands—perhaps millions—of business firms, government agencies, and private organizations. Their economic activity involves millions of products and services, millions of corresponding prices and many thousands of banks and monetary instruments. Micro theory has necessarily been highly abstract and consequently not of much help in modeling whole economies at the microeconomic level. It was salience that led theorists to a higher level of aggregation.

One of the salient facts motivating macroeconomics is the prolonged expansion of production in Europe and the United States. John Maynard Keynes, who is best known for his macroeconomic theory of recessions and the use of monetary and fiscal policy to deal with them, was impressed by economic growth in the market economies. He estimated that between the years 1580 when Sir Francis Drake returned to England with the spoils of the Spanish treasure fleet and 1930 when Keynes' article *The Treatise on Money* was published, the average standard of living in Europe and the United States had increased about four-fold. He observed further that the Depression was a "temporary phase of maladjustment . . . and predicted that the standard of life one hundred years hence [that is, in 2030] would be between four and eight times as high as it was in 1930." Actually, real GDP per person in the United States since 1930 had already increased five-fold by 2003, so a standard well above that might be achieved by 2030.

Adam Smith (1776) had observed that the output of society depends on the productivity of its workers, on the causes of its improvement (in particular the division of work into specialized tasks), and on the accumulation of capital. Keynes' young colleague, Frank Ramsey, using an intertemporal optimizing model based on some of Keynes' ideas, published the first mathematical theory of economic growth and the accumulation of wealth. About the same time C.W. Cobb, a mathematician, and Paul H. Douglas, an economist, developed a method for measuring the relative contribution of a nation's capital and labor to its aggregate output. Some 20 years later, Robert Solow augmented the Cobb-Douglas method to estimate the contribution of productivity improvements in a paper aimed at understanding economic growth in terms of a mathematical model.[8] To do this, he abstracted from the short-run problems of unemployment, excess capacity, and the role of government policy, using instead an approach that assumed, as Ramsey had, that the economy worked in a competitive equilibrium each and every period. Although he emphasized that such an assumption could be justified only as an approximate condition, he showed that such a model explains how the economy grows and why it tends to grow along a *balanced growth path* in which the aggregate capital/labor ratio remains approximately constant.

Subsequently, equilibrium growth theory was embraced by Robert Lucas[9] who articulated a vision, described in his book, *Models of Business Cycles*, of a decentralized market economy, all of whose economic "agents" perfectly understand themselves and the entire system, who take into account the causal implications of their actions over an infinite future, and who find a state of perfect coordination at every moment in time. To implement that vision at the macroeconomic level, the entire economy came to be represented, not by aggregate supply and demand relationships (that might in principle be derived from individual households and firms), but as if it were a single "representative agent" who plans production, consumption, and investment optimally for the entire future, making optimal adjustments in response to random "shocks" that temporarily perturb the underlying relationships in the economy, in this way remaining at all times in a competitive equilibrium in spite of the external disturbances coming from outside the economy. Empirical research following this approach was pioneered by Kydland and Prescott in a development known generally as the "real business cycle" or RBC theory. It has come to dominate many academic journals and texts. Important collections of studies based on it will be found in Barro and in Cooley and Prescott.[10]

Growth, however, was not the only salient fact that intrigued Keynes. As previously noted, he was optimistic about the future of the market economy but the drastic state of imbalance in the industrialized economies in the 1930s concerned Keynes deeply in spite of his belief that it was a temporary malady. At existing prices and wages there was a serious oversupply of labor or, equivalently, a serious deficiency in the demand for labor. In the United States it reached an unemployment rate of 24 percent in 1933. Even though employment increased after that, the problem remained: unemployment was still 14 percent of the labor supply when the United States entered World War II in December 1941—12 years after the stock market crash of 1929 ushered in the Great Depression. Nothing could have stood out more boldly or more urgently commanded an explanation. Here was salience indeed!

Keynes modified existing equilibrium theory in order to explain how such a situation might occur and persist, and how government policy could help eliminate it. His primary break with prevailing theory was to abandon the widely held assumption—in spite of overwhelming evidence to the contrary—that market prices always adjust to equate supply and demand *for all goods all the time*. Instead, he recognized the fact that prices and wages were "sticky" and especially slow to adjust downward in the presence of excess supply. And when inventories piled up excessively, businesspeople might reduce output instead of lowering prices. As a result, demand for labor might sometimes be insufficient to employ everyone who wanted to work at existing wages.

Keynes introduced a concept of demand—not defined for a single good—but for aggregates of goods: the total demand for consumer goods by households and the total demand for investment goods by firms. With the inclusion of interest the money market was seen to play a potential role, one not given much attention in the standard economic theories of the time. Finally, Keynes introduced government expenditure and taxation explicitly as exogenous variables influencing aggregate demand. This made it possible to incorporate the fiscal and monetary instruments as integral parts of the entire system that policy-makers could potentially influence.

Although his analytical derivations were static and focused on a persistent unemployment, excess capacity situation, Keynes had in mind a dynamic theory and fully intended to explain the tendency of the market economy to fluctuate due to the interactions between the monetary and real goods sectors. But in spite of its deficiencies, his partially developed framework was obviously relevant. A large body of work followed that was aimed at reducing these deficiencies, work that continues in the present.[11]

Keynes' ideas also inspired a large number of economists who gave more detailed and rigorous versions of ideas that were merely sketched in the *General Theory* (1935), implementing them in highly detailed econometric models using real world data, including Jan Tinbergen (1968) of the Netherlands and Lawrence Klein (1941) of the United States. Models of this kind are still being studied, for example, by Fair and Godley.[12] Highly detailed versions of them are currently used by the Council of Economic Advisors and the Federal Reserve.

In summary: modern macroeconomics can be divided into two contrasting ways of explaining and interpreting events at the macroeconomic level. The first one derives from an equilibrium view of economic change. The second derives from the out-of-equilibrium concept of economic change. The equilibrium models approximate average behavior in the market economies over extended periods of time fairly well and are useful for characterizing aggregate productivity, for roughly explaining average growth rates, and for indicating something about the "preferences" of society as a whole. The out-of-equilibrium approach can also explain economic growth and is necessary for understanding fluctuations in employment, capital utilization, and in the rate of growth. Moreover, because it incorporates the role of government and the monetary system variables, it is useful for describing the impact of fiscal and monetary policy on the private business and household sectors.

8.5 From simple macroeconomic theory to complex behavior

8.5.1 The analogic point of view

The thrust of the preceding discussion is the necessity of specifying structure at a level in the hierarchy of phenomena where relatively simple relationships can be formulated and understood in themselves and that can mimic salient behavior of the real world at that level. Newton's gravitational theory provides the archetype of this process, simple enough to be completely understood theoretically and empirically relevant enough to provide practical guidance for human action. The early development of macroeconomic theory was similarly motivated and constructed. It explains salient facts and provides at least some practical guidance.

The basic growth models explain the role of investment and improving productivity in economic growth.[13] Of course, the theoretical parameters themselves are not explained: why the fraction invested and the rate of productivity improvement are different from one country to another or from one historical era to another. But the measurement of these parametric differences suggests where to look for explanations in variations among institutions and cultural characteristics among countries and historical eras, in this comparative way pointing to possible policy implications. In particular, the optimal growth theory points to the importance of time preference in determining investment rates, a psychological variable from the microeconomic point of view, but a cultural attribute at the macro level that can actually be estimated, as shown in Day and Yang (2005), using the ingenious method explained by Cooley and Prescott (1995).

But this theory pays a heavy price for its insights concerning economic growth. It portrays the economy as a perfectly coordinated one, one that tends to grow at an exponential rate forever with no excess capacity and no unemployment. But the latter facts are the ones that dominated the Great Depression era. Moreover, they continue to concern policy-makers and the general public when they increase more than usual or even where there is *fear* that they might. To deal with these salient facts bears its own costs in terms of increased numbers of variables and the potential for more complex behavior, behavior that is more difficult to understand yet whose understanding is crucial if we are to understand why macroeconomic variables behave as they do and why fiscal and monetary policy issues cannot be avoided.

Progress can be made by using computer simulation techniques to study the detailed econometric equations. This kind of activity, however, does not lend itself to theoretical understanding using analytical methods. To do that requires returning to simplified versions of out-of-equilibrium macroeconomic processes or slightly more complicated versions of standard macroeconomic growth models. That was the strategy taken in Day (1981), Day and Shafer (1987), and more recently in Day and Pavlov (2004). It involves explicitly representing crucial nonlinearities and dynamic elements in basic macroeconomic theory, then using the methods of nonlinear dynamics to derive the properties of model solutions. This approach is analogic and can produce irregular (complex) behavior somewhat like real world data on the basis of very much simplified but relevant characteristics of actual economic structures.

This methodological discussion is not the place to go into mathematical details. These can be found elsewhere. What follows here is a brief description of two examples that illustrate how crucial sources of complexity in quite simple macroeconomic models lead to complex behavior.

8.5.2 *Equilibrium macroeconomic growth*

The Solow equilibrium growth model can be represented by the efficiency capital accumulation equation,

$$k_{t+1}^e = \theta(k_t^e)\frac{1}{(1+n)\,(1+b)}((1-\delta)k_t^e + j(k_t^e)), \tag{8.1}$$

where k_t^e is per worker capital stock measured in efficiency units, where n and b are, respectively, the rates of growth in the labor supply and productivity, and where $j(k_t^e)$ is the investment function.[14]

The production function in efficiency units is

$$q_t^e = (k_t^e)^\beta \tag{8.2}$$

where q_t^e is output in efficiency units. Solow assumed that investment is a constant fraction, φ, of output so $j(k_t^e) = \varphi(k_t^e)^\beta$. Given these assumptions, efficiency capital at time $t+1$ is a monotonically increasing function of capital at time t and is easily shown to converge to a unique positive fixpoint, $\tilde{k}^e$, a property that implies that output (and income) per worker converges to a path growing exponentially at the rate of growth of productivity. The United States does crudely follow such a path. Recent results, however, show that the modern era, 1929–2005, can be broken into at least four separate "growth eras," each of which is approximated by its own distinct growth path. This finding suggests that actual macroeconomic growth switches phase from time to time.[15]

The optimal equilibrium growth model is based on a utility function that exponentially discounts future consumption streams. It implies a concave, monotonically increasing investment function, $j^*(k_t^e)$, also, but one that depends on the time preference discount parameter. Like the Solow model, all trajectories of per capita output and capital must converge to exponential paths. Both imply the simple dynamics of monotonic, balanced growth.

Now imagine a society that exhibits wealth saturation, that is, a point at which any further accumulation is seen to be undesirable even to the point of allowing existing capital stock to deteriorate. Such behavior might not be entirely implausible if we are thinking of a generational time period where one generation might inherit so much capital that it would see no point in accumulating more, even if it meant that its heirs would be less wealthy than themselves.[16]

Capital would then decumulate. The return on investment by the next generation would increase, perhaps motivating an increase in investment. Thus, an overshoot of the steady state could occur so as to satisfy the conditions for the existence of chaotic trajectories of the efficiency capital-labor ratio, which would imply irregular output, investment, and capital accumulation from one generation to the next.

8.5.3 Out-of-equilibrium growth

As previously noted, equilibrium growth assumes that capital and labor are fully employed and that savings equals investment; in other words, that all components in the economy are in a perfectly coordinated state—even if the paths are chaotic. The out-of-equilibrium approach drops these assumptions. It can be illustrated with a dynamic aggregate demand and supply model that is designed to make direct comparison with the equilibrium approach possible (Day and Yang, 2008). Household, business, monetary, and government sectors are distinguished; consumption and investment demand are determined independently; investment depends on both output and the real interest rate; the real interest rate is a real money rate—not the marginal productivity of physical capital—and depends on output, the real money supply, and the rate of inflation; output is determined by demand. Government demand for public consumption and capital goods is represented exogenously.

The trick employed above converts the variables to efficiency units. It can be used to the same effect in the out-of-equilibrium theory if the following extreme properties are assumed: the money supply in efficiency units and the general price level grow (or decline) at a constant rate. The per capita exogenous government spending grows at the productivity rate of growth. By assuming that real income is equal to the real value of output, the demand-driven output generation equation is

$$q_{t+1}^e = a^i\,[(c^{ge} + j^{ge} + x^{ge}) + h(q_t^e)]. \qquad (8.3)$$

The first term on the right, a^i, is a non-negative constant "multiplier" that depends on the consumption demand parameters and the tax rate. The now single-humped, private investment function, $h(\cdot)$, is the resultant of a positive, direct income effect and a negative, *in*direct income effect that derives from the monetary sector. It increases at low levels of output at a declining rate, reaches a maximum, then declines and eventually reaches or converges to zero. Evidently, the type of nonlinearity that can lead to chaos is present—here in the demand-driven output generation equation. In this model the capital accumulation equation is

$$k^e_{t+1} = \frac{1}{(1+n)(1+b)}[(1-\delta)k^e_t + j^{g^e} + h(q^e_t)] \tag{8.4}$$

where q^e_t is determined not by k^e_t, but by equation (8.4) (with a lag). Its dynamics now depends on the nonlinear behavior of demand. Fluctuations, if they occur, are induced by the properties of the money demand function and the money supply. They can, in principle, occur even if the money supply grows at the constant rate determined by the population, productivity, and inflation rates of growth.

The out-of-equilibrium character of the model arises because of the distinction between the amount of capital accumulated and the amount actually utilized in production. If k^{eu}_t is the utilized capital/employed labor ratio in efficiency units, then actual national aggregate supply of output is also equal to national aggregate demand for output,

$$E_tB_tf(k^{eu}_t) = Q_t = N_tq_t, \tag{8.5}$$

where $f(k^{eu}_t)$ is the usual Cobb-Douglas form in efficiency units (8.2). This implies that employment,

$$E_t = N_tq_t/(B_tf(k^{eu}_t)), \tag{8.6}$$

depends on population, the utilized capital/labor ratio, and on the dynamics of demand.

The utilized capital/labor ratio, k^{eu}_t, is not given by the theory in the incomplete form presented here. In equilibrium it is determined by the equilibrium wage/capital rental ratio. Out-of-equilibrium it is determined by labor market supply and demand adjustments and product market price adjustments from which we abstract for simplicity. Given that ratio, utilized capital is

$$K^u_t = E_tk^{eu}_t.$$

Consequently, if L_t is the exogenously given labor supply, then the employment ratio is E_t/L_t and capacity utilization ratio is K_t^u/K_t or $E_t k_t^{eu}/(N_t k_t^e)$.

Our simplifying assumptions obscure the practical utility of the underlying model. The important potential policy instruments are: (1) government demand, $c_t^g + f_t^g$; (2) the tax rate, τ, which plays an implicit role in the definition of the "multiplier," a^i; and (3) the nominal money supply, m_t, which can influence private investment. The exploration of these effects would require a considerably more detailed description of the components of aggregate demand than presented here and would carry us beyond our present limited purpose.

8.6 Conclusions

I introduced my remarks by commenting on the roles of simplicity and complexity in science in order to stress the obvious fact that successful scientific inquiry must deal with manifold complexity by fashioning decomplexifying strategies. The discussion that followed was intended to emphasize the role that those strategies play in macroeconomic research. Relative simplicity is made possible by the construction of macro data that are not themselves observable. They are composed from observed micro data. The causal relationships among the resulting index numbers arise out of microeconomic activities but they must be identified at the macroeconomic level and cannot be derived directly from the micro. Where natural nonlinearities are incorporated explicitly in the causal relationships then, even in macroeconomic models so simple as to permit graphical illustration, complex behavior is potential.

A concluding admonition is in order. In general, the greater the simplification, the more crude the approximation. The more crude the approximation, the less complete is the understanding acquired. Scientific progress is therefore always a kind of dialectic trade-off between complexifying detail and decomplexifying method.

Notes

1. That is, whose behavior cannot be described as steadily growing, steadily shrinking or repeating a given pattern over and over.
2. Honoré Balzac, *The Rise and Fall of César Birotteau* (1837).
3. Day (2004).
4. Cyert and March (1992), Chamberlain (1962).
5. Leontief (1953), Jorgenson (1996), Day (2004).
6. Fair (2004), Godley, Izurieta and Zegza (2004), Forrester (1972).
7. Deep philosophical ideas are involved here. For an interesting discussion of some of them, see Velupillai (2005).
8. Ramsey (1928), Cobb and Douglas (1928), Solow (1956, 1957).
9. Lucas (1987).
10. Kydland and Prescott (1982), Barro (1989), Cooley and Prescott (1995).
11. The importance of lags in the income and expenditure adjustments was explored by

Lundberg (1937) and Robinson (1958), work that inspired an analysis by Metzler (1941) of inventory adjustments in a macroeconomic model of aggregate business fluctuations. Moreover, out-of-equilibrium growth as an explicitly dynamic process was investigated by Kaldor (1986), Kaleki ([1933] 1971), Goodwin (1993), and subsequently Flaschel, Franke, and Semmler (2003) and Chiarella, Flaschel, and Franke (2005).

12. Fair (2004). Godley's model has not yet been published but has been described in a series of policy-oriented studies by the Levy Institute of Bard College. See, for example, Godley, Izurieta, and Zegza (2004). The current use of macroeconomic models in economic policy was described in oral remarks by Ben Bernanke at the conference in honor of Paul Samuelson, spring 2005.
13. That is, the models of Cobb and Douglas (1928), Solow (1956, 1957), Swan (1956), Lucas (1987), Kydland and Prescott (1982).
14. Efficiency variables are obtained by dividing per capita variables by the productivity variable, $B_t = (1 + b)^t B_0$. Thus, $k_t^e - k_t/B_t$ where $k_t = K_t/E_t$, where K_t is aggregate social (private + public) capital stock and E_t aggregate employment. Both K_t and E_t are assumed to be their full employment values.
15. Day and Yang (2004).
16. This kind of behavior would imply a different preference ordering of possible trajectories than the one usually assumed in the optimal growth literature. Or it might involve an inability to forecast accurately future rates of return on investment, which might diminish more than anticipated on the basis of current and past experience, as shown in Day and Dawid (2007).

References

Barro, R. (ed.) (1989), *Modern Business Cycle Theory*, Cambridge, MA: Harvard University Press.

Chamberlain, Neil W. (1962), *The Firm: Microeconomic Planning and Action*, New York: McGraw-Hill Book Company, Inc.

Chiarella, C., P. Flaschel, and R. Franke (2005), *Foundations for a Disequilibrium Theory of the Business Cycle*, Cambridge, UK: Cambridge University Press.

Cobb, C.W. and P.H. Douglas (1928), "A Theory of Production," *American Economic Review*, **18**(Supplement), 139–65.

Cooley, T.F. and E.C. Prescott (1995), "Economic Growth and Business Cycles," in T.F. Cooley (ed.), *Frontiers of Business Cycle Research*, Princeton: Princeton University Press, Ch. 1.

Cyert, R. and J. March (1992), *A Behavioral Theory of the Firm*, 2nd edn, Oxford: Blackwell Publishers.

Day, R.H. (1981), "Emergence of Chaos from Neoclassical Growth," *Geographical Analysis*, **13**(4), 315–27.

Day, R.H. (2004), *The Divergent Dynamics of Economic Growth: Studies in Adaptive Economizing, Technological Change and Economic Development*, Cambridge, UK: Cambridge University Press.

Day, R.H. and H. Dawid (2007), "Sustainable Standards of Living in Economic Growth," *Journal of Economic Dynamics and Control*, **31**, 2374–97.

Day, R.H. and O. Pavlov (2004), "Computing Economic Chaos," *Computational Economics* **23**(4), 289–301.

Day, R.H. and W. Shafer (1987), "Ergodic Fluctuations in Deterministic Economic Models," in A. Medio (ed.), *Advances in Dynamic Economics* (Special issue of the *Journal of Economic Behavior and Organization*) **8**(3), 339–62.

Day, R.H. and C. Yang (2004), "A Dynamic Analysis of the Bush Fiscal Policy," in L.J.S. Alen, B. Aulbach, S. Elaydi, and R. Sacker (eds), *Difference Equations and Discrete Dynamical Systems*, New Jersey: World Scientific.

Day, R.H. and C. Yang (2005), "Economic Growth and Revealed Social Preference," in *Studies in Nonlinear Dynamics and Econometrics*, Berkeley, CA: Berkeley Electronic Press.

Day, R.H. and C. Yang (2008), "An Encompassing Theory of Macroeconomic Growth and Fluctuation," P. Flaschel and M. Landesmann (eds), *Mathematical Economics and the Dynamics of Capitalism: Goodwin's Legacy Continued*, Routledge Frontiers of Political Economy, London: Routledge.

Fair, R.C. (2004), *Estimating How the Macro Economy Works*, Cambridge, MA: Harvard University Press.

Flaschel, P., R. Franke, and W. Semmler (2003), *Dynamic Macroeconomics*, Cambridge, UK: Cambridge University Press.

Forrester, J.W. (1972), *World Dynamics*, Cambridge, MA: The MIT Press.

Godley, W., A. Izurieta, and G. Zezza (2004), "Prospects and Policies for the U.S. Economy," in *Strategic Analysis*, The Levy Institute of Bard College, Cambridge Endowment for Research in Finance.

Goodwin, R. (1993), "A Marx-Keynes-Schumpeter Model of Economic Growth and Fluctuations," in R. Day and P. Chen (eds), *Nonlinear Dynamics and Evolutionary Economics*, Oxford: Oxford University Press.

Jorgenson, D.W. (1996), *Capital Theory and Investment Behavior*, Cambridge, MA: The MIT Press.

Kaldor, N. (1986), *Nonequilibrium Economics*, New Haven, CT: Yale University Press.

Kaleki, M. [1933] (1971), "Outline of a Theory of the Business Cycle," in *Selected Essays on the Dynamics of the Capitalist Economy*, Cambridge, UK: Cambridge University Press.

Klein, L. (1941), *Economic Fluctuations in the United States, 1921–1941*, Cowles Commission for Research in Economics, New York: John Wiley & Sons.

Kydland, F. and E.C. Prescott (1982), "Time to Build and Aggregate Fluctuations," *Econometrica*, **50**(6), 1345–70.

Leontief, W. (1953), "Dynamic Analysis," in W. Leontief (ed.), *Studies in the Structure of the American Economy*, New York: Oxford University Press.

Lucas, R.E., Jr. (1987), *Models of Business Cycles, Structural Change and Economic Dynamics*, Oxford: Basil Blackwell, Ltd.

Lundberg, E. (1937), *Studies in the Theory of Economic Expansion*, Stockholm Economic Studies 6, London: P.S. King & Son.

Metzler, L. (1941), "The Nature and Stability of Inventory Cycles," *Review of Economic Studies* **23**(1), 101–29.

Ramsey, F. (1928), "Optimal Growth," *Economic Journal*, **38**, 543–59.

Robinson, E.A.G. (1958), *The Structure of Competitive Industry*, Chicago: University of Chicago.

Samuelson, P.A. (1948), *Foundations of Economic Analysis*, New York: Harvard University Press.

Smith, A. (1776), *An Inquiry into the Nature and Causes of the Wealth of Nations*, London: Methuen & Co.

Solow, R. (1956), "A Contribution to the Theory of Economic Growth," *Quarterly Journal of Economics*, **70**, 65–94.

Solow, R. (1957), "Technical Progress and Productivity Change," *Review of Economics and Statistics*, **39**, 312–20.

Swan, T.W. (1956), "Economic Growth and Capital Accumulation," *Economic Record*, **32**, 334–61.

Tinbergen, J. (1968), *Statistical Testing of Business Cycles*, New York: Agathon Press.

Velupillai, K. (ed.), (2005), *Computability, Complexity and Constructivity in Economic Analysis*, Oxford: Blackwell Publishers.

PART IV

ECONOPHYSICS AND FINANCIAL MARKETS

9. Applications of statistical physics in finance and economics

*Thomas Lux**

9.1 Introduction

"The economy" easily comes to one's mind when looking for examples of a "complex system with a large ensemble of interacting units". The layperson usually feels that terms like "out-of-equilibrium dynamics", "critical states" and "self-organization" might have a natural appeal as categories describing interactions in single markets and the economy as a whole. When dealing with the economy's most opalescent part, the financial sphere with its bubbles and crashes, "life at the edge of chaos" and "self-organized criticality" equally easily enter the headlines of the popular press. However, this proximity of the keywords of complexity theory to our everyday perception of the economy is in contrast to the relatively slow and reluctant adaptation of the ideas and tools of complexity theory in economics. While there has been a steady increase of interest in this topic from various subsets of the community of academic economists, it seems that the physicists' wave of recent research on financial markets and other economic areas has acted as an obstetrician for the wider interest in complexity theory among economists.

Physicists entered the scene around 1995 with the ingenious invention of the provocative brand name of *econophysics* for their endeavors in this area. Both the empirical methodology and the principles of theoretical modeling of this group were in stark contrast to the mainstream approach in economics so that broad groups of academic economists were initially quite unappreciative of this new current. While the sheer ignorance of mainstream economics by practically all econophysicists already stirred the blood of many mainstream economists, the fact that they seemed to have easy access to the popular science press and as representatives of a "hard science" were often taken more seriously by the public than traditional economists, contributed to increased blood pressure among their opponents.[1] At the other end of the spectrum, the adaptation of statistical physics methods has been welcomed by economists critical of some aspects of the standard paradigm. Econophysics, in fact, had a close proximity to attempts at allowing for heterogeneous interacting agents in economic models. It is in this strongly increasing segment of academic economics where complexity theory and econophysics have made the biggest impact.

In the following I will review the econophysics contribution to various areas of economics/finance and compare it with the prevailing traditional economics approach.

9.2 Power laws in financial markets: phenomenology and explanations

9.2.1 Financial power laws: fat tails and volatility clustering as scaling laws

Scaling laws or power laws (that is, hyperbolic distributional characteristics of some measurements) are the most sought imprint of complex system behavior in nature and society. Finance luckily offers a number of robust scaling laws that are well accepted among empirical researchers. The most pervasive finding in this area is that of a ubiquitous power-law behavior of large price changes that had been confirmed for practically all types of financial data and markets. In applied research, the quantity one typically investigates is relative price changes or returns: $r_t = (p_t - p_{t-1})/p_{t-1}$ (p_t denoting the price at time t). For daily data, the range of variability of r_t is roughly between -0.2 and $+0.2$, which allows replacement of r_t by log-differences (called continuously compounded returns) $r_t \cong \ln(p_t) - \ln(p_{t-1})$, which for high-frequency data would practically obey the same statistical laws. Statistical analysis of daily returns offers overwhelming evidence for a hyperbolic behavior of the tails:

$$Pr(|r_t| > x) \sim x^{-\alpha}. \tag{9.1}$$

Figure 9.1 illustrates this finding with a selection of stock indices and foreign exchange rates. As one can see the linearity in a log-log plot imposed by equation (9.1) is a good approximation for a large fraction of both the most extreme positive and negative observations. Obviously, the power law of large returns is of utmost importance not only for researchers in complex system theory, but also for anyone investing in financial assets: equation (9.1) allows a probabilistic assessment of the chances of catastrophic losses as well as the chances for similarly large gains and, therefore, is extremely useful in such mundane occupations like risk management of portfolios. To be more precise, our knowledge concerning the scaling law equation (9.1) can be concretized as follows:

- The overall distribution of returns looks nicely bell-shaped and symmetric. It has, however, more probability mass in the center and the extreme regions (tails) than the benchmark bell-shaped Normal distribution.

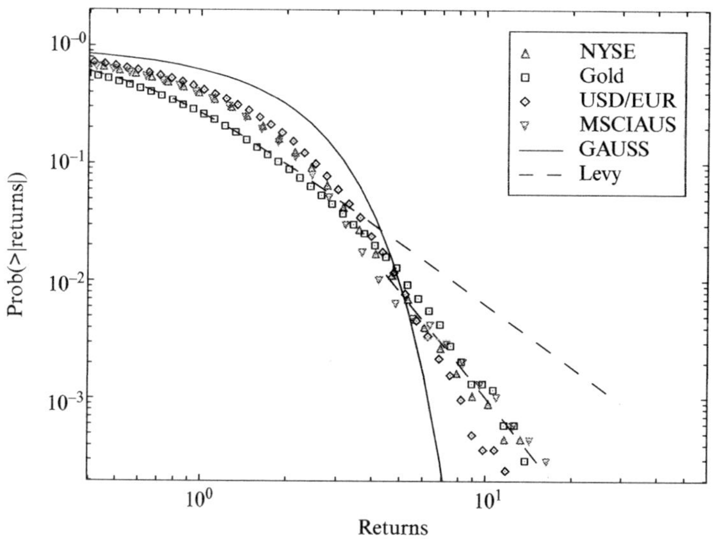

Note: Log-log plot of the complement of the cumulative distribution of daily returns from a sample of representative financial markets: the NYSE composite index, the MSCI index of the Australian stock market, the price of gold and the USD against euro exchange rate (pre-1999 the DEM was used instead of the euro). All series cover the period 1979 to 2004. Despite some variations between these series, their tail regions are all close to a scaling law with index $\alpha \approx 3$ (demarcated by the broken line). This universal behavior of financial returns is intermediate between the exponential decline of the Normal distribution and the more pronounced tail fatness of members of the Levy stable family. Our example of the latter family of distributions has $\alpha = 1.7$, a value characteristically obtained when estimating the parameters of these distributions for financial data.

Source: Datastream.

Figure 9.1 The scaling law of large returns

- The tails have a hardly disputable hyperbolic shape starting from about the 20 to 10 percent quantiles at both ends.
- The left- and right-hand tails have a power-law decline with about the same decay factor α (differences are mostly not statistically significant).
- For different assets, estimated scaling parameters hover within a relatively narrow range around $\alpha = 3$. Figure 9.1 exhibits this benchmark of a "cubic law" of large returns together with a sample of empirical data scattered around it.

The literature on this *scaling law* is enormous. It starts with Mandelbrot's (1963) and Fama's (1963) observation of leptokurtosis in cotton futures and their proposal of the Levy distributions as a statistical model for asset returns (implying a power-law tail with exponent $\alpha < 2$). For 30 years, the empirical literature in finance has discussed evidence in favor and against this model. A certain clarification has been achieved (in the view of most scientists involved in this literature) by moving from parametric distributions to a semi-parametric analysis of the tail region. Pertinent studies (for example, Jansen and de Vries, 1991; Lux, 1996) have led to a rejection of the stable distribution model demonstrating that α is typically significantly above 2. While this controversy was going to be settled in the empirical finance literature, the emergent econophysics approach had repeated the 30-year development in economics within a shorter time interval. Both an early paper by Mantegna (1991) and one of the first widely acknowledged econophysics papers by Mantegna and Stanley (1995) have advocated the Levy distribution, but subsequent work by the same group pointed out "the universal cubic law" of asset returns (Gopikrishnan et al., 1998).

The finding of a power law according to equation (9.1) is remarkable as it identifies a truly *universal* property within the social universe. Note also that in contrast to many other power laws claimed in social sciences and economics (cf. Cioffi, 2008, for an overview), the statistical basis of this law compares favorably to those of similar universal constants in the natural sciences: financial markets provide us with huge amounts of data at all frequencies and the power-law scaling has been confirmed over space and time without any apparent exception.

The power law in the vicinity of $\alpha = 3$ to 4 is also remarkable since it implies a kind of universal pre-asymptotic behavior of financial data at certain frequencies. In order to see this, note that according to the central limit law, random variates with $\alpha > 2$ fall into the domain of attraction of the Normal distribution, while random variates with $\alpha < 2$ would have the Levy stable distributions as their attractors. Under aggregation, returns with their leptokurtotic shape at daily horizons should, therefore, converge to a standard Gaussian. Aggregation of returns generates returns over longer time horizons (weekly, monthly), which, in fact, appear to be the closer to the Normal the higher the level of aggregation (time horizon). On the other hand, our benchmark daily returns can be conceived as aggregates of intra-daily returns. Since the tail behavior should be conserved under aggregation, the scaling laws at the daily horizon should also apply to intra-daily returns, which is nicely confirmed by available high-frequency data.

The power law for large returns has as its twin a similarly universal feature, which also seems to characterize all available data sets without exception: hyperbolic decay of the auto-covariance of any measure of *volatility* of returns. The simplest such measures are *absolute* or *squared* returns, which preserve the extent of fluctuations but disregard their direction. Taking absolute returns as an example, this second pervasive power law can be characterized by

$$Cov(|r_t|, |r_{t-\Delta t}|) \sim \Delta t^{-\gamma}. \tag{9.2}$$

The estimated values of γ have received less publicity than those of α, but reported statistics also show remarkable uniformity across time series with $\gamma \cong 0.3$ being a rather typical finding. It is worthwhile pointing out that equation (9.2) implies very strong correlation of volatility over time. Hence, expected fluctuations of market prices in the next periods would be the higher the more volatile today's market is. Visually, one observes typical switches between tranquil and more turbulent episodes in the data ("volatility clustering"). This dependency can be exploited for prediction of the future development of volatility, which would also be important information for risk and portfolio management. Again, the literature on this topic is huge. For quite some time, the *long-term dependency* inherent in power-law decline of equation (9.2) had not been properly taken into account. Available models in financial econometrics like the legacy of GARCH models (Engle, 1983; Bollerslev, 1986) have rather modeled the volatility dynamics as a stochastic process with exponential decay of the autocovariance of absolute (or squared) returns. Long-term dependence has been demonstrated first by Ding, Engle and Granger (1993) in the economics literature and, independently, by Liu et al. (1997) and Vandewalle and Ausloos (1997) in contributions in physics journals. The measurement of long-range dependence in the econophysics publications is mostly based on estimation of the Hurst exponent from Mandelbrot's R/S analysis or the refined detrended fluctuation analysis of Peng et al. (1994). The financial engineering literature has taken long-term dependence into account by moving from the original GARCH to FIGARCH and long-memory stochastic volatility models (Breidt, Crato and de Lima, 1998), which allow for hyperbolically decaying autocorrelations.

Besides the two above universal features, the literature has also pointed out additional power-law features of financial data. From the wealth of statistical analyses it seems that long-range dependence of *trading volume* is as universal as long-term dependency in volatility (Lobato and Velasco, 2000). Although exponents do not appear to be entirely identical, it is likely that the generating mechanism for both should be related (since trading volume is the ultimate source of price changes and volatility).

Additional power-laws have been found for high-frequency data from the US stock market (Gopikrishnan et al., 2001):

1. The *unconditional* distribution of volume in this data is found to follow a scaling law with exponent ~ 1.5.
2. The number of trades per time unit has been claimed to follow a power law with index ~ 3.4.

9.2.2 Possible explanations of financial power laws

Gabaix et al. (2003) have offered a theoretical framework in which the above findings are combined with the additional observation of a Zipf's law for the size distribution of mutual funds (that is, power law with index ~ 1) and a square root relationship between transaction volume (V) and price changes (Δp): $\Delta p \sim V^{0.5}$. In this theory the power law of price changes is derived from a simple scaling arithmetic: combining the scaling of portfolios of big investors (mutual funds) with the square root price impact function and the distribution of trading volume in US data, one obtains a cubic power law for returns. Although their model adds some behavioral considerations for portfolio changes of funds, in the end the unexplained Zipf's law is at the origin of all other power laws. Both the empirical evidence for some of the new power laws and the power law arithmetic itself are subject to a controversial discussion in recent econophysics literature (for example, Farmer and Lillo, 2004). In particular, it seems questionable whether the power law with exponent 1.5 for volume is universal (it has not been confirmed in other data; cf. Farmer and Lillo, 2004; Eisler and Kertész, 2005) and whether the above linkage of power laws from the size distribution of investors to volume and returns is admissible for processes with long-term dependence à la equation (9.2).

It is worthwhile emphasizing that the power laws in the financial area would, in this theory, be due to other power laws characterizing the size distribution of investors. The latter would probably have to be explained by a more complete theory of the economy along with the distribution of firm sizes and other macroeconomic characteristics. This somewhat subordinate role of the financial market in Gabaix et al. (2003) is certainly at odds with perceptions of "criticality" and "phase transitions" displayed in this market. The derivative explanation is also in contrast to what economists call the "disconnect paradox", that is, the observation that share markets and foreign exchange markets seem to develop a life of their own and at times appear entirely disconnected from their underlying economic fundamentals. Aoki and Yoshikawa (2007, Ch. 10) point out that the power-law behavior of financial returns is not shared by macroeconomic data that are rather characterized by exponentially distributed increments. They argue that the wedge between the real economy and financial markets stems from the higher level of activity of the latter. They demonstrate that, when modeling the dynamics of economic quantities as truncated Levy fights, different limiting distributions can emerge depending on the frequency of elementary events. Beyond a certain threshold, the limiting distribution switches from exponential to power law. The conjecture, then, is that this dependency on the number of contributing random events is responsible for the difference between exponential increments of macroeconomic data and power-law tails in financial markets. From an economic perspective the excess of relevant micro events in the financial sphere would be due to the decoupling from the real sector and the autonomous speculative activity in share and foreign exchange markets.

Most models proposed in the behaviorally orientated econophysics literature attempt to model this speculative interaction via simple models that are designed along certain prototypical behavioral types found in financial markets. Behavioral models of speculative markets have been among the first publications inspired by statistical physics. However, contrary to some claims from the physics community, physicists have not been the first and foremost in simulating markets. Earlier examples in the economics literature include Stigler (1964) and Kim and Markowitz (1989). The earliest econophysics example is Takayasu et al. (1992) who in a continuous double auction let agents' bid and ask prices change according to given rules and studied the statistical properties of the resulting price process. A similar approach has been pursued by Sato and Takayasu (1998) and Bak, Paczuski and Shubik (1997). Independently, Levy, Levy and Solomon (1994, 1995, 2000) have developed a multi-agent model inspired by statistical physics, which, at first view, looks more conventional than the previous ones: agents possess a well-defined utility function, which they attempt to maximize by choosing an appropriate portfolio of stocks and bonds. They adopt a particular expectation formation scheme (expected future returns are assumed to be identical to the mean value of past returns over a certain time horizon), and impose short-selling and credit constraints as well as idiosyncratic stochastic shocks to individuals' demand for shares. Under these conditions, the market switches between periodic booms and crashes whose frequency depends on agents' time horizons. Although this model and its extensions produce spectacular price paths, their statistical properties are not really in line with the empirical findings outlined above, nor are those of the other early models (cf. Zschischang and Lux, 2001). Somewhat ironically, these early econophysics papers on financial market dynamics have been, in fact, similarly ignorant of the stylized facts (that is, the scaling of equations (9.1) and (9.2)) like most of the traditional finance literature.

The second wave of models was more directly influenced by the empirical literature and had the declared aim of providing candidate explanations for the observed scaling laws. Mostly, they performed simulations of "artificial" financial markets with agents obeying a set of plausible behavioral rules and demonstrated that pseudo-empirical analysis of the generated time series yields results close to empirical findings. To our knowledge, the model by Lux and Marchesi (1999, 2000) has been the first that generated both the (approximate) cubic law of large returns and temporal dependence of volatility (with realistic estimated decay parameters) as emergent properties of their market model. This model had its roots in earlier attempts at introducing heterogeneity into stochastic models of speculative markets. It had drawn some of its inspiration from Kirman's (1993) model of information transmission among ants, which had already been used as a model of interpersonal influences in a foreign exchange market in Kirman (1991). While Kirman's model had been based on pair-wise interaction, Lux and Marchesi had a mean-field approach in which an agent's opinion was influenced by the average opinion of all other traders. Using statistical physics methodology, it could be shown that a simple version of this model was capable of generating bubbles with over- and undervaluation of an asset as a reflection of the emergence of a majority opinion among the pool of traders. Similarly, periodic oscillations and crashes could be explained by the breakdown of such majorities and the change of "market sentiment" (Lux, 1995). A detailed analysis of second moments can be found in Lux (1997) where the explanatory power of stochastic multi-agent models for time-variation of volatility has been pointed out (Ramsey, 1996, also emphasizes the applicability of statistical physics methods for deriving macroscopic laws for second moments from microscopic behavioral assumptions).

The group dynamics of these early interaction models have been enriched in the simulation studies by Lux and Marchesi (1999, 2000) and Chen, Lux and Marchesi (2001) by allowing agents to switch between a chartist and fundamentalist strategy in response to differences in profitability of both strategies. Interpersonal influences enter via chartists' attempts to trace out information from both ongoing price changes as well as the observed "mood" of other traders. Assuming that the market is continuously hit by news on fundamental factors, one could investigate how far price changes would reflect incoming information (the traditional view of the efficient market paradigm) or would be disconnected from fundamentals. The answer to this question turned out to have two different aspects: on the one hand, the speculative market on average kept close track of the development of the fundamentals. All new information was incorporated into prices relatively quickly as otherwise fundamentalist traders would have accepted high bets on reversals towards the fundamental value. On the other hand, however, upon closer inspection, the output (price changes) differed quite significantly from the input (fundamental information) in that price changes were always characterized by the scaling laws of equations (9.1) and (9.2) even if the fundamental news were modeled as a white noise process without these features. Hence, the market was never entirely decoupled from the real sphere (the information), but in processing this information it developed the ubiquitous scaling laws as *emergent properties* of the macroscopic market statistics from the distributed activity of its independent subunits.

This result could also be explained to some extent via an analysis of approximate differential equations for the mean value dynamics of state variables derived from the mean-field approach (Lux, 1998; Lux and Marchesi, 2000). In particular, one finds that, in a steady state, the composition of the population is *indeterminate*. The reason is that, in a stationary environment, the price has to equal its fundamental value and no price changes are expected by agents. In such a situation, neither chartists nor fundamentalists would have an advantage over the other group as neither mispricing of the asset nor any discernible price trend prevails. In the vicinity of such a steady state, movements between groups would, then, only be governed by stochastic factors that would lead to a *random walk in strategy space*. However, in this model (and in many related models), the composition of the population determines stability or instability of the steady state. Quite plausibly (and in line with a large body of literature in behavioral finance), a dominance of chartists with their reinforcement of price changes will be destabilizing. Via bifurcation analysis one can identify a threshold value for the number of chartists at which the system becomes unstable. The random population dynamics will lead to excursions into the unstable region from time to time, which leads to an onset of severe fluctuations. The ensuing deviations of prices from the fundamental value, however, will lead to profit differentials in favor of the fundamentalist traders so that their number increases and the market moves back to the stable subset of the strategy space.

As can be seen from Figure 9.2, the joint dynamics of the population composition and the market price has a close resemblance to empirical records. With the above mechanism of intermittent switching between stability and (temporal) instability the model does not only exhibit interesting *emergent properties*, but it also can be characterized by another key term of complexity theory: *criticality*. Via its stochastic component, the system approaches a critical state where it temporally loses stability and the ensuing out-of-equilibrium dynamics give rise to stabilizing forces. One might note that "self-organizing criticality" would not be an appropriate characterization as the model does not have any systematic tendency towards the critical state. The trigger here is a purely stochastic dynamics without any preferred direction.

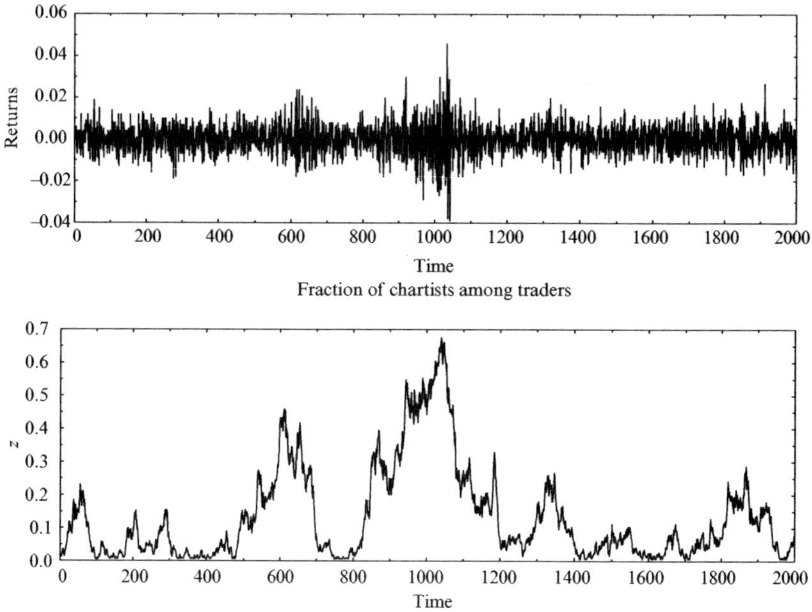

Note: The upper panel exhibits returns (relative price changes between unit time intervals), the lower panel shows the simultaneous changes of the fraction of chartists (z) within the population. Note that the remaining part of the population follows a fundamentalist strategy. As can be seen a higher fraction of chartists leads to an increase in the volatility of price changes.

Figure 9.2 A snapshot of the evolution of prices and the composition of the pool of traders in the microscopic market model proposed by Lux and Marchesi (1999)

Lux and Marchesi argue that, irrespective of the details of the model, indeterminateness of the population composition might be a rather general phenomenon in a broad range of related models (because of the absence of profitability of *any* trading strategy in *any* steady state). Together with dependency of stability on the population composition, the intermittent dynamics outlined above should, therefore, prevail in a broad class of microscopic interaction models. Support for this argument is offered by Lux and Schornstein (2005) who investigate a multi-agent model with a very different structure. Adopting the seminal Kareken and Wallace (1981) approach to exchange rate determination, they consider a foreign exchange market embedded into a general equilibrium model with two countries and overlapping generations of agents. In this setting, agents have to decide simultaneously on their consumption and savings together with the composition of their portfolio (domestic vs. foreign assets). Following Arifovic (1996), agents are assumed to be endowed with artificial intelligence (genetic algorithms), which leads to an evolutionary learning dynamics in which agents try to improve their consumption and investment choices over time. This setting also features a crucial indeterminacy of strategies: in a steady state, the exchange rate remains constant so that holdings of domestic and foreign assets would earn the same return (assuming that returns are only due to price changes). Hence, the portfolio composition would be irrelevant as long as exchange rates do not change (in steady state) and any configuration of the genetic algorithm for the portfolio part would have the same pay-off. However, out-of-equilibrium different portfolio weights might well lead to different performance as an agent might profit or lose from exchange rate movements depending on the fraction of foreign or domestic assets in his or her portfolio. The resulting dynamics again shares the scaling laws of empirical data. Similarly, Giardina and Bouchaud (2003) allow for more general strategies than Lux and Marchesi (1999) but also found a random walk in strategy space to be at the heart of emergent realistic properties.

A related branch of models with critical behavior has been launched by Cont and Bouchaud (2000). Their set-up also focuses on interaction of agents. However, they adapt the framework of percolation models in which agents are situated on a lattice with periodic boundary conditions. In percolation models, each site of a lattice might initially be occupied (with a certain probability p) or empty (with probability $1-p$). Clusters are groups of occupied neighboring sites (various definitions of neighborhood could be applied). In Cont and Bouchaud, occupied sites are traders and trading decisions (buying or selling a fixed number of assets or remaining inactive) are synchronized within clusters. Whether a cluster buys or sells or does not trade at all is determined by random draws. Given the trading decisions of all agents, the market price is simply driven by the difference between overall demand and supply. Being modeled closely along the lines of applications of percolation models in statistical physics, it follows immediately that the distribution of returns (price changes) is connected to the scaling laws established for the cluster size distribution. Therefore, if the probability for connection of lattice sites, say q, is close to the so-called percolation threshold q_c (the critical value above which an infinite cluster will appear), the distribution will follow a power law. As detailed in Cont and Bouchaud, the power-law index for returns at the percolation threshold will be 1.5, some way apart from the "cubic law".

As shown in subsequent literature, finite-size effects and variations of parameters could generate alternative power laws, but a cubic law would emerge only under particular model designs (Stauffer and Penna, 1998). Autocorrelation of volatility is entirely absent in these models, but could be introduced by sluggish changes of cluster configurations over time (Stauffer, de Oliveira and Bernardes, 1999). If clusters dissolve or amalgamate after transactions, more realistic features could be obtained (Eguiluz and Zimmerman, 2000). As another interesting addition, Focardi, Cincotti and Marchesi (2002) consider latent connections that only become active in times of crises.

Alternative lattice types have been explored by Iori (2002) who considers an Ising-type model with interactions between nearest neighbors. This approach appears to generate more robust outcomes and seems not to suffer from the percolation models' essential need to fine-tune the parameter values at criticality for obtaining power laws. Another recent alternative is a cellular automaton model of percolation proposed by Bartolozzi and Thomas (2004). In this model each cell is occupied by one trader who might buy, sell or remain inactive at any time step. Traders influence their neighbors, become inactive or are activated spontaneously with certain probabilities. It is shown that time series from this model have realistic properties if the probability for natural influence among traders is sufficiently high. If traders are subjected to strong interpersonal influences, relatively large clusters of homogeneous trading activity will emerge and these clusters of agents will lead to clusters of volatility.

As long as no self-organizing principles are offered for the movements of the system towards the percolation threshold, the extreme sensitivity of percolation models with respect to parameter choices is certainly unsatisfactory. Sweeping these systems back and forth through a critical state is an interesting variation (explored by Stauffer and Sornette, 1999) that gets rid of the necessity for fine-tuning of parameters. In the context of a stock market model, Stauffer and Sornette are able to get a robust cubic power law for returns. However, the behavioral underpinnings for such sweeping dynamics remain to be elucidated.

9.3 Other applications in financial economics

The contributions of physicists to financial economics are voluminous. A great part of it is of a more applied nature and does not necessarily have any close relationship to the methodological view expressed in the manifesto of the Boston group of pioneers in this field:

> Statistical physicists have determined that physical systems which consist of a large number of interacting particles obey laws that are independent of the microscopic details. This progress was mainly due to the development of scaling theory. Since economic systems also consist of a large number of interacting units, it is plausible that scaling theory can be applied to economics. (Stanley et al., 1996a)

However, rather than investigating the underlying forces responsible for the universal scaling laws of financial markets, a relatively large part of the econophysics literature mainly adopts physics tools of analysis to more practical issues in finance. This line of research is the academic counterpart to the work of "quants" in the financial industry who mostly have a physics background and are occupied in large numbers for developing quantitative tools for forecasting, trading and risk management. The material published in the journal *Quantitative Finance* (launched in 2000) provides ample examples for this type of applied work. Similarly, some of the monographs and textbooks from the econophysics camp have a strong focus on applied quantitative work in financial engineering. A good example is the well-known monograph by Bouchaud and Potters (2000) whose list of contents covers an introduction to probability and the statistics of financial prices, portfolio optimization and pricing of futures and options. While the volume provides a very useful and skilled introduction to these subjects, it has only cursory references to a view of the market as a complex system of interacting subunits. Much of this literature, in fact, fits well into the mainstream of applied and empirical research in finance although one often finds a scolding of the carefully maintained "straw man" image of traditional finance. In particular, ignoring decades of work in dozens of finance journals, it is often claimed that "economists believe that the probability distribution of stock returns is a Gaussian", a claim that can easily be refuted by a random consultation of any of the learned journals of this field. In fact, while the (erroneous) juxtaposition of scaling (physics!) via Normality (economics!) might be interpreted as an exaggeration for marketing purposes, some of the early econophysics papers even gave the impression that what they attempted was a first quantitative analysis of financial time series ever. If this was, then, performed on a level of rigor way below established standards in economics (a revealing example is the analysis of supposed day-of-the-week effects in high-frequency returns in Zhang, 1999),[2] it clearly undermined the standing of econophysicists in the economics community.

However, among the (sometimes reinventive and sometimes original) contributions of physicists to empirical finance, portfolio theory and derivative pricing, a few strands of research stand out that certainly deserve a more detailed treatment. These include the intricate study of the microstructure of order book systems, new approaches to determining correlations among assets, the proposal of a new type of model for volatility dynamics (so-called multifractal models), and the much promoted attempts at forecasting financial downturns.

9.3.1 The dynamics of order books

The impact of the institutional details of market organization is the subject of market microstructure theory (O'Hara, 1995). According to whether traders from the demand and supply side are getting into direct contact with each other or whether trades are carried out by intermediaries (called market-makers or specialists) one distinguishes between order-driven and quote-driven markets. The latter system is characteristic of the traditional organization of the US equity markets in which trading has been organized by designated market-makers whose task it was and still is to ensure continuous market liquidity. This system is called quote-driven since the decisive information for traders is the quoted *bid* and *ask prices* at which the market-makers would accept incoming orders. In most European markets, these active market-makers did not exist and trading was rather organized in a continuous *double auction* in which all orders of individual traders are stored in the *order book*. In this system, traders could either post limit orders that would have to be carried out when a pre-specified limiting price is reached over time and are stored in the book until execution, or market orders that are carried out immediately. The order book, thus, covers a whole range of limit orders on both the demand and supply sides with a pertinent set of desired transaction volumes and pertinent prices. This information can be viewed as a complete characterization of the demand and supply schedules with the current transaction price and volume being determined at the intersection of both curves. Most exchanges provide detailed data records with all available information on the development of the book, that is, time-stamped limit and market orders with their volumes, limit bid and ask prices and cancellation or execution times. The recent literature contains a wealth of studies of order book dynamics, both empirical analyses of the abundant data sets of various exchanges, as well as numerical and theoretical studies of agents' behavior in such an institutional framework.

Empirical research has come up with some insights on the distributional properties of key statistics of the book. The distribution of incoming new limit orders had been found to obey a power law in the distance from the current best price in various studies. There is, however, disagreement on the coefficient of this scaling relationship: while Farmer and Zovko (2002) report numbers around 1.5 for a sample of 50 stocks traded at the London Stock Exchange, Bouchaud, Potters and Mézard (2002) find a common exponent of ~ 0.6 for three frequently traded stocks of Paris Bourse. The average volume in the queue of the order book was found to follow a gamma distribution with roughly identical parameters for both the bid and ask side. This hump-shaped distribution with a maximum at a certain distance from the current price can be explained by the fact that past fluctuations might have thinned out limit orders in the immediate vicinity of the mid-price while those somewhat further away had a higher survival probability.

A recurrent topic in empirical studies of both quote-driven and order-driven systems had been the shape of the price impact function: as has been reported above, Plerou, Gopikrishnan and Stanley (2003) found a square-root dependency on volume in NYSE data: $\Delta p \sim V^{0.5}$. Conditioning on *volume imbalance* (Ω), that is, the difference between demand and supply, Plerou, Gopikrishnan and Stanley (2003) found an interesting bifurcation: while the conditional density of Ω on its first absolute moment (Σ) was uni-modal for small Σ it developed into a bi-modal distribution for larger volume imbalances. They interpret this finding as indication of two different phases of the market dynamics: an *equilibrium phase* with minor fluctuations around the current price and an out-of-equilibrium phase in which a predominance of demand or supply leads to a change of the mid-price in one or the other direction. However, Matia and Yamasaki (2005) show that this feature appears quite naturally in simulation experiments if the distribution of volume follows a power law simply because large positive and negative realizations of Ω give rise to a bi-modal distribution. This feature can, therefore, be explained almost mechanically and need not be due to the alleged presence of critical phenomena. Matia and Yamasaki also criticize the sloppy use of the concept of a phase transition in Plerou, Gopikrishnan and Stanley's *Nature* paper (2003): While phase transitions in physics have an independent variable as the control parameter, here it is a moment of the order parameter itself.

The empirical work on order book dynamics is often accompanied by theoretical work or simulation studies trying to explain the observed regularities. Some of the earliest models in the econophysics literature already contained simple order book structures with limit orders being posted according to some simple stochastic rule. In Bak, Paczuski and Shubik (1997), bid and ask prices of individual agents change randomly over time with equal probabilities for upward and downward movements. If bid and ask prices cross each other, a trade between two agents will be induced. The two agents' bids and asks are subsequently cancelled. The agents are then reinjected into the market with randomly chosen new limit orders between the current market price and the maximum ask or minimum bid, respectively. Like in many early models this stochastic design of the market amounts to a process that has been studied before (it is isomorphic to a reaction-diffusion process in chemistry). For this process, the time variation of the price can be shown to follow a scaling law with Hurst exponent 1/4. Since this is clearly an unrealistic behavior, the authors expand their model by allowing for volatility feedback (the observed price change influencing the size of adjustment of bid and ask prices). In this case $H = 0.65$ is estimated for simulated time series, which would rather speak for long-term dependence in the price dynamics. Although it is plausible that the volatility feedback could lead to this outcome, this is also different from the well-known martingale behavior of financial markets with $H = 0.5$ (Bak, Paczuski and Shubik, 1997, quote some earlier econometric results that indeed found $H \approx 0.6$, but these are viewed as being due to biases of their estimation procedure nowadays).

A number of other papers have followed this avenue of analyzing simple stochastic interaction processes without too many behavioral assumptions: Tang and Tian (1999) provided analytical foundations for the numerical findings of Bak, Paczuski and Shubik (1997). Maslov (2000) seemed to have been the first to attempt to explain fat tails and volatility clustering from a very simple stochastic market model. His model is built around two essential parameters: in every instant a new trader appears in the market who with probability q places a limit order and with the complementary probability $1 - q$ trades at the current market price. New limit orders are chosen from a uniform distribution with a support on $[0, \Delta_m]$ above or below the price of the last transaction. Slanina (2001) provides theoretical support for a power-law decline of price changes in this model. The mechanics of volatility clustering in this set-up might be explained as follows: if prices change only very little, more and more new limit orders in the vicinity of the current mid-price built up, which leads to persistence of low levels of volatility. Similarly, if price movements have been more pronounced in the past, the stochastic mechanism for new limit orders generates a more dispersed distribution of entries in the book, which also leads to persistence of a high-volatility regime. Very similar models have been proposed by Smith et al. (2002) and Daniels et al. (2003) whose main message is that a concave price impact can emerge from such simple models without any behavioral assumptions.

What is the insight from this body of empirical research and theoretical models? First, the analysis of the huge data sets available from most stock markets might allow us to identify additional stylized facts. So far, however, evidence for robust features, applying to more than one market, appears sparse. It rather seems that some microstructural features do vary between markets such as, for example, the distribution of limit orders within the book. Second, the hope of simple interaction models is to explain stylized facts via the organization of the trading process. In a sense, this line of research is similar to earlier work in economics on markets with *zero-intelligence traders* (Gode and Sunder, 1993) and, in fact, physicists have often adopted this label for their pertinent research. However, the zero-intelligence literature in economics had a clear interest in the allocative efficiency of markets in the presence of agents without any understanding of the market mechanism. Such a criterion is absent in the above models: while one gets certain distributions of market statistics under certain assumptions on arrival probabilities of traders and the distribution of their limit orders, it is not clear how to compare different market designs. A clear benchmark both for the evaluation of the explanatory power of competing models as well as for normative conclusions to be drawn from their outcomes is entirely absent. As concerns explanatory power, most models feature some stylized facts. However, what would be a minimum set of statistical properties and how robust they would have to be with respect to slight variations of the distributional assumptions has not been specified in this literature. Any normative evaluation, for example with respect to excessive volatility caused by certain market mechanisms, is impossible simply because prices are not constrained at all by factors outside the pricing process. A recent paper by Chiarella and Iori (2002) has made some progress in this perspective by considering different trading strategies (chartist, fundamentalist) in an order book setting. They note that incorporation of these behavioral components is necessary in their model for generating realistic time series.

9.3.2 *Analysis of correlation matrices*

The study of cross-correlations between assets has attracted a lot of interest among physicists. This body of research has a strong resemblance to portfolio theory in classical finance. Consider the portfolio choice problem of an investor in an economy with an arbitrary number N of risky assets. One way to formulate this problem is to minimize the variance of the portfolio for a given required expected return $\bar{r}$. Solving this quadratic programming problem for all $\bar{r}$ leads to the well-known efficient frontier that depicts the trade-off the investor faces between the expected portfolio return and its riskiness (that is, the variance). A central but problematic ingredient in this exercise (the so-called Markowitz problem, Markowitz, 1952) is the $N \times N$ covariance matrix. Besides its sheer size (when including all assets of a developed economy or, as one should do in principle, all assets available around the world's financial markets), stability and accuracy of historical estimates of cross-asset correlations to be used in the Markowitz problem are problematic in applied work. Furthermore, the formulation of the problem assumes either quadratic utility functions (so that investors only care about the first and second moments) or Normally distributed returns (so that the first and second moments are sufficient statistics for the entire shape of the distribution). Of course, both variants are easily criticized: returns are decisively non-Normal at least at daily frequency and developments like value-at-risk are a clear indication of more complex objective functions than mean-variance optimization.

The econophysics literature has contributed to the literature at various ends: first, some papers took stock of theoretical results from random matrix theory. Random matrix theory allows us to establish bounds for the eigenvalues of a correlation matrix under the assumption that the matrix has random entries. As has been shown, only a few eigenvalues "survive" above the noise bands (Laloux et al., 1999). In a comprehensive study of the US stock market, Plerou et al. (2000) found that the deviating non-random eigenvalues were stable in time and that the largest eigenvalue corresponded to a common influence on all stocks (in line with the market portfolio of the capital asset pricing model). Various studies have proposed methods for identification of the non-random elements of the correlation matrix (Galluccio, 1998; Laloux et al., 1999; Noh, 2000). It can easily be imagined that efficient frontiers from the original correlation matrix might differ strongly from those generated from a correlation matrix that has been cleaned by eliminating the eigenvalues within the noise band. Quite plausibly, the incorporation of arguably unreliable correlations may lead to an illusory high efficient frontier. According to the underlying argument, standard covariance matrix estimates might then vastly overstate the chances of diversification so that better performance could be expected from using cleaned-up matrices. An interesting recent contribution uses random matrix theory for complexity reduction in large multivariate GARCH models (Rosenow, 2008). As demonstrated in this paper, determination of the small number of significant components allows us to easily estimate multivariate models with hundreds of stocks and to forecast portfolio volatility on the base of these estimates.

A closely related branch of empirical studies attempts to extract information on hierarchical components in the correlation structure of an ensemble of stocks. This line of research was pioneered by Mantegna (1999) who used an algorithm known as *minimum spanning tree* to visualize the correlation structures between stocks in a connected tree. Alternative methods for cluster identification have been proposed by Kullmann, Kertész and Kaski (2002) and Onnela et al. (2003). A visualization is provided in Figure 9.3 adopted from Onnela et al. From an economics point of view these approaches are germaine to so-called *factor models* that incorporate common risk factors (for example, sector-specific or country-specific ones) into asset pricing models (Chen, Roll and Ross, 1986). The clustering algorithms could, in principle, provide valuable inputs for the implementation of such factor models. Unfortunately, the major weakness of available research in this area is that it has confined itself to illustrating the application of a particular methodology. However, it had hardly ever tried a rigorous comparison of refined methods of portfolio optimization or asset pricing based on random matrix theory or clustering algorithms (a remarkable exception is the mentioned contribution by Rosenow, 2008). There seems to be some cultural difference between the camps of

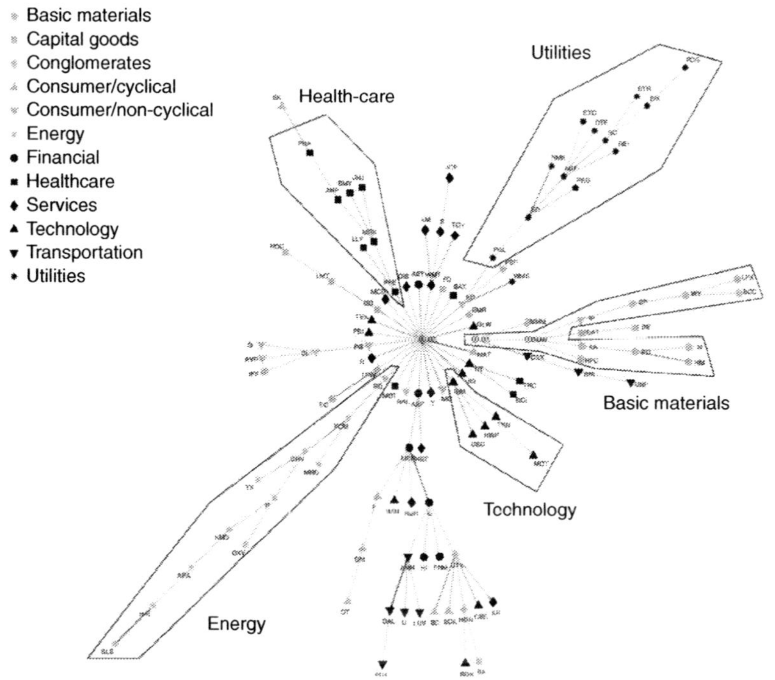

Note: This taxonomy of a sample of 116 stocks has been obtained by constructing a so-called minimum spanning tree for the mean correlation coefficients of stock returns over a certain time window (1996 to 1999 in the present case).

Source: By courtesy of J.-P. Onnela. Reprinted with permission from Onnela et al. (2003), ©2003 by the American Physical Society.

Figure 9.3 The hierarchical structure of the major US stocks as indicated by a cluster identification algorithm

economists/statisticians and physicists that makes the former insist on rigorous statistical tests while the latter inexplicably shy away from such evaluations of their proposed theories and methods.

9.3.3 Forecasting volatility: the multifractal model

There is, however, one area of application of statistical physics methods, in which researchers have rather successfully connected themselves to the mainstream of research in empirical finance: the small literature on multifractal models of asset returns. The introduction of so-called multifractal models (MF) as a new class of stochastic processes for asset returns was mainly motivated by the findings of their *multi-scaling* properties.

Multi-scaling (often also denoted as multifractality itself) refers to processes or data that are characterized by different scaling laws for different moments. Generalizing equation (9.2), these defining features can be captured by dependency of the temporal scaling parameter on the pertinent moment, that is,

$$E\left[\left|r_t^q r_{t-\Delta t}^q\right|\right] \sim \Delta t^{-\gamma(q)}. \tag{9.3}$$

The phenomenology of equation (9.3) has been described in quite a number of early econophysics papers. A group of authors at the London School of Economics, Vassilicos, Demos and Tata (1993), deserves credit for the first empirical paper demonstrating multi-scaling properties of financial data. Other early work of a similar spirit includes Ausloos and Vandewalle (1998) and Ghashghaie et al. (1996). The latter contribution estimates a particular model of turbulent processes from the physics literature and has stirred a discussion about similarities and differences between the dynamics of turbulent fluids and asset price changes (cf. Vassilicos, 1995; Mantegna and Stanley, 1996).

Note that equation (9.3) implies that different powers of absolute returns (which all could be interpreted as measures of volatility) have different degrees of long-term dependency. In the economics literature, Ding, Engle and Granger (1993) had already pointed out that different powers have different dependence structures (measured by their ensemble of autocorrelations) and that the highest degree of autocorrelation is obtained for powers around 1. However, standard econometric models do not capture this feature of the data. Baseline models like GARCH and so-called stochastic volatility models rather have exponentially declining autocorrelations. While these models have been modified so as to allow for hyperbolic decline of the autocorrelation function according to equation (9.2),[3] no models have existed in the econometrics toolbox prior to the proposal of the MF model that generically could give rise to multi-scaling à la equation (9.3). However, since data from turbulent flows also exhibit multi-scaling, the literature on turbulence in statistical physics had already developed models with these characteristics. These are known as multifractal cascade models and are generated via operations on probability measures. To model the break-off of smaller eddies from bigger ones one starts with a uniform probability measure over the unit interval [0, 1]. In the first step, this interval is split up into two subintervals of equal length (smaller eddies), which receive fractions p_1 and $p_2 = 1 - p_1$ of their "mother intervals". In principle, this procedure is repeated *ad infinitum* for the resulting subintervals; cf. Figure 9.4. What it generates is a heterogeneous structure in which the final outcome after n steps of emergence of ever smaller eddies

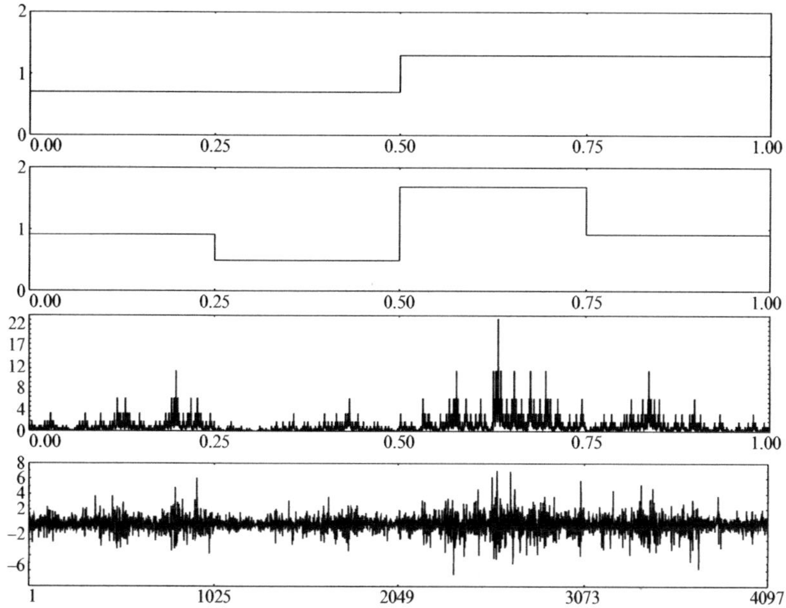

Note: The first panel illustrates the segmentation of the unit interval into two segments of equal length receiving fractions $p_1 = 0.65$ and $p_2 = 0.35$ of the overall mass. The second panel shows the second stage of the Binomial cascade, while the third panel shows the result after 12 iterations of this process with a total of $2^{12} = 4096$ segments. Using these segments as time transformations in the sense of equation (9.4) with $H = 0.5$ generates returns with heterogeneous volatility (lower panel).

Figure 9.4 The construction of a multifractal cascade and its use as a time transformation

can take any of the values $p_1^m p_2^{n-m}, 0 \leq m < n$. This process is highly autocorrelated since neighboring values have on average several joint components. In the limit of $n \rightarrow \infty$, "strict" multifractality according to equation (9.3) can be shown to hold.

The literature on turbulent flows has investigated quite a number of variants of the above algorithm. The above multifractal measure is called a Binomial cascade. However, instead of taking the same probabilities, one could also have drawn random numbers for the multipliers. An important example of the latter class is the Log-normal model in which the two probabilities of the new eddies are drawn from a Log-normal distribution. Note that in this case, the overall mass of the measure is not exactly preserved (as in the Binomial), but is maintained only in expectation (upon appropriate choice of the parameters of the Log-normal distribution). While the mean is, thus, constant in expectation over different steps, other moments might converge or diverge. Other extensions imply transition from the case of two subintervals to a higher number (trinomial, quadranomial cascades) or using irregularly spaced subintervals.

How do we apply these constructs as models of financial data? While the multifractal measure generated in Figure 9.4 does not exhibit too much similarity with price charts, we know that by its very construction it shares the multi-scaling properties of absolute moments of returns. Since multi-scaling applies to the *extent of fluctuations* (volatility), one would, therefore, interpret the non-observable process governing volatility as the analog of the multifractal measure. The realizations over small subintervals would, then, correspond to local volatility. A broadly equivalent approach is to use the multifractal measure as a transformation of chronological time. Assuming that the volatility process is homogeneous in transformed time, then, means that via the multifractal transformation, time is compressed and retarded so that the extent of fluctuations within chronological time steps of the same length becomes heterogeneous. This idea was formulated by Mandelbrot, Fisher and Calvet (1997), Calvet, Mandelbrot and Fisher (1997), and Fisher, Calvet and Mandelbrot (1997) in three seminal Cowles Foundation working papers, which for the first time went beyond a mere phenomenological demonstration of multi-scaling in financial data. They assumed that log price changes follow a compound stochastic process in which the distribution function of a multifractal measure Θ serves as the directing process (transforming chronological time into business time) and the subordinate process is fractional Brownian motion B_H,

$$r(t) = B_H[\Theta(t)]. \tag{9.4}$$

In contrast to GARCH and stochastic volatility models, this model is scale-free so that one and the same specification can be applied to data of various sampling frequencies. Mandelbrot, Fisher and Calvet show how the stochastic properties of the compound process reflect those of the directing multifractal measure. They also introduce a so-called scaling estimator for the parameters of the process and apply it to both daily and intra-daily data of the US \$-DEM foreign exchange market. A more systematic analysis of the underlying estimation procedure and additional empirical applications can be found in Calvet and Fisher (2002).

Unfortunately, the process as specified in equation (9.4) has serious drawbacks that limit its attractiveness in applied work: due to its combinatorial origin, it is bounded to a prespecified interval (which in economic applications might be a certain length of time) and it suffers from non-stationarity. Application of many standard tools of statistical inference would, therefore, be questionable and the combinatorial rather than causal nature limits its applicability as a tool for forecasting future volatility.

These restrictions do not apply to a time series model by Calvet and Fisher (2001), which preserves the spirit of a hierarchically structured volatility process but has a much more "harmless" format. Their Markov-switching multifractal process (MSM) can be interpreted as a special case of both Markov-switching and stochastic volatility models. Returns over a unit time interval are modeled as:

$$r_t = \sigma_t \cdot u_t \tag{9.5}$$

with innovations u_t drawn from a standard Normal distribution $N(0, 1)$ and instantaneous volatility σ_t being determined by the product of k volatility components or multipliers $M_t^{(1)}, M_t^{(2)}, \ldots, M_t^{(k)}$ and a constant scale factor σ:

$$\sigma_t^2 = \sigma^2 \prod_{i=1}^{k} M_t^{(i)}. \tag{9.6}$$

Each volatility component is renewed at time t with probability γ_i depending on its rank within the hierarchy of multipliers. Calvet and Fisher propose the following flexible form for these transition probabilities:

$$\gamma_i = 1 - (1 - \gamma_1)^{(b^k - 1)} \tag{9.7}$$

with parameters $\gamma_1 \in [0, 1]$ and $b \in (1, \infty)$. This specification is derived by Calvet and Fisher (2001) as a discrete approximation to a continuous-time multifractal process with Poisson arrival probabilities and geometric progression of frequencies. They show that when the grid step size of the discretized version goes to zero, the above discrete model converges to the continuous-time process.

Estimation of the parameters of the model involves γ_1 and b as well as those parameters characterizing the distribution of multipliers. If a discrete distribution is chosen for the multipliers (for example, a Binomial distribution with states p_1 and $1 - p_1$ like in our combinatorial example above), the discretized multifractal process is a well-behaved Markov-switching process with 2^k states. This framework allows estimation of its parameters via maximum likelihood (ML). ML estimation of this process comes along with identification of the conditional probabilities of the current states of the volatility components, which can be exploited for computation of one-step and multi-step forecasts of the volatility process using Bayes' rule. The Markov-switching multifractal model, thus, easily lends itself to practical applications. Calvet and Fisher (2004) demonstrate that the model allows for improvements over various GARCH-type volatility processes in a competition for the best forecasts of exchange rate volatility in various currency markets. A certain drawback of the ML approach is that it becomes computationally unfeasible for a number of volatility components beyond 10. Its applicability is also limited to MSM specifications with a finite state space so that it can not be applied to processes where multipliers are drawn from a continuous distribution (for example, the Log-normal).

Recent additions to extant literature introduce alternative estimation techniques that allow us to deal with these cases: Calvet, Fisher and Thompson (2006) consider a simulated maximum likelihood approach based on a particle filter algorithm, which allows the estimation of both models with continuous state space and a new bivariate MSM (which would be computationally too demanding for exact ML). Lux (2008) proposes a generalized method of moments technique based on a particular selection of analytical moments together with best linear forecasts along the lines of the Levinson-Durbin algorithm. Both papers also demonstrate the dominance of the multifractal model over standard specifications in some typical financial applications. Financial applications of a different formalization of multifractal process can be found in Bacry, Kozhemyak and Muzy (2008).

The relatively small literature that has emerged on multifractal processes over the last decade could be seen as one of the most significant contributions of physics-inspired tools to economics and finance. In contrast to some other empirical tools, researchers in this area have subscribed to the level of rigor of empirical work in economics and have attempted to show how far their proposed innovations provide an advantage over standard tools in crucial applications. Somewhat ironically, this literature is both better known and has had more of an impact in economics than in the econophysics community itself.

Available literature on MF models is altogether empirical in orientation and is not very informative on the origin of multifractality.[4] However, the empirical success of the multifractal model suggests that their basic structural set-up, a multiplicative hierarchical combination of volatility components, might be closer to the real thing than earlier additive models of volatility. Some speculation on the source of this multi-layer structure can be found, for example, in Dacorogna et al. (2001) who argue that different types of market participants with different time horizons are at the heart of the data-generating mechanism. To substantiate such claims would offer a formidable challenge to agent-based models. While there are few papers that demonstrate multi-scaling of artificial data from particular models (for example, Castiglione and Stauffer, 2001, for a particular version of the Cont/Bouchaud model), it seems clear that most behavioral models available so far do not really have the multi-frequency structure of the stochastic MF models.

9.3.4 Problematic prophecies: predicting crashes and recoveries

While the success of MF volatility models has only received scant attention beyond the confines of financial econometrics, attempts at forecasting the time of stock market crashes from precursors became a notorious and highly problematic brand of econophysics activity. This strand of activity started with a number of papers offering ex-post formalizations of the dynamics prior to some major market crashes, for example, the crash of October 1997 (Sornette, Johansen and Bouchaud, 1996; Vandewalle and Ausloos, 1998; Sornette and Johansen, 1997; Johansen and Sornette, 1999b). Adapting a formalization similar to that of precursor activity of earthquakes in geophysics, it was postulated that stock prices follow a log-periodic pattern prior to crashes that could be modeled by a dynamic equation of the type:

$$p_t = A + B\left(\frac{t_c - t}{t_c}\right)^{-m}\left[1 + C\cos\left(\omega \ln\frac{t_c - t}{t_c}\right) + \varphi\right] \tag{9.8}$$

for $t < t_c$. This equation generates fluctuations of accelerating frequency around an increasing trend component of the asset price. Such a development culminates in the singularity at the *critical time* t_c. Since the log-periodic oscillation breaks down at t_c this is interpreted as the estimate of the occurrence of the subsequent crash. Note that A, B, C, m, ω, t_c, and φ are all free parameters in estimating the model without imposing a known crash time t_c. A voluminous literature has applied this model (and slightly different versions) to various financial data discovering – as it had been claimed – dozens of historical cases to which the log periodic apparatus could be applied. This business had subsequently been extended to "anti-bubbles", mirror-imaged log-periodic downward movements, which should give rise to a recovery at criticality. Evidence for this scenario has first been claimed for the Nikkei in 1999 (Johansen and Sornette, 1999a) and had also been extended to various other markets shortly thereafter (Johansen and Sornette, 2001b).

Somewhat unfortunately, the details of the estimation algorithm for the many parameters of the highly nonlinear log-periodic equation have not been spelled out exactly in all this literature and an attempt at replicating some of the published estimates reported that the available information was not sufficient to arrive at anything close to the authors' original results (Feigenbaum, 2001a, b). Eventually, the work in this area culminated via an accelerating number of publications and log-periodicity of increasing publicity in its own critical rupture point: Sornette and Zhou (2002)

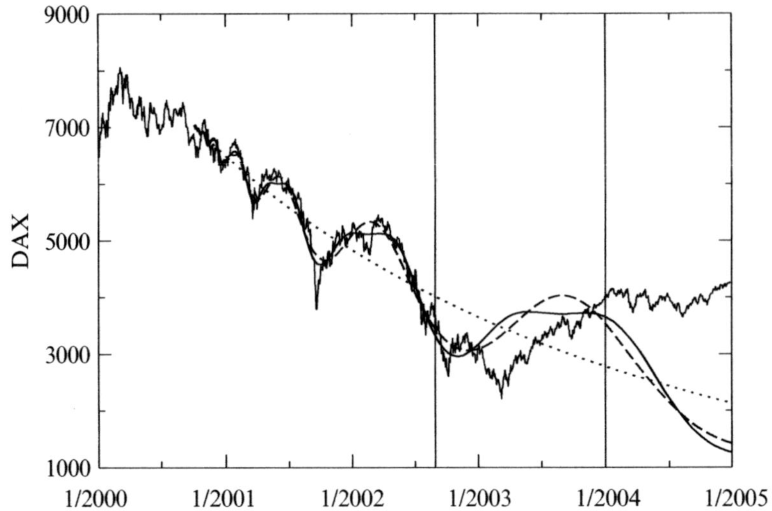

Note: The figure compares the predictions by Zhou and Sornette (2003) and the subsequent development of the index.

Source: By courtesy of J. Voit. Reprinted with permission from Voit (2005). ©2005 Springer-Verlag.

Figure 9.5 Log-periodic predictions

published a prediction that the US stock market would follow a downward log-periodic pattern for the years to come, culminating in a sharp fall in the first half of 2004. Similar predictions were subsequently issued for other important markets (Zhou and Sornette, 2003). However, not many of these predictions materialized. As can be seen in Figure 9.5 for the case of the German DAX, the predicted log-periodic evolution was quite different from the actual market development. While the in-sample fit (up to early 2003) seems quite good, the predicted and actual changes appear virtually uncorrelated.

The bubble of log-periodicity would certainly constitute an interesting episode for a deeper analysis of sociological mechanisms in scientific research. Within a few years, publications in learned journals (all authored by a very small group of scientists) on this topic reached almost three-digit numbers and the prospect of predicting markets created enormous excitement both in the popular press as well as among scientists. At the same time, almost no one had apparently ever successfully replicated these results. While physicists have often been sympathetic to this approach (due to its foundation in related work in geophysics), economists coming across the log-periodic hypothesis have always been conscious of the amount of "eye-balling" statistics involved. After all, inspecting a time window with a crash event, one is very likely to see an upward movement prior to the crash (otherwise the event would not qualify itself as a crash). Furthermore, it is well-known that the human eye has a tendency to "detect" spurious periodicity even in entirely random data, so that inspection of data prior to a crash might easily give rise to the impression of apparent oscillations with an upward trend. Because of this restriction to an endogenously selected subperiod of the data, a true test of log-periodicity would be highly demanding. On the other hand, one might have the feeling that the idea of a built-up of intensifying pressure and exuberance that can only be sustained for some time and eventually leads to a crash has some appeal. Unfortunately, the literature has not produced behavioral models in which such log-periodic patterns occurred.

The decline in the interest in log-periodic models was due to the poor performance of their predictions. There had, in fact, been strong emphasis within the econophysics community on producing *point predictions* of future events that would confirm the superiority of the underlying models.[5] While this aim is perhaps understandable from the importance of such predictions in the natural sciences, it might be misleading when dealing with economic data. The reason is that it neglects both the stochastic nature of economic systems (due to exogenous noise as well as the endogenous stochasticity of the large number of interacting subunits) as well as their self-referential nature. Rather than testing theories in a dichotomic way in the sense of a clear yes/no evaluation, the approach in economics is to evaluate forecasts statistically via their average success over a larger *out-of-sample* test period or a number of different cases. Unfortunately, the log-periodic theory like many other tools introduced in the econophysics literature has hardly ever been rigorously scrutinized in this manner.[6]

9.4 The distribution of wealth and income

Although the predominant subjects of the econophysics literature have been various strands of research on financial markets, some other currents exist. Maybe the area with the highest number of publications next to finance is work on microscopic models of the emergence of unequal distributions of wealth and pertinent empirical work.

The frequency distribution of wealth among the members of a society has been the subject of intense empirical research since the days of Vilfredo Pareto (1897) who first reported power-law behavior with an index of about 1.5 for income and wealth of households in various countries. Empirical work initiated by physicists has confirmed these time-honored findings (Levy and Solomon, 1997; Fujiwara et al., 2003; Castaldi and

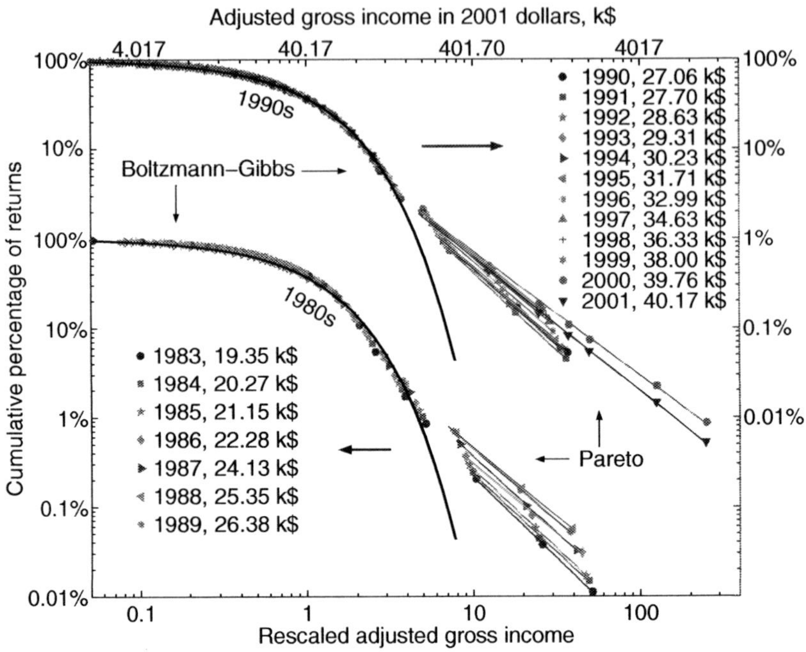

Note: The decomposition shows a pronounced crossover from the bulk of observations to a Pareto tail for the highest incomes. The numbers on the left-hand side give the average income per year.

Source: By courtesy of V. Yakovenko. Reproduced with permission from Yakovenko Silva (2005). ©2005 by Springer-Verlag.

Figure 9.6 The distribution of gross income in the United States compiled from tax revenues over the period 1983–2001

Milakovic, 2005). While Pareto as well as most subsequent researchers have emphasized the power-law character of the largest incomes and fortunes, the recent literature has also highlighted the fact that a crossover occurs from exponential behavior for the bulk of observations and Pareto behavior for the outmost tail. A careful study of US income data locates the crossover at about the 97 to 99 percent quantiles (Silva and Yakovenko, 2005) as illustrated in Figure 9.6 taken from this source. It seems interesting to note that this scenario is similar to the behavior of financial returns that also exhibit an asymptotic power-law behavior in the tails and a relatively well-behaved bell shape in the center of the distribution. The difference between the laws governing the majority of the small and medium-sized incomes and fortunes and the larger ones might also point to different generating mechanisms underlying these two segments of the distribution.

In economics, the emergence of inequality had been a hot topic up to the 1950s and 1960s. Several authors have proposed Markov processes that under certain conditions would lead to emergence of a Pareto distribution. The best-known contribution to this literature is certainly Champernowne (1953): his model assumes that an individual's income develops according to a Markov chain with transition probabilities between a set of income classes (defined over certain intervals). As a basic assumption, transitions were only allowed to either lower income classes or the next higher class, and the mean change for all agents was assumed to be a reduction of income (which is interpreted as a stability condition). Champernowne showed that the equilibrium distribution of this stochastic process is the Pareto distribution in its original form. Variations on this topic can be found in Whittle and Wold (1957), Mandelbrot (1961) and Steindl (1965), among others. Over the 1960s and 1970s, the literature on this topic gradually died out due to the rise of the representative agent approach as the leading principle of economic modeling. From the point of view of this emergent new paradigm, the behavioral foundations of these earlier stochastic processes seemed too nebulous to warrant further research in this direction. Unfortunately, a representative agent framework – quite obviously – does not offer any viable alternative for investigation of distributions among agents. As a consequence, the subject of inequality in income and wealth has received only scant attention in the whole body of economics literature for some decades and lectures in the "theory of income distribution and wealth" eventually disappeared from the curricula of economics programs.[7]

The econophysics community recovered this topic in 2000 when three very similar models of "wealth condensation" (Bouchaud and Mézard, 2000) and the "statistical mechanics of money" (Chakraborti and Chakrabarti, 2000; Dragulescu and Yakovenko, 2000) appeared. While these attempts at microscopic simulations of wealth formation among interacting agents received an enthusiastic welcome in the popular science press (Buchanan, 2002; Hayes, 2002), they were actually not the first to explore this seemingly unknown territory. The credit for a much earlier analysis of essentially the same type of structures has to be given to sociologist John Angle. In a series of papers starting in 1986 (Angle, 1986, 1993, 1996, among many others), he explored a multi-agent setting that draws inspiration from two quite distinct sources: particle physics and human anthropology. Particle physics motivates the modeling of agents' interactions as collisions from which one of both opponents emerges with an increase of his or her wealth at the expense of the other. Human anthropology provides a set of stylized facts that Angle attempts to explain with this "inequality process".

In particular, he quotes evidence from archeological excavations that inequality among the members of a society first emerges with the introduction of agriculture and the prevalence of food abundance. Once human societies proceed beyond the hunter and gatherer level and production of some "surplus" becomes possible, the inequality of a "ranked society" or "chiefdom" appears. Since this ranked society persists through all levels of economic development, a very general and simple mechanism is required to explain its emergence. The "inequality process" proposes a mechanism for this stratification of wealth from the following ingredients (Angle, 1986): within a finite population, agents are randomly matched in pairs. A random toss, then, decides which of both agents comes out as the winner of this encounter. In the baseline model, both agents have the same probabilities 0.5 of winning but other specifications have also been analyzed in subsequent papers. If the winner is assumed to take away a fixed portion of the other agent's wealth, say ω, the simplest version of the process leads to a stochastic evolution of wealth of two individuals i and j bumping into each other according to:

$$w_{i,t} = w_{i,t-1} + D_t \omega w_{j,t-1} - (1 - D_t) \omega w_{i,t-1},$$

$$w_{j,t} = w_{j,t-1} + (1 - D_t) \omega w_{i,t-1} - D_t \omega w_{j,t-1}. \tag{9.9}$$

Time t is measured in encounters and $D_t \in \{0, 1\}$ is a binary stochastic index that takes the value 1 (0) if $i(j)$ is drawn as the "winner". Angle (1986) shows via microscopic simulations that this process leads to a limiting distribution that can be reasonably well fitted by a Gamma distribution. Later papers provide a theoretical analysis of the process, various extensions as well as empirical applications (see Angle, 2006, for a summary).

The econophysics papers of 2000 proposed models that are almost undistinguishable from Angle's. Dragulescu and Yakovenko (2000) begin their investigation with a model in which a constant "money" amount is changing hands rather than a fraction of one agent's wealth. They show that this process leads to a Boltzmann-Gibbs distribution $P(w) \sim e^{-w/T}$ (with T "effective temperature" or average wealth). Note that this variant of the inequality process is equivalent to a simple textbook model for the exchange of energy of atoms. One generalization of their model allows for a random amount of money changing hands, while another considers the exchange of a fraction of wealth of the losing agent, that is, Angle's inequality process depicted in equation (9.9).

Chakraborti and Chakrabarti (2000) have a slightly different set-up, allowing agents to swap a random fraction ε of their total wealth, $w_{i,t} + w_{j,t}$. A more general variant of the wealth exchange process can be found in Bouchaud and Mézard (2000) whose evolution of wealth covers simultaneous interactions between all members of the population. Cast into a continuous-time setting, agent *i*'s wealth, then, develops according to:

$$\frac{dw_{i,t}}{dt} = \eta_i(t)\, w_{i,t} + \sum_{j(\neq i)} J_{ij} w_{j,t} - \sum_{j(\neq i)} J_{ji} w_{i,t} \qquad (9.10)$$

with: η_i a stochastic term and the matrix J_{ij} capturing all factors of redistribution due to interactions within the population. Solving the resulting Fokker-Planck equation, for the case of identical exchange parameters $J_{ij} = J/N$, the authors show that the equilibrium distribution of this model obeys a power law with the exponent depending on the parameters of the model (J and the distributional parameters of η_i).

In the rich literature following Dragulescu and Yakovenko and Chakraborti and Chakrabarti one of the main goals was to replace the baseline models with their exponential tail behavior by refined ones with power-law tails. Power laws have been found when introducing "savings" in the sense of a fraction of wealth that is exempted from the exchange process (Chatterjee, Chakraborti and Manna, 2003) or asymmetry in interactions (Sinha, 2005).

What is the contribution of this literature? As pointed out by Lux (2005b) and Anglin (2005), economists (even those subscribing to the usefulness of agent-based models) might feel bewildered by the sheer simplicity of this approach. Taken at face value, it would certainly be hard to accept the processes surveyed above as models of the emergence of inequality in market economies. A first objection would be that the processes, in fact, do model what has been called "theft and fraud" economies (Hayes, 2002). The principles of voluntary exchange to the mutual benefit of both parties are entirely at odds with the model's main building blocks. Human agents with a minimum degree of risk aversion would certainly prefer not to participate at all in this economy. The models also dispense with all facets of *collaborative activity* (that is, production) to create wealth and merely focus on redistribution of a constant, given amount of wealth (although there is a point to Angle's implicit view that the universality of inequality for all advanced societies may allow the abstraction from wealth creation). What is more and what perhaps is at the base of economists' dissatisfaction with this approach is that wealth is a *derived* concept rather than a primitive quantity. Tracking the development of the distribution of wealth, then, requires to look at the more basic concepts of quantities of goods traded and the change of evaluation of these goods via changes of market prices.

Luckily, a few related papers have been looking at slightly more complicated models in which "wealth" is not simply used as a primitive concept, but agents' wealth is derived from the valuation of their possessions. Silver,

Slud and Takamoto (2002) consider an economy with two goods and an ensemble of agents endowed with Cobb-Douglas preferences:

$$U_{i,t} = x_{i,t}^{f_{i,t}} y_{i,t}^{1-f_{i,t}}. \tag{9.11}$$

Equation (9.11) formalizes the utility function of agent i at time t whose message is that the agent derives pleasure from consuming (possessing) goods x and y and their overall contribution to the agent's well-being depends on the parameter $f_{i,t}$. This parameter is drawn independently, for each agent in each period, from a distribution function with support in the interval [0, 1]. This stochasticity leads to changing preferences for both goods that induce agents to exchange goods in an aggregate market. Summing up demand and supply over all agents one can easily determine the relative price between x and y in equilibrium at time t as well as the quantities exchanged between agents. Changes of quantities and prices over time lead to emergence of inequality. Starting from a situation of equal possessions of all agents, wealth stratification is simply due to the favorable or unfavorable development of agents' preferences vis-à-vis the majority of their trading partners (for example, if one agent develops a strong preference for one good in one particular period, he or she is likely to pay a relatively high price in terms of the other good and might undergo a loss in aggregate wealth if his or her preferences shift back to more "normal" levels in the next period). Note that exchange is entirely voluntary in this economy and allows all agents to achieve their maximum utility possible in any period with given resources and preferences. Silver, Slud and Takamoto show via both simulations and theoretical arguments that this process converges to a limiting distribution that is close to the Gamma distribution. A somewhat similar result is already reported in passing in Dragulescu and Yakovenko (2000, p. 725) who, besides their simple wealth exchange models reviewed above, had also studied a more involved economic model with a production sector.

It, therefore, seems that a certain tendency prevails both in simple physics-sociological models and in more complicated economic models of wealth formation to arrive at an exponential distribution for large fortunes. The analogy to the Boltzmann-Gibbs theory for the distribution of kinetic energy might be at the heart of this (almost) universal outcome of various simple models. All the relevant papers consider *conservative* systems (in the sense of a given amount of "wealth" or otherwise given resources) governed by random reallocations. The limiting distribution in such a setting, then, reflects the maximization of entropy through the random exchange mechanisms. The important insight from this literature is that the bulk of the distribution can, in fact, be explained simply by the influence of random forces. While the primitive models à la equations (9.9) and (9.10) are the purest possible formalization of this randomization, the economically more refined version of Silver, Slud and Takamoto demonstrates that their results survive in a setting with more detailed structure of trading motives and exchange mediated via markets.

This leaves the remaining Pareto tail to be explained by other mechanisms. Although some power laws have been found in extended models, these seem to depend on the parameters of the model and do not necessarily yield the apparently universal empirical exponents. In the view of the above arguments, it might also seem questionable whether one could find an explanation of Pareto laws in conservative systems. Economists would rather expect capital accumulation and factors like inheritance to play a role in the formation of big fortunes. Extending standard representative agent models of the business cycle to a multi-agent setting, a few attempts have been made recently to explore the evolution of wealth among agents. A good example of this literature is Krusell and Smith (1998) who study a standard growth model with intertemporally optimizing agents. Agents have to decide about consumption and wealth accumulation and are made heterogeneous via shocks in their labor market participation (that is, they stochastically move in and out of unemployment) and via shocks to their time preferences (that is, preferences for consumption vis-à-vis savings). The major contributions of this paper are: the development of a methodology to derive rational (that is, consistent) expectations in a multi-agent setting and the calibration of their model with respect to selected quantiles of the US Lorenz curve.

Alternative models with a somewhat different structure are to be found in Huggett (1996) and Castañeda, Díaz-Giménez and Ríos-Rull (2003). All these models, however, restrict themselves to matching selected moments of the wealth dispersion in the United States. It is, therefore, not clear so far whether their structures are consistent with a power-law tail or not. While the unduly neglected topic of the emergence of inequality in modern societies has been approached from various sides, none of these new developments has come out with an explanation for the Pareto tails so far. It seems, therefore, to be a worthwhile undertaking to bridge the gap between the extremely simple wealth exchange processes proposed in the econophysics literature and the much more involved emergent new literature on wealth formation in economics. An appropriate middle way might provide useful insights into the potential sources of power-law tails.

9.5 Macroeconomics and industrial organization

Much of the work done by physicists on non-financial data is of an exploratory data-analytical nature. Most of it focuses on the detection of power laws that might have gone unrecognized by economists. Besides high-frequency financial data, another source of relatively large data sets is cross-sectional records of firms' characteristics such as sales, number of employees and so on. One such data set, the Standard and Poor's COMPUSTAT sample of US firms has been analyzed by the Boston group around G. Stanley in a sequence of empirical papers. Their findings include:

1. The size distribution of US firms follows a Log-normal distribution (Stanley et al., 1995).
2. A linear relationship prevails between the log of the standard deviation σ of growth rates of firms and the log of firm size, s (measured by sales or number of employees; cf. Stanley et al., 1996b). The relationship is, thus,

$$\ln \sigma \approx \alpha - \beta \ln s \tag{9.12}$$

   with estimates of β around 0.15. This finding has been shown by Canning et al. (1998) to extend to the volatility of GDP growth rates conditioned on current GDP. Due to this surprising coincidence, the relationship has been hypothesized to be a universal feature of complex organizations.
3. The conditional density of annual growth rates of firms $p(r_t \mid s_{t-1})$ with s the log of an appropriate size variable (sales, employees) and r its growth rate, $r_t = s_t - s_{t-1}$, has an exponential form

$$p(r_t|s_{t-1}) = \frac{1}{\sqrt{2}\sigma(s_{t-1})}\exp\left(-\frac{\sqrt{2}|r_t - \bar{r}(s_{t-1})|}{\sigma(s_{t-1})}\right); \tag{9.13}$$

cf. Stanley et al. (1996b), Amaral et al. (1997).

Log-normality of the firm size distribution (finding no. 1), is, of course, well-known as Gibrat's law of proportional effect (Gibrat, 1931): if firms' growth process is driven by a simple stochastic process with independent, Normally distributed growth rates, the Log-normal distribution governs the dispersion of firm sizes within the economy. The Log-normal hypothesis has earlier been supported by Quandt (1966). However, other studies suggest that the Log-normal tails decrease too fast and that there is excess mass in the extreme part of the distribution that would rather speak in favor of a Pareto law. Pareto coefficients between 1.0 and 1.5 have already been estimated for the size distribution of firms in various countries by Steindl (1965). Okuayama, Takayasu and Takayasu (1999) also report Pareto coefficients around 1 (between 0.7 and 1.4) for various data sets. Probably the most comprehensive data set has been used by Axtell (2001) who reports a Pareto exponent close to 1 (hovering between 0.995 and

1.059 depending on the estimation method) for the total ensemble of firms operating in 1997 as recorded by the US Census Bureau.[8]

Finding no. 2 has spawned work in economics trying to elucidate the sources of this power law. Sutton (2002) shows that one arrives at a slope coefficient between −0.21 and −0.25 under the assumption that the growth rates of constituent businesses within a firm are uncorrelated. The difference between these numbers and the slightly flatter empirical relationship would, then, have to be attributed to joint firm-specific effects on all business components.

From a broader perspective, a number of researchers have shown the emergence of several empirically relevant statistical laws in artificial economies with a complex interaction structure of their inhabitants. Axtell (1999) building upon the "sugarcube economy" of Epstein and Axtell (1996) allows agents to self-organize into productive teams. Cooptation of additional workers to existing teams is advantageous because of increasing returns, but also provides the danger of suffering from free-riding of some group members who might reduce the level of effort invested in team production. This latter effect limits the growth potential of firms since agents have less and less incentives to supply effort in growing teams because of the decreasing sensitivity of overall output to individual contributions. In an agent-based model in which workers have to decide adaptively on the formation and break-off of teams, the evolving economy exhibits a number of realistic features: log growth rates of firms (in terms of the number of employees) follow a Laplace distribution (finding no. 3), and the size distribution of firms is skewed to the right. Estimation of the Pareto index yields 1.28 for employees and 0.88 for the distribution of output.

Delli Gatti et al. (2003) arrive at a very similar replication of empirical stylized facts for firm sizes and growth rates. However, their starting point is a framework in which the basic entities are the firms themselves and the heterogeneity of the ensemble of firms with respect to market and financial conditions is emphasized. Focusing on the development of firms' balance sheets, the financial conditions of the banking sector and allowing for bankruptcies, their model generates business cycle fluctuations driven by the financial sphere of the economy. Simulations and statistical analyses of the synthetic data reveal a reasonable match not only of some of the stylized facts above, but also conformity with other aspects of macroeconomic fluctuations. A third independent approach that not only reproduces stylized facts from industrial organization but also a Pareto wealth distribution is the model by Wright (2005). Wright considers a computational model with both workers and firm owners. His framework covers stochastic processes for consumption, hiring and firing decisions of firms and the distribution of agents on classes. Despite the relatively simple behavioral rules for all these components, the resulting macroeconomy seems remarkably close to the empirical data in its statistical features.

While so far the number of papers on agent-based artificial economies is extremely limited, the fact that computational models with very different building blocks have been shown to reproduce stylized facts seems encouraging. Clearly, these promising results still leave a long agenda of investigations in the robustness and generating mechanisms of the macroeconomic power laws.

The agent-based approach to macroeconomic modeling has also been pursued by Aoki in a long chain of publications, most of which are summarized in his recent books (Aoki, 1996, 2002; Aoki and Yoshikawa, 2007). His approach had initially been rather technically orientated, advocating the use of tools from statistical physics like mean-field approximations, Master equations and clustering processes. In some of his work, he had nicely illustrated the potential usefulness of these techniques by revisiting well-known economic models. An example is Diamond's (1982) model of a search economy with multiple equilibria (cf. Aoki, 2002, Ch. 9). With a mean-field approach, the assumption of an infinite population can be dispensed with and one arrives at new results on cyclicity and equilibrium selection in this benchmark model of the neo-Keynesian macroeconomics literature.

Recent work by Aoki and Yoshikawa makes an even stronger point for replacing the representative agent paradigm in macroeconomics by an agent-based approach. Most interestingly, the proposed new models have a strong Keynesian flavor, revisiting such concepts like the liquidity trap, the role of uncertainty in macroeconomics and the possibility of a slowdown of economic growth due to demand saturation. With their focus on analytical tractability, the models proposed by Aoki and Yoshikawa are more stylized than the computational approaches reviewed above. They are not analyzed from a power-law perspective, but rather from the perspective of other well-known macroeconomic laws like Okun's (a decrease of unemployment by 1 percent comes along with an additional increase of GDP by 2.5 percent). Nevertheless, their approach is very similar to that of Axtell, Delli Gatti et al. and Wright in that well-known statistical relationships on the macro level are explained as *emergent* results of a multisectoral industrial dynamics.

One particular interesting innovation in Aoki and Yoshikawa's recent work is the application of *ultrametric structures* as an ingredient in a labor market model. Ultrametric structures are tree-like, hierarchical structures pretty similar to the hierarchical structure of the multifractal volatility model exhibited in Figure 9.4. Such structures are applied here to measure the distance in terms of specialization of different occupations. A worker

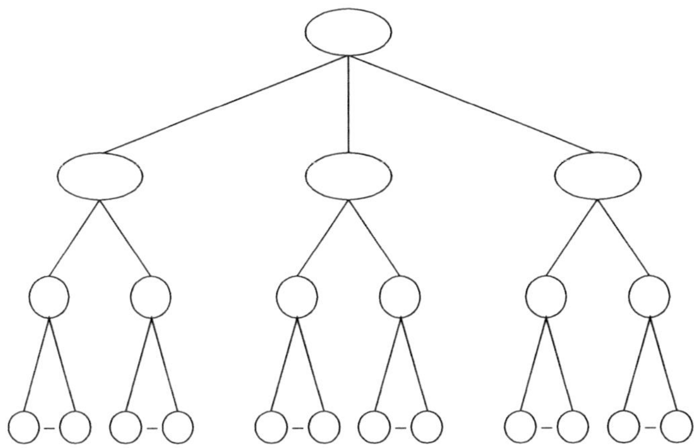

Note: Such a structure could be contemplated as a formalization of the proximity of professional specializations. In a macroeconomic setting, the ultrametric structure of industries would, then, determine the costs of relocating resources from one sector to another. Note the formal similarity of hierarchical trees to multifractal cascades (depicted in Figure 9.5). The cluster formation algorithm underlying Figure 9.3 is also based upon an ultrametric concept of distance between companies.

Figure 9.7 Example of hierarchical structure in an ultrametric space

at one end node of the tree model has a very similar specialization to that of his or her neighbor if their branch stems from the same mother nodes at higher hierarchic levels, but they might as well have a large "ultrametric distance" if they originate from different mother nodes (cf. Figure 9.7). This hierarchy provides an avenue for explaining the differences in adaptability of certain workers to new jobs offered, the time needed for retraining and the likelihood to find employment in a different occupation. With high ultrametric differences, restructuring of the labor force in the presence of structural change might be a sluggish process. The model, therefore, provides an avenue towards modeling of the much discussed *hysteresis* phenomenon in labor markets: the long-lasting influence of transitory shocks to employment that is held responsible for high levels of unemployment in European countries.[9]

9.6 Concluding remarks

While there had been some crossover of ideas from the econophysics literature into economics and finance, much of the current research still lives in a kind of parallel society that is largely unheard of in the native population of economics departments. Where it had become known, exaggerated claims of the superiority of econophysics and the uselessness of traditional economic thought (McCauley, 2006) together with a sometimes amateurish use of terminology and concepts from economics have inhibited fruitful communication. Economists also often found the empirical analyses in the log-log style to represent substandard methodology compared with the refined methodology developed in econometrics. However, the development of, for example, the literature on multifractal models in econometrics demonstrates that new concepts from statistical physics can be successfully adapted for economic applications and integrated into the econometrician's toolbox. It is particularly remarkable that in this area progress was exactly due to the more rigorous development of methods of statistical inference and forecasting instead of simple copying of the formalism inherited from the turbulence literature. It is worth emphasizing that applications of these models in the economics literature go far beyond contemporaneous econophysics publications that still confine themselves to only demonstrating some scaling laws of empirical data. It could be possible that the methodological developments in this area feed back to the original subject and we will see applications of Markov-switching multifractal processes on turbulent flows in the near future. Other methods brought to the attention of economists via the econophysics literature might undergo a similar transformation.

While the dissemination of various methodological concepts that have been unfamiliar to economists so far is certainly an important aspect of "econophysics", there might be an even more seminal influence in its natural emphasis on economies and markets as dispersed systems of interacting units. After the disappointing insights in the (near) impossibility of deriving stable macroeconomic (or macroscopic) behavioral correspondences as the aggregate of individual decisions, much of mainstream economic theory has simply side-stepped this issue by evoking representative agents as the (one or two) single actors in macroscopic models. However, "there is no plausible formal justification for the assumption that the aggregate of individuals, even maximizers, acts itself like an individual maximizer" (Kirman, 1992), "macro activity is essentially the result of the *interactions between agents* and as such is not usefully represented by a single 'optimizer' that by definition eliminates all trade between agents and thereby ignores the interactions between them" (Ramsey, 1996). Behavioral work in econophysics typically starts out from the interactions of the elementary units of a system whose macroscopic regularities are emergent properties of the overall dynamics of the system. In empirical research, instead of postulating *ad hoc* the existence of meaningful macro variables, one can let the data themselves speak and reveal its stable properties. It might well be the case that some scaling laws are more robust characterizations of economic data than the behavior of a simple average of some measurement. The prevalence of Pareto laws in income, wealth, firm size and financial returns supports the view that the scaling view of statistical physics could be fruitful in economics, too. In any case, these emergent properties seem to be much more stable (even quantitatively so) than many of the well-known hypothesized relationships between macro variables in economic theory (take money demand as a striking example; cf. Knell and Stix, 2006, for a recent survey). Since economics deals with statistical ensembles of microscopic configurations, whose exact realization cannot be determined, what can be said about the system as a whole must be based on the statistical laws governing the entire ensemble. These ensemble averages are objects of study in their own right and will – except for trivial cases – not correspond to the behavioral laws of individual members of the ensemble. A satisfactory theory will, therefore, typically require the analysis of both time-varying population averages and their dispersion (second moment). In many cases, even the investigation of the co-evolution of means and (co-)variances of sensible macroscopic measurements might be too rough an approximation and one might want to extend the analysis to higher moments like skewness and kurtosis.[10] Since statistical physics has developed a formal apparatus for dealing with collective phenomena in non-human systems, it provides a rich source of inspiration for the analysis of collective behavior in markets and other areas of social interaction.

Notes

* I am indebted to Simone Alfarano, Jack Angle, Mishael Milakovic, Dietrich Stauffer and Friedrich Wagner for many intense discussions on the relationships between physics and economics. I also wish to thank Maren Brechtefeld, Claas Prelle, Dietrich Stauffer and the editor, J. Barkley Rosser, for their careful reading of a previous version of this chapter and many useful and important comments. Financial support by the European Commission under STREP contract no. 516446 is greatfully acknowledged.

1. The author of this review once received a referee report including several pages of refutation of the econophysics approach. Strangely enough, the paper under review was a straight econometrics piece and the referee's scolding seemed only to have been motivated by the author's association with some members of the econophysics community in other projects.
2. The reader might compare this paper with the more or less simultaneous paper by Sullivan, White and Golomb (2001), which is quite representative of the state-of-the-art in this area in empirical finance.
3. The most prominent example is fractionally integrated GARCH; cf. Baillie, Bollerslev and Mikkelsen (1996).
4. However, Calvet, Fisher and Thomson (2006) relate low-frequency volatility components to certain macroeconomic risk factors.
5. In relation to Zhou and Sornette's prediction of a steep decline of the US stock market in 2003/04, Stauffer (2002), among others, had emphasized the importance of such "non-trivial statements . . . published . . . before the event is over" as a kind of litmus test for the significance of econophysics research. While Zhou's and Sornette's predictions are quite remarkably rejected by the data, it is worthwhile noting that quite a variety of actual developments could have been claimed as supporting evidence. The upshot of the log-periodic prediction was, in fact, summarized more in the style of an investors'

newsletter than a rigorous scientific statement: "in the next two years, we predict an overall contribution of the bearish phase, punctuated by local rallies" and so on; cf. Sornette and Zhou (2002, p. 468). Luckily, the lack of success of stock market predictions also casts doubts on the validity of subsequent far-fetched doomsday scenarios derived from a log-periodic study of non-financial socioeconomic data (Johansen and Sornette, 2001a).

6. Chang and Feigenbaum (2006) make an effort on rigorous statistical tests of the log-periodic model. Their results are hardly supportive.
7. Another explanation of the decline of interest in distributional issues is that this was not a politically opportune topic in Western countries during the Cold War era with its juxtaposition of communist and market-oriented systems.
8. The Zipf's law for the size distribution of firms is reminiscent of the well-known Pareto law for the distribution of city sizes; cf. Nitsch (2005) for a review of the evidence and Gabaix (1999) for a potential explanation.
9. While the notion of hysteresis stems from physics and engineering, it had become the standard technical term for this phenomenon in economics already some 20 years ago; cf. Cross (1988).
10. Note that the exponent of a scaling law also gives the highest existing moment of the underlying time series.

References

Amaral, L.A.N., S.V. Buldyrev, S. Havlin, P. Maass, M.A. Salinger, H.E. Stanley and M.H.R. Stanley (1997), "Scaling behavior in economics: The problem of quantifying company growth", *Physica A*, **244**(1), 1–24.

Angle, J. (1986), "The surplus theory of social stratification and the size distribution of personal wealth", *Social Forces*, **65**(2), 293–326.

Angle, J. (1993), "Deriving the size distribution of personal wealth from 'The rich get richer, the poor get poorer'", *Journal of Mathematical Sociology*, **18**, 27–46.

Angle, J. (1996), "How the gamma law of income distribution appears invariant under aggregation", *Journal of Mathematical Sociology*, **31**, 325–58.

Angle, J. (2006), "The inequality process as a wealth maximizing process", *Physica A*, **367**, 388–414.

Anglin, P.M. (2005), "Econophysics of wealth distribution: A comment", in A. Chatterjee et al. (eds), *Econophysics of Wealth Distribution*, Milan: Springer-Verlag Italia, pp. 229–38.

Aoki, M. (1996), *New Approaches to Macroeconomic Modeling: Evolutionary Stochastic Dynamics, Multiple Equilibria, and Externalities as Field Effects*, Cambridge, MA: Cambridge University Press.

Aoki, M. (2002), *Modeling Aggregate Behavior and Fluctuations in Economics*, Cambridge, MA: Cambridge University Press.

Aoki, M. and H. Yoshikawa (2007), *A Stochastic Approach to Macroeconomics and Financial Markets*, Cambridge, MA: Cambridge University Press.

Arifovic, J. (1996), "The behavior of the exchange rate in the genetic algorithm and experimental economies", *Journal of Political Economy*, **104**(3), 510–41.

Ausloos, M. and N. Vandewalle (1998), "Multi-affine analysis of typical currency exchange rates", *European Physical Journal B*, **4**(2), 257–61.

Axtell, R.L. (1999), "The emergence of firms in a population of agents: Local increasing returns, unstable Nash equilibria and power law size distribution", Brookings Institution, Center for Social and Economic Dynamics, *Working Paper*.

Axtell, R.L. (2001), "Zipf distribution of U.S. firm sizes", *Science*, **293**(5536), 1818–20.

Bacry, E., A. Kozhemyak and J.-F. Muzy (2008), "Continuous cascade models for asset returns", *Journal of Economic Dynamics and Control*, **32**(1), 156–99.

Baillie, R.T., T. Bollerslev and H. Mikkelsen (1996), "Fractionally integrated generalized autoregressive conditional heteroskedasticity", *Journal of Econometrics*, **74**(1), 3–30.

Bak, P., M. Paczuski and M. Shubik (1997), "Price variations in a stock market with many agents", *Physica A*, **246**, 430–53.
Bartolozzi, M. and A.W. Thomas (2004), "Stochastic cellular automata model for stock market dynamics", *Physical Review E*, E69(4), 046112.
Bollerslev, T. (1986), "A generalized autoregressive conditional heteroskedasticity", *Journal of Econometrics*, **31**(3), 307–27.
Bouchaud, J.-P. and M. Mézard (2000), "Wealth condensation in a simple model of economy", *Physica A*, **282**, 536–45.
Bouchaud, J.-P. and M. Potters (2000), *Theory of Financial Risks: From Statistical Physics to Risk Management*, Cambridge, UK: Cambridge University Press.
Bouchaud, J.-P., M. Potters and M. Mézard (2002), "Statistical properties of stock order books: Empirical results and models", *Quantitative Finance*, **2**(4), 251.
Breidt, F., N. Crato and P. de Lima (1998), "On the detection and estimation of long memory in stochastic volatility", *Journal of Econometrics*, **83**(1–2), 325–48.
Buchanan, M. (2002), "Wealth happens", *Harvard Business Review*, **80**(4), 49–54.
Calvet, L.E. and A. Fisher (2001), "Forecasting multifractal volatility", *Journal of Econometrics*, **105**(1), 27–58.
Calvet, L.E. and A. Fisher (2002), "Multifractality in asset returns: Theory and evidence", *The Review of Economics and Statistics*, **84**(3), 381–406.
Calvet, L.E. and A. Fisher (2004), "How to forecast long-run volatility: Regime switching and the estimation of multifractal processes", *Journal of Financial Econometrics*, **2**(1), 49–83.
Calvet, L.E., A. Fisher and S.B. Thompson (2006), "Volatility comovement: A multifrequency approach", *Journal of Econometrics*, **131**(1–2), 179–215.
Calvet, L.E., B. Mandelbrot and A. Fisher (1997), "Large deviations and the distribution of price changes", Mimeo: Cowles Foundation for Research in Economics.
Canning, D., L.A.N. Amaral, Y. Lee, M. Meyer and H.E. Stanley (1998), "A power law for scaling the volatility of GDP growth rates with country size", *Economics Letters*, **60**(3), 335–41.
Castaldi, C. and M. Milakovic (2007), "Turnover activity in wealth portfolios", *Journal of Economic Behavior and Organization*, **63**(3), 537–52.
Castañeda, A., J. Díaz-Giménez and J.-V. Ríos-Rull (2003), "Accounting for the US earnings and wealth inequality", *The Journal of Political Economy*, **111**(4), 818–57.
Castiglione, F. and D. Stauffer (2001), "Multi-scaling in the Cont-Bouchaud microscopic stockmarket model", *Physica A*, **300**(3), 531–8.
Chakraborti, A. and B. Chakrabarti (2000), "Statistical mechanics of money: How saving propensities affects its distribution", *European Physical Journal B*, **17**, 167–70.
Champernowne, D.G. (1953), "A model of income distribution", *The Economic Journal*, **63**, 318–51.
Chang, G. and J. Feigenbaum (2006), "A Bayesian analysis of log-periodic precursors to financial crashes", *Quantitative Finance*, **6**(1), 15–36.
Chatterjee, A., B. Chakrabarti and S.S. Manna (2003), "Money in gas-like markets: Gibbs and Pareto laws", *Physica Scripta*, **106**, 36–38.
Chen, S.-H., T. Lux and M. Marchesi (2001), "Testing for non-linear structure in an artificial market", *Journal of Economic Behavior and Organization*, **46**(3), 327–42.
Chen, N., R. Roll and S.A. Ross (1986), "Economic forces and the stock market", *Journal of Business*, **59**(3), 383–403.
Chiarella, C. and G. Iori (2002), "A simulation analysis of the microstructure of double auction markets", *Quantitative Finance*, **2**(5), 346–53.
Cioffi, C. (2008) (ed.), *Power Laws in the Social Sciences: Discovering Complexity and Non-equilibrium Dynamics in Social Universe*, in preparation.
Cont, R. and J.-P. Bouchaud (2000), "Herd behavior and aggregate fluctuations in financial markets", *Macroeconomic Dynamics*, **4**(2), 170–96.
Cross, R. (ed.) (1988), *Hysteresis and the Natural Rate Hypothesis*, Oxford: Blackwell.
Dacorogna, M., R. Gencay, U. Muller, R. Olsen and O. Pictet (2001), *An Introduction to High-frequency Finance*, San Diego: Academic Press.

Daniels, M.G., J.D. Farmer, L. Gillemot, G.Iori and E. Smith (2003), "Quantitative model of price diffusion and market friction based on trading as a mechanistic random process", *Physical Review Letters*, **90**(10), 108102(4).
Delli Gatti, D., M. Gallegati, G. Giuleoni and A. Palestrini (2003), "Financial fragility, patterns of firms' entry and exit and aggregate dynamics", *Journal of Economic Behavior and Organization*, **51**(1), 79–97.
Diamond, D.W. (1982), "Aggregate demand management in search equlibrium", *Journal of Political Economy*, **90**(5), 881–94.
Ding, Z., R. Engle and C. Granger (1993), "A long memory property of stock market returns and a new model", *Journal of Empirical Finance*, **1**(1), 83–106.
Dragulescu, A.A. and V.M. Yakovenko (2000), "Statistical mechanics of money, income, and wealth", *European Physical Journal B*, **17**(4), 723–9.
Eguiluz V.M. and M.G. Zimmermann (2000), "Transmission of information and herd behavior: An application to financial markets", *Physical Review Letters*, **85**(26), 5659–62.
Eisler, Z. and J. Kertész (2005), "Size matters: Some stylized facts of the stock market revisited", *European Physical Journal B*, **51**(1), 145–54.
Engle, R. (1983), "Autoregressive conditional heteroskedasticity with estimates of the variance of U.K. inflation", *Econometrica*, **50**(4), 987–1008.
Epstein, J.M. and R.L. Axtell (1996), *Growing Artificial Societies: Social Science from the Bottom Up*, Cambridge, MA: MIT Press.
Fama, E. (1963), "Mandelbrot and the stable Paretian hypothesis", *Journal of Business*, **36**(4), 420–29.
Farmer, J.D. and F. Lillo (2004), "On the origin of power law tails in price fluctuations", *Quantitative Finance*, **4**(1), C7–C11.
Farmer, J.D. and I.I. Zovko (2002), "The power of patience: A behavioral regularity in limit order placement", *Quantitative Finance*, **2**(5), 387–92.
Feigenbaum, J.A. (2001a), "A statistical analysis of log-periodic precursors to financial crashes", *Quantitative Finance*, **1**(3), 346–60.
Feigenbaum, J.A. (2001b), "More on a statistical analysis of log-periodic precursors to financial crashes", *Quantitative Finance*, **1**(5), 527–32.
Fisher, A., L.E. Calvet and B. Mandelbrot (1997), "Multifractality of Deutschemark/US Dollar exchange rates", Mimeo: Cowles Foundation for Research in Economics.
Focardi, S., S. Cincotti and M. Marchesi (2002), "Self-organization and market crashes", *Journal of Economic Behavior and Organization*, **49**(2), 241–67.
Fujiwara, T., W. Souma, H. Aoyama, T. Kaizaji and M. Aoki (2003), "Growth and fluctuations of personal income", *Physica A*, **321**(3–4), 598–604.
Gabaix, X. (1999), "Zipf's law for cities: An explanation", *The Quarterly Journal of Economics*, **114**(3), 739–767.
Gabaix, X., P. Gopikrishnan, V. Plerou and H.E. Stanley (2003), "A theory of power-law distributions in financial market fluctuations", *Nature*, **423**, 267–70.
Galluccio, S., J.-P. Bouchaud and M. Potters (1998), "Rational decisions, random matrices and spin glasses", *Physica A*, **259**, 449–56.
Ghashghaie, S., W. Breymann, D. Peinke, P. Talkner and Y. Dodge (1996), "Turbulent cascades in foreign exchange markets", *Nature*, **381**, 767–70.
Giardina, I. and J.-P. Bouchaud (2003), "Bubbles, crashes and intermittency in agent based market models", *European Physical Journal B*, **31**(3), 421–37.
Gibrat, R. (1931), *Le Inégalités Economiques*, Paris: Librairie du Recueil.
Gode, D.K. and S. Sunder (1993), "Allocative efficiency of markets with zero-intelligence traders: Market as a partial substitute for individual rationality", *Journal of Political Economy*, **101**(1), 119–37.
Gopikrishnan, P., M. Meyer, L.A.N. Amaral and H.E. Stanley (1998), "Inverse cubic law for the probability distribution of stock price variations", *European Journal of Physics B*, **3**, 139–40.
Gopikrishnan P., V. Plerou, X. Gabaix, L.A.N. Amaral and H.E. Stanley (2001), "Price fluctuations, market activity and trading volume", *Quantitative Finance*, **1**, 262–70.

Hayes, B. (2002), "Follow the money", *American Scientist*, **90**(5), 400–405.

Huggett, M. (1996), "Wealth distribution in life-cycle economies", *Journal of Monetary Economics*, **38**(3), 469–94.

Iori, G. (2002), "A micro-simulation of traders' activity in the stock market: The role of heterogeneity of agents' interactions and trade-friction", *Journal of Economic Behavior and Organization*, **49**(2), 269–85.

Jansen, D. and C. de Vries (1991), "On the frequency of large stock returns: Putting booms and busts into perspective", *The Review of Economics and Statistics*, **73**(1), 18–24.

Johansen, A. and D. Sornette (1999a), "Financial 'anti-bubbles': Log-periodicity in gold and Nikkei collapses", *International Journal of Modern Physics C*, **10**(7), 563–75.

Johansen, A. and D. Sornette (1999b), "Predicting financial crashes using discrete scale invariance", *Journal of Risk*, **1**(4), 5–32.

Johansen, A. and D. Sornette (2001a), "Finite-time singularity in the dynamics of the world population and economic indices", *Physica A*, **294**(3–4), 405–502.

Johansen, A. and D. Sornette (2001b), "Bubbles and anti-bubbles in Latin-American, Asian and Western stock markets: An empirical study", *International Journal of Theoretical and Applied Finance*, **4**(6), 853–920.

Kareken, J. and N. Wallace (1981), "On the indeterminacy of equilibrium exchange rates", *The Quarterly Journal of Economics*, **96**, 207–22.

Kim, G. and H. Markowitz (1989), "Investment rules, margins, and market volatility", *Journal of Portfolio Management*, **16**(1), 45–52.

Kirman, A. (1991), "Epidemics of opinion and speculative bubbles in financial markets", in M. Taylor (ed.), *Money and Financial Markets*, London: Macmillan.

Kirman, A. (1992), "Whom or what does the representative agent represent?", *Journal of Economic Perspectives*, **6**(2), 117–36.

Kirman, A. (1993), "Ants, rationality, and recruitment", *The Quarterly Journal of Economics*, **108**(1), 137–56.

Knell, M. and H. Stix (2003), "Three decades of money demand studies: Similarities and differences", *Applied Economics*, **38**(7), 805–18.

Krusell, P. and A. Smith Jr. (1998), "Income and wealth heterogeneity in the macroeconomy", *Journal of Political Economy*, **106**(5), 867–96.

Kullmann, L., J. Kertész and K. Kaski (2002), "Time-dependent cross-correlations between different stock returns: A directed network of influence", *Physical Review E*, **66**(2), 026125.

Laloux, L., P. Cizeau, M. Potters and J.-P. Bouchaud (2000), "Random matrix theory and financial correlations", *International Journal of Theoretical and Applied Finance*, **3**(3), 391–7

Levy, M. and S. Solomon (1997), "New evidence for the power-law distribution of wealth", *Physica A*, **242**(1), 90–94.

Levy, H., M. Levy and S. Solomon (1994), "A microscopic model of the stock market: Cycles, booms, and crashes", *Economics Letters*, **45**(1), 103–11.

Levy, H., M. Levy and S. Solomon (1995), "Simulations of the stock market: The effects of microscopic diversity", *Journal de Physique I*, **5**(8), 1087–107.

Levy, H., M. Levy and S. Solomon (2000), *Microscopic Simulation of Financial Markets: From Investor Behavior to Market Phenomena*, San Diego: Academic Press.

Liu, Y., P. Cizeau, M. Meyer, C.-K. Peng and G. Stanley (1997), "Correlations in economic time series", *Physica A*, **245**, 437–40.

Lobato, I.N. and C. Valasco (2000), "Long memory in stock market trading volume", *Journal of Business and Economic Statistics*, **18**(4), 410–27.

Lux, T. (1995), "Herd behavior, bubbles and crashes", *The Economic Journal*, **105**(431), 881–96.

Lux, T. (1996), "The stable Paretian hypothesis and the frequency of large returns: An examination of major German stocks", *Applied Financial Economics*, **6**(6), 463–75.

Lux, T. (1997), "Time variation of second moments from a noise trader/infection model", *Journal of Economic Dynamics and Control*, **22**(1), 1–38.

Lux, T. (1998), "The socio-economic dynamics of speculative markets: Interacting agents, chaos, and the fat tails of return distributions", *Journal of Economic Behavior and Organization*, **33**(2), 143–65.
Lux, T. (2005a), "Financial power laws: Empirical evidence, models, and mechanisms", *Working Paper*, University of Kiel.
Lux, T. (2005b), "Emergent statistical wealth distributions in simple monetary exchange models: A critical review", in A. Chatterjee et al. (eds), *Econophysics of Wealth Distributions*, Milan: Springer-Verlag Italia, pp. 51–90.
Lux, T. (2008), "The Markov-switching multifractal model of asset returns: GMM estimation and linear forecasting of volatility", *Journal of Business and Economics Statistics*, **26**(3), 194–210.
Lux, T. and M. Marchesi (1999), "Scaling and criticality in a stochastic multi-agent model of a financial market", *Nature*, **397**, 498–500.
Lux, T. and M. Marchesi (2000), "Volatility clustering in financial markets: A microsimulation of interacting agents", *International Journal of Theoretical and Applied Finance*, **3**(4), 675–702.
Lux, T. and S. Schornstein (2005), "Genetic algorithms as an explanation of stylized facts of foreign exchange markets", *Journal of Mathematical Economics*, **41**, 169–96.
McCauley, J. (2006), "Response to 'worrying trends in econophysics'", *Physica A*, **371**(2), 601–9.
Mandelbrot, B. (1961), "Stable Paretian random functions and the multiplicative variation of income" *Econometrica*, **29**(4), 517–43.
Mandelbrot, B. (1963), "The variation of certain speculative prices", *Journal of Business*, **26**(4), 394–419.
Mandelbrot, B., A. Fisher and L.E. Calvet (1997), "A multifractal model of asset returns", Mimeo: Cowles Foundation for Research in Economics.
Mantegna, R.H. (1991), "Levy walks and enhanced diffusion in Milan stock exchange", *Physica A*, **179**, 232–42.
Mantegna, R. (1999), "Hierarchical structure in financial markets", *European Physical Journal B*, **11**, 193–7.
Mantegna, R.H. and H.E. Stanley (1995), "Scaling behaviour in the dynamics of an economic index", *Nature*, **376**, 46–9.
Mantegna, R.H. and H.E. Stanley (1996), "Turbulence and financial markets", *Nature*, **383**, 587–8.
Markowitz, H. (1952) "The utility of wealth", *The Journal of Political Economy*, **60**(2), 151–8.
Maslov, S. (2000), "Simple model of a limit order-driven market", *Physica A*, **278**(3), 571–8.
Matia, K. and K. Yamasaki (2005), "Statistical properties of demand fluctuations in the financial markets", *Quantitative Finance*, **5**(6), 513–17.
Nitsch, V. (2005), "Zipf zipped", *Journal of Urban Economics*, **57**(1), 86–100.
Noh, J.D. (2000), "Model for correlations in stock markets", *Physical Review E*, **61**(5), 5981–2.
O'Hara, M. (1995), *Market Microstructure Theory*, Oxford: Blackwell Business.
Okuayama, R., M. Takayasu and H. Takayasu (1999), "Zipf's law in income distribution of companies", *Physica A*, **269**(1), 125–31.
Onnela, J.-P., A. Chakraborti, K. Kaski, J. Kertesz and A.Kanto (2003), "Dynamics of market correlations: Taxonomy and portfolio analysis", *Physical Review E*, **68**(5), 056110.
Pareto, V. (1897), *Cours d'Economie Politique*, Lausanne: F. Rouge.
Peng, C.K., S.V. Buldyrev, S. Havlin, M. Simons, H.E. Stanley and A.L. Goldberger (1994), "Mosaic organization of DNA nucleotides", *Physical Review E*, **49**, 1685–9.
Plerou, V., P. Gopikrishnan and H.E. Stanley (2003), "Two-phase behavior of financial markets", *Nature*, **421**, 130.
Plerou, V., P. Gopikrishnan, B. Rosenow, L.A.N. Amaral and H.E. Stanley (2000), "A random matrix theory approach to financial cross-correlations", *Physica A*, **287**, 374–82.

Quandt, R.E. (1966), "On the size distribution of firms", *American Economic Review*, **61**(3), 416–32.

Ramsey, J. (1996), "On the existence of macro variables and macro relationships", *Journal of Economic Behavior and Organization*, **30**(3), 275–99.

Rosenow, B. (2008), "Determining the optimal dimensionality of multivariate volatility models with tools from random matrix theory", *Journal of Economic Dynamics and Control*, **32**(1), 279–302.

Sato, A.-H. and H. Takayasu (1998), "Dynamical models of stock market exchanges: From microscopic determinism to macroscopic randomness", *Physica A*, **250**, 231–52.

Silva, A.C. and V.M. Yakovenko (2005), "Temporal evolution of the 'thermal' and 'superthermal' income classes in the USA during1983–2001", *Europhysics Letters*, **69**(2), 304–10.

Silver, J., E. Slud and K. Takamoto (2002), "Statistical equilibrium wealth distributions in an exchange economy with stochastic preferences", *Journal of Economic Theory*, **106**(2), 417–35.

Sinha, S. (2005), "The rich are different! Pareto law from asymmetric interactions in asset exchange models", in A. Chatterjee et al. (eds), *Econophysics of Wealth Distributions*, Milan: Springer-Verlag Italia, pp. 177–83.

Slanina, F. (2001), "Mean-field approximation for a limit order-driven market model", *Physical Review E*, **64**(5), 056136.

Smith, E., J.D. Farmer, L. Gillemot and S. Krishnamurthy (2002), "Statistical theory of the continuous double auction", *Quantitative Finance*, **3**(6) 481–514.

Sornette, D. and A. Johansen (1997), "Large financial crashes", *Physica A*, **245**(3–4), 411–22.

Sornette, D. and W.-X. Zhou (2002), "The US 2000–2002 market descent: How much longer and deeper?", *Quantitative Finance*, **2**(6), 468–81.

Sornette, D., A. Johansen and J.-P. Bouchaud (1996), "Stock market crashes, precursors and replicas", *Journal de Physique I*, **6**(1), 167–75.

Stanley, M.H.R., S.V. Buldyrev, S. Havlin, R.N. Mantegna, M.A. Salinger and H.E. Stanley (1995), "Zipf plots and the size distribution of firms" *Economic Letters*, **49**(4) 453–57.

Stanley, M.H.R., L.A.N. Amaral, S.V. Buldyrev, S. Havlin, H. Leschhorn, P. Maass, M.A. Salinger and H.E. Stanley (1996a), "Can statistical physics contribute to the science of economics?", *Fractals*, **4**(3), 415–25.

Stanley, M.H.R., L.A.N. Amaral, S.V. Buldyrev, S. Havlin, H. Leschhorn, P. Maass, M.A. Salinger and H.E. Stanley (1996b), "Scaling behavior in the growth of companies", *Nature*, **379**, 804–6.

Stauffer, D. (2002), "How to get rich with Sornette and Zhou", *Quantitive Finance*, **2**(6), 408.

Stauffer, D. and T. Penna (1998), "Crossover in the Cont-Bouchaud percolation model for market fluctuations", *Physica A*, **256**, 284–90.

Stauffer, D. and D. Sornette (1999), "Self-organized percolation model for stockmarket fluctuations", *Physica A*, **271**(3–4), 496–506.

Stauffer, D., P. de Oliveira and A. Bernardes (1999), "Monte-Carlo simulation of volatility clustering in a market model with herding", *International Journal of Theoretical and Applied Finance*, **2**(1), 83–94.

Steindl, J. (1965), *Random Processes and the Growth of Firms: A Study of the Pareto Law*, London: Griffin.

Stigler, G. (1964), "Public regulation of the securities markets", *Journal of Business*, **37**(2), 117–42.

Sullivan, R., H. White and B. Golomb (2001), "Dangers of data mining: The case of calendar effects in stock returns", *Journal of Econometrics*, **105**(1), 249–86.

Sutton, J. (2002), "The variance of firm growth rates: The scaling puzzle", *Physica A*, **312**(3), 577–90.

Takayasu, H., H. Miura, T. Hirabayashi and K. Hamada (1992), "Statistical properties of deterministic threshold elements – the case of market price", *Physica A*, **184**, 127–34.

Tang, L.H. and G.-S. Tian (1999), "Reaction-diffusion-branching models of stock price fluctuations", *Physica A*, **264**(3), 543–50.
Vandewalle, N. and M. Ausloos (1997), "Coherent and random sequences in financial fluctuations", *Physica A*, **246**, 454–9.
Vandewalle, N. and M. Ausloos (1998), "How the financial crash of October 1997 could have been predicted", *The European Physical Journal*, **4**(2), 139–41.
Vassilicos, J.C. (1995), "Turbulence and intermittency", *Nature*, **374**, 408–9.
Vassilicos, J.C., A. Demos and F. Tata (1993), "No evidence of chaos but some evidence of multifractals in the foreign exchange and the stock market", in A.J. Crilly, R.A. Earnshaw and H. Jones (eds), *Applications of Fractals and Chaos*, Berlin: Springer.
Voit, J. (2005), *Statistical Mechanics of Financial Markets*, 3rd edn, Berlin: Springer.
Whittle, P. and H.O.A. Wold (1957), "A model explaining the Pareto distribution of wealth", *Econometrica*, **25**(4), 591–5.
Wright, I. (2005), "The social architecture of capitalism", *Physica A*, **346**(3–4), 589–620.
Yakovenko, V. and C. Silva (2005), "Two-class structure of income distribution in the U.S.A.: Exponential bulk and power-law tail", in A. Chatterjee, S. Yarlagadda and B. Chakraborti (eds), *Econophysics of Wealth Distribution*, Berlin, Springer.
Zhang, Y.-C. (1999), "Towards a theory of marginally efficient markets", *Physica A*, **269**(1), 30–44.
Zhou, W.-X. and D. Sornette (2003), "Evidence of a worldwide stock market log-periodic anti-bubble since mid-2000", *Physica A*, **330**(3–4), 543–83.
Zschischang, E. and T. Lux (2001), "Some new results on the Levy, Levy and Solomon microscopic stock market model", *Physica A*, **29**, 563–73.

10. On the analysis of time series with nonstationary increments

*Joseph L. McCauley, Kevin E. Bassler and Gemunu H. Gunaratne**

10.1 Introduction

The finance and physics literature contains many papers claiming scaling via Hurst exponents on the one hand, and fat tail scaling on the other. We can identify as the 'central dogma of econophysics' the widespread expectations of Hurst exponent scaling and fat-tailed distributions. Some dynamical models that have been postulated or (much better) inferred from empirical data are Markovian, others are not. That is, there are very strongly contradictory claims in the literature about the underlying market dynamics, although various 'stylized facts' have been widely accepted.

The inference of Markov dynamics (diffusive dynamics with no memory) from empirical data would seem to be a reasonable approximation to reality because normal financial markets are very hard to beat, while a Markovian market would be impossssible to beat. That is, we expect finance markets to be Markovian to lowest order. But what exactly do we mean by 'lowest order', and why is the Markov approximation not a 'stylized fact'?

We've recently constructed a new theoretical analysis (McCauley, Bassler and Gunaratne, 2008) based on our recent foreign exchange (FX) data analysis (Bassler, McCauley and Gunaratne, 2008) that defines below precisely what 'lowest order' means. We will explain that the 'central dogma of econophysics', Hurst exponent scaling and fat tails, fails to be realized in FX markets. We will exhibit explicitly why most existing data analyses are wrong: most data analyses make a single wrong assumption that generates both a Hurst exponent $H_s = 1/2$ and fat tails as *spurious stylized facts*, where Hurst exponents are denoted by H and fat tail exponents are denoted by μ.

We can think of finance market dynamics as a stochastic process $x(t)$ (McCauley, 2004), and the analysis of this chapter can be seen as a tale told of two variables: first, there is what *we* now define (Bassler, McCauley and Gunaratne, 2008; McCauley, Bassler and Gunaratne, 2008) as the *log return*

$$x(t) = \ln p(t)/p_c(t) \tag{10.1}$$

where $p(t)$ is the price of a stock, bond, or foreign exchange at time t, and $p_c(t)$ can be understood as 'value' (McCauley, Gunaratne and Bassler, 2005), the most probable price, the price that locates the peak of the one-point returns density $f_1(x,t)$ at time t. Then, there is what most theorists mean by the 'log return',

$$x(t, T) = x(t + T) - x(t) = \ln p(t + T)/p(t), \qquad (10.2)$$

but which is clearly a *log increment*. We will explain that the log return $x(t)$ is always a 'good' variable, both in theory and data analysis, and then we will explain why the use of the log increment $x(t, T)$ in data analysis leads to spurious stylized facts, to both $H_s = 1/2$ and spurious fat tails in a wrongly extracted one-point returns density f_s, where the subscript 's' denotes (generated via using a) 'sliding window'. We will show that the one-point returns density $f_1(x, t)$ correctly extracted from market time series does not scale with H over a time scale of a day or a week, and has no fat tails in intraday trading. We speculate that stock prices, in contrast, may perhaps exhibit fat tails (but not Hurst exponent scaling) over those same time scales, but we haven't done the required stock returns analysis.

Markov processes generate uncorrelated increments that are generally nonstationary: $\langle x(t, T)x(t, -T)\rangle = 0$ where $x(t, -T) = x(t) - x(t - T)$, and the mean square fluctuation $\langle x^2(t, T)\rangle$ about a specific point $x(t)$ depends on the starting time t. The latter condition guarantees nonstationarity of the increments. In FX (and in most other) data analyses, stationary increments are implicitly assumed via the use of a technique called 'sliding windows'. A 'sliding window' is used to build histograms that, in the presence of nonstationary increments, cannot reflect $f_1(x, t)$, and can at best reflect a spurious density $f_s(z, t, T)$, by reading a time series using $z = x(t, T)$ while fixing T and sliding the starting time t along the series. The increments in intraday finance data are *not* stationary (Bassler, McCauley and Gunaratne, 2008) so that the sliding window method produces spurious stylized facts. We emphasize intraday statistics because, even with a six-year time series, there simply are not enough points at each time t to calculate ensemble averages meaningfully over the time scale even of one week.

Another conclusion that we draw is that scaling doesn't matter anyway, scaling gives us no information whatsoever about either the underlying market dynamics or memory. The purpose of this chapter is to explain these assertions, and to indicate how to analyze random time series correctly without generating spurious stylized facts. Our method and conclusions are not restricted to finance data but have application to the analysis of any random time series, whether in physics, economics, biology, or elsewhere. We should emphasize that this is a completely new viewpoint in the theory of stochastic processes and in data analysis.

10.2 Hurst exponent scaling

We define scaling, meaning self-similarity, starting from the mathematicians' standpoint (Mandelbrot and van Ness, 1968; Embrechts and Maejima, 2002) and then show that their definition is equivalent to our recent definition (Bassler, Gunaratne and McCauley, 2006; McCauley, Gunaratne and Bassler, 2007a) in terms of densities, so long as the moments of the one-point density are finite.

A stochastic process $x(t)$ is said be self-similar with scaling exponent H, $0 < H < 1$, if (Embrechts and Maejima, 2002)

$$x(t) = t^H x(1), \tag{10.3}$$

where by equality we mean equality 'in distribution'. Note first that scaling trajectories necessarily pass through the 'filter' $x(0)=0$; trajectories with $x(0) \neq 0$ cannot scale. Second, a method designed by Hurst to detect trends was originally used to define a different scaling exponent that he called K, and which Mandelbrot and Taqqu (1979) called the Joseph exponent J. However, the notation 'H' was used by Mandelbrot and van Ness (1968) to describe fractional Brownian motion (fBm), a self-similar process that *does* produce the trends of the Hurst-Mandelbrot 'Joseph effect' via long time pair correlations arising from stationarity of the increments. Mandelbrot and Taqqu distinguished H from J on the basis of Hurst's R/S construction, and noted that while $H = J$ for fBm, for example, for processes without long time increment autocorrelations, like Levy processes (and, we should add, drift-free Markov processes), $H \neq J = 1/2$. Embrechts and Maejima (2002) denote the self-similarity exponent by H, but stop short of writing *H(urst)*. Because of the confusion in the literature, wherein $H \neq 1/2$ is too often but wrongly thought to imply long time pair correlations, we will call the self-similarity exponent H 'the Hurst exponent' and emphasize that self-similarity, taken alone, does not and cannot produce (drift-free) trends in the form of long time pair correlations. We will introduce another exponent, the 'spurious Hurst exponent', which we denote by H_s, and will see that H_s plays essentially the same role as the Joseph exponent: $H \neq H_s = 1/2$ whenever there is self-similarity without long time pair correlations, but $H = H_s \neq 1/2$ in the presence of long time pair correlations. The essential requirement for long time pair correlations will be seen to be stationarity of the increments, not self-similarity (equation 10.3).

Self-similarity and stationarity of the increments are confused together into an unhealthy soup too often in the literature (see, for example, the definition of the Hurst exponent in Wikipedia, http://en.wikipedia.org/wiki/Hurst_exponent, where the note added October 2007 is ours). Now for the definition of self-similarity in terms of probability densities, which explains what is meant by asserting that $x(t) = t^H x(1)$ 'in distribution'.

The one-point density $f_1(x, t)$ reflects the statistics collected from many different runs of the time evolution of $x(t)$ from a specified initial condition $x(t_o)$, say $x(0) = 0$, but cannot describe correlations or the lack of same. Given a dynamical variable $A(x,t)$, absolute (as opposed to conditional) averages of A are calculated via

$$\langle A(t) \rangle = \int^{\infty} A(x, t) f_1(x, t) dx. \tag{10.4}$$

From (10.1), the moments of x must obey

$$\langle x^n(t) \rangle = t^{nH} \langle x^n(1) \rangle = c_n t^{nH}. \tag{10.5}$$

Combining this with

$$\langle x^n(t) \rangle = \int X^n f_1(x, t) dx \tag{10.6}$$

we obtain (Bassler, McCauley and Gunaratne, 2008)

$$f_1(x,t) = t^{-H} F(u), \tag{10.7}$$

where the scaling variable is $u = x/t^H$ (Bassler, Gunaratne and McCauley, 2006).

In contrast, conditional averages $\langle A(x, t) \rangle_{\text{cond}}$ would require the two-point density

$$f_2(x, t + T; y, t) = p_2(x, t + T | y, t) f_1(y, t), \tag{10.8}$$

or, more to the point, the two-point transition density $p_2(x, t + T: y, t)$ (McCauley, Bassler and Gunaratne, 2008).

If the absolute average of $x(t)$ vanishes, then the variance is simply

$$\sigma^2 = \langle x^2(t) \rangle = \langle x^2(1) \rangle t^{2H}. \tag{10.9}$$

This explains what is meant by Hurst exponent scaling, and also specifies what's meant by (10.1) holds 'in distribution'. Vanishing of the absolute average of x does not mean that there's no conditional trend: in fractional Brownian motion (fBm), for example, the conditional average of x does not vanish and depends on t. In a Markov process, scaling requires that the drift rate depends at worst on t (is independent of x) and has been subtracted, that by 'x' we really mean the detrended variable $x(t) - \int R(s)ds$. Markov processes with x-independent drift can be trivially detrended, but fBm cannot be detrended because the 'trend' is due to long time correlations, not to an additive drift term (McCauley, Bassler and Gunaratne, 2008).

Empirically, the best evidence for scaling would be a data collapse of the form $F(u) = t^H f_1(x, t)$. A weaker altenative is to look for scaling of a finite number of the moments $\langle x^n(t)\rangle$. It's important to understand that Hurst exponent scaling, taken alone, tells us nothing about the underlying stochastic dynamics. More to the point, a one-point density tells us nothing about the dynamics (Hänggi et al., 1978; McCauley, 2007; McCauley, Bassler and Gunaratne, 2008), and scaling is at best a characterization of one-point densities: even if scaling holds at the one-point level, as in fBm, the two-point density (the transition density p_2) and the pair corelations $\langle x(t + T)x(t)\rangle$ do *not* scale, and it's the transition density p_2 that's required to give us any idea at all of the underlying dynamics. In particular, scaling, taken alone, implies neither the presence nor absence of autocorrelations in increments/displacements taken over nonoverlapping time intervals. That is, scaling has nothing whatsoever to say about whether a market is effectively efficient (hard to beat), or is easily beatable, in contrast to what one of us incorrectly assumed earlier (McCauley, 2004; McCauley, Gunaratne and Bassler, 2005).

10.3 Stationary vs. nonstationary processes

A necessary but insuffcient condition for a stationary process $x(t)$ is a normalizable, time-independent one-point density $f_1(x)$ (Stratonovich, 1963; McCauley, 2004). The mean and variance and all other moments are constants. A stationary process represents statistical equilibrium, a state of maximum Gibbs entropy. Stationary processes have never been observed in financial markets, nor has convincing evidence been presented for asymptotic stationarity (an approach to equilibrium) in *any* market, financial or nonfinancial. In financial markets the variance is strongly time-dependent, we see no asymptotic approach to statistical equilibrium. We should therefore forget about equilibrium and stationary processes in order to understand real markets.

Self-similar processes (10.1) are strongly nonstationary: by (10.4), the moments do not approach constants; rather, the one-point density necessarily spreads in width forever, reflecting the continual loss of information about where $x(t)$ lies. But a nonstationary process may have either stationary or nonstationary *increments* (Stratonovich, 1963). Stationarity of the increments is the crucial point for understanding long time autocorrelations that would make a market easily beatable in principle. A hard-to-beat market will have pair correlations that look Markovian, but memory may be present in higher-order correlations. Such a market is described by a martingale stochastic process $x(t)$ (McCauley, Bassler and Gunaratne, 2008).

In the financial economics literature one can find many wrong claims about financial time series. In Fama (1970), for example, the claim is made that returns are uncorrelated, $\langle x(t + T)x(t)\rangle = 0$. More recently, Rickles (2007, 2008) reports the claim that prices are random (by 'random' we should here understand 'uncorrelated') but returns are not random. The correct statements, explained below, are that neither prices nor returns are uncorrelated, $\langle p(t + T)p(t)\rangle \neq 0, \langle x(t + T)x(t)\rangle \neq 0$, but *increments* in returns are approximated zero after a trading time of 10 minutes: $\langle x(t, T)x(t, - T)\rangle \approx 0$ for $T \geq 10$ minutes of trading (Bassler, McCauley and Gunaratne, 2008). The latter is basically the effectively efficient market hypothesis: one cannot make money systematically by trading on either simple averages or pair correlations (McCauley, Bassler and Gunaratne, 2008).

10.4 Stationary vs. nonstationary increments

Stationary processes are often confused with stationary increments in the literature (see Bassler, Gunaratne and McCauley, 2006 for a discussion). Stationary increments are implicitly assumed without prior justification in data analyses whenever a sliding window method is used, and the sliding window method is quite commonly found in the literature (Borland, 1998; Dacorogna et al., 2001; D. Matteo, Aste and Dacorogna, 2003; McCauley and Gunaratne, 2003). We define stationary and nonstationary increments and exhibit their implications for the question of long time autocorrelations, or complete lack of autocorrelations. We show that the question of stationary increments, not scaling, is central for the existence of long time correlations.

By increments, we mean displacements $x(t, T) = x(t + T) - x(t)$. Stationary increments of a nonstationary process $x(t)$ are defined by (Stratonovich, 1963; Embrechts and Maejima, 2002)

$$x(t + T) - x(t) = x(T), \tag{10.10}$$

'in distribution', with $x(0) = 0$, and by nonstationary increments (Stratonovich, 1963; McCauley, Gunaratne and Bassler, 2007a; McCauley, Bassler and Gunaratne, 2008) we mean that

$$x(t + T) - x(t) \neq x(T) \tag{10.11}$$

in distribution (again, taking $x(0)=0$ here). The implications of this distinction for data analysis, and for understanding Hurst exponents, are central. In the latter case the density of increments $z = x(t, T)$ must be obtained from the two-point density, and must be obtained from $f_2(x(t), x(t+T); t, t+T)$ and depends on starting time t,

$$f(z, t, t+T) = \int dxdy f_2(y, t+T; x, t)\delta(z - y + x), \quad (10.12)$$

whereas for stationary increments this one-point density is independent of t, $f(z, t, t+T) = f_s(z, 0, T)$. Since the series are nonstationary, there is no convergence theorem to suggest that histograms obtained from sliding a window should reflect the correct increment density.

By the efficient market hypothesis (EMH) (Skjeltorp, 2000; McCauley, Bassler and Gunaratne, 2008) is often meant that the market is impossible to beat, that there are no correlations at all (no systematically repeated price/returns patterns) that can be exploited for profit. Such a market is necessarily uncorrelated noise, albeit not simply uncorrelated Gaussian noise. A Markov market satisfies the condition of an impossible-to-beat market. Because real markets are very hard (if not necessarily impossible) to beat, models that generate no autocorrelations in increments are a good zeroth order approximation to real markets (McCauley, Bassler and Gunaratne, 2008). In such models, the autocorrelations in increments $x(t, T)$ and $x(t, -T)$ vanish

$$\langle (x(t_1) - x(t_1 - T_1))(x(t_2 + T_2) - x(t_2)) \rangle = 0, \quad (10.13)$$

if there is no time interval overlap,

$$[t_1 - T_1, t_1] \cap [t_2, t_2 + T_2] = \varphi, \quad (10.14)$$

where Φ denotes the empty set on the line. This is a much weaker and more pregnant condition than would be asserting that the increments are statistically independent. Condition (10.14) is in fact a martingale condition in weak disguise. Equation (10.14) means that nothing that happened in an earlier time interval can be used to predict systematically the returns in a later time interval at the level of (simple averages and) pair correlations. That is, the market is 'effectively efficient' in the sense that simple averages and pair correlations look Markovian, unlike fBm there is no memory in pair correlations to be exploited. This does not rule out higher-order correlations that could be used for arbitrage/technical trading. That is, a Markovian market is 'efficient' in the strictest sense, is impossible to beat, whereas a martingale market looks Markovian to lowest order (at the level of simple averages and pair correlations), but might be systematically beatable at some higher level of insight. This defines precisely what we mean by 'lowest order'.

Consider a stochastic process $x(t)$ where the increments are uncorrelated. From this condition we easily obtain the autocorrelation function for returns $x(t)$

$$\langle x(t)x(s)\rangle = \langle (x(t) - x(s))x(s)\rangle + \langle x^2(s)\rangle = \langle x^2(s)\rangle > 0, \quad (14.15)$$

since $x(s) - x(t_o) = x(s)$, so that $\langle x(t)x(t + T\rangle = \langle x^2(t)\rangle^2 = \sigma^2(t)$ is simply the variance in x. *This is a martingale condition,*

$$\langle x(t + T)\rangle_{\text{cond}} = x(t), \quad (10.16)$$

or

$$\int \mathrm{d}y y p_2(y, t + T|x, t) = x. \quad (10.17)$$

We next obtain a simple but very important result. Combining

$$\langle (x(t + T) - x(t))^2\rangle = +\langle (x^2(t + T)\rangle + \langle x^2(t)\rangle - 2\langle x(t + T)x(t)\rangle \quad (10.18)$$

with (10.14), we get

$$\langle (x(t + T) - x(t))^2\rangle = \langle x^2(t + T)\rangle - \langle x^2(t)\rangle \quad (10.19)$$

which depends on both t and T, excepting the rare case where the variance $\langle x^2(t)\rangle$ is linear in t. *Martingale increments are uncorrelated and are generally nonstationary*. That is, we must expect nonstationary increments in effectively efficient markets.

Consider next the class of all stochastic processes with stationary increments, $x(t, T) = x(0, T)$ 'in distribution'. Here, we begin with

$$-2\langle x(t + T)x(t)\rangle = \langle (x(t + T) - x(t))^2\rangle - \langle (x^2(t + T)\rangle - \langle x^2(t)\rangle, \quad (10.20)$$

and then using (10.8) on the right-hand side of (10.18) we obtain

$$-2\langle x(t + T)x(t)\rangle = \langle (x^2(T)\rangle - \langle (x^2(t + T)\rangle - \langle x^2(t)\rangle, \quad (10.21)$$

which differs from (10.13). The increment autocorrelation function is

$$2\langle (x(t) - x(t - T))(x(t + T) - x(t))\rangle = \langle x^2(2T)\rangle - 2\langle x^2(T)\rangle, \quad (10.22)$$

which vanishes iff the variance $\langle x^2(t)\rangle$ is linear in t. *Stationary increments are typically strongly correlated.* For example, if scaling (10.3) holds then we obtain the prediction of infinitely long time autocorrelations

$$\langle (x(t) - x(t - T))(x(t + T) - x(t))\rangle = \langle x^2(T)\rangle(2^{2H-1} - 1). \tag{10.23}$$

characteristic of fBm (Mandelbrot and van Ness, 1968; McCauley, Gunaratne and Bassler, 2007a). This autocorrelation vanishes iff $H = 1/2$, otherwise the autocorrelations are strong for all time scales T. Such fluctuations violate the EMH, especially if H cannot be approximated as $H = 1/2$, and therefore could at best occur as higher-order effects in finance markets. Note that scaling is not the essential point, is in fact irrelevant: stationarity of the increments, reflected in the t-independent pair correlations (10.21), is the central requirement for long time increment autocorrelations.

Summarizing, the Hurst exponent H, taken alone, tells us nothing whatsoever about autocorrelations in increments, tells us nothing whatsover about the underlying dynamics apart from scaling itself, and tells us nothing whatsoever about the effficiency or lack of same of a market. In the next two sections we will sharpen the distinction by exhibiting both scaling Markov processes and fBm where $H \neq 1/2$.

10.5 Markov processes

An arbitrary stochastic process may have memory. By 'finite memory' we mean a 'filtration' $(x_{n-1}, x_{n-2}, \ldots, x_1)$ that every trajectory must pass through. The two-point transition density then depends on n points, and the hierarchy of transition densities obeys

$$p_{k-1}(x_k, t_k|x_{k-2}, t_{k-2}; \ldots; x_1, t_1) = \int dx_{k-1} p_k(x_k, t_k|x_{k-1}, t_{k-1}; \ldots; x_1, t_1)$$
$$p_{k-1}(x_{k-1}, t_{k-1}|x_{k-2}, t_{k-2}; \ldots; x_1, t_1) \tag{10.24}$$

with $k = 2, \ldots, n$. In particular,

$$p_2(x_3, t_3|x_1, t_1) = \int dx_2 p_3(x_3, t_3|x_2, t_2; x_1, t_1) p_2(x_2, t_2|x_1, t_1). \tag{10.25}$$

A Markov process is a stochastic process without memory (Wang and Uhlenbeck, 1954; Stratonovich, 1963; Durrett, 1984): the conditional probability density for $x(t_n)$ in a time series $\{x(t_1), x(t_2), \ldots x(t_n)\}$ depends only on $x(t_{n-1})$, and so is independent of all earlier trajectory history $x_1, \ldots, x_{n-2}$. In this case

$$p_k(x_k, t_k|x_{k-1}, t_{k-1}; \ldots; x_1, t_1) = p_2(x_k, t_k|x_{k-1}, t_{k-1}) \tag{10.26}$$

and so

$$p_2(x_3, t_3|x_1, t_1) = \int dx_2 p_2(x_3, t_3|x_2, t_2) p_2(x_2, t_2|x_1, t_1). \tag{10.27}$$

All knowledge of the dynamics is contained in the two-point transition density depending on two points. This means that the drift diffusion coefficients of a Markov process cannot depend on any memory at all, including not on the initial condition. The drift and diffusion coefficients may depend on the present point $(x(t), t)$ alone and on no other points. This delineates drift-free Markov processes from martingales. In a martingale there can be memory of one or more points in the two-point transition density, and this memory can then appear in the diffusion coefficient, which is constructed from the two-point transition density depending on $n - 1$ points (McCauley, Bassler and Gunaratne, 2008). FBm, in contrast, has stationary increments and depends on the entire past history and so cannot be constructed via a *finite* filtration of the past.

For martingales, including drift-free Markov processes (meaning that Markov processes with trivial drift coefficients $R(t)$ are allowed), we know already that we have vanishing increment autocorrelations, $\langle x(t_2, T)x(t_1, -T)\rangle = 0$, for nonoverlapping time intervals $t_1 < t_2$ with $T > 0$.

For an Ito process, a martingale plus drift, the drift and diffusion coefficients are defined by

$$R(x, t; \textit{history}) = \frac{1}{T}\langle x(t + T) - x(t)\rangle$$
$$\approx \frac{1}{T}\int (y - x)p_2(y, t + T|x, t; x_{n-1}, t_{n-1}; \ldots; x_1, t_1)dy \tag{10.28}$$

and

$$D(x, t; \textit{history}) = \frac{1}{T}\langle (x(t + T) - x(t))^2\rangle$$
$$\approx \frac{1}{T}\int dy(y - x)^2 p_2(y, t + T|x, t; x_{n-1}, t_{n-1}; \ldots; x_1, t_1) \tag{10.29}$$

as T vanishes. But one never knows the transition density in advance. Rather, one must deduce a model diffusion coefficient $D(x, t)$ empirically (Bassler, McCauley and Gunaratne, 2008).

As an aside, we see that Markov processes with variance scaling with $H \neq 1/2$ will generate nonstationary, uncorrelated increments.

10.6 Scaling Ito processes

We review scaling Ito processes (Durrett, 1984; Bassler, Gunaratne and McCauley, 2006) in order to contrast increment-uncorrelated drift-free Gaussian-Markov processes with fBm, which is a Gaussian process with stationary increments.

Here, we restrict to the one-point density $f_1(x, t) = p_2(x, t; 0, 0)$, the full transition density does not scale (pair correlations do not scale with H even if $x(t) = t^H x(1)$!). Therefore, only trajectories with $x(0) = 0$ can occur.

An Ito process is generated locally by the stochastic differential equation (SDE) (Gunaratne and McCauley, 2005)

$$\mathrm{d}x = R(x,t) + \sqrt{D(x,t)}\mathrm{d}B(t) \tag{10.30}$$

where $B(t)$ is the Wiener process (McCauley, Gunaratne and Bassler, 2007a; McCauley, Bassler and Gunaratne, 2008). The Wiener process is a drift-free uncorrelated Gaussian process scaling with $H = 1/2$, so that the increments are stationary and (from Ito's theorem [Friedman, 1975; McCauley, 2004]) $\mathrm{d}B^2 = \mathrm{d}t = \langle(\mathrm{d}B)^2\rangle$. Iff $R(x, t) = R(t)$ is independent of x can we detrend all trajectories once and for all by replacing $x(t)$ by $x(t) - \int R(s)\mathrm{d}s$. With this substitution, the Ito process is a martingale. Finite memory may be present but we will not write the possible memory explicitly. Instead, we will use the notation of a Markov process for simplicity. So, the absolute average gives $\langle x(t)\rangle = 0$ and there is no trend.

The variance can be calculated from (10.29) as

$$\sigma^2 = \int_0^t \mathrm{d}s \int_{-\infty}^{\infty} \mathrm{d}x f_1(x, s) D(x, s), \tag{10.31}$$

where $x(0) = 0$, so that scaling of the density and the variance imply that the diffusion coefficient scales as well (Bassler, Gunaratne and McCauley, 2006):

$$D(x, t) = t^{2H-1} D(u), u = x/t^H. \tag{10.32}$$

Note that scaling of D does not imply scaling of the transition density $p_2(x, t + T; x_o, t)$ because the limit of vanishing T and the integration over x_o in (10.28) cannot be interchanged.

We can think of (10.31) as the global volatility (McCauley, 2004). Using the fact that $f_1(x, 0) = \delta(x)$, we obtain the 'local volatility' for the case where t is near zero,

$$\sigma^2 \approx D(x, t)\Delta t. \tag{10.33}$$

We can also write the mean square fluctuation about an arbitrary point $x(t)$ globally as

$$\langle (x(t+T) - x(t))^2 \rangle$$
$$= \int_t^{t+T} ds \int_{-\infty}^{\infty} dx f_1(x,s) D(x,s) = \langle x^2(1) \rangle ((t+T)^{2H} - t^{2H}) \quad (10.34)$$

and locally as

$$\langle (x(t+T) - x(t))^2 \rangle \approx t^{2H-1} D(u) T. \quad (10.35)$$

Both the global and local mean square fluctuations will prove to be useful in data analysis (Section 10.10).

Hurst exponent scaling for Markov processes is possible with $R(t)$ independent of x, but not with arbitrary drift $R(x, t)$. For example, the drift $R(x, t) = r - D(x, t)/2$ that would in principle be required for risk-neutral, or Martingale option pricing (McCauley, Gunaratne and Bassler, 2006) does not scale. One can derive a scaling requirement for a general drift $R(x, t)$, but such scaling is generally not satisfied. We assumed a time-dependent drift $R(t)$ that has been removed, so that by $x(t)$ we mean $x(t) - \int R(t)dt$. The empirical evidence for this approximation will be discussed below. This means that we can work with the drift-free Fokker-Planck partial differential equation (PDE)

$$\frac{\partial p_2}{\partial t} = \frac{1}{2} \frac{\partial^2}{\partial x^2} (D p_2), \quad (10.36)$$

where scaling may occur at best only for $f_1(x, t) = p_2(x, t{:}\ 0, 0,)$.

Scaling solutions for Markov processes are easily calculated (Durrett, 1984; Alejandro-Quinones et al., 2006; Bassler, Gunaratne and McCauley, 2006). With

$$f_1(x, t) = t^{-H} F(u); u = x/t^H \quad (10.37)$$

and

$$D(x, t) = t^{2H-1} D(u), u = x/t^H \quad (10.38)$$

the Fokker-Planck PDE (10.32) yields

$$2H(uF(u))' + (D(u)F(u))'' = 0, \quad (10.39)$$

which we integrate to obtain

$$F(u) = \frac{C}{D(u)} e^{-2H\int u\mathrm{d}u/D(u)}. \tag{10.40}$$

For $H \neq 1/2$ all of these processes generate nonstationary increments. If

$$D(u) = 1 + |u| \tag{10.41}$$

then

$$F(u) \frac{C}{(1 + |u|)^{1-2H}} e^{-2H|u|}, \tag{10.42}$$

yielding a pure exponential density iff $2H = 1$.

We can also study the class of quadratic diffusion coefficients

$$D(u) = \mathrm{d}'(\varepsilon)(1 + \varepsilon u^2), \tag{10.43}$$

which yields the two parameter (ε, H) class of Student's-*t*-like densities

$$F(u) = C'(1 + \varepsilon u^2)^{-1 - H/\varepsilon \mathrm{d}'(\varepsilon)} \tag{10.44}$$

with tail exponent $\mu = 2 + 2H/\varepsilon \mathrm{d}'(\varepsilon)$, and where H and ε are independent parameters to be determined empirically. This shows where Student's-*t*-like distributions come from (Bassler, Gunaratne and McCauley, 2006). Here, we generate all fat tail exponents $2 < \mu < \infty$, and obtain a finite variance (10.1) scaling as $\sigma^2 = ct^{2H}$ whenever $\mu > 3$ (for $2 \leq \mu \leq 3$ the variance is infinite).

In particular, the choice $D(\mathrm{u}) = D =$ constant yields the Gaussian returns model $F(u) = (H/\pi)^{1/2}\exp(-Hu^2/D\langle x^2(1)\rangle) - (1/2\pi\langle x^2(1)\rangle^{1/2}$ $\exp(u^2/2\langle x^2(1)\rangle)$ with $0 < H < 1$. Gaussian-Markov processes with $H \neq 1/2$ generate nonstationary increments. But there are Gaussian processes that are not Markovian.

10.7 Fractional Brownian motion

FBm is defined to be a stationary increment Gaussian process with Hurst exponent scaling, $0 < H < 1$ (Embrechts and Maejima, 2002). We now explicitly construct the one- and two-point Gaussian densities of fBm. In general, infinitely many transition densities in the hierarchy p_k, $k = 1, 2, \ldots, n, \ldots$ are required to characterize fBm, but all those transition densities are known once the pair correlation is specified (this is peculiar to a Gaussian process). The pair correlation function $\langle x(t)x(t + T)\rangle$ is completely specified by two separate conditions: (1) increment stationarity, and (2) scaling.

Fractional Brownian motion is not an Ito process; Ito processes admit at worst finite filtrations. But we can obtain non-Ito-type scaling (10.1) from integrals of the type (McCauley, Gunaratne and Bassler, 2007a)

$$x_H(t+T) - x_H(t) = \int_{-\infty}^{T} k(T,s)\mathrm{d}B(s) = x_H(T) \tag{10.45}$$

if the kernel scales, $k(t, s) = t^{H-1/2}k(1, s/t)$, *and* if the lower limit of integration is, as shown, at $s = -\infty$ or is $t = 0$. Long-time correlations for increments over nonoverlapping time intervals (10.21) follow iff the increments of (10.45) are stationary, and this requires that the lower limit of integration in (10.45) is $t = -\infty$. Mandelbrot and van Ness (1968) have provided us with a specific scaling model *with stationary increments*,

$$\begin{aligned} x_H(t) = HK\int_{-\infty}^{0} [(t-s)^{H-1/2} - (-s)^{H-1/2}]\mathrm{d}B(s) \\ + \int_{0}^{t} [(t-s)^{H-1/2}\mathrm{d}B(s), \end{aligned} \tag{10.46}$$

a model of fBm with $\sigma^2(t) = K\langle x^2(1)\rangle t^{2H}$. Deleting the first integral in (10.46) would yield a scaling process with *nonstationary* increments.

We can construct the two-point Gaussian density that defines fBm. Any two-point Gaussian density (Wang and Uhlenbeck, 1954) is given by

$$f_2(x,t) = \frac{1}{2\pi \det B} e^{-x^{+}B^{-1}x} \tag{10.47}$$

where

$$B_{kl} = \langle x_k x_l \rangle \tag{10.48}$$

defines the autocorrelation matrix. Without specifying the pair correlations (10.48), one cannot say whether the process $x(t)$ is Markovian or not. The autocorrelation

$$\langle x(s)x(t)\rangle = \frac{\langle x^2(1)\rangle}{2}(|s|^{2H} + |t|^{2H} - |s-t|^{2H}) \tag{10.49}$$

enforces stationary increments and therefore will enforce the long time autocorrelations of fBm in the increments. Scaling of $x(t)$ with H is also asssumed in agreement with (10.45), but note that $\langle x(t)x(t+T)\rangle$ does *not* scale with either t or $s = t + T$. The resulting two-point density of fBm can be written as[1]

$$f_2(x(s),s;x(t),t) = \frac{1}{2\pi\sigma_1\sigma_2(1-\rho^2)^{1/2}} e^{-(x^2(s)/\sigma_1^2 + x^2(t)/\sigma_2^2 - 2\rho x(s)xs(t)/\sigma_1\sigma_2/2(1-\rho^2)^2} \tag{10.50}$$

where $\sigma_1\sigma_2\rho = \langle x(t)x(s)\rangle$, $\sigma_1^2 = \langle x^2(1)\rangle |s|^{2H}$ and $\sigma_2^2 = \langle x^2(1)\rangle |t|^{2H}$ and

$$\rho = (|s|^{2H} + |t|^{2H} - |t-s|^{2H})/2|st|^H. \tag{10.51}$$

If we integrate over the earlier variable $x(s)$, taking $s < t$, then we obtain the one-point density f_1,

$$f_1(x, t, -\infty) = \frac{t^{-H}}{\sqrt{2\pi\langle x^2(1)\rangle}} e^{-x^2/2\langle x^2(1)\rangle t^{2H}}, \tag{10.52}$$

which scales with H, and is identical with the density for a scaling martingale process. This merely reflects the fact (Hänggi et al., 1978; McCauley, 2007) that a one-point density tells us nothing whatsoever about the underlying dynamics.

The implication of this chapter, so far, for the analysis of time series is: the two central questions are those of nonstationary vs. stationary increments, and correlated vs. uncorrelated increments. Uncorrelated increments are nonstationary with a variance nonlinear in t, whereas stationary increments exhibit long time autocorrelations for a variance nonlinear in t. These separate points are confused together into an inedible soup in the econophysics and finance literature.

10.8 Liquidity, noise traders, and crashes

An essential implicit assumption for the applicability of continuous (x, t) stochastic processes is that the market is an adequate 'liquidity bath', meaning a very liquid market. By a liquid market we mean the following: a liquidity bath is assumed, in part analogous to the heat bath in statistical physics, where approximately reversible trades are possible via your discount broker in real time over the shortest time intervals Δt on the order of a few seconds on your iBook or PC. This assumption is represented by the noise term $\sqrt{D(x,t)}dB(t)$, which describes the behavior of the 'noise traders'. Noise traders (Black, 1986) provide the liquidity/entropy (McCauley, 2004) in the market. Mathematically seen, noise traders *are* the market 'with measure one' in a continuous in (x, t) stochastic process where all discrete effects are ignored. Noise traders, uncertain about 'value', buy and sell frequently: a financial market is essentially noise because most traders don't have inside or other useful knowledge to trade on.

Fat tails do not describe market crashes. Markets with or without fat tails crash in the same way: fat tails describe large returns that occur during very liquid markets. In contrast, a market crash is a *liquidity drought*, where the noise traders can't sell because there are effectively no buyers, and is described qualitatively to zeroth order by $R << 0$ and $D(x, t) \approx 0$.

10.9 Defining 'value' dynamically

Note that the diffusion coefficients for scaling martingale processes defined in Section 10.4 have minima where the scale invariant part $F(u)$ of the density peaks, at $u = 0$. But remember that 'x' is a martingale, the average drift was subtracted. If we replace x by $x - Rt$ then we obtain one-point densities $f_1(x, t)$ of the stochastic process that peak instead at $x = Rt$, and the diffusion coefficients correspondingly have minima there. For example, for the linear diffusion model with scaling,

$$D(x, t) = t^{2H-1}(1 + |x - Rt|/t^{1/2}). \tag{10.53}$$

Now, were equilibrium possible, then the time-invariant definition of 'value' would be the most probable price, the price where $f_1(x)$ is a maximum. Either the average price or the most probable price could be used in that case to define value. We can generalize this and identify 'value' dynamically as the price $p_c(t)$ where $f_1(x, t)$ peaks, because that is the price that most traders agree on at time t. This is essentially the same as the consensus price p_c given by the average return $\langle x(t) \rangle = Rt$, so that we identify the price p_c in $x = \ln p(t)/p_c$ as the most probable price, or 'value' at $t = 0$. We see from (10.53) that value evolves in time as $p_c(t) = p_c e^{-Rt}$, where, in $f_1(x, t)$ and $D(x, t)$, we can write $x - Rt = \ln(p(t)/p_c(t))$. This generalizes the neo-classical definition of value to nonstationary markets (McCauley, Gunaratne and Bassler, 2005).

The price p_c defines the 'consensus price' because it is the most widely agreed-upon price of the financial instrument at time t. Unfortunately, the average rate of return R in $\langle x(t) \rangle \approx Rt$ of $f_1(x, t)$ does not stand still, it can shift suddenly in a market crash and even in normal intraday or intraday trading: the expected return R can change discontinuously with sudden changes in noise traders' sentiments. In other words, 'value' is a very strongly and discontinuously time-dependent notion, it depends on what most noise traders believe about an instrument at any given time. In particular, 'value' is generally not accurately predictable in advance. This is an example of complexity. We can only know accurately what value was at different times in the past. This means that notions like 'overvalued' and 'undervalued' are knowable only at the present time or historically, but usually cannot be predicted with any degree of confidence for the future. Most technical traders use past data (charts) to try to anticipate the future value, while some few exceptional traders like George Soros do something entirely different.

Fischer Black (1986) believed, apparently uncritically, in the neoclassical notion of stable market equilibrium (so did Merton and Scholes, as the history of long-term capital management [LTCM; Dunbar, 2000] makes clear): Black argued that prices will deviate from 'value' but will always tend to return to 'value' (1986). Here, he was wrong: there is no tendency at all for prices to 'return to value'. Because market dynamics are unstable/nonstationary, price always diffuses away from 'value', there being no 'springs' in the market to pull prices back to value (McCauley, 2004). In contrast, Soros' (1998) words are correct: financial markets are dynamically unstable.

10.10 FX market facts vs. spurious 'stylized facts'

For the typical expectations of theorists about FX markets we repeat here the 'observed stylized facts' stated by Hommes (2002): (1) asset prices are persistent and have, or are close to having, a unit root and are thus (close to) nonstationary; (2) asset returns are fairly unpredictable, and typically have little or no autocorrelations; (3) asset returns have fat tails and exhibit volatility clustering and long memory. Autocorrelations of squared returns and absolute returns are significantly positive, even at high-order lags, and decay slowly; (4) trading volume is persistent and there is positive cross-correlation between volatility and volume. This is the standard picture. Next, we contrast those expectations with the results of our recent FX data analysis (Bassler, McCauley and Gunaratne, 2008). Our analysis is based on six years of euro/dollar exchange rates taken at one-minute intervals. Using those results, we can now correct Hommes' mis-statements of the facts of finance markets.

In point (1) 'unit root' means martingale and we've established that, correspondingly (prices and) returns are highly nonstationary. Prices are not 'persistent', prices are just as unpredictable as returns (the one is a simple coordinate transformation on the other). (2) Both prices and returns have positive autocorrelation, $\langle x(t+T)x(t)\rangle = \langle x^2(t)\rangle > 0$, and autocorrelations in increments are approximately zero after 20 minutes of trading, $\langle x(t, T)x(t,-T)\rangle \approx 0$. (3) Asset returns have martingale autocorrelations and therefore uncorrelated increments. We find no fat tails (or Hurst exponent scaling) on the time scale of a day or a week, and a seven-year. FX time series is far too short to indicate what may happen on the time scale of a month, much less a year. Although we do not exhibit it here, volatility clustering does not indicate 'long memory' but is explained as a purely Markovian phenomenon for variable diffusion processes, stochastic processes with diffusion coefficients $D(x, t)$ where the (x, t) dependence is inherently nonseparable. About point (4) above, we offer no comment in this chapter.

Osborne's Gaussian returns model and Mandelbrot's Levy distribution (Cootner, 1964) provided the first finance market models. The Gaussian returns model was used by Black, Scholes and Merton to make the first falsifiable option pricing model (Black and Scholes, 1973; Merton, 1973). The model was falsified because returns are not approximately Gaussian. Since the advent of econophysics, newer data analyses have suggested other statistical distributions to describe finance market data, including truncated Levy distributions (Mantegna and Stanley, 2000), scaling Markov dynamics with $D(x, t)$ linear in x/t^H (McCauley, Gunaratne and Bassler, 2003; McCauley, 2004), models with the diffusion coefficient quadratic in x/t^H (Borland, 2002; Bassler, Gunaratne and McCauley, 2006), and other models with variable diffusion coefficients (Renner, Peinke and Friedrich, 2001). All of those studies disagree on details but report that the returns distribution is non-Gaussian, scales with Hurst exponent H $f(x, t) = t^{-H}F(u)$, and has fat tails for large returns $f(x, t) \approx x^{-\mu}$ for $x >> 1$. Some studies report fat tails, but with multi-affine Hurst exponent scaling (Dacorogna et al., 2001; Di Matteo, Aste and Dacarogna, 2003) (generally mislabeled as 'multifractal' scaling [McCauley, 2002]), indicating that $f(x, t) \neq t^{-H}F(u)$. Here's the central point: all of the data analyses suggesting those models have used a technique called 'sliding windows' (Bassler, McCauley and Gunaratne, 2008), and the point of this section is to explain that sliding windows produce spurious results because FX data do not have stationary increments. One previous data analysis (Galluccio et al., 1997) showed that sliding windows lead to a spurious Hurst exponent $H = 1/2$ when applied to nonstationary increments. We explain this observation theoretically below.

Here's what's meant by the sliding window method: one *attempts* to construct histograms representing $f_1(x, T)$ for increments $z = x(t, T)$ at different times T by reading a time series of returns $x(t)$, where the asumption is that $x(t, T) = x(0, T)$ so that $z = x$ with $x(0) = 0$. One starts at initial time t and forms a window at time $t + T$. One implicitly assumes that the increment $z = x(T, t) = x(t + T) - x(t)$ generates a density f_1 that is independent of t by sliding the window along the entire length of the time series, increasing t by one unit at a time while holding T fixed. For a long time series, one of at least $t_{max} \approx$ several years in length, this method is expected to produce good statistics because it picks up a lot of data points. Again, there is no known reason to assume convergence of the sliding window histograms to $f_1(x, T)$ even if the increments would be stationary, and intraday FX increments are not stationary.

In all that follows, both the simulation and market data have been detrended. The trend in FX data since 1999 is tiny and could have been neglected altogether without changing our conclusions.

To illustrate how spurious results are generated by using sliding

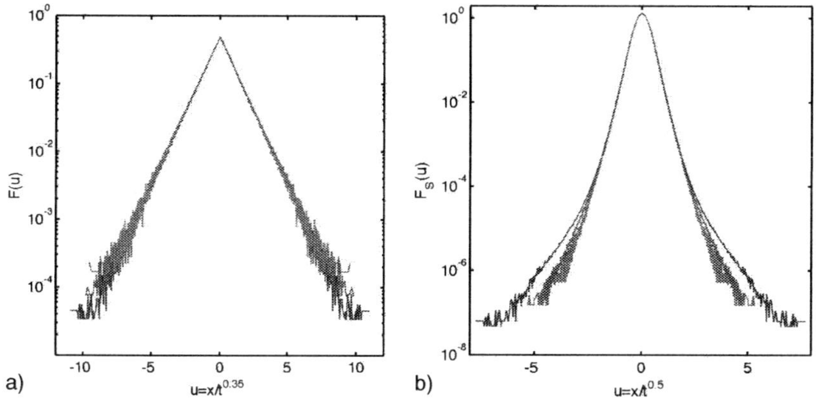

Figure 10.1a and b (a) The scaling function $F(u)$ is calculated from a simulated time series generated via the exponential model, $D(u) = 2H(1 + |u|)$ with $H = 0.35$. 5 000 000 independent runs of the exponential stochastic process were used. (b) The 'sliding window scaling function' $F_S(u_s)$, $u_s = x_s(T)/TH^S$ was calculated for the same simulated data. Note that F_S has fat tails whereas F does not, and that $H_S=1/2$ appears contradicting the fact that H = 0.35 was used to generate the time series

windows in data analysis, we apply that method to a time series with uncorrelated nonstationary increments, one with no fat tails and with a Hurst exponent $H = 0.35$, namely, a time series generated by the exponential density (10.16) with $H = 0.35$ (Figure 10.1a) and linear diffusion (10.41). Figure 10.1a was generated by taking 5,000,000 independent runs of the Ito process, each starting from $x(0) = 0$ for $T=10$, 100, and 1000. The sliding window result is shown as Figure 10.1b. In this case, the sliding windows appear to yield a scale-free density $F_s(u_s)$, $u_s = x_s(T)/T^{Hs}$, from an empirical average over t that one cannot formulate theoretically, because for a nonstationary process there is no ergodic theorem. Note that F_s is badly behaved for large u, but as we have stated above, the assumption that a scale-free density $F_s(u_s)$ $u_s = x(T)/T^{Hs}$ exists independently of the starting time t is completely wrong. Summarizing the main points, not only are fat tails generated artificially, but we get a spurious Hurst exponent $H_S = 1/2$ as well. This is the method that has been used to generate 'stylized facts' in nearly all existing finance data analyses.

Next, we describe our study of a six-year time series of euro/dollar exchange rates from Olsen & Associates (Bassler, McCauley and Gunaratne, 2008). The increments $x(t, T) = x(t + T) - x(t) = \ln(p(t + T)/p(t))$ are

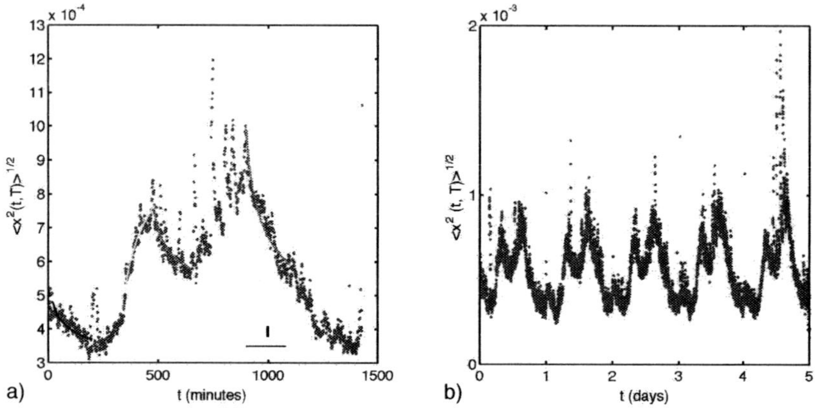

Figure 10.2a and b (a) The root mean square fluctuation $\langle x^{\beta}(t,T)\rangle^{1/\beta}$ *of the daily euro/dollar exchange rate is plotted against time of day t, with T = 10 minutes to insure that autocorrelations in increments have died out (Figure 10.3). (b) We showed by calculating ensemble averages that the same intraday stochastic process occurs during each trading day. Both of the plots (a) and (b) would be flat were the increments x(t, T) stationary. Instead, the root mean square fluctuation of x(t, T) varies by a factor of 3 each day as t is varied, showing strong nonstationarity of increments. Note in (a) that we get scaling with H at best in the four disjoint regions shown by a line, and with different values of H in each region*

nonstationary, as is shown by the root mean square fluctuation in increments plotted against t in Figure 10.2a, where $T = 10$ minutes to insure that there are no autocorrelations in increments (Figure 10.3). Second, note that the returns data do not scale with a Hurst exponent H or even with several Hurst exponents over the entire day. Figure 10.2b shows that the same stochastic process is repeated on different days of the week, so that we can assume a *single*, definite intraday stochastic process $x(t)$ in intraday returns. In Figure 10.1a we see that scaling is observed at best within four disjoint time intervals during the day, and even then with four different Hurst exponents ($H < 1/2$ in three of the intervals, $H > 1/2$ in the other). That is, the intraday stochastic process $x(t)$ generally does not scale and is instead complicated.

Within the largest of the four time intervals where we could fit the data using a scaling collapse $F(u) = t^H f(x, t)$, we chose the longest interval. There, we see that the scaling function $F(u)$ has no fat tails, is instead

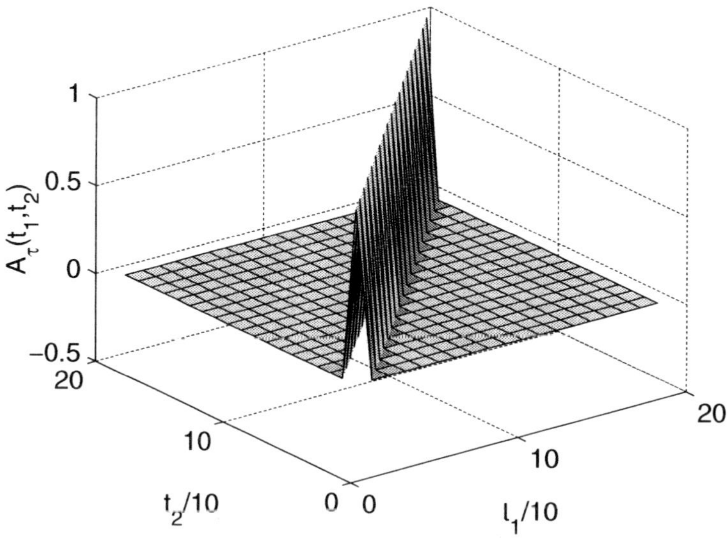

Figure 10.3 *Normalized autocorrelations in increments* $A_T(t_1, t_2) = \langle x(t_1, T)x(t_2, T)\rangle / (\langle x^2(t_1)x^2(t_2)\rangle)^{1/2}$ *for two nonoverlapping time intervals* $[t_1, t_1 + T]$, $[t_2, t_2 + T]$ *decay rapidly toward zero for* $T \geq 10$ *minutes of trading. This implies a martingale stochastic process*

approximately exponential (Figure 10.4a). If we apply the method of sliding windows to the finance time series within the interval I shown in Figure 10.2a, then we get Figure 10.4b, which has artificially generated fat tails and also a spurious Hurst exponent $H_S - 1/2$, just as with our numerical simulation using time series generated via the exponential density to generate a Markov time series (Figure 10.2a and b). This shows how sliding windows can generate artificial fat tails and a Hurst exponent of 1/2 in data analysis. That is, the use of sliding windows generates 'spurious stylized facts' when the increments are nonstationary. Again, this is because sliding windows implicitly assume stationary increments. This observation has far reaching consequences for the analysis of random time series, whether in physics, economics/finance, or biology.

Next, we emphasize the features of the intraday stochastic process that allow us to infer a general class of models. The goal is to try to infer the class of stochastic models describing the intraday data. We've checked that the autocorrelations of increments over nonoverlapping time intervals vanish for $T > 10$ minutes of trading time by calculating $\langle x(t, T)x(t, -T)\rangle$ (Figure 10.3). Vanishing autocorrelations of the increments rules out fBm.

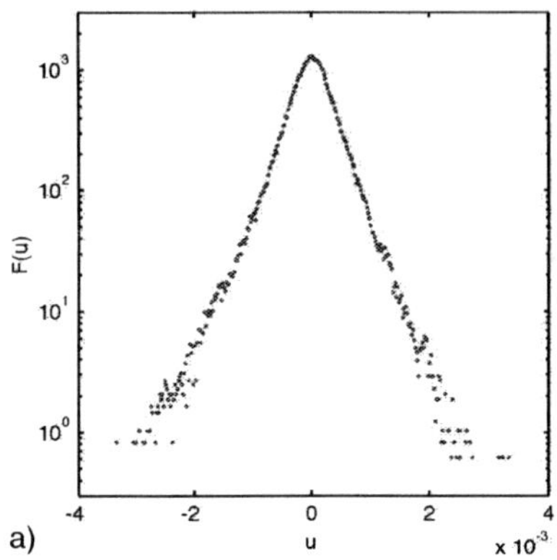

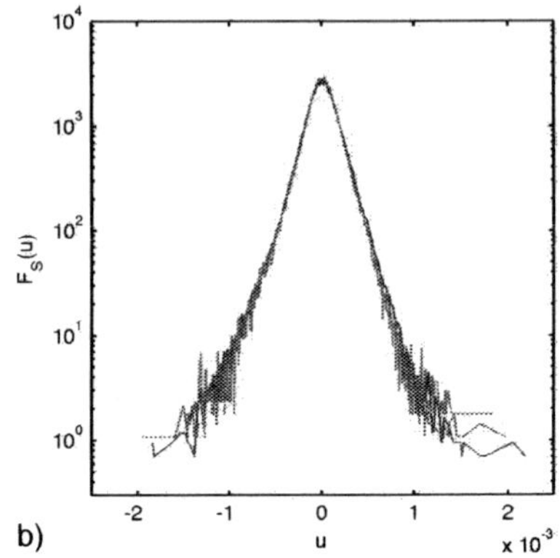

Figure 10.4a and b (a) Our scaling analysis focuses on the interval I shown in Figure 10.2a. We plot the scaling function $F(u)$ for $H = 0.35$ with 10 minutes $\leq T \leq$ 160 minutes. Note that $F(u)$ is slightly asymmetric and is approximately exponential, showing that the variance is finite. (b) The 'sliding interval scaling function' $F_s(u_s)$, $u_s = x_s(T)/T^{H_s}$, is constructed empirically from the same interval I for T=10, 20 and 40 minutes. Note that fat tails have been generated spuriously by the sliding windows, and that a spurious Hurst exponent H_s=1/2 has been generated as well, just as in the simulation data shown as Figure 10.2a and b.

Second, the variance is finite, as is shown in Figures 10.2 and 10.4a, and the histograms (Figure 10.4a) have no fat tails, ruling out Levy distributions. Does the density $f(x, t)$ scale within the three regions where the mean square fluctuation scales with t? That is, is there a scaling function $F(u)$, $u = x/t^H$, in the scaling regions? By studying $\langle x^\beta(t, T)\rangle^{1/\beta}$, varying t while T is fixed at T = 10 minutes for different β, we rule out multi-affine scaling (Figure 10.5). This indicates that there should be a data collapse $F(u) = t^H f(x, t)$ within the four separate scaling regions indicated in Figure 10.2a, but without sliding windows the error bars on the empirically constructed histograms are too large to verify this claim directly. That's why we've studied the moments of the increments instead of the histograms. Putting all of this together, a martingale process is indicated, one with variable diffusion coefficient $D(x, t)$. Martingale memory beyond the level of pair correlations is not ruled out. Next, we show how H_s = 1/2 arises from sliding a window.

Using the short time behavior for $T/t << 1$, we obtain from the short time ($T << t$) approximation (10.35) to the mean square fluctuation (10.34) obeys

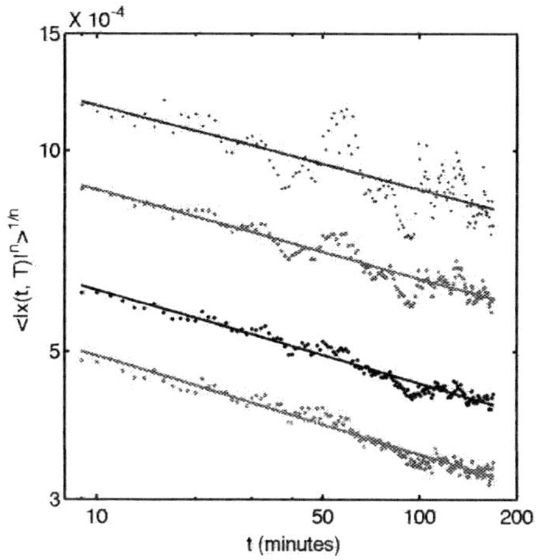

Figure 10.5 *A log-log plot of* $\langle x^{\beta}(t, T)\rangle^{1/\beta}$ *for* $\beta = 0.5, 1.0, 2.0$, *and 3.0 shows power law scaling* $t^{-\eta}$ *for each index* β *with* $\eta \neq 0.15$, *yielding* $H = 1 - \eta \approx 0.35$, *ruling out multi-affine scaling. The time t is local NY time starting at 9a.m. The error magnitude estimates for our values* $\eta \approx 0.13$–0.15 *range from 0.02 to 0.08 from nonlinear fits*

$$\langle x^2(t, T)\rangle \approx D(x, t)T = t^{2H-1}D(u)T. \tag{10.54}$$

With T fixed at 10 minutes, we vary t to find, for example, that $H \approx 0.35$ in the scaling region I shown in Figure 10.3. That is, for Figure 10.4a the diffusion coefficient is given approximately by (10.41) with $H = 0.35$. We can use this result explain $H_S = 1/2$.

With uncorrelated nonstationary increments, in a scaling region we have more generally from (10.34) that

$$\langle x^2(t, T)\rangle = \langle (x(t + T) - x(t))^2\rangle = \langle x^2(1)\rangle[(t + T)^{2H} - t^{2H})] \tag{10.55}$$

independent of the details of the diffusion coefficient $D(x, t)$, the result (10.54) being a very short time lag approxmiation. In most existing data analyses we generally have $T/t << 1$ when sliding windows are applied to the increments $x(T, t)$, yielding

$$\langle x^2(t, T)\rangle \approx \langle x^2(1)\rangle 2Ht^{2H-1}T. \tag{10.56}$$

Sliding windows then average empirically over t,

$$\langle x^2(t, T)\rangle_S \approx \langle x^2(1)\rangle 2H\langle t^{2H-1}\rangle_S T \tag{10.57}$$

yielding $\langle x^2(t, T)\rangle \approx T^{2H_S}$ with $2H_S = 1/2$. Hurst exponents $H_S = 1/2$ have been reported several times in the literature (Borland, 2002) for Markov models that scale with $H \neq 1/2$, but without any correct explanation of how they arise. That $H_S = 1/2$ is a consequence of using sliding windows was first reported by Galluccio et al. (1997) in a paper that we did not appreciate at all until we rediscovered the implications of nonstationary increments for ourselves. Until recently, there was no theory available as guide.

The reader may ask why we don't analyze returns over a week or a month. Weekly returns in Figure 10.2b show that the intraday behavior is systematically repeated over the days of the week, but because we have not yet understood the stochastic process that generates intraday data we are not prepared to speculate about an interday stochastic process. Here, in order to get good statistics from data with nonstationary increments, we have been forced to think of each trading day as a rerun of the same stochastic process: with the sliding window method disqualified, all histograms are sparse, especially those for large T. As T is increased beyond 10 minutes, one obtains big error bars in the graphs from which the density $f_1(x, t)$ must be inferred. That is, with $T \approx$ one week or one month the modeling would inherently be wildly nonunique, it would be too easy to 'fit' sparse, uncertain data via many different (and wrong!) model classes.

10.10.1 Note added 29 March 2008

We've shown why, in Bassler, Gunaratne and McCauley (2008), two-point densities and therefore transition densities cannot scale, even if the time series scales with H. The conflict between efficient markets and hypothetical stationary markets is exhibited in McCauley (2008). In McCauley, Bassler and Gunaratne (forthcoming) we show the limitations of integration I(d) and cointegration, and explain why 'integration I(d)' fails for finance data. Correspondingly, we suggest therein why the neoclassically expected equilibrium relationships between FX rates and relative price levels is not observed.

Notes

* KEB is supported by the National Science Foundation through grants #DMR-0406323 and #DMR-0427938, and the Air Force Research Lab. GHG is supported by the NSF through grant #DMS-0607345 and by Texas Learning and Computation Center. JMC thanks Eduardo Roman, Enrico Scalas and Harry Thomas for helpful e-mail discussions.

1. This corrects a mis-statement about fBm in Bassler, McCauley and Gunaratne (2008).

References

Alejandro-Quinones, A.L., K.E. Bassler, M. Field, J.L. McCauley, M. Nicol, I. Timofeyev, A. Török and G.H. Gunaratne (2006), 'A Theory of Fluctuations in Stock Prices', *Physica A*, **363**(2), 383.

Bassler, K.E., G.H. Gunaratne and J.L. McCauley (2006), 'Hurst Exponents, Markov Processes, and Nonlinear Diffusion Equations', *Physica A*, **369**(1), 343.

Bassler, K.E., G.H. Gunaratne and J.L. McCauley (2008), 'Empirically Based Modeling in Financial Economics and Beyond: Spurious Stylized Facts', *International Review of Financial Analysis*, **17**(5), 767–83.

Bassler, K.E., J.L. McCauley and G.H. Gunaratne (2007), 'Nonstationary Increments, Scaling Distributions, and Variable Diffusion Processes in Financial Markets', *PNAS*, **104**, 17297, 23 October.

Black, F. (1986), 'Noise', *J. of Finance*, **41**(3), 529.

Black, F. and M. Scholes (1973), 'The Pricing of Options and Corporate Liabilities', *J. Political Economy*, **81**(3), 637.

Borland, L. (1998), 'Microscopic Dynamics of the Nonlinear Fokker-Planck Equation: A Phenomenological Model', *Phys. Rev.*, **E57**(6), 6634.

Borland, L. (2002), 'Option Pricing Formulas Based on a Non-Gaussian Stock Price Model', *Phy. Rev. Lett.*, **89**(9).

Cootner, P. (ed.) (1964), *The Random Character of Stock Market Prices*, MIT, Cambridge, MA.

Dacorogna, M.M., G. Ramazan, U.A. Müller, R.B. Olsen and O.V. Picte (2001), *An Introduction to High Frequency Finance*, Academic Press, NY.

Di Matteo, T., T. Aste and M.M. Dacorogna, 'Scaling Behaviors in Differently Developed Markets', *Physica A*, **324**(1–2), 183.

Dunbar, N. (2000), *Inventing Money, Long-term Capital Management and the Search for Risk-free Profits*, Wiley, New York.

Durrett, R. (1984), *Brownian Motion and Martingales in Analysis*, Wadsworth, Belmont.

Embrechts, P. and M. Maejima (2002), *Selfsimilar Processes*, Princeton University Press, Princeton.

E. Fama (1970), 'Efficient Capital Markets, a Review of Theory and Empirical Evidence', *J. Finance*, **25**(2), 383–417.

Friedman, A. (1975), *Stochastic Differential Equations and Applications*, Academic, New York.

Galluccio, S., G. Caldarelli, M. Marsilli and Y.-C. Zhang (1997), 'Scaling in Currency Exchange', *Physica A*, **245**(3), 423.

Gunaratne, G.H. and J.L. McCauley (2005), 'Variable Step Random Walks, Self-similar Distributions, and Pricing of Options', *Proceedings of SPIE Conference on Noise & Fluctuations*, **5848**, 131.

Hänggi, P., H. Thomas, H. Grabert and P. Talkner, 'Note on Time-evolution of Non-Markov Processes', *J. Stat. Phys.*, **18**, 155.

Hommes, C.H., (2002), 'Modeling the Stylized Facts in Finance Through Simple Nonlinear Adaptive Systems', *PNAS*, **99**(3), 7221.

Mandelbrot, B. and M.S. Taqqu (1979), 'Robust R/S analysis of long-run serial correlation', *Proceedings of the 42nd Session of the International Statistical Institute of Manila*, **XLVIII**(2), 69–99.

Mandelbrot, B. and J.W. van Ness (1968), 'Fractional Brownian Motions, Fractional Noises, and Applications', *SIAM Rev.*, **10**(2), 422.

Mantegna, R. and H.E. Stanley, (2000), *An Introduction to Econophysics*, Cambridge Univ. Pr., Cambridge.

McCauley, J.L. (2002), 'Are Galaxy Distributions Scale Invariant? A Perspective from Dynamical Systems Theory', *Physica A*, **309**(1–2), 183.

McCauley, J.L. (2004), *Dynamics of Markets: Econophysics and Finance*, Cambridge University Press, Cambridge, MA.

McCauley, J.L. (2007), 'Markov vs. nonMarkovian processes: A Comment on the Paper

"Stochastic Feedback, Nonlinear Families of Markov Processes, and Nonlinear Fokker-Planck Equations" by T.D. Frank', *Physica A*, **382**, 445.
McCauley, J.L. (2008), 'Nonstationarity of Efficient Financial Markets: FX Market Evolution from Stability to Instability', *International Review of Financial Analysis*, **17**(5), 820–37
McCauley, J.L. and G.H. Gunaratne (2003), 'Finance Market Dynamics with Option Pricing, *Physica A*, **329**, 178.
McCauley, J.L., K.E. Bassler and G.H. Gunaratne (2008), 'Martingales, Detrending Data, and the Efficient Market Hypothesis', *Physica A*, **387**(12), 2802–8.
McCauley, J.L., K.E. Bassler and G.H. Gunaratne (forthcoming), 'Integration I(d) of Nonstationary Time Series', submitted 2009.
McCauley, J.L., G.H. Gunaratne and K.E. Bassler (2005), 'What Economists Should Learn from Econophysics', in *Dynamics of Complex Interconnected Systems, Networks and Bioprocesses*, A.T. Skjeltorp and A. Belyushkin (eds), Springer, NY, pp. 191–202.
McCauley, J.L., G.H. Gunaratne and K.E. Bassler (2007a), 'Hurst Exponents, Markov Processes, and Fractional Brownian Motion', *Physica A*, **379**(1), 1–9.
McCauley, J.L., G.H. Gunaratne and K.E. Bassler (2007b), 'Martingale Option Pricing', *Physica A*, **380**, 351.
Merton, R.C. (1973), 'Theory of Rational Option Pricing', *Bell Journal of Economics and Management Science*, **4**(1), 141.
Renner, C., J. Peinke and R. Friedrich (2001), *Physica A*, **298**, 49.
Rickles, D. (2007), 'Econophysics for Philosophers', *Studies in History and Philosophy of Modern Physics*', **38**(4), 948–78.
Rickles, D. (2008), 'Econophysics and the Complexity of Financial Markets', in J. Collier and C. Hooker (eds), *Handbook of the Philosophy of Science, Vol. 10: Philosophy of Complex Systems*, North-Holland, Elsevier.
Skjeltorp, J.A. (2000), 'Fractal Scaling Behavior in the Norwegian Stock Market', *Physica A*, **283**, 486.
Soros, G. (1998), *The Crisis of Global Capitalism*, Little, Brown & Co., NY.
Stratonovich, R.L. (1963), *Topics in the Theory of Random Noise*, Gordon & Breach: NY.
Wang, M.C. and G.E. Uhlenbeck (1954), 'On the Theory of Brownian Motion II', in N. Wax. (ed.), *Selected Papers on Noise and Stochastic Processes*, Dover: NY.

PART V

INTERNATIONAL ECONOMICS

11. Exchange rate dynamics: a nonlinear survey

Frank H. Westerhoff

11.1 Introduction

The foreign exchange market is the broadest and most active financial market in the world. Trading volume is enormous. According to the Bank for International Settlement (2005), the global turnover in traditional foreign exchange market segments reached an estimated daily average of USD1.9 trillion in April 2004. Such a high trading volume clearly dwarfs that of other (financial) markets. The nature of foreign exchange markets seems to be highly speculative. The overwhelming part of the trading volume reflects very short-term transactions. For example, operations of intraday traders account for about 75 percent of the market volume. Moreover, international trade transactions represent only a small fraction of the total volume. Speculative transactions are roughly 20 times higher than the sum of world trade and international portfolio investment. Not surprisingly, the fast and hectic trading is also reflected in the dynamics of exchange rates. Foreign exchange markets are characterized by a very high volatility. For instance, the DEM/USD exchange rate changed by about 0.5 percent per day between 1974 and 1998. Even more important, the distribution of the returns displays fat tails. Extreme price changes, say above 3 percent, appear much more frequently than predicted by the normal distribution.

Is such evidence in line with the efficient market hypothesis? The efficient market hypothesis states that prices always reflect their fundamental values. Hence, price changes are due to unexpected fundamental shocks. Clearly, if we observe an exchange rate movement by 5 percent, then this should correspond to a 5 percent shock in the fundamentals. Given also the fact that exchange rates change on a second-to-second basis, it is difficult to imagine where all these fundamental shocks should come from. Note also that other stylized facts such as volatility clustering must also be caused by the news arrival process. All in all, this perspective appears not very convincing and consequently new approaches to model the behavior of exchange rates have emerged.

Our goal is to provide an elementary introduction to and a survey of the so-called chartist-fundamentalist approach, which may be regarded as a promising part of the currently burgeoning field of behavioral finance (see, for example, Hirshleifer, 2001; Shiller, 2003; or Lo, 2004). The chartist-fundamentalist approach has strong empirical roots, since it takes into account the observation that professional foreign exchange market participants rely on both technical and fundamental trading strategies when determining their speculative investment positions. Technical analysis aims at identifying trading strategies out of past price movements. Since technical analysis typically suggests going with the current price trend, these trading rules are likely to add a positive feedback to the dynamics. Fundamental analysis bets on a reduction of the mispricing in the market. For instance, when the exchange rate is below its fundamental value, then fundamental analysis suggests buying the undervalued currency. In general, fundamental trading rules add a negative feedback to the dynamics.

A central insight of the chartist-fundamentalist approach is that non-linear deterministic interactions between positive and negative feedback rules may create complex endogenous dynamics and thus contribute to the turbulent behavior of foreign exchange markets. For recent general reviews of such models see Hommes (2006), LeBaron (2006) or Lux (2006). Moreover, if one adds random shocks to these models, then at least some of them have the potential to replicate certain statistical features of actual exchange rate fluctuations quite well. Put differently, simulated and actual exchange rate time series share the same statistical properties and it is quite hard to tell whether a time series is real or whether it is artificial. Overall, these models may improve our understanding of what is going on in foreign exchange markets. Although still in the beginning stage, this research area may also be useful to design more efficient trading environments and help us to evaluate the effectiveness of certain regulatory mechanisms.

To obtain a preliminary taste of the models discussed here, let us take a quick glance at the dynamics such models may produce. Suppose that a market is dominated by destabilizing technical traders. Then it is likely that the exchange rate will be driven away from its long-run equilibrium value. This process may continue for some time since technical analysis is likely to be profitable. But the more the exchange rate deviates from its fundamental value, the more traders will realize that a fundamental price correction must eventually set in. At least some traders may therefore abandon technical analysis and opt for fundamental analysis. And in fact, if sufficient traders employ fundamental analysis, the exchange rate will revert towards its long-run equilibrium value. But this may not necessarily be the end of the story. When the misalignment has vanished, potential gains from fundamental analysis appear weak. Speculators may therefore switch back to technical analysis and kick off the next temporary bubble. We will see that such patterns may repeat themselves over and over again, yet in an intricate way. It is worthwhile stressing that the dynamics may emerge completely endogenously, that is, it is not necessary to assume repeated exogenous shifts in fundamentals. All trading signals needed to keep the process going are generated by the traders themselves.

The remainder is organized as follows: in Section 11.2, we briefly review some important stylized facts of exchange rate dynamics. In Section 11.3, we investigate the trading behavior of professional foreign exchange market participants and also sketch the essence of technical and fundamental analysis. In Section 11.4, we explore several nonlinear deterministic models with interacting chartists and fundamentalists that have the power to produce endogenous complex dynamics. In Section 11.5, we show that if such models are buffeted with dynamic noise, quite realistic exchange rate dynamics may be generated. In Section 11.6, we debate some policy issues and discuss some open problems and potential avenues for future research. The last section concludes the chapter.

11.2 Some stylized facts

In recent years, it has become clear that the price statistics across a wide range of quite different speculative markets exhibit certain universal properties. For in-depth accounts of these stylized facts see, for example, Guillaume et al. (1997), Mantenga and Stanley (2000), Cont (2001), Lux and Ausloos (2002), Johnson, Jefferies and Hui (2003) or Sornette (2003). We will focus on the following five features:

- Foreign exchange markets regularly produce significant bubbles and crashes. If exchange rates always reflected their fundamental values, crashes ought to correspond to really bad shocks. However, thorough ex-post analyses of crashes are in many cases inconclusive as to what this dramatic piece of new information might have been. Empirical studies suggest that many crashes occur endogenously due to market instabilities.
- Exchange rate volatility is too high to be justified by fundamental shocks. As just mentioned, distinct changes in exchange rates often appear to be unrelated to the arrival of significant new information. Excess volatility is also reflected in the fact that exchange rates typically move on a second-to-second basis whereas news hits the market less frequently.
- The distribution of the returns deviates significantly from the normal distribution and possesses fat tails. Fat-tailedness may be quantified by estimating the so-called tail index. For many different exchange rates, the tail index hovers between 3 and 4, implying that the fourth moment of the distribution of the returns (that is, the kurtosis) does not exist.

- Exchange rate increments are uncorrelated. For instance, the autocorrelation function of raw returns is essentially zero for all time lags. As a result, the evolution of exchange rates resembles a random walk.
- Periods of low volatility alternate with periods of high volatility. The autocorrelation function for absolute returns is positive and decays slowly. Temporal correlation in volatility may last several months.

Figures 11.1 and 11.2 seek to illustrate these properties for DEM/USD and JPY/USD exchange rates, respectively. The time window ranges from 1974 to 1998, so that we have 6264 daily observations for each time series. The first panels present the exchange rates in the time domain. One of the most popular examples of a bubble-and-crash pattern is given by the path of the DEM/USD exchange rate in the 1980s. Over the period 1981–84, when real interest rates in the United States rose above those among trading partners, the dollar appreciated from DEM 1.93 to DEM 2.67. At times, however, the path of the dollar departed from what would be expected on the basis of macroeconomic fundamentals. The most dramatic episode is the period from June 1984 to February 1985. The dollar appreciated further from DEM 2.67 to DEM 3.46 over this interval, even though the real interest differential had already begun to fall. Other observable factors at that time were also moving in the wrong direction to explain the dollar rise. Taking these observations into account, one may argue that a substantial fraction of the appreciation was due to nonfundamental forces. After February 1985, the bubble burst. By the end of 1987, the exchange rate dropped below DEM 1.60.

The second panels of Figures 11.1 and 11.2 show the evolution of the returns, that is, the changes in log exchange rates. Note that extreme returns may be as large as 5 percent. Between 6–8 October 1998, the JPY/USD exchange rate even made a spectacular cumulative jump of about 14 percent. A common proxy for volatility is given by the average absolute return, which is about 0.5 percent per time step for the two time series. Although we do not have exact knowledge of the variability of the fundamentals, such volatility estimates appear to be too high to be justified solely by fundamental shocks. In addition, at least some of the more distinct exchange rate changes appear to be unrelated to any new information.

The third lines of panels of Figures 11.1 and 11.2 depict the distributions of the returns. The dotted lines indicate the corresponding normal distributions, represented by identical mean and variance. The left-hand panels contain the plain histograms of the returns. Note that the shapes of the distributions appear well behaved: the histograms are unimodal, almost symmetric and bell-shaped. The right-hand panels contain log-linear plots

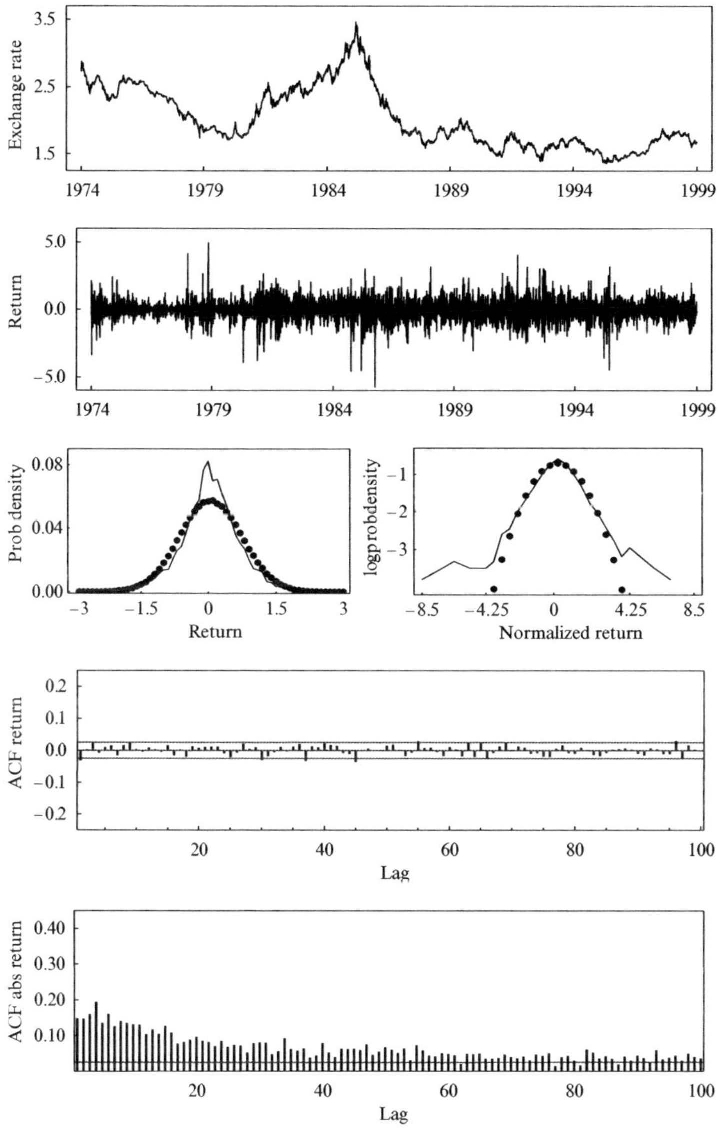

Note: The panels show from top to bottom the exchange rates, the returns, the probability density function of the returns (the dotted line indicates the normal distribution), the autocorrelation function of raw returns and the autocorrelation function of absolute returns, respectively.

Figure 11.1 The dynamics of daily DEM/USD exchange rates from 1974 to 1998

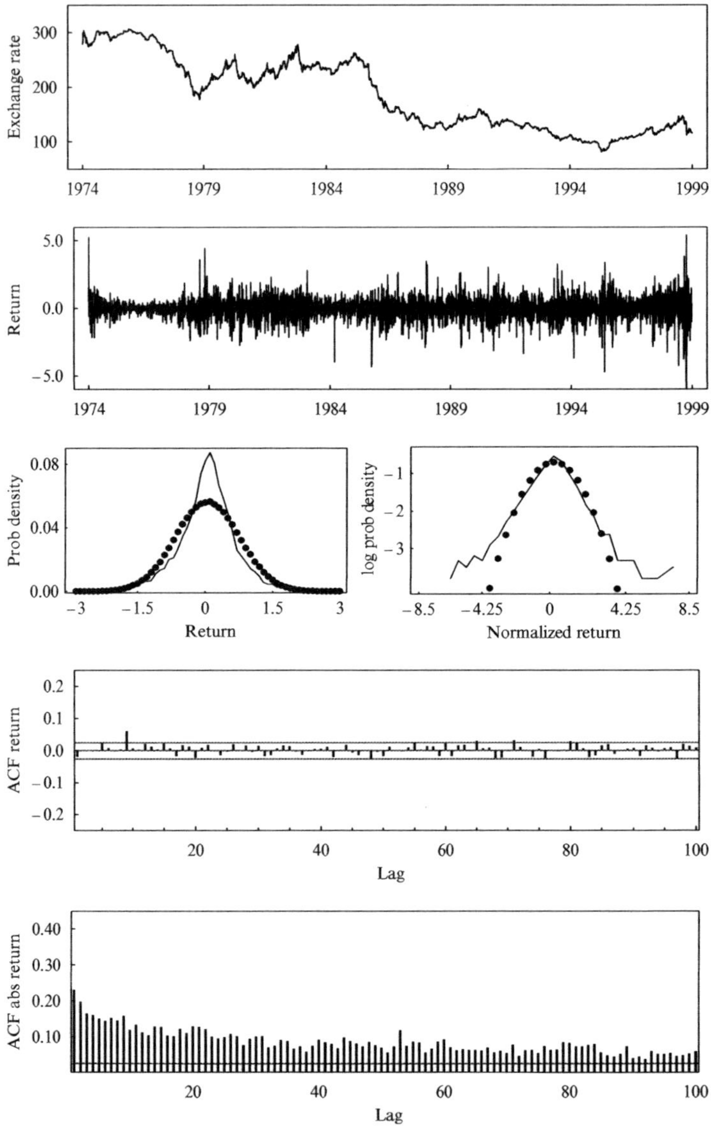

Note: The panels show from top to bottom the exchange rates, the returns, the probability density function of the returns (the dotted line indicates the normal distribution), the autocorrelation function of raw returns and the autocorrelation function of absolute returns, respectively.

Figure 11. 2 The dynamics of daily JPY/USD exchange rates from 1974 to 1998 of the distribution of the normalized returns. The returns are normalized by dividing by the standard deviation. The right-hand panels clearly show that extreme returns occur more frequently than warranted by the normal distribution. Overall, we may conclude that the distributions of exchange rate returns are more concentrated around the mean, have thinner shoulders and possess more probability mass in the tails.

The bottom two panels of Figures 11.1 and 11.2 display the autocorrelation function of raw returns and of absolute returns, respectively. The dotted lines indicate 95 percent confidence bands. Note that for almost all lags, the autocorrelation of raw returns is not significant. Hence, the evolution of exchange rates is close to a random walk. A different picture emerges when one explores the autocorrelation function of absolute returns. The autocorrelation coefficients for the first 100 lags are positive and significant, clear evidence of volatility clustering.

11.3 Trader behavior

Since Simon (1955), a considerable amount of empirical evidence has been collected that impressively demonstrates that people generally lack the computational power to derive fully optimal actions. But this does not imply that they are completely irrational. In fact, people strive to do the right thing. Their behavior may better be described as rule-governed behavior. As argued by psychologists Kahneman, Slovic and Tversky (1986), people tend to follow simple heuristics that have proven to be useful in the recent past. Natural selection pressure apparently limits the number of applied rules. If a certain strategy repeatedly fails to satisfy people, they will, of course, stop using it. Note that this may be an important observation: if we are able to identify the agents' main heuristics, then we may be able to model and explore their behavior. But how do professional foreign exchange traders behave in reality? Fortunately, empirical studies give us a quite clear description of their activity.

Due to Smith (1991), who pioneered the use of laboratory financial market experiments, we are nowadays able to observe investor behavior in a well-defined and controlled environment. In such experiments, each participant typically receives an initial portfolio of cash and assets and is free to trade. Trading is conducted by computer through local networks and thus mimics trading in real financial markets quite well. When all participants have entered their action, the next period's price is revealed. The experiments indicate that the participants use simple forms of forecast rules such as (destabilizing) extrapolative or (stabilizing) regressive predictors. Furthermore, they frequently drove prices far above fundamentals, after which the markets crashed. Bubble-and-crash sequences appear to be quite robust, even when all agents know the true fundamental value of the market (Caginalp, Porter and Smith, 2001; Sonnemans et al., 2004). Hommes et al. (2005), who have particularly designed their experiments to study the agents' expectation formation process, find that agents tend to coordinate on some popular prediction strategies. Such coordination behavior furthermore suggests that the number of applied financial trading rules may be rather limited, at least at certain times.

Laboratory experiments are typically conducted with students. A related strand of literature explores the behavior of professional market participants who have repeatedly been asked over an extended period of time to forecast the course of exchange rates for different time horizons (for example, Frankel and Froot, 1987; Ito, 1990; Takagi, 1991). These studies report that expectations of foreign exchange market participants are not rational. Instead, standard models such as extrapolative or regressive expectation formation models obtain significant empirical support (which is in agreement with the laboratory results mentioned above). Interestingly, short-term expectations are quite different from long-term expectations. Destabilizing bandwagon expectations dominate on short-term horizons: when there is an exchange rate trend, it is then believed that this trend will continue. On long-term horizons, expectations tend to be stabilizing. For instance, the respondents predicted reversals of exchange rate trends or adjustments towards long-run equilibrium values.

Finally, professional market participants have also been directly asked how they form their prediction. As reported by Taylor and Allen (1992), Menkhoff (1997) and Lui and Mole (1998), professional foreign exchange market participants rely on both technical and fundamental analysis when they determine their orders. Most professional traders are familiar with both concepts. With respect to long-term horizons, the vast majority of respondents prefer fundamental analysis as a prediction instrument. However, foreign exchange markets are dominated by short-term transactions. For short-term horizons, say up to one week, technical and fundamental analyses are judged as equally important. Which rule is applied in a given situation seems to depend on market circumstances.

Let us briefly sketch the key elements of these trading strategies. Fundamental analysis is the study of economic and political conditions in an effort to determine the intrinsic (fundamental) value of a currency. A typical benchmark for the fundamental value might be derived from the purchasing power parity condition or more elaborate structural macroeconomic models. A fundamentalist believes that an exchange rate may deviate from its intrinsic value in the short run, but converges to it in the long run. Thus, the idea is to buy undervalued currencies and to sell overvalued currencies in the hope of a future price correction. From an economist's point of view, such behavior – which is basically equivalent to forming regressive expectations – appears to be reasonable.

Rather than attempting to compute intrinsic values, chartists instead look for price patterns that may indicate the future direction of exchange rates. Standard manuals of technical analysis include Edwards and Magee (1966), Pring (1991) and Murphy (1999). Technical analysis is a prediction method founded in the belief that current prices represent all necessary information about an asset. Studying price action is thus all that is required. The most basic concept of technical analysis is that markets have a tendency to follow trends, hence the saying 'the trend is your friend'. In general, technical trading rules suggest buying when prices increase, and vice versa. Positive feedback trading obviously corresponds to forming extrapolative expectations.

Many economists are skeptical of the usefulness of technical analysis, yet empirical work indicates that at least some technical analysis rules have been profitable in the past (Brock, Lakonishok and LeBaron, 1992; LeBaron 1999; Lo, Mamaysky and Wang, 2000). The profitability of technical analysis is an interesting issue. What is more important, however, is the observation that many professional traders are indeed using these strategies. And since they influence the evolution of exchange rates, we should try to understand their impact on the price formation process.

11.4 Deterministic models

The last section has revealed that speculators rely on simple technical and fundamental trading rules to determine their orders. The goal of this section is to explore what happens when these trader types clash together in foreign exchange markets. In Section 11.4.1, we start for pedagogical reasons with a linear exchange rate model. In the following subsections, we then investigate various nonlinear mechanisms that may stimulate endogenous dynamics.

11.4.1 A simple linear model

We develop a simple exchange rate model with chartists and fundamentalists. Since its law of motion is given by a two-dimensional linear difference equation, the dynamics of the model is easy to characterize. The price adjustment process is modeled according to a so-called price impact function. A price impact function relates the amount of foreign currency bought or sold in a given time interval to the price change caused by these orders. One may therefore express the log of the exchange rate P in period $t + 1$ as

$$P_{t+1} = P_t + A_t(W_t^C D_t^C + W_t^F D_t^F), \tag{11.1}$$

where A captures the (positive) price adjustment speed with respect to the excess demand, W^C stands for the fraction of chartists, W^F denotes the fraction of fundamentalists, D^C are the orders generated by technical trading rules, and D^F are the orders generated by fundamental trading rules. Note that when excess demand is positive (negative), the exchange rate increases (decreases).

Technical analysis rules extrapolate past price trends. Orders triggered by technical trading rules may be formalized as

$$D_t^C = b(P_t - P_{t-1}), \tag{11.2}$$

where b is a positive reaction parameter. A buying signal is given when the exchange rate increases and a selling signal is given when it decreases.

Fundamental analysis aims at exploiting the mispricing in the market. Orders generated by fundamental trading rules may be written as

$$D_t^F = c(F - P_t), \tag{11.3}$$

where c is a positive reaction parameter and F represents the log of the fundamental value. When the exchange rate is below (above) its fundamental value, buying (selling) is suggested.

For $A_t = a$, $W_t^C = W^C$ and $W_t^F = W^F$ the law of motion of the exchange rate is a two-dimensional linear difference equation

$$P_{t+1} + (acW^F - abW^C - 1)P_t + abW^C P_{t-1} = acW^F F. \tag{11.4}$$

Rewriting Schur's stability conditions shows us that the unique fixed point $P = F$ is stable if (1) $acW^F > 0$, (2) $acW^F < 2 + 2abW^C$ and (3) $abW^C < 1$. Since all parameters are by definition positive, condition (1) is always fulfilled, yet conditions (2) and (3) impose true restrictions. Stability may be lost when either the total market impact of the fundamentalists (given by acW^F) or the total market impact of the chartists (given by abW^C) exceeds a certain critical threshold. Note also that condition (2) implies that in the presence of some chartists ($0 < abW^C < 1$), the stability requirement for the fundamentalists is less strict than when there are no chartists. In this sense, a positive but not too high fraction of chartists may be beneficial for market stability.

Figure 11.3 shows a simulation run for $a = 1$, $b = 1.5$, $c = 2$, $F = 1$, $W^C = W^F = 0.5$ and an initial exchange rate shock of 1 percent. In an efficient market, the exchange rate would jump back towards its fundamental value in the next period without any transactions. But this does not happen in our case: the first panel reveals that the exchange rate fluctuates with

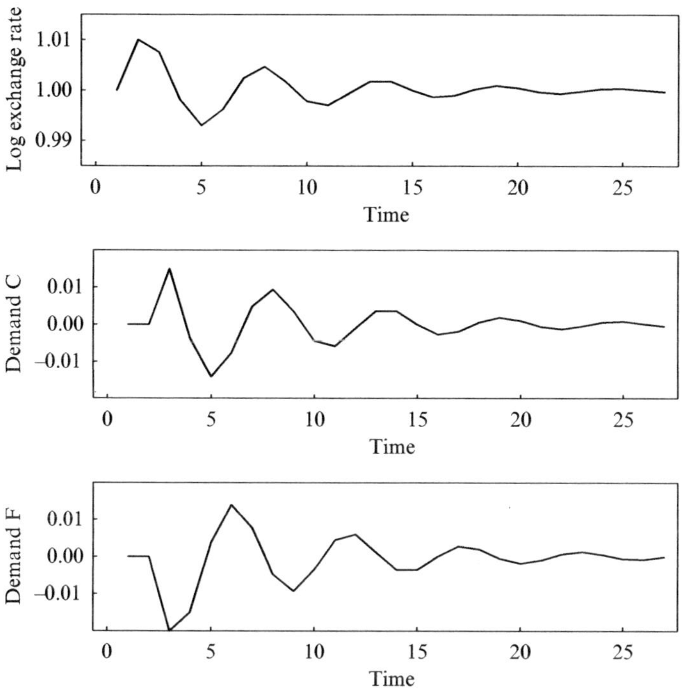

Note: The panels show from top to bottom the log of the exchange rates, the demand of the chartists and the demand of the fundamentalists, respectively.

Figure 11.3 A linear model

a decreasing amplitude around its fundamental value. The bottom two panels display the corresponding orders of the chartists and fundamentalists, respectively. Depending on the resulting excess demand, the exchange rate may go up or down. After about 25 periods, the dynamics has more or less died out. Within linear models, a single impulse may only trigger temporary exchange rate movements. This, however, already contributes to the excessive behavior of exchange rates and also to the high trading volume, as observed in real markets.

11.4.2 Nonlinear price impact function

In the previous section, we applied a log-linear price impact function. One might imagine that such a function is a general description of a more complex limit order book mechanism (see, for example, Chiarella and Iori, 2002 for such a modeling approach) or reflects a stylized representation of the behavior of market-makers. The market-maker scenario is a popular and also realistic description of the actual price adjustment in foreign exchange markets (see Lyons, 2001 for an empirical account). Market-makers are large market participants who stand ready to absorb imbalances between buyers and sellers. They supply excess demand from their inventory or accumulate inventory when there is an excess supply. Market-makers adjust prices by paying attention to two kinds of information. On the one hand, they react to excess demand. When excess demand is positive (negative), prices go up (down). On the other hand, they closely watch their inventory. Market-makers dislike large inventory imbalances and thus may quote prices that help to unwind their positions. While the first aspect is captured by the price impact function, the second aspect is often neglected. One exception is Westerhoff (2003a), who develops a simple exchange rate model in which the market-makers control their positions by quoting exchange rates that provoke offsetting orders of technical and fundamental traders. Such behavior may amplify trading volume and exchange rate variability. Similar results are reported by Gu (1995), who argues that market-makers have an incentive to churn the market in order to raise profits.

The price impact function may also be nonlinear for another important reason. Trading volume in foreign exchange markets is not constant over time. According to the Bank for International Settlement (2005), which estimates the trading volume in foreign exchange markets every three years, average daily turnover dropped from USD1.6 trillion in April 1998 to USD1.4 trillion in April 2001. In April 2004, however, average daily trading volume was recorded at a record high of USD1.9 trillion. The price adjustment may thus also depend on market depth: a given transaction may cause a larger price change when market depth is low than when it is high. In this section, we focus on this aspect. We will see that even slight variations in the price adjustment speed may lead to endogenous exchange rate motion.

To be precise, the price adjustment is now modeled as

$$P_{t+1} = P_t + A_t(W_t^C D_t^C + W_t^F D_t^F), \tag{11.5}$$

with

$$A_t = \begin{cases} x \text{ for } |W_t^C D_t^C| + |W_t^F D_t^F| > z \\ y \text{ otherwise.} \end{cases} \tag{11.6}$$

Depending on whether trading volume is above or below a certain threshold level z, the price adjustment speed is high or low, that is, $0 < x < y$. Westerhoff (2004a) discusses the case in which the price adjustment function is smooth with respect to liquidity.

The remainder of the model is as in the previous section. The weights of chartists and fundamentalists are fixed. Chartists extrapolate past price trends

$$D_t^C = b(P_t - P_{t-1}), \tag{11.7}$$

while fundamentalists bet on mean reversion

$$D_t^F = c(F - P_t). \tag{11.8}$$

The reaction coefficients b and c are positive and the fundamental value is constant.

Figure 11.4 presents a simulation run of the model for $x = 1.33$, $y = 1.35$ and $z = 0.01$. As before, we set $b = 1.5$, $c = 2$, $F = 1$ and $W^C = W^F = 0.5$. The only difference between the two simulation runs is thus given by the price adjustment speed. Note that in the linear model, market stability requires that $a < 1.\bar{3}$, which is in between the assumed values for x and y. The panels of Figure 4.11 show from top to bottom the evolution of the log of the exchange rate, the demand of the chartists, the demand of the fundamentalists, and the price adjustment speed, respectively. Visual inspection reveals that the exchange rate does not settle down at its fixed point but continuously moves up or down.

What is driving the dynamics of the model? Note that the market switches back and forth between two regimes. When liquidity is high, the market is stable and price fluctuations decline. But low price fluctuations indicate only weak trading signals and thus the transactions of the speculators decrease. As liquidity decreases, however, the price responsiveness of a given trade increases. The market therefore becomes unstable and price fluctuations increase again. Consequently, traders perceive stronger trading signals and trading volume goes up. When trading volume exceeds a critical value, the price responsiveness of a given trade decreases again. Although differences in x and y are quite small, everlasting exchange rate fluctuations are the result.

11.4.3 Nonlinear trading rules

One major reason for endogenous complex foreign exchange dynamics may be that the trading rules of the market participants are nonlinear. In fact, there are numerous nonlinear technical trading rules. Prominent examples include head-and-shoulders patterns or filter rules. Nonlinear technical trading has been explored by, for example, Chiarella (1992), Farmer (2002), Farmer and Joshi (2002), Chiarella, Dieci and Gardini (2002) and Westerhoff (2006). But fundamental trading rules may also be nonlinear. A famous model that considers this aspect is Day and Huang

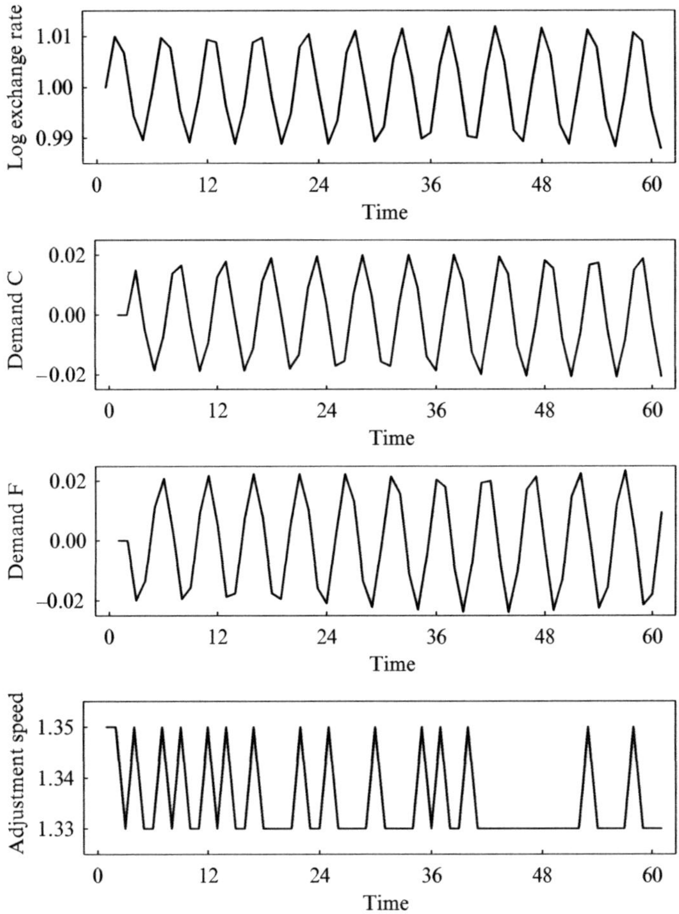

Note: The panels show from top to bottom the log of the exchange rates, the demand of the chartists, the demand of the fundamentalists and the price adjustment speed, respectively.

Figure 11.4 A nonlinear price impact function

(1990). Variations of this theme are discussed in Huang and Day (1993) and He and Westerhoff (2005). The goal of this subsection is to illustrate the dynamics of such models. We focus on nonlinear fundamental trading rules.

11.4.3.1 A nonlinear fundamental trading rule We assume a log-linear price impact function. The exchange rate for period t+1 is given as

$$P_{t+1} = P_t + a(W^C D_t^C + W^F D_t^F). \tag{11.9}$$

The price adjustment speed and the fractions of the chartists and the fundamentalists are fixed. The chartists again use a linear trading rule and extrapolate past price trends

$$D_t^C = b(P_t - P_{t-1}), \tag{11.10}$$

where b is a positive reaction coefficient.

The fundamentalists use a nonlinear trading rule. Their orders are determined by

$$D_t^F = c(F - P_t)\sqrt{|F - P_t|}. \tag{11.11}$$

Since the reaction coefficient c is positive, fundamentalists buy when the exchange rate is below its fundamental value and sell when the exchange rate is above its fundamental value. Due to the square root expression, the strength of trading activity is time-dependent: the larger the misalignment in the market, the higher the confidence of the fundamentalists in the usefulness of their trading strategy, and thus their activity level increases. Such changes in confidence may be justified by the fact that profit opportunities of fundamental trading rules increase with the misalignment (Day and Huang, 1990).

Note again that all other aspects are as in our linear benchmark model. How does the nonlinear fundamental trading rule influence the dynamics of our model? Figure 11.5 presents a simulation run for $a = 1, b = 2, c = 38$, $F = 1$, $W^C = W^F = 0.5$ and an initial exchange rate shock of 1 percent. The panels display from top to bottom the log of the exchange rate, the demand of the chartists and the demand of the fundamentalists, respectively. Visual inspection reveals that the exchange rate fluctuates around its fundamental value without any apparent tendency to converge.

The story of the dynamics is quite easy to grasp. When the exchange rate is far away from its fundamental value, the fundamentalists are quite confident of their trading strategy and trade rather aggressively. Their orders dominate those of the chartists and drive the exchange rate back towards fundamentals. However, when the exchange rate is close to fundamentals, fundamental analysis is not regarded as very attractive and thus its market impact is relatively weak. In this situation the market is governed by the destabilizing orders of the chartists, who create the next temporary bubbles. The process then repeats itself.

11.4.3.2 Variation 1: Emergence of bull and bear markets One might argue that the behavior of the exchange rate depicted in Figure 11.5 does

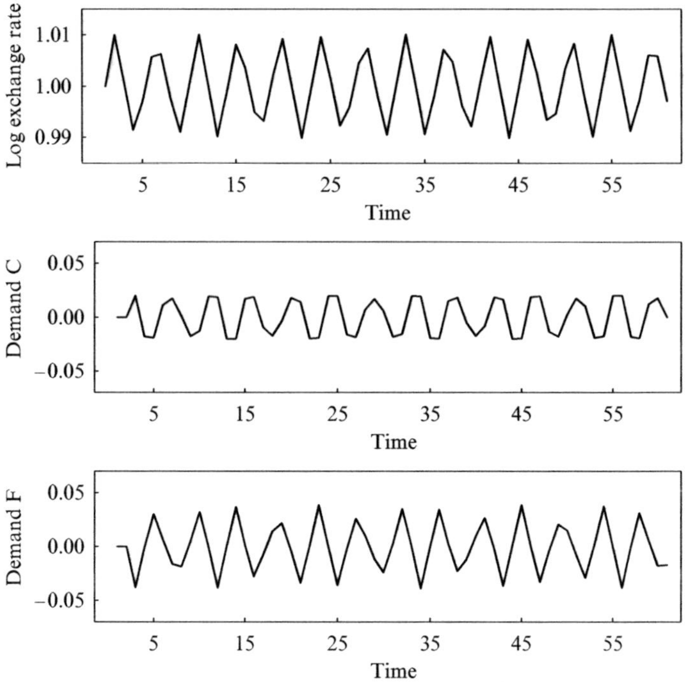

Note: The panels show from top to bottom the log of the exchange rates, the demand of the chartists and the demand of the fundamentalists, respectively.

Figure 11.5 A nonlinear fundamental trading rule

not look very spectacular. However, this may change when we modify the behavior of the chartists. As in Day and Huang (1990), we now assume that the chartists believe in the persistence of either bull or bear markets. Their orders are now approximated by

$$D_t^C = b(P_t - F), \tag{11.12}$$

where b is a positive reaction coefficient. Accordingly, the chartists submit buying orders when the market is overvalued, in the belief that the market will further increase. In a bear market, the chartists are pessimistic and submit selling orders to the market.

Figure 11.6 shows a simulation run for $a = 1$, $b = 12$, $c = 18$, $F = 1$, $W^C = W^F = 0.5$. From top to bottom we see the evolution of the log of the exchange rate, the orders of the chartists and the orders of the fundamentalists, respectively. Now the dynamics looks spectacular! We observe the

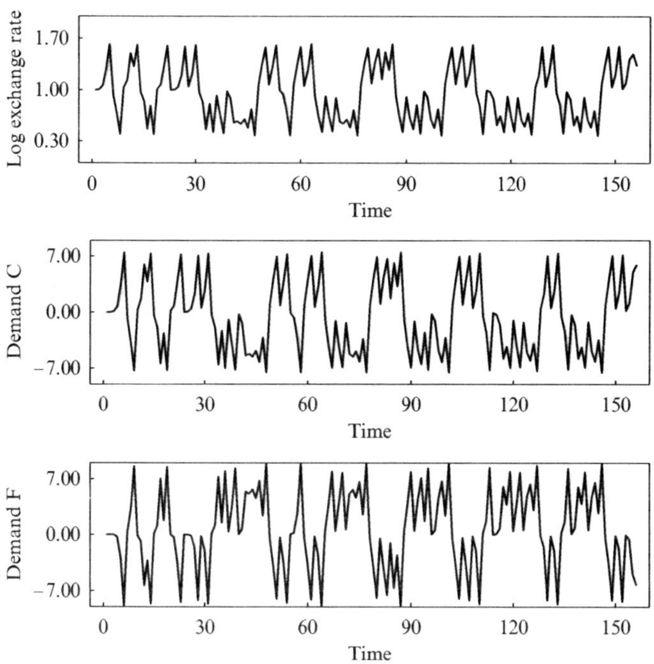

Note: The panels show from top to bottom the log of the exchange rates, the demand of the chartists and the demand of the fundamentalists, respectively.

Figure 11.6 A simple variation of the previous model

emergence of bull and bear markets, intricate switching between bull and bear markets and irregular motion within bull or bear markets.

The dynamics of the model may be sketched as follows. Suppose that the exchange rate is slightly above its fundamental value. Then chartists dominate the market and drive the exchange rate up. However, the larger the mispricing, the stronger the trading activity of the fundamentalists. At some point in time they are stronger than the chartists and push the exchange rate back towards fundamentals. But then the chartists are back in charge and the exchange rate increases again. This explains the apparent random evolution of the exchange rate in the bull market. The same story holds, of course, in the bear market. What causes a shift from a bull to a bear or a bear to a bull market? Suppose that the exchange rate is extremely high. Then the chartists are still buying but the fundamentalists are selling strongly. Their selling pressure may not only drive the exchange rate down but may cause a severe crash in which the exchange rate is pushed below its fundamental value. Then a bull market turns into a bear market.

11.4.3.3 Variation 2: Decreasing impact of fundamental analysis In the previous two models we have assumed that the confidence of the fundamentalists in their trading rules increases as the distance between the exchange rate and its fundamental value grows. The motivation was that profit opportunities increase with the misalignment. But one should note that as long as the exchange rate runs away from its fundamental value, the fundamentalists mispredict the direction of the exchange rate and their trading strategies are highly unprofitable. One might therefore also assume that the fundamentalists lose confidence in fundamental analysis in such a situation. Let us briefly explore what may happen then. We use the same model as in Section 11.4.3.1 but now assume that the orders of the fundamentalists are determined by

$$D_t^F = c(F - P_t)/\sqrt{d + |F - P_t|}. \tag{11.13}$$

Since parameters c and d are positive, the fundamentalists are still betting on a reduction of the mispricing, yet their aggressiveness decreases with the misalignment.

Figure 11.7 illustrates the dynamics for $a = 1$, $b = 2$, $c = 2.4$, $d = 0.001$, $F = 1$ and $W^C = W^F = 0.5$. The nonlinear interactions between the chartists and the fundamentalists again create a complex development of the exchange rate. Remember from Section 11.4.1 that the fundamentalists may also be a source of market instability when they trade too aggressively. This is here the case close to the fundamental value. The size of the orders of the fundamentalists is so strong that it causes an overshooting of the exchange rate. Fortunately, their market impact weakens when the exchange rate disconnects from fundamentals such that the market does not explode. The role of the chartists is that they contribute to the turbulence. If their behavior is excluded, more regular motion sets in.

Is such a scenario completely out of the blue? Westerhoff and Reitz (2003) present empirical evidence that the market impact of the fundamentalists may indeed decrease with the misalignment. A similar theoretical argument is made by Frankel and Froot (1986, 1990), who claim that fundamental analysis will be used less forcefully when the exchange rate traces out a bubble path. This brings us to the next section in which we discuss models where agents may select their trading strategies.

11.4.4 Endogenous selection of trading strategies

In the majority of models, the fraction of chartists and fundamentalists is determined endogenously. Quite different mechanisms have been proposed. Frankel and Froot (1986, 1990) discuss a model in which a portfolio

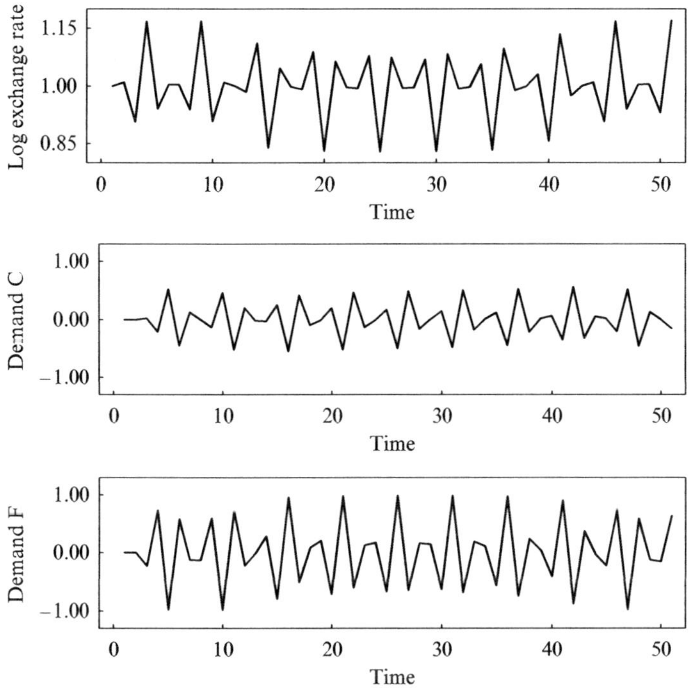

Note: The panels show from top to bottom the log of the exchange rates, the demand of the chartists and the demand of the fundamentalists, respectively.

Figure 11.7 A different nonlinear fundamental trading rule

manager uses a weighted average of the predictions of chartists and fundamentalists. The better a group predicts the course of the exchange rate, the larger its weight becomes. Brock and Hommes (1997, 1998) develop a framework in which the fraction of technical and fundamental trading rules depends on their evolutionary fitness: a given strategy gains in popularity when it produces profits. Lux (1995, 1997, 1998) and Lux and Marchesi (2000) present a related mechanism in which the impact of technical and fundamental analysis depends on profit differentials. The goal of this section is to illustrate a few of these interesting ideas.

11.4.4.1 Selection of strategies according to misalignment Let us start with a simple model. Suppose that the log of the exchange rate is quoted as

$$P_{t+1} = P_t + a(W_t^C D_t^C + W_t^F D_t^F), \qquad (11.14)$$

where $a > 0$ captures the price adjustment speed. The fractions of chartists W_t^C and fundamentalists W_t^F are now time-dependent. As in our benchmark model, chartists extrapolate the exchange rate trend

$$D_t^C = b(P_t - P_{t-1}), \tag{11.15}$$

while fundamentalists expect a mean reversion

$$D_t^F = c(F - P_t). \tag{11.16}$$

The parameters b and c are positive and the log of the fundamental value F is constant.

In each period, traders choose between technical and fundamental analysis rules. The traders seek to exploit bull and bear market situations but they are also aware that such behavior is risky. The more the exchange rate deviates from its fundamental value, the more traders come to the conclusion that the bull or bear market might collapse. As a result, an increasing number of them opt for fundamental analysis, which appears superior. The market share of technical traders is defined as

$$W_t^C = \frac{1}{1 + e(F - P_t)^2}. \tag{11.17}$$

Since the market shares add up to one, the weight of the fundamentalists is $W_t^F = 1 - W_t^C$. Note that the higher parameter $e > 0$ is, the faster the agents switch to fundamental analysis as the misalignment increases.

A typical simulation run for $a = 1, b = 9, c = 0.2, e = 20000$ and $F = 1$ is presented in Figure 11.8. The panels show the log of the exchange rate, the demand of the chartists, the demand of the fundamentalists and the fraction of chartists, respectively. As can be seen, the exchange rate circles in a complex manner around its fundamental value. Note that the fraction of chartists varies strongly. When the exchange rate is close to its fundamental value, most traders prefer technical analysis, and the exchange rate is consequently driven away from its fundamental value. However, the weight of the chartists decreases with increasing misalignments. When the majority of traders rely on fundamental analysis, a period of convergence sets in until this process repeats itself.

Such switching behavior is, for example, stressed by Hommes (2001). A model along these lines is discussed in Westerhoff (2003b). Similar models are due to de Grauwe and Dewachter (1992, 1993). They also present a very interesting alternative explanation for the above switching model. In their approach, fundamentalists are heterogeneous. They perceive the fundamental value correctly, but only on average. When the exchange

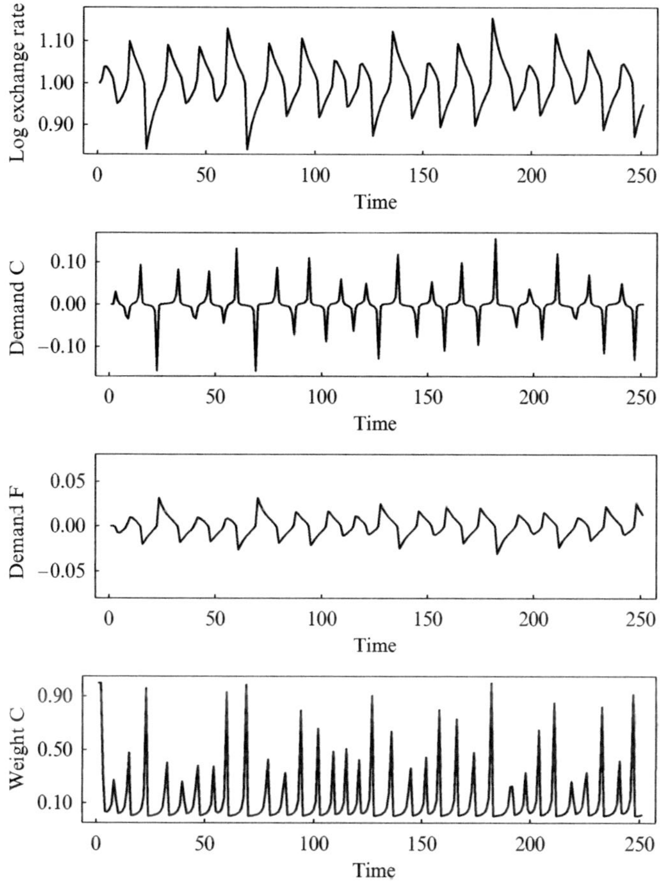

Note: The panels show from top to bottom the log of the exchange rates, the demand of the chartists, the demand of the fundamentalists and the fraction of chartists, respectively.

Figure 11.8 Selection of trading rules depending on misalignment

rate is equal to its fundamental value, half of the fundamentalists view the exchange rate as overvalued and half as undervalued. As a result, the orders of the fundamentalists cancel out each other. However, when the exchange rate disconnects from its fundamental value, more and more fundamentalists agree on the direction of the future exchange rate path and thus their net impact increases. When the orders of the fundamentalists cancel out each other, the market impact of the chartists is obviously maximal and when all fundamentalists agree on the future direction of the exchange rate, the market impact of chartists is minimal.

Moreover, de Grauwe, Dewachter and Embrechts (1993) demonstrate that other technical trading rules may easily increase the complexity of the exchange rate process. They suggest modeling the orders of chartists as

$$D_t^C = b((P_t - P_{t-1}) - 0.5(P_t - P_{t-3})). \tag{11.18}$$

Accordingly, the chartists rely on what is called a double-crossover method. Such a method combines two moving averages. When a short-term moving average of the past exchange rates crosses a long-term moving average of the past exchange rates from below (above), then a buying (selling) signal is triggered. The strength of trading depends on $b > 0$. For simplicity, the short-term moving average is a two-period change and the long-term moving average a three-period change. Higher lag structures may, of course, intensify the dynamics.

Figure 11.9 shows how such trading behavior modifies the dynamics of the model. The simulation run is generated with $a = 1$, $b = 10$, $c = 0.25$, $e = 5000$ and $F = 1$. The panels show the log of the exchange rate, the demand of the chartists, the demand of the fundamentalists and the fraction of chartists, respectively. Compared with Figure 11.8, the dynamics now appears to be much more intricate. The exchange rate may, for instance, remain for some periods above or below its fundamental value. However, the story behind the dynamics is essentially the same.

11.4.4.2 Selection of strategies according to evolutionary fitness measures What investors care most about is profits. It thus seems reasonable to base the agents' choice of trading rules on the rules' past performance. Here we consider a simple example that is closely related to the Brock and Hommes (1997, 1998) framework. The log of the exchange rate in time step t11 is announced as

$$P_{t+1} = P_t + a(W_t^C D_t^C + W_t^F D_t^F), \tag{11.19}$$

with

$$D_t^C = b(P_t - P_{t-1}) \tag{11.20}$$

as the orders of technical trading rules and

$$D_t^F = c(F - P_t) \tag{11.21}$$

as the orders of fundamental trading rules. Parameters a, b and c are again positive and the fundamentals are constant.

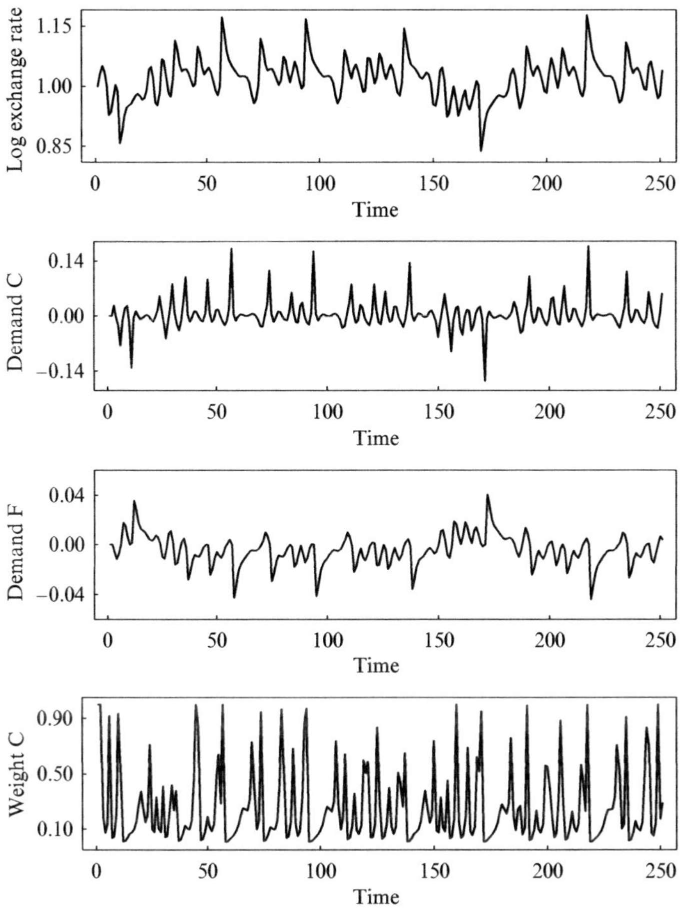

Note: The panels show from top to bottom the log of the exchange rates, the demand of the chartists, the demand of the fundamentalists and the fraction of chartists, respectively.

Figure 11.9 A simple variation of the previous model

The impact of a trading strategy depends on its evolutionary fitness. The fitness of technical analysis is defined as

$$K_t^C = (\text{Exp}[P_t] - \text{Exp}[P_{t-1}])D_{t-2}^C, \tag{11.22}$$

while the fitness of fundamental analysis is given as

$$K_t^F = (\text{Exp}[P_t] - \text{Exp}[P_{t-1}])D_{t-2}^F. \tag{11.23}$$

Obviously, the fitness of the trading strategies depends on their most recent performance. The time structure of the model is as follows. Orders submitted in period $t - 2$ are filled at prices in period $t - 1$. Whether or not a transaction will produce a (myopic) profit then depends on the realized price in period t. One may further consider that the agents do not forget the fitness values of past trading periods, that is, that they possess a memory.

The higher the fitness of a strategy, the more agents will rely on it. The fraction of agents deciding on technical analysis is

$$W_t^C = \frac{\mathrm{Exp}[gK_t^C]}{\mathrm{Exp}[gK_t^C] + \mathrm{Exp}[gK_t^F]}. \tag{11.24}$$

The fraction of agents selecting fundamental analysis is

$$W_t^F = \frac{\mathrm{Exp}[gK_t^F]}{\mathrm{Exp}[gK_t^C] + \mathrm{Exp}[gK_t^F]}. \tag{11.25}$$

The parameter $g > 0$ captures how sensitive the mass of agents is to select the most attractive strategy. The higher g is, the more agents will select the strategy with the highest fitness. In this sense, g may also be interpreted as a rationality parameter.

The dynamics of the model are depicted in Figure 11.10, where we assume that $a = 1$, $b = 2.9$, $c = 1.225$, $g = 150$ and $F = 1$. We see from top to bottom the log of the exchange rate, the demand of the chartists, the demand of the fundamentalists and the fraction of chartists, respectively. A permanent evolutionary competition between the trading rules causes endogenous exchange rate dynamics.

In a stylized way, the dynamics evolves as follows. During an exchange rate trend, technical analysis is profitable. However, technical analysis produces strong forecast errors at turning points. When the exchange rate reverts towards its fundamental value, fundamental analysis becomes profitable. The profitability of technical and fundamental analysis continously varies as the exchange rate oscillates around its fundamental value. Hence, the dynamics may not die out but continue.

11.4.5 Interactions between markets

Until now, speculators have been active in one market only. In reality, however, speculators may wander around markets. This aspect has only recently received attention. It should be obvious that if traders can switch between markets, this may lead to intricate dynamics since the composition of technical and fundamental traders on a market may change over time. First set-ups in this direction have been suggested by Westerhoff (2004b), Chiarella, Dieci and Gardini (2005) and Westerhoff and Dieci (2006).

Here we discuss the approach of Westerhoff and Wieland (2004)

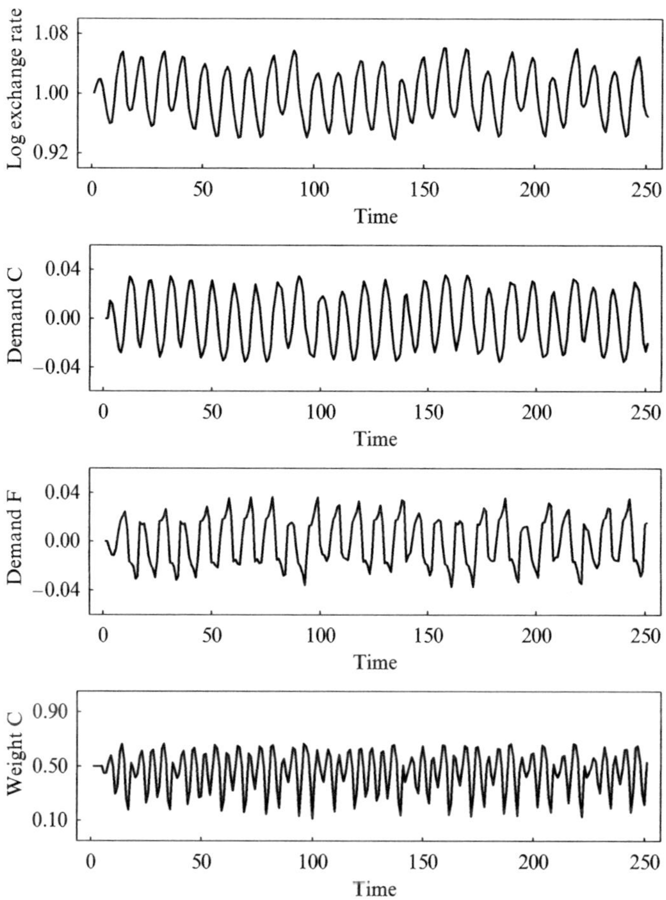

Note: The panels show from top to bottom the log of the exchange rates, the demand of the chartists, the demand of the fundamentalists and the fraction of chartists, respectively

Figure 11.10 Selection of trading rules depending on past fitness

who consider $h = 1, 2, \ldots, H$ foreign exchange markets in their model. Fundamentalists are regarded as experts who specialize in one market and thus remain in that market. Since chartists use rather flexible trading rules, they may easily switch between markets. The chartists seek to exploit price trends but strongly dislike misaligned markets. The log of the exchange rate in market h at time step $t + 1$ is quoted as

$$P_{t+1}^{h} = P_t^h + a^h(W_t^{C,h} D_t^{C,h} + D_t^{F,h}). \tag{11.26}$$

The orders of technical trading rules in market h depend on the observed exchange rate trend

$$D_t^{C,h} = b^h(P_t^h - P_{t-1}^h). \tag{11.27}$$

The orders of the fundamental trading rules in market h increase with the mispricing

$$D_t^{F,h} = c^h(F^h - P_t^h). \tag{11.28}$$

Parameters a^h, b^h and c^h are all positive.

The chartists seek to profit from exchange rate trends. But, as is well known, eventually every bubble bursts. Chartists identify the risk of being caught in a bursting bubble as

$$K_t^h = \mathrm{Log}\frac{1}{1 + j^h(F^h - P_t^h)^2}. \tag{11.29}$$

This fitness function is bell-shaped and bounded between minus infinity and zero. Note that the larger the distance between the exchange rate and its fundamental value, the lower the fitness of a market. How quickly the fitness of a market changes depends on $j^h > 0$.

The fraction of chartists entering market h is determined by

$$W_t^{C,h} = \frac{\mathrm{Exp}[g^h K_t^h]}{\sum_{h=1}^{H} \mathrm{Exp}[g^h K_t^h]}. \tag{11.30}$$

The higher the attractiveness of a market, the more chartists will enter that market. Parameter g^h may again be regarded as a rationality parameter since it captures how sensitive the mass of traders is to selecting the most attractive market.

All h markets involve the same key currency (say the US dollar). Implicitly, the model fixes several cross-rates. Figure 11.11 displays a simulation run for $H = 5$ symmetric markets and $a = 1$, $b = 5$, $c = 0.2$, $g = 1.2$, $j = 500000$ and $F = 1$. The panels show from top to bottom the log of the exchange rate in market 1, the log of the exchange rate in market 2 and the log of the cross-rate between markets 1 and 2, respectively.

The exchange rates in markets 1 and 2 and also the cross-rates fluctuate around their fundamental values in a complex manner. For some periods, the markets are relatively stable. At other times, volatility is elevated. When elevated, all markets usually display strong exchange rate fluctuations. What is going on here? Suppose that a market is dominated

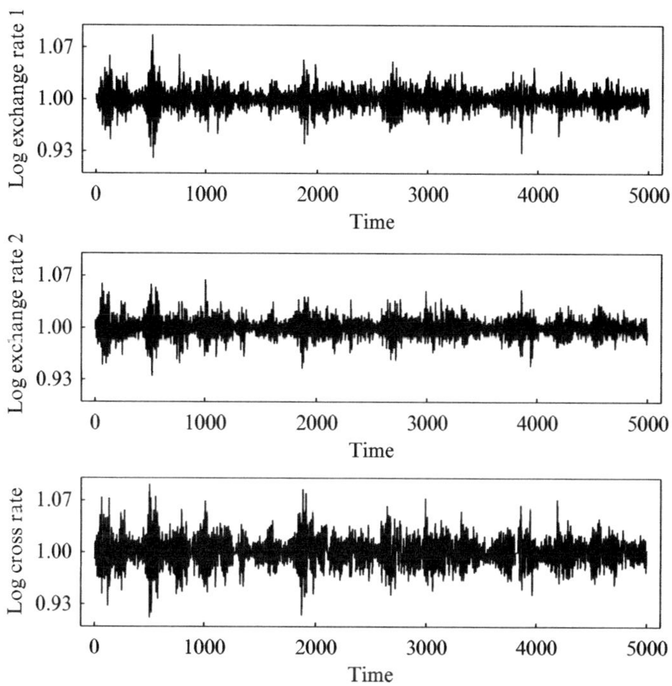

Note: The panels show from top to bottom the log of the exchange rates in market 1, the log of the exchange rates in market 2 and the log of the cross-rates between markets 1 and 2, respectively.

Figure 11.11 Interactions between markets

by chartists. Then it is likely that the exchange rate is driven away from its fundamental value. However, this decreases the fitness of the market for the chartist. The chartists leave the market (they enter another market, which will then be destabilized) and thus the fundamentalists drive the exchange rate back to fundamental values. This increases the fitness of the market and the chartists are likely to return soon.

11.4.6 Summary and some additional mechanisms

The goal of Section 11.4 is to illustrate some important nonlinear mechanisms that may contribute to the complex behavior of exchange rates. From these examples it should have become clear by now that nonlinear motion is rather the rule than the exception. Let us mention some other nonlinear approaches. Kaizoji (2002) develops a model in which both technical and fundamental trading rules are nonlinear. Li and Rosser

(2001, 2004) present a model in which traders may switch between a linear technical trading rule and a nonlinear fundamental trading rule. In Chiarella and He (2001, 2005), the dynamics is further complicated by the fact that the agents' wealth changes over time. When certain trader types become wealthier, they obtain a stronger impact on prices. De Grauwe and Grimaldi (2006, 2007) focus on the mean reversion pressure that results from the goods markets. Due to transaction costs, mean reversion pressure from the goods markets may be absent. But when it kicks in, fundamentalists may take this into account and trade more aggressively. Last but not least, Rosser, Ahmed and Hartmann (2003) explore what may happen when the evolution of the fundamental value itself is a chaotic process. Clearly, fundamentals are not constant over time but may change with respect to (nonlinear) macroeconomic developments. When traders react to changes in the fundamentals, quite intricate dynamics may arise.

So far we have illustrated the dynamics of the models by plotting them in the time domain. However, part of the models' complexity is better revealed in a phase space representation. The eight panels of Figure 11.12 show the dynamics of the eight nonlinear models discussed so far in phase space, that is, the log of the exchange rate in period $t + 1$ is plotted against the log of the exchange rate in period t. As can be seen, the models may produce so-called strange attractors, which indicate that the underlying dynamics may indeed be chaotic. It should be noted that there exists a large battery of quite sophisticated numerical and analytical tools that allow the investigation of the dynamics of the models in much more detail. The interested reader may consult, for instance, Gandolfo (1985), Puu (1989), Medio (1992) or Rosser (2000).

11.5 Stochastic models

In Section 11.4, we reviewed several prominent mechanisms that may lead to complex foreign exchange dynamics. One important mechanism that is still missing is herding behavior. Herding behavior will be discussed in Section 11.5.1. Another goal of the current section is to show that models with heterogeneous interacting agents that are buffeted with dynamic noise may produce quite realistic exchange rate movements. Although the models discussed in Section 11.4 are able to mimic some stylized facts of exchange rates, the dynamics typically contains too much structure. With the help of some exogenous disturbances, however, the stylized facts presented in Section 11.2 might be replicated quite well. In Section 11.5.2 we also comment on more sophisticated agent-based computational models.

11.5.1 A simple herding model

We present a simplified version of Kirman's herding model (1991, 1993). A central feature of this model is that the agents' selection of trading rules is

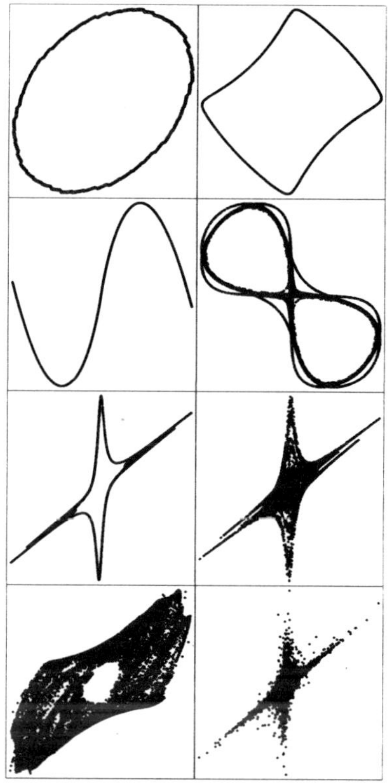

Note: The log of the exchange rate of period t is plotted against the log of the exchange rate in period $t-1$ for the eight nonlinear models of Section 11.4.

Figure 11.12 The dynamics in phase space

due to stochastic social interactions. In fact, market participants regularly talk to each other and this may influence their selection of trading rules. Besides becoming 'infected' due to communication, the agent's choice of a trading rule may also change exogenously. We will see that when the majority of market participants rely on technical trading rules, the market displays bubbles and crashes. But when the majority of them opt for fundamental analysis, the market becomes rather stable.

In Kirman's herding model there are two prevalent views of the world, and each agent holds one of them. View 1 corresponds to being a chartist and view 2 to being a fundamentalist. Overall, there are N agents. Denote by K_t the number of agents who hold view 1 in time step t. The state of the system may be defined by the number K_t of agents holding view 1, that is, $K_t \in \{0, 1, \ldots, N\}$. The system evolves as follows: two individuals meet at random. The first is converted to the second's view with probability $(1 - \delta)$. Moreover, there is a small probability ε that the first will change his or her opinion independently (for example, an existing agent is replaced by a new one who does not share the same view). The dynamic evolution of the process is given by

$$K_t = K_{t-1} + \begin{cases} 1 & \text{with probability } p_{t-1}^1 \\ -1 & \text{with probability } p_{t-1}^2 \\ 0 & \text{with probability } 1 - p_{t-1}^1 - p_{t-1}^2, \end{cases} \tag{11.31}$$

where

$$p_{t-1}^1 = \left(1 - \frac{K_{t-1}}{N}\right)\left(\varepsilon + (1 - \delta)\frac{K_{t-1}}{N - 1}\right), \tag{11.32}$$

and

$$p_{t-1}^2 = \frac{K_{t-1}}{N}\left(\varepsilon + (1 - \delta)\frac{N - K_{t-1}}{N - 1}\right). \tag{11.33}$$

With probability p_{t-1}^1, K_{t-1} increases by $+1$ and with probability p_{t-1}^2, K_{t-1} changes by -1. With probability $1 - p_{t-1}^1 - p_{t-1}^2$, K_{t-1} remains constant.

The proportion of the time the system will spend in each state depends on the relative values of ε and $(1 - \delta)$. There are two interesting cases: when the probability of self-conversion is relatively high, and the probability of being converted by another agent is relatively low (for example, $\varepsilon = 0.15$, $1 - \delta = 0.7$, $N = 100$), the state of the system fluctuates around $K = 50$ so that most of the probability mass is located in the center. But when the probability of self-conversion is relatively low and the probability of being converted by another agent is relatively high (for example, $\varepsilon = 0.005$, $1 - \delta = 0.99$, $N = 100$), the system spends most of the time in the extremes. Then nearly all agents hold the same view for some time, but suddenly the whole crowd may switch to the other view. In neither example does the system converge to any particular state K, that is, none of the states $K \in \{0, 1, \ldots, N\}$ is, itself, an equilibrium.

Let us now turn to the exchange rate model. The log of the exchange rate adjusts as

$$P_{t+1} = P_t + a(W_t^C D_t^C + W_t^F D_t^F), \tag{11.34}$$

where $a > 0$ reflects the price adjustment speed with respect to excess demand. The fractions of agents who use technical analysis is defined as

$$W_t^C = K_t/N. \tag{11.35}$$

The remaining fraction of agents relies on fundamental analysis

$$W_t^F = (N - K_t)/N. \tag{11.36}$$

The chartists extrapolate the exchange rate trend. Depending on $b > 0$, their orders are given as

$$D_t^C = b(P_t - P_{t-1}) + \beta_t. \tag{11.37}$$

In reality, there exists an ocean of different technical trading rules. To capture part of the variety of technical analysis rules, we add a noise term β, which is normally distributed with mean zero and constant standard deviation σ^β.

The orders of the fundamentalists depend on the expected mean reversion

$$D_t^F = c(F - P_t) + \chi_t. \tag{11.38}$$

The reaction parameter c is positive and the log of the fundamental value is denoted by F. Again we add a normally distributed noise term with mean zero and constant standard deviation σ^χ, which may reflect that agents use slightly different fundamental trading rules or commit little errors when determining their investment positions.

The dynamics of the model is illustrated by Figure 11.13. We set $a = 1$, $b = 0.05$, $c = 0.02$, $\sigma^\beta = 0.017$, $\sigma^\chi = 0.004$, $F = 1$, $\varepsilon = 0.005$ and $\delta = 0.5$. Moreover, 100 time steps in the herding part of the model correspond to one time step in the exchange rate model. The panels show from top to bottom the fraction of chartists, the log of the exchange rate, the returns, the probability density function of the returns, the autocorrelation function of raw returns and the autocorrelation function of absolute returns, respectively. Does the model match the stylized facts of financial markets? A comparison of Figures 11.1, 11.2 and 11.13 reveals some striking similarities: we find bubbles and crashes, a high exchange rate variability, fat tails for the distribution of the returns, the absence of autocorrelation in raw returns and temporal dependence in volatility.

All in all, the simple herding model produces quite realistic dynamics. The reason for this is partially revealed by the top panel of Figure 11.13. Changes in opinion may occur quite quickly. The chartists are typically responsible for high exchange rate volatility and may also create bubbles. But due to random interactions among market participants, the market

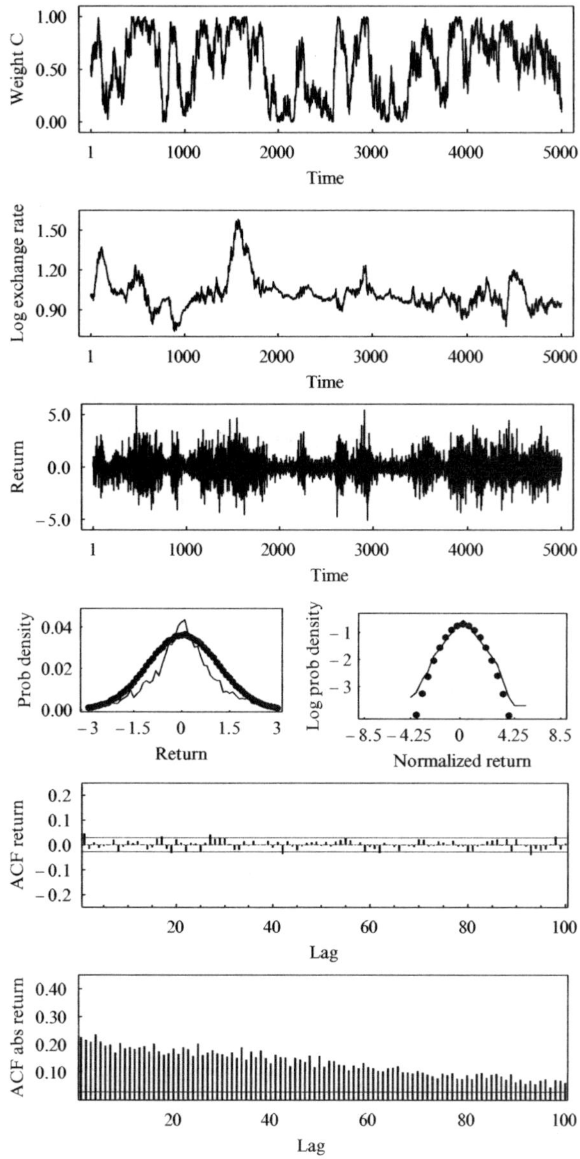

Note: The panels show from top to bottom the fraction of chartists, the log of the exchange rates, the returns, the probability density function of the returns, the autocorrelation function of raw returns and the autocorrelation function of absolute returns, respectively.

Figure 11.13 The dynamics of a simple stochastic herding model impact of chartists may abruptly decrease. Fundamentalists then push the exchange rate back to fundamental values and the market becomes less volatile. Switching between the trading rules thus also causes volatility clustering. Since the behavior of the traders is partially noisy, the exchange rate returns are uncorrelated.

11.5.2 Artificial foreign exchange markets

Up to now, we concentrated on relatively simple models in which agents rely on a particular technical and a particular fundamental trading rule. Due to nonlinearities, interesting dynamics may evolve. In reality, agents naturally use a much larger set of trading rules. So-called agent-based computational models seek to take this into account. To illustrate the philosophy of such models, we briefly address the main features of its most prominent member, namely the Santa Fe approach of Palmer et al. (1994), Arthur et al. (1997) and LeBaron, Arthur and Palmer (1999). They propose a theory of price formation based on heterogeneous traders. Each agent at any time possesses a multiplicity of forecast rules and uses those that are both best suited to the current state of the market and have recently proved most reliable. Agents learn by discovering which of their predictors prove best, and by developing new ones from time to time.

More specifically, each predictor is a condition-forecast rule that contains both a market condition that may at times be fulfilled by the current state of the market and a forecasting formula for the price of the next period. Each agent holds a given number of individual predictors in mind and uses the most accurate of those that are active. Thus, each agent has the ability to recognize different sets of states of the market. For example, if a head-and-shoulders pattern has a high performance, a trader will not use it until he or she has really detected a head and shoulders pattern. If a head-and-shoulders pattern emerges, the forecasting part of the predictor triggers a trading position.

The market price is driven by the trading activity of the agents. Once the market clearing price is revealed, the traders update the accuracy of the active predictors. In addition, the traders continually explore new forecasting rules. That is, from time to time they drop rules that perform badly, and create new ones. Learning takes place in two ways: on a rapid base as agents learn which of their predictors are accurate and worth acting upon, and which should be ignored, and at a slower time scale as non-performing predictors are discarded and new ones are invented.

The model generates very realistic price dynamics. Stylized facts such as excess volatility, fat tails for the distribution of the returns or volatility clustering are replicated. Another important result is that technical trading rules are not forced to exist but endogenously persist in the market. For instance, technical analysis can emerge if trend-following predictors are generated by chance in the population, and if random perturbations activate them and subsequently validate them.

The agent-based computation approach has both advantages and disadvantages. On the one hand, agents are allowed to explore a fairly wide range of possible forecasting rules. In addition, they have flexibility in using and ignoring different pieces of information. On the other hand, it is often difficult to pin down causalities acting inside the market. Suppose that a model includes 25 traders, each relying on a set of 100 predictors. Then 2500 different predictors can be used at a given time step. As time proceeds, the traders constantly explore new rules. For alternative set-ups see, for example, Raberto et al. (2001) or Chen and Yeh (2001). In Lawrenz and Westerhoff (2003), the traders only follow a set of six time-invariant trading rules. The selection of trading rules is modeled via genetic algorithm learning. Their model still allows the development of an intuitive understanding of what is going on in such market models.

11.6 Discussion

Models with heterogeneous interacting agents have the potential to match the stylized facts of foreign exchange markets quite well. In this sense, they also help us to develop a better understanding of the behavior of exchange rates. Since the models are obviously quite powerful, we may use them as computer laboratories to design better trading environments and to explore the effectiveness of certain regulatory mechanisms. Here we briefly discuss preliminary results concerning the workings of central bank interventions and transaction taxes.

Central banks frequently intervene in foreign exchange markets. Such interventions are motivated by the desire to check short-run trends or to correct longer-term deviations from fundamental values. Accordingly, central banks either trade against the current exchange rate trend and thus counter the behavior of chartists or they trade in the direction of the fundamental value and thus act like fundamentalists. These simple strategies are called leaning against the wind and targeting long-run fundamentals. Although central banks seem to believe in the power of intervention operations, both the theoretical and the empirical literature remain skeptical about their usefulness. Westerhoff and Wieland (2004) explore the effectiveness of central bank interventions in a system of linked foreign exchange markets (see Section 11.4.5). They find that central bank interventions may, in principle, be able to stabilize exchange rate fluctuations. However, unexpected spillover effects may also arise. If many destabilizing chartists leave the intervention market, then other markets may display stronger exchange rate fluctuations.

How may transaction taxes influence the stability of foreign exchange markets? Westerhoff and Dieci (2006) develop a model in which agents may trade in two different markets, using both technical or fundamental trading rules. In addition, the agents are free to trade, that is, they may become inactive. If a central authority imposes a transaction tax in one market only, then the taxed (untaxed) market becomes stabilized (destabilized). The main reason is that some (destabilizing) traders migrate from the taxed market to the untaxed market. If a uniform transaction tax is imposed in both markets, then both markets become less volatile and distorted. The analysis also reveals that technical traders are more punished by a transaction tax than fundamental traders. The profits of technical traders are to some degree random and based on a strong trading intensity.

Let us finally stress some open problems and potential avenues for future research. We have modeled the price adjustment by assuming a fixed relation between excess demand and consecutive price changes. One may interpret this as a stylized description of the activity of market-makers. However, a more detailed underpinning would be desirable. For instance, how do market-makers adjust prices with respect to their inventory? The fundamental value is typically set at constant or modeled as a simple random walk. It would be very interesting to see how other types of processes of the fundamental value may affect interactions between heterogeneous agents. In addition, we have always assumed that the agents perceive the fundamental value correctly. That is, of course, a rather strong assumption. People may have some knowledge about the fundamental value but are not aware of its true law of motion. A theory of how agents perceive fundamentals is missing. A related question is how agents react to the arrival of new information. Most models only focus on financial markets. However, there exist important spillover effects between real and financial markets. One may try to connect a two-country macroeconomic model with a heterogeneous agent financial market model. This may then also be a promising way to endogenize the fundamental value and let the agents learn the fundamental value from macroeconomic data. Finally, the models are calibrated such that they are able to mimic certain stylized facts. What is needed, however, is a more direct empirical validation of these models, that is, one should try to estimate the models' structure and parameters with real data.

11.7 Conclusions

The foreign exchange market is characterized by a quite turbulent dynamics. Its market participants are, of course, responsible for this outcome. Guided by empirical evidence, the chartist-fundamentalist approach explores the interactions between heterogeneous speculators. A main finding is that complex foreign exchange dynamics may arise due to the nonlinear interplay between technical and fundamental traders. There exist several natural reasons why this interplay may be nonlinear, in particular (1) trading rules may be nonlinear, (2) agents may select between trading strategies, or (3) agents may switch between markets. Buffeted with dynamic noise, models with heterogeneous agents may also match some important stylized facts of financial markets, including uncorrelated price increments, fat tails for the distribution of the returns and volatility clustering. Overall, the chartist-fundamentalist approach may help us understand what is going on in foreign exchange markets and may thus hopefully also be beneficial for designing better trading institutions in the long run.

References

Arthur, B., Holland, J., LeBaron, B., Palmer, R. and Tayler, P. (1997), 'Asset pricing under endogenous expectations in an artificial stock market', in Arthur, B., Durlauf, S. and Lane, D. (eds), *The Economy as an Evolving Complex System II*, Addison-Wesley: Reading, pp. 15–44.

Bank for International Settlement (2005), *Triennial Central Bank Survey of Foreign Exchange and Derivative Market Activity 2004*, BIS: Basle.

Brock, W. and Hommes, C. (1997), 'A rational route to randomness', *Econometrica*, **65**(5), 1059–95.

Brock, W. and Hommes, C. (1998), 'Heterogeneous beliefs and routes to chaos in a simple asset pricing model', *Journal of Economic Dynamics Control*, **22**(8–9), 1235–74.

Brock, W., Lakonishok, J. and LeBaron, B. (1992), 'Simple technical trading rules and the stochastic properties of stock returns', *Journal of Finance*, **67**(5), 1731–64.

Caginalp, G., Porter, D. and Smith, V. (2001), 'Financial bubbles: Excess cash, momentum, and incomplete information', *Journal of Psychology and Financial Markets*, **2**(2), 80–99.

Chen, S.-H. and Yeh, C.-H. (2001), 'Evolving traders and the business school with genetic programming: A new architecture of the agent-based artificial stock market', *Journal of Economic Dynamics and Control*, **25**(3–4), 363–93.

Chiarella, C. (1992), 'The dynamics of speculative behavior', *Annals of Operations Research*, **37**(1–4), 101–23.

Chiarella, C. and He, X.-Z. (2001), 'Asset price and wealth dynamics under heterogeneous expectations', *Quantitative Finance*, **1**(5), 509–26.

Chiarella, C. and He, X.-Z. (2005), 'An asset pricing model with adaptive heterogeneous agents and wealth effects', in, Lux, T., Reitz, S. and Samanidou, E. (eds), *Nonlinear Dynamics and Heterogeneous Interacting Agents*, Springer: Berlin, pp. 269–85.

Chiarella, C. and Iori, G. (2002), 'A simulation analysis of the microstructure of the double auction market', *Quantitative Finance*, **2**(5), 1–8.

Chiarella, C., Dieci, R. and Gardini, L. (2002), 'Speculative behavior and complex asset price dynamics: A global analysis', *Journal of Economic Behavior and Organization*, **49**(2), 173–97.

Chiarella, C, Dieci, R. and Gardini, L. (2005), 'The dynamic interaction of speculation and diversification', *Applied Mathematical Finance*, **12**(1), 17–52.

Cont, R. (2001), 'Empirical properties of asset returns: Stylized facts and statistical issues', *Quantitative Finance*, **1**(2), 223–36.

Day, R. and Huang, W. (1990), 'Bulls, bears and market sheep', *Journal of Economic Behavior and Organization*, **14**(3), 299–329.

De Grauwe, P. and Dewachter, H. (1992), 'Chaos in the Dornbusch model of the exchange rate', *Kredit und Kapital*, **25**(1), 26–54.

De Grauwe, P. and Dewachter, H. (1993), 'A chaotic model of the exchange rate: The role of fundamentalists and chartists', *Open Economies Review*, **4**(4), 351–79.
De Grauwe, P. and Grimaldi, M. (2006), 'Heterogeneity of agents, transactions costs and the exchange rate', *Journal of Economic Dynamics and Control*, **29**(4), 691–719.
De Grauwe, P. and Grimaldi, M. (2007), 'Exchange rate puzzles: A tale of switching attractors', *European Economic Review*, **50**(1), 1–33.
De Grauwe, P., Dewachter, H. and Embrechts, M. (1993), *Exchange Rate Theory – Chaotic Models of Foreign Exchange Markets*, Blackwell: Oxford.
Edwards, R. and Magee, J. (1966), *Technical Analysis of Stock Trends*, John Magee: Boston.
Farmer, D. (2002), 'Market force, ecology, and evolution', *Industrial and Corporate Change*, **11**(5), 895–953.
Farmer, D. and Joshi, S. (2002), 'The price dynamics of common trading strategies', *Journal of Economic Behavior and Organization*, **49**(2), 149–71.
Frankel, J. and Froot, K. (1986), 'Understanding the U.S. dollar in the eighties: The expectations of chartists and fundamentalists', *Economic Record*, **62**(special issue), 24–38.
Frankel, J, and Froot, K. (1987), 'Using survey data to test standard propositions regarding exchange rate expectations', *American Economic Review*, **77**(1), 133–53.
Frankel, J. and Froot, K. (1990), 'Chartists, fundamentalists and the demand for dollars', in Courakis, A. and Taylor, M. (eds), *Private Behavior and Government Policy in Interdependent Economies*, Clarendon Press: Oxford, pp. 73–126.
Gandolfo, G. (1985), '*Economic Dynamics: Methods and Models*, North-Holland: Amsterdam.
Gu, M. (1995), 'Market mediating behavior: An economic analysis of the security exchange specialists', *Journal of Economic Behavior and Organization*, **27**, 237–56.
Guillaume, D., Dacorogna, M. Dave, R., Müller, U., Olsen, R. and Picet, O. (1997), 'From the bird's eye to the microscope: A survey of new stylized facts of the intra-daily foreign exchange markets', *Finance Stochastics*, **1**, 95–129.
He, X.-Z. and Westerhoff, F. (2005), 'Commodity markets, price limiters and speculative price dynamics', *Journal of Economic Dynamics and Control*, **29**(4), 1577–96.
Hirshleifer, D. (2001), 'Investor psychology and asset pricing', *Journal of Finance*, **56**(4), 1533–97.
Hommes, C. (2001), 'Financial markets as nonlinear adaptive evolutionary systems', *Quantitative Finance*, **1**(1), 149–67.
Hommes, C. (2006), 'Heterogeneous agent models in economics and finance', in Tesfatsion, L. and Judd, K. (eds), *Handbook of Computational Economics Vol. 2: Agent-based Computational Economics*, North-Holland: Amsterdam.
Hommes, C., Sonnemans, J., Tuinstra, J. and van de Velden, H. (2005), 'Coordination of expectations in asset pricing experiments', *Review of Financial Studies*, **18**(3), 955–80.
Huang, W. and Day, R. (1993), 'Chaotically switching bear and bull markets: The derivation of stock price distributions from behavioral rules', in Day, R. and Chen, P. (eds), *Nonlinear Dynamics and Evolutionary Economics*. Oxford University Press: Oxford, 169–82.
Ito, T. (1990), 'Foreign exchange rate expectations: Micro survey data', *American Economic Review*, **80**(3), 434–49.
Johnson, N., Jefferies, P. and Hui, P. (2003), *Financial Market Complexity*, Oxford University Press: Oxford.
Kahneman, D., Slovic, P. and Tversky, A. (1986), *Judgment under Uncertainty: Heuristics and Biases*, Cambridge University Press: Cambridge, MA.
Kaizoji, T. (2002), 'Speculative price dynamics in a heterogeneous agent model', *Nonlinear Dynamics, Psychology and Life Sciences*, **6**(2), 217–29.
Kirman, A. (1991), 'Epidemics of opinion and speculative bubbles in financial markets', in Taylor, M. (ed.), *Money and Financial Markets*, Blackwell: Oxford, pp. 354–68.
Kirman, A. (1993), 'Ants, rationality, and recruitment', *Quarterly Journal of Economics*, **108**(1), 137–56.
Lawrenz, C. and Westerhoff, F. (2003), 'Modeling exchange rate behavior with a genetic algorithm', *Computational Economics*, **21**(3), 209–29.

LeBaron, B. (1999), 'Technical trading rule profitability and foreign exchange intervention', *Journal of International Economics*, **49**(1), 125–43.

LeBaron, B. (2006), 'Agent-based computational finance', in Tesfatsion, L. and Judd, K. (eds), *Handbook of Computational Economics Vol. 2: Agent-based Computational Economics*, North-Holland: Amsterdam.

LeBaron, B., Arthur, B. and Palmer, R. (1999), 'Time series properties of an artificial stock market', *Journal of Economic Dynamics and Control*, **23**(9–10), 1487–516.

Li, H. and Rosser, B. (2001), 'Emergent volatility in asset markets with heterogeneous agents', *Discrete Dynamics in Nature and Society*, **6**(3), 171–80.

Li, H. and Rosser, B. (2004), 'Market dynamics and stock price volatility', *European Physical Journal B*, **39**(3), 409–13.

Lo, A. (2004), 'The adaptive markets hypothesis: Market efficiency from an evolutionary perspective', *Journal of Portfolio Management*, **30**(1), 15–29.

Lo, A., Mamaysky, H. and Wang, J. (2000), 'Foundations of technical analysis: Computational algorithms, statistical inference, and empirical implementation', *Journal of Finance*, **55**, 1705–65.

Lui, Y.-H. and Mole, D. (1998), 'The use of fundamental and technical analysis by foreign exchange dealers: Hong Kong evidence', *Journal of International Money and Finance*, **17**, 535–45.

Lux, T. (1995), 'Herd behavior, bubbles and crashes', *Economic Journal*, **105**(431), 881–96.

Lux, T. (1997), 'Time variation of second moments from a noise trader/infection model', *Journal of Economic Dynamics and Control*, **22**(1), 1–38.

Lux, T. (1998), 'The socio-economic dynamics of speculative markets: interacting agents, chaos, and the fat tails of return distributions', *Journal of Economic Behavior and Organization*, **33**(2), 143–65.

Lux, T. (2006), 'Financial power laws: Empirical evidence, models and mechanisms', in Cioffi-Revilla, C. (ed.), *Power Laws in the Social Sciences: Discovering Complexity and Non-equilibrium Dynamics in the Social Universe*.

Lux, T. and Ausloos, M. (2002), 'Market fluctuations I: Scaling, multiscaling, and their possible origins', in Bunde, A., Kropp, J. and Schellnhuber, H. (eds), *Science of Disaster: Climate Disruptions, Heart Attacks, and Market Crashes*, Springer: Berlin, pp. 373–410.

Lux, T. and Marchesi, M. (2000), 'Volatility clustering in financial markets: A micro-simulation of interacting agents', *International Journal of Theoretical and Applied Finance*, **3**(4), 675–702.

Lyons, R. (2001), *The Microstructure Approach to Exchange Rates*, MIT Press: Cambridge, MA.

Mantegna, R. and Stanley, E. (2000), *An Introduction to Econophysics*, Cambridge University Press: Cambridge, UK.

Medio, A. (1992), *Chaotic dynamics*, Cambridge University Press: Cambridge, UK.

Menkhoff, L. (1997), 'Examining the use of technical currency analysis', *International Journal of Finance and Economics*, **2**(4), 307–18.

Murphy, J. (1999), *Technical Analysis of Financial Markets*, New York Institute of Finance: New York.

Palmer, R., Arthur, B., Holland, J., LeBaron, B. and Tayler, P. (1994), 'Artificial economic life: A simple model of a stock market', *Physica D*, **75**(1–3), 264–74.

Pring, M. (1991), *Technical Analysis Explained*, McGraw-Hill: New York.

Puu, T. (1989), *Nonlinear Economic Dynamics*, Springer: Berlin.

Raberto, M., Cincotti, S., Focardi, S. and Marchesi, M. (2001), 'Agent-based simulation of a financial market', *Physica A*, **299**(1–2), 319–27.

Rosser, J.B. (2000), *From Catastrophe to Chaos: A General Theory of Economic Discontinuities*, 2nd ed. Kluwer Academic Publishers: Boston.

Rosser, B., Ahmed, E. and Hartmann, G. (2003), 'Volatility via social flaring', *Journal of Economic Behavior and Organization*, **50**(1), 77–87.

Shiller, R. (2003), 'From efficient markets theory to behavioral finance', *Journal of Economic Perspectives*, **17**(1), 83–104.

Simon, H. (1955), 'A behavioral model of rational choice', *Quarterly Journal of Economics*, **69**(1), 99–118.
Smith, V. (1991), '*Papers in Experimental Economics*, Cambridge University Press: Cambridge, UK.
Sonnemans, J., Hommes, C., Tuinstra, J. and van de Velden, H. (2004), 'The instability of a heterogeneous cobweb economy: A strategy experiment on expectation formation', *Journal of Economic Behavior and Organization*, **54**(4), 453–81.
Sornette, D. (2003), *Why Stock Markets Crash*, Princeton University Press: Princeton.
Takagi, S. (1991), 'Exchange rate expectations: A survey of survey studies', *IMF Staff Papers*, **38**(1), 156–83.
Taylor, M. and Allen, H. (1992), 'The use of technical analysis in the foreign exchange market', *Journal of International Money and Finance*, **11**(3), 304–14.
Westerhoff, F. (2003a), 'Market-maker, inventory control and foreign exchange dynamics', *Quantitative Finance*, **3**(6), 363–93.
Westerhoff, F. (2003b), 'Expectations-driven distortions in the foreign exchange market', *Journal of Economic Behavior and Organization*, **51**(3), 389–412.
Westerhoff, F. (2004a), 'Market depth and price dynamics: A note', *International Journal of Modern Physics C*, **15**, 1005–12.
Westerhoff, F. (2004b), 'Multiasset market dynamics', *Macroeconomic Dynamics*, **8**(05), 596–616.
Westerhoff, F. (2006), 'Technical analysis and the power of trading breaks', *International Journal of Theoretical and Applied Finance*, **9**(2), 227–44.
Westerhoff, F. and Dieci, R. (2006), 'The effectiveness of Keynes-Tobin transaction taxes when heterogeneous agents can trade in different markets: A behavioral finance approach', *Journal of Economic Dynamics and Control*, **30**(2), 293–22.
Westerhoff, F. and Reitz, S. (2003), 'Nonlinearities and cyclical behavior: The role of chartists and fundamentalists', *Studies in Nonlinear Dynamics and Econometrics*, **7**(4).
Westerhoff, F. and Wieland, C. (2004), 'Spillover dynamics of central bank interventions', *German Economic Review*, **5**(4), 435–50.

12. Complex systems modeling and international development

*Hans-Peter Brunner and Peter Allen**

12.1 Society and its economy as a complex system

As Matutinovic (2005, p. 873) states:

> An economy is a complex system consisting of a myriad of agents that may be placed in three broad categories: firms, households, and government. Agents' interactions come under the broad umbrella of cooperation and competition while their production and consumption activities constitute the functional fabric of the economic system. Economic activities often span several hierarchical levels of functional interdependence.

Complex systems are highly networked systems. They achieve their stability with the existing interdependencies of economic agents. Large-scale disruptions through intervening external agencies can destroy the web of interdependencies that exist in the socioeconomic system already, and introduce a simple dependency on the intervention and the funds associated with it, that can do more harm than good. This also means that the existing interactions are an evolved expression of the working of the system, and therefore external change agents will encounter resistance from the system to introduce change unless the intervention is designed sufficiently broadly and in a way that it is compatible with the existing system (Bar-Yam, 2004). Hence, international development is about the stimulation of a society's and economy's innate autocatalytic/self-organizing processes through interventions at the meso level of hierarchy (mostly the intermediary institutional level, and not at the individual agent or at the macro level). The interventions have to engage with the agents within the system, be sizeable enough to be deemed worthy of a response, but not so large that they overwhelm the system.

This chapter explains the autocatalytic nature of a change process, and it describes the network structure of complex societies. With illustrations of traditional development efforts and with examples that take a complex systems view of society, the chapter makes a plausible case for appropriate, practitioner-friendly development approaches. The choice of analytical framework and of concepts not only helps in selecting the best use of funds by international agencies, but facilitates international development intervention more likely to lead to desirable outcomes.

12.2 The autocatalytic, self-organizing nature of a process of change

"Autocatalysis" refers to "any cyclical concatenation of processes wherein each member has the propensity to accelerate the activity of the succeeding link" (Ulanowicz, 1999, pp. 41–55). Autocatalysis in an economic system presumes a variety of economic actors (= vertices or nodes of a network) interacting in a network of economic links. The network structure of interaction will be detailed in a following section. Economists have used positive and negative feedback loops to model the autocatalytic nature of economic change. Brunner (1994) has formalized mechanisms underlying the creation of populations of economic actors such as firms leading to macroeconomic change. Productivity change is driven by diverse exploratory behavior and fluctuating population size within an institutional setting for economic rules. Firms are subjected to variations in frequencies of events and performance characteristics. The frequency of firm attributes in a population is the result of a stochastic process of innovation and imitation. This view provides a common basis for the complexity science approach to economics (Allen, 1997, 2001; Allen and Strathern, 2004; Allen, Strathern, and Baldwin, 2006) and that of Schumpeter's "creative destruction" (Foster and Kaplan, 2001) and evolutionary economics (Nelson and Winter, 1982). In this view, productivity increase can be detected and felt at the higher, macro level, but the change is the outcome of variations of individual behavior that is guided by very limited knowledge concerning outcomes, and that is susceptible to three distinct forces (Brunner and Allen, 2005), competition and cooperation in networks, technological diversity, and "appropriability" conditions (the legal and institutional frame, for instance intellectual property rights). In positive and negative feedback loop models, autocatalysis streamlines energy, material, and financial flows towards more efficient members of the population. Heterogeneous agents continually adjust to the macro situation they create collectively. The whole population is ratcheted up on the macroeconomic level until the constituent members of a population touch a physical or spatial constraint and a negative feedback loop constrains growth (Matutinovic, 2005, p. 872).

12.3 Traditional development efforts and their outcome

Traditional equilibrium development theory is based on full information, complete networks and systems such that disturbances at any node spread evenly in the system. Moreover, when explanation happens at the macro level, agents are assumed to be of an average quality and consistent with aggregate behavior (Arthur, 2006), and change impacts on all agents evenly. As Potts (2001) shows in detail, the traditional microeconomic development framework is based on "field theory,"[1] whereas a complex systems approach does not define all connections between nodes or points in a field as complete. In this non-traditional way the explanatory focus becomes the change in the structure of an incomplete system to a less complete or more complete (complex) system as a result of a development intervention. What is to be explained in socioeconomic systems is the structural change in terms of degree of heterogeneity of agent populations in space, the modularity and hierarchy of a system, and other aspects of composite structural existence. According to Potts (2001, pp. 14, 19), the economic concept of a field is the extreme and unrealistic case of the geometry of economic space. If a set of interactions cannot be collapsed to a field of actions as in traditional development theory, then the geometry of development space must be mapped by a set of specific network connections among agents.

Traditional economic development theory posits an equilibrium setting, with an economy generally being in equilibrium or in a steady state, then being disturbed by random shocks returns to different equilibrium or steady states. Change is not the result of the complex system's innate, self-organizing properties of populations of heterogeneous agents. Very central to the approach is the market clearing mechanism of supply or demand imbalances over the price or quantity adjustment mechanism. Events are explained at a macro level usually contra-positioning supply and demand, savings, and investment and so on, without recognizing the underlying complex microeconomic autocatalytic processes inducing supply and demand, savings, and investment imbalances. As a result the traditional approach relies conveniently and exclusively on tractable mathematical, numerical methods of representation, for instance on the use of difference or differential equations.

The savings and investment imbalances in traditional theory arise from price changes as a result of factor substitution when supply and demand of factors change as a result of exogenous forces such as a larger educated population or more efficient techniques that allow for more use of capital-intensive production. A production function is used to reflect in equilibrium models the changes in factor proportion in terms of movement around a production function with given technology, and to reflect a production function shift toward a "known" technology frontier as a result of the exogenous adoption of efficient techniques. In complex, evolutionary systems and development theory, investment is related to technology progress, and this relationship is expressed in a technology progress function (Metcalfe, Foster, and Ramlogan, 2006), which replaces the need for a production function. A technology progress function links the productivity variable to growth.

Very widespread is the application of the two-gap differential equation model of economic growth where growth is constrained by either domestic savings or foreign exchange earnings from exports. A development intervention shocks a constrained-growth equilibrium by releasing a growth constraint, thereby moving the macro system onto a higher development equilibrium. It is a mechanistic approach based on field theory. Thus, the conventional model approach leads development policy to mechanistically direct resources to increase investment, or to change relative factor prices, or to increase factor endowments.

Conventional recommendations for trade policy, for instance to remove a foreign exchange gap, are based on models with constant or diminishing returns in technological capabilities (Arthur, 1990, p. 98). Such models settle for single equilibrium points (in contrast to autocatalytic or positive feedback approaches, which can lead to multiple equilibria, some of which can be undesirable. Traded goods settle at a fixed world price ("law of one price") as conditions of zero transaction and information costs prevail. The traditional Ricardian model of trade excludes all transaction costs. No institutions, no transport is necessary. Information and knowledge about products, markets, and so on, is transmitted instantly and costlessly. Because of these field-theory assumptions, the traditional Ricardian model of trade allows simply for the numerical analysis of the effect of changing relative factor prices on the structures of production.

The venerated Heckscher-Ohlin approach is the neoclassical prototype equilibrium model. In all such trade models the location of production is determined by relative (comparative) advantages based on factor endowments on a macro level. When, however, resources are created by different, heterogeneous market participants in different locations, and by a dynamic process of competition and cooperation leading to innovation and imitation, then it is far from obvious that patterns of trade are determined by changing relative prices, or factor endowments. Induced micro-dynamics in an adequate institutional setting, where policy interventions do not overwhelm the system but stimulate innate autocatalytic processes of productivity improvements lead to new trade patterns. When trade patterns shift, we encounter the complexity of an out-of-equilibrium economy, and international development design needs to be based on a model different from the mechanistic and purely numerical one. Only a complex systems approach to international development will help us calibrate interventions to a complex system such that an intervention stimulates enough for significant and positive change, without creating systems dependency on it. International development thus leads to more desirable outcomes with the complex systems approach.

12.4 The "small-world network" structure of economy interactions and relationships

One example of autocatalytic, self-organizing structure formation in an economy is the formation of cities and economic hubs of specialized industries and services in a network of supply and value chains. According to Barabasi (2002) the economic hubs play a special role in the stability of an evolving economic network. Structure formation and international development result from a change of the economic interactions and of the functional relationships in trade connections of economic actors. Such trade connections can be represented as a directed network ("small-world network"), where incoming links k_a refer to supply flows and outgoing links k_b to selling flows, so that the degree of an actor or vertex in network terms is the total number of its connections, $k = k_a + k_b$ (see Matutinovic, 2005, pp. 873–77 for a detailed description of an economy as "small-world network"). A small-world network is characterized by short average paths connecting any two agents in the economy, by a small number of hubs populated with few firms that have a large total number of connections in the network. Firms are connected to their suppliers, buyers, and other firms in cooperation; households are connected to consumer product markets and service categories; government provides services both to firms and households and is linked to a large total number of supplies incoming from firms. In small-world networks, economic flows among firms are highly skewed, where a few relationships make for most of the interactions. This is the well-know 80/20 pattern, where 80 percent of business is conducted with 20 percent of suppliers and customers. Product markets and service categories are defined by a dense topology of connections that represent supply and value chains.

12.5 Examples of recent approaches

Recent approaches to international development take a complex systems and network view. Microeconomic behavior of economic agents, when constrained by institutions and expectations, interact with each other to produce macroeconomic outcomes. Firms are economic actors and they make constrained rational decisions about production, investment, and marketing strategy among others. Firms operate in an environment of procedural and substantial uncertainty and their behavior is dominated by trial and error, learning is a continuing process (Nelson and Winter, 1982; Brunner, 1994; Matutinovic, 2005). New goals, skills, and technology result in new behavior. Novelty arises spontaneously in response to problems—novelty diffuses among a population of firms and through networks of interaction. New solutions lead to new problems. Fluctuations and novelty at the macroeconomic level arise from a nonlinear dynamic process among market actors.

Brunner and Allen (2005) present development policy experiments with the help of complex system, evolutionary trade models. Such models combine the mathematic, numeric approach where differential equations determine macroeconomic outcomes, with a logic (time-indexed) sequence model that defines the trade network interaction of heterogeneous economic agents at the micro level. Development intervention is enacted at the meso (institutional) level of a hierarchically structured economic system. In those experiments trade is foremost influenced by the policy-induced change in capability of economic agents to engage in trade. Economic agents use their trading power to buy further technological capability. A technological progress function is used. Trade is productivity-driven and the evolutionary trade models in this book link productivity change to structural differences occurring in terms of export product variety and quality. Structural changes in trade are linked to increases in employment, incomes, and in growth rates. In the models, export success feeds back into a positive loop, or (nonlinear) autocatalytic process of increased productivity leading to increasing economies of scale and agglomeration effects.

Economic agents are approximated as actors in networked geographic space. Each geographic cell in a cellular automaton (CA) establishes trade with the neighboring cells, mainly based on the productive capability of an export-oriented firm within the cell. Put into an agent space of the CA, the economic model combines a numerical mathematical model with a logic time-indexed sequence of agent states. Each geographic space thus produces output and consumes at the same time (no explicit demand function here, it could be added in a more complex model). Producers earn rent for their efforts. Consumers earn wages. Production and consumption can temporarily diverge in a particular location, thus leading to trade with neighbors. Firms compete with other firms in the same sector, and get selected for their success. Firms cooperate in networks of suppliers of inputs, knowledge providers, consultants, marketing, industry, and service cooperatives and associations. Trade networks emerge. The whole combination of factors in a variety of trade services is characterized by a combined "transaction technology," which is incorporated in export unit values of South Asian exports to OECD countries (import data of the OECD countries). Emerging trade networks encapsulate knowledge. In evolutionary trade theory, variation and selection among agents re-coordinates knowledge. Development intervention is directed at structure change.

These ideas are further extended by the introduction of a non-equilibrium model (Brunner and Allen, 2005), with a population and labor force as well as natural resource sub-model. From the view of spatial structure, the demographic, economic, and environment variables in the modeling framework are disaggregated into those of different regions and sectors, similar to the CA structure in the previous model. The extended model introduces three dynamic drivers that are represented through the use of three "attractivities." These are the demand attractiveness, the migration attractiveness, and investment attractiveness. These attractivities affect the decision-making of the actors (individuals, firms, investors and so on) within the model and capture their responses to differences in price, reward, and productivity. As a result, initially small differences can be amplified through autocatalytic processes and eventually lead to a spatial restructuring of the system, and a change in the trading pattern across zones. Economic incentives emanating from the development interventions and investment attractivities create the opportunity of employment, increase vacancies, and raise labor productivity, which causes the increase of jobs and wages. Improved or decreased income earning opportunities will alter relative economic conditions among the regions and sectors, changing the pattern of attraction and flow of the workforce between regions. This will in turn alter patterns of demand for services and the relative investment behavior of sectors.

This model allows an exploration and understanding of the different potential futures of a developing region, where on the one hand investment can lead to further incentives favoring further investment in the region, which can in turn lead to further migration from other regions. On the other hand, the further growth of population could lead to the degradation of the environment, particularly of water supply, waste disposal, congestion, and increased utility costs in this region. The potential degradation could lead a decrease in comparative advantages with regard to further increases in economic activity and population. Instead of a model of inter-regional trade that moves towards a single, predictable outcome of equity or structured activity, in our model there exist a combination of positive and negative feedback loops that can lead to different spatial structures of economic activity and population depending on the order and rapidity of responses of the different agents, and their abilities to innovate and to trade successfully. The balance of advantages can potentially evolve in different directions, and change the spatial pattern of economic activity and population migration.

Let us present a practical application in order to illustrate how the new ideas can be used to illuminate the probable consequences of possible infrastructural projects, with a view to ascertaining how worthy they are of support, and what the impacts on poverty and society are likely to be.

12.6 Non-equilibrium spatial model in West Bengal

The example is taken from a study commissioned by the Asian Development Bank (ADB) concerning some possible infrastructural projects in West Bengal. A dynamic, spatial model was developed using 33 different spatial zones of West Bengal that were chosen by the main consultants on the project, Halcrow-Fox, for its transportation study of the region. In addition, each of these zones was linked to activities in Orissa, the Indian South and Central States, Bihar (Ranchi) and Bihar (Patna), the Indian North- and Northwestern States, Assam, Sikkim, the Indian Northeastern States, Bangladesh North, Bangladesh Central and Bangladesh South, Nepal and Bhutan. There were 46 in all.

The transportation study provided information concerning the flows of goods and commodities between these zones, along the transport infrastructure of West Bengal (WB). This information concerned the volume and value, by 24 different sectors and thc origins and destinations. Four different types of flow can be distinguished:

- purely internal flows within any zone;
- flows between any two zones or WB;
- flows between a zone in WB and any of the external zones;
- flows between two external zones that transit WB.

What we can suppose is that the flows reflect the current relative prices, and that these prices include the transport costs (generalized). In general, any money flow between one place and another will reflect the price of the goods times the quantity, and the latter will reflect the relative attractiveness of the zone i compared with other possible alternatives, as viewed by consumers at j.

$$Flow£(i,j) = \frac{P^k(i)}{(P^k(i) + transcost(i,j))} \cdot Demand^k(j) \frac{A^{ij}}{\sum_{i'} A^{i'j}}$$

Where:

- $flow£^k(i, j)$ is the value of financial flow associated with goods of sector K arriving at i from demand coming from j;
- $P^k(i)$ is the price (factory gate) of a unit of goods k (unit value) in zone i;
- $transcost(i, j)$ is the cost per "ton" of transporting k from i to j;
- $demand^k(j)$ is the demand (in money) in zone j that will be spent on goods of type k. A^{ij} is the attractiveness of the goods coming from i, resulting usually from their price including transport costs.

In fact the key piece of information that is needed to drive the model is the actual cost of transporting goods between the zones, and the manner in which this will be changed by any particular transportation investment project. It is these changes in cost that will affect the prices charged at the points of consumption, and will therefore confer an economic benefit on consumers.

Halcrow has provided matrices for the existing costs per truck of delivering goods between the different zones. These are given for 24 different sectors, and the matrix is not filled completely. Only the main flows have been sampled.

The model will consider how the lower prices of delivery result in consumers spending their gains on extra consumption that, in turn, generates more jobs. The model therefore responds to the reduced prices by examining how much the different income classes are affected, and how they may choose to spend the resulting income. Savings will affect income groups differently, as those that spend more save more in absolute terms, but the poor will be able to buy more food, and also if jobs available in the industrial and service sectors increase, then this will also increase the income of some of the poor.

The model uses three sectors for its operation: agriculture, industry, and services. One of the first steps therefore has been to aggregate the data concerning transport into these categories.

Matrices were constructed of the flows of agricultural and industrial goods between the zones. These gave the daily flows, in tons, and also in value. These flows result from the decisions made by both final and intermediate product consumers concerning the quantity of goods that they wish to buy. This reflects the possible sources of such goods, and the relative prices charged for them.

The demand arising in a particular zone results from several origins:

- Households of each type spend their income. The types considered are poor, medium, and rich.
- The buying of commodities and components by economic activities located in the zone. Each economic sector has its own pattern of input requirement, and the figures for this are taken from the input–output tables for India.

The demand is generated by the splitting of their income into demand for agricultural, industrial goods, and services coming from different types of household. These are called poor, medium, and rich households. They have half, average, and twice the average wages, and in the absence of hard data have been represented as in Table 12.1.

In other words the different sectors generate different proportions of poor, medium, and rich wage households. This can be further weighted by the district GDP/head compared with the average for West Bengal. So, in a poor district the proportions of poor households are increased, and in a rich one they are decreased. Once we know the number of poor, medium,

Table 12.1 Households in different sectors

Household Demand	Poor	Medium	Rich
Agriculture	50%	30%	20%
Industry	30%	50%	60%
Services	20%	20%	20%

Table 12.2 Proportion of household demand

Household Demand	Poor (0.5)	Medium (1)	Rich (2)
Agriculture	60%	40%	10%
Industry	20%	30%	40%
Services	20%	30%	50%

and rich households in a zone, we can construct the demand for each sector by assuming the relative proportions of their demand (Table 12.2).

The flows of goods are generated by the fact that the spatial distribution of demand does not coincide with that of supply. For example, the city of Calcutta clearly requires large quantities of food, but has no agricultural land available to produce it. The costs of transportation, however, act as a "net loss" to the "utility" of consumers, since they must pay for it, but only because they want the goods that it brings.

12.6.1 Modeling the impact of changes in transport costs

When the costs of taking a truck from origin to destination are reduced, then we can calculate how much this benefits each type of consumer, and this allows us to establish the pattern of immediate benefit. This reduction in costs is then credited to the different consumers at the point, and they allocate the income thus released to buying more goods.

The model tracks this to the points of production, and increases demand for goods. Over time this results in an increase in production, requiring more labor, and more inputs. In the case of agricultural goods, it is not clear that there is more land that can be farmed, and so on the whole more jobs are not created. The model takes into account the available space, and the space requirements per unit of production.

Consider the changes that may be expected in the $Flow£^k(i, j)$ resulting from some infrastructure investment on the route between them. If the transport cost, $transcost^k(i, j)$, is modified by a percentage reduction, then we will have:

$$transcost^k(i,j) \rightarrow transcost^k(i,j).(1 - \%reduction^k)$$

This new value of the flow of k to j from i means that more money arrives at i for each ton of goods flowing. In turn this means that the fraction "wasted" in transportation becomes smaller, and that extra money can now be used by consumers at j to buy more goods than they could before. This assumes that when the costs fall,

$$NewFlow£^k(i,j) = \frac{P^k(i)}{P^k(i) + \%reduction^k transcost(i,j))} \cdot Demand^k(j) \frac{A_k^{ij}}{\sum_{i'} A_k^{i'j}}$$

prices fall by that amount, and the consumer population spend the same amount of money as before on that sector. This will not arise if the producers simply keep the extra profits resulting from the transport cost reduction, and we also need to know the amount charged for any toll on the new section of road. So, if competition is weak, extra profits will be retained at i, while if it is strong, extra production will occur at i to justify extra income. The assumption made in our model is that competition is sufficiently strong to make sure that the benefit is passed on to consumers.

Clearly, if the reduced transportation costs from i to j also reduce the costs from i' to j then there will be little relative effect. Otherwise, there will be a competitive gain by i and it will attract more customers. This is what really underlies what economists refer to as "elasticity." It concerns the increase or decrease in volume of trade that would result from a given price change.

$$Vol(P(i)) = Vol(P_0)\left(\frac{P_0}{P(i)}\right)^e$$

So, for example, if $e = 1$, then if price halves, volume doubles, and if price doubles, then volume halves. However, in reality, this should result from people making decisions to consume or not consume the product according to the price. Clearly, however, people can only consume if they have enough income, and so really this kind of simplification will be incorrect, particularly in the case of India, where poverty is so general. We need therefore to calculate the changes in volumes from the mathematics of the re-directed choices, taking into account the conservation of income, rather than from some assumed elasticity.

The model allows us to follow the manner in which the increased demand from each point falls onto the different zones of production and leads to the possibility of increased production. This, in turn requires jobs to be created and filled, which means that people must be available to fill them. The demographic increase in each zone provides a growing number

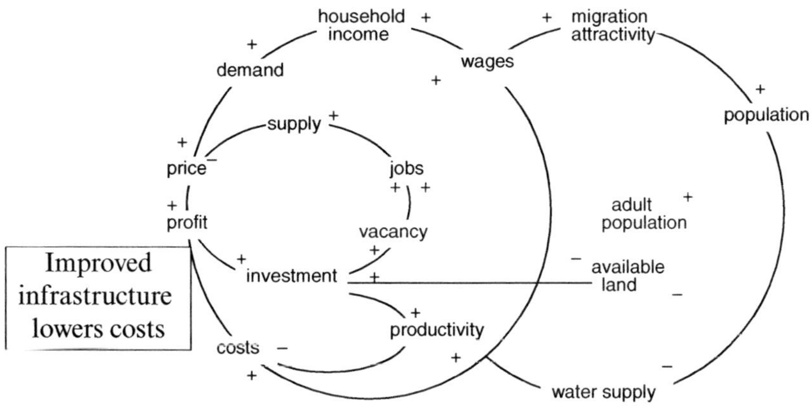

Figure 12.1 *Improvements in transport infrastructure reduces costs and all the multipliers act on this*

of people seeking jobs, but this may be insufficient in some zones, and too many in others. The actual growth of active, filled jobs therefore reflects the changing distribution of population between the zones, and the migratory flows that tend to reflect the job opportunities. Also, different wage levels available in the sectors will also allow growth in a higher-paying sector at the expense of a lower-paying one. Another factor that is important is the availability of land for economic activities. For example, clearly there is a very large demand for agricultural products in Calcutta, but there is no space to make fields and grow crops and so instead, jobs are not created and filled (despite the demand) and food is transported into the city.

The model takes into account these different factors, and calculates where economic growth will occur, by sector and zone. This allows us to track the changes in employment for the 33 different spatial zones in West Bengal, and to use this as a base for a comparison with the changes that occur when different transport infrastructure projects are implemented (see Figure 12.1).

Transport costs reduce the "transmission" of demand from the consumer to the producer, and reduce the overall development feedback loop.

The model runs these mechanisms over the 33 different spatial zones, and also for the different sectors of the economy. Population is attracted to places of perceived employment opportunity and this allows vacancies to be transformed into jobs. This increases the local income, and hence the demand emanating from the zone. The demand for each sector (agriculture, industry, and services) is calculated from the household income distribution. This arises from the employment present in the zone, but agriculture generates more very low incomes than industry and services, and so the proportion of poor, medium, and rich income groups is dependent on the distribution of employment types, and the numbers of jobs to households.

Demand emanating from a zone is:

$$Demand(l, i, j) = \sum_k \beta_k^l . Income^k \cdot \frac{A_{ij}^l}{\sum_{i'} A_{i'j}^l}$$

where k corresponds to poor, medium, and rich income groups, and β_l^k to the fraction of income of group k spent on sector l. Income k is the income in the zone that is spent by group k. The attractivities A_{ij}^l express the attraction of the zone i, as viewed from j as a source for the goods sector l. This is simply given by the function:

$$A_{ij}^l = \exp(-R^*(Price(l, i) + transcost(l, i, j))$$

where *Price(l,i)* is the price of the good in sector l in zone i, and *transcost(l,i,j)* the cost of transporting it from i to j. The term R expresses the homogeneity of the decision-making at j, and the clarity of information available. If R is high, then the information is totally clear and the product and the populations homogeneous. If R is low, then the products and the population may be more heterogeneous and information less clear.

The value of the demand arriving at zone i from j is diminished by the amount spent on transportation, and will only be:

$$Value(l, i, j) = \frac{Price(l, i)}{(Price(l, i) + Transcost(l, i, j))} {}^*Demand(l, i, j)$$

The sum of this over all points j is the income arriving at i from the production of goods l at i.

In turn the production of goods at i will be the number of *jobs(l, i)* * *productivity(l, i)* (tons/year), which in value will be this multiplied by the price charged, *Price(l,i)*.

As shown in Figure 12.1, if supply does not equal demand, then the price will adjust. If in any zone the demand is greater than supply, the price will increase, and it will decrease if the opposite is true. If the price is greater than the cost of production, then profits are made, which can allow for expansion and maintenance of production at i. If more jobs are contemplated, then they can only be filled if there is space, and people available. The model checks for these, and then increases the number of jobs, and the supply at the point.

The population is also changing as a result of demographic increase and also of migration. The model does not provide a detailed spatial dynamic model of migration, but merely favors migration towards the zones with higher job opportunities.

This completes the feedback mechanisms presented in Figure 12.1. The dynamic model will adapt the relative prices in different zones to adjust supply and demand to equality, and so the distribution of jobs will reflect the relative locations of the demand and of transportation costs. By running the model with no modifications in the transportation matrix costs, we can generate a "base scenario." This can then be compared with a run in which the costs of transportation have been changed as a result of some investment in an infrastructure project.

The model can then compare various differences between the two simulations. First, there is the amount of "extra income" available for spending at any particular zone. This can further be broken down into that arising for the poor, medium, and rich income groups. In addition however, we can see the difference in the distribution of jobs over time. This changes the income distribution within each zone and changes the proportions of the different income groups. It also changes the overall income generated in a zone, and hence contributes to the benefits.

12.6.2 Running the model

The program reads in the initial values of population, employment, and productivity for the three sectors for each of the 33 zones. Productivity is a value in tons/year (unit value), and the value of the output per worker is simply productivity multiplied by the price per ton.

The program then opens the Excel file displaying the average cost of transportation of 1 ton of goods between each of the 33 zones. This matrix has been produced by averaging the costs for 24 different commodities that were generated by the Halcrow consultants. The "agricultural sector" corresponds to commodities 1 to 9 of the 24 different types studied by Halcrow, and the "industrial" sector averages the sectors 10–24.

It is assumed that there is a fixed cost associated with any production and that in addition to this there will be a variable cost related to the input materials and the labor costs. The total turnover of each sector for the entire economy is:

- 125 550 million rupees/year in agriculture;
- 100 440 million rupees/year in industry;
- 136 390 million rupees/year in services; and there are
- 15.775 million workers in agriculture;
- 5.749 million workers in industry;
- 6.257 million workers in services, which sets a base for our simulation.

It is possible to calculate the total income generated in a zone by considering the total amount of wages paid, and the contribution arising from the fixed costs. We also assume the values for demographic growth that correspond to a birth rate of 0.022 and a death rate of 0.007 per year, per individual. In addition to this we shall identify three different types of household. These will be of low, medium, or high income, and as a result they will have different patterns of spending as mentioned in the earlier section. There is also an elasticity for the expansion or contraction of employment in a zone, and this will influence how fast growth and decline of jobs responds to the changing potential.

Another factor in the model is the demand for production coming from other producers. This intermediate demand has been assumed to be described by the parameters characteristic for India as a whole. This may not be quite accurate for West Bengal but should be not too wrong. In the equations this is expressed as being the tons of one sector output required in the production of 1 ton of the other. The program also opens a file corresponding to the values of various variables at the end of the previous run. This allows comparisons to be made in the output.

The system operates on a weekly time-step. It calculates the changes in supply, demand, prices, flows, costs, jobs, wages, population, and so on for each zone each week. The dynamics allow us to run 15- or 25-year simulations by simply following the succession of changes that occur each week.

The cost of production of sector l in zone i is the sum of the fixed and variable costs. The development of jobs does depend on there being available space and so these constraints must be assumed, so that for example, Calcutta cannot undergo growth in agriculture simply because there is a demand for it. Initially then the space available is made equal to that used, allowing for the different spatial requirements per job of agriculture, industry, and services.

The program then starts to take weekly steps and calculate the changes that occur. We assume some slow increase in productivity over time, as technology improves. However, we also allow a 3 percent annual increase in available space for economic activities, except for agriculture in Calcutta. The program then calculates the total income at a zone, and then the ratio of this spending that will be "decided" by poor, medium, and rich households respectively. For this we assume that in a zone, the contribution of the different sector employment to the different income groups is not the same. The agricultural jobs give more "poor households" than industrial or service jobs. We also assume that what we mean by "poor" is an average of half the average income for the zone. While "rich" means an average of twice the average income for the zone. Medium households have simply the average income for the zone. From these assumptions we can calculate the demand emanating from a zone, and coming from these different types of household.

In making the spatial choices about "where" to buy goods and services from, we calculate the relative attractiveness of possible sources, and take the one that is best. This calculation allows us to say what fraction of the total demand at *j* for a given sector *l* will be "directed" at zone *i*. This will depend on the "factory gate prices" charged, plus the transport costs incurred in getting the goods from *i* to *j*.

We can calculate the factory gate costs by considering each factor in turn. First, there is the cost of inputs. These must also be brought from wherever it is most cheaply available and so we have an equation of the form:

$$Inputcost/ton(l, ll, i, j)$$
$$= cross(l, ll)*(price(ll, j) + transcost(ll, j, i)*\, att(ll, j, i)/sumatt(ll, i)$$

where *cross(l,ll)* is the tons of *ll* required per ton of *l*. *Price(ll,j)* is the cost/ton of *ll* at *j*, *transcost(ll,j,i)* is the cost/ton of transporting it from *j* to *i*, and the *att(ll,j,i)/sumatt(ll,i)* term gives the relative attractiveness of *j* as a source for a producer at *i*.

The program then goes on to add in the cost of labor to this, to arrive at a cost of production for *l* at *i*. The next important step is to calculate the demand falling on *i* from the population situated at and around *i*. This is done by considering the demand for a sector *l*, coming from the different households in *j*, which is attracted to the production at *i*. The demand coming from production situated at *j* is then added. The amount of demand "leaving" *j* is not what arrives at *i*. This is reduced by the amount needed to pay the transportation costs.

The supply situated at *i* is known from the number of jobs and their productivity. Knowing the supply and the demand falling on *i* allows us to calculate the change in the price that is being charged at *i*. The program then calculates the changes in the numbers of jobs at each zone using the difference between the price and the cost of production to generate either expansion or contraction. Expansion does require that there be sufficient available space however, which would reflect the input of investment by entrepreneurs who had spotted the possibilities.

The jobs can only be filled also if there are sufficient people available in the zone to fill the vacancy. The capacity may come either from the natural demography, or also from the migration flows, which are affected by the spatial distribution of opportunities.

The screen displays the growth in jobs that are occurring in Calcutta (sum of zones 1 to 12) and for the other 13 to 33 zones. The jobs are in agriculture, industry, and services. The first run sets a base, and the second run allows a comparison, for example, following the implementation of the infrastructure projects. In the output displays there is a first presentation of the income gains to each zone as result of the reduced transport costs. The second shows differences in employment in the three sectors per zone. The third display is that of the gain per household of type poor, medium, or rich for each zone of West Bengal. This is probably the most important one since it shows how the "poor" are affected by the transportation infrastructure.

12.6.3 Output of the model

Data for the effect on transport between the different zones has been calculated for 24 different commodities. These have then been averaged out for agriculture, industry, and services and the reductions in cost inserted into the model described above. The model changes the relative attractiveness of various locations for growth of employment. The money saved by consumers increases demand and so jobs and income grow. The patterns of growth of jobs with and without the transportation infrastructure investment can be compared, and in this way a view of the overall impacts of the investments can be obtained. The output of the computer model is displayed either on maps or in tables for the different zones.

The data supplied was the comparative transportation costs in 2015, with or without the projects, and again in 2025 with and without the projects. The differences reveal the spatial distribution of consequences of the projects, the impacts on employment, and on the different income groups of the zone.

12.6.4 Result for the projects up to 2015

In Table 12.3 we can see the results of the model calculations for the impacts of the projects scheduled up to 2015. The population has grown according to the demographic predictions and the productivity and production has grown too. However, by comparing the simulations made with the transportation projects with those made without it, we can show the geographical distribution of economic effects.

The overall gain is some 40,000 jobs. However, the multipliers are still operating and so the results after 25 years reflect not only the effects of the extra projects executed in the intervening period, but also the continuation of the economic multiplier introduced by the earlier investments.

These extra jobs can immediately translate into a gain for the poor of each zone. This is because these are "new jobs" in addition to those that would have existed without the infrastructure investment. If we multiply the 40,000 by the average wages per job, then we find about 600 million

Table 12.3 Impacts of infrastructure projects 2000–15: output table (1) additional jobs

	Agriculture	Industry	Services
Calcutta	0.00	4689.97	−112.55
13. South Parganas	240.09	184.52	0.95
14. North Parganas	−17.02	7173.06	−684.02
15. Hugli	633.36	135.57	−24.91
16. Nadia	163.08	262.19	−8.29
17. Barddhaman	−6.91	−26.58	22.65
18. Durgapur	0.11	−29.30	8.76
19. Murshidabad	67.11	78.35	7.00
20. Maldah	29.09	1126.48	−71.64
21. Dakshin Dinajpur	56.30	0.71	1.08
22. Utta Dinajpur S.	330.27	48.73	−0.96
23. Utta Dinajpur N.	46.49	7.19	1.18
24. Darjeeling	177.82	1293.60	−168.23
25. Jaipalguri, Koch Bihar	875.06	3764.60	−315.55
26. Birbhum	−2.15	−24.48	10.94
27. Bankura Purulia	0.00	−41.19	24.94
28. N. Medinipur	1.31	4.02	21.76
29. S. Medinipur	48.16	94.86	4.95
30. Hoara	1.55	46.88	18.78
31. Haldia Dock	0.31	12575.81	9.00
32. Haldia, Balughata	0.22	7545.71	6.57
33. Kulaghat Pansura	−0.28	−0.79	0.99

rupees per year. In addition to this, there are the effects on external trade, and also the savings in consumption costs as a result of the cheaper transportation.

The effects on income are also calculated as the result of reduced costs of goods for the different income groups in each zone (×1000 (Table 12.4)).

12.6.5 Results for 2025 after full project

The extra jobs are now about 117,000, which are worth about 1.7 billion rupees. This corresponds roughly to $34 million per year, and so to a return of 5 percent just in these new jobs alone.

Distribution of extra jobs by 2025 (Table 12.5): There are around 117,000 additional jobs resulting from the increased spending power of consumers in West Bengal and the surrounding region.

Shown in Table 12.6 are the savings going to the different income groups of each zone. The results demonstrate the potential of the methods outlined in this section. An overall evaluation can be made of the future impacts

Table 12.4 Impacts of infrastructure projects 2000–15: output table (2) the distribution of savings by income group; in 1000 rupees/ year in 2015

	Poor	Medium	Rich
Calcutta	42802	255771	215000
13. South Parganas	463	1415	1263
14. North Parganas	1391	5370	4710
15. Hugli	400	1472	1782
16. Nadia	1732	2665	927
17. Barddhaman	0	0	0
18. Durgapur	0	0	0
19. Murshidabad	1931	4366	4902
20. Maldah	1852	4562	5102
21. Dakshin Dinajpur	154	278	360
22. Utta Dinajpur S.	1262	1316	949
23. Utta Dinajpur N.	0	0	0
24. Darjeeling	4854	12432	6964
25. Jaipalguri, Koch Bihar	12629	28113	21552
26. Birbhum	0	0	0
27. Bankura Purulia	0	0	0
28. N. Medinipur	3820	8521	9233
29. S. Medinipur	3951	14077	16499
30. Hoara	159	749	767
31. Haldia Dock	5	24	26
32. Haldia, Balughata	3405	15162	16868
33. Kulaghat Pansura	20	73	88

of infrastructure investments, with both the impact of poverty in different zones, and also the overall benefits for the regional economy. The gains generated by the investment, together with the additional external trading gains, argue the case for the transport infrastructure investments.

12.7 Summary

The important point that we must underline concerning this work and the application of the ideas of complex systems science to social and economic phenomena is that the models recognize the reality of non-equilibrium interactions and responses within the system. Essentially, equilibrium assumes that the variables describing the incomes, costs, wages, and employment of each region can be successfully explained and described by a set of simultaneous equations relating their values at each moment. Because complexity science recognizes that real, evolved systems are a product of successive events and processes, where only the non-viable elements are

Table 12.5 Impacts of infrastructure projects 2000–25: output table (3) the distribution of additional jobs by the year 2025

	Agriculture	Industry	Services
Calcutta	0.00	4 218.28	−78.53
13. South Parganas	859.38	1 24.28	8.70
14. North Parganas	−37.37	5 364.66	−400.07
15. Hugli	2 094.51	80.14	−94.35
16. Nadia	554.20	156.64	−3.16
17. Barddhaman	−28.19	−17.91	45.00
18. Durgapur	0.03	−16.72	17.64
19. Murshidabad	211.95	40.08	17.23
20. Maldah	95.13	732.85	−36.84
21. Dakshin Dinajpur	192.91	0.60	0.75
22. Utta Dinajpur S.	1 326.20	24.20	−5.26
23. Utta Dinajpur N.	175.65	6.20	1.24
24. Darjeeling	454.29	1 103.94	−233.29
25. Jaipalguri, Koch Bihar	2 844.21	2 312.42	−271.68
26. Birbhum	−9.30	−13.52	19.34
27. Bankura Purulia	−0.24	−32.90	74.27
28. N. Medinipur	5.48	15.71	48.22
29. S. Medinipur	147.64	68.49	19.43
30. Hoara	3.70	54.30	49.23
31. Haldia Dock	2.15	58 750.51	195.38
32. Haldia, Balughata	1.83	34 976.78	142.28
33. Kulaghat Pansura	−0.77	1.16	2.15

removed by "selection," and hence the explanation can only be in terms of the changes that occur at each moment. In other words, changes in the system can only be described by dynamic equations linking the changes and responses of the agents involved. The most important point therefore that the chapter makes is that it is possible to build dynamic, spatial models that can be used to support policy analysis in problems of social and economic development.

The analysis presented above allows us to give an estimate of the spatial economic impacts of the transportation infrastructure projects that have been proposed. The results are by no means predictions, but represent the "natural" spatial effects in the absence of any specific spatial plans or policies applied over the period. Also, they naturally assume a continuation of present trends, and of the present economic structure. The most important point, however, is that each output simulation shows the difference between results obtained under these assumptions with and without the projects. Because of this, the actual scenario of economic development that

Table 12.6 Impacts of infrastructure projects 2000–25: output table (4) the consumer surplus (rupees/year) made by different income groups in each zone in 2025

	Poor	Medium	Rich
Calcutta	56 509 188	346 379 536	288 283 354
13. South Parganas	573 014	1 989 218	1 661 303
14. North Parganas	1 618 788	6 734 306	5 758 251
15. Hugli	447 591	1 853 328	2 130 734
16. Nadia	2 019 716	3 510 507	1 150 213
17. Barddhaman	0	0	0
18. Durgapur	0	0	0
19. Murshidabad	2 201 962	5 598 482	5 929 405
20. Maldah	2 159 130	6 041 217	6 415 234
21.Dakshin Dinajpur	182 560	358 046	436 271
22. Utta Dinajpur S.	1 441 929	1 556 974	1 093 500
23. Utta Dinajpur N.	0	0	0
24. Darjeeling	5 779 175	16 393 038	8 855 106
25. Jaipalguri, Koch Bihar	14 58 8074	36 681 176	26 603 852
26. Birbhum	0	0	0
27. Bankura Purulia	0	0	0
28. N. Medinipur	4 593 080	11 440 077	11 785 125
29. S. Medinipur	4 423 926	17 832 758	19 797 470
30. Hoara	184 208	944 780	936 560
31. Haldia Dock	6 281 898	29 126 200	31 538 234
32. Haldia, Balughata	3 909 483	17 488 620	19 419 784
33. Kulaghat Pansura	23 531	97 415	112 005

West Bengal will actually experience is not very significant for the results. Considerably different economic development paths are entirely possible. However, what the simulations show is the effect of having better transportation available, and lower costs, and how these gains will generate spatial multipliers throughout the system. These will be approximately true for a very broad range of actual histories that might occur, and therefore provide a good basis for comparing different possible schemes, and for assessing the overall benefit of the projects.

The full implementation of the project leads to a growing number of extra jobs. Very soon after the completion of the project these have reached over 117,000, and are alone worth about 1.7 billion rupees extra activity in the West Bengal economy. Because these jobs are "in addition" to whatever other jobs arise, then we may say that they directly help the poor, since even if jobs in fact "filter down" it still means that there will be 117,000 new jobs provided for those otherwise without them. However, the job difference is growing and so in reality the cheaper transport and extra jobs are leading to an additional annual rate of increase of jobs that is very high. Without the project, the extra congestion and transportation costs would lead to a significant loss of competitivity for trade and commerce, and to increasing costs and losses of jobs and of revenue.

The method developed here must be considered as a preliminary attempt to carry out a poverty impact assessment. Issues such as the impacts on migration, land prices, and the availability of space and of appropriate facilities and so on, could all be included in an improved version. But greater resources would be required to perform this more thorough job. However, despite these limitations the method provides a new basis for an estimation of the spatial impacts of economic development, and of the multipliers set in motion by such investments.

One of the notable characteristics of the complex system approach is that the economic models are built upon an inter-regional matrix. The economic variables, such as demand and supply, import and export, productivity accumulation and consumption, costs, wages, and profits, link directly with the inter-regional matrix or input–output system. The flow equations are then calculated in the simulation models, thus enabling adequately calibrated development intervention and effective use of economic resources. Since the economic sectors of different regions are differentiated there is a constant tendency to instability mediated by market mechanisms, mainly prices. So, this inter-regional matrix that is suggested here establishes the relationship between the whole economy, the regional/sector economy and local decision-making process, that is, the relationship between "macro" economic behavior and "micro" economic structure.

This chapter has canvassed some practitioner-friendly approaches to international development. Development is about interventions in a highly complex system—society. Complex systems are change resistant and intervention requires understanding the autocatalytic self-organizing processes that shape an economy across micro, meso, and macro scales. In positive and negative feedback loop models, autocatalysis streamlines energy, material, and financial flows towards more efficient economic actors and agents. Heterogeneous agents are located and linked in space and geography. What makes for structural change, and thus development, is the reconfiguration and filling-in of economic network connections among agents. In the complex systems way the explanatory focus becomes the change in the structure of an incomplete system. In traditional equilibrium theory a priori complete networks ("field theory") spread change equally across the system composed of homogeneous "average" actors. In a complex systems approach, microeconomic, autocatalytic processes lead to macroeconomic, aggregate behavior of the system, and the evolving macro scale of the system constrains in turn the behavior of heterogeneous actors. Traditional equilibrium theory does not link micro processes to the macro scale of an economy. In evolutionary complex systems, scales are linked, because both numeric models and logic algorithms are combined, not so in traditional theory. Moreover, the complex systems models canvassed in the chapter do not employ as part of the numeric model traditional production functions, instead technology progress functions are incorporated into the models.

Notes

* The assessments and opinions expressed are solely those of the authors and should not be attributed to any of the organizations with which they are affiliated. The authors thank the participants of the 6th International Conference on Complex Systems in Boston for their valuable inputs.

1. A field is a space in which all points are connected to all other points in the space, thus conjuring full information among agents.

References

Allen, P.M. (1997), *Self-organizing Cities and Regions: Models of Complexity*, London: Taylor and Francis.

Allen, P.M. (2001), "A Complex Systems Approach to Learning, Adaptive Networks," *International Journal of Innovation Management*, **5**(2), 149–80.

Allen, P.M. and M. Strathern (2004), "Evolution, Emergence and Learning in Complex Systems", *Emergence*, **5**(4), 8–33.

Allen, P.M. and M. Strathern (2005), "Models, knowledge creation and their limits," *Futures, Special Issue "Complexity and the Limits of Knowledge,"* Guest eds, P.M. Allen and P.M. Torrens, **37**(7–8), 729–44.

Allen P.M., M. Strathern, and J.S. Baldwin (2006), "Evolutionary Drive: New Understanding of Change in Socio-economic Systems," *Emergence Complexity & Organization*, **8**(2), July.

Arthur, Brian (1990), "Positive Feedbacks in the Economy," *Scientific American*, 92–9.

Arthur, Brian (2006), "Out-of-equilibrium Economics and Agent-based Modeling," in *Handbook of Computational Economics, Vol.2: Agent-based Computational Economics*, K. Judd and L. Tesfatsion (eds), Amsterdam: Elsevier/North-Holland.

Barabasi, Albert (2002), *Linked: The New Science of Networks*, Cambridge, MA: Perseus Publishing.

Bar-Yam, Yaneer (2004), *Making Things Work*, Cambridge, MA: New England Complex Systems Institute Knowledge Press.

Brunner, Hans-Peter (1994), "Technological Diversity, Random Selection in a Population of Firms, and Technological Institutions of Government," in *Evolutionary Economics and Chaos Theory*, L. Leydesdorff and P. van den Besselaar (eds), London: Pinter.

Brunner, Hans-Peter and Peter Allen (2005), *Productivity, Competitiveness and Incomes in Asia: An Evolutionary Theory of International Trade*, Cheltenham, UK and Northampton, MA, USA: Edward Elgar Publishing.

Foster, R. and S. Kaplan (2001), *Creative Destruction: Why Companies that are Built to Last Underperform the Market – and how to Successfully Transform Them*, New York: Currency.

Matutinovic, Igor (2005), "The Microeconomic Foundations of Business Cycles: From Institutions to Autocatalytic Networks," *Journal of Economic Issues*, **39**(4), 867–98.

Metcalfe, J. Stan, John Foster, and Ronnie Ramlogan (2006), "Adaptive Economic Growth", *Cambridge Journal of Economics*, **30**(1), 7–32.

Nelson, Richard and Sidney Winter (1982), *An Evolutionary Theory of Economic Change*, Cambridge, MA, Harvard University Press.
Potts, Jason (2001), *The New Microeconomics*, Cheltenham, UK and Northampton, MA, USA: Edward Elgar Publishing.
Ulanowicz, Robert (1999), "Life after Newton: An Ecological Metaphysic," *BioSystems*, **50**(2), 127–42.

PART VI

EVOLUTIONARY AND ECOLOGICAL-ENVIRONMENTAL ECONOMICS

13. Subgame perfection in evolutionary dynamics with recurrent perturbations

*Herbert Gintis, Ross Cressman, and Thijs Ruijgrok**

13.1 Introduction

A fundamental property of evolutionary systems governed by the replicator dynamic (Taylor and Jonker, 1978) is that every stable equilibrium is a Nash equilibrium of the underlying stage game (Nachbar, 1990; Samuelson and Zhang, 1992). Since some Nash equilibria are dynamically unstable (Samuelson, 1997), stability with respect to the replicator dynamic serves as an equilibrium selection technique. However, this technique is not very effective when the game is given in extensive form. For instance, for every perfect information game (that is, an extensive form where each player decides what action to take with complete knowledge of the previous decisions by all players), Cressman and Schlag (1998) (see also Cressman, 2003) show that every pure Nash equilibrium is Lyapunov stable in the replicator dynamic. They also show that, if this pure Nash equilibrium is not subgame perfect, then its Nash equilibrium component is never stable in the replicator dynamic since the subgame perfect equilibrium is contained in any interior asymptotically stable set. This latter result suggests that subgame perfection can be justified on dynamic grounds. Unfortunately, the subgame perfect Nash equilibrium need not be stable either, as elementary examples exist (Cressman and Schlag, 1998) where the subgame perfect component is not even locally attracting in the replicator dynamic.

A heuristic argument why the replicator dynamic fails to select subgame perfection in perfect information games is that this is a monotonic selection dynamic (Samuelson and Zhang, 1992) and so is characterized by negligible selection pressure towards higher pay-off actions at decision points off the subgame perfect equilibrium path.

This intuition led to dynamic models that combine a discrete-time deterministic selection process with a small stochastic effect whereby players sometimes make mistakes and do not choose better strategies. Informally, a stochastically stable state is then a strategy for each player that persists as the mutation rate goes to zero (Young, 1993). A particularly relevant model for us is the one developed by Hart (2002) who showed that, with a specific non-monotonic selection dynamic, there is always convergence to the subgame perfect equilibrium as population size increases and the mutation rate goes to zero in such a way that the per-period number of mutations is bounded away from zero. That is, the subgame perfect equilibrium is the unique stochastically stable state for Hart's model.[1] Hart speculated that a similar result would not hold for an underlying monotonic dynamic, though he provided no counterexample. In this chapter, we provide analytical counterexamples based on the (continuous-time) replicator dynamic and with mutations modeled as recurrent perturbations. Our analysis shows that these games have a unique dynamically stable Nash equilibrium that does not converge to the subgame perfect equilibrium of the underlying game as the perturbation rates tend to zero. Moreover, our numerical simulations for a wide variety of simple games with perfect information suggest this same result holds quite generally.

We assume throughout that Γ is a finite n-player extensive form game of perfect information with a unique subgame perfect Nash equilibrium, and there are no moves by nature. Evolutionary dynamics are defined through the corresponding n-player normal form of Γ (also called the stage game) where player i has a finite number of pure strategies $s_{i1} \ldots s_{ik_i} \in S_i$. Let α_{kl} be the fraction of population k using pure strategy $s_{kl} \in S_k$. Then the pay-off to strategy j of player i, assuming one member of each of the other $n - 1$ populations is chosen at random to play the stage game, is given by

$$\pi_{ij} = \sum_{s_{kl_k} \in S_k, k \neq i} \left(\prod_{k \neq i} \alpha_{kl_k} \right) \pi_i(s_{1l_1}, \ldots, s_{i-1\,l_{i-1}}, s_{ij}, s_{i+1\,l_{i+1}}, \ldots, s_{nl_n}).$$

The average pay-off to a member of population i is then

$$\bar{\pi}_i = \sum_{j=1,\ldots,k_i} \alpha_{ij}\pi_{ij}.$$

The standard replicator equations governing the dynamics of the population are given by

$$\dot{\alpha}_{ij} = \alpha_{ij}(\pi_{ij} - \bar{\pi}_i), \quad i = 1,\ldots,n, j = 1,\ldots,k_i - 1. \tag{13.1}$$

The results presented in this chapter were anticipated by Binmore, Gale, and Samuelson (1995), who added a low level of "drift" to the replicator equations for the "ultimatum game," and found a locally stable equilibrium near the non-subgame perfect component of the game. Ponti (2000) showed by means of simulation that if agents are forced to adopt strictly mixed strategies, however close to pure, in the three-legged "centipede game" there may be no stable equilibria, and the dynamics may exhibit

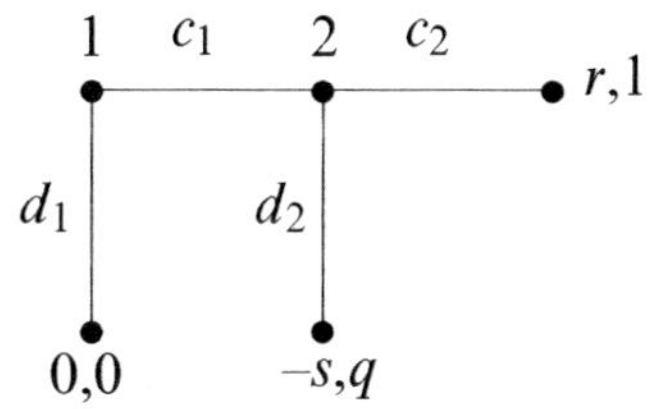

Figure 13.1 *The two-move centipede game*

limit cycles. This chapter is a generalization of their result to other games and analyzes the limiting behavior of the system as the perturbation rate goes to zero.

13.2 The two-move centipede game

Figure 13.1 depicts the extensive form of a two-move centipede game. We assume $q > 1$ and $r, s > 0$. Player 2 has a weakly dominant strategy d_2 and the Nash equilibria consist of the move d_1 by player 1 and any mixed strategy of player 2 that places at least probability $r/(r + s)$ on d_2. The unique subgame perfect Nash equilibrium is (d_1, d_2).

Let α be the frequency of d_1, let β be the frequency of d_2, let μ_1 be the probability per unit time that player 1 spontaneously changes strategy, and let μ_2 be the corresponding probability for player 2. The replicator equations (13.1) for this game are then given by:

$$\dot{\alpha} = (1 - \mu_1)(1 - \alpha)\alpha((s + r)\beta - r) + \mu_1(1 - 2\alpha)$$
$$\dot{\beta} = (1 - \mu_2)(q - 1)(1 - \alpha)\beta(1 - \beta) + \mu_2(1 - 2\beta). \qquad (13.2)$$

Figure 13.2 shows the phase diagram for equations (13.2), with $r = 1$, $s = 2$, $q = 2$ and $\mu_1 = \mu_2 = 0$. With these parameter values, system (13.2) is not structurally stable. In particular, a generic perturbation will destroy the continuum of fixed points on the line $\alpha = 1$, leaving a finite number of fixed points and possibly limit cycles. For convenience, we will take $r = 1$, $s = 2$, $q = 2$ in the following, although the results can be easily generalized.

Theorem 1 Consider the dynamical system given by equations (13.2) for $\mu_1, \mu_2 > 0$.

a. The attracting set is contained in A (see Figure 13.3).
b. The set A contains an attracting, 1-dimensional invariant manifold.
c. The flow in the invariant manifold contains one attracting fixed point. This fixed point is the limit point for all orbits starting in $[0, 1] \times [0, 1]$.

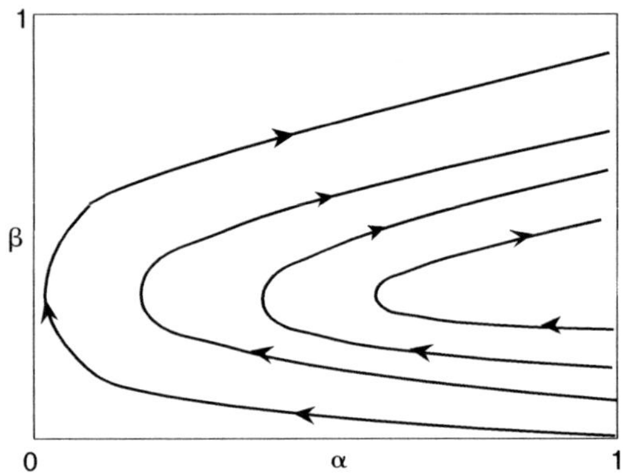

Figure 13.2 Phase diagram for equation (13.2), with $r = 1$, $s = 2$, and $q = 2$ and $\mu_1 = \mu_2 = 0$

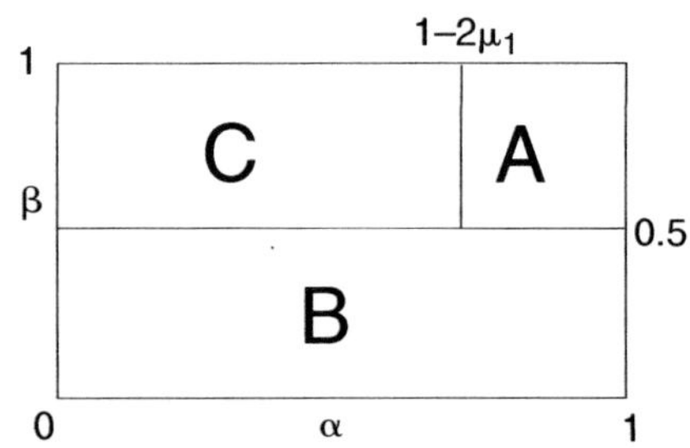

Figure 13.3 Partitioning of the phase space

d. The α-component of the unique fixed point is equal to one when the mutation terms go to zero. The β-component of the unique fixed point can take on any value between 0.5 and 1 when the mutation terms go to zero. The final value depends on the relative rates with which μ_1 and μ_2 go to zero. For instance, if $\mu_1 = \mu_2$, then β tends approximately to 0.773.

Proof: Assume $\mu_1, \mu_2 > 0$.

a. It is easy to check that $[0, 1] \times [0, 1]$ is invariant for the flow of (13.2). When $\beta < 0.5$, we see that $\dot{\beta} = (1 - \alpha)\beta(1 - \beta)(1 - \mu_2) + \mu_2(1 - 2\beta) > 0$, so there can be no fixed points or limit cycles in B. When $\alpha < 1 - 2\mu_1$, then $(1 - \alpha)\alpha/2 > \mu_1$. So, for $(\alpha, \beta) \in C$, we have that $\dot{\alpha} = (1 - \alpha)\alpha(3\beta - 1)(1 - \mu_1) + \mu_1(1 - 2\alpha) > (1 - \alpha)\alpha(1 - \mu_1)/2 + \mu_1(1 - 2\alpha) > \mu_1(1 - \mu_1) + \mu_1(1 - 2\alpha) = 2\mu_1(1 - \alpha) - \mu_1^2 > 0$, for sufficiently small μ_1. It follows that there can be no fixed points or limit cycles in C for sufficiently small μ_1. Therefore, the attracting set of the flow of (13.2) must lie in A for sufficiently small μ_1.

b. For the unperturbed equation, the manifold S_0 consisting of the points with $\alpha = 1, 0 < \beta < 0.5$ is invariant, 1-dimensional, locally attracting and normally hyperbolic (all solutions approach it non-tangentially). According to a theorem by Fenichel (1971), for sufficiently small perturbations, there will be a manifold $S\mu$ in the perturbed system with the characteristics mentioned above and close to S_0, although no longer consisting of fixed points. The manifold $S\mu$ can be described by $\alpha = 1 + h(\beta, \mu_1, \mu_2)$ with $h(\beta, \mu_1, \mu_2)$ a C^∞ function such that $h(\beta, 0, 0) = 0$.

For $(\alpha, \beta) \in S_\mu$, we must have $(\partial h/\partial\alpha)\dot{\alpha} + (\partial h/\partial\beta)\dot{\beta} = 0$. This leads to the equation (we have abbreviated $h(\beta, \mu_1, \mu_2) = h(\beta)$):

$$-(1-\alpha)\alpha(3\beta-1)(1-\mu_1)+\mu_1(1-2\alpha)$$
$$+\,h'(\beta)\,[(1-\alpha)\beta(1-\beta)(1-\mu_2)+\mu_2(1-2\beta)]=0.$$

Substituting $\alpha = 1 + h(\beta)$ yields the equation for $h(\beta)$:

$$-h(\beta)\,(1+h(\beta))(3\beta-1)(1-\mu_1)$$
$$-\mu_1(1+2h(\beta))+h'(\beta)[h(\beta)\beta(1-\beta)(1-\mu_2)+\mu_2(1-2\beta)]=0$$

Since $h(\beta, \mu_1, \mu_1)$ is small for small μ_1 and μ_2, the first order approximation gives $-h(\beta)(3\beta - 1) - \mu_1 = 0$, so $h(\beta, \mu_1, \mu_2) = -\mu_1/(3\beta - 1)$, so the invariant manifold S_μ is given to first order by $\alpha = 1 - \mu_1/(3\beta - 1)$.

c. To first order, the flow in the invariant manifold S_μ is given by

$$\begin{aligned}\dot{\beta} &= (1-\alpha)\beta(1-\beta)+\mu_2(1-2\beta)\\ &= -h(\beta)\beta(1-\beta)+\mu_2(1-2\beta)\\ &= \mu_1\frac{\beta(1-\beta)}{3\beta-1}+\mu_2(1-2\beta)\end{aligned}\tag{13.3}$$

The flow of (13.2) on $[0, 1] \times [0, 1]$ is given in Figure 13.4. The flow in A is shown in Figure 13.5.

d. Equation (13.3) has only one fixed point when $\beta > 0.5$, and it is easy to check that it is an attractor in S_μ, and therefore an attractor for the full equation (13.2). Let $\beta^*(\mu_1, \mu_2)$ be the fixed point. Let $\mu_1, \mu_2 \to 0$ in such a way that $\lambda = \mu_1/\mu_2$ remains constant. Then $\beta^*(\mu_1, \mu_2)$ converges to $\beta^*(\lambda)$, where $\beta^*(\lambda)$ is the solution of

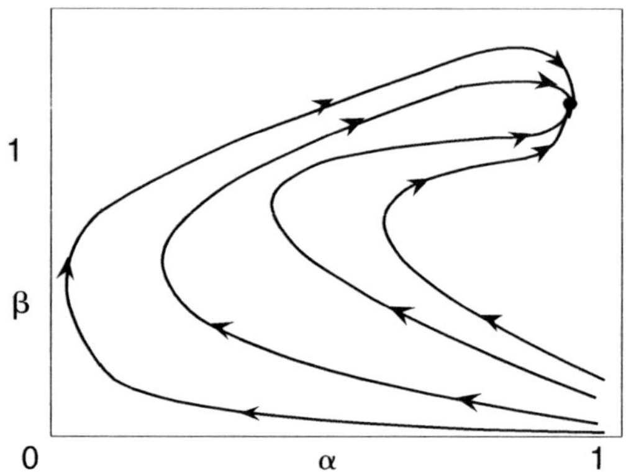

Figure 13.4 Phase diagram for equation (13.2), with r = 1, s = 2, and q = 2 and $\mu_1 = \mu_2 = 0.01$

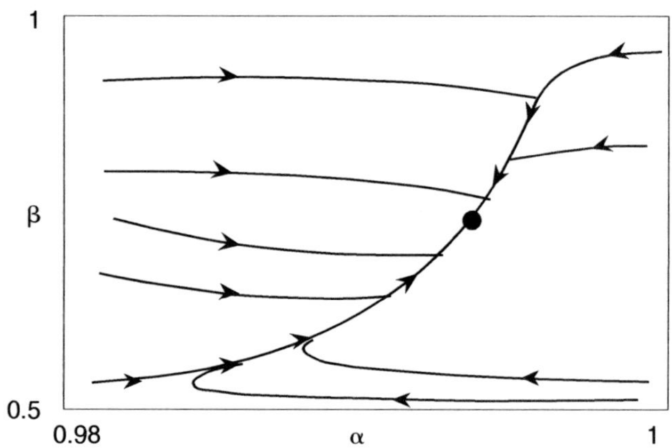

Figure 13.5 Flow within the set A and the invariant manifold S_μ

$$\lambda\frac{\beta(1-\beta)}{3\beta-1} + (1-2\beta) = 0$$

In Figure 13.6 $\beta(\lambda)$ is plotted, showing that every limiting value of β is possible, when the mutation terms go to zero. Solving this equation when $\lambda = 1$ yields $\beta = 0.773$.

The behavior of system (13.2) can be explained as follows. Initially, the logic of backward induction applies, whereby player 2 consistently reduces his or

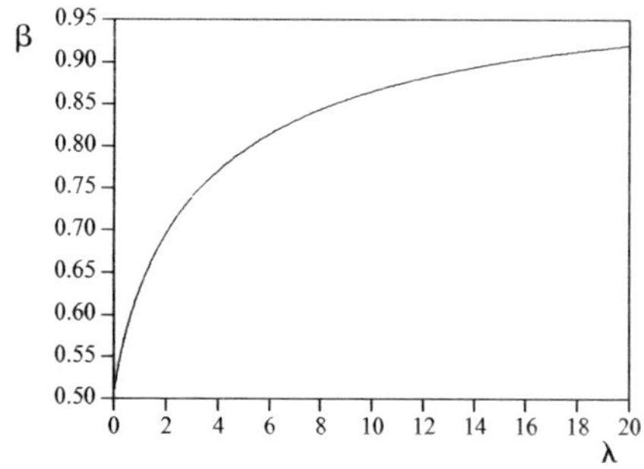

Figure 13.6 Value of $\beta^*(\lambda)$

her probability of playing c_2 and consequently player 1 will more and more use strategy d_1. However, when the system is in a state in set A, a different mechanism takes over. Suppose α and β are both close to 1. Then it pays for player 2 to play c_2 more often, as it entices player 1 to start playing c_1 more. This situation corresponds to a trajectory in Figure 13.4, where α initially increases, but close to the line $\alpha = 1$ starts to decrease again as β starts to decrease also. However, player 2 needs to be helped by random perturbations, or mistakes, to discover this mechanism. Without mutations, he or she would simply not discover that if player 1 plays d_1 almost always, it becomes profitable for him or her to increase the frequency of c_2.

At a certain point, however, the tendency of increasing c_1 and c_2 stops again, namely when it becomes more profitable for player 2 to play d_2 again. This mixed strategy by player 2, teasing and punishing in a certain proportion, is only successful because the mutations in player 1's strategy guarantees a steady trickle of hopeful c_1 plays. We note that the final outcome only benefits player 2, and these benefits are only of order μ.

The only possibility that the subgame perfect solution can be stable is when the mutation rate μ_2 of player 2 is negligible compared with that of player 1. In that case, player 2 simply takes advantage of the small number of c_1 plays by player 1, by eventually playing only d_2. Only when his or her mutation rate increases, will player 2 discover that by being less greedy (in the form of playing c_2 more often) he or she can increase the frequency of c_1 by player 1, and on balance profit from the increase in non-trivial interactions.

13.3 Three-move centipede game: agent extensive form

Figure 13.7 depicts the agent extensive form of a three-move centipede game (that is, players 1 and 3 have the same pay-offs and information, so are in effect one player), assuming $r, s, q > 0$. The unique subgame perfect Nash equilibrium is (d_1, d_2, d_3), although there are many other Nash equilibria.

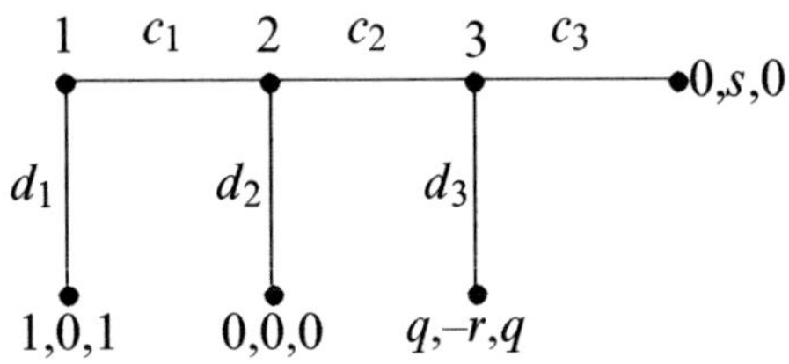

Figure 13.7 Three-move centipede game: agent extensive form

The replicator equations with recurrent perturbations, with equal perturbation constant μ for all players, are given by:

$$\begin{aligned}\dot{\alpha} &= \alpha(1-\alpha)(1-q(1-\beta)\gamma)(1-2\mu)+\mu(1-2\alpha)\\ \dot{\beta} &= \beta(1-\alpha)(1-\beta)((r+s)\gamma-s)(1-2\mu)+\mu(1-2\beta)\\ \dot{\gamma} &= q\gamma(1-\alpha)(1-\beta)(1-\gamma)(1-2\mu)+\mu(1-2\gamma),\end{aligned} \tag{13.4}$$

where α is the frequency of d_1, β is the frequency of d_2 and γ is the frequency of d_3.

For $\mu = 0$, the equations have a two-dimensional invariant set

$$I = \{(\alpha, \beta, \gamma)|\alpha = 1, 0 \leq \beta, \gamma \leq 1\},$$

consisting of fixed points.

The fixed points in $S_0 \subset I$ for which additionally $1 - q(1-\beta)\gamma > 0$ are locally attracting. There are no other attracting fixed points.

The manifold S_0 is in fact *globally* attracting. This can be seen by noting that a conserved quantity can be derived from equations (13.4). Let

$$Q(\beta, \gamma) = \beta^q(1-\gamma)^r\gamma^s, \tag{13.5}$$

then

$$\frac{d}{dt}Q(\beta, \gamma) = \frac{\partial Q}{\partial \beta}\dot{\beta} + \frac{\partial Q}{\partial \gamma}\dot{\gamma} = 0,$$

as can easily be checked.

The phase space is therefore foliated by invariant two-dimensional manifolds $Q(\beta, \gamma) =$ constant, as shown in Figure 13.8. These invariant manifolds do not contain any fixed points, so the only possible dynamics within such a manifold is that all solutions flow to a fixed point in S_0, as depicted in Figure 13.9. This shows that S_0 is globally attracting, or, to put

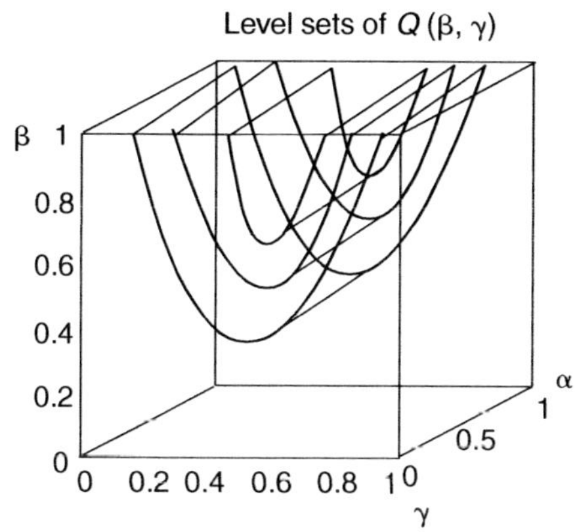

Figure 13.8 Foliation of two-dimensional manifolds without fixed points: three-dimensional view

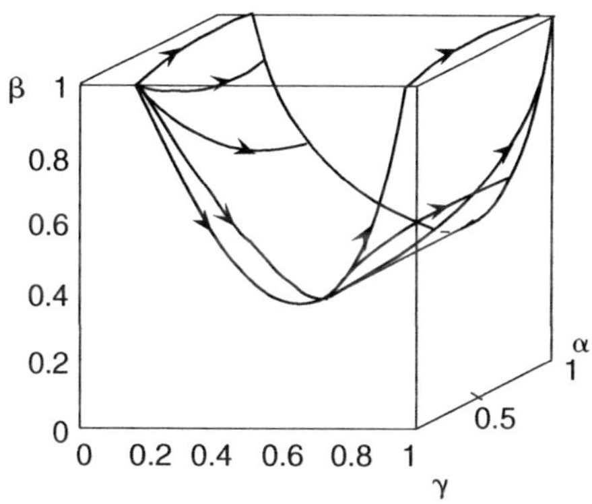

Figure 13.9 Flow within an invariant manifold $Q(\beta, \gamma) = c$

it in another way, that the stable manifold of S_0 is the whole of the phase space.

For sufficiently small $\mu > 0$, Fenichel's theorem guarantees the existence of a locally attracting two-dimensional invariant manifold S_μ, close to S_0, but not consisting of fixed points. The same theorem also states that locally, the stable manifold of S_μ is close to, and of the same dimension as, the stable manifold of S_0. The small perturbation does not affect the topology of the flow outside a neighborhood of S_0. Therefore, in the perturbed system all solutions will tend to a neighborhood of S_μ. From there, all solutions will be attracted to S_μ itself, since all solutions starting in its neighborhood will converge to S_μ.

As in the previous example, S_μ can be defined through $\alpha = 1 + h(\beta, \gamma, \mu)$. Inserting this expression in (13.4) leads, to first order, to

$$h(\beta, \gamma, \mu) = \frac{-\mu}{1 - q(1 - \beta)\gamma} \tag{13.6}$$

The dynamics within S_μ can be derived by inserting (13.6) in (13.4). This yields, to first order,

$$\dot{\beta} = \frac{\beta(1 - \beta)\,((r + s)\gamma - s)}{1 - q(1 - \beta)\gamma} + (1 - 2\beta)$$

$$\dot{\gamma} = \frac{q\gamma(1 - \beta)\,(1 - \gamma)}{1 - q(1 - \beta)\gamma} + (1 - 2\gamma) \tag{13.7}$$

The phase space of (13.7) is shown in Figure 13.10. From this diagram, it follows that there is one attracting fixed point within S_μ. From the above considerations we conclude that this fixed point is the unique global attractor.

The replicator equations without perturbations for the fixed point (β^*, γ^*) are

$$(1 - 2\beta^*)(1 - q(1 - \beta^*)\gamma^*) + \beta^*(1 - \beta^*)(r\gamma^* - s(1 - \gamma^*)) = 0 \tag{13.8}$$

$$(1 - 2\gamma^*)(1 - q(1 - \beta^*)\gamma^*) + q(1 - \beta^*)\gamma^*(1 - \gamma^*) = 0. \tag{13.9}$$

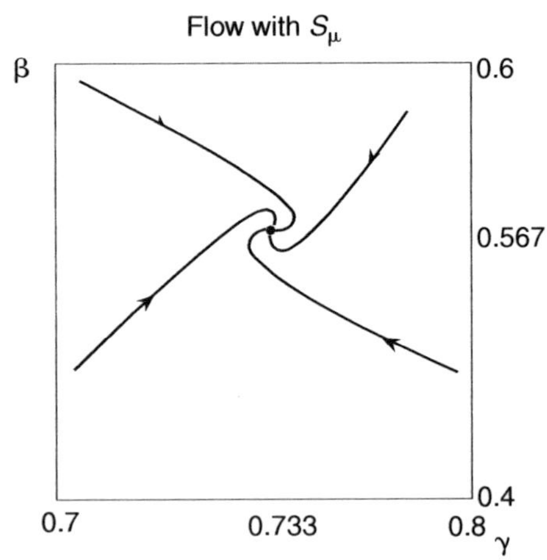

Figure 13.10 Phase space of (13.8), (13.9) in the invariant manifold near $\alpha = 1$

These equations can be solved in closed analytical form, but the result is uninteresting, comprising many hundreds of lines of mathematical symbols. The more interesting result is that the subgame perfect equilibrium cannot be among the solutions, since both left-hand sides evaluate to -1 when $\beta^* = \gamma^* = 1$. Evaluating the solutions at $r = 1$, $s = 2$, $q = 2$ gave the approximations $\beta^* = 0.566588$ and $\gamma^* = 0.732637$. Clearly, our limit $(1, \beta^*, \gamma^*)$ is far from the subgame perfect equilibrium. The subgame perfect Nash pay-offs obtain, however, as $\alpha^* = 1$ since, in fact, $(1, \beta^*, \gamma^*)$ is a mixed strategy Nash equilibrium of Figure 13.7.

13.4 Multi-move centipede game

The examples above can be generalized to the multi-move centipede game in Figure 13.11. The equations for the multi-move centipede game with n moves, general pay-offs and $\mu = 0$, are:

$$\dot{\alpha} = \alpha(1 - \alpha)\,(a_1 - (a_2x_2 + a_3(1 - x_2)x_3 + \ldots a_{n+1}(1 - x_2)\ldots(1 - x_n)))$$
$$\dot{x}_j = x_j(1 - \alpha)\ldots(1 - x_j)\,(c_j - (c_{j+1}x_{j+1} + c_{j+2}(1 - x_{j+2})x_{j+2} + \ldots$$
$$\ldots + c_{n+1}(1 - x_{j+1})\ldots(1 - x_n)))\; j = 2,\ldots n - 1.$$
$$\dot{x}_n = x_n(1 - \alpha)\ldots(1 - x_n)\,(a_n - a_{n+1}(1 - x_n)), \tag{13.10}$$

where $c_j = a_j$ if j is odd and $c_j = b_j$ if j is even. The above equation is for the case that n is odd. When n is even, the letter a in the last equation must be replaced with a b. In these equations, α is the frequency of d_1, x_j is the frequency of d_j, $j = 2, \ldots n$. To ensure that the subgame perfect equilibrium of this game is the solution whereby all players play d, we must impose the condition

$$a_1 > a_2,\, b_2 > b_3,\, a_3 > a_4, \ldots, a_n > a_{n+1} \tag{13.11}$$

(see Cressman, 2003, p. 255). Equations (13.10) have a hierarchy of invariant manifolds, all consisting of fixed points, and all fixed points are

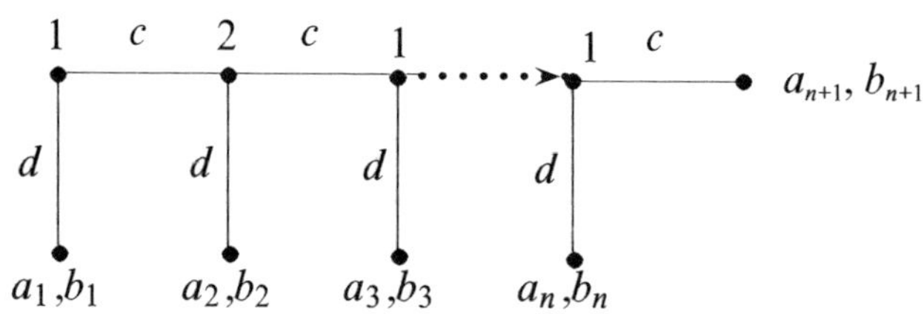

Figure 13.11 Centipede game of length n

contained in one of these manifolds. V_{n-1} is the $(n-1)$-dimensional manifold of points for which $\alpha = 1$, V_{n-2} is the $(n-2)$-dimensional manifold of points for which $\alpha = 0$ and $x_2 = 1$, and in general V_{n-k} is the $(n-k)$-dimensional manifold of points for which $\alpha = 0, x_2 = 0, \ldots, x_{k-1} = 0, x_k = 1$.

V_{n-1} has a subset of fixed points that are stable, namely those points $(x_1, \ldots, x_n)$ for which

$$a_1 - (a_2x_2 + a_3(1 - x_2)x_3 + \ldots + a_{n+1}(1 - x_2)\ldots(1 - x_n)) > 0. \quad (13.12)$$

All fixed points in the other invariant manifolds are unstable. For V_{n-2}, this can be seen by linearizing around such a fixed point. If we write $\alpha = y_1$ and $(x_2 = 1 + y_2$, with y_1 and y_2 small, then to first order the equation for y_1 is given by: $\dot{y}_1 = (a_1 - a_2)y_1$. It follows from condition (13.11) that this solution is unstable. Similarly, it follows from (13.11) that every point in V_{n-k} is unstable in the x_{k-1} direction.

The equations for x_{n-1} and x_n are:

$$\dot{x}_{n-1} = x_{n-1}(1 - \alpha)\ldots(1 - x_{n-1})\,(c_{n-1} - (c_nx_n + c_{n+1}(1 - x_n)))$$

$$\dot{x}_n = x_n(1 - \alpha)\ldots(1 - x_n)\,(a_n - a_{n+1}(1 - x_n)). \quad (13.13)$$

By "dividing out" the common term $(1 - \alpha)\ldots(1 - x_{n-1})$, we can derive a conserved quantity $Q_n(x_{n-1}, x_n)$. Using this expression and the equations for x_{n-2} and x_{n-1}, a second, independent conserved quantity $Q_{n-1}(x_{n-2}, x_{n-1})$ can be derived. This process can be continued to yield $n - 2$ independent integrals of motion. The existence of these integrals of motion implies that the phase space is foliated by 2-dimensional manifolds defined by $Q_n(x_{n-1}, x_n) = c_n$, $Q_{n-1}(x_{n-2}, x_{n-1}) = c_{n-1}, \ldots Q_3(x_2, x_3) = c_3$. Since there are no interior fixed points, the flow on these invariant manifolds is straightforward: all solutions converge to the hyperplane $\alpha = 1$.

Using Fenichel's theorem, we can show, by extending the methods of Sections 13.2 and 13.3, that for $\mu > 0$, there will be a globally attracting $(n-1)$-dimensional manifold near the hyperplane $\alpha = 1$. However, it is not a priori clear that for $n > 3$, all solutions in this invariant manifold will converge to a unique fixed point, as in the previous examples.

13.5 Four-move centipede game: agent extensive form

In the case of $n = 4$ we do find convergence to a fixed point. As in the previous examples, the subgame perfect equilibrium is never among the solutions to the set of equations determining this fixed point. For instance, for the game depicted in Figure 13.12 with $r = 1$, $s = 4$ and $q = 2$, the

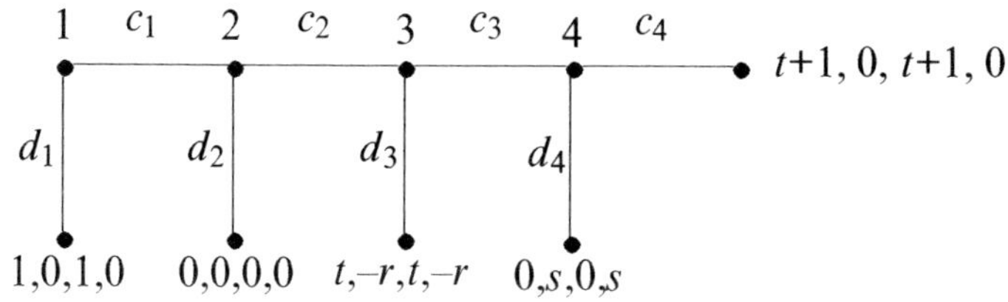

Figure 13.12 Four-move centipede game

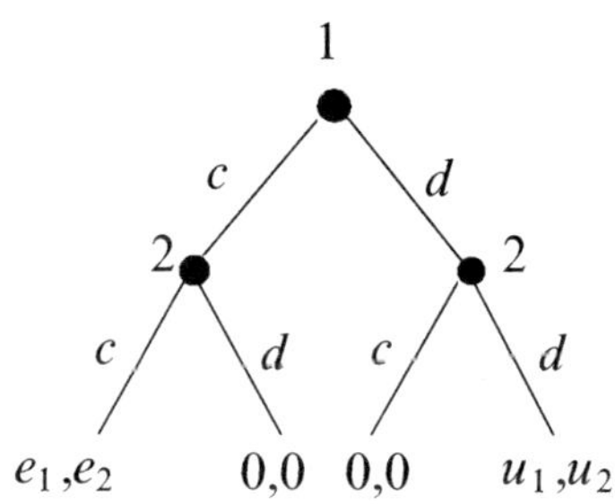

Figure 13.13 Ultimatum game

equations have one fixed point given by $\beta^* = 0.516$, $\gamma^* = 0.786$, and $\delta^* = 0.606$. Evaluation of the Jacobian of the system in a neighborhood of this equilibrium confirms that it is locally stable. Note that if player 3 defects, he or she gets $q = 2$, whereas if he or she cooperates he or she gets $(q + 1)(1 - \delta^*) = 1.182$, so he or she should defect. But, if he or she defected, player 2 should defect, to get zero as opposed to $-r = -1$. If player 3 cooperates, then so should player 2, so the latter can get the 1.182 also. However, player 3 defects with probability $\gamma^* = 0.786$, so player 2 actually gets $1.182(1 - \gamma^*) - \gamma^* = -0.533$ by cooperating. Why doesn't he or she just defect? Because the random walk of the perturbation leads him or her to cooperate with probability 1/2, and the cost of cooperation only reduces this rate by about 10 percent.

13.6 The ultimatum game

Figure 13.13 depicts the ultimatum game where player 1 (the Proposer) has two strategies, c (cooperate) and d (defect). Player 2 (the Responder) has four strategies $\{cc, cd, dc, dd\}$ where xy means do x if Proposer plays d and do y if Proposer plays c. The pay-offs are $\pi_i(d, dd) = \pi_i(d, dc) = u_i$, $\pi_i(d, cd) = \pi_i(c, cd) = 0$, $\pi_i(c, dc) = \pi_i(c, cc) = e_i$, $i = 1, 2$. We assume $u_i, e_i > 0$, $u_1 > \max(u_2, e_1)$, and $u_1 + u_2 = e_1 + e_2 = 10$. Cooperating thus means offering $e_2 > u_2$ for the Proposer, and accepting e_2 while rejecting u_2 for the Responder. All other moves are defection. The unique subgame perfect Nash equilibrium is (d, dc), but any combination of dd and dc is a best response for the Responder. Another Nash equilibrium component is given by $(c, pdc + (1-p)cc)$ for $p \leq e_1/u_1$.

Let α be the probability the Proposer plays d. Numerical simulations show that as $\mu \to 0$, all trajectories converge and that, along a particular trajectory, either $\alpha^* \to 1$ or $\alpha^* \to 0$, and both limits are possible. In particular, unlike the result in Hart (2002), some trajectories do not converge to the subgame perfect equilibrium pay-offs. When $\alpha^* \to 1$, we can write the replicator equations as

$$\dot{\alpha} = \mu(1 - 2\alpha) + \alpha(1 - \alpha)(u_1(\beta + \gamma) - e_1(1 - \beta - \delta))(1 - 2\mu) \tag{13.14}$$

$$\dot{\beta} = \mu(1 - 4\beta + \beta(u_2\alpha A - e_2B(1 - \beta - \delta))(1 - 4\mu)) \tag{13.15}$$

$$\dot{\gamma} = \mu(1 - 4\gamma + \gamma(u_2\alpha A - e_2B(\beta + \delta))(1 - 4\mu)) \tag{13.16}$$

$$\dot{\delta} = \mu(1 - 4\delta) - \delta(e_2(1 - \alpha)(1 - \beta - \delta) + u_2\alpha(\beta + \gamma))(1 - 4\mu), \tag{13.17}$$

where β is the probability the responder plays dd, γ is the probability the responder plays dc, and δ is the probability the responder plays cd, and $A = (1 - \beta - \gamma)/\mu$, $B = (1 - \alpha)/\mu$. Since $\alpha^* = 1$, from (13.15), letting $\mu \to 0$, we find $\beta^* + \gamma^* = 1$. Now, β^* and γ^* are determined by the following equations:

$$1 - 4\beta + \beta(Au_2 - Be_2(1 - \beta)) = 0 \tag{13.18}$$

$$1 - 4\gamma + \gamma(Au_2 + Be_2\beta) = 0 \tag{13.19}$$

$$\beta + \gamma = 1 \tag{13.20}$$

$$\beta + \gamma B(u_1 - \gamma e_1) = 1. \tag{13.21}$$

These equations have closed form solutions, but it is not illuminating to exhibit them. Assuming $u_1 = 9$, $u_2 = 1$, $e_1 = e_2 = 5$, we find $\beta^* = 0.4$ and $\gamma^* = 0.6$. Evaluation of the Jacobian of the system in a neighborhood of this equilibrium confirms that it is locally stable. Clearly, this is not the subgame perfect equilibrium. Indeed, it is clear that for all parameter values, the subgame perfect equilibrium does not obtain.

Suppose $\alpha^* = 0$. Then we can write the replicator equations as

$$\dot{\alpha} = \mu(1 - 2\alpha + A(1 - \alpha)(u_1(\beta + \gamma) - e_1(1 - \beta - \delta)))(1 - 2\mu) \tag{13.22}$$

$$\dot{\beta} = \mu(1 - 4\beta - B(u_2\alpha(-1 + \beta + \gamma) + e_2(1 - \alpha)(1 - \beta - \delta))(1 - 4\mu) \tag{13.23}$$

$$\dot{\gamma} = \mu(1 - 4\gamma + \gamma(u_2A(-1 + \beta + \gamma) - e_2(1 - \alpha)((B + D)))(1 - 4\mu)) \tag{13.24}$$

$$\dot{\delta} = \mu(1 - 4\delta - D(u_2\alpha(\beta + \gamma) + e_2(1 - \alpha)(1 - \beta - \delta))(1 - 4\mu)), \tag{13.25}$$

where $A = \alpha/\mu$, $B = \beta/\mu$, and $D = \delta/\mu$. Assuming A, B and D remain bounded as $\mu \to 0$, we have $\beta^* = \delta^* = 0$ and the following four equations hold:

$$A(u_1\gamma^* - e_1) + 1 = 0 \tag{13.26}$$

$$1 - De_2 = 0 \tag{13.27}$$

$$1 - Be_2 = 0 \tag{13.28}$$

$$1 - 4\gamma^* - \gamma^*(u_2A(1 - \gamma^*) + e_2(B + D)) = 0. \tag{13.29}$$

These equations reduce to a complicated quadratic equation for A and γ^*. Assuming $u_1 = 9$, $u_2 = 1$, $e_1 = e_2 = 5$, we have $\gamma^* = 0.1604$.

13.7 Conclusion

We have shown that generally, the subgame perfect equilibrium is not a solution of the corresponding replicator equation when small recurrent perturbations are taken into account. From the extensive form examples considered in this chapter with non-singleton Nash equilibrium components, it seems clear that evolutionary dynamics with recurrent perturbations do not converge to the subgame perfect equilibrium as the perturbation rate approaches zero. This contrasts with the result in Hart (2002). In fact, for the ultimatum game, which has two Nash equilibrium components, we see that some trajectories even converge to the non-subgame perfect component. On the other hand, for centipede games of arbitrary length (whose only Nash equilibrium component includes the subgame perfect equilibrium), we have shown that, as the perturbation rate goes to zero, the pay-offs approach that of the unique subgame perfect equilibrium, but the frequencies of strategies off the equilibrium path are quite different from the subgame perfect Nash equilibrium.

Notes

* We thank Ken Binmore, Drew Fudenberg, and Sergiu Hart for helpful comments.

1. Hart (2002) used "evolutionarily stable" in place of "stochastically stable." We avoid this former phrase since it is potentially misleading if it is confused with the static concept of an evolutionarily stable strategy (ESS) that was introduced by Maynard Smith and Price (1973) and forms a cornerstone of evolutionary game theory.

References

Binmore, Kenneth G., John Gale, and Larry Samuelson (1995), "Learning to be Imperfect: The Ultimatum Game," *Games and Economic Behavior*, **8**(1), 56–90.

Cressman, Ross (2003), *Evolutionary Dynamics in Extensive Form Games*, Cambridge, MA: The MIT Press.

Cressman and Karl Schlag (1998), "The Dynamic (In)Stability of Backwards Induction," *Journal of Economic Theory*, **83**(2), 260–85.

Fenichel, N. (1971), "Persistence and Smoothness of Invariant Manifolds for Flows," *Indiana University Mathematics Journal*, **21**(3), 193–225.

Hart, Sergiu (2002), "Evolutionary Dynamics and Backward Induction," *Games and Economic Behavior*, **41**(2), 227–64.

Maynard Smith, John and G.R. Price (1973), "The Logic of Animal Conflict," *Nature*, **246**(5427), 15–18.

Nachbar, John H. (1990), "'Evolutionary' Selection Dynamics in Games: Convergence and Limit Properties," *International Journal of Game Theory*, **19**(1), 59–89.

Ponti, Giovanni (2000), "Cycles of Learning in the Centipede Game," *Games and Economic Behavior*, **30**(1), 115–41.

Samuelson, Larry (1997), *Evolutionary Games and Equilibrium Selection*, Cambridge, MA: MIT Press.

Samuelson, Larry and Jianbo Zhang (1992), "Evolutionary Stability in Asymmetric Games," *Journal of Economic Theory*, **57**(2), 363–91.

Taylor, Peter and Leo Jonker (1978), "Evolutionarily Stable Strategies and Game Dynamics," *Mathematical Biosciences*, **40**(1–2), 145–56.

Young, H. Peyton (1993), "An Evolutionary Model of Bargaining," *Journal of Economic Theory*, **59**(1), 145–68.

14. Complex dynamics in ecologic-economic systems

J. Barkley Rosser, Jr.

> A Public Domain, once a velvet carpet of rich buffalo-grass and grama, now an illimitable waste of rattlesnake-bush and tumbleweed, too impoverished to be accepted as a gift by the states within which it lies. Why? Because the ecology of the Southwest happened to be set on a hair trigger. (Aldo Leopold, 1933, "The Conservation Ethic," *Journal of Forestry*, **31**(6), 636–7)

14.1 Introduction and definitions

The question of what constitutes complex dynamics is multi-faceted and complicated, with a variety of definitions being offered. For purposes of this discussion we shall focus on the dynamic definition of complexity provided by Day (1994) and discussed in connection with alternatives by Rosser (1999, Chapter 3 this volume). This definition posits that systems are dynamically complex if they fail to converge to either a point, a limit cycle, or an exponential expansion or contraction due to endogenous causes. The system generates irregular dynamic patterns of some sort, either sudden discontinuities, aperiodic chaotic dynamics subject to sensitive dependence on initial conditions, multi-stability of basins of attraction, or other such irregular patterns. Combined ecologic-economic systems seem to be especially prone to such dynamics, with the resulting problems arising from these becoming serious problems for policy-makers (Rosser, 2001). In this chapter we shall focus on the complex dynamics of fisheries, forests, the global climatic-economic system, and hierarchical systems.

Without doubt, prior to the appearance of human beings, ecological systems experienced discontinuities in their dynamic paths, if only due to dramatic exogenous shocks such as meteorite strikes or volcanic eruptions that probably triggered the episodes of mass extinctions known to have occurred in geological time. We also now know that in contrast to Darwin's (1859, p. 166) view that "*natura non facit saltum*" ("nature does not take a leap") evolution may well have proceeded in a more discontinuous, "saltationalist," manner via punctuated equilibria, with long periods of little change alternating with periods of very rapid change (Gould, 2002). However, it is also likely that these periods of rapid evolutionary change were driven by sudden changes in broader environmental conditions such as climate.

Of somewhat greater interest are the fluctuations and discontinuities that arise in an endogenous manner from within ecosystems. The Lotka-Volterra predator-prey cycle is perhaps the most famous and widespread such phenomenon, although it does not involve discontinuities per se (Lotka, 1925). Two (or more) species interact in a coupled oscillation whose swings can be so great that they can appear to be almost discontinuous at certain points, as in the famous hare-lynx example of the Hudson Bay (Odum, 1953).[1] An even more dramatic example is the spruce budworm dynamics in Canadian forests (Holling, 1965; May, 1977; Ludwig, Jones, and Holling, 1978; Ludwig, Walker, and Holling, 2002), the roughly 40-year cycle marked by discontinuous outbreaks of the budworm population.[2] This latter clearly involves a situation of multiple equilibria with possible hysteresis cycles between them. Furthermore, predator-prey cycles and more complicated interspecies relationships can lead to chaotic dynamics (Schaffer, 1984; Brauer and Soudack, 1985; Doveri et al., 1993)[3] even if it has been argued that truly such dynamics are only rarely observed among natural populations in the wild (Zimmer, 1999)[4] in contrast to laboratory populations (Hassell, Lawton, and May, 1976).

Other strictly ecological systems that exhibit such multiple equilibria with accompanying discontinuities as systems move from one basin of attraction to another include coral reefs (Done, 1992; Hughes, 1994), kelp forests (Estes and Duggins, 1995), and potentially eutrophic shallow lakes (Schindler, 1990; Scheffer, 1998; Carpenter, Ludwig, and Brock, 1999; Carpenter, Brock, and Ludwig, 2002; Wagener, 2003), although these latter can be affected by human input of phosphorus. A more particular phenomenon involves situations when species invade ecosystems leading to sudden disruption as in some grasslands (D'Antonio and Vitousek, 1992), although increasingly these invasions have been triggered by humans transporting species across Wallace's realms (Elton, 1958). A further complication with multiple basins of attraction arises when these basins may have fractal boundaries, thereby increasing the degree of complexity of possible dynamics, with this shown as a possibility for predator-prey systems under certain conditions (Gu and Huang, 2006).

The problem of lake eutrophication due to phosphorus loadings from human activity noted above is another important example as is the problem of overgrazing of ecologically fragile rangelands that can be taken over by woody vegetation (Noy-Meir, 1973; Walker et al., 1981; Ludwig, Walker, and Holling, 2002). A fundamental concept in all this is the stability-resilience trade-off first posited by Holling (1973), with true discontinuities being associated with crossing from one basin of attraction to another in a failure of resilience.[5]

14.2 Complex fishery dynamics

Colin W. Clark (1985, p. 6) lists species that have experienced relatively sudden population collapse in fisheries: Antarctic blue whales, Antarctic fin whales, Hokkaido herring, Peruvian anchoveta, Southwest African pilchard, North Sea herring, California sardine, Georges Bank herring, and Japanese sardine. While some of these have since recovered, yet others have since collapsed, most dramatically the Georges Bank cod (Ruitenbeck, 1996). Needless to say these events have drawn much study and effort with many approaches being used, including catastrophe theory for the Antarctic blue and fin whale cases (Jones and Walters, 1976).[6] A more general approach has been developed (Clark, 1990; Rosser, 2001; Hommes and Rosser, 2001) based on the study of open access fisheries by Gordon (1954), combined with the yield curve model of Schaefer (1957) and drawing on the insight of Copes (1970) that the supply curve in many fisheries may be backward-bending. However, this analysis will also apply to closed access fisheries managed in an optimal manner, the open and closed access cases coinciding for the case where the discount rate for the future is infinite, that is, the future is not counted at all.

Let x = fish biomass, r = intrinsic growth rate of the fish, k = ecological carrying capacity, t = time, h = harvest, and $F(x) = \mathrm{d}x/\mathrm{d}t$ the growth rate of the fish without harvest. Then a sustained yield harvest is given by

$$h = F(x) = rx(1 - x/k). \tag{14.1}$$

Let E = catch effort in standardized vessel time, q = catchability per vessel per day, a constant marginal cost = c, p = price of fish, and δ = the time discount rate. The basic harvest yield is

$$h(x) = qEx. \tag{14.2}$$

Hommes and Rosser (2001) show that the optimal discounted supply curve is then given by

$$x\delta(p) = k/4\{1 + (c/pqk) - (\delta/r) + [(1 + (c/pqk) - (\delta/r)^2 + (8c\delta/pqkr)]^{1/2}\}. \tag{14.3}$$

This entire system is depicted in Figure 14.1, with the backward-bending supply curve in the upper right and the yield curve in the lower right. It must be noted that if the discount rate is low enough, then there is no backward bend, although it will do so for discount rates exceeding 2 percent, which is not very high. The maximum backward bend will occur with a

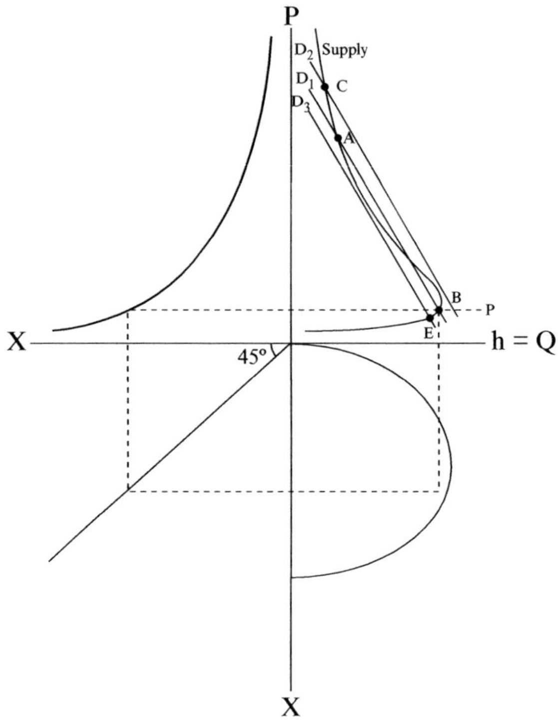

Source: Rosser (2001, p. 27).

Figure 14.1 Gordon-Schaefer-Clark fishery model

discount rate of infinity, in which the future is not counted at all, which coincides with the open access case.

The basic collapse story occurs as a sufficiently inelastic demand curve gradually shifts outward. This is also shown in Figure 14.1, and it can be seen that as the demand curve shifts outward, the system will go from a single equilibrium with a low price and large fish stock and harvest through a zone of three equilibria, and then will suddenly jump to another single equilibrium case of high price and low fish stock and harvest as the demand curve continues to move outwards (Anderson, 1973). Needless to say this scenario is more likely for the case of open access with its known propensity for overexploitation of a natural resource.

If one posits adaptive behavior by fishers, then the dynamics vary considerably as the discount rate varies. At low discount rates, the system will stay on the lower section of the supply curve, with high quantities and low prices. At very high discount rates, the opposite will occur, with prices

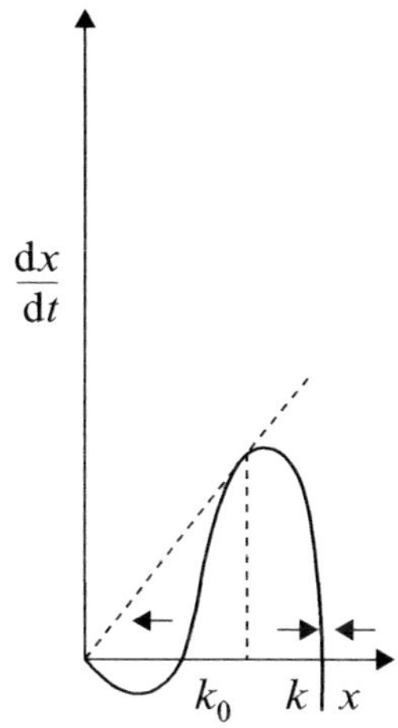

Source: Rosser (2001, p. 29).

Figure 14.2 Critical depensation yield function

being high and quantities low. However, Hommes and Rosser (2001) in studying this system showed that for intermediate ranges of the discount rate, chaotic dynamics can arise, essentially involving fishers jumping back and forth between the lower and upper ranges of the supply curve. They also show that the fishers can "learn to believe in chaos" and adapt to an underlying chaotic dynamic using simple rules of thumb along lines studied by Hommes and Sorger (1998), following their concept of consistent expectations equilibria.[7] While not using this framework, Conklin and Kohlberg (1994) have also demonstrated the possibility of chaotic dynamics for fisheries.

Now this set-up does not generate a complete collapse of the fishery to zero. This can happen if the yield function exhibits the character of depensation (Allee, 1931; Clark and Mangel, 1979). The yield function and the harvest yield curve for the critical depensation case is shown in Figure 14.2. In this case a complete collapse of the population to zero can happen. This is the situation when a species has a minimum number below which it will fail to reproduce.

The potential for complete collapse of a fishery can also arise from the phenomenon of capital stock inertia (Clark, Clarke, and Munro, 1979). This is exacerbated in practice by the unwillingness of many fishers to give up their lifestyle and the tendency for many to belong to isolated minority groups with strong identities who resent policy efforts by outsiders (Charles, 1988). It is well known that if the fishers themselves can organize themselves to manage their fisheries and control access then this is a superior outcome (Walters, 1986; Durrenberger and Pálsson, 1987; Ostrom, 1990; Bromley, 1991; Sethi and Somanathan, 1996). However, game-theoretic approaches are relevant in the analysis of conflicts over access, especially in connection with fisheries spilling across national boundaries (Okuguchi and Szidarovsky, 2000; Bischi and Kopel, 2002). The problem is not "common property," as was thought in the period of Gordon (1954), but is of control of access (Ciriacy-Wantrup and Bishop, 1975).

Yet another potential source for the collapse of a fish species involves interactions between competitive species. Gause (1935) developed the competitive species version of the Lotka-Volterra model. Let s = intrinsic growth rate of the y species and L its carrying capacity, with all other variables defined as above, this is given by

$$\mathrm{d}x/\mathrm{d}t = rx(1 - x/k) - \alpha xy \tag{14.4}$$

$$\mathrm{d}y/\mathrm{d}t = sy(1 - y/L) - \beta xy. \tag{14.5}$$

An isocline for x to remain constant is given by

$$Y = (r/\alpha)(1 - x/k) - (q/\alpha)E. \tag{14.6}$$

As E increases the system can bifurcate with a collapse of x occurring. This will coincide with its competitive replacement by y when $E = s/\beta$ (Clark, 1990). Murphy (1967) analyzed the collapse of the Pacific sardine fishery in the late 1940s and its replacement by the anchoveta as a likely example of such a competitor-driven collapse. Figure 14.3 depicts this case, with x collapsing while its yield-effort curve is still increasing.

In contrast to the competitor species case there is the question of dynamics in the predator-prey case. This case with harvesting of the predator species has been studied by Brauer and Soudack (1979). They find a stable case and an unstable case, with the latter emerging as the harvest rate increases. In both cases there are two equilibria. In the stable case, one equilibrium is stable while the other is an unstable node from which the dynamics move to the stable equilibrium. In the unstable case, the formerly stable equilibrium destabilizes, with the possibility of the collapse of the predator population occurring. This situation is depicted in Figure 14.4, with (a) the stable case and (b) the unstable case. Brauer and Soudack (1985) suggest various strategies for stabilizing the unstable case.

The problem of managing fisheries with such predator-prey interactions has also been studied by Walters (1986). More particularly he has considered the problem of preserving trout in Lake Superior after their

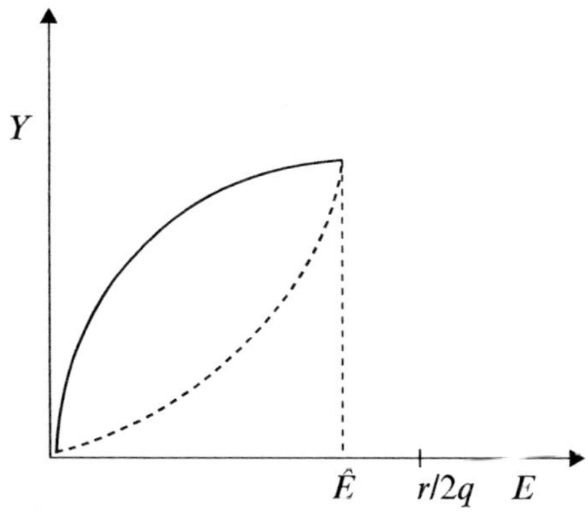

Source: Rosser (1991, p. 250).

Figure 14.3 Fishery collapse with competitor species

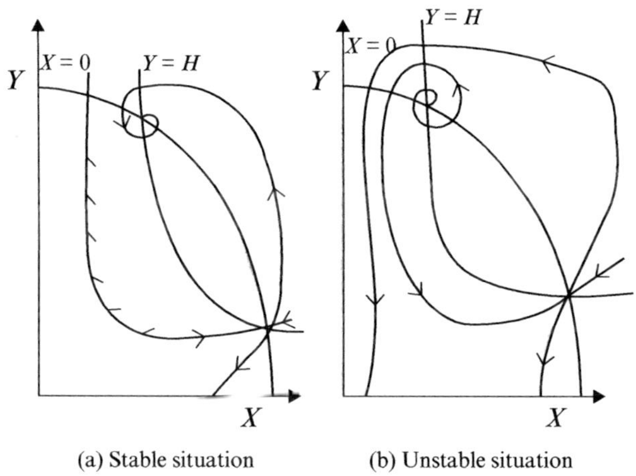

Source: Rosser (1991, p. 251).

Figure 14.4 Complex predator-prey dynamics with harvesting

devastation by the lamprey, which invaded through the St. Lawrence Seaway. He has suggested that in an effort to maximize yield while avoiding catastrophic collapse one may have to "surf" near the edge of the system as in (a) in Figure 14.5. Fishers face the trade-off between too little information but a higher and safer yield versus more information but the danger of a catastrophic collapse of the wild trout population as in (b) in Figure 14.5.

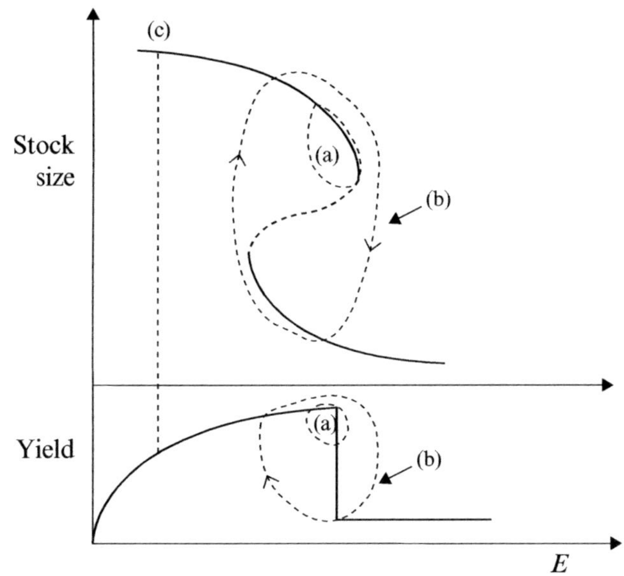

Source: Rosser (1991, p. 253).

Figure 14.5 Great lakes trout dynamics under alternative strategies

14.3 Complex forestry dynamics

Above we noted the case of the spruce budworm cycle and the influence that distant human activities can have on it (Holling, 1988). We shall now consider certain situations where more direct human management of forests can lead to discontinuities of various sorts. In this analysis we shall assume that the forest managers are optimizing agents. While in some cases this optimization may take the form of simple wealth maximization based on future expected income streams from timber harvesting or grazing of species with economic pay-offs, it can be generalized to managers of publicly owned forests who are valuing benefits that do not have marketed economic value such as various forms of recreation, carbon sequestration, biodiversity preservation, or others.

Following the pioneering work of Faustmann ([1849] 1968) that focused strictly on the optimal rotation period of a forest being utilized strictly for timber and replanted after harvesting, Hartman (1976) expanded this to include non-timber amenities. Let $f(t)$ be the growth function of the trees, p the price of timber (assumed constant),[8] r the real market rate of interest, c the marginal cost of timber harvesting, e the base of the natural logarithms, $g(t)$ the time pattern of the value of the non-timber amenities, and T the optimal rotation period (the period the forest is allowed to grow before being cut and replanted), then the infinite horizon optimization gives the following solution:

$$pf'(T) = rpf(T) + r[(pf(T) - c)/(erT - 1)] - g(T). \qquad (14.7)$$

This implies that if the non-timber amenities continue to have positive value over time, then the optimal rotation will be longer than for a forest being managed solely for its timber value. Indeed, if $g(t)$ continues to grow over time and is sufficiently high, it can become optimal not to cut the trees, even though they have timber value.

However, if the $g(t)$ is high early in the life of the forest and declines, this can lead to quite a different solution. Thus, many forests possess grazing benefits in early stages. Swallow, Parks, and Wear (1990) have studied this case for national forests in western Montana, which possess cattle grazing benefits in the early stages of forest growth. They estimated parameter values for the following grazing function

$$g(t) = \beta_0 \exp(-\beta_1 t). \qquad (14.8)$$

The value of this is maximized at $T = 1/\beta_1$, which for the case of cattle grazing in the western Montana forests was found to be at 12.5 years. The function they estimated is shown in Figure 14.6.

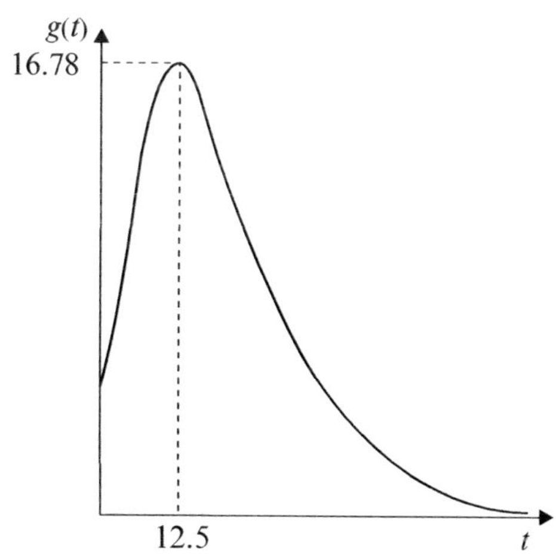

Source: Swallow, Parks, and Wear (1990).

Figure 14.6 Grazing benefit function

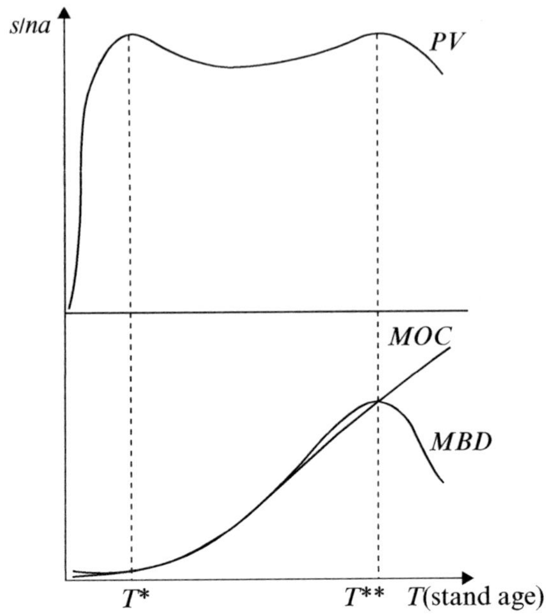

Source: Swallow, Parks, and Wear (1990).

Figure 14.7 Optimal Hartman rotation

Figure 14.7 depicts for this case the present value of the forest at different ages and also the comparison between the marginal benefit of delaying harvest (*MBD*) and the marginal opportunity cost (*MOC*) of doing so. Clearly there are multiple solutions, although in this case the later local optimum is clearly superior. Nevertheless, for this case it occurs at an earlier time than the pure Faustmann solution would indicate in the absence of this early grazing benefit. Implicit here is the possibility of a discontinuity arising from a change in the market rate of interest, *r*, which influences both the *MBD* and the *MOC*. Thus, there could be drastic changes in harvest policy at a critical interest rate, with the optimal rotation suddenly jumping to a very different value.[9]

A more non-market type of benefit is hunting. Figure 14.8 depicts the time pattern of $g(t)$ for hunting in the George Washington National Forest in Virginia as estimated by Rosser (2005) based on data gathered during a land-use planning exercise as part of the FORPLAN process in the early 1980s (Johnson, Jones, and Kent, 1980). This shows three separate peaks of hunting value at different times after a clearcut of these largely deciduous forests. The first occurs about six years after the cut when deer hunting

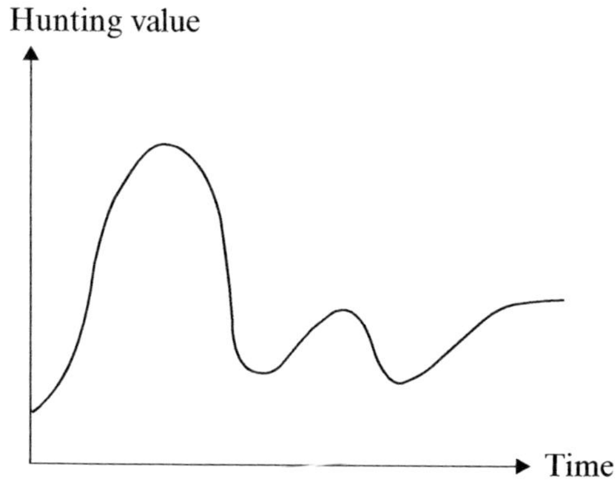

Source: Rosser (2005, p. 198).

Figure 14.8 Virginia deciduous forest hunting amenity

is maximized. This is somewhat analogous to the cattle grazing example noted above, with the deer liking the clearcut zones with small trees and especially the edges of such zones. The next peak occurs around 25 years after the cut and is associated with hunting of wild turkeys and grouse. This is approximately the period of maximum biodiversity of this forest as the succession from oaks to successor species begins and there is much underbrush. Finally after about 60 years the forest becomes "old growth" and bear hunting is maximized, basically increasing in value with the age of the forest as the bears like large fallen-down trees.[10] Needless to say, such a pattern simply opens the door to even more possible discontinuities.

Although there will be no further detailed analysis of the various time patterns of them in forests, the list of other potential non-timber amenities that can (or should) be accounted for is quite long. They include a variety of biodiversity amenities (Perrings et al., 1995), carbon sequestration (Alig, Adams, and McCarl, 1998), and reduced flooding and soil erosion (Plantinga and Wu, 2003). By and large most of these tend to favor longer rotation periods for most forests.

Probably the most dramatic discontinuities in forestry management involve stability-resilience trade-offs (Holling, 1973). We have noted above the case of pest management in regard to the spruce budworms, with efforts to control the budworms in the late stages of their cycle by spraying generally only aggravating their eventual population explosion and the resulting collapse of the spruce forest, this leading to a pattern of hysteresis cycles (Holling, 1965; 1986; 1988). He has documented several other cases besides this one where similar patterns arise (1986).

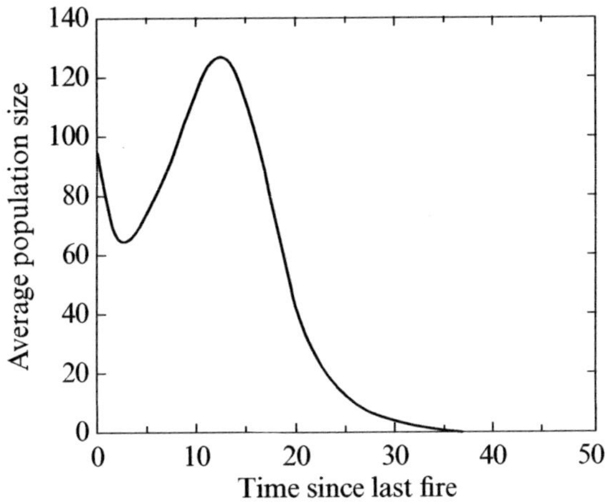

Source: Clark and Margel (2000, p. 178).

Figure 14.9 Average population path

Somewhat similar is the problem facing forestry managers regarding fire management. Longstanding policy in the US national forests was to vigorously suppress almost all fires, even those naturally occurring due to lightning strikes. However, it is now understood that this policy achieved short-term stability at the risk of long-term lack of resilience as underbrush build-up can set a forest up for a truly devastating large-scale fire as happened in Yellowstone National Park. Muradian (2001) argues that the relationship between fire frequency and vegetative density is one of multiple states (Dublin et al., 1990). This supports the idea of the possibility of catastrophic dynamics as we have seen.

Besides the vegetation issue there are also implications for preservation of endangered species, with some doing best in the wake of fires at mid-range successional stages, such as the eastern bristlebird in the US (Pyke, Saillard, and Smith, 1995). Clark and Mangel (2000, pp. 176–81) offer an analysis of this sort of case. Figure 14.9 depicts the time path of an endangered population after a fire. They argue that from the perspective of maximizing such an endangered species, controlled fires should be set when the population is the largest, which could entail relatively frequent fires. Of course, controlled fires can get out of control, which has been a problem in recent years also.

Finally with respect to forests there is the issue of the size of harvest cuts, another matter of great controversy. Generally timber companies prefer to do large-sized clearcuts as they are less expensive in simple economic terms. However, aside from externalities such as flooding, soil erosion, or plain

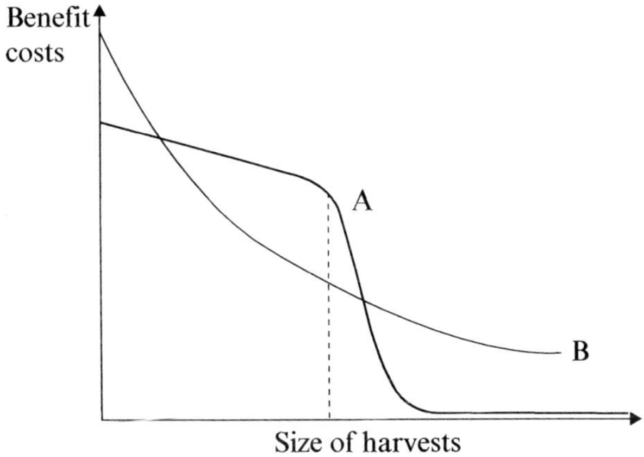

Source: Rosser (2005, p. 202)

Figure 14.10 Harvest cut and habitat damage

unsightliness, there are implications for endangered species management as well. Thus, it has been argued that there are nonlinear relations between largest patch size of habitat and the general degree of habitat destruction or fragmentation. The larger the harvest cut the more likely the resulting patch size may be smaller. More particularly it is argued that below a certain habitat patch size there is a collapse of the fragile species population (Bascompte and Solé, 1996; Muradian, 2001).[11] The implications of this potential for population collapse in conjunction with the declining costs of harvesting larger-sized cuts is depicted in Figure 14.10. The A curve represents the population able to be maintained as a function of the size of the harvest cut, while the B line represents the average costs of the cut. The case for somewhat smaller cuts (but not too small) is clear.

14.4 Complex dynamics in the global climatic-economic system

An example of how the globally coupled climatic-economic system might behave chaotically has been studied by Chen (1997), even though each of the sub-systems does not behave chaotically by itself uncoupled from the other sub-system within this model. The basics of it are quite simple, arguably much simpler than reality.

The climate model used by Chen is due to Henderson-Sellars and McGuffie (1987). It assumes that global average temperature is a linear function of the level of global manufacturing output, given by

$$T_{t+1} = (1 - c)(T_t - T_n) + T_n + gX_{mt}, \qquad (14.9)$$

where $c \varepsilon (0,1)$, T_n is normal global average temperature, t and $t+1$ subscripts indicate time periods, $g > 0$, and X_{mt} is global manufacturing output in time t.

The economic model has two sectors, agriculture, a, and manufacturing, m. Optimization occurs based on a CES utility function of the levels of consumption of agriculture and manufacturing, given by

$$U(C_{at}, C_{mt}) = (C_{at}^{\rho} + C_{mt}^{\rho})^{1/\rho}, \tag{14.10}$$

with $C_{it} = X_{it}$ and the elasticity of substitution $\sigma = 1/(1 - \rho) < 1$. Outputs in each sector are linear in sectoral labor, l_{it}, with total labor supply constant and normalized to sum to unity. Furthermore, agricultural output is a quadratic function of average global temperature. Thus, given that α, β, and b are all positive constants we have

$$X_{at} = (-\alpha T_t^2 + \beta T_t + 1) l_{at} \tag{14.11}$$

$$X_{mt} = b l_{mt}. \tag{14.12}$$

This system generates a market clearing price, p, given by

$$P_t = (-\alpha T_t^2 + \beta T_t + 1)/b. \tag{14.13}$$

All this then provides an equilibrium law of motion of global temperature, which is given by

$$T_{t+1} = (1 - c) T_t + g[(bp_t^{1-\sigma})/(1 + p_t^{1-\sigma})]. \tag{14.14}$$

Chen simulated this model for parameter values $\sigma = 0.5$, $\alpha = 8$, $\beta = 7$, $b = 1$, and $g = 0.6$. The crucial control parameter is c, the adjustment factor for global temperature, which has a critical bifurcation value of 0.233. Above that value, the system converges to a steady state, but goes through period-doubling bifurcations as c declines below that value, with 0.209 being the value below which aperiodic chaotic dynamics appear. In that range the system exhibits sensitive dependence on initial conditions, aka, the "butterfly effect." Matsumoto and Inaba (2000) extend this model to the case of world population varying endogenously to economic conditions and show the possibility of chaotic long-wave fluctuations with the possibility of population crashes.

Now we emphasize that these chaotic dynamics occur for a model in which the climate sub-system on its own is not chaotic. However, it has long been widely believed that the climate system is chaotic on its own.

Indeed, the butterfly effect was first posited for global climate by Lorenz (1963) based upon his study of a three-equation model of global climatic dynamics. This would be capsulized in the famous remark that a butterfly flapping its wings in Brazil could cause hurricanes in Texas (Lorenz, 1993).

Indeed, subsequent studies of the climatic system have made us aware of even a broader range of possible nonlinearities, such as the albedo feedback effect and possible effects regarding oceanic responses to climatic change, which increase substantially not only the possibility of chaotic dynamics but also of even more complicated dynamics, including patterns exhibiting fat tails and higher probabilities of extreme events and outcomes. Weitzman (2007) has warned of this possibility as the most serious problem that must be considered in formulating global climate policy, and Rosser (2001) emphasizes the need to consider the precautionary principle in light of this.

14.5 Hierarchy and complex dynamics

One of the deeper and more unresolved problems is how these discontinuous dynamics operate within the context of ecologic-economic hierarchies. There has been considerable study of this problem from the strictly ecological perspective (Allen and Starr, 1982; O'Neill et al., 1986; Holling, 1992) with Simon (1962) providing a more general foundation. A standard argument has been that higher levels constrain lower levels, but that lower levels do not do so in reverse. However, this has come into question in more recent years. Inspired by the analysis of Diener and Poston (1984) of the "revolt of the slaved variables," Rosser et al. (1994) studied how events at lower levels could trigger changes at higher levels, especially discontinuous ones, a view also advocated by Gunderson et al. (2002, p. 13). They also drew on the theory of hierarchical entrainment of Nicolis (1986) to show how the "anagenetic moment" could arise, where a new level of hierarchy could emerge in a self-organizing manner out of lower levels.[12]

A related approach is that of Aoki (1996). He draws on the mean field theory of Brock (1993) to study how externalities in a hierarchical system can bring about higher level coherences and emergent structures. Fixed points in the coarse graining or aggregation of microunits are associated with sudden structural changes in the dynamical hierarchical system. Sequences of phase transitions can arise in this model as sequences of clusters of equilibria. A key to stability and a lack of such general hierarchical restructurings may be the existence of critical levels of a hierarchy whose stability ensures a broader order in the system, much like the role played by a keystone species in a more general ecosystem (Vandermeer and Maruca, 1998).

Another matter that can arise in hierarchical systems is chaotic dynamics. In combined ecologic-economic systems these couplings can produce particularly complicated patterns that are hard to analyze or predict or manage. Such structures and systems have been extensively studied by Kaneko and Tsuda (1996). These structures of coupled predator-prey systems can feed into the higher-order dynamics of evolution itself. Thus, macroevolution of entire systems can occur with chaotically oscillating patterns of phenotype and genotype that happen over long periods of evolutionary change (Solé and Bascompte, 2006; Sardanyès and Solé, 2007). This formulation resembles to some degree the chaotic long-wave evolutionary dynamics studied by Goodwin (1986).

Within combined ecologic-economic hierarchies, questions of management involve assignment of property rights and the careful assessment of appropriate policies related to the appropriate level. Rosser (1995) argues that the property rights should be assigned to the relevant level of the combined hierarchy in order to facilitate appropriate policies. The importance of this is seen by considering situations where this has not happened. Thus, Wilson et al. (1999) have shown how fisheries attempting to manage from too high a level of scale can lead to overfishing of crucial local stocks and their destruction, with broader implications for the ecosystem in question at multiple levels. This reminds us again that social and economic organization by those most knowledgeable and in touch with a situation or system is often the best way to go. The breakdown of traditional management systems of common property through higher-level interventions has a long and tragic history (Rosser and Rosser, 2006). Likewise, attempting to manage a higher level from a lower level can be ultimately frustrating as the ongoing failure to seriously grapple with global climatic change reminds us.

14.6 Conclusion

In ecologic-economic systems there are many situations in which dynamic discontinuities appear. Many of these are of an undesired sort, especially when they involve the collapse or even extinction of a species or the more general destruction of an ecosystem. While we have noted a large variety of situations where such discontinuities occur, we have focused most of our discussion on the problems of fisheries and forests, both under broad and serious pressure from mismanagement by human beings. It is somewhat ironic that such discontinuities can sometimes arise when humans are trying to account for broader sets of concerns and phenomena than merely simple economics, although certainly sometimes it is the emphasis on the latter that can be the source of problems.

We should note here a point made by Rosser (2001) regarding the policy implications of different kinds of complex dynamics. Thus, the catastrophic discontinuities suggest a focus on the precautionary principle. Chaotic dynamics pose different kinds of problems. In particular, chaotic dynamics are bounded, which means that as long as the bounds are within thresholds of resilience, they may not indicate problems for the system. However, if the fluctuations are too severe, then some sort of method of controlling chaos may be called for (Ott, Grebogi, and Yorke, 1993), although such techniques tend to involve a very high degree of exact knowledge of the dynamics of the system, which is generally lacking in ecologic-economic systems.

In any case, the broader concerns must be dealt with. Hence a more vigorous effort needs to be made to reform institutions and decision-making systems to insure that awareness of critical thresholds of a damaging sort are properly understood and accounted for. There really is no excuse anymore for the heedless destruction of ecologic-economic systems.

Notes

1. For a dissenting view that such cycles are really driven by maternal effect dynamics in the prey population see Ginzburg and Colyvan (2004).
2. Holling (1986, 1988, 1994) has noted that human activities at some distance such as tropical deforestation and disrupting the waterholes of migratory birds that prey on the budworms can strongly influence this cycle. He has favored encouraging control of the budworms through birds rather than spraying, which he sees as simply aggravating an eventual breakdown of resilience in a failed effort to maintain stability.
3. For an overview of chaotic dynamics in predator-prey models, see Solé and Bascompte (2006, pp. 38–42). Chaotic dynamics of predator-prey models also underlie chaotic dynamics in many agricultural systems (Sakai, 2001).
4. Claimed examples of chaotic dynamics in natural populations have included Finnish voles and lemmings (Ellner and Turchin, 1995; Turchin, 2003).
5. For further discussion of specifically discontinuous dynamics in ecologic-economic systems, see Rosser (2008).
6. For a more thorough discussion of the application of catastrophe theory in economic models see Rosser (1991, 2007).
7. Foroni, Gardini, and Rosser (2003) have also shown that the Hommes-Rosser model can generate multiple basins of attraction that possess fractal boundaries.
8. Constancy of price is a non-trivial assumption. When price can change stochastically options pricing theory can be used, which considerably complicates the analysis (Arrow and Fisher, 1974; Zinkhan, 1991; Saphores, 2003).
9. This is reminiscent of how discontinuities can arise when capital-theoretic paradoxes such as reswitching occur in cases where time patterns of costs and benefits are irregular over time (Porter, 1982; Rosser, 1983; Prince and Rosser, 1985).
10. The supervisor of the forest at that time made clear to this author that the biggest single conflict he had to deal with between different groups in the public was that between the deer hunters and the bear hunters, both very well organized and articulate groups, whose interests regarding how much timber harvesting should occur were (and are) very much at odds. In many less developed countries the hunting and fishing in forests may be for subsistence of aboriginal peoples (Norgaard, 1994; Kant, 2000).
11. For broader perspectives on species extinction dynamics see Clark (1973), Solé and Manrubia (1996), and Newman and Palmer (2003).
12. These ideas can be seen as more recent expressions of the British "emergentist" school

that was influential early in the 20th century (Lloyd Morgan, 1923) and whose roots can be traced back to John Stuart Mill (1843).

References

Alig, R.J., D.M. Adams, and B.A. McCarl (1998), "Ecological and Economic Impacts of Forest Policies: Interactions across Forestry and Agriculture," *Ecological Economics*, **27**, 63–78.

Allee, W.C. (1931), *Animal Aggregations*, Chicago: University of Chicago Press.

Allen, Timothy F.H. and Thomas B. Starr (1982), *Hierarchy: Perspectives for Ecological Complexity*, Chicago: University of Chicago Press.

Anderson, L.G. (1973), "Optimum Economic Yield of a Fishery Given a Variable Price of Output," *Journal of the Fisheries Research Board of Canada*, **30**, 509–13.

Aoki, Masanao (1996), *New Approaches to Macroeconomic Modelling: Evolutionary Stochastic Dynamics, Multiple Equilibria, and Externalities as Field Effects*, Cambridge, UK: Cambridge University Press.

Arrow, Kenneth J. and Anthony C. Fisher (1974), "Preservation Uncertainty and Irreversibility," *Quarterly Journal of Economics*, **87**(3), 312–19.

Bascompte, J. and R. Solé (1996), "Habitat Fragmentation and Extinction Thresholds in Spatially Explicit Models," *Journal of American Ecology*, **65**(4), 465–73.

Bischi, Gian-Italo and Michael Kopel (2002), "The Role of Competition, Expectations and Harvesting Costs in Commercial Fishing," in Tönu Puu and Irina Sushko (eds), *Oligopoly Dynamics: Model and Tools*, Heidelberg: Springer-Verlag, pp. 85–109.

Brauer, Fred and A.E. Soudack (1979), "Stability Regions and Transition Phenomena for Harvesting Predator-Prey Systems," *Journal of Mathematical Biology*, **7**, 319–37.

Brauer, Fred and A.E. Soudack (1985), "Optimal Harvesting in Predator-Prey Systems," *International Journal of Control*, **41**(1), 111–28.

Brock, William A. (1993), "Pathways to Randomness in the Economy: Emergent Nonlinearity in Economics and Finance," *Estudios Económicos*, **8**(1), 3–55.

Bromley, Daniel W. (1991), *Environment and Economy: Property Rights and Public Policy*, Oxford: Basil Blackwell.

Carpenter, Stephen R., William A. Brock, and Donald Ludwig (2002), "Collapse, Learning, and Renewal," in Lance H. Gunderson and C.S. Holling (eds), *Panarchy: Understanding Transformations in Human and Natural Systems*, Washington: Island Press, pp. 173–93.

Carpenter, Stephen R., Donald Ludwig, and William A. Brock (1999), "Management of Eutrophication for Lakes Subject to Potentially Irreversible Change," *Ecological Applications*, **9**(3), 751–71.

Charles, Anthony T. (1988), "Fishery Socioeconomics: A Survey," *Land Economics*, **64**(3), 276–95.

Chen, Zhiqi (1997), "Can Economic Activity Lead to Climate Chaos? An Economic Analysis on Global Warming," *Canadian Journal of Economics*, **30**(2), 349–66.

Ciriacy-Wantrup, S.V. and Richard C. Bishop (1975), "'Common Property' as a Concept in Natural Resources Policy," *Natural Resources Journal*, **15**(4), 713–27.

Clark, Colin W. (1973), "Profit Maximization and the Extinction of Animal Species," *Journal of Political Economy*, **81**(4), 363–72.

Clark, Colin W. (1985), *Bioeconomic Modelling and Fisheries Management*, New York: Wiley-Interscience.

Clark, Colin W. (1990), *Mathematical Bioeconomics: The Optimal Management of Renewable Resources*, 2nd edn, New York: Wiley-Interscience.

Clark, Colin W. and Marc Mangel (1979), "Aggregation and Fishery Dynamics: A Theoretical Study of Schooling and the Purse Seine Tuna Fisheries," *Fisheries Bulletin*, **77**, 317–37.

Clark, Colin W. and Marc Mangel (2000), *Dynamic State Variables in Ecology: Methods and Applications*, New York: Oxford University Press.

Clark, Colin W., F.H. Clarke, and G.R. Munro (1979), "The Optimal Exploitation of

Renewable Resource Stocks: Problems of Irreversible Investment," *Econometrica*, **47**(1), 25–49.
Conklin, James E. and William C. Kolberg (1994), "Chaos for the Halibut," *Marine Resource Economics*, **9**(2), 159–82.
Copes, Parzival (1970), "The Backward-bending Supply Curve of the Fishing Industry," *Scottish Journal of Political Economy*, **17**(1), 69–77.
D'Antonio, C.M. and P.M. Vitousek (1992), "Biological Invasions by Exotic Grasses, the Grass-fire Cycle, and Global Change," *Annual Review of Ecology and Systematics*, **23**, 63–87.
Darwin, Charles (1859), *On the Origin of Species by Means of Natural Selection or the Preservation of Favored Races in the Struggle for Life*, London: John Murray.
Day, Richard H. (1994), *Complex Economic Dynamics: An Introduction to Dynamical Systems and Market Mechanisms, Vol. I*, Cambridge, MA: MIT Press.
Diener, Marc and Tim Poston (1984), "The Perfect Delay Convention, or the Revolt of the Slaved Variables," in Hermann Haken (ed.), *Chaos and Order in Nature*, 2nd edn, Berlin: Springer-Verlag, pp. 249–68.
Done, T.J. (1992), "Phase Shifts in Coral Reef Communities and their Ecological Significance," *Hydrobiology*, **247**(1), 121–32.
Doveri, F., M. Scheffer, S. Rinaldi, S. Muratori, and Y.A. Kuznetsov (1993), "Seasonality and Chaos in a Plankton-Fish Model," *Theoretical Population Biology*, **43**(2), 159–83.
Dublin, H.T., A.R.E. Sinclair, and J. McGlade (1990), "Elephants and Fire as Causes of Multiple Stable States in the Serengeti-Mara Woodlands," *Journal of Animal Ecology*, **59**(1), 1147–64.
Durrenberger, E. Paul and Gisli Pálsson (1987), "Resource Management in Icelandic Fishing," in B.J. McCay and J.M. Acheson (eds), *The Question of the Commons*, Tuscon: University of Arizona Press, pp. 370–92.
Ellner, S. and Peter Turchin (1995), "Chaos in a Noisy World: New Methods and Evidence from Time Series Analysis," *American Naturalist*, **145**(3), 343–75.
Elton, Charles S. (1958), *The Ecology of Invasions by Plants and Animals*, London: Methuen.
Estes, J.A. and D. Duggins (1995), "Sea Otters and Kelp Forests in Alaska: Generality and Variation in a Community Ecological Paradigm," *Ecological Monographs*, **65**(1), 75–100.
Faustmann, Martin [1849] (1968), "On the Determination of the Value which Forest Land and Immature Stands Possess," (originally in German) English translation in M. Gane (ed.), *Martin Faustmann and the Evaluation of Discounted Cash Flow*, Oxford University Paper No. 42.
Foroni, Ilaria, Laura Gardini, and J. Barkley Rosser, Jr. (2003), "Adaptive and Statistical Expectations in Renewable Resource Markets," *Mathematics and Computers in Simulation* **63**(6), 541–67.
Gause, G.J. (1935), *La Théorie Mathématique de la Lutte pour la Vie*, Paris: Hermann.
Ginzburg, Lev and Mark Colyvan (2004), *Ecological Orbits: How Planets Move and Populations Grow*, New York: Oxford University Press.
Goodwin, Richard M. (1986), "The Economy as an Evolutionary Pulsator," *Journal of Economic Behavior and Organization*, **7**, 341–9.
Gordon, H. Scott (1954), "Economic Theory of a Common Property Resource: The Fishery," *Journal of Political Economy*, **62**(2), 124–42.
Gould, Stephen Jay (2002), *The Structure of Evolutionary Theory*, Cambridge, MA: The Belknap Press of Harvard University.
Gu, En-Guo and Yibing Huang (2006), "Global Bifurcations of Domains of Feasible Trajectories: An Analysis of a Discrete Predator-Prey Model," *International Journal of Bifurcations and Chaos*, **16**(9), 1601–13.
Gunderson, Lance H., C.S. Holling, Lowell Pritchard, Jr., and Garry Peterson (2002), "Understanding Resilience: Theory, Metaphors, and Frameworks," in Lance H. Gunderson and Lowell Pritchard, Jr. (eds), *Resilience and the Behavior of Large-scale Systems*, Washington: Island Press, pp. 3–20.

Hartman, R. (1976), "The Harvesting Decision when a Standing Forest has Value," *Economic Inquiry*, **14**, 52–8.
Hassell, M.P., J.H. Lawton, and R.M. May (1976), "Patterns of Dynamical Behavior of Single-species Populations," *Journal of Animal Ecology* **45**(2), 471–86.
Henderson-Sellars, A. and K. McGuffie (1987), *A Climate Modeling Primer*, New York: John Wiley & Sons.
Holling, C.S. (1965), "The Functional Response of Predators to Prey Density and its Role in Mimicry and Population Regulation," *Memorials of the Entomological Society of Canada* **45**, 1–60.
Holling, C.S. (1973), "Resilience and Stability of Ecological Systems," *Annual Review of Ecology and Systematics*, **4**, 1–24.
Holling, C.S. (1986), "Resilience of Ecosystems: Local Surprise and Global Change," in W.C. Clark and R.E. Munn (eds), *Sustainable Development of the Biosphere*, Cambridge, UK: Cambridge University Press, pp. 292–317.
Holling, C.S. (1988), "Temperate Forest Insect Outbreaks, Tropical Deforestation and Migratory Birds," *Memoirs of the Entomological Society of Canada*, **146**, 22–32.
Holling, C.S. (1992), "Cross-scale Morphology, Geometry, and Dynamics of Ecosystems," *Ecological Monographs*, **62**, 447–502.
Holling, C.S. (1994), "An Ecologist's View of the Malthusian Conflict," in K. Lindahl-Kiesslking (ed.), *Population-Environment Development*, Stockholm: Beijer International Institute of Ecological Economics, pp. 43–59.
Hommes, Cars H. and J. Barkley Rosser, Jr. (2001), "Consistent Expectations Equilibria and Complex Dynamics in Renewable Resource Markets," *Macroeconomic Dynamics*, **5**, 180–203.
Hommes, Cars H. and Gerhard Sorger (1998), "Consistent Expectations Equilibria," *Macroeconomic Dynamics*, **2**(3), 287–321.
Hughes, T.P. (1994), "Catastrophes, Phase Shifts, and Large-scale Degradation of a Caribbean Coral Reef," *Science*, **265**(5178), 1547–51.
Johnson, K.N., D.B. Jones, and B.M. Kent (1980), *A User's Guide to the Forest Planning Model* (FORPLAN), Fort Collins: USDA Forest Service, Land Management Planning.
Jones, Dixon D. and Carl J. Walters (1976), "Catastrophe Theory and Fisheries Regulation," *Journal of the Fisheries Resource Board of Canada*, **33**, 2829–33.
Kaneko, Kunihiko and Ichiro Tsuda (1996), *Complex Systems: Chaos and Beyond, A Constructive Approach with Applications in Life Sciences*, Berlin: Springer.
Kant, Shashi (2000), "A Dynamic Approach to Forest Regimes in Developing Economies," *Ecological Economics*, **32**(2), 287–300.
Lloyd Morgan, C. (1923), *Emergent Evolution*, London: Williams and Norgate.
Lorenz, Edward (1963), "Deterministic Non-periodic Flow," *Journal of Atmospheric Science*, **20**(2), 130–41.
Lorenz, Edward (1993), *The Essence of Chaos*, Seattle: University of Washington Press.
Lotka, Alfred J. (1925), *Elements of Physical Biology*, (reprinted in 1945 as *Elements of Mathematical Biology*), Baltimore: Williams and Wilkins.
Ludwig, Donald, Dixon D. Jones, and C.S. Holling (1978), "Qualitative Analysis of Insect Outbreak Systems: Spruce Budworm and Forest," *Journal of Animal Ecology*, **47**(1), 315–32.
Ludwig, Donald, Brian H. Walker, and C.S. Holling (2002), "Models and Metaphors of Sustainability, Stability, and Resilience," in Lance H. Gunderson and Lowell Pritchard, Jr. (eds), *Resilience and the Behavior of Large-scale Systems*, Washington: Island Press, pp. 21–48.
Matsumoto, A. and T. Inaba (2000), "Endogenous Global Warming in a Simple Economic Model," in *Proceedings of the First International Symposium on Trade and Environmental Risk in Regional and Global Systems*, Tokyo: Science Council of Japan, pp. 95–102.
May, Robert M. (1977), "Thresholds and Breakpoints in Ecosystems with a Multiplicity of Stable States," *Nature*, **269**(5628), 471–7.
Mill, John Stuart (1843), *A System of Logic: Ratiocinative and Inductive*, London: Longmans Green.

Muradian, R. (2001), "Ecological Thresholds: A Survey," *Ecological Economics* **38**(1), 7–24.
Murphy, G.I. (1967), "Vital Statistics of the Pacific Sardine," *Ecology*, **48**(5), 731–6.
Newman, Mark and Richard Palmer (2003), *Modeling Extinction*, New York: Oxford University Press.
Nicolis, John S. (1986), *Dynamics of Hierarchical Systems: An Evolutionary Approach*, Berlin: Springer-Verlag.
Norgaard, Richard B. (1994), *Development Betrayed: The End of Progress and a Coevolutionary Revisioning of the Future*, London: Routledge.
Noy-Meir, I. (1973), "Desert Ecosystems: Environment and Producers," *Annual Review of Ecology and Systematics*, **4**, 355–64.
Odum, Eugene P. (1953), *Fundamentals of Ecology*, Philadelphia: W.B. Saunders.
Okuguchi, K. and F. Szidarovsky (2000), "A Dynamic Model of International Fishing," *Keio Economic Studies*, **13**(4), 471–6.
O'Neill, R.V., D.V. De Angelis, J.B. Waide, and T.F.H. Allen (1986), *A Hierarchical Concept of an Ecosystem*, Princeton: Princeton University Press.
Ostrom, Elinor (1990), *Governing the Commons: The Evolution of Institutions for Collective Action*, Cambridge, UK: Cambridge University Press.
Ott, Edward, Celso Grebogi, and James A. Yorke (1990), "Controlling Chaos," *Physical Review Letters*, **64**(II), 1196–9.
Perrings, Charles, Karl-Göran Mäler, Carl Folke, C.S. Holling, and Bengt Jansson (eds) (1995), *Biodiversity Loss: Economic and Ecological Issues*, Cambridge, UK: Cambridge University Press.
Plantinga, A.J. and J. Wu (2003), "Co-benefits from Carbon Sequestration in Forests: Evaluating Reduction in Agricultural Externalities from an Afforestation Policy in Wisconsin," *Land Economics*, **79**(1), 74–85.
Porter, Richard C. (1982), "The New Approach to Wilderness Through Benefit–Cost Analysis," *Journal of Environmental Economics and Management*, **9**(1), 59–80.
Prince, Raymond and J. Barkley Rosser, Jr. (1985), "Some Implications of Delayed Environmental Costs for Benefit Cost Analysis: A Study of Reswitching in the Western Coal Lands," *Growth and Change*, **16**, 18–25.
Pyke, G.H., R. Saillard, and J. Smith (1995), "Abundance of Bristlebirds in Relation to Habitat and Fire History," *Emu*, **95**, 106–10.
Rosser, J. Barkley, Jr. (1983), "Reswitching as a Cusp Catastrophe," *Journal of Economic Theory*, **31**(1), 182–93.
Rosser, J. Barkley, Jr. (1991), *From Catastrophe to Chaos: A General Theory of Economic Discontinuities*, Boston: Kluwer Academic.
Rosser, J. Barkley, Jr. (1995), "Systemic Crises in Hierarchical Ecological Economies," *Land Economics*, **71**(2), 163–72.
Rosser, J. Barkley, Jr. (1999), "On the Complexities of Complex Economic Dynamics," *Journal of Economic Perspectives*, **13**(4), 169–92.
Rosser, J. Barkley, Jr. (2001), "Complex Ecologic-Economic Dynamics and Environmental Policy," *Ecological Economics*, **37**(1), 23–37.
Rosser, J. Barkley, Jr. (2005), "Complexities of Dynamic Forest Management Policies," in Shashi Kant and R. Albert Berry (eds), *Sustainability, Economics, and Natural Resources: Economics of Sustainable Forest Management*, Dordrecht: Springer, pp. 191–206.
Rosser, J. Barkley, Jr. (2007), "The Rise and Fall of Catastrophe Theory Applications in Economics: Was the Baby Thrown out with the Bathwater?", *Journal of Economic Dynamics and Control*, **31**, 3255–80.
Rosser, J. Barkley, Jr. (2008), "Dynamic Discontinuities in Ecologic-Economic Systems," in Craig R. Allen and C.S. Holling (eds), *Discontinuity Theory in Ecosystems and Other Complex Systems*, New York: Columbia University Press, pp. 179–92.
Rosser, J. Barkley, Jr. and Marina V. Rosser (2006), "Institutional Evolution of Environmental Management under Global Economic Growth," *Journal of Economic Issues*, **40**(2), 421–9.
Rosser, J. Barkley, Jr., Carl Folke, Folke Günther, Heikki Isomäki, Charles Perrings, and

Tönu Puu (1994), "Discontinuous Change in Multi-level Hierarchical Systems," *Systems Research*, **11**(3), 77–94.
Ruitenbeck, H.J. (1996), "The Great Canadian Fishery Collapse: Some Policy Lessons," *Ecological Economics*, **19**(2), 103–6.
Sakai, K. (2001), *Nonlinear Dynamics and Chaos in Agricultural Systems*, Amsterdam: Elsevier.
Saphores, J. (2003), "Harvesting a Renewable Resource under Uncertainty," *Journal of Economic Dynamics and Control*, **28**(3), 509–29.
Sardanyès, Josep and Ricard V. Solé (2007), "Chaotic Stability in Spatially-revolved Host-Parasite Replicators: The *Red Queen* on a Lattice," *International Journal of Bifurcations and Chaos*, **17**(2), 589–606.
Schaefer, M.B. (1957), "Some Considerations of Population Dynamics and Economics in Relation to the Management of Marine Fisheries," *Journal of the Fisheries Research Board of Canada*, **14**(5), 669–81.
Schaffer, M.W. (1984), "Stretching and Folding in Lynx Fur Returns: Evidence for a Strange Attractor in Nature," *American Naturalist*, **124**(6), 796–820.
Scheffer, Merten (1998), *Ecology of Shallow Lakes*, London: Chapman and Hall.
Schindler, D.W. (1990), "Experimental Perturbations of Whole Lakes as Tests of Hypotheses Concerning Ecosystem Structure and Function," *Oikos*, **57**, 25–41.
Sethi, Rajiv and Eswaran Somanathan (1996), "The Evolution of Social Norms in Common Property Resource Use," *American Economic Review*, **86**(4), 766–88.
Simon, Herbert A. (1962), "The Architecture of Complexity," *Proceedings of the American Philosophical Society*, **106**(6), 467–82.
Solé, Ricard V. and Jordi Bascompte (2006), *Self-organization in Complex Ecosystems*, Princeton: Princeton University Press.
Solé, R.V. and S.C. Manrubia (1996), "Extinction and Self-organized Criticality in a Model of Large-scale Evolution," *Physical Review E*, **54**(1), R42–R45.
Swallow, S.K., P.J. Parks, and D.N. Wear (1990), "Policy-relevant Nonconvexities in the Production of Multiple Forest Benefits," *Journal of Environmental Economics and Management*, **19**(3), 264–80.
Turchin, Peter (2003), *Complex Population Dynamics: A Theoretical/Empirical Synthesis*, Princeton: Princeton University Press.
Vandermeer, J. and S. Maruca (1998), "Indirect Effects with a Keystone Predator: Coexistence and Chaos," *Theoretical Population Biology*, **54**, 38–43.
Wagener, Florian O.O. (2003), "Skiba Points and Heteroclinic Bifurcations with Applications to the Shallow Lake System," *Journal of Economic Dynamics and Control*, **27**(9), 1533–61.
Walker, Brian H., Donald Ludwig, C.S. Holling, and R.M. Peterman (1981), "Stability of Semi-arid Grazing Systems," *Journal of Ecology*, **69**(2), 473–98.
Walters, Carl J. (1986), *Adaptive Management of Renewable Resources*, New York: Macmillan.
Weitzman, Martin L. (2007), "A Review of the *Stern Review on the Economics of Climate Change*," *Journal of Economic Literature*, **45**(3), 686–702.
Wilson, J., B. Low, R. Costanza, and E. Ostrom (1999), "Scale Misperceptions and the Spatial Dynamics of a Social-Ecological System", *Ecological Economics*, **31**, 243–57.
Zimmer, C. (1999), "Life after Chaos," *Science*, **284**(5411), 83–6.
Zinkhan, F.C. (1991), "Option Pricing and Timberland's Land-use Conversion Option," *Land Economics*, **67**, 317–25.

PART VII

BROADER HISTORICAL PERSPECTIVES

15. Complexity and Austrian economics*

Roger Koppl

15.1 Introduction

Austrian economics is a school of thought within the broader complexity movement in economics. The characteristic feature of Austrian economics is often thought to be its supposed rejection of mathematics. Complexity theory, by contrast, is often equated with the mathematical tools used by complexity researchers. Thus, the intersection of Austrian economics and complexity theory might seem to be empty. There are, however, rather deep connections between complexity theory and Austrian economics. Some of the basic features of Austrian economics are also defining characteristics of complexity theory. These common features make Austrian economics a particular school of thought within the broader complexity movement in economics.

I will briefly indicate what I mean by "Austrian economics," before reviewing some of the historical connections between complexity theory and Austrian economics. I will then discuss the substantive connections and the contributions of Austrian economics to complexity economics.

15.2 What is Austrian economics?

"Austrian economics" is the school of economic thought that began with Carl Menger's 1871 classic, *Gründsätze der Volkwirtschaftsleher*, or *Principles of Economics* ([1871] 1981). Menger was an Austrian national who taught at the University of Vienna. Thus, the school of thought he founded was called the "Austrian school" of economics. Menger's book made him one of the three traditionally cited co-creators of marginal utility theory and neoclassical economics. William Stanley Jevons and Marie Esprit Léon Walras were the others. Unlike the other two founders of neoclassical economics, however, Menger did not use equations or mathematical notation.

Menger's version of marginal utility contained a detailed analysis of how "economizers" plan. Ever since, the "Austrian" economists have been very interested in how things look *from the actor's perspective*. They want to be sure that all the things their theories say about how individuals act are reasonable things to say about real people. Consider the theory that inflation is caused by a wage-price spiral. This theory implies that people do not care how much their money holdings can buy. Since people *do* care about their real cash balances, Austrians reject such "cost-push" theories of inflation. Austrians call such agent-based reasoning "subjectivism."

After World War II, members of the Austrian school stuck to their literary style and "subjectivist" principles. The rest of the profession grew ever more mathematical. It also grew more and more attached to statistical techniques, even when there was no way to connect those techniques to the actor's perspective. These developments occurred partly under the influence of the Keynesian-neoclassical synthesis. Over time, the Austrians grew so far apart from the mainstream that by about 1970 they finally began to see themselves as a separate, heterodox school.

The mathematical and statistical tools of post-war economic orthodoxy were particularly ill suited to Austrian subjectivism. The Bourbakian mathematics of Debreu (1959) and others was well suited to finding fixed points that one might interpret as equilibria. It was not well suited, however, to investigating the processes that might lead decentralized heterogeneous agents toward or away from cooperative outcomes. The dominant econometrics of the post-war period required one to sharply divide a simple and invariant "structural" model from an assumed and invariant noise term (Sutton, 2000, p. 18). Such econometric practices were not well suited to investigating the evolution of open-ended systems driven by the local decision making of heterogeneous agents. It is no wonder, then, that the Austrian school grew alienated from the mainstream of economics. Austrian theory represented markets as complex processes that produce their order from the bottom up. The methods of the mainstream, however, were suited to relatively simple top-down systems. Today, complexity theorists use mathematical and statistical tools appropriate for the sort of open-ended evolving systems described in Austrian economics. Today, therefore, the Austrians are in a position to regain their traditional position as a distinct school within the broader mainstream of economic thought (Koppl, 2006). (The methods of experimental economics are also well suited to Austrian themes and should, I believe, be pursued energetically. That topic, however, would carry us too far from the main themes of this chapter.)

Friedrich Weiser and Eugen Böhm-Bawerk were early followers of Menger. F.A. Hayek and Ludwig von Mises were their students. Mises was an important influence on Hayek and the leader of the school from about 1920 to his death in 1973. Israel Kirzner was the leader of the Austrian school until his recent retirement from New York University. The leader of the school today is Peter Boettke of George Mason University. Nobel Laureate Vernon Smith should probably be considered an adoptive member of the Austrian school. Although not originally trained in the Austrian tradition, Smith's research program led him in an increasingly

Austrian direction. He is a close follower of Hayek, whose work formed the basis of Smith's Nobel speech (2003) and recent book (2008).

15.3 Historical links between complexity theory and Austrian economics

Historically, the founder of the Austrian school, Carl Menger, had a theory of complexity that had important points of contact with modern complexity theory. Menger's theory of the evolution of money, for example, can be modeled using a characteristic tool of complexity economics, nonlinear Pólya urn processes (Klein and Selgin, 2000; Selgin, 2003). Menger explicitly sought to "reduce the complex phenomena of human economic activity to the simplest elements that can still be subjected to accurate observation" and "to investigate the manner in which more complex economic phenomena evolve from their elements according to definite principles" (Menger [1871] 1981, pp. 46–47). Citing Menger, Hayek dubbed this the "compositive method" (1952a, p. 67 n. 4. See also pp. 61–76).

In his *Problems of Economics and Sociology*, Menger (1963) expanded at length on the compositive method, particularly as applied to "organic" social phenomena. "Law, language, the state, money, markets, all these social structures," Menger argues, "are to no small extent the unintended result of social development" (p. 147). We must treat "prices of goods, interest rates, ground rents, wages and a thousand other phenomena of social life" in a way "analogous to the unintentionally created social institutions" (ibid.). In Menger's compositive method we derive complex phenomena as the unintended outcome of heterogeneous agents pursuing local ends. Order emerges bottom up as the unintended consequence of individual action. It would probably exaggerate to call Menger a complexity theorist, but we might well consider him a precursor.

Hayek, who explicitly adopted the compostive method in his own work, may have been Menger's most faithful methodological follower. Rosser (1999) calls Hayek "an early and independent developer of complexity theory in something resembling its current form, albeit without computers" (p. 186, n. 11). Rosser further reports that Hayek "had significant communication with both Ilya Prigogine and Hermann Haken, respectively the founders of the Brussels and Stuttgart schools" (p. 185, n. 11). It is rumored that Haken was responsive and engaged Hayek with some enthusiasm, whereas Prigogine seems to have found Hayek to be an entirely curious and somewhat dubious figure. Unfortunately, I do not know of any evidence to support these rumors. Bruce Caldwell (2003, especially pp. 361–9) also emphasizes the role of complexity in Hayek's thought.

Complexity theorists trace their origins in part to Ludwig von Bertalanffy's work on systems theory and to the cybernetics of Norbert Wiener. Hayek cites both Bertalanffy and Wiener. In *The Fatal Conceit* Hayek explains that he has been researching "the formation of complex structures in terms of processes transcending our capacity to observe all several circumstances operating in the determination of their particular manifestations" (1988, p. 9). He continues:

> When I began my work I felt that I was nearly alone in working on the evolutionary formation of such highly complex self-maintaining orders. Meanwhile, researches on this kind of problem – under various names, such as autopoiesis, cybernetics, homeostasis, spontaneous order, self-organisation, synergetics, systems theory, and so on – have become so numerous that I have been able to study closely no more than a few of them. (Ibid.)

Hayek had a serious knowledge of and interest in systems theory and cybernetics. He even produced a book in 1952 (Hayek, 1952b), based on his student essay of 1920, in which he described the central nervous system as a complex adaptive system. (Hayek cites Hebb's similar theory, but developed his ideas independently.) Though he did not use the phrase "complex adaptive system," Hayek often used the words "complex" and "complexity." He even wrote an essay entitled "The Theory of Complex Phenomena" (1967a). He sounds like a product of the Santa Fe Institute when he describes "[t]he 'emergence' of 'new' patterns as a result of the increase in the number of elements between which simple relations exist" (p. 26). Hayek's choice of subjects, his theoretical sources, and his very language are all surprisingly close to other strands of complexity theory, such as Santa Fe complexity.

The most characteristic feature of Hayek's system of thought is probably his notion of "spontaneous order." A spontaneous order is a complex adaptive system. It is Adam Smith's idea of the "invisible hand." Models of spontaneous orders are sometimes called "invisible-hand explanations" (Ullmann-Margalit, 1978). Hayek coined this term to describe the "grown order," the "self-generating or endogenous order" (1973, p. 37). Spontaneous orders in society are "the Results of Human Action, but not of Human Design" (1967b). The study of spontaneous orders, Hayek argued, was originally the province of economics. But biology "from its beginnings has been concerned with that special kind of spontaneous order we call an organism" (1973, p. 37). It was not until the arrival of "cybernetics [as] a special discipline" that the physical sciences came to discuss these "self-organizing or self-generating systems" (ibid.).

I think it is reasonable to say that Hayek's notion of spontaneous order is, at a minimum, similar to the complexity theorists' notion of "complex adaptive system." Hayek claims that such orders "result from their elements obeying certain rules of conduct" (1973, p. 43). Each "agent" follows a set of rules and responds to local information. The interaction of many such agents produces an overall order that was not planned by any of the agents who produced it. If the number of agents is large enough, this order may be very complex even when the rules governing each individual are quite simple. Hayek is an evolutionary theorist whose evolutionary ideas are based, in part, on a cognitive psychology similar to the sorts of things discussed at complexity conferences. As with the complex adaptive systems of the Santa Fe group, Hayek recognizes that there is "no global controller" (Arthur, Durlauf, and Lane, 1997, p. 4) of the economy or any other complex adaptive system.

I argue below that Hayek's theory of complexity is also closely related to the algorithmic complexity theory of Kolmogorov, Solomonoff, and Chaitin, which, though related to other branches of complexity theory, including Santa Fe complexity, represents a distinct complexity tradition that is currently undervalued in economics.

While the historical connections between Austrian economics and complexity theory are interesting and important, the substantive links are more important.

15.4 Substantive links between complexity theory and Austrian economics

The substantive links between Austrian economics and the rest of the complexity movement come mostly in the form of five characteristics shared by complexity economics and modern Austrian economics, namely, bounded rationality, rule following, institutions, cognition, and evolution. When listed in this order, they suggest the acronym BRICE. It is true that, with some exceptions (for example, Koppl and Rosser, 2002 and Mulligan, 2004), Austrian economists do not use the mathematical tools characteristic of modern complexity theory. Although I believe Austrian economists would do well to use such tools more often, I do not believe method worship produces truth. The defining characteristics of BRICE economics are descriptive of complexity theory, but they do not require any particular mathematical tools or exclude so-called literary economics. As I have hinted above, modern Austrian economics shares with another branch of complexity theory, algorithmic complexity theory, an important characteristic sometimes neglected in the rest of complexity economics, namely, computability. Markose (2005) notes that Hayek "was one of the first economists who explicitly espoused the Gödelian formalist incompleteness and impossibility limits on calculation," whereas most other economists have paid "scant attention" to "the epochal non-computability issues" first raised by Gödel (1967). In both "computable economics" (Velupillai, 2005) and Austrian economics, such issues are taken seriously.

The B in BRICE stands for *bounded rationality*. Both Austrian economists and complexity economists tend to assume that people have only "bounded rationality." (For a leading example see Sargent, 1993.) The term was coined by Herbert Simon, who is probably viewed by most observers as the one great pioneers of bounded rationality in economics. And he was indeed a great pioneer. Austrians, however, recognize that both von Mises and Hayek assumed bounded rationality and derived many consequences from it, especially in the debate over socialist calculation. Adam Smith assumed bounded rationality as well. Indeed, the assumption of unbounded rationality is a peculiarity of certain strands of neoclassical economics, namely, the strands that entered the "neoclassical synthesis" of post-war Anglo-American economics. Today, the great majority of economists agree that agents should be modeled as having, in some sense, only "bounded rationality."

Hayek's *The Sensory Order* (1952b) includes a theory of bounded rationality. In Hayek's theory, the bounds to human rationality have a logical and meta-mathematical dimension, and are not merely a contingent empirical fact about limited powers of cognition. The mind would have to be more complex than itself to fully explain itself to itself (ibid., pp. 186–90). As Hayek notes, this is a Gödelian and Cantorian point (Hayek, 1967a, p. 61, n. 49).

Recently, a literature on "computable economics" has emerged in which it is shown that many results of standard theory depend on the implicit assumption that agents can rapidly compute functions that cannot be computed at all by the mathematicians' ideal type of a computer, a universal Turing machine (Velupillai, 2005). Hayek anticipated computable economics, as Markose seems to recognize when she correctly notes that Hayek "was one of the first economists who explicitly espoused the Gödelian formalist incompleteness and impossibility limits on calculation which he referred to as the limits of constructivist reason" (Markose, 2005, p. F165). Barkley Rosser and I have attempted to relate this sort of reasoning to arguments made by Morgenstern, Hayek, and Keynes (Koppl and Rosser, 2002). Koppl (2008) uses a review of Velupillai (2005) as a vehicle to survey the mathematical tools of this branch of complexity economics.

The R in BRICE stands for *rule following*. Both Austrian economists and complexity economists tend to model people as rule followers. (For a leading example, see Arthur, 1994.) Hayek viewed action as rule following, saying, "Man is as much a rule-following animal as a purpose-seeking one" (Hayek, 1973, p. 11). One of the central difficulties of implementing a rule-following framework is squaring it with the economic principle that individuals tend to seek out their interests cunningly. I have argued that rule following can be defined "objectively" with the aid of information theory, in particular the concept of mutual information (Koppl, 2002a). Sensitive to computability issues, Austrians generally prefer simple rules to discretion. This is why classical liberals favor the "rule of law." I address this issue in Koppl (2002b).

The I in BRICE stands for *institutions*. Both Austrian economists and complexity economists compare economic performance under alternative institutions. (For a leading example see Howitt and Clower, 2000.) While it is commonplace to seek microfoundations for macroeconomics, the complexity economist David Colander (1996) has emphasized the importance of macroeconomic foundations of microeconomics. Colander thereby points to the importance of institutions for shaping microeconomic behavior.

From the beginning, Austrian economists recognized that institutions matter and included close institutional analysis in their work. Carl Menger's theory of the evolution of money is the standard example of an Austrian theory of institutions. Menger, by the way, traces the theory back through Mill and Smith to John Law ([1705] 1966). The importance of institutional analysis in the Austrian theory led von Mises and Hayek to a position in the socialist calculation debate quite different from that of scholars who adopted a more narrowly Walrasian framework of analysis. And Austrians have always understood the importance of institutional details. Hayek, for example, objected to the legal rules allowing one corporation to own another. Because a large minority shareholder may exercise effective control over a corporation, this legal rule permits a kind of telescoping action that puts power in the hands of a managerial elite, which comes to acquire a high degree of autonomy (Hayek, 1967b). Unfortunately, this important argument has not been taken up by others or updated in the light of the literature on the market for corporate control.

The C in BRICE stands for *cognition*. Both Austrian economists and complexity economists pay close attention to cognition. (For a leading example, see Arthur et al., 1997.) Once the assumption of bounded rationality is introduced, it is hard to avoid entering into cognitive psychology. Complexity economists take cognitive psychology seriously. Like floodwaters, the level of interest in cognitive psychology is high and rising. Hayek's *The Sensory Order* is a still-neglected source that should be of special interest to complexity economists (1952b). His theory of complexity is rooted in the theory of mind articulated in the book. In the final "philosophical" chapter of that work, Hayek uses his theory of mind to spin out a defense of "*verstehende* psychology." Hayek's vocabulary points directly to the "understanding" tradition of Max Weber and others. His reasoning is directly based on the sort of Gödelian and Cantorian considerations characteristic of algorithmic complexity theory. Thus, we have in Hayek an interesting attempt to base "humanistic" social science on the "scientific" foundations of complexity theory and the theory of mind.

Today, Austrian economists tend to defend the use of "*verstehende* psychology" in the social sciences (Koppl and Whitman, 2004). An understanding of understanding is salient among all that the Austrian school has to offer in exchange with the rest of complexity economics. A distinguishing feature of Austrian economics is precisely that it brings the *Verstehen* tradition of Wilhelm Dilthey, Max Weber, Ludwig von Mises, and Alfred Schutz into contact with the concepts and mathematical tools of complexity theory. This unusual combination of "humanistic" and "scientific" methods derives directly from Hayek's theory of complexity. It may be worth noting that the *Verstehen* tradition is also related to the biological concept of a "theory of mind module." (See Appendix 1 of Koppl, 2002b.) I discuss *Verstehen* at greater length below.

Hayek's view of cognition is strikingly similar to views expressed by two important complexity theorists, namely John Holland and Stuart Kauffman. For Kauffman, "adaptive systems" make piecemeal adjustments to their environments. To do so successfully, they must respond to their environments; they must engage in "computation and adaptation" (1993, p. 232). Adaptive systems must "*interact* with and internally *represent* other entities of their environment" (ibid., emphasis in original):

> In other words, complex living systems must "know" their worlds. Whether we consider E. coli swimming upstream in a glucose gradient, a tree manufacturing a toxin against a herbivore insect, or a hawk diving to catch a chick, organisms sense, classify, and act upon their worlds. In a phrase, organisms have internal models of their worlds which compress information and allow action. (Ibid.)

This view of cognition as classification is close to that of Hayek and might be identical. Like Hayek, Kauffman finds the classification in the response patterns of the organism. In the case of E. coli, for example, Kauffman says, "I permit myself the word 'classified' because we may imagine that the bacterium responds more or less identically to any ligand binding the receptor, be it glucose or some other molecule" (p. 233).

Holland (1992) too, uses the example of bacteria. A "bacterium moves in the direction of a chemical gradient, implicitly predicting that food lies in that direction" (p. 197). He also uses Hebb's connectionist model to describe the central nervous system (pp. 58–65). Hebb's model is very close to that of Hayek, as Hayek himself noted. Like Hayek, Holland notes that the operations of the central nervous system are too complex to be captured in a simple stimulus-response framework.

The E in BRICE stands for *evolution*. Both Austrian economists and complexity economists construct models of economic evolution. (For a leading example, see Epstein and Axtell, 1996.) One of the standard defenses of rational maximizing, Milton Friedman's essay on positive economics, relies on evolution (Friedman, 1953). The solution of the maximization model, Friedman says, describes what the agent must do if it is to survive market competition. This defense is widely recognized to have merit. But it leaves unexamined the evolutionary mechanisms at work in economic life (Nelson and Winter, 1982, pp. 139–41; Langlois, 1986, pp. 241–7). Besides, although evolution sometimes approximates an optimal solution, it does not always do so. The Austrian school is notable for its evolutionary theory of institutions, which I have already mentioned. The engine of change in an Austrian theory of evolving institutions is, of course, the Kirznerian entrepreneur (Kirzner, 1973).

15.5 Austrian contributions to the complexity tradition

It is clear, I think, the broader complexity movement has much to offer Austrian economists. I have argued this point before Austrian audiences in the past (Koppl, 2006). The Austrian school also has many contributions to make to the broader complexity tradition. For example, it provides a useful reinterpretation of pre-war marginalism as complexity economics (Koppl, 2000) and it brings to the complexity movement a long tradition of policy analysis based on complexity themes. It has two further contributions to make that I will comment on at some length. It offers a better picture of the limits of economic analysis and it connects complexity economics to the *Verstehen* tradition.

15.5.1 The limits of economic analysis

Following Hayek, Austrian complexity theorists are sensitive to the limits of economic analysis. Complexity matters, in part, because it imposes limits on our knowledge. "It is high time," Hayek argued, "that we take our ignorance more seriously" (1967a, p. 39). Economists have taken complexity seriously and the profession has changed as a result. If economists were to take our ignorance seriously, too, it would effect further salutary changes in economic theory, modeling techniques, and policy recommendations. "It would represent great progress indeed," Bruce Caldwell argues, "if some leading members of the profession would emphasize the limitations of economic science in their statements to the public and, perhaps more important, in their recommendations concerning pedagogy" (2003, p. 401).

The humble attitude of Hayek and other Austrian economists contrasts with the ambitions of at least some other complexity theorists. John Holland (1992), for example, expresses optimism about what computer simulations can do. "It should be possible," he says, "to take a first step toward a general theory of complex adaptive systems by formalizing a framework based on" the mechanisms of parallelism, competition, and recombination (pp. 197–8). Next, he believes, we can "incorporate a mathematics that emphasizes process over end points" (p. 198). This second step would bring us close to Holland's ultimate goal. "At that point," he explains, "the incipient theory should begin to provide the guidelines that make the computer-based experiments more than uncoordinated forays into an endlessly complex domain. Once we get that far, we come at last to a rational discipline of complex adaptive systems providing genuine predictions" (ibid.). In his semi-popular work *Hidden Order*, Holland makes the policy thrust of his predictive ambitions more explicit. The right "amalgam" of mathematical models and computer programs "offers hope for a unified approach to the difficult problems of complex adaptive systems that stretch our resources and place our world in jeopardy" (1995, p. 172).

In Hayek's theory of complexity, predictions of the sort Holland desires are out of reach. When dealing with complex phenomena, we are in a position to generate "pattern predictions," telling us that "in certain general conditions a pattern of a certain kind will appear" (1967a, p. 24). We are not generally in a position to make highly specific predictions, even when we have detailed knowledge of initial conditions.

Hayek seems to have viewed this result as "practical" and not "theoretical" (1967a, p. 34). He felt he had a general proof only for the proposition that "the conception of the mind fully explaining itself involves a logical contradiction" (p. 34), but not for the more general claims about complex adaptive systems in general. Since Hayek wrote, however, computable economics has provided theoretical foundations for his "practical" conclusion. The best book-length introduction to computable economics is Velupillai (2005). Velupillai seems to have coined the phrase "computable economics." He is the founder and most important contributor to this branch of complexity economics. In Koppl (2008) I have attempted to provide an introductory survey of computable economics that does not presume familiarity with this field's characteristic mathematical tools of computability, constructivity, and algorithmic information theory.

Computable economics has started to make economists aware of just how pervasive non-computability is. It is surprising to learn just how little we can figure out about the mathematical world even of classical analysis. The mathematicians da Costa and Doria (2005) favorably cite "Wolfram's conjecture" that "undecidability exists everywhere, even in trivial physical theories" (p. 18). They show that even finite games can be undecidable. This almost bizarre result merits attention.

In one sense any finite game is trivially decidable. If we have a finite number of players, each of whom has a finite number of strategies, then we can list every strategy combination and its corresponding pay-off vector. We can simply run down this finite list and see which entries, if any, are Nash equilibria. Citing Prasad (1991) and quoting Tsuji, da Costa, and

Doria, 1998, da Costa and Doria say "by brute force comparison we end up with the desired equilibria" (2005, p. 36). So far so good. But this result, they point out, assumes we have a complete list of all strategies and pay-offs "without the mediation of any formal language" (ibid.). Often, however, we have no such list available to us. Instead we describe strategies and pay-offs obliquely through formal language. Again quoting Tsuji, da Costa, and Doria, 1998, they offer the following deep and important remark: "Formalized theories are about strings of symbols that purport to represent our intuitions about concrete objects" (p. 36). Thus, finite games that seem so trivially decidable can be described with "complicated expressions, which may be the case when we are dealing with a 'model' . . . of some market" (p. 37), and for some games so described, it is not possible to compute the Nash equilibria (ibid.).

The algorithmic information theory of Kolmogorov, Chaitin, and Solomonoff strengthens the point. The "common insight" of Kolmogorov, Solomonoff, and Chaitin, McCall (2005) tells us, "was that complexity can be measured by algorithmic information content, which is the size of the shortest algorithm generating the number of objects being studied. A sequence of numbers is random if it is not subject to any algorithmic compression" (p. 113). This definition makes randomness every bit as ubiquitous as undecidability.

Under such notions of randomness, "uncertainty resides in mathematics," including number theory. In particular, Chaitin produced the strange result that "most integers are random" (p. 114). Does God play dice with the universe? Nothing and everything is random to God because he can decide everything without resort to algorithmic compression, but all possible worlds are deeply random for the finite creatures living in them (if such there be) because they will be able to compress only a small part of the data of their world.

To intervene successfully in a complex adaptive system we must be able to predict to the behavior of the system in the wake of alternative possible interventions. To make such predictions, we would have to compress the data generated by such a system. Algorithmic information theory helps us to see just how little data we can compress and how little, therefore, we can predict about the behavior of complex adaptive systems under alternative policy interventions.

As Wolpert (1996) has shown, even when some desired information about a system is perfectly computable, our "prediction" may come too late. If the system we are trying to predict has about as much computational prowess as the computer we are programming, it may be impossible to generate our predictions ahead of time. See Koppl and Rosser (2002, pp. 354–8) for a discussion.

Computable economics may be bringing us formal foundations for Hayek's "practical" recognition of the limits of prediction in economics. These limits do not say "You can't predict!" They do, however, limit our predictions, for the most part, to Hayekian "pattern prediction." Vernon Smith notes that the hub-and-spoke system brought on by airline deregulation was not predicted (2003, p. 472). It was not hard to predict that airline deregulation would produce the general patterned result of increased efficiency and lower ticket prices, but even so general a pattern as the hub-and-spoke system proved too specific to predict.

Austrian economists are accustomed to warn against "market interventions" on the grounds that their consequences are hard to predict. We are less accustomed to issuing equally cogent warnings, however, about the dangers of deregulation. Vernon Smith once again provides a salient example, namely, deregulation in the wholesale electric energy market. Deregulation, Smith explains, is "effected as a planned transition with numerous political compromises." The political compromises may contain hidden dangers. "In California," he explains, political compromise "took the form of deregulating wholesale markets and prices while continuing to regulate retail prices at fixed hourly rates over the daily and seasonal cycles in consumption" (ibid.). The disastrous result was the California energy crisis of 2000 and 2001. "Deregulation" is not necessarily good, even when "regulation" is bad. Our epistemic limits imply the need for caution and humility.

Humility, caution, and moderation in the pursuit of liberty are an integral part of the liberal political tradition claimed by most Austrian economists. In *Liberalism: In the Classical Tradition*, Ludwig von Mises traces the origins of liberalism as a well-formed system of ideas to David Hume, Adam Smith, and Jeremy Bentham (1985, p. 194). In his *The History of England*, Hume clearly expresses an aversion to violent political changes of all sorts, saying at one point, "a regard to liberty, though a laudable passion, ought commonly to be subordinate to a reverence for established government" (1983, vol. VI, p. 533). Humean status quo bias warns us against incautious or precipitate deregulation of markets. Such caution should be viewed as an implication of Austrian epistemic arguments perfectly parallel to Austrian warnings about the dangers of regulation and control.

15.5.2 Complexity and the Verstehen *tradition*

The same arguments that led Hayek, in *The Sensory Order*, to the notion of pattern prediction led him to defend "*verstehende* psychology" (1952b, p. 192). Hayek was defending, in other words, the "understanding" tradition of Wilhelm Dilthey and Max Weber. This is the tradition of "hermeneutics," which Dilthey defined as "the methodology of the interpretation of written records" (Dilthey, 1976, p. 249). Following Hans Albert (1985), Koppl and Whitman (2004) carefully distinguish the "classical hermeneutics" defended by Hayek from the "universal hermeneutics" of Martin Heidegger and his followers. I share the perplexity of many economists with the strange and oracular pronouncements of universal hermeneutics, such as, "the movement of human existence . . . issue[s] in a relentless inner tension between illumination and concealment" and "interpretation is always on the way" (Gadamer, 1981, pp. 104 and 105). The "*verstehende* psychology" Hayek defended, however, is merely the straightforward recognition that we cannot describe human action without reference to human meanings.

The point may be expressed in the language of algorithmic information theory. Because other humans are about as complex as we are, we cannot so greatly compress the data describing them as to dispense with the use of words and concepts such as "intention," "motive," "love," and "hate." We cannot "reduce" human action to physics because human action is too complex for that. In principle, perhaps, emergent mental phenomena are "merely" physical processes obedient to known laws of physics. Any attempt to describe human action in purely physical terms, however, will not capture all the information embodied in "humanistic" descriptions that use words referring to mental processes. "The conclusion to which our theory leads us," Hayek explains, "is thus that to us not only mind as a whole but also all individual mental processes must forever remain phenomena of a special kind which, although produced by the same principles which we know to operate in the physical world, we shall never be able to fully explain in terms of physical laws" (1952b, p. 191).

Hayek's defense of classical hermeneutics matters because it opens communication between "humanistic" and "scientific" approaches to the study of human action. Clearly, if humanistic tools and arguments are viewed as substitutes for scientific analysis, we must neglect them and stick with science. But if they are complements, then we may hope to find room in science for the insights generated by humanistic approaches to the study of society. Fritz Machlup (1952) may be the leading example of a "scientific" economist who nevertheless used "humanistic" methods and arguments when appropriate. The theory of economic expectations is but one area in which it seems reasonable to hope for insights from social science in the "understanding" tradition (Koppl, 2002b).

15.6 Summary

The Austrian school of economics is a distinct school of thought within the broader complexity movement in economics. Austrians share several characteristic features with other complexity economists as reflected in the acronym BRICE. They assume their agents have *bounded rationality* and engage in *rule following*. They have a theory with *institutions* and a theory of institutions. Their research is informed by considerations of *cognition*. Finally, they produce theories and models of economic *evolution*. Although Austrians often express themselves without the aid of mathematics, they have important contributions to make to the larger complexity tradition, including a clear recognition of the limits of economic analysis and the integration of "humanistic" and "scientific" economics.

Note

* This chapter borrows shamelessly from Koppl (2000, 2006, and 2008).

References

Albert, Hans (1985), *Treatise on Critical Reason*, Princeton: Princeton University Press.

Arthur, Brian (1994), "Inductive Reasoning and Bounded Rationality," *American Economic Review*, **84**(2), 406–11.

Arthur, W. Brian, Steven N. Durlauf, and David A. Lane (1997), "Introduction," in *The Economy as an Evolving Complex System II*, Reading, MA: Addison-Wesley.

Arthur, W. Brian, John H. Holland, Blake LeBaron, Richard Palmer, and Paul Taylor (1997), "Asset Pricing Under Endogenous Expectations in an Artificial Stock Market," in Arthur, W. Brian, Steven N. Durlauf, and David A. Lane (eds), *The Economy as an Evolving Complex System II*, Reading, MA: Addison-Wesley.

Caldwell, Bruce (2003), *Hayek's Challenge: An Intellectual Biography of F.A. Hayek*, Chicago: The University of Chicago Press.

Colander, David (1996), "The Macrofoundations of Micro," in Colander David (ed.), *Beyond Microfoundations: Post Walrasian Macroeconomics*, Cambridge, MA: Cambridge University Press, pp. 57–68.

da Costa, N.C.A. and F.A. Doria (2005), "Computing the Future," in Velupillai, Vela (ed.), *Computability, Complexity and Constructivity in Economic Analysis*, Oxford: Blackwell.

Debreu, Gérard (1959), *Theory of Value*, New Haven and London: Yale University Press.

Dilthey, W. (1976), "The development of hermeneutics," in Rickman, H.P. (ed.), *W. Dilthey: Selected Writings*, Cambridge, UK: Cambridge University Press, pp. 246–63.

Epstein, Joshua M. and Robert L. Axtell (1996), *Growing Artificial Societies from the Bottom Up*, Washington, DC: Brookings Institute Press.

Friedman, Milton (1953), "The Methodology of Positive Economics," in *Essays in Positive Economics*, Chicago: The University of Chicago Press.

Gadamer, Hans-Georg (1981), *Reason in the Age of Science*, translated by F.G. Lawrence, Cambridge, MA: The MIT Press.

Gödel, Kurt (1967), "On Formally Undecidable Propositions of *Principia Mathematica* and Related Systems I," in Heijenoort, Jean van (ed.), *From Frege to Gödel: A Source Book in Mathematical Logic, 1879–1931*, Cambridge, MA: Harvard University Press.

Hayek, F.A. von (1952a), *The Counter Revolution of Science: Studies in the Abuse of Reason*, Chicago: University of Chicago Press.

Hayek, F.A. von (1952b), *The Sensory Order*, Chicago: University of Chicago Press.

Hayek, F.A. von (1967a), "The Theory of Complex Phenomena," in *Studies in Philosophy, Politics and Economics*, Chicago: University of Chicago Press.

Hayek, F.A. von (1967b), "Rules, Perception and Intelligibility," in *Studies in Philosophy, Politics and Economics*, Chicago: University of Chicago Press.

Hayek, F.A. von (1973), *Law, Legislation and Liberty, Volume I: Rules and Order*, Chicago: University of Chicago Press.

Hayek, F.A. von (1988), *The Fatal Conceit: The Errors of Socialism*, Chicago: The University of Chicago Press.
Holland, John H. (1992), *Adaptation in Natural and Artificial Systems: An Introductory Analysis with Applications to Biology, Control, and Artificial Intelligence*, Cambridge, MA: The MIT Press.
Holland, John (1995), *Hidden Order: How Adaptation Builds Complexity*, Reading, MA: Addison-Wesley Publishing Company, Inc.
Howitt, Peter and Robert Clower (2000), "The Emergence of Economic Organization," *Journal of Economic Behavior and Organization*, **41**(1), 55–84.
Hume, David (1983), *The History of England from the Invasion of Julius Caesar to the Revolution in 1688*, Indianapolis, IN: Liberty Fund.
Kauffman, Stuart A. (1993), *The Origins of Order: Self-organization and Selection in Evolution*, New York and Oxford: Oxford University Press.
Kirzner, I.M. (1973), *Competition and Entrepreneurship*, Chicago: The University of Chicago Press.
Klein, Peter and George Selgin (2000), "Menger's Theory of Money: Some Experimental Evidence," in John Smithin (ed.), *What is Money?*, London and New York: Routledge, pp. 217–34.
Koppl, Roger (2000), "Teaching Complexity: An Austrian Approach," in Colander, David (ed.), *The Complexity Vision and the Teaching of Economics*, Cheltenham, UK and Northampton, MA, USA: Edward Elgar.
Koppl, Roger (2002a), "Custom and Rules: Comments on Ekkehart Schlicht's on Custom in the Economy," *American Journal of Economics and Sociology*, **61**(2), 531–7.
Koppl, Roger (2002b), *Big Players and the Economic Theory of Expectations*, London and New York: Palgrave Macmillan.
Koppl, Roger (2006), "Austrian Economics at the Cutting Edge," *Review of Austrian Economics*, **19**(4), 231–41.
Koppl, Roger (2008), "Thinking Impossible Things: A Review Essay," *Journal of Economic Behavior and Organization*, **66**, 837–47.
Koppl, Roger and Rosser, J. Barkley Jr. (2002), "All That I Have to Say Has Already Crossed Your Mind," *Metroeconomica*, **53**(4), 339–60.
Koppl, Roger and Douglas Glen Whitman (2004), "Rational-choice Hermeneutics," *Journal of Economic Behavior and Organization*, **55**(3), 295–317.
Langlois, Richard N. (1986), "Rationality, Institutions, and Explanation," in Langlois (ed.), *Economics as a Process: Essays in the New Institutional Economics*, Chicago: The University of Chicago Press.
Law, John [1705] (1966), *Money and Trade Considered, With a Proposal For Supplying The Nation With Money*, New York: Augustus M. Kelley Publishers.
Machlup, Fritz (1952), *The Economics of Sellers' Competition: Model Analysis of Sellers' Conduct*, Baltimore: The Johns Hopkins Press.
Markose, Sheri M. (2005), "Computability and Evolutionary Complexity: Markets as Complex Adaptive Systems (CAS)," *The Economic Journal*, **115**(504), F159–F192.
McCall, John J. (2005), "Induction: Algorithmic and Exchangeable Aspects," in Velupillai, Vela (ed.), *Computability, Complexity and Constructivity in Economic Analysis*, Oxford: Blackwell.
Menger, Carl (1963), *Problems of Economics and Sociology*, translated by Francis J. Nock, edited by Louis Scheider, Urbana, Illinois: University of Illinois Press.
Menger, Carl [1871] (1981), *Principles of Economics*, translated by James Dingwell and Bert F. Hoselitz, New York: New York Universtiy Press.
Mulligan, Robert F. (2004), "Fractal Analysis of Highly Volatile Markets: An Application to Technology Equities," *Quarterly Review of Economics and Finance*, **44**(1), 155–79.
Nelson, Richard R. and Sidney G. Winter (1982), *An Evolutionary Theory of Economic Change*, Cambridge, MA: Harvard University Press.
Prasad, K. (1991), "Computability and Randomness of Nash Equilibria in Infinite Games," *Journal of Mathematical Economics*, **20**(5), 429–42.

Rosser, J. Barkley Jr. (1999), "On the Complexities of Complex Economic Dynamics," *Journal of Economic Perspectives*, **13**(4), 169–92.
Sargent, Thomas J. (1993), *Bounded Rationality in Macroeconomics*, Oxford: Oxford University Press.
Selgin, George (2003), "Adaptive Learning and the Transition to Fiat Money," *Economic Journal*, **113**(484), 147–65.
Smith, Vernon (2003), "Constructivist and Ecological Rationality in Economics," *American Economic Review*, **93**(3), 465–508.
Smith, Vernon (2008), *Rationality in Economics: Constructivist and Ecological Forms*, Cambridge, UK and elswhere: Cambridge University Press.
Sutton, John (2000), *Marshall's Tendencies: What Can Economists Know?*, Cambridge, MA: MIT Press.
Tsuji, M., N.C.A. da Costa and F.A. Doria (1998), "The Incompleteness of Theories of Games," *Journal of Philosophical Logic*, **27**(6), 553–68.
Ullmann-Margalit, Edna (1978), "Invisible Hand Explanations," *Synthèse*, **39**(2), 263–91.
Velupillai, Vela (ed.) (2005), *Computability, Complexity and Constructivity in Economic Analysis*, Oxford: Blackwell.
von Mises, Ludwig (1985), *Liberalism: In the Classical Tradition*, Irvington-on-Hudson, NY: Foundation for Economic Education, Inc.
Wolpert, David H. (1996), "An Incompleteness Theorem for Calculating the Future," *Santa Fe Institute Working Paper* No. 96-03-008.

16. Complexity and the history of economic thought*

David Colander

16.1 Introduction

The history of thought is a set of patterns that we superimpose on the development of ideas and theories from our current perspective. History is much like a magic eye picture: change one's perspective and one changes what seems important in history. Thus, our account of the history of economics tells us about ourselves and our current views, as well as about what previously transpired.

Since all patterns do not fit equally well, the pattern view of history does not mean that anything goes; some histories fit the pattern of events better than others. But, inevitably, fitting the pieces of an historical pattern together into a composite whole requires forceful and fast writing on the part of the author, and some gullibility on the part of the reader. What this means is that there will often be three or four lenses that can reasonably be used to look at the history of economics to convey quite different patterns. That is certainly the case for economics.

Most histories of economic thought, mine included (Landreth and Colander, 2002) are written from the perspective of developments in general equilibrium theory being the pinnacle of development. This chapter takes a different tack, thus providing an example of this pattern view of history; it considers the history of economic thought from a different perspective than do most contemporary histories of economic thought. Specifically it highlights the contribution of various economists and schools of thought as seen from a complexity view of economics.

I begin by explaining what I mean by a complexity view of economics, and how it differs from what might be called the simplicity view of economics. Then, I discuss the pattern way of looking at history, briefly summarizing the story told in the standard history of thought texts. Having done that I sketch out, in broad outlines, some of the changes that I believe occur in the history of economic thought when one's underlying vision of economics changes from a "structural simplicity" vision to a "complexity" vision.[1] In doing so it briefly considers whether major economists' ratings would rise or fall as our perspective changes. It also briefly discusses two economists who generally do not show up prominently in current history of thought texts, but who would show up prominently in one written from a complexity vision.

16.2 Alternative visions of economics

All economists know the economy is complex—very complex. That is one of the reasons why society needs economists—to try to make that complexity somewhat simpler and more understandable. In that endeavor conventional economics has seen itself as a conventional science; it takes complexity and simplifies it by finding a formal structural analytic model—an equation, or set of equations—that fits the data. The model is then tested by comparing the predictions of the model with the empirical data, using formal statistical techniques. These models are generally linear and static, since they are only ones with unique, deterministic solutions. To test the models classical statistical tests are generally used.

To believe that such a model exists before it has been discovered and tested requires a leap of faith; science, at the edge, is necessarily a combination of art and religion. It requires dedicated researchers who are operating on faith until sufficient empirical verification can be achieved so that we will tentatively accept that our understanding embodied in the model has gone beyond faith, and become what we call fact. In many areas, that faith has been borne out; conventional science has numerous successes. In other areas it has been less successful.

Formal models do not develop from a void. The beginnings of science in all areas involve developing informal insights into how some aspect of reality operates. Scientists then begin work on simplifying those informal insights into formal models. All science works on such simplification: the questions in such a simplification process are how to simplify, and whether the simplifications lose important elements of the informal knowledge; they are not about whether to attempt to simplify.

Since formal analytic models compress the data more efficiently than informal models, formal models are preferable as long as they do not lose insights of the informal models that led to them, and which allowed a broader set of explanatory variables and more of a sense of the importance of faith. In most areas where individuals think science has been successful, there has been a general belief that the formal models do not lose insights of the informal model. Where that belief is not generally shared, there is more debate about how successful science has been.

16.3 Complexity: Extending the boundaries of science

The conventional view of science has been that if one decides that formal structural models lose more insights than they gain, one has decided that science is not relevant to that area. For example, we have no science of love; we rely on our informal understanding. Recently, however, a group of scientists, whom I call complexity scientists, have questioned whether that conventional structural simplification process is the best way of understanding highly complex phenomena. They have suggested that such phenomena might best be approached from an alternative perspective. In doing so they have added a new way in which science might approach complex phenomena.

A number of points should be emphasized about this complexity approach to science. First, those following it are committed to science; they accept structural simplicity whenever it can be achieved. But they argue that there are areas—highly complex phenomena—where structural simplicity cannot be achieved, but where science may nonetheless have something to say.

Second, complexity scientists accept that the purpose of science is simplification. Where they differ from standard scientists is not in the desire for simplification, but in the proposed simplification process. They suggest that for complex systems, a simplification process centered around iterative processes, not structure, may be best. This new approach has come to be called the complexity approach to science. Let me give an example. Say you are trying to understand how ice forms. In conventional science one looks for laws that govern the formation of ice, and, in principle, finds a structural relationship explaining why a molecule changes from a liquid to a solid state. One then expands the analysis from the molecule to the whole. In complexity science, one looks for simple iterative processes that, under certain circumstances, lead to a large-scale transformation of water from a liquid state to a solid state.

A leap of faith that complexity scientists make is that they assume that all complex phenomena are subject to similar forces—that, as complexity increases, transformations take place in which large numbers of interactions all work simultaneously to form a pattern that would otherwise be unpredictable. What should be chaos is actually an ordered pattern. Thus, they study the general development of these patterns, and then apply the results of that general study to specific cases.

The study of complexity is highly mathematical and statistical. Where it differs from what I call conventional science is in the nature of the mathematics and statistics it uses. Instead of trying to find a formal analytical model, with a formal solution for these complex phenomena, complexity theory looks for patterns that develop when nonlinear processes are repeated for long periods of time. The mathematics used is nonlinear dynamics, and the models generally are open models with no unique deterministic solution. Many solutions are possible; which one is arrived at depends upon initial conditions and the path the model follows. What complexity scientists have shown is that, given certain dynamic relationships, certain patterns can develop, and that sudden changes in these patterns can occur.

The laws of complexity science are statistical probabilistic laws. They refer to large groups of actors and are not reducible to laws of individual actors. Complexity allows that aspects of reality can emerge from chance and the law of large numbers. Even though the individual components of a complex system are chaotic and indeterministic, and the movement of individuals within the body may appear random, the sum of the parts—the whole—can be deterministic. This structural determinism undermines the development of a deductive microfoundation of the aggregate. It means that composites of elements of smaller components are indecomposible, and must be treated as a separate entity and not as the sum of their parts. As complex systems evolve, new patterns can emerge, and these patterns can take on an existence and life of their own.

The complexity approach to science is highly controversial. Some (see especially Horgan, 1996) argue that it is ill-defined, and far too grandiose; it is attempting to be a science of everything. These critics object to its attempt to extend the boundaries of science. Others argue that complexity science offers little new, that it is non-empirical, and simply speculative. My view of these criticisms can be understood by classifying all phenomena into three types: (1) those areas for which most people believe that standard science sheds insight, (2) those areas where there is debate about how much insight standard science provides, and (3) those areas where standard science does not tread.

In category (1), where structural simplification has been shown to be useful, such as particle physics or chemistry, for me, there is no debate; these are the realms of standard science. In category (2), within which I classify economics and other social sciences, there is much less scientific agreement about the gains we have achieved from structural simplification; in these fields complexity is challenging the standard approaches to these fields, and the debate is about which simplification process is preferable. Since standard science and scientific methods are being used, complexity science is simply an alternative approach. The critics of complexity science have had little to say about its use in these areas, because, to say anything useful, one would have to compare the success of the complexity approach with the standard approach.

The broad criticism of the complexity approach, such as Horgan's, deals primarily with the third category—the category in which complexity theory is used to analyze areas that conventional science does not touch. Some of the extensive claims that have been made for complexity science—that it will add insight into these areas—have been overdone and are too far-reaching; the critics are probably right for these areas. Complexity science is a long way from unlocking the essence of the development of life. But such criticisms are not relevant for the application of complexity to economics since they do not, in any way, undermine the possibility that complexity science can be useful in analyzing the second category, where economics is found.

I have no definitive view on whether what is currently known as the complexity approach is going to succeed or not. I am drawn to it nonetheless because of my belief that, in economics, we have been unsuccessful in following a standard structural simplification approach. To achieve our current structural models we are assuming away too many important aspects of our complex economy. Whether the new work in complexity will eventually improve our knowledge of physical phenomena and the economy remains to be seen, but the vision that underlies the complexity approach seems strong. Regardless of whether it is successful or not, complexity provides a general framework within which to think about complex systems that is quite different than the conventional approach and is worth considering.

16.4 Complexity science and economics

The history of economics has been a history of methodological fights—the famous *Methodenstreit* (fight about method) is one well-known example. One of the major reasons for these fights is that it is not clear where economics fits in as a science; usually on one side of the methodological fight have been those who are arguing that the simplifications being used do not do justice to the field, and on the other side is a group who argue that simplification is absolutely necessary, even if bought at the cost of assumptions that do not fit reality. This fight has often been portrayed as a mathematical approach versus a non-mathematical historical/institutional approach, and that division has been a dividing line between mainstream and heterodox approaches. Complexity changes that; it is highly mathematical, and, as I stated above, accepts the need for simplification. But it argues that the mathematics needed to simplify economics often involves nonlinear dynamic models that have no deterministic solution.

In earlier time periods, such a statement would be equivalent to saying that there is no feasible mathematical approach to dealing with economics, but recently that has changed. Developments in computers have made it possible to deal with models that are far more complicated than previously could be dealt with. One can simulate, and, through rote computer power, gain insight into models with no analytic solution. Thus, computers and simulations are the foundation of the complexity approach.

The use of computers and simulations to gain insight into problems involves an enormous technological change in the way economists do economics. Complexity advocates take the position that such a change is a natural shift to new technology. For them those who are not moving toward solving models with computers are demonstrating Luddite tendencies in an attempt to protect their rents. Thus, complexity advocates find themselves on both sides of the fence in the standard methodological debates; they are agreeing with critics that standard science is lacking, but they favor moving to a new, even more complicated mathematics and statistics than standard economics uses, and are arguing that ultimately it is mathematics that will provide the formal insights into institutions and history that is needed for economics to be a science.

Let me give an example of how complexity economics differs from standard economics. Say one is trying to understand an interaction between investment and changes in income. Standard economics would develop a simple analytically solvable model—for instance, the Samuelson multiplier/accelerator model—that has a set of deterministic solutions, and then use that to study a variety of cases. In the complexity approach, one would try hundreds of variations of nonlinear models, many with no deterministic solution, which capture the dynamic interactions and rely on the computer to show which model best fits the data. One would, of course, study the general properties of nonlinear models, but whether the models have analytic solutions would not be a relevant choice criterion as it is now; the choice criteria would be "fit with the data." Elegance and analytic solvability of models are de-emphasized.

There are, of course, limits to what we can discover through simulations, and there is much methodological work to be done before the complexity approach becomes one that can be generally used. But the complexity vision is that this is the important work, and that, as computing costs continue to fall, analytic solutions in mathematics will be less and less important. Similarly in econometrics; Monte Carlo and bootstrap methods will replace analytic methods of testing in many cases.

Because the complexity approach involves even more focus on mathematics and statistics than does standard economics, the complexity method may seem even less compatible with many of the heterodox approaches and with the study of the history of thought than is mainstream economics. That, however, is only partly true. Low cost of computing lowers the value of theories. The complexity approach demotes theory to a lower level and replaces it with conjectures and patterns that temporarily fit. Determining whether these patterns are meaningful requires a knowledge of history and of the history of economics. Whereas in standard economics the latest theory includes the best of the past, in complexity economics patterns can fluctuate and a variety of theories will be constantly tested. In complexity economics one is not searching out the truth; one is simply searching for a statistical fit that can be temporarily useful in our understanding of the economy. If these fits become good, then we can develop a law, but, because of the way dynamic equations work, the laws can change, and they can change suddenly. One period may be quite different than the period before, and, instead, be much more related to a much earlier period.

16.5 Conventional histories of economic thought

Conventional histories of science are stories of how thinking progressed from informal stories and verbal metaphors that capture aspects of reality to more formal structural models. For example, a standard history of physics might go as follows: Kepler discovered informally that planets follow elliptical orbits around the sun, but did not formalize his understanding. Newton compressed Kepler's understanding of the astronomical data into an inverse square law. Newton's compression was supplemented and extended by Einstein's theory and models that reduced the relationship of energy and mass to $E = mc^2$. Each of these laws and models is an example of structural simplicity. It is formal and reducible into a simple equation or set of equations.

Just as conventional economics follows standard science, so too conventional histories of economic thought tell the story of how economists have formalized Adam Smith's informal understanding of how competition guides people to serve the common good. Most conventional histories agree that economics is not as far along as is physics, but they see the search for a more formal simple structural model as the right one, and present the history of economics accordingly. Thus, they see the formalization of supply and demand, production functions, general equilibrium theory, national income accounting, and the concepts of capital and labor as structural simplifications that have marked progress in economics.

A two-paragraph conventional history of economic thought written for the layperson would go as follows: it all began with Adam Smith's insight of the invisible hand. Classical economics (Ricardo and Mill are usually highlighted) developed that insight, attempting to derive an acceptable theory of value based on all costs, or on labor alone. It failed in that attempt, but in the process developed the seeds of many ideas that were later expanded by neoclassical economists. Neoclassical economics differs from classical economics in that it stopped looking for value only on the cost side, and developed a supply/demand theory of value in which both supply and demand considerations together determined value (Marshall and Walras are usually highlighted). Although this supply/demand approach was developed by a variety of economists, Walras' contribution is seen as providing the beginnings of the most general theory—that of general equilibrium.

In the 1930s, Keynes developed an alternative macro theory, but by the 1990s that had fallen by the wayside. Modern economics (Hicks and Samuelson are usually highlighted) has developed general equilibrium theory and in 1954 that development reached its apex in the Arrow/Debreu theory of general equilibrium. Since then, general equilibrium theory has been further simplified, and expanded upon. It has incorporated many variations, but it remains the centerpiece of modern economists' understanding of the world. Along the way to this understanding, there have been many side roads followed, (Malthus, Marx, Robinson, Hayek, Veblen, and Keynes are often mentioned briefly) but these are primarily detours; the centerpiece of economic theory is general equilibrium theory.

How one tells the above story depends on the methodological approach one takes to economics. Relativist historians of economic thought, who see economics as reflecting the problems of the time, see little development of a grand theory; they emphasize the side roads, arguing that there is no overall thread of development in thinking. Absolutist historians, sometimes called Whig historians, see economics as conventional science; they tell the story emphasizing the main lines of development and give much less shrift to the side roads. But, within conventional economics, the trunk is still there. It is a story of the search for simplicity in structure as found in general equilibrium theory.

16.6 A complexity perspective on the history of economic thought

The complexity perspective provides a different pattern to be placed on the history of economic thought. It specifically does not accept that the gains from simplicity of structure have been worth the costs in terms of what we have lost in our informal knowledge. It sees an economics that has found a simple structure, but only at the cost of assumptions that make the theory difficult, if not impossible, to relate to empirical reality. Important elements of economic processes—path dependency, increasing returns, multiple equilibria, and technology are downplayed, and the importance of institutional structure is almost lost. The complexity approach to economics is trying to remedy that. It sees the economy as a complex system that follows the same laws as all complex systems. Complexity theory developed spontaneously, in a search for the laws of complex dynamics. The hope is that insight into large complex systems will come from the study of iterative processes involving nonlinear dynamics.

The advantage of seeing economics as the result of such iterative processes is that it allows a more direct inclusion of increasing returns and institutions than does the standard approach. Complexity theory differs from conventional theory in that it holds that the complexity of the economy precludes the far-sighted rationality assumed of individuals in conventional theory. If the economy is truly complex, then individuals cannot rationally deal with every part of it, making any model based on full global rationality inconsistent with the complex structure of the model. People will develop institutions to deal with the world, and these institutions will change their behavior. Thus, the data reduction program in economics cannot be held together by a general equilibrium system that assumes far-sighted rationality.

Where the complexity approach challenges conventional economics most is in its explanation of macro phenomena. In a highly complex system, the connection between micro and macro that economics has been searching for cannot be discovered. With this view the complexity approach calls into question the entire line of general equilibrium research that is the centerpiece of standard economics.

The complexity interpretation of the history of economic theory is different from the standard heterodox interpretation of the history of thought for a number of reasons. First, the complexity interpretation fits better in the absolutist approach than in the relativist approach that most heterodox economics takes. By that I mean that the complexity approach sees economics as having a grand theory, and sees the purpose of economic science as finding that theory. It differs from the standard histories in that it sees multiple potential patterns of simplification, but it is, in many ways, an absolutist history with a twist. It sees conventional economics as having followed a reasonable, but ultimately wrong, path in its search for simplicity of structure as the central trunk of the story. Instead, it suggests that there is another trunk, which finds simplification in dynamics, not in static structure.

Second, the complexity approach also takes a much more sympathetic view of the earlier development of standard economics than do most heterodox approaches to the history of economics. The reason is that, until recently, the high-powered computers and mathematics to explore the alternative complexity simplification path did not exist, so the complexity approach was not viable. What makes it viable now is the development of computer technology that has so increased our ability to get numerical solutions to complicated nonlinear equations, and to see the implications of iterative processes involving nonlinear equations, that it changes the way it is reasonable to look for patterns in data. The point is often made with the "12-cent Ferrari" example. Had the same degree of increases in technology occurred in the automobile industry as has occurred in the computer industry, automobiles would be essentially free and a Ferrari would cost 12 cents. That would change our transportation pattern; shouldn't the change in computer technology also change our research pattern?

Before advances in computers made dealing with more complex systems possible, it was only reasonable to explore the alternative structural simplicity path. Thus, from a complexity perspective many economists may have had a complexity perspective, but they did not follow up on it in their formal work because they did not have the tools to do so. Numerous examples can be given. Consider Joseph Schumpeter's discussion of multiple equilibria. He writes:

> Multiple equilibria are not necessarily useless, but from the standpoint of any exact science the existence of a uniquely determined equilibrium is, of course, of the utmost importance, even if proof has to be purchased at the price of very restrictive assumptions; without any possibility of proving the existence of (a) uniquely determined equilibrium—or at all events, of a small number of possible equilibria—at however high a level of abstraction, a field of phenomena is really a chaos that is not under analytical control. (Schumpeter, 1954)

John Hicks had a similar understanding of the problem. He writes that serious consideration of increasing returns could lead to the "wreckage of the greater part of general equilibrium theory" (1946, p. 84). My point is that many earlier economists understood the implications of complexity, of which increasing returns and multiple equilibria are important elements, but they also recognized that they did not have the tools to deal with it formally, and therefore did not work on such issues. The role of Kenneth Arrow, one of the economists who made a major contribution to general equilibrium theory, but who also was central in establishing the Santa Fe Institute that has explored complexity within economics, is another example.

Any history of thought told from a complexity perspective must also recognize that while conventional economics used general equilibrium theory as its core organizing feature, much of the development of applied economics was not dependent on general equilibrium theory. Other avenues developed, including much work that considered increasing returns, and much of the complexity work will build on that work. It is not the standard practice of economics, but the formal general equilibrium centerpiece of economics, that complexity challenges.

16.7 Conventional wisdom and our intellectual predecessors

Now that I have given a general discussion of how switching to a complexity perspective changes the way we view economics, let me consider how previous writers fare in the changed perspective. I consider the issue in three separate sections. First, I consider general schools of economics; next I consider some economists who would move up or down in my rankings. Finally, I briefly discuss two individuals who, from our current standpoint, are relegated to footnotes, but who would enter into the panoply from a complexity perspective. I should make it clear that the discussion is a "reporter's treatment" of the field, not a specialist's treatment.

16.7.1 Assessment of schools of thought

In the standard history of economics text, the mainstream, or neoclassical, school is given primary focus, but students are introduced to various other schools including the German historical school, the Austrian school, American institutionalists, and the radical-Marxian school. The general views of each of these schools are presented, and contrasted with the mainstream development from classical to neoclassical to modern.

In a history of thought told from a complexity perspective, the story told about these heterodox schools would be much the same as is currently told, but told a bit more sympathetically. Many of the heterodox objections to standard economics would be presented as precursors of the modern complexity school's objections: the German historical school opposed the equilibrium method, believing instead that history mattered, and that different periods could be unique; the institutionalists opposed neoclassical theory as too simple; Austrians saw the market mechanism as an example of spontaneous order, again providing a precursor to the complexity focus on emergent order; radicals saw that there was more than a single way of looking at the economy.

The above argument deals with the presentation. But the assessment of these heterodox schools of thought would not significantly change. Although one can find many areas where the schools were precursors of complexity work, complexity economics did not develop from these schools. Complexity economics developed out of standard economics, and is best seen as a natural evolution—the economics field responding to the changing technology. The complexity approach shares with standard economics a focus on formal mathematics and maintaining a formal scientific approach. Most modern institutionalists argue against the use of formal mathematics, radicals replaced a neoclassical ideological bias with an alternative bias, claiming that bias was inherent in science; Austrians relied on deduction to the almost total exclusion of induction; and the German historical school was anti-formalist in almost all the forms.[2] Thus, in my view, none of these schools would have led to complexity economics. They would have likely led standard economics elsewhere. Thus, from a complexity perspective, these heterodox schools are seen in roughly the same light that they are seen now by sympathetic interpreters—as schools that had some of the important insights, but which were ahead of their time.

16.7.2 Assessment of individual economists

While the assessment of schools may not change much, the assessment of individual economists will. Table 16.1 provides my fast and dirty overview of selected economists' change in rankings when they are considered within

Table 16.1 Overview of economists' change in rankings

Economist	Change in Ranking
Smith	Up
Malthus	Neutral
Ricardo	Down
Mill	Up
Marx	Up
Walras	Down
Marshall	Up
Hayek	Up
Keynes	Neutral

a complexity framework. The discussion below the table gives a brief justification for that assessment.

16.7.2.1 Adam Smith Smith goes up in the rankings because of his recognition of the problems of complexity, his emphasis on increasing returns, and his vent for surplus argument, all of which can be seen as leading to ideas that are consistent with the complexity perspective. In the conventional texts Smith is presented as "the father of economics"—the person who codified economic thinking—but he is also presented as a fuzzy thinker whose informal reasoning allowed many inconsistencies. He had a variety of theories of value, a confused presentation of the price level, and unclear policy prescriptions. Later classical economists had to clarify these. From the complexity perspective, Smith is still inconsistent, but there is good reason for that inconsistency since the mathematical techniques had not yet developed to handle the issues that he recognized were important. His emphasis on vent for surplus, increasing returns, and the need for a broader setting for economics fits well with the complexity vision, as do his unclear policy prescriptions—the complexity approach to economics does not lead to definitive policy prescriptions.

16.7.2.2 Thomas Malthus Malthus stays neutral in the ranking, but it is a neutrality that results from his rising in one dimension and falling in another. He rises because of his work on population; Malthus saw that the interesting issue in understanding economics was in iterative processes. His ideas on population were central in the development of Darwin's ideas, which has a close tie-in with the complexity perspective. He falls in the rankings because the dynamic process that he emphasized was one that focused on diminishing returns. He did not allow for the development of ongoing endogenous growth. He further falls in the ranking because his macro argument that general gluts were possible fails to use any of the insights of complexity, and thus helped reinforce the view that if one approaches the macro economy logically, there can be no unemployment.

16.7.2.3 David Ricardo Ricardo is seen in many ways as the hero in the structural simplicity vision; he took Smith's ambiguous ideas and formalized them into economic laws. The standard history of thought emphasizes how his theory of comparative advantage is one of the greatest developments in economics. It is also generally acknowledged that he developed the labor theory of value as far as it could be developed (the 93 percent labor theory) and clarified the argument for trade. With his theory of rent, he was a precursor of the neoclassical marginal productivity theory.

In part Ricardo falls because, with his current high ranking, there is nowhere to go but down. While his formalization helped make Smith's ideas specific, that same formalization led economists to the focus on structural simplicity, and took away the emphasis found in Smith on increasing returns. Ricardo's search for value within a unique equilibrium system made the theory simpler than it otherwise would have been and directed economic researchers away from taking seriously the complexity of the economy.

16.7.2.4 John Stuart Mill Mill is generally presented as the mature classical economist who had little to add to formal classical thought. He made a few contributions: he pulled classical economics towards a humanist mode; he led classical economics away from the wages fund theory; and he drew a distinction between the social laws of distribution and the technical laws of production. With these insights he moved away from the labor theory of value, but he did not abandon it. In the standard view, he receives high ranking, but not at Ricardo's level. From the complexity perspective, Mill's ranking increases. His focus on social laws of distribution was an important development in recognizing the complexity of the economy. He recognized that social and economic phenomena couldn't be divided. He saw the importance of path dependency in a way that Ricardo did not. His nervous breakdown can be seen as a natural reaction of an individual trying to fit the complex world into too simple a structure.

16.7.2.5 Karl Marx Marx is generally presented as a classical economist who did not share the mainstream ideological views. He turned the labor theory of value into a theory of exploitation, and, in doing so, showed some deeper problems with it. He focused on increasing returns, the tendency of economies to grow, and how distribution was tied into that growth process.

Marx's ranking improves from a complexity perspective not only because of his formal analysis, but also because of his informal analysis of class, and his emphasis that individuals' rationality is shaped by the social situation around them. His failure to see social relations evolving to maintain stability in the economy still limits his being considered a precursor of complexity economics.

16.7.2.6 Léon Walras The standard view of Walras is that he led economics into general equilibrium theory as well as that he developed marginalism. He receives high marks for both. In the complexity perspective, since general equilibrium and marginalism fall in the ranking, it is not surprising that Walras also falls. Walras directed economics into a particular mathematical structure that did not fit.

16.7.2.7 Alfred Marshall In the standard history Marshall receives a positive, but subdued, treatment. He played a key role in introducing supply and demand concepts, but he simultaneously failed to formalize theory. Thus, he is often accused of following the "zigzag windings of the flowery path of literature," and his work is characterized by Paul Samuelson as having "paralyzed the best brains in the Anglo-Saxon branch of our profession for three decades."[3] In his Principles of Economics (1890) Marshall struggled with how to include both the classical focus on dynamics and growth—which called for explicit treatment of increasing returns—and the neoclassical focus on diminishing marginal returns in the production of goods.

As Marshall typically did when faced with conflicts, he used what might be called "the Marshallian Straddle" to circumvent them. He discussed each but never integrated them. Still, his stature rises somewhat relative to Walras because the reason he refused to formalize was precisely that his perception of the economy was that it was complex, and that the tools were not up to formalizing the insights; he recognized the limitations that Walras did not. He rejected any simple specification of general equilibrium and in Note 21 in *Principles* argued that the true foundation of aggregate economics was to be found in thermodynamics, an idea that clearly places him in the complexity perspective.

16.7.2.8 Frederick Hayek Hayek usually receives only a short mention in the standard history of thought, in part because he lived until the 1980s and his work was continually evolving, and, in part, because he did not fit the standard mold. Starting in the 1940s with his publication of *Abuse of Reason* (1940) Hayek's work was evolving outside of the Austrian tradition of Ludwig von Mises. As it did, it better fits a complexity tradition. In his vision, Hayek came very close to the modern definition of complexity; however, he did not conduct any deeper empirical or analytic research into the field of complexity.

Hayek understood the nature of complex phenomena and correctly associated them with the economy. His emphasis on spontaneous organization has complexity written all over it, as does his focus on prices as storing systemic information that individuals did not have and could not compute. In his Nobel address in 1974 he developed the arguments in his earlier work and argues that the reductionist approach of economics, which is mimicking that of the pure sciences, is inapplicable to economics since economics studies phenomena of "essential complexity, i.e. with structures whose characteristic properties can be exhibited only by models made up of relatively large numbers of variables" (Hayek, 1989, p. 4). In the same address Hayek also recognizes that "organized complexity" is dependent on the "manner in which the individual elements are connected with each other" at least as much as the individual properties of the agents in the system. Thus, Hayek, especially, in his later writings, will significantly move up in the rankings.

16.7.2.9 John Maynard Keynes Keynes stays neutral in the rankings in large part because he currently gets such high ratings. His questioning of econometrics, his emphasis on the nonergodicity of the economy, and his work on probability all can be seen as a positive from a complexity perspective. But, in policy, he never shied away from the simple static models that were developed to capture his views, and never made clear that his analysis rested on a complexity perspective, even though he had opportunities to do so. Thus, the foundations of his *General Theory* ([1936] 1991) were ambiguous, and, despite many possibilities in which he could have laid its foundations in complexity, he did not do so. His primary interest in policy took him away from theoretical issues, and his willingness to accept standard theory, if it arrived at the policy result he wanted, leaves him unchanged in my rankings.

16.7.3 Two economists who move from footnotes to the main text

In this final section I consider two economists, Charles Babbage and John von Neumann, who seldom show up prominently in standard histories of economic thought, but who have a significant place in a history told from a complexity perspective. As Nathan Rosenberg (2000) nicely points out, Babbage applied complexity reasoning to the economy as he expanded Smith's ideas to the industrial age. He emphasized nonlinear costs and thought of the economy within a complexity perspective. Had economics focused on his work rather than Ricardo's its history likely would have been quite different.

Unlike Babbage, who is hardly ever mentioned at all in histories of economic thought, John von Neumann frequently gets a short section in history of economics texts for his work on game theory. That work, however, is not what earns the main focus from a complexity perspective. Instead, it is his work on self-replicating systems. That work, which is a precursor to work in artificial intelligence, and is related to the development of the computer, is central in the development of the complexity perspective, and places von Neumann as a pivotal figure in any history of economic thought told from a complexity perspective.

The importance of John von Neumann to economics should come as no surprise. He is already considered by many to be one of the most brilliant minds of the 20th century. He contributed significantly to numerous branches of science, including mathematics, quantum mechanics, and computer science. In standard economics he is known for his development of game theory, which pushes the analytic approach to economics as far as it can be pushed. But it is not game theory that would be emphasized in a complexity history of thought; it is his work on self-replicating systems, where he developed the logic of what was necessary. Specifically he specified the minimum requirements needed for self-replicating systems in his theory of automata (see Von Neumann, 1966). That theory is an important cornerstone in complexity theory, and is particularly useful in trying to understand and simulate artificial life, which is central for understanding and simulating iterative processes.

An automaton is a general-purpose universal machine that can execute the instructions of any algorithm. There are natural automata, such as the nervous system, and artificial ones, such as computers. Von Neumann argued that, similarly to natural living systems, artificial systems should also be able to reproduce themselves. He imagined a machine floating on the surface of a lake, where a lot of machine parts float as well. Following instructions, the machine—a universal constructor—assembles another machine. It can reproduce itself if it has a blueprint of itself within itself. Reproducing automata are description copiers—they include a blueprint of each machine they construct within it. The "genetic" information of the machine is thus both interpreted as an algorithm to be followed, and as genetic material copied uninterpreted, as a piece of the machine being copied.[4] That work is far from standard economics but it lies at the heart of complexity theory.

16.8 Conclusion

This quick and dirty overview of the history of thought is delivered from a complexity perspective. In many ways the most interesting part of the story is its relation to heterodox economics, many of whose practitioners have had something close to a complexity vision. But the complexity approach did not develop from heterodox economics. The line of descent is through standard economics. The complexity approach developed from the standard approach to economics for two reasons. The first is the limitations and problems with the standard approach; it simply did not provide a meaningful model of the aggregate economy. But that failure was not enough to cause the mainstream of economics to abandon the approach, and those who did became known as heterodox economists. What was necessary for the mainstream of economics to consider the complexity vision was the second reason, a change in research technology, primarily the computer, which allowed economists to study dynamic systems that previously were beyond analytic study.

The methodology of complexity economics is quite consistent with the methodology of standard economics and, as such, does not fit well with many heterodox traditions. Still, many heterodox economists have had a complexity vision, and thus complexity economics can be seen as a melding of heterodox vision with standard scientific methods, which is only now coming of age.

Notes

* This paper is adapted from Colander (2000). For additional discussion of the issues see that book.

1. Having spent much of my time during the last 20 years writing textbooks, I have learned the importance of simplifications, and have also learned the enormous injustice such simplifications do to the various writers. The ideas of the writers discussed in this chapter, and the history of economics it conveys, are much more complex than this chapter suggests.
2. The schools did not necessarily start that way, and it can be argued convincingly that early heterodox economists were simply waiting for the right mathematics to come along. But there seems to be a path-dependency argument. Arguing against current mathematical approaches attracts followers who oppose math, and thus these heterodox schools did not attract the individuals who developed complexity theory.
3. See Edgeworth (1925, II, p. 282) and Samuelson (1967, p. 109).
4. It is interesting to note that only later it was discovered that DNA within all natural living organisms has the same dual function, and that natural systems reproduce according to von Neumann's abstract method.

Bibliography

Colander, David (ed.) (2000), *Complexity and the History of Economic Thought*, London and New York: Routledge.

Edgeworth, F.Y. (1925), *Paper Relating to Political Economy*, New York: Burt Franklin.

Hayek, F.A. (1940), *The Counter-revolution of Science: Studies on the Abuse of Reason*, Glencoe: Il: Free Press.

Hayek, F.A. (1989), "The Pretense of Knowledge," *The American Economic Review*, **79**(6), 4 (reprint of Nobel address).

Hicks, John Richard, Sir (1946), *Value and Capital; An Inquiry into Some Fundamental Principles of Economic Theory*, 2nd edn, Oxford: Clarendon Press.

Horgan, John (1996), *The End of Science: Facing the Limits of Knowledge in the Twilight of the Scientific Age*, Reading, MA: Addison-Wesley.
Keynes, John Maynard [1936] (1991), *The General Theory of Employment, Interest, and Money*, San Diego: Harcourt, Brace, Jovanovich.
Landreth, Harry and David C. Colander (2002), *History of Economic Thought*, 4th edn, Boston: Houghton-Mifflin.
Rosenberg, Nathan (2000), "Charles Babbage in a Complex World," in Colander (2000).
Samuelson, Paul (1967), "The Monopolistic Competition Revolution," in *Competition Theory*, (ed.) Kuene, R.E., New York: John Wiley.
Schumpeter, Joseph Alois (1954), *History of Economic Analysis*, New York, Oxford University Press.
Von Neumann, John (1966), *Theory of Self-reproducing Automata*, Urbana: University of Illinois Press.
Von Neumann, John (1961–63), *Collected Works*, New York. Pergamon Press.

Index